VISIBLE AND INVISIBLE REALMS

VISIBLE AND

INVISIBLE REALMS

Power, Magic, and Colonial Conquest in Bali

Margaret J. Wiener

THE UNIVERSITY OF CHICAGO PRESS
CHICAGO & LONDON

MARGARET J. WIENER is assistant professor in the
Department of Anthropology at the University of
North Carolina at Chapel Hill.

The University of Chicago Press, Chicago 60637
The University of Chicago Press, Ltd., London
© 1995 by Margaret Wiener
All rights reserved. Published 1995
Printed in the United States of America
04 03 02 01 00 99 98 97 96 95   5 4 3 2 1

ISBN (cloth): 0-226-88580-1
ISBN (paper): 0-226-88582-8

Library of Congress Cataloging-in-Publication Data

Wiener, Margaret J.
    Visible and invisible realms : Power, magic, and
colonial conquest in Bali / Margaret J. Wiener.
        p.   cm.
    Includes bibliographical references and index.
    ISBN 0-226-88580-1 — ISBN 0-226-88582-8 (pbk.)
    1. Bali Island (Indonesia)—History.   I. Title.
DS647.B2W48   1995
959.8'6—dc20   94-25826
                                          CIP

⊗ The paper used in this publication meets the minimum
requirements of the American National Standard for Information Sciences—Permanence of Paper for Printed Library
Materials, ANSI Z39.48-1984.

It is impossible to represent an alien ideological world adequately without first permitting it to sound, without having first revealed the special discourse peculiar to it. After all, a really adequate discourse for portraying a world's unique ideology can only be that world's own discourse, although not that discourse in itself, but only in conjunction with the discourse of an author.

Bakhtin, *The Dialogic Imagination*

If the value of a drama lay merely in its final scene, the drama itself would be a very long, crooked and laborious road to the goal; and I hope history will not find its whole significance in general propositions, and regard them as its blossom and fruit. On the contrary its real value lies in inventing ingenious variations on a probably commonplace theme, in raising the popular melody to a universal symbol and showing what a world of depth, power, and beauty exists in it.

Nietzsche, *The Use and Abuse of History*

Contents

Illustrations

Preface

In the last twenty years or so, colonialism has emerged as a locus for rethinking relations between knowledge and power, both within anthropology (Asad 1973) and without (Said 1979). Indeed, discussions of European discourses about colonized others and the politics of representation increasingly challenge more and more subtle forms of Euro-American ethnocentrism, while serving to destabilize the categories used to make sense of the world. Among anthropologists, whose object of knowledge has typically been colonized or formerly colonized peoples, this has led to a salutary turn to history. Many key works in recent anthropology have been concerned with the "encounter" between Europeans and non-Europeans and with the effect of European colonizers on the lives and worldviews of the colonized (Cohn 1987; Comaroff and Comaroff 1991; Dirks 1992; Sahlins 1985; Taussig 1987).

Current anthropological interest in colonialism, however, is often still constructed within master narratives that grant to Europeans the determining agency in both enacting and narrating global history. The colonized appear to have in one way or another either accepted the identities imposed upon them by their colonizers or resisted them. While this clearly oversimplifies often subtle and illuminating analyses, it is nonetheless striking that there are few accounts of how conquest and the colonizing process appeared to the colonized. If, as Inden (1990) suggests, the challenge at present is to provide alternative accounts of human agencies, this would appear to be an important arena to do so. There is, perhaps, some reason to despair of providing such accounts, for increasingly it seems we discover how ethnocentric, in the end, are even those attempts to be least so. Yet to preclude trying seems more problematic yet.

This, then, is a work of anthropological history focused upon the "commonplace theme" of colonialism. In it, in addition to decentering colonial representations, I have presented an alternative history of one colonial encounter, deriving from indigenous accounts and attending insofar as possible to "the special discourse peculiar to" a Balinese world. Indigenous narratives do not represent the "truth" of what happened any more than colonial accounts do. But they do suggest how people made sense of events we often think can only be understood in one way.

Most of the issues central to discussions of Bali were set by the discourse of the colonial era. One of my purposes in writing this book is to deconstruct colonial discourse, rather than perpetuate it. Here I have found Sahlins's (1976) caution about seeing ourselves too much in others—of assuming that what motivates Euro-Americans is universal—critical. No account, however self-conscious, is utterly without presuppositions. But by attempting not to take much for granted, I have tried to undermine the power of old stereotypes, and by trying to attend to what people I knew in Bali were actually saying (and by striving to become attuned as well as their silences), I have attempted to avoid creating too many new ones.

Translation, the saying goes, is treason; in writing about one culture in the language of another it is impossible to avoid distortion. But there is another problem with translation, and that is that the most difficult of all things is to learn something new. Interpretations and analyses necessarily begin with analogies: we understand something unfamiliar by comparison with what is. However, provisional analogies can become petrified as "truths," a problematic process that becomes more so when they bring associations that may not fit the case at hand. Moreover, analogies, commonly made in the context of unequal relations of power, can enable agendas of domination. To call someone else's forms of political agency "feudal" or even refer to political agents as "kings" has a political effect. It is even more troubling to designate other people's ideas as "beliefs" rather than "knowledge," especially given the notorious philosophical difficulties of identifying what knowledge is.

Thus opacity may be a virtue. Why should understanding be easy? It is easy only if we see patterns we already know. In the same way, to contextualize the stories I heard in Klungkung too firmly within current theoretical and disciplinary concerns would make them conform to what is already comfortably familiar, and potentially prevent readers from being affected by them, from actually hearing and learning anything. This is one reason why we keep discovering that our descriptions of others really describe ourselves.

THIS ACCOUNT is based upon numerous trips to Bali, which began with nearly three years of fieldwork from February 1984 through December 1986. I was able to clarify some of the issues that confused me through visits in 1988, 1989–90, 1992, and 1993. I also conducted two periods of research in colonial archives: the first, from June through August of 1985, at the Algemeen Rijksarchief in the Netherlands, after I had spent fifteen consecutive months in Bali; the second, six weeks in the fall of 1986 at the Arsip Nasional in Jakarta, at the end of my field research. To the staffs of both of those institutions, especially de Heer de Graaff of the Algemeen Rijksarchief, I gratefully acknowledge my thanks. I also thank Christopher Wake, for guiding me through the mysteries of the Rijksarchief, and Henk Schulte Nordholt, for providing numerous unpublished documents.

The research could never have been accomplished without the aid of the Indonesian Academy of Sciences (LIPI) and the sponsorship of Udayana University in Bali. I wish to thank especially Dr. Gusti Ngurah Bagus, for his warm friendship and support. Many thanks are also due to Drs. Wayan Geria, Drs. Wayan Warna, Drs. Ida Bagus Narayana, Drs. Anak Agung Wirawan, and the staffs of the Gedong Kirtya in Singaraja, the Museum Bali in Denpasar, and the office of the Bupati in Klungkung, especially the staff of KESRA. The Indonesian Department of Education provided sponsorship and funds toward an invaluable year's study of the Balinese language. Finally, life was made ever so much easier by the extraordinary competence of Kristina Melcher, then consular agent in Bali, and Nelly Paliama of USIS.

I gratefully acknowledge the financial support provided for my research in Indonesia and the Netherlands by grants from IIE/Fulbright-Hays, the USED Fulbright-Hays program, the Joint Committee on Southeast Asia of the Social Science Research Council and the American Council of Learned Societies (with funds provided by the Ford Foundation and the National Endowment for the Humanities), and the Institute for Intercultural Studies. A Charlotte W. Newcombe Award from the Woodrow Wilson Fellowship Foundation provided me a year's funding for writing up the results.

I am most fortunate in having friends, colleagues, and teachers who generously read through and commented on this book at various stages of its production, or who kept me thinking with their stimulating conversation. I particularly want to thank Jane Bestor, Bernard Cohn, Hildred Geertz, Jim Hevia, Mark Hobart, Anjana Mebane-Cruz, James Peacock, Marshall Sahlins, Pam Schmoll, Edie Turner, Valerio Valeri, and Roy Wagner. Mark Hobart's critical eye proved especially invaluable in final revisions. I also wish to extend a special thank-you to my mother, Estelle Wiener, for her constant and loving encouragement while I completed what often seemed to both of us a daunting task.

There are too many persons in Klungkung and Peliatan to whom I am indebted—for being kind enough to share with me their memories and thoughts; for their warmth, generosity, and humor—to name them all here. I want to mark out for special notice the late Anak Agung Niang Kudar and her husband, the late Anak Agung Pekak Gaci, of Puri Bedulu; the late Gusti Sobo; Ida Bagus Gedé Aji of Geria Sengguan; Ida Pedanda Gedé Kenitén of Dawan Kelod; Ratu Dalem Pemayun and his wives, especially Jero Ketut; Cokorda Isteri Agung and her parents (particularly the late Cokorda Lingsir), Cokorda Isteri Oka (especially for lending me her late father's writings), and the late Cokorda Isteri Biang Sayang of Puri Anyar; Anak Agung Aji Widia;

the late Dadong Ribek of Losan; I Madé Regeg of Pasinggahan; the late Pedanda Madé Gélgél and Pedanda Isteri Rai and her family of Geria Sengguan; the late Madé Kanta and the late Kaki Cetig, both of Klungkung; and the late Anak Agung Niang Bagus of Gélgél. It saddens me to have to append "late" before so many of their names. I hope all of them will pardon me for the deficiencies of this work, for *"ten wenten luput ring salah."*

To Ida Bagus Jagri and Dayu Alit, the two people from whom I learned the most—and not only or even most importantly about matters Balinese—mere words of thanks are inadequate. When I think of Bali, I see Dayu Alit's foot moving up and down on the treadle of her sewing machine, or Ida Bagus Jagri's face glistening with beads of holy water as he listens to a client's problems. Here I simply acknowledge my gratitude to them both, for sharing "hot and cold" with me as families do, and for collaborating with me in producing this work.

When a Balinese author begins inscribing a historical chronicle, he begins by petitioning those about whom he writes not to curse him for his audacity in evoking their names. Indeed, he asks that they grant him and all of his descendants long life and happiness. In beginning this book, so filled with references to persons long ago, I follow that practice.

The spelling of all Balinese terms and names follows the conventions formulated by the Balinese Office of Education in 1978 and employed in its Balinese-Indonesian dictionary, except when quoting older sources. I have also followed the Balinese practice of not indicating plural forms; therefore *keris* may indicate one *keris* or many. Finally, all translations from Balinese, Indonesian, Kawi, Dutch, and French are my own.

PART ONE

Power and Knowledge

ONE

Introduction

On the morning of 28 April 1908, four companies of the Netherlands Indies army marched north from the sea toward the capital of Klungkung, the paramount realm on the island of Bali. Hostilities between the Dutch and Klungkung, one of only two Balinese realms still independent of colonial rule, had broken out barely two weeks earlier when a Dutch lieutenant was shot during a routine march through the town of Gélgél. The attack had been ordered by the lord of Gélgél, who opposed his king's attempt to maintain nominal independence by a policy of appeasement. The Dutch retaliated by destroying Gélgél and bombarding the capital itself from the sea for over a week. Their ultimatum, giving the king until noon on the twenty-eighth to surrender, had been answered by requests for more time; their advice to at least send the women and children of his family elsewhere for safety was greeted by silence. To the commanders of the Dutch expedition, it was clear that Klungkung's king had resolved on a fight to the death, what Balinese referred to as a *puputan,* or "finishing."

The soldiers reached Klungkung by early afternoon, having encountered no one during their slow and hot march. Heavy field ordnance was rolled into the crossroads, just across from the high brick walls of the royal residence known as Smarapura, abode of the god of love. It was only then that a cluster of Balinese men and boys appeared, all dressed entirely in white. They charged forward, brandishing lances and *keris* (wavy-bladed daggers). As rifles and howitzers loosed volleys of fire, the Balinese fell in bloody and mangled heaps before managing to so much as scratch an enemy soldier with their weapons. Moments later they were replaced by other white-clad figures, intent upon the same end. Among them were women, resplendent in gold and jewels, many leading children by the hand or carrying them in their arms. They too fell before the relentless guns as they advanced toward the Dutch troops, and so the massacre continued until nearly two hundred Balinese lay dead or wounded on Klungkung's main road. At last the king himself appeared, together with his remaining lords. One more round and it was over: an era in Balinese history had ended. From now on, Klungkung, once the 3 center of the signifying and material practices that produced a Balinese reality, would be simply a marginal corner of more global cultural and political formations.

THE FIRST ACCOUNTS of Klungkung's conquest were written by and for its conquerors. Reports by colonial officials to their bureaucratic superiors and newspaper accounts in the Dutch-language press represented what transpired at Klungkung as an unfortunate tragedy, motivated by a feudal concern with honor and precipitated by fanatics who pushed a weak-willed king into an inevitably bloody confrontation with the superior military and moral force of the Dutch. While an event as dramatic as the puputan could hardly fail to make an impression upon the European imagination, for the most part it constituted a minor footnote in colonial discourse about Bali and Klungkung. The puputan was absorbed as an anomaly in an essentially benevolent European conquest, a heroic gesture that was basically meaningless. For the most part, Klungkung's fall was surrounded by silence.

Such silence was not without its motivations. Only a year and a half before, word of the death of four hundred men, women, and children under similar circumstances during the conquest of the South Balinese realm of Badung scandalized politicians in the Netherlands who justified such annexations as promoting the welfare of indigenous people.¹ It was mostly due to that reaction (so reported several journalists) that Klungkung had not been annexed then and there. Small wonder, then, that the death of what was reported as a quarter of that number at Klungkung seemed hardly worth mentioning—in his telegram to the Governor General reporting the Dutch victory, the Resident refers dismissively to a "little puputan"—and it was only good politics to play it down.

Quite apart from public opinion, the colonial government had other reasons for treating Klungkung's conquest as a minor event. By this time in the history of Dutch imperialism, indigenous sovereigns were regarded as despots and parasites, who exploited their subjects and expended their lives and resources in petty wars. That mostly aristocrats participated in the puputan at Klungkung, and that there was no opposition to colonial rule in its aftermath, was read as confirmation of such claims. Not long after the bodies were burned and surviving members of the ruling class exiled to Lombok, a new Dutch Resident noted in a letter to the Governor General that the people of Klungkung were so indifferent to the death of their king that they even allowed his shrines to go untended.²

Silence, then, existed on the Balinese side as well. But this silence was by no means the affirmation of colonial authority that the Dutch chose to believe. It is true that, from the perspective of a colonial administration concerned with the maintenance of "peace and order," the Balinese were satisfactorily compliant colonial subjects. There were no rebellions and nothing that could be obviously identified as resistance. But Klungkung was what Sahlins (1985) calls a "heroic polity": there were no grounds for resistance with its king dead and all possible successors dead or exiled. And where people could once have fled to another realm rather than live under new rulers to whom they had no ties of clientage, in colonial Bali there was no place left to go. As one man ruefully remarked, remembering the days following the puputan: "People were *bé cundang,* cocks defeated in a fight. They knew they had lost. They surrendered to the Dutch, who had the right to kill them, but they refused." Moreover, people were not indifferent to the loss of their leaders; there were those in Klungkung, looking back from the perspective of an equally kingless present, who imagined the numbing sense of abandonment following the Dutch victory as "everyone had to look after himself, take care of himself." Without a king, I was told, things feel different, "wobbly," and "adrift." Another man reflected that a realm without a king is like a snake with its head cut off (and that he spoke of snakes and heads was significant, as we will see); it still moves, at least momentarily, but with no direction.

Dadong Ribek, a former palace servant who actually lived through these events, provided the most vivid sense of the immediate impact of the conquest. Not quite an adolescent in 1908, she had been ordered by the slightly older crown prince to wait inside the palace when he went to meet his death. She was still waiting there when she was discovered by a friend:

> My Betara [literally, gods; here it refers to members of the royal family] had already died, all of them. I waited and stood guard there. There was a servant, I Pica:
> "Kembar, why are you still here, at home? Haven't your Betara already 'finished,' already gone home? Come along, come outside."
> "My lord Déwa Agung Gedé Agung [the crown prince] told me to wait. If I leave, won't I be wrong?"
> "No, he has already 'gone home' [died]."
> That's how it was. Her name was I Pica. The rifles were firing only now and then. They [those who participated in the puputan] walked out [of the palace] like that, and went over there to sleep, they walked out there and went to sleep. My Betara were sleeping at the very bottom. "Elder Sister, Elder Sister," that's what I said to the servant, "what is going on? Why are they all sleeping there? Why don't they get up, Elder Sister?" "Those people have died," that's what the servant said. "*Méh,* now where will we go? It's so empty like this." One of their betel-quid containers was standing there, deserted . . .
> There were still rifles going off now and then. I went east of Puri Kajanan, and then I headed north. My friend said to me,

"Ah, the bullets aren't touching us. Come, let's run away. Come on. Why stay here, running this way and that, if we're not going to be hit by the bullets."

"All right. Wherever you go, Elder Sister, I'll follow."

There were about eleven who came with me, servants [*parekan*] from who knows where. I ran away there, east of Puri Kaléran, and then headed north. I went with her to Besang. *Méh*, none of [us] could sleep, the servants of my Betara. There in Besang. There were those who cried, there were those . . . Ah, I was small. A child.

I slept overnight in Besang Kawan. The next day I went there [to Klungkung]. Good lord! There were bodies all the way to Bendul. My Betara were all there, in the cockfight pavilion. At the *penalikan* [an apparatus for counting out the hours of the day]. They were laid out. I was terrified. I saw their faces, their blood scattered. (Interview in Losan, February 1986)

The silence colonial officials reported, then, was caused not by apathy but by shock and fear, mixed with uncertainty about what manner of beings these Dutchmen were and what they might do next. Several old people recalled a rumor about the Dutch that circulated just after Klungkung was taken: "The news that came was this. They were looking for those who hadn't yet had their teeth filed. Their heads. They were going to use them as the foundation for a bridge on the Unda, it was said." The man who told me this laughed and added, "That wasn't really true." True or not, such rumors are ample evidence of a mood. Thirty years into the colonial era, many villagers still had misgivings about Europeans: Margaret Mead, in Bali at that time, was struck by how afraid Balinese children were of white people, who, their mothers suggested to them, were akin to tigers, scorpions, witches, and dangerous spirits (1942:31).[3] As we will see, the nineteenth-century rulers of Klungkung regarded the Dutch in similar ways.

The meaning of the conquest to the Balinese, however, lay beyond the horizon of colonial premises about Bali. From the first colonial embassy, the Dutch interpreted the actions of Bali's rulers in terms of their own understandings of power and authority. This had especially important consequences for colonial interactions with the rulers of Klungkung, paramount lords of the island. Seen through the lens of the colonial government, Klungkung's kings appeared to be either ineffective Oriental despots, full of intrigues but ultimately incapable of enforcing their authority, or insignificant "spiritual overlords," removed from the political arena. The king's response to the Dutch attack in 1908 seemed merely another expression of the same impotence. And so matters have continued to be seen by scholars. Thus Geertz describes the puputan as the desperate act of a symbolic kingship, a "strange ritual . . . in the most

illustrious state of all, Klungkung, the nominal 'capital' of traditional Bali . . .
[which] expired as it had lived: absorbed in a pageant" (1980:11–12).

MEMORIES OF the puputan play an important role in contemporary Klungkung. When I arrived there in 1984, Klungkung had just celebrated the first of
what was planned to be an annual commemoration of the puputan. It was an
important time in Klungkung, when an official history was just in the process
of being constructed, and an oral history possibly on the brink of disappearing.

Official interest in the puputan and the forms in which that interest were
expressed need to be understood against a background of national hegemony
and political peripheralization. The history such celebrations make, for example, is a nationalist one. Jakarta encourages an interest in local history, as
long as it focuses upon the struggle against colonial domination out of which
the Indonesian republic had been born. As examples of anticolonial resistance, such histories, it is claimed, engender a sense of a common past and a
feeling for national unity necessary for the development of the nation.

Klungkung itself had begun to become a peripheral corner of the nation-
state under colonialism, for under the colonial administration Klungkung was
treated as only one of eight equal realms. But the end of colonial rule exacerbated Klungkung's decline into marginality, by eliminating kingship and
bringing into contestation the principles upon which it was based. In addition, since the 1960s the capital of the island has been an increasingly urbanized Badung. Badung is not only the center of government; its economy is
booming as well, with three beach resorts at Kuta, Sanur, and the newly built
Nusa Dua. More to the point, Badung has replaced Klungkung as the center
for the production of hegemonic discourses—including discourses about art,
religion, and history.

For the first celebration of Puputan Day, the office of the *bupati* (the head
of the regional government) had commissioned a committee to produce a
book narrating Klungkung's history up to its conquest. That its authorship
was multiple, and that there were public seminars to discuss the results of their
research, was no accident, for the effort to represent Klungkung's past generated considerable local tension. Old enmities, dating from the nineteenth
century, mingled with postcolonial conflicts over the value of tradition and
the nature of modernity, as different parties with a stake in Klungkung's past
and present sought to impose their points of view. The composition of the
committee reflected some of the tensions, for it included persons whose ancestors had played a role in the events, who were widely seen as representing
their own familial concerns. In addition, while the authority of some committee members stemmed from their legitimation as scholars by modern academic institutions, others had been selected for their expertise in more traditional forms of knowledge, namely, as interpreters of historical chronicles.

The book their collaboration produced was a history of Klungkung "from Smarapura to the puputan," as the subtitle put it (Sidemen et al. 1983). It actually began some centuries earlier, with the founding of the Klungkung dynasty, and its preface, which described the authors' aims and methods, placed it quite squarely in the present of New Order Indonesia. Written in Indonesian, in a neutral, authoritative tone, the text reconstructed major events in the precolonial past of the kingdom, placing the emphasis on politics. An entire chapter was devoted to the administrative structure of the realm: its territorial boundaries, chains of command, economic base, and mode of succession. Another chapter evaluated Klungkung's position within Bali as a whole, based largely upon the evidence of a series of Balinese documents collected by colonial officials who considered them to be "treaties" concluded between Bali's various princes. Mainly, however, the book dwelt upon Klungkung's relations with the Dutch—the treaties signed, the first military confrontations, and finally the puputan.

In a sense the book represented the final act of colonial conquest. Relying heavily upon colonial newspaper reports, Dutch publications, and colonial documents from the National Archives, the book was shaped by the preoccupations of Klungkung's conquerors. The language (replete with terms like "feudal" and "guerilla war"), the emphasis on a certain vision of politics and economics, the "just the facts, ma'am" use of even Balinese sources: except for the anticolonialist inflections and the stress on Balinese heroes as opposed to Dutch ones, it could almost have been the work of a scholarly committee in Leiden, rather than Klungkung. And in today's Leiden even these differences might be muted. But then resistance is sometimes only the flip side of domination; all too often, they speak the same language, but with the signs reversed.

I soon discovered, however, that almost no one in Klungkung was happy with the book. The committee, some people told me darkly, had not dared write "the truth," had not wanted to name names for fear of retaliation by neighbors and kin. The "truth," however, was not just a history of accusations, although these were part of it. Those who complained most of being ignored by the committee did indeed tell tales and legends that named names, rarely in flattering terms. But villainy was a minor part of their stories. More to the point, they told stories about the power of the rulers of Klungkung. Those stories proved to be common knowledge in Klungkung, despite the fact that they were ignored by the committee writing Klungkung's history. And it was because they were indignant at not having been consulted during the writing of the book that some people began to tell me their versions of them.

These stories form part of a rather different discourse than the one that informed the committee's labors. Like the book, this discourse also includes accounts of the origin of the dynasty, the constitution of its authority, and the history of its relations with the Dutch. But it is primarily a discourse of magic, portraying a world where bullets fly about by themselves to destroy colonial generals, where spirit armies bring victory against apparently hopeless odds, where river sprites, properly petitioned, prevent downpours from destroying special ritual events.

Given that these stories were common knowledge in Klungkung, it is striking that the only reference to them in the book was a footnote referring to local stories about a magical gun (Sidemen et al. 1983:100). That such stories were relegated to a single footnote suggests a great deal about the politics of magic in late twentieth-century Bali. Certain postcolonial elites who pride themselves on their "modernity" find references to sorcerers, spirits, or powerful persons vestiges of an embarrassing way of thinking; discourses of magic are in the process of becoming what Foucault termed "subjugated knowledges" (1980:82). It is by no means clear, however, that everyone who embraces the modern finds much reason in Euro-American styles of rationalization, and as elsewhere in the world (see Taussig 1980 and 1987), the opportunities and constraints of a changing political economy provide a fertile soil for magical tales and practices. Indeed, it is hard to imagine situations more conducive to the jealousies and envies that motivate sorcery than competition for the limited places in the civil service or for the patronage of the tourists who never come in sufficient numbers to fill all of the homestays Balinese have built on once productive rice fields. But such concerns are not broadcast in public and official discourses.

Despite the fact that they were ignored, Klungkung stories formed more of an oppositional and anticolonial discourse than the book. They were not taken from colonial sources. They did not even grant the colonial government much agency in the fall of the realm. Ignoring the Dutch and the kind of history they made, they focused on an entirely Balinese drama. And they situated Bali's struggles with Dutch imperialism within a radically different set of preconceptions about power than those that shaped colonial or nationalist interpretations.

Unlike the celebrations, the stories did not focus on the puputan itself. The conquest was represented as only one moment in a larger narrative concerning the encounter between Klungkung's rulers and the colonial government. Typically, stories contrasted the conquest to an event people called the Kusamba War: the first clash between Klungkung and the armies of the Netherlands Indies, which concluded the Third Bali Expedition of 1849. This earlier engagement, in which the commander of the colonial forces was killed, was represented as a Klungkung victory, attributed to the "magical power" (*kasaktian*) of Klungkung's ruler. Tales centered around the magical weapon that killed the Dutch general, one of many such weapons belonging to Klung-kung's royal clan. According to these stories, it was only because these weapons were no longer efficacious (and what interested most narrators was why) that the Dutch had been able to defeat Klungkung in 1908. But stories did not end in defeat. Narrators went on to speak of Klungkung's last ruler, a survivor of the puputan appointed by the colonial government twenty years after the conquest. He had died in the mid-1960s, shortly before the coup that led to the establishment of Suharto's New Order, but his power and benevolence were still legendary.

The motifs that wove these tales together, particularly the focus on weapons with supernatural capacities, were of a piece with another set of stories, both widely known and more official, about earlier Klungkung rulers, collected in a text called the *Babad Dalem*. Taking the form of a chronicle, this text is one of the charters of Balinese society, and episodes from it are often performed during large rituals and other occasions. Indeed, this text appeared to provide a background for stories about the colonial encounter, as well as serving as the source for much that the first colonial envoys reported—filtered through a very different screen of assumptions—about precolonial Klung-kung. And since both the *Babad Dalem* and occasional remarks in colonial documents suggested that nineteenth-century Balinese shared many of their descendants' assumptions about power and agency, their stories also provided insights into history.

Together, the *babad* and the narratives form a single discourse, a set of practices and representations concerned with the *kasaktian*, loosely glossable as "power," of the royal house of Klungkung and with its transformation as a result of colonialism. *Kasaktian*, which results from the generation or reproduction of connections between a person and the invisible world, especially the gods, corresponds poorly to Euro-American political concepts; but neither may it be described as a "religious" concept. From a Balinese perspective, power is enmeshed not merely in the visible world of social relations but also in the invisible world of "spiritual" relations. It is in fact the latter that makes the authority of a person in the former possible at all.

That the practices of the precolonial Balinese ruling class implicated ideas of power quite distinct from that of European political theory has of course been advanced by Geertz. But Geertz's distinction between the expressive and the instrumental obscures Balinese intentions. And while ritual was central to Balinese statecraft, its purpose was not, as Geertz claims, status competition. Geertz's conclusion, that Balinese cultural models were in contradiction with "real" social structures, is itself an artifact of an analytical position that does not take indigenous discourses seriously into account. As a consequence, Geertz ends up recapitulating many of the claims made by Dutch colonial officials.

Balinese models of power are especially salient to representations concerning Klungkung. While precolonial Bali was divided into eight or nine principalities, Klungkung, the smallest realm, was paramount. The Dutch, with their own ideas about authority, had trouble understanding just how; in the end they concluded that Klungkung's overlordship was nominal rather than actual, a claim made real under colonial rule and endlessly reproduced in the scholarly literature on Bali.

There are many reasons to call such conclusions into question. But whether or not Klungkung was politically supreme by colonial standards, it is crucial for understanding the way power could be discussed or enacted in precolonial Bali.

At the time the Dutch first appeared on the scene, Klungkung was the center and source of a hegemonic discourse produced through chronicles, ritual, etiquette, and architecture. All of Bali's nobles asserted and expressed their claims to authority in terms of this discourse, which was most fully elaborated for and totalized in Klungkung. This is not to say that there may not have been counterhegemonic discourses operating in precolonial Bali. No doubt there were. But without clearly delineating the primary discourse of power and identifying the institutions and practices through which it was promulgated, it is impossible to recognize them. Because scholars take the received colonial wisdom about Klungkung for granted, recent claims about Balinese kingship strike me as simplistic. These contrast a cultural model, exemplified by Klungkung and purportedly characterized by "Indic" or "divine" kings, with the secular and military *realpolitik* of other realms, which disputed or ignored Klungkung's claim to domination (e.g., Boon 1977; Guermonprez 1985, 1989; Schulte Nordholt 1988). Accounts of "divine" kingship, however, usually repeat stereotypes that have, on inspection, very little to do with Balinese practices or representations. Moreover, discourses of power constructed in and around Klungkung are much more complex than conventional representations of Klungkung assume, and they include the military motifs commonly attributed to other and "later" kingships. Finally, to the extent that challenges to Klungkung were made in the language of Klungkung hegemony, they do not escape it but show themselves, ultimately, to be subsumed by it.

This hegemony is precisely what made Klungkung's defeat culturally consequential. As the culmination of a colonial encounter that began in 1817, it marked the turning point between the time "when the world was steady"—when the production and reproduction of Balinese society and culture centered on the enunciative capacity of its kings—and the Dutch, Japanese, and "modern" eras that followed, during which former hegemonies were challenged as Bali was drawn into more global relationships of power. Small wonder, then, that a rich oral tradition developed in Klungkung concerning the relation between Klungkung's rulers and the colonial government, a discourse that weighted past events with cultural content. The puputan was less the object of this discourse than its grounds, for with the conquest Klungkung lost the ability to frame the world.

VISIBILITY AND INVISIBILITY

The "invisible realms" of my title originally referred to the panoply of divinities, demons, and spirits that play a major role in the discourse of history making in Klungkung. In writing about Klungkung and its history, however, I came to see that Klungkung itself was invisible. Therefore this book is in part an exploration of silences and silencings, of the various ways in which Klungkung has been constructed as an invisible realm: by colonial and Balinese practices of power and knowledge, and by colonial and postcolonial policies and politics.

Klungkung's invisibility to Euro-Americans has complex historical and cultural roots. I have already referred to the effects of its peripheralization, first by colonial policies and then by the postcolonial state. Klungkung's invisibility also stems, however, from the ascendancy of certain forms of knowledge in Euro-American discourse. It is impossible to understand the actions and words of Balinese without appreciating how much the invisible world is both taken for granted and intimately implicated in Balinese agencies. In a profound way, Balinese matter-of-factness about such things highlights the complicity between European representations and domination; scholars either dismiss such indigenous discourses as false consciousness or—and this is fundamentally the same thing—reinterpret them to show they are "really" about something we already know. Such certainties about the nature of the world make it singularly difficult to appreciate what Balinese are saying and doing.

Klungkung has also been invisible because the kind of power attributed to Klungkung rulers is not spoken of in explicit terms. If Klungkung's power was invisible to the Dutch in part because the Dutch were looking at and for different things, it was also invisible because Balinese speech and practices concerned with the invisible world are hedged by culturally patterned silences.

Visibility and invisibility, therefore, are tropes that refer to competing epistemologies and constructions of the real, as well as to things colonial officials did and did not see and to matters Balinese would and would not reveal. It is therefore important to attend to both the politics of Balinese magical discourses and the magic of Dutch political discourse—for the Dutch conjured reality so successfully that their representations still exert power on the way Bali and its past are known.

This book focuses on the conceptual and practical construction of power in and concerning the realm of Klungkung and with that region's historical transformation from paramount realm of precolonial Bali to a marginal corner of the Indonesian nation-state. Klungkung's rulers are generally asserted to have been the "nominal" overlords of precolonial Bali but to have had no "real" power. As described in the literature, Klungkung seems the paradigmatic "theater-state," its rulers immobile symbols. But at best this describes a colonial kingship, when the arenas in which kings could act were limited to ritual, and even here it is questionable, since that ritual was not merely an expressive activity.

I challenge assumptions about Klungkung's impotence in three ways. First, I historicize the stereotypes, showing under what conditions they developed. I demonstrate that such representations of Klungkung were historically created in conjunction with and as part of the process of colonial domination. Klungkung's ruler was initially described by a series of analogies as Bali's "emperor" or "spiritual overlord," or by reference to Central Javanese rulers. Later colonial discourse focused less overtly on the nature of his power and more upon its extent, but the implicit model for evaluating this was the hierarchical structure of the colonial civil service. It was only around 1900 that what is now taken for granted became authoritative, but by then, after sixty years of colonial interventions, Klungkung hegemony had been seriously challenged, and the Dutch, embarked upon a new phase of imperial expansion, regarded indigenous authority with contempt.

Second, I counterpoise colonial discourses with Balinese ones, which provide a different perspective on the nature and meaning of power, and on the encounter between Klungkung's kings and imperial agents. In this way I seek to denaturalize colonial mythologies. In Bali power is acquired by producing or reproducing connections with the invisible world of spirits. Certain places and objects (especially keris) are imbued with spiritual energies, and the practices of royal power centered around such objects (acquired from superior agents, including divinities) and places (marked by shrines). It is therefore significant that contemporary Klungkung is described by its inhabitants as a place filled with spirits, and that accounts of Klungkung's rulers associate them with particular objects, temples, and divinities.

Third, both Dutch and scholarly claims about Klungkung's impotence are based upon a superficial understanding of the nature of power and agency and upon an inadequate analysis of the evidence. The forms power took in Bali were not readily recognizable to Europeans, for they involved neither the contractual relations presupposed by the juridical ideologies that dominated European political theory, nor the surveillance that increasingly informed the disciplinary practices of European state institutions (Foucault 1979 and 1980).

The emphasis in part 1 is on knowledge and its production. I begin undermining stereotypes of precolonial Klungkung by tracing a genealogy of the colonial categories used to discuss Klungkung and its power (chapter 2) and then presenting some examples of contemporary Klungkung discourses and practices, which introduce a different perspective on power (chapter 3). After a discussion of Balinese and Dutch practices of making history, I end part 1 with a look at specific constructions of the power of the rulers of Klungkung in the *Babad Dalem* (chapter 5). In part 2, I trace two histories of the colonial encounter between the Netherlands Indies government and Klungkung's kings. The first of these histories, narrated in chapters 6 and 8, is largely structured by the reports of colonial officials, and it focuses upon social and political relations—in Balinese parlance, the "visible world." The second history represents Klungkung versions of the same events as expressions of relations between Klungkung's kings, the Dutch, and the invisible world of gods, spirits, and demons. Balinese narratives speak of those relationships in terms of named heirloom weapons. These objects were not merely "symbols"; the practices associated with such things produced (and reproduced) power, in articulating, for example, royal ideology with warfare, prosperity, and social constructions of gender.

COLLABORATION

That ethnographies and histories are inherently partial has been forcefully stated over the past decade (e.g., Clifford and Marcus 1986) but is still underappreciated. Specificity is especially important in writing about precolonial Bali, where political and epistemological authority were dispersed. The ways in which even the most codified forms of knowledge were created and reproduced mitigate against easy generalization. Only in New Order Indonesia have institutional structures appeared that enable the development of doctrines or orthodoxies.

In this book, therefore, I make no claims to represent "the Balinese point of view." Nor, given how complexly mediated knowledge is by culture and history, can I make any pretense to representing Bali as it "really" was or is. In any event, claims about objectivity usually reveal themselves over time to be ineluctably situated. Therefore, I want to position my account from the start. What I present is a picture of Klungkung based on observations and conversations from 1984 to 1992, mainly with aristocrats and Brahmanas in Klungkung. While discussions with persons from elsewhere in Bali, and with lower-status persons in Klungkung, suggest that this picture may not be limited to them, I leave it to others to demonstrate or refute this. I have attempted to report accurately what I was told in Klungkung and to rethink colonial sources from what I came to understand as a Klungkung perspective.

That the perspective I offer on the encounter between Klungkung and the

Dutch is an elite one is hardly surprising given the subject. As the persons most directly affected by the conquest were aristocrats, it is only to be expected that their descendants had the greatest interest in recalling events connected to it. Although the stories they told were also known to commoners, I encountered such persons largely by chance or by following out ties—of service or marriage—that began at the court. Thus even when I extended my investigations beyond elite circles, my contacts were mainly with persons who were part of the court network: former dependents, village heads, and temple priests.

Contributing to the elite perspective was the fact that my understanding of what I learned in Klungkung was mediated by two Balinese collaborators, a Brahmana couple from Gianyar named Ida Bagus Jagri and Dayu Alit.[4] Since they play a major role in my understanding of Balinese discourses, I want to introduce them here and explain our collaboration.

I met Ida Bagus Jagri and Dayu Alit in 1984 when I came to Bali to spend a year learning Balinese. Not yet having clearance to conduct research, I was concerned that living in Klungkung might compromise my relations with local administrators. I decided to live in Peliatan, in the foothills of Gianyar, which was both reasonably close to the university in Denpasar, where I was officially enrolled, and (unlike Denpasar) pleasantly rural. In making that decision, however, I did not realize that the Peliatan area was a center for a distinctive form of tourism. During the colonial era, expatriate artists had settled in the region and encouraged the development of new forms of painting, carving, and dancing, from which many Balinese still make their living. Both the historical precedents and present production attract many foreign connoisseurs and students of those arts. People naturally assumed I was one of them. As people were used to conversing with such visitors in Indonesian, this hampered my efforts to learn Balinese. For two discouraging months I took language lessons from local men who had instructed other researchers, but progress was slow, for the language of instruction was Indonesian and their emphasis was more on reading and writing than on speaking.

My luck turned, appropriately enough, on the day sacred to Saraswati, the goddess of learning, which is celebrated in Brahmana households. An American couple I had come to know had Brahmana friends and managed to include me in an invitation to their compound. And so, dressed in the *pakaian adat* (Indonesian for "traditional clothes," a category that contrasts such dress with "modern" skirts and pants) regarded as respectful of local mores, I entered for the first time a tiny yard, where I was greeted by a delicately boned, smiling man in his early forties. This was Ida Bagus Jagri. Delighted I could speak Indonesian, he immediately began to elucidate the symbols associated with the goddess. Such spontaneous exegesis overwhelmed me. When I explained that

I had come from America to learn Balinese, he invited me to visit whenever I wanted to practice speaking. I was there the next day, and the next, and every day thereafter.

His wife, Dayu Alit, at first could not understand my interest in them. From her point of view, they had little to offer. They were poor, possessing no rice land and living in pavilions with rickety woven bamboo walls and leaking thatched roofs. Ida Bagus Jagri made woodcarvings he mainly sold to a Chinese middleman, and she sewed patchwork bedspreads and clothing for export on a treadle-operated sewing machine. While Ida Bagus Jagri was un-usually interested in religion (as both felt was proper to his status as the head of a Brahmana household), he had no official role—as bureaucrat or teacher or priest—that gave him the authority to tell me things. And then too, as he himself said many times in those first months, in one of the few English phrases he knew, "I think alone."

That, of course, was what appealed to me. Despite the poster of Sukarno on the wall, he defiantly described himself as "old-fashioned," to emphasize that he had come to take the ways of his ancestors—as he knew these from texts and tales—very seriously. Yet while he was, as he said, a man who "liked to study," he could not manage to "be still" as students of the invisible world are supposed to be, and he was both outspoken and opinionated. While there were matters that he would not discuss (which he learned from texts that bore the warning "this must not be revealed"), usually he responded to my inter-minable questions and attempts at interpretation with enthusiasm.

His position in Peliatan was anomalous. Dayu Alit had grown up in the village, in a compound just across the road, and her mother was the village Brahmana priest. Ida Bagus Jagri, a kinsman, was from the more cosmopolitan town of Sanur in Badung, where they had lived virilocally, following Balinese practice, for several years after their marriage. At that time Ida Bagus Jagri traded antiques in Java and had little interest in religion, but this changed when he became mysteriously ill. They moved in with Dayu Alit's family so his priestly mother-in-law could take him to sacred springs for purifications, and decided to stay in Peliatan permanently when it became evident that re-turns to Sanur resulted in a relapse. It was only then that he had begun to study, and in doing so had healed himself. At the time I met them, they had been living in Peliatan at least twelve years.

Initially I hoped for nothing more of our friendship than a chance to speak and hear Balinese. They knew in a vague way I was there to "study," but not much else. But one day, after the Americans brought a parade of other friends over to meet them, Ida Bagus asked me sharply what all of us *wanted* in Bali anyway. When I protested that I could not speak for everyone, he said, "What do you want, then?" Sure I would alienate him, I talked about anthro-pology and my research, though at that moment both seemed of dubious value. He listened closely (not only, I would guess, to my words), then re-laxed and smiled. Later he told me that he had been testing me. A long time after, I asked what would have happened had I failed. He said he would have still been friendly, but he would not have told me things. As it was he told me much.

During my daily visits, Ida Bagus Jagri and his wife began to regard me as their responsibility. They told me how sorry they felt for me, being so far from home and on my own, and it was not long before they hesitantly invited me to move in. I too hesitated but decided to accept. And with that I began to become—to the astonishment of us all—a member of the family.

By then the government had approved my research, and I was anxious to make contacts in Klungkung. To my surprise, they offered help. Ida Bagus Jagri claimed that he had family in Klungkung, very important people. And so he did—for the subclan to which they belonged had its core in the Klung-kung village of Kamasan; indeed, this turned out to be the priestly house (*geria*) that had traditionally performed royal rituals. In their company, I went to Klungkung and met several Brahmana priests, most important among them Pedanda Gedé Kenitén of Dawan, *bagawanta* (court priest) of Klungkung's last king.

My Balinese, however, was not yet fluent enough for me to handle in-terviews. Ida Bagus Jagri and Dayu Alit had instructed me in refined or "high" Balinese (the polite form of the language, used to address or refer to priests, aristocrats, and other persons of status)—in fact, to help me achieve facility, everyone in the household good-humoredly used high Balinese—but as a consequence I understood little ordinary Balinese, which such people often spoke back to me. And Klungkung speech patterns seemed at least twice as fast as those in Gianyar and Badung. So Ida Bagus Jagri and Dayu Alit spoke for me when I found myself at a loss, while I ran my tape recorder so I could go over what had been said, slowly and with a dictionary, at my leisure. Since only if they understood what I wanted to know could they tell whether or not my questions had been answered, they became increasingly involved in my research. And when I would go over my tapes and wonder how from those words they had come up with that interpretation, they patiently did their best to explain to me contexts and connotations.

During this period I met Ratu Dalem Pemayun,[5] eldest son of Klungkung's last king, who invited me to stay in his courtyard in the east wing of the Puri Agung, the core-line royal compound (*puri* is generally translated as "palace"). When I made the move to Klungkung, my Peliatan family decided that Dayu Alit should come with me, at least for a while, to continue to help and to keep me company. But I missed my long philosophical discussions with Ida Bagus Jagri, and he was not comfortable having us "ask for rice" at the puri, accepting hospitality he could not repay. Finally we reached an agreement: if

I were willing to support the family in Peliatan and if we could find a place to set up a temporary household in Klungkung, they would help me with my research full-time. We moved into an empty house in a corner of a Brahmana priest's compound in Banjar Sengguan, an area that reminded Ida Bagus Jagri of his neighborhood in Sanur because everyone on the street was a kinsman to everyone else. They were even, it turned out, his kinsmen, members of the same subclan.

Both Dayu Alit and Ida Bagus Jagri played an active role in the research. Dayu Alit accompanied me all over Klungkung. Warm and outgoing, she delighted the older men and women we met with her teasing, and I encouraged her to do most of the talking even after I could understand people's answers by myself. Ida Bagus Jagri transcribed interviews, copied texts that we borrowed, and joined us at rituals or when he felt his expertise and/or status as a male might be useful—on interviews with high priests, for example, or with men who, like himself, "studied."[6] Since both were familiar with what people told me, I could check my impressions, ask about points I found puzzling, fill in contexts, and explore subtleties and nuances of interpretation. Although Dayu Alit deferred to her husband when he claimed she was wrong (his authority was based partly on gender, partly on his studies), she had strong opinions of her own, and the disparities only made matters more interesting.

The impression that Dayu Alit and Ida Bagus Jagri (and, by partial extension, I) made upon people in Klungkung was based upon a number of social facts. First of all, they were Brahmanas, members of the highest, priestly "caste."[7] Moreover, they were Brahmanas of the Kenitén subclan, which had close connections to Klungkung's court.[8] Finally, although they lived in Peliatan, they regarded themselves (and described themselves) as being "from" Sanur, a place with a reputation throughout Bali for magic.

That they were Brahmana Kenitén was mainly relevant to royal and priestly informants, who often remarked that "Kenitén" was really *kanataan,* from the root *nata* (king), and noted the close connection between Brahmana Kenitén and the court. Some explained this by reference to the Kenitén apical ancestress, a princess from Blambangan who was kin to Klungkung's rulers (see Rubinstein 1991). Members of the royal family also mentioned a vow an early king had made to always "remember" the Brahmana Kenitén—that is, have them perform royal rituals—as a reward for an especially admirable display of ritual power by the first Kenitén priest. For commoners, it was the fact that they were Brahmanas that mattered, since it invested interactions with a degree of formality. Their status encouraged some to talk about the invisible world, something Brahmanas are supposed to know about; on the other hand, for the same reason, others were more reticent in their presence. Somewhat more difficult to specify was the impact of their Sanur origins. When my friends so identified themselves, people would often laugh knowingly and say, "Well, Sanur, everyone there is said to be powerful."

Our different kinds of outsideness were also important. Had I been alone I would have heard only a fraction of what I did. When people directed remarks to me they tended to take shortcuts, for there were too many things that foreigners were not expected to understand. Then too, some Balinese react to mass tourism by repeating the stereotypes through which Bali is marketed. As Balinese, Ida Bagus Jagri and Dayu Alit could be expected to understand things, all the more as they were Brahmanas; but, not being from Klungkung, they were sufficiently outsiders that matters specific to Klungkung needed to be spelled out. Such "ethno-ethnography" is in fact an indigenous form of discourse, even between Balinese from different villages. Even those people who would have talked openly to me without them (for certain people very much wanted what they had to say recorded, and others thought that as a foreigner I could be objective) could take more enjoyment in telling me things knowing that there was a greater chance that I would be able to appreciate the nuances given such evidence of my intimacy with matters Balinese. At the same time, without me, Ida Bagus Jagri and Dayu Alit would have just been ordinary people, to whom there would have been no reason to speak of such things; my presence not only provided the occasion but lent them prestige.

That Dayu Alit and I were both women no doubt also affected what I was told. It made it easier to talk to other women, and women often knew more stories and were more comfortable telling them. Several of the most eloquent people I met were elderly women whose fathers had been politically prominent in precolonial Klungkung. Strongly attached to them, they had listened attentively to their stories and reminiscences and had a much greater interest in family history than their husbands, brothers, and sons. They were proud of their knowledge and concerned that it be passed on. But in the context of a national culture that valued "modernity" they were perceived as "old-fashioned" (*kolot*, an Indonesian word and concept) and credulous. To them I represented a way of both transmitting what they knew to their descendants and validating its worth.

An additional advantage to having Dayu Alit and Ida Bagus Jagri as my "patrons" was that it provided a certain distance from the royal clan itself, which had its own internal politics. For example, through Ratu Dalem Pemayun I had been introduced to Cokorda Isteri Agung of Puri Anyar, who became another good friend, and she was the one who introduced us to members of other branch-line houses. There were historical roots to our relationship, for since the end of the nineteenth century Puri Anyar has played the major role in mediating between Klungkung's royal house and foreigners. It was in Puri Anyar that colonial officials were lodged in the years just prior to conquest, and a prince of that house was the king's envoy to the Dutch. During the colonial era, Cokorda Anom, Cokorda Isteri Agung's own grandfather, was considered the family expert on the royal house, and in that capacity he was consulted by anthropologists such as Roeloef Goris and Jane Belo. (This same Cokorda Anom copied the manuscript of the *Babad Dalem* now treated as authoritative by the core line, as well as the text for Geria Pidada I use as the basis for the analysis in chapter 5.) More recently still, other foreign researchers had stayed with Cokorda Isteri Agung and her family. Puri Anyar's role in Klungkung history was not limited to contacts with foreigners, however. Its rise to prominence in the nineteenth century had occasioned enmities that rankled still. Often, as Dayu Alit and I came to know better the people to whom Cokorda Isteri Agung had originally introduced us, they made certain we heard of these, so that I would not take as truth what they assumed I was being told there.

There were, of course, others in Klungkung with whom I conferred as well. One forum for especially stimulating discussions arose from an arrangement with other aims entirely. Many Balinese texts are written in a mixture of Balinese and a literary language called Kawi. Gusti Sobo, one of Klungkung's experts on Kawi, was an affine of my landlord and lived around the corner. He agreed to come by in the evenings to help me with the language. But Ida Bagus Jagri was also interested in learning Kawi, and Ida Bagus Gedé Aji, another neighbor, came to listen in, and I soon found myself part of a spontaneous, informal Balinese reading/translation club (see Zurbuchen 1987). Indeed, from the start Gusti Sobo took the practices of such clubs as a model of how to proceed. He—or occasionally Ida Bagus Jagri—would recite a line of text in Kawi and then provide a Balinese gloss. Periodically we would stop to discuss obscure points or drink coffee, which often led to more general conversation about America and Bali, reminiscences about Klungkung in earlier days, and further elaborations and comments upon what I had heard from others, in which my neighbors were keenly interested.

My collaboration with Ida Bagus Jagri and Dayu Alit, however, did not end with fieldwork. Most of this book was written and rewritten at their home on return visits to Bali, and during that time I frequently discussed what I had read in colonial archives with them, especially with Dayu Alit. Their reactions to and interpretations of what colonial officials reported about the words and acts of nineteenth-century Balinese illuminated past events in unexpected ways, while rendering the documents as strange to me as they were to them.

However much my interpretations originated in dialogue, the selection of themes and tropes and the emplotment of these as history are clearly my own. As ballast to my own interpretive voice, I cite liberally and extensively from my sources: oral accounts from Klungkung and the writings of Dutch colonial officials. I have tried to translate and edit Balinese narratives so that they may be intelligible yet still retain some flavor of the original.

I should note that my understanding was generated not only by certain kinds of talk but by specific genres of text. Other Balinese texts concerned with power and rule, such as moral tracts or texts on temples, might offer a different perspective than *babad* and were equally relevant to the self-conceptions of nineteenth-century rulers.[9] In addition, my Dutch sources consisted largely of official reports and accounts of Bali. A different side of colonial discourse is found in gossip, fiction, traveler's tales, magazines, and the rumors reported by colonial newspapers (Taylor 1983), which include Dutch fantasies about the magic of indigenous people, often in a nightmare version of the invisible world (Wiener 1993). The Dutch certainly deserve more attention, particularly given that the burgeoning literature on colonial discourse and Orientalism has focused entirely on "Anglo-French imperial formations" (e.g., Said 1979; Inden 1990); there are grounds for thinking that Dutch relations of power/knowledge differed in interesting ways (Day 1986; Wiener 1994). My concern here, however, is narrower: to show how certain images of Klungkung were created and to challenge their hegemony.

That Klungkung stories about the conquest led back to the 1840s is only fitting. For it was in that decade that the colonial government first began to take an active interest in Klungkung, and it was in that period that perduring images of Bali began to emerge from the pens of Orientalists. Foreigners have produced images of Bali without end ever since. It seems only just that these stories reveal something of what Balinese made of the foreigners.

By juxtaposing postcolonial Balinese narratives with colonial Dutch ones, I hope to explode the power of colonial discourse, with its bias toward a historically particular form of rationality. Regarding it as presumptuous to assume Euro-American discourse has the capacity to clarify all modes of being in the world, my concern is less with explaining these stories than with exploring the way they are constructed—the distinctions, categories, and experiences out of which they are built and their intertextual relations. At the very least such narratives show that there is more than one way of experiencing the world.

TWO

Colonial Representations
of Klungkung

Tucked into the southeast corner of the island of Bali, tiny Klungkung is awash with paradoxes. According to prevailing ideas about Balinese political history, until the seventeenth century Bali consisted of a single kingdom, centered in Gélgél. When Gélgél collapsed, the polity dissolved into multiple, competing, warring kingdoms, of which Klungkung, whose ruler was heir to the Gélgél kings, was only one. As described in the literature, Klungkung was in fact the smallest of the nine principalities making up precolonial Bali, the others being Badung, Tabanan, Karangasem, Gianyar, Mengwi, Buléléng, Jembrana, and Bangli (see fig. 1). The ruler of Klungkung, whose title was Déwa Agung (literally, Great God), is acknowledged to have been the highest ranking and most respected. But this rank has been said to have had nothing to do with actual political power, and the respect accorded to Klungkung was, so it is claimed, purely formal.

That this image seems so natural to modern scholars and even to their Balinese informants may be due to the fact that it conformed to twentieth-century experience. The colonial administration gave this understanding of Balinese political structure institutional reality: in 1938 the Dutch created a federation of Balinese rulers, called by the colonial government the Asta Negara (Eight Countries).[1] Each of these rulers had a vote in a "council of rajas," and they differed from one another mainly in their titles, which were established by colonial fiat. This sociopolitical structure lasted into the early years of the Republican period, and under the postcolonial Indonesian state Bali is still divided into "eight countries"—now called *kabupaten* rather than *negara*. But was the relationship between cultural forms and social institutions quite so attenuated in the days before the Dutch were masters of Balinese ceremonial?

To question Klungkung's place in precolonial Bali nearly a century after the colonial conquest raises difficulties. The problem is that precolonial Bali can only be known through representations, and representations are always culturally and historically mediated. Twentieth-century scholars tell us that the Déwa Agung was a figurehead, given status and deference, but without power. The same claims (in almost the same words) are repeated in one account after another. That this vision of Klungkung's authority is so common

22

Figure 1. Map of Bali.

might be good reason to balk at challenging it. The weight of scholarly tradition is on its side. And this tradition has its origins in the opinions and
evaluations of persons who had direct experience of precolonial Bali. But the
question is whether the scholarly reproduction of such images is anything
more than a hall of mirrors, each faithfully reflecting a previous one back to
an original that is presumed to provide an undistorted picture of reality. At
the basis of such scholarly praxis is the familiar positivist notion that knowledge is an unmediated mirror of nature.

    Yet two decades of scholarly critique show that to treat colonial represen-
tations as simple descriptions is untenable (see especially Asad 1973; Guha
1983; Inden 1990; and Said 1979). In the unfamiliarity of their modes of
political praxis, their resistance to colonial projects, and their rejection of
European superiority Klungkung's rulers posed a problem for colonial administrators, a problem at once theoretical and practical. What is reflected in the
scholarly mirror is only one of a number of rather different images produced
by administrators to resolve that problem at various points in time.

In the precolonial era, colonial interpretations of Klungkung's power were highly unstable, oscillating back and forth between the two poles of a pair of oppositions. One pair concerned the nature of Klungkung's power; the other its extent. Some officials regarded Klungkung's ruler as Bali's emperor, a supreme political authority to whom all others were (at least ideally) subordinate. Other officials, however, characterized the Déwa Agung as Bali's "spiritual overlord," and even a kind of high priest, commanding deference by virtue of his ritual preeminence. But whatever might have been the source or nature of Klungkung's claims to overlordship, the more immediate issue for the colonial government was the success of its rulers in achieving it. Here too verdicts diverged. At various times, Klungkung's power was asserted to be mere empty pretension; Bali's other rulers, so it was said, went their own way without any regard for the Déwa Agung, however much he may have exercised domination at some distant point in the past. On other occasions, officials claimed that he had a great influence on the actions and attitudes of other Balinese princes: the Dutch found this highly alarming when he took a position contrary to their own interests; at other moments still they tried to exploit this influence, especially in attempting to convince recalcitrant Balinese lords to accept new and unpalatable decrees.

The contradictory nature of such descriptions suggests the inadequacy of European categories to encompass Balinese realities. This is hardly surprising, since the categories available to Dutch officials came, of course, from their own past experiences and cultural institutions. No one has ever seriously questioned, however, whether the routines and rhetorics that signaled relations of power and dependency to nineteenth-century Dutchmen and those relevant to nineteenth-century Balinese were in any sense commensurate. Instead, Dutch images of an imperfectly understood reality at particular moments in its history have generally been accepted as simple and transparent mirrors of that reality rather than the complex cultural constructions they really are.

The question that must be asked is what it means to say that Klungkung's authority was nominal. Who says this? On what grounds?

To address these issues in the depth that they deserve would take us too far afield. However, a sufficient challenge to the transparency of the received opinion can be offered by a glance at a number of documents, in which officials explicitly or implicitly presented their superiors with a reading of the nature of Klungkung's authority in Balinese political life.

Taken "archaeologically" (to borrow Foucault's metaphor) these accounts reveal layered strata of colonial views of Klungkung. The earliest strata are closest to Balinese representations; they are in fact prefiltered through Balinese eyes, derived secondhand. The Klungkung they present is paradoxical, but in a way congenial to Balinese understandings of power.

The epistemological soil changes hue with Huskus Koopman, who in 1840 was one of the first imperial agents to meet the Déwa Agung face to face. With Huskus Koopman a new discourse begins, marked by efforts to translate the Déwa Agung's position into terms meaningful to the colonial authorities. But these efforts introduce analytical distinctions foreign to Balinese practice. The ensuing "contradictions" become the central problem about Klungkung in nineteenth-century Dutch eyes: Does the Déwa Agung exercise political power or merely spiritual authority? Is he a priest, a god? Was he powerful once but no longer?

For the rest of the century, these same questions are reiterated and reproduced, despite a succession in Klungkung and a frequent turnover of colonial bureaucrats. But as Balinese territories come under the authority of the colonial state, Dutch interest shifts from a concern with the kind of power the Déwa Agung has to an interest in how much power he wields. About this there is equally little consensus until their colonial presence creates such disturbances in Balinese affairs that they are able to resolve the enigmas, by restructuring the conditions of Balinese praxis. And so we come to the upper layers of the test pit, which extend all the way to the surface of the present where scholars are busy creating new layers. These exhibit little doubt about Klungkung's rulers: they were impotent.

OVERVIEW OF NINETEENTH-CENTURY BALINESE-DUTCH RELATIONS

The story begins in the second decade of the nineteenth century. Although contacts between Balinese and Europeans date back to the very first Dutch voyages of exploration in the archipelago, it was not until 1817 that the Dutch made their first real efforts to comprehend Balinese political relations. During the seventeenth and eighteenth centuries, references to Bali appear only sporadically in the registers of the Dutch East India Company (Vereenigde Oost-Indische Companie, or VOC). Compared to elsewhere in the archipelago, Bali was of little commercial or strategic importance to the Company's attempts to monopolize the spice trade or to produce goods such as sugar and coffee for European markets. Bali's rulers certainly purchased Indian textiles and other luxury goods from the Company, but there were no anchorages in Bali suitable for large ships. As far as the Company was concerned, the most valuable product Bali's rulers had to offer was people; there was a great demand in Batavia for Balinese slaves, who were known as hard workers, desirable concubines, and fearless soldiers. The Company's policies radically altered local political economies, and Bali was undoubtedly affected—Bali may have played more of a role in the Asia trade prior to the Company's monopoly, for example, and as Company control spread east from Batavia the Dutch checked Balinese interests in East Java—but apart from various attempts to enlist one another in temporary military alliances, Company merchants and Balinese rulers had little to do with one another.

Bali came to the attention of the Dutch largely as a result of nineteenth-century European conflicts. At the turn of the eighteenth century, events in France—first the Revolution, then Napoleon's rise to power—were shaking up European political institutions and cultural certainties. In 1795 revolutionary French troops invaded the Netherlands and the Dutch established a Batavian Republic. Not long after, a Dutch colonial empire was established when the Republic took over the debts and assets of the bankrupt VOC, but the Dutch had more immediate concerns than overseas colonies. It was only after Napoleon established his brother as ruler of the Netherlands that a Governor General was finally dispatched to Java, to begin administering the Indies on behalf of the Dutch government.

Since Great Britain and France were enemies, having the Indies come under the French sphere of interest worried British merchants. Arguing that a French presence along the sea route between India and Australia could jeopardize trade, the British East India Company sent troops to occupy Java. Sir Thomas Stamford Raffles was dispatched from Calcutta to serve as Lieutenant Governor.

Raffles's five years in Java were to have important consequences both for European representations of Balinese culture and society and for later colonial policies. Raffles brought with him from India an interest in ancient Hindu-Buddhist culture. He was an enthusiastic Orientalist who launched investigations into Javanese culture and history and who decided that Bali preserved something of the formerly glorious Javanese past. Raffles's relations with Bali were by no means purely scholarly; there were clashes between the British and the ruler of North Bali in 1814.

But the more important effect of Raffles on Bali's history was an indirect result of his growing conviction of the strategic importance of the archipelago to British interests. He was grievously disappointed when, after Napoleon's defeat and the establishment of the Kingdom of the Netherlands, the British government gave Java back to the Netherlands. But he was able to achieve a permanent British presence in the region when, as Lieutenant Governor of the British-controlled region of Benkulen in Sumatra, he managed in 1819 to acquire a small island just off the Malay coast called Singapore. In a treaty signed between the British and the Dutch in 1824, Britain exchanged its archipelago possessions, including Benkulen, for Dutch territories on the mainland, which included Malacca. Singapore was all that remained of Raffles's dreams of British hegemony in the Indies, but it was more than enough to concern the Dutch. Not only did Singapore quickly become important to archipelago trade, threatening to supplant the Dutch ports of Batavia and

Surabaya, but it provided a base from which the Dutch feared the British might expand into unclaimed portions of the archipelago.

In 1817, shortly after the Dutch regained Java from the British, they sent an envoy to Bali to learn more about the island. But the British interregnum, particularly the negative effect of Raffles's policies on the lucrative slave trade (Schulte Nordholt 1981:20), had not left Bali's rulers well disposed toward Europeans, and the Dutch envoy, van den Broek, was given a cool reception.

It was less as a result of this inhospitable encounter than due to the fact Bali was peripheral to colonial concerns that little further transpired for another decade. The major consideration of the Netherlands government at this time was the profitability of those regions that were already Dutch possessions. Colonial policies led, however, to conflicts with indigenous populations in West Sumatra, South Sulawesi, and especially Central Java, where a prince named Diponegoro led a rebellion against them. It was precisely these wars that led the Netherlands Indies government to make its next overtures to Bali's rulers, for the Dutch needed soldiers to fight in their army. In 1827 Pangeran Said Hassan, a Javanese prince, was sent to Bali to discuss the possibility of establishing an agent there to negotiate recruitments. The princes of Badung were amenable, and the agent, Pierre Dubois, remained in Kuta under their patronage from 1828 to 1831. Since the "recruits" were criminals, debtors, and prisoners of war, who had little say in the matter, and the princes who provided them were paid, in essence this was a revival of the slave trade (Schulte Nordholt 1981).

As long as the colonial government's relations with Bali were largely commercial, there was little reason to have anything to do with Klungkung and its ruler. Lacking an important harbor, Klungkung was at this time relatively isolated from European contact. Boats did dock at its port at Kusamba, but trade there was insignificant when compared to Singaraja in Buléléng, or Kuta in Badung. It was through the latter port in particular that the Dutch first came to know Balinese—and from the former that they extended their knowledge until Bali's final conquest.

In the mid-1830s, however, the colonial government's interest in Bali began to take on political overtones. An Englishman, George King, was managing trade on behalf of one of the Balinese rulers on the island of Lombok. (Lombok had been conquered at the end of the eighteenth century by Karangasem; the princes on Lombok were kinsmen of the prince of Karangasem). In the office of the Ministry of Colonies this aroused familiar concerns about British intentions; merchants were all too often followed by consulates and armies. King's activities might bode ill for Dutch interests in the archipelago, especially after King's patron succeeded in eliminating his rivals. Moreover, both Bali and Lombok, which at this point were producing large surpluses of rice, were engaged in a lively trade with Singapore, from which the rice was shipped to China. It was time to take a more active interest in Java's nearest neighbor.

The first overtures made by the colonial government were commercial. Granpré Molière, the Surabaya agent of the Netherlands Trading Society (Nederlands Handels Maatschappij), was dispatched to Bali in 1838 to discover if Bali's rulers would be amenable to having a factory on the island. The response was favorable, and an agent was established in Kuta the following year. Not long after, the government sent an envoy, J. H. Huskus Koopman, to negotiate treaties by which Bali's rulers would formally acknowledge the sovereignty of the Netherlands Indies government over the island, thus forestalling any future moves by the British. In the several years it took Huskus Koopman to succeed in persuading Balinese rulers—including the ruler of Klungkung—to sign such documents, an additional clause had been added, abolishing a custom that the colonial government referred to as the "plundering" of ships wrecked on the reefs off Bali's coast. By 1843 the Dutch thought they had finally achieved a satisfactory agreement with Bali's and Lombok's rulers.

Almost immediately, however, differences between the government and Bali's rulers regarding the interpretation of their relationship led to conflict. In 1846 the colonial government organized the First Bali Expedition, to "punish" the ruler of Buléléng in North Bali for continual violations of their treaty. The Dutch were victorious, but he ignored his promises to them as soon they withdrew their forces. A second expedition in 1848 was also aimed at Klungkung and Karangasem (ruled by Buléléng's kinsman and ally), but the colonial army got no farther than Buléléng before retreating in chaos. The following year yet a third expedition was launched. This time, both Buléléng and Karangasem were conquered. The Dutch also attacked Klungkung, but the engagement ended in a draw, and both sides agreed to make peace. New treaties signed in 1849 authorized regular diplomatic relationships between the colonial government and the Balinese.

Although the Dutch did not initially administer the territories they had conquered themselves, within a few years they had stationed a controleur, or district officer—P. L. van Bloemen Waanders—in North Bali. In addition to his administrative duties in Buléléng, he also made regular visits to the courts south of the mountains. Van Bloemen Waanders was soon promoted to Assistant Resident, and other Europeans—lower-ranking officials, journalists, missionaries, scholars—settled in the north as well. The Dutch began by seeking an epistemic mastery over South Bali; political domination followed later.

Despite the establishment of a Residency in Buléléng in 1882, Bali and regions like it remained peripheral to politicians in The Hague for most of the nineteenth century. The major debate in Netherlands Indies colonial policy concerned whether or not the government should promote free enterprise in its colonial possessions. Those in favor (known as the liberals) also tended to urge reforms of indigenous legal, political, and economic institutions to bring them into conformity with European values, including those of rational administration and good business; their opponents (the conservatives) argued for the preservation of indigenous practices (van Niel 1963). At first the question was which would bring greater profit to the Netherlands; later, which would be more beneficial to the welfare of the natives. These were not necessarily regarded as separate issues: the capitalists, who hoped at first to produce export crops and later sought markets for manufactured goods, tended to ally themselves with those promoting intervention on humanitarian grounds. As this group increasingly came to dominate public opinion, the government began to intercede in the affairs of indigenous states that offered no obvious commercial benefits. By the end of the first decade of the twentieth century, the entire archipelago was in Dutch hands.

While it took the Netherlands Indies fifty years to annex South Bali, the colonial presence in the north played a crucial part in a concatenation of conflicts among the southern realms, as well as in their resolution. It was these conflicts that indirectly led to events the colonial government used to justify the conquest of Lombok in 1894, which brought Karangasem's ruler under the wing of the Netherlands Indies empire as a Viceroy (*Stedehouder*) of the government. The same conflicts led Gianyar to come voluntarily under colonial rule as a second Viceroy soon after. Bangli's ruler achieved the same status in 1908, after the Dutch had conquered the three remaining realms of Badung, Tabanan, and—last of all—Klungkung.

FIRST GLIMPSES OF KLUNGKUNG

The first description of Klungkung comes from van den Broek, the first envoy to visit the island. Discussing each of the Balinese dominions in turn, he begins his account of Klungkung as follows:

> The principality Kalonkong, sufficiently in the center of the island, is the smallest and least populated of all. With a population of only 75 to 80,000 souls, it cannot muster more than 14–15,000 able-bodied men; but the royal house is of the oldest and most respected origins, and, so I believe, was the very first ruling house after the annihilation of the original inhabitants of Bali, called Raxassas (monsters) (van den Broek 1835:181).

Van den Broek then describes some of the ways in which respect toward Klungkung was manifested:

> The King is named Dewa-agong, that is to say great God or highest Divinity; all the other Princes have an unlimited and idolatrous reverence

for that of Kalonkong, and style him, in speaking as well as in their correspondence, "father," although the present Sovereign is an insignificant youth who, when I was on Bali, had only reached the age of eighteen years. Also he never has to fear any invasion in his land, and is never involved in wars unless it be that he himself chooses one or another party, in which case the opposing party does not hesitate to act defensively against him (1835:181–82).

Van den Broek's description of Klungkung immediately locates it at the center of a paradox: Klungkung is at once an empty and tiny land, yet its ruler is the most respected on the island, viewed with "an unlimited and idolatrous reverence," despite his years. With somewhat less confidence (". . . so I believe . . ."), van den Broek traces the prestige of Klungkung's royal house to a piece of legendary history, which clearly had been communicated to him by a Balinese. But it is unlikely that he heard the legend in Klungkung itself, as there is reason to think he never actually visited that realm.

During his short sojourn on the island, van den Broek lived in Badung, venturing forth from there to some of the neighboring realms. He managed to get as far as Gianyar (he describes a strenuous journey by horseback) and Mengwi (where he spent, he claims, one of the unhappiest days of his life), and his ship stopped in Jembrana and passed Buléléng on its way from East Java. It is less clear whether he actually journeyed to any of the other realms, although he may have sent subordinates to collect information.

If I linger on the matter of an actual visit it is because of the claim he makes that Klungkung is "at the center of the island." This it is not; at least not geographically. A further description—he comments that the land in Klungkung is not especially fertile, since it is "stony and hilly"—reiterates the point, as if Klungkung were indeed located in the central mountainous regions. Accounts by Dutchmen who later journeyed to Klungkung, on the contrary, describe a capital ringed by rice fields (van Bloemen Waanders 1870; van Kol 1914). Van den Broek's statement about Klungkung's centrality, therefore, probably stemmed from a Balinese assertion rather than a Dutch observation.

As described by van den Broek, Klungkung's political relations with the rest of Bali were enveloped in an idiom of kinship and religion, in both of which an ideal hierarchy manifested itself: in comparison to other rulers the Déwa Agung was a "father" and the "highest divinity." Again these characterizations are clearly Balinese in origin, though the author leaves unexamined the implications of such paternity and divinity. His claim that Klungkung's ruler may initiate war, but is never directly challenged by his underlings, was another important statement concerning Balinese hierarchy.

Somewhat later, van den Broek returns to discuss the origin of the Balinese princes, which he has already suggested was closely tied to the esteem in which the ruler of Klungkung was held. He notes that the population of Bali originally came from Java. Prior to that,

> it appears that . . . Bali was inhabited by a savage and wild people, who had the custom of devouring prisoners of war. . . . These original inhabitants are still seen portrayed in stone by the Balinese of the present day, in their shadow puppets (*wayangs*) as well as in the palaces of the Princes and in the inner squares of the temples, with tigers' heads and very large protruding teeth, and bear the name of Raxassas.
>
> The Monarchs and Priests relate, that these man-eaters were the original inhabitants of Bali; that they really had extraordinarily large teeth, and devoured a man with the same ease as a tiger; . . . that the Diwas, a sort of God, finally offended by them, had made war on them and entirely destroyed them, whereupon they had brought forth the Balinese Kings and Priests; and it is on these grounds, that both of these castes are fancied as being of divine descent, which is not imbued with the least doubt by the common Balinese. If the Kings really believe this is a question which I don't dare decide; but it is certain that it advances their political interest at the least to accept the appearance thereof, and to reinforce their subjects in this belief (1835:185–86).

As we will see later, this story establishes a set of distinctions (ferocious, fanged monsters versus divinities; indigenes versus foreigners) and conjunctions (between princes, priests, and divinities) through which Klungkung's power was articulated. But while dutifully reporting it, van den Broek registers his skepticism, seeing in such claims mainly an ideology for domination.

A similar cynicism regarding Klungkung in particular is expressed some thirteen years later by Pierre Dubois, the commercial agent for the Netherlands Indies:

> As the prince of *Klonkong* exercised on earth . . . charitable works . . . toward his subjects, the Brahmanas decided in regard to him to confer the title of *Dewa*, which in a single word signifies: *terrestrial prince, as perfect, wise and virtuous as a God*. This is then indeed a *compliment*, devised to flatter, and perhaps also for political reasons: for each time that one addressed this title to the prince of Klungkung, one recalled to him his duty to be clement, good, charitable.[2]

Like van den Broek, Dubois suggests that the Balinese have a theory of "divine kingship," at least in regard to Klungkung, the ruler of which is encouraged to act like a god. However, Dubois's view of the behavior expected from gods colors his description, painting the portrait of Klungkung's "divine king" with a decidedly European and Christian palette.

On the whole Dubois's description of Klungkung in 1830 is strikingly similar to, if more elaborate than, van den Broek's:

The town of *Klongkong* . . . lies on a mountain which overlooks all of the other dwelling places on the island.[3]

The *Nateeng*[4] *Willa Tika* [a literary name for Majapahit], having finally conquered *Balie*, chose, in order to establish there the seat of his new empire, the summit of a mountain situated in the east part of the island, near, but to the west, and only halfway up, *Mount Agong*, named *Besoeké*, and there he built the capital town of *Klonkong*. The *Brahmanas* settled on a hump of the supreme mountain a little less [illegible] than Mount Besoeké; and the captains of the armies were disseminated in the plain.[5]

As with van den Broek, this description suggests that despite his lengthy stay on the island Dubois never visited Klungkung himself.[6] Besakih is a village, not a mountain, but it is indeed about halfway up the slopes of Mount Agung. It is famous as the location of the most important temple in Bali, Pura Besakih, a temple that had intimate links with the power of the Déwa Agung. But the town of Klungkung where the Déwa Agung resided is at a considerable distance from the temple and is much closer to the sea than it is to the summit of Agung—all of which only serves to make this thoroughly mistaken description even more interesting. For if Dubois is not reporting an empirical fact, he is faithfully recording a social one: Klungkung's "elevation," which has much to do with the temple of Besakih, is social rather than physical. In short, Dubois seems to be repeating something that he has been told: that Klungkung is "high," its ruler elevated above both priests and other rulers, and that it is associated with Besakih.

Dubois continues, describing what is clearly a very idealized image of Klungkung:

Still the province of *Klongkong* is famous *as the land consecrated to virtue*, according to the style [?(*devoir*)] of the Balinese; indeed, in the moral deterioration occasioned by the introduction of *opium* to *Bali*, *Klonkong* has not degenerated at all, for the reason that this deadly drug was always prohibited there. . . .

 . . . The princes of the country *Klonkong* [are] decorated with titles which compare them to divinities, [which] indeed spurs them, and [they] develop a habit of exercising toward their vassals a completely paternal benevolence. . . .

All of the social customs, then, all of the moral rules, all of the acts of people great and small in this principality feel the benign influence of the court. Marriages, which in all of the other provinces operate mostly by means of a voluntary, and sometimes violent, abduction, are ordinarily contracted by legal means in *Klonkong*. Cockfights, which are practiced daily in a profane sense elsewhere, are only held in *Klonkong* in order to fulfill religious formalities.[7]

Here Dubois again reads implications that stem from European theology and morality into the "religious" character of the king whose title is Great God. His claim that the Déwa Agung's rule exemplifies legality and benevolence has a Balinese ring to it (and note again the reference to "paternity"), as we will see; but an interdiction on opium on moral grounds does not.

Both of these vignettes appear to be secondhand, based on hearsay rather than derived from things seen and heard in Klungkung itself. Dubois's identification of Klungkung with Besakih, and van den Broek's assertion that it is at the center of the island, report not empirical facts but cultural ones. These are Balinese claims about Klungkung, albeit filtered through European understandings.

The source of these descriptions was probably the rulers of Badung. Of the ports at which trade between Europeans and Balinese took place, Kuta in Badung was by far the most important until 1849. It was in Kuta that van den Broek stayed in 1817, Dubois lived from 1828 to 1831, and Schuurman, agent for the Netherlands Trading Society, set up shop in 1839. Badung's rulers were clearly amenable to intercourse with foreigners. Indeed, a Danish trader named Mads Lange, who settled at Kuta shortly before Schuurman's arrival and played an important role in Balinese-Dutch relations in the 1840s, even became harbormaster for one of Badung's princes.[8] When Huskus Koopman arrived in Bali in 1839 to begin diplomatic negotiations, he too went first to Kuta, where Schuurman served as his liaison with Badung's rulers. Knowledge of other rulers, however, was minimal and largely mediated through Badung. And so the first glimpses we have of Klungkung in colonial records are filtered through the perceptions and opinions of Badung's princes. But this makes it all the more striking that Klungkung is described in such exalted terms, as relations between Klungkung and Badung were strained during these years; indeed, in the 1840s the Dutch even regarded Badung's princes as their allies against the Déwa Agung. These descriptions suggest that at the very least Klungkung's ruler exercised an ideological hegemony over the island.

THE DÉWA AGUNG: KEIZER OR POPE?

In the shift from commerce to colonialism, the Dutch suddenly found themselves face to face with a phenomenon hitherto largely invisible to them: Klungkung. That they were aware that Klungkung was something that had to be dealt with is evident by the fact that in 1838 when Granpré Molière was sent to Bali and Lombok on behalf of the Netherlands Trading Society he not only went to Badung, as was usual, and to Lombok, which had after all initially attracted Dutch attention to these islands, but also to Klungkung.[9]

Molière was possibly the first colonial agent to appear before the Déwa Agung. He was not, however, the first European. Both King and Lange frequently visited the Balinese courts in the course of their trading ventures, and Lange and the Déwa Agung supported the same side in the affair on Lombok.

The Déwa Agung received Molière with warmth, even presenting him with a black horse as a gift (of the kind, Molière noted, that only princes were allowed to ride in Bali) and asking in return if the Dutch could provide him with a rhinoceros, or at least its meat, blood, and hide, for use in an upcoming ritual. Indeed, Molière was sufficiently delighted with his reception in Klungkung to recommend Kusamba, Klungkung's harbor, as a possible location for the Dutch factory. The Déwa Agung apparently liked the idea, since Molière reports that he offered to improve the facilities to make it easier for large ships to anchor there. But the Trading Society decided to place their agent Schuurman in Kuta. He did bring the rhinoceros with him and eventually, after much grief, managed to have it delivered to Klungkung. As a commercial agent he, like Lange and King, visited Klungkung as a matter of course, but he was able to conduct very little trade there. Hearing rumors that the Déwa Agung was angry at the ruler of Mataram on Lombok (George King's patron), he even tried offering help with troops but was refused (Lekkerkerker 1923).

It was J. H. Huskus Koopman, the envoy sent to convince Bali's rulers to acknowledge Dutch sovereignty and reject relations with other European governments, who first recognized Klungkung's importance. Huskus Koopman prepared for his embassy not only by reading everything available about Bali in the government archives but also by speaking to everyone who had ever been to the island. The Javanese Pangeran Said Hassan al Habashy told him that "the prince of Klonkong is the most esteemed on Balie" and suggested that negotiations with him might bring Huskus Koopman's task to its quickest and happiest conclusion. A meeting with Mads Lange pointed in the same direction; Lange even informed him that the princes of Mengwi and Gianyar were directly under Klungkung's control.[10]

On the basis of these preliminary reports, before even setting foot on the island, Huskus Koopman began to refer to the hitherto little-known Déwa Agung in both his journal and in letters as the "keizer" of Bali and Lombok.[11] The Dutch version of the treaties of 1849 also designates Klungkung's king by this title. Although almost immediately thereafter the appellation was dropped, the colonial government continued to refer to the Déwa Agung as Susuhunan (a title used as the Malay translation of *keizer* in the treaties) of Bali and Lombok until 1904.

What *keizer* or *susuhunan* meant to Dutchmen of the time is far from clear.

Although *keizer* derives from the Latin for *emperor*, until Germany's attempt to assert political mastery over Europe—to become a "keizer" in the original Roman sense—it may have connoted rather less in the way of political power. Its primary mid-nineteenth-century referent was probably the Holy Roman Emperor, whose power had a history and an ambivalence of meanings similar to that which the Dutch came to attribute to the Déwa Agung: sanctioned by religion but declining from a position of actual to symbolic rule, a fall from real power to mere respect.

Susuhunan is, if anything, an even more problematic nomination. On the one hand, it is close to a Balinese term, *sesuunan*, which literally means "that which is carried on the head"—especially (though not exclusively) objects treated with reverence, such as objects in which ancestors or deities sit. *Sesuunan* may also refer to the deities themselves, or to whatever is revered, respected, treated as sacred. The term was, in the Balinese context, an appropriate one for Klungkung's ruler, and the Déwa Agung both referred to himself and was referred to by other Balinese as Susuhunan, at least from the 1840s on.[12]

For colonial officials, *susuhunan* had a more reifed referent: it was the title of the ruler of Surakarta in Central Java. This Susuhunan shared the rule of Central Java with the Sultan of Jogjakarta but was considered to have an older and more prestigious claim to authority. Both courts existed, however, on the sufferance of the colonial authorities, with considerable limits to their power (see, e.g., Rickleffs 1974). If Klungkung's position put Dutch officials in mind of Surakarta, what they meant to suggest by the use of the title is ambiguous. An 1856 document, for example, glosses *susuhunan* as "spiritual overlord," whereas another in 1874 defines it as "supreme king."[13] If Surakarta is the reference point for either gloss, it is difficult to see in what respect Klungkung might parallel it: if the Susuhunan of Surakarta was Java's supreme king, he was a king without much effective say in mid-nineteenth-century colonial Java; and if he was a spiritual overlord, the differences between Islamic Java and Hindu Bali suggest such an analogy was likely to be misleading.

Huskus Koopman clearly regarded the Déwa Agung as a political figure, as a supreme ruler. Various other officials, at various later points in time, did the same. But when the situation in Bali did not fit the expectations this raised, other officials challenged the idea that the Déwa Agung was a ruler, asserting that his authority was merely nominal.

The major grounds for such challenge stemmed from the observation that other realms acted independently of his wishes. While in matters of etiquette and custom, so it was proclaimed, the Déwa Agung was treated with deference by other rulers, this could be explained solely by reference to his greater nobility. Such deference, however, had little to do with the serious matter of command and obedience.

Such assessments of Klungkung were not in fact new. A visitor to Buléléng at the time of Dubois's sojourn on the island described Klungkung as follows:

> Kalongkong . . . is the oldest and most important state of Bali, the king of it assuming a precedence and superiority over all the states, which is acceded to in matters of form and ceremony but by no means in business of high interest and moment (Anonymous [Medhurst] 1830:23–24).

Here we have the basic terms of the familiar characterization: Klungkung's "superiority over all the states, which is acceded to in matters of form and ceremony but by no means in business of high interest and moment." What might be considered "high interest and moment" is left unspecified but clearly does not include "matters of form and ceremony."

The "ceremony" invoked could well have been religious. For as the glosses of *susuhunan* show, the primary alternative to the view that the ruler of Klungkung was Bali's supreme political authority was that he was the island's spiritual overlord. I have found no reports that specify exactly what was meant by "spiritual overlord," although scattered remarks in colonial reports suggest something of the evidence that led to this conclusion. There are, for example, numerous references to the king's involvement in ritual, since he frequently used this as an excuse not to meet with colonial envoys or answer letters by the dates they wished.[14] That he was often consulted by other rulers concerning large rituals they were planning also made an impression: Huskus Koopman, for example, mentions that in 1840 Pamecutan's new ruler went to Klungkung to discuss with "the keizer, as supreme priest" upcoming ceremonies for the cremation of his predecessor.[15] Then there was the way people referred to him. Take, for example, the following remarks in published accounts of the Bali expeditions:

> The king of Klonkong is by hereditary right the head of all of the priests of the island [a footnote adds: As such, he bears the title of Dewa Agong Betara]: also the other princes give him the honors which assure him a kind of supremacy over all the sovereigns of Bali, under the title of Tjoekoerda (Gerlach 1859:560).

And another, similar characterization:

> The king of the Balinese realm Kelongkong is the general head of the religion of the whole island. As such he bears the title of Dewa Agoeng Betara, and he enjoys much prestige and honors. Also temporally, with the title of Tjoekoerda, he is regarded as supreme ruler of Bali, at least in name (Klinkert 1870:195).

These remarks suggest that at this time the Déwa Agung's position was interpreted in the colonial world as being something like that of a pope. Note that these writers divide what to the Dutch are distinguishable strands of the Déwa Agung's high status under the different titles by which he is known, assuming that *Cokorda* signifies a political office (*Betara*, which is another term for *Divinity*, clearly does not in their opinion). But they also agree that his religious position is preeminent, and any political influence merely secondary.

Such colonial descriptions had practical implications. If the Déwa Agung was Bali's emperor, then he had to be the focus of diplomacy, since his cooperation would ensure the cooperation of all. If he was, on the other hand, a kind of supreme priest or (not necessarily the same thing) spiritual overlord, he might have influence over Bali's rulers but was in no position to impose his will upon them: spiritual overlordship implied a certain political peripherality. As we will see, power in Bali was much more ambiguous than this; in particular, there were no divisions between sacred and secular of the kind the Dutch assumed. Colonial officers were not interested in ethnographic niceties, however, but in political utilities. If his authority was mainly exercised over ritual matters, he could safely be ignored.

There is every evidence, as we will see, that the Déwa Agung's power did have something to do with ritual. But it by no means went unexpressed in what Europeans considered "temporal" contexts: in, for example, war. The colonial government first had to take stock of this following the First Bali Expedition, when it became clear that Buléléng had been aided by troops from elsewhere in Bali, by order of the Déwa Agung. Nor was such mobilization restricted to wars against foreigners. As colonial records show, Klungkung rulers exercised such authority from at least the late eighteenth century until the 1890s.[16] Hence the compromise by Dutch military historians: the Déwa Agung filled two separate offices, marked by distinct titles, simultaneously.

But at the same time that these images generated by the three Bali expeditions were being absorbed, P. L. van Bloemen Waanders, the newly established Controleur of North Bali, was in the process of rejecting the idea that the Déwa Agung had either temporal *or* spiritual power. As he wrote in 1856:

> In 1855 it was still maintained that the *Dewa Agong* of *Klongkong* should be spiritual overlord or Soesoehoenan of *Bali* and *Lombok*, as he is recognized as such by the princes of the island, and concerning this no change has occurred. That such a thing is *not possible* with the institutions of Bali and the ideas existing there concerning the priestly caste was already discussed at length in the Report of 1854.[17]
>
> However, according to custom [adat] . . . the *Dewa Agong* is the supreme prince of these islands, and the remaining princes are nothing other than *mantja agong*, that is, *rijksbestierder* [governor].

He adds that while the other princes were supposed to take an oath of loyalty to Klungkung annually, the custom had waned: only Badung, Gianyar, and Mengwi had done so. Thus, he concluded, while the Déwa Agung, by virtue of his birth, is "the first person of the land, [he] exercises absolutely no power over the remaining princes of Bali and Lombok, except for Mengwi," which was regarded as an actual vassal state.[18]

Here even the spiritual overlordship of the Déwa Agung is rejected, and on the grounds of van Bloemen Waanders's authority as an expert on Balinese culture. While the position of Déwa Agung was, after all, properly one of temporal mastery, holders of the title no longer exercised any power. While van Bloemen Waanders's authoritative dismissal of the idea that the Déwa Agung was a religious figure did not stop later officials from continuing to characterize Klungkung's ruler as a spiritual overlord, it did begin to refocus the issue of Klungkung around the extent of the Déwa Agung's authority rather than its nature.

THE EMERGENCE OF A CONSENSUS

Despite van Bloemen Waanders's opinions, the idea that the Déwa Agung wielded no real power did not solidify for the Dutch as "fact" until the 1890s: precisely when the Netherlands Indies government began to annex South Balinese territory, both actively and passively.

In consequence of this shift, activities of the Déwa Agung were interpreted as attempts to usurp prerogatives that did not belong to him. Increasingly, the Déwa Agung was seen as only one Balinese ruler among others:

> The Kloengkoeng government . . . up to the present day continually in all sorts of ways extends its authority at the cost of that of the other self-rulers. . . . Efficacious improvement will therefore be able to be attained if the Kloengkoeng rulers are forced to occupy themselves exclusively with the rule of their own territory.[19]

More and more the "spiritual" dimensions of the Déwa Agung's position drop out of commentaries. He is increasingly portrayed as a political agent, and a failed one at that. One of the most forceful expressions of the shift appears in an account written in 1903 by van Kol, a socialist member of the Dutch parliament who made several trips to Bali:

> The Dewa-Agoeng Poetra still considers himself as the Sovereign of Bali and Lombok, and still continually aspires to absolute power, although his prestige has strongly decreased in the last years and the size of his realm has become extremely insignificant. Although he may address the other Princes of Bali in low Balinese, the only bond which joins them is fear of our spirit of annexation. In the Treaty concluded with Kloengkoeng in 1849 he is named by us "the keizer of Bali and Lombok," but

in the Treaty of 1853 with the latter land we have simply spirited away that title and the suzerainty. In his letters he still titles himself "Soesoehoenan of Bali and Lombok," and he is pretentious enough to avoid as much as possible every contact with the Controleur of the Civil Service, as such an official in his eyes is of too low rank to come into contact with him (van Kol 1903:478).

For van Kol, the title of Susuhunan of Bali and Lombok (which he clearly regards as political) was patently out of touch with reality. And when this Déwa Agung died not long after, and was succeeded by a son who proved to be the last of Klungkung's precolonial rulers, Resident Eschbach formally brought up this matter of titles with his superiors in Batavia.

The Resident wrote to recommend that in its official acknowledgment of the succession the colonial government should modify the Déwa Agung's title "to bring it into accord with his present position, which is not Soesoehoenan of Bali and Lombok":

> When the political treaties were signed the independent ruler of Kloengkoeng still had had some sovereignty over both islands or his supremacy was recognized by the remaining radja's; at present such is no longer the case, at least not in the territories standing under direct rule.[20]

While the change was deemed unnecessary (since "the title of Soesoehoenan of Bali and Lombok only has an historical significance, and from it no rights or attributes are derived"), the Council of the Indies did suggest that official documents not refer to "Kloengkoeng and dependencies,"

> because by doing so the well-known aspirations of the Dewa Agoeng to a certain measure of supremacy over the other Balinese self-governing realms, probably can arouse the idea that this supremacy was recognized by our Government to a certain degree.[21]

In the end, however, the Resident got his way: during the few years that he ruled, this Déwa Agung was referred to in Dutch documents by the title of Susuhunan of Klungkung.

And in those final years, comments in bureaucratic reports suggested that even this title had little to do with what the Dutch recognized as the exercise of power. For when the Déwa Agung tried to enforce Dutch commands in the regions belonging to him, he seemed to have no better success in marshaling obedience than he had over the island as a whole.

CHANGING PERCEPTIONS

It is clear at this point that more than one image of Klungkung may be found in colonial records. The difference between van den Broek's description of the

Déwa Agung in 1817 and van Kol's in 1903 might, however, simply be attributed to the effects of increasing knowledge. In 1817 what little the colonial government knew of Klungkung came from hearsay. From 1854 on, however, the administration had regular and relatively unimpeded access to the realm, through the annual visits of colonial officials, and therefore had reliable empirical evidence of how things "really" were: the title and status of Déwa Agung were merely empty pretensions.

Apparently confirming this, it was officials such as van Bloemen Waanders, officials who spent considerable time on Bali and who actually visited Klungkung, who insisted that Klungkung's power was minimal and argued strenuously against those who, perhaps bewitched by his title, suggested the colonial government support Klungkung's ruler as Bali's overlord. Thus an administrator who enthusiastically promoted the Déwa Agung (see chapter 8) was said to have based his opinions of the man on vague "reports," clearly deriving from Balinese. For the government, then, there was a difference between reality and Balinese ideology.

But why accept that what colonial officials saw with their own eyes provided a better picture of Klungkung than what they heard from Balinese? Why presume that their descriptions and conclusions were any less ideological? For one thing, the colonial government had a very direct interest in the matter: political decisions hinged upon what administrators chose to accept as true. To acknowledge the Déwa Agung as Bali's sovereign potentially meant supporting him in that role and directly or indirectly providing opportunities that might allow him to unify Bali in a manner more consistent with Dutch ideas of authority. And such unification, whatever it might have meant to the other rulers of Bali, was ultimately not in Dutch interests, as administrators repeatedly noted.

Moreover—and more important—if officials increasingly were able to make observations based upon a direct experience of Klungkung and of Bali, their observations were grounded upon and filtered through a complex set of preconceptions.

The distinction between sacred and secular power is only one of these, although it is the most prominent. It is noteworthy that the more officials encountered evidence of the Déwa Agung's involvement in what they recognized as political matters the less likely they were to describe him as a spiritual overlord. I am tempted to think that they were influenced by the connotations of *spirituality* to Europeans—piety, Christian morality, unworldliness; taking at least the English term more literally (as an involvement with *spirits*) brings one somewhat closer to the Balinese view of things.[22]

Colonial perceptions of Klungkung's power were also shaped by European ideas about kingship. Royalty in Holland had never been as potent as in France or England—indeed, the Netherlands did not even have a king until

after the Congress of Vienna—but even in the latter realms the nineteenth
century saw the transformation of European sovereigns into constitutional
monarchs, figureheads with only symbolic authority. If it occurred to colonial authorities to see Balinese rulers as powerful in name only, they may in
part have been projecting their own still inchoate experience of European
monarchy.

However, one must proceed with caution in moving from changes in
Europe to perceptions in the colonies. Dutch colonial officers may have been
citizens of the Netherlands, but they often had little direct experience of their
homeland. Many were born in the Indies or lived there most of their lives.
Thus their sense and understanding of monarchy was filtered even further.
Their colonial experience in the archipelago as a whole, and particularly in
Java, provided more immediate contexts for evaluating indigenous political
systems. In Java the effects of the colonial presence led to an increasingly
ceremonial form of kingship (Ricklefs 1974). As already noted, Dutch officials
frequently took Central Java as the model for describing the position of the
Déwa Agung; to cite van Bloemen Waanders again: "In regard to the leaders
and people of these islands [he] stands in no other relationship, than the
Keizer of Soerakarta with respect to the people of Java."[23]

But if colonial descriptions of Klungkung were on the one hand a reflex
of the shaping of experience by ideology and ideology by experience, they
also reflect the effects of colonial intervention itself. We will see in chapter 8,
for example, that symbolic forms of domination—in the guise of an etiquette
for court visits—constituted one means by which colonialism subtly altered
the ways in which power could be expressed. More broadly, by acting or
not acting upon various descriptions of Klungkung, the Dutch had an impact
upon Balinese projects.

Thus if the ambiguities, contradictions, and disjunctures in colonial descriptions of Klungkung in part reflect the inability of Dutch categories to
encompass Balinese realities, these descriptions must also be read diachroni-
cally: they show how Klungkung's rulers attempted to work out the cultural
possibilities open to them in the context of a problematic European presence.
Whatever the changes in perception traceable to increasing access to information, the cumulative effect of interactions between Balinese and the colonial
government was a real shift in the power of Klungkung. As will be seen in
chapter 6, there is reason to think that in the 1840s the Déwa Agung was *not*
just a nominally powerful figurehead; by 1908, however, the Déwa Agung's
authority was seriously contested.

There is, then, evidence that the conventional characterization of Klungkung is an anachronistic projection of the outcome of a historical process
involving complex relationships among the Dutch, the rulers of Klungkung,
and the lords of Bali, and the interplay between both Dutch and Balinese

representations. The conditions under which this image of Klungkung could emerge were established when colonial officials attempted to grasp Balinese realities in terms of Dutch distinctions—emperor versus priest, temporal versus spiritual, powerful versus powerless. But it took more than fifty years to develop its now familiar form, and only conquest finally solidified it. If it appears that an accumulation of knowledge made it possible for officials to finally fix Klungkung's image, this knowledge was a reflex of power, expressed and constructed through interactions.

Colonial accounts do not provide simple and transparent reflections of Balinese realities. The Balinese past that may be seen in them is mediated through the understanding of outsiders, who could not always speak the language, had their own ideas about the nature of the world, were representatives of a system that had a set of definite interests to implement, and in many instances were recording their impressions within the confines of a very particular cultural form: the bureaucratic report.

If their descriptions are not "mirrors" of Bali, colonial reports nonetheless reflect recurrent images that appear to have a certain stability. Clearly the power attributed to Klungkung had something to do with both "history" and "religion," more specifically with the Majapahit empire and the temple of Besakih. It is equally apparent that Bali was divided into multiple kingdoms but that in relation to other rulers the Déwa Agung was "father" and "eldest." Colonial descriptions also show a king whose position is in a symbolic space "above" others, and we shall see they reveal a set of behaviors characterized by relative immobility and silence. Thus for all of their limitations, Dutch descriptions of Klungkung remain priceless: in the interstices of colonial reports can be glimpsed a different Klungkung, a Klungkung closer to the one known to Balinese.

THREE

The View from Klungkung:
Power and the Invisible World

A visitor to modern Klungkung would find little to attract his or her attention. It appears to be a typical Indonesian town, the sights and sounds along its main road a familiar mix of old and new. On the one hand, there are banks and television repair shops, not to mention a cinema topped with an enormous billboard advertising the current feature in day-glo colors. The streets are congested with motorcycles, tourist buses, passenger vans, and especially with trucks, carrying goods east from Java and construction materials west to Denpasar. On the other hand, there are the pigeons, bells tied to their feet, whirring and wheeling in the sky; the occasional cart, drawn by a sturdy pony with tinkling bells on his harness, ferrying matrons laden with ducks, fruit, and packages of coffee and sugar from the market; peddlers hawking herbal remedies and good luck charms near the main crossroads. In the shopping district east of the market, Chinese, Arab, and Indian merchants perch on stools inside the open fronts of their shops waiting for customers to buy the cloth, gold, and consumer goods they offer for sale. Yet further east, in the Islamic quarter, girls dressed in long green skirts, their hair covered with white shawls, giggle to one another as they walk past the Masjid Al Hikmah from which, five times a day, summonses to the faithful echo out across the town. The same things could be seen and heard almost anywhere in Indonesia.

The regency (*kabupaten*) of Klungkung consists of four administrative units (*kecamatan*): Banjarangkan, Klungkung, Dawan, and the island group Nusa Penida. According to the 1980 census, only about 150,000 people lived in the entire regency, some five hundred people per square kilometer. There were 96 buildings of more than one story, 550 shops, 1,017 handicraft businesses, and only 8 restaurants or homestays, the fewest anywhere in Bali.

People in Klungkung know quite well that theirs is the smallest regency in Bali. Indeed, its inhabitants delight in a joking pun on the name of their region: Klungkung, they say, is only *aklingkungan*, a mere bend in the road— turn a corner and you're already somewhere else. But a basic theme of discourse about Klungkung in Klungkung is that things are not what they seem.

In precolonial Klungkung, size per se mattered little. Labor, not land, was what counted in Southeast Asian political economies. A ruler's strength was measured less by the extent of his territory and more by the number of persons he could mobilize to fight his wars and prepare offerings for his rituals (Errington 1983; Gullick 1958), and in the nineteenth century Klungkung's rulers could rely on human labor well beyond their own borders to achieve their goals (see chapter 6). But when Pedanda Gedé Kenitén chuckled over the tiny size of the realm, and indicated that the emptiness of the hills bordering Karangasem to the east and north belied Klungkung's true strength, he was not referring to such potential to enlist the aid of its allies and vassals in other realms. He was alluding to other allies, other vassals.

When in the 1890s Karangasem attacked Klungkung, his father and uncle sat on a bamboo platform reciting mantras to add an invisible fortress to the fortifications already in place. The troops from Karangasem boasted victory would be easy; by noon, they said, they would be in the palace, gorging themselves on delicious foods. But when they crossed the border into Klungkung, out of nowhere they suddenly found themselves confronted by endless streams of platoons: from one side a company dressed entirely in green, down to the green umbrellas of rank held over the heads of its commanders; from another, a company all in red, with red umbrellas; over there yet another, this one entirely in yellow. Terrified, the Karangasem soldiers turned and ran back over the border to the safety of their own territory. The Pedanda, when he told me this, shook his head in delight and laughed. The hills, he said, only appear to be empty; actually, they are filled with "people." Klungkung may be small, he added, but Sang Hyang Widhi, one Balinese name for the highest manifestation of Divinity, dwells there.

ENTERING THE MAGIC KINGDOM

The Pedanda's story is a fairly typical episode in Klungkung history. But such miracles are by no means thought to be a thing of the past. Indeed, it is because they are so congruent with present experience that stories like this make such good sense of past events to people in Klungkung.

Shortly after I met her, Cokorda Isteri Agung told me the following anecdote—a lesson, really—about what things are like in Klungkung. It seems that when Mount Agung erupted in 1963, an engineer was sent to inspect the bridge over the Unda River. He was warned by a local resident to take care, as the bridge was not very sturdy. Proud of his expertise, he scornfully replied, "This bridge won't collapse until after I die." He had barely finished speaking when a rock spewed from the mountain struck him on the head, killing him instantly: shortly thereafter, a stream of lava destroyed the bridge. His boast had come true, though hardly in the way he expected. Bad enough to have spoken so arrogantly; everyone knows that this sort of speech is dangerous. But, said Cokorda Isteri Agung, to have been so thoughtless right on the Unda was truly foolhardy.

Rivers are generally populated with spirits, so that was not what was unusual about this tale. The Unda, however, seemed rather more densely populated than usual (tales abound of mysterious encounters on its banks), and the speed with which the hapless engineer met his fate made it quite clear that in Klungkung invisible forces were not to be trifled with.

I would not have appreciated how unusual this was had I not been accompanied on my forays into Klungkung's inner world by Dayu Alit and Ida Bagus Jagri. Both set about "inventing" Klungkung for themselves by comparing its customs to those more familiar to them from Gianyar and Badung and systematizing their perceptions of the differences (Wagner 1975). What struck them almost immediately was that not only Pedanda Gedé Kenitén and Cokorda Isteri Agung but nearly everyone we met seemed to matter-of-factly pass along some tale involving a dramatic demonstration of the presence of supernatural beings.

On the road where we lived, for example, at the northeast end of the town of Klungkung, a road that ended at a complex of several temples, it was not uncommon for people foolhardy enough to venture forth at night to encounter a giant named Panji Landung, the spirit "owner" of that stretch of road.[1] Next to a ravine in the west end of town was a shrine the late king had built for Jero Nyoman, a spirit with power over rain. Then there was the pair of wooden slit-gongs that sounded by themselves whenever illness threatened Klungkung. The priest responsible for the spirits of these gongs nearly fainted one day when, late in placing offerings in their accustomed place, he happened to glance down the road from his perch next to the door of the royal palace to the crossroads at the center of town: setting out in his direction was a horrific long-fanged, bulging-eyed ghoul. People spoke as well of casual meetings with acquaintances from the village that houses the temple Goa Lawah, near Klungkung's eastern border, only to discover, days later, that their acquaintance had been nowhere near the place at the time in question: they had been chatting with a spirit. Even worse, in the midst of conversation, the "friend" might suddenly vanish into thin air. The army troops that frequently marched past another temple were, its priest informed us, also spirits, and he made certain to be diligent in setting out offerings so they would leave him alone.

In short, Klungkung appeared to be positively overrun with spirits, especially of the sort called *tanana*—literally, "not there." But then, as victors over the demonic ruler of the island of Nusa Penida (which remained always in Klungkung's domain and was a place for exiling political enemies and criminal transgressors), the Déwa Agungs held dominion over that ruler's spirit minister, Jero Gedé Macaling, "the Fanged Lord" who dwells in the temple of Péd, and his thousands of spirit subjects.[2] During the rainy season between the sixth and ninth lunar months, these minions bring illness and death from Nusa Penida to all of South Bali. But according to stories in Klungkung, to Klungkung's ruler they provided protection, turning out in the form of ghostly battalions (the famous *bala samar* mentioned by Pedanda Gedé Kenitén) to fight his wars.

In contrast to Klungkung, such spirits are rarely seen in Badung or Gianyar, or at least so my companions informed me. Instead, small signs occasionally indicate their presence: close to a ravine one might hear the music of their gamelan orchestras, or smell their cooking fires. Now and again a spirit becomes infatuated with a human, who disappears or is found wandering dreamily in the wastelands such spirits favor, but this is a rare occurrence. The only other place that my friends had ever been so constantly aware of the presence of the invisible world had been Sanur—but there sorcerers rather than spirits formed the main topic of such talk.

But it was not only these (rather alarming) spirits who lived in Klungkung. The more time we spent there, the more impressed we became by evidence of more awesome presences. According to local inhabitants, these were inscribed in the very geography of the place. Northeast of the village of Akah is a *penyampuan*, a confluence of rivers, called the Tri Sakti, "Threefold Power." This is a name for Divinity when it manifests itself in the form of Brahma, Wisnu, and Iswara, which is exactly what it seems to do at this joining of waters. For like the god Wisnu, the water of the Telaga Waja is dark, and it flows from Wisnu's direction, the north; the Masih is cloudy white and comes from the east, both attributes of the god Iswara; and the Unda, which flows south from there to the sea, is reddish, the direction and color of the god Brahma: a strange and wondrous thing.

In Klungkung discourse, then, invisible forces appear unusually close to the world of humans. It was not only in such talk, however, but also in practice that Klungkung's identity as a "spiritual" domain was constructed by its inhabitants. All of the invisible beings generate a continuous (if quiet) hum of ritual activity. Given the size of its population, there is a remarkably high ratio of Brahmana priests, who are kept unusually busy (at least in the eyes of my Brahmana friends) by nearly daily visits from clients asking for holy water—and not just holy water in general, but a spectrum of specific varieties, each with very different properties and uses. This too was different from Gianyar and Badung, where, Ida Bagus Jagri and Dayu Alit claimed, people only seek holy water (and then only of the generic sort) when planning a ritual.

Dayu Alit was also struck by the offerings that people in Klungkung brought to temple rituals. Despite their apparently infinite variety, all Balinese offerings consist at core of a combination of cooked rice, fruits, sweet rice cakes, meats, flowers, ingredients used for chewing betel nut, and palm leaves cut into various shapes and sewn together with bamboo pegs. In Gianyar, where she was from, a chicken leg or a mere morsel of certain confections is frequently used to represent an entire cooked animal or complete cake in an offering piled high with magnificent and abundant layers of fruits and more decorative confections. Klungkung offerings, Dayu Alit remarked, are rarely as elaborate as those in Gianyar, but what they lack in flourish they make up for in integrity. There is no skimping on the basic and essential elements: never just a bit of meat, but an entire grilled chicken, even for the simplest of occasions. Gianyar offerings, she noted, are more splendid, but ritual is sacrificed to art (*seni*). There is, then, a characteristic "flavor" to Klungkung ritual practice: modest in scale, but "complete" (Indonesian, *lengkap*).

Something of the same sort goes on in Klungkung temple structures as well. In general, the central shrine of any Balinese temple, dedicated to the god or gods of the locality, takes the form of a small pavilion, sometimes with a stack of pagoda-like roofs (the number, always odd, depends upon the importance of the divinity and the rank of the persons who worship there). This shrine carries what could be termed the main "semantic load" of the temple. Occasionally there are similar shrines to other divinities, and often a shrine in the form of a high stone seat for certain divinities who are called upon to serve as "witnesses" of ritual acts. Such is the basic temple of Gianyar or Badung. But in Klungkung, Dayu Alit was amazed to see, there were even house-temples full of shrine-types that in Gianyar or Badung would be found in only the most important temples of the realm: *mascari-mascatu* (a nearly identical pair, distinguished only by the shapes of the inverted pottery-piece that crowns their top), dedicated to the rice goddess; *sapta patala* (shaped like a throne, its stone "arms" carved into crowned serpents), representing the seven layers that form the foundation of the world; *padmasana* (a higher throne), for the high gods, and so forth. One might say that in Klungkung the meaning of these shrines was more grammatical than semantic; they were part of what made in Klungkung the "well-formed temple." Repeated in all Klungkung temples that we saw, such shrines have a different importance than they do elsewhere, since they can no longer code a distinction between temples at different levels. Instead what they conveyed to my friends was a sense that people in Klungkung paid attention to the forces of the entire universe in their ritual spaces. Another way of analyzing them is that they signaled the difference between Klungkung, encompassing and totalizing, and other realms.[3]

Such completeness made sense to my friends because to most Balinese Klungkung is associated with *kawitan*, "sources," and sources are totalizing centers. In texts Klungkung is sometimes referred to as *sanggah Bali-pulina*, the

ancestral shrines or sacred place of the island of Bali. A great many of the
ancestral temples, origin points (*kawitan*) of important Balinese clans, are located in Klungkung (most of the rest are part of the temple complex called
Besakih); hence Balinese often come to Klungkung with ritual in mind. People
also come to Klungkung to seek their *kawitan*, for "forgetting" one's ancestors
(failing to make offerings at the proper temples) is a common cause of afflic-
tion. Clues about ancestors come through consultations with trance mediums,
but their cryptic communications must then be matched to geography and
written genealogical chronicles. And most genealogical experts belong to the
various priestly and royal houses of Klungkung. In fact, Klungkung's last ruler
would often tell people who their ancestors were without consulting texts at
all; he simply "knew," though his proclamations were confirmed (and inscribed) by a more scholarly cousin, who did rely on chronicles. Nowadays
Ratu Dalem, the eldest of his sons, produces not only genealogical texts but
temple images for a steady stream of petitioners from all over Bali. Klungkung
is still in some spheres an enunciative center.

If Klungkung temples reiterated for my friends the theme of completeness
and connected it to history, another comparison they made between Klungkung and Gianyar involved the value of modesty, which Balinese associate
with superior age and understanding. In certain respects Klungkung had less
ritual activity than Gianyar. For example, Gianyarese conduct two annual
rites that are not part of Klungkung practice at all: a procession (*melasti*) of all
temple deities to the sea to be ritually cleansed, and a rite called *nangluk merana*
to keep away epidemics and pests, also conducted at the sea. Moreover, in
Gianyar monthly offerings to demons are made by every household during
the inauspicious rainy season from the sixth to the ninth months, culminating
in a larger ritual to mark the end of the period in each village and at the
capital of the regency.

These same ritual functions are otherwise addressed in Klungkung. It is
not deemed necessary to purify temple deities at the sea annually, but only
when they are to be honored with an unusually large ritual. Like the towering
temple offerings so beloved in Gianyar, an annual procession looks to Klungkung eyes excessive and baroque. A certain economy of action is stressed, a
stance appropriate, explained Ida Bagus Jagri, to one who is "older" and "understands things," and suggestive as well of greater power.

As for annual rites to ward off unfavorable forces, or monthly rites in
each compound, Klungkung has other ways to deal with those, mainly centering around the royal house. Precolonially, magical weapons belonging
to the king helped protect against forces responsible for illness and crop failure. Only one royal regalia still remains—the wooden slit-gongs mentioned
above, onomatopoeically named Depang (Let It Be) and Tulung (Help)—but
these at least give warning, by sounding when danger is near. Hearing their

voices, people promptly bring offerings to their shrine in the royal residence and receive in return protective amulets from the shrine's priest. As for monthly offerings to demons, in Klungkung these are replaced by a single, grand (at one time royally sponsored) version of the ritual at the end of the rainy season, called the Taur Agung (Great Payment).

The general tendency in Klungkung even in the 1990s is to collectivize ritual and concentrate it in royal hands. While the court is no longer financially responsible for the Taur Agung or rites at the temple of Besakih, members of the royal family are important participants in both. They organize the Taur Agung, which is held on the open field outside one of the core-line royal residences. Most of the offerings are manufactured by women of the royal clan, who expect and receive no compensation. Certain large offerings at Besakih's annual All the Gods Descend ritual are also contributed by the Klungkung royal house.

Another type of ritual consolidation was also made clear by my friends' comparisons. In Gianyar or Badung people who wish to be purified—to serve as healers or performers, or simply to study texts or otherwise come safely into contact with invisible forces—do so in private ceremonies, conducted in the house-temple of their hereditary Brahmana priest. In Klungkung all such rites are performed collectively, during the great ritual works (*karya*) held annually in Pura Dasar and Pura Kentel Gumi, two of Klungkung's four state temples. The royal family's own priests officiate, and members of the royal family must be present as witnesses.

To Ida Bagus Jagri and Dayu Alit, there was clearly a connection between the stories told in Klungkung concerning spirits and this abundance of ritual attention to invisible forces. On the one hand, the continual evidence of the proximity of invisible beings in Klungkung experience led to an intensity of Klungkung's ritual life, for if spirits manifest their presence they can scarcely—or not safely—be ignored; on the other, the ritual diligence of Klungkung's populace also drew the interest of spirits. All things considered, it was hardly surprising that Klungkung *felt* different, more *tenget,* than other places. Both the diligence and the density of spirits were, however, ineluctably tied to Klungkung's past and the power of its kings.

THE CONSTITUENTS OF THE INVISIBLE WORLD

For Balinese, there is more to what happens than ordinary experience would suggest. Like Azande, Balinese are not content to conclude that a van collided with a truck because a driver was careless. People are just as unlikely to attribute the wealth of a neighbor merely to her diligence. Balinese regard such phenomena as outcomes of relationships to agents who cannot be seen, but whose favors may be actively solicited: the wealthy neighbor wears a ring set with a stone that attracts business; the driver failed to place small offerings on his dashboard before setting off on his journey, or leave others at shrines at major crossroads or bridges.

Every Balinese knows that in addition to the *sekala*—the palpable, material, concrete reality perceptible to the senses—there is the *niskala*, numinous and invisible. There is little of human importance that does not partake of the *niskala*. But it can usually only be known by signs of its impingement upon the ordinary world.

The invisible world is characterized in a variety of ways. It is, first, *sunia*, empty, quiet. The idea of *sunia* encapsulates the paradoxes of an intangible reality, which influences everything yet is emptiness and absence. The invisible world is also *suksma*, hidden, secret, inaccessible to normal perception, but capable of being sensed by those gifted with power.

At their most literal, *sekala* and *niskala* have nothing to do with visibility. But if the idiom of sight is not the only one Balinese use to explain these concepts, it seems to be the most common.[4] Thus certain mantras or powerful persons are said to have the ability to make visible what is normally not visible. Betara Surya, the sun, source of the light and clarity that signals the presence of the benevolent *niskala*, is also spoken of as the daily witness of human actions. His mortal equivalent is the Brahmana priest, the Surya of his clients (those who ask him for holy water); certain offerings are also forms of this divinity. (The priest is called the *Surya sekala*, the offerings the *Surya niskala*).[5] In high Balinese the eye (*penyurian*) is the sun (*surya*) of the body—or (at one register of linguistic politeness down) that which witnesses (*penyaksian*).

Balinese play upon the theme of visibility in their ritual practices. The temples of Bali have few images; mainly they contain god-houses, miniature pavilions complete with roofs and doors. Behind those doors may be a pair of golden statuettes, one male and one female, or a male and female duo with painted wooden faces and bodies made from Chinese coins stitched together into triangular forms. But there may be only a neatly folded pile of white or yellow cloth, or a mysterious, never-opened box. It is in such odd objects that the gods, say Balinese, "sit" during rituals. Of course it is only to ordinary people that such objects appear to be mere objects. A person with power may see a glow that marks the presence of the numinous, or even—but this is truly extraordinary—actually see the divinity who sits there.

The gods, however, rarely manifest themselves (at least in this era) in visible forms. Divinity in its highest form could not, for it is a mass of contradictions—as people liked to say, "the one whose body is invisible, He [or She; the pronoun *ida* is gender neutral] is short, He is tall and large; if you say He is small, He is small. He wears new clothing, He is naked." If Divinity does take immanent form, it is necessarily mediated. For example, the Brahmana priest's daily liturgy enables him to become a temporary receptacle for the god Surya/Siwa and imbue water with the power to bring whatever it touches into contact with the numinous.

A further paradox of Divinity is that it is both singular and encompassing and multiple and partial. Balinese metaphysics is emanationist: the divinity who is the emptiness that brought forth the universe exists simultaneously with the lesser divinities who are its partial manifestations, sometimes identified as its "children."[6] Names by which the supreme divinity are known include Divine Oneness (Sang Hyang Tunggal), the Inconceivable (Acintya), and the Slippery One (Sang Hyang Licin). As the source of what exists in the world, this divinity is also known as the Divine Creator or Poet (Sang Hyang Kawi) and, especially common nowadays, Divine Order (Sang Hyang Widhi).

In slightly more tangible form, Divinity becomes the god of the sun (Betara Surya), witness to all worldly activity. When paired with his consort, the goddess of the moon (Betari Ratih), he is known as Betara Smara, and the two are responsible for all forms of love, attraction, pleasure, and delight. In relation to humans and all of the other gods that are his lesser manifestations, he is also the Divine Teacher or Father (Betara Guru), and in this form he encompasses the deified ancestors of human beings, who were, as parents, versions of him.

For those attracted to cosmological speculation, the most important lesser manifestations of Divinity are conceived as the underlying order of the visible world. In certain texts, dimensions of time, space, matter, and energy are represented as arranged in neat coherent patterns, which are particularly pertinent to ritual processes meant to influence the invisible world. Here gods are associated with cardinal directions, days of the week, colors, elements, bodily organs, syllables, animals, and mythological weapons. When Divinity is apprehended in this form, it is given the names of the great Hindu gods. The divinity from which all emanates is known as Siwa and conceived as forming the center; Wisnu, the preserver, to the north, is associated with the color black and with water; Brahma, the creator, is associated with the color red, south, and fire. To the east Siwa takes the form of Iswara, the god of whiteness and purity; to the west he takes the form of Mahadéwa, whose color is yellow. The system may be contracted (to the threefold Brahma-Wisnu-Siwa scheme, briefly mentioned earlier) or expanded (to a system of nine gods or even eleven).

The three major gods also have female consorts. Giriputri/Durga, Siwa's consort, receives homage in the Pura Dalem that is found in every Balinese village; Sri, consort of Wisnu and goddess of rice, is worshipped in the ubiquitous water temples; Saraswati, Brahma's consort and the goddess of the arts and learning, dwells in the letters inscribed on palm-leaf texts. Siwa, Wisnu, and Brahma seem more abstract and less localized than their consorts and have more tenuous material abodes. Unlike the brick and stone shrines for Sri and Durga, theirs tend to be temporary and of necessity reconstructed. Summoned by mantras, they come to sit in towering bamboo shrines (*sanggar tawang*), erected anew for each occasion, to witness great rituals.[7]

Although growing in importance in the last twenty-five years as attempts are made to reconcile Balinese practices with the principle that all Indonesians believe in one supreme deity, for the most part these forms of Divinity are primarily relevant to priests and others interested in metaphysics. Most Balinese are far more concerned with the deities worshipped in, and known as the gods of, specific, local temples, especially the gods of their village temples and the deified ancestors in each compound's house-temple. People pay much less attention to the Hindu pantheon than they do to the idiosyncrasies of the god of the local Pura Dalem, and while there are those who refer to that deity by Hindu names, most simply speak of "the goddess of the Dalem."[8] Such neighborhood deities often have characteristic ways of making their presence known: through strong winds or rain, for example, whenever they are brought down from their shrines, or by causing whoever bears their seat to break into a run. Differences in ritual practice from village to village are tangible expressions of a deep feeling that numinous beings impinge on the visible world in peculiarly individualized and localized ways.

So far, discussion has focused on divinities. But the invisible forces affecting human affairs are not always benevolent, and indeed it is impossible to understand Balinese ritual practice unless others are also taken into account. Most important of these are the *buta-kala*, "demons," malign or destructive aspects of the invisible world.

There is a certain ambiguity here in Balinese usage. Although *niskala* may refer to all nonvisible agents, the term more often is used in a marked sense, to designate benevolent forces. Indeed, *niskala* could be literally translated as "without kala," what exists in the absence of suffering and want. According to their Sanskrit roots, *buta* and *kala* could even be glossed as time and the elements (in Balinese *kala* means "time," as Ida Bagus Jagri liked to point out), suggesting that *niskala* might refer to the experience of those no longer attached to the material world. However, such esoterica has little to do with the common view of *buta* and *kala*. Ordinarily they are regarded as invisible agents that have a negative effect on human harmony and well-being.

The *buta-kala* are the immediate cause of all that is injurious to human joy and comfort, physical and mental, natural and social. Wars, epidemics, catastrophes, arguments, anger, confusion, greed, sadness, or other disturbances are signs of their presence. People under the influence of *buta* or *kala* behave badly: they steal, or attack others, or otherwise cause harm. On several occasions I heard people observe that *buta* also means "blind," "and when people are angry, aren't they blind?" The *buta-kala* are everywhere, but their influence is felt mainly in the absence of Divinity; they define human experience when the gods are distant, or when human neglect or wrong-doing has alienated Divinity, leaving humans at the mercy of less benevolent forces. A rash of epidemics or disasters—natural catastrophes, quarrels among those living in the same compound, the sudden appearance of strange insects or parasitic growths in a houseyard—is an omen, evidence of the need for a demon offering.

The relationship between the benevolent and malevolent aspects of the invisible world, however, is actually complex. Divinities may take frightening forms, as *buta* and *kala*, when angry at humans (especially if forgotten and neglected) or when testing them (see below). The commander of all demons (some say superior even to Sang Hyang Kala, the destructive aspect of her husband Siwa) is the goddess Durga, the terrible form of Giriputri. Moreover, *buta* and *kala* may also serve the gods, and carry out their orders.

Nor are *buta* and *kala* entirely negative. They can, when remembered with offerings, actually help humans achieve important goals. Ida Bagus Jagri told me that without them people could not live, for they are also responsible for basic human appetites. Then too, Balinese cannot imagine the attraction of a life that has no pain in it whatsoever; how, I was asked, would you then recognize when things were good?

Benevolent divinities are represented (in texts, paintings, or shadow theater) as attractive, fine-featured humans. So are other beings who, while not strictly speaking divinities, keep company with them: *widiadara* and *widiadari*, celestial children of Indra, king of the gods, are the essence of beauty and are ritually called upon to "sit" in adolescents. By contrast, *buta* and *kala* are depicted as either inadequately human, usually in bodily integrity—thus certain *buta* are portrayed as body parts, a head with one arm, for example, or with heads below their groins—or, like *kala*, as excessively so, with exaggerated and uncontrollable passions and emotions, especially greed and anger, represented by fangs, bulging eyes, and potbellies.[9]

In addition to "gods" and "demons," the world is also populated by a host of lesser invisible creatures, the spirits apparently so abundant in Klungkung, which are referred to generically as *tanana*, a felicitous expression that means something like "not there."[10] Like the term *niskala*, *tanana* may be used to designate the whole invisible world. But generally it refers to these shape-shifters, who are something between nature spirits and ghostly sprites.

There are many kinds of *tanana*, among them *tonya*, *samar*, *jin*, *sétan*, and *gamang*. *Tonya* and *gamang* inhabit ravines and large trees, especially banyan trees. *Samar* (part of the same paradigm of sight, the word means "obscure") make up the invisible spirit armies referred to earlier, which have their head-quarters in the precincts of temples. Some say the various types of *tanana* are hierarchically ranked (as are gods, demons, and persons), but precisely how various kinds of *tanana* differ from one another is not something most people spend much time wondering about. Like the *buta-kala*, to which they are in-ferior (just as the *buta-kala* are inferior to humans, and humans to gods), *tanana* have a commander: the Fanged Lord of Pura Péd. They also may be instru-ments of greater agencies.

Tanana, which make themselves visible now and again, look just like people. Some, in fact, were once people, who died bad deaths as suicides, in childbirth, or in accidents. While waiting for their liberation, they live in a limbo betwixt and between the visible and invisible worlds.

Like other invisible agents, *tanana* help their favorites, but their general disposition is impish. Beggars and other eccentric people, especially if en-countered at bridges, may really be *tanana*. It is dangerous to ignore them, for they are likely to cause accidents to those who annoy them. To be safe, people give something, however small, to whomever asks. *Tanana* (particularly those which haunt trees and ravines) are usually amenable to accepting offerings and, so placated, may offer protection and aid. While some think it best to have as little to do with them as possible (although no one would reject their overtures altogether; the prudent ask of them only to be safe and well), there are those who establish more long-term relationships with them. Healers, for example, may have *tanana* familiars, and then there were the spirit armies of Klungkung's kings. Occasionally a person becomes infatuated with a spirit (or vice versa) and disappears; summoned back by concerned kinsmen, he may tend thereafter to stare dreamily into space and periodically wander off to the banks of a nearby river. Things as well as people may be taken by *tanana*; they are the ones responsible when something was "just there, a minute ago," al-though they may replace it if promised their favorite things: a certain kind of snack, not unlike a small pancake, and scented oils.

It is difficult, and misleading, to render what Balinese have to say about divinities, demons, or spirits in systematic form. For one, Balinese do not normally talk about such matters. To mention invisible forces may be suffi-cient to invoke them, a foolhardy business for those without ritual prepa-ration or knowledge. And knowledge is always directed toward pragmatic as opposed to theoretical ends. Balinese are inclined to neither theology nor starry-eyed mysticism. In general, establishing relationships to the in-visible world interests Balinese far more than reflecting upon it. When peo-ple do study about invisible beings—which largely comes down to learning their various names and the offerings and mantras associated with them—they do so in order to enlist their aid. Indeed, even texts that address the most esoteric cosmological themes have a practical intent: to enable their student to achieve some form of power.

INTERSECTIONS BETWEEN VISIBLE
AND INVISIBLE REALITIES

Although people say that Sang Hyang Widhi is present whenever someone concentrates upon him, people usually do so in places (and with the aid of objects) imbued with high concentrations of *niskala* energies. Such places are called *tenget*, and to those who concern themselves with such matters they have a recognizable feel, something of which is captured by English terms such as "enchanted" or "haunted." *Tenget* places include mountaintops, forests, beaches, the ravines and trees favored by *tanana*, and springs and artificial pools (where *widiadari* like to bathe). Temples, priestly houses, and palaces are often built in such regions, or on any land where there are signs of numinosity such as the presence of certain species of trees, or a luminescence, fragrance, or pleasurable feeling of well-being.[11]

One may also attract invisible beings to spaces that are made suitable to them: in laying out a house compound, the east corner facing the mountains (in Balinese, the *kaja-kangin* corner) is by convention set aside for shrines for the deified ancestors of the house. Once the shrines are consecrated, plants favored by *niskala* beings often sprout spontaneously nearby.

Objects, both natural and manufactured, can also mediate between the visible and invisible worlds. Certain objects appear to be endowed with the power of the places in which they are found: for example, odd artifacts found in the sea, which purifies by absorbing into itself negative energies, are often efficacious in healing. Objects through which a connection to the invisible world may be effected may also be made by those with special knowledge.[12] Often taking the form of weapons, god figures, and masks, such objects are ideally made out of materials either attractive to or already imbued with invisible forces. Thus trees favored by *tanana* are good sources of wood for masks and slit-gongs; to be really powerful the wood chosen would have been seen to glow.

The potency of such objects, which might be described as simultaneously sacred and magical, depends in part on the spiritual power of their creators. Throughout the process of manufacturing such things, offerings rest at the artisan's side, and at various stages he invokes invisible forces with mantras, sacred syllables, seeking to join their power with that of his creation. When the labor is complete, the object is "finished" (*puput*) by rituals: a purification (*mlaspasin*) to eliminate any harmful influences deriving from the manufacturing process itself and to bring it to life, and a *masupatin* (from the root *pasupati*, a name for Siwa), in which invisible forces are invited to "sit" in it and make it useful (*maguna*). Such objects may be passed down in a family as heirlooms (*pusaka*) or kept in temples. In either case, they are treated with reverence and periodically cleaned, dressed, and "fed" with offerings, for without such treatment the invisible forces within them will vanish and they will become mere things. The possession of such fragments of the numinous, which are both the physical casing for invisible forces and indices of their presence, provides a conduit to power.

That certain activities in the *sekala* realm have impact upon the *niskala* is the basis for the effectiveness of offerings and meditation. The idea is to bring the *niskala* in its positive aspects close, to attract the gods so one may petition them to bring one's wishes to fruition. Positive *niskala* forces are drawn to fragrant smells, harmonious sounds, profusions of color, and whatever is clean and pure and still. The flowers and incense used in prayer are themselves instances of an invisible reality whose temporal and spatial existence is ephemeral.

THE ROYAL RITUAL ORDER

If invisible forces are placated and petitioned through rituals, those forces that affect large numbers of people are the object of collective rites. In precolonial Bali authority over such rituals was vested in kings and their priests. Bali was a Hocartian polity, organized by a concern for a prosperity controlled by spirits, gods, and demons (Hocart 1970). Balinese rulers were responsible for the well-being of their dependents and their land. Thus kings were referred to in texts as *sang nata*, a phrase meaning "protector and refuge" (Zoetmulder 1982:1177). What they protected against in particular were *buta-kala* and other forces that manifested themselves in—and were responsible for—shared human suffering. Power entailed a capacity to mediate with invisible forces on behalf of one's followers.

In practice, rulers discharged their responsibility by maintaining particular temples and ensuring the regular performance of their rites, mainly celebrations of the anniversary of the date on which the temple was consecrated. A ruler was also informed of large rituals within his domain in his followers' homes, village shrines, or family temples, at which his presence as witness was considered auspicious. But the quintessential royal rituals were large ceremonies to placate the *buta-kala*, which rulers both organized and witnessed.[13]

These rites were only loosely tied to the temple system; instead they were keyed to significant periodicities in the astronomical/cosmological year. Balinese use two major systems for establishing auspicious and inauspicious occasions for the performance of significant human activities. The first consists of a lunar-solar calendar of twelve months of thirty days apiece, with an intercalary month added when (in the opinion of the Brahmana priests who advised the king) it was merited; here the significant days are the full and new moons. The second was a 210-day calendar of thirty seven-day weeks of named days and ten interlocking periodicities (see Goris 1960). While most temple rituals were birthdays ordered by the 210-day calendar, many realm rituals were keyed to lunar and solar patterns. One of the most important tasks of court priests was to coordinate ritual activities on behalf of the realm by selecting auspicious dates on which these could occur, determining on what day in the 210-day cycle the full and new moons of what months of the lunar-solar calendar would fall.[14] This involved an interpretive tacking back and forth between natural signs (for example, the blooming of certain flowers) and textual ones. Since texts and their interpretation varied from priest to priest and realm to realm, the calendars of different realms were rarely in sync with one another; in one realm it might be the year 1820 and in the next 1822.

The most important realm ceremony was an annual exorcism at the end of the rainy season. The rainy season from the sixth to ninth months of the solar year was an inauspicious time when certain divinities and dangerous spirits (including the minions of the Fanged Lord) had the right to afflict or claim persons who had offended them. On the new moon of the ninth month, the inauspicious season was brought to a close with a great ritual at the public square before the royal residence of each realm, the rite known as the Taur Agung in Klungkung. This ritual also marked the beginning of a new year.

In addition to temple rituals and annual exorcisms, special rites were organized when signs such as epidemics suggested that negative forces were improperly in ascendancy in the realm. When such signs were brought to his attention, the king would see to it that no rituals were celebrated until the initiating cause—for example, the birth of twins to commoners (see Belo 1970)—had been properly addressed. Natural catastrophes (earthquakes, mudslides, epidemics, crop failures) and social disruptions (continual fighting, improper sexual relations, thefts) could also be signs: that the realm had become "hot," for example, and that either additional rituals needed to be made or the Taur Agung needed to be larger than usual. In short, events in the world, the result of positive or negative attentions of invisible forces, were interpretable as messages.

But whether a particular event was taken to be a message and, if so, of what, was not predetermined. Not all interpreters and not all texts agreed that particular events were signs or were in accord over what they meant. It was up to the ruler to ensure that messages were understood and properly answered. Palm-leaf manuscripts belonging to the ruler and his priests identified the spirits responsible for various catastrophes and, more important, the offerings that could be made to restore well-being. However, manuscripts, not to mention the opinions of those interpreting them, might differ. Ultimately decisions about whether to hold rituals, and what rituals these might be, rested with the king.

Royal authority rarely derived from a mastery of texts. It rested instead upon the ruler's special relationship to specific deities, demons, ancestors, and spirits. Semidivine figures, kings were sometimes referred to by their subjects as Betara Sekala or Betara Katon, "visible deities," or even Betara Nyeneng—a god come to life. In making decisions, a king could be guided by the promptings of the gods, which he would experience as a *kleteg ring kayun*—literally, a feeling or sensation affecting his thoughts, intentions, and desires; the closest English approximation might be "intuition." Such power was in part inherited, but it had to be actively augmented by a variety of practices, among them rituals, private meditation at temples, and manufacturing or otherwise obtaining magical objects.

THE MEANING AND SOURCES OF POWER

The ways that people in Klungkung speak of Klungkung are in part ways of talking about the power of Klungkung's rulers. Power, *kasaktian*, results from the generation or maintenance of connections between a person and the invisible world, especially (though not exclusively) the gods. In the broadest sense, *kasaktian* is the ability to achieve *any* goal (as noted by Cole 1983); it is synonymous with efficacy. Since the ultimate agent of such potency is *niskala*, there is a cultural emphasis on modesty; it is never really the self that accomplishes things but invisible forces working through the self. Usually, however, *kasaktian* suggests more than normal human capacities: an ability to prevent rain, say; or, to take another kind of example, to know (and potentially affect) the bodies and feelings of others. Phenomena Euro-Americans would ascribe to chance, coincidence, luck, or charisma—words whose English definitions are essentially confessions of ignorance—are treated as meaningful messages to and about persons with power. Persons with endless good luck, whose presence is sought by others who happily do their bidding, are regarded as attuned to the invisible world or *sakti* (roughly, one is *sakti*; one has *kasaktian*).

Persons obviously differ in the strength of their connection to the invisible world, and thus in their power. Balinese say that a capacity for power is in part foreordained. People are born with "letters" written on their foreheads, which determine (among other things) if their lives will be easy or difficult. In addition, the day of birth itself brings specific facilities, and characteristic obstacles as well. Surviving a perilous entry into the world demonstrates a capacity to transcend ordinary human abilities; breech births, cesareans, babies born with a caul—all have a potential for power.

Generally, however, power is constructed through both a material culture and an ensemble of practices. This is the case even with apparently heritable power. Balinese expect, for example, that more often than not power and rank will coincide. But one reason for this is that high-ranking people are more likely to have many rituals performed for them (and with greater attention to details) during their lifetimes, thus establishing closer relations to the invisible world. The proper appeasement of negative spirits and attention to positive ones during rites of marriage will also aid in conceiving a child beloved by the invisible world. Such distinctions are reinforced over time since if a person is the reincarnation of a powerful ancestor he will have an easier time acquiring power himself, and high-ranking people are more likely to have powerful ancestors than low-ranking ones.

To be powerful, however, it is not necessary to be born an aristocrat. Low-ranking persons may also be loved by the gods. Stories are told about powerful men who, recognizing signs of grace in commoner women (such as urine attractive to honeybees and butterflies), marry them, knowing their offspring will also be powerful (e.g., *Babad Ksatria;* Worsley 1972). Certain texts also advise how to produce an exceptional child: there are calendrically auspicious days for sexual relations, mental images upon which to focus during the sexual act, and rules for both parents to follow during pregnancy (the major one being that both should try to keep their thoughts free of disturbances).

But whatever one's ancestry, or the signs observed or rituals performed in the early years of life, these still only index a potential for power, rather than ensuring its achievement. To fulfill that potential requires an exploit of self-creation, the production of a certain kind of experience. Power is only achieved through practices that alter the subject. Ultimately *kasaktian* must be actively achieved in the course of a life.

Routes to power are roughly ranked. The most inferior is to have, unsought, some extraordinary experience involving the invisible world, to receive a "call." Most often commoners and women, people "called" by the gods typically have an unnerving or unusual experience that requires expert interpretation. For example, they may one day find their hair has coalesced into a single mass, which cannot be separated (if they cut it off, as the parents of one woman I know tried to do for their daughter several times, it simply grows back in the same unnatural way). A long illness, even a period of madness, may also index the interest of the invisible world. A more pleasant "call" is to *polih nyambut,* to find a powerful object, often one capable of bringing good fortune or protection, in an unusual or powerful place: temples are most common, but I heard of one man who found a gem inside a rice cake.[15] There may even be a direct encounter with a spirit. Such events are usually brought to a trance medium or Brahmana for interpretation. Frequently persons troubled by such incidents end up undergoing purification ceremonies and becoming temple priests or healers. Their lives are ever after changed, for persons who have been purified must maintain their state through food taboos and other restrictions or suffer unpleasant consequences.

Power acquired in this way may, however, prove ephemeral. Often such power—or the object that embodies it—brings dazzling fame and fortune for a time and then vanishes as mysteriously and suddenly as it appeared. To retain power requires something more active than grace: discipline. This is why other paths to power are regarded as superior.

The most enduring form of power, and the one felt most appropriate to Brahmanas, is acquired through the study of texts, accompanied by meditation, fasting, and other austerities (*mabrata*). Power based on knowledge not only cannot vanish but can be carried into future incarnations. But the path of knowledge also involves the greatest obstacles. People who study must not only undergo the rituals of purification already mentioned, with the same consequences, but may betray themselves with their own cleverness: they may quibble, waver, be too skeptical, succumb to boredom. The gods, say Balinese, prefer those who are stupid but honest.

But there is another path to power, one particularly relevant to Klungkung history, for in precolonial Bali it was a common practice of the ruling class: to "ask for a gift" (*nunas ica*) at a temple at night, to *nakti*, or *nyéwa-seraya*. It is difficult to imagine a person with any form of traditional authority who had never tried to *nakti*. While undoubtedly practiced by all rulers, it was probably critical for those whose claims to office were problematic, or those whose ambitions outstripped their circumstances.

Night visits to temples exemplify the key psychological attitudes, the phenomenology, of royal *kasaktian*: firmness of purpose and a mastery of fear To seek a gift involved a transformation of subjectivity that was indeed productive of social power. In the end to become powerful is to achieve a certain disposition, produced by and as a disciplined intent and calm indifference, a transformation that is then in complex ways socially validated. *Nakti*'ing is both paradigmatic of power and best illustrates its meaning.[16]

To "ask for a gift" one must pick an auspicious night, such as the full or new moon, and an appropriate temple.[17] Most commonly this will be the local Pura Dalem, whose goddess is especially inclined to confer gifts of power, both good and bad. According to stories told in Klungkung, that region's rulers and some of its greatest lords commonly prayed in Klungkung's state temples (especially Klotok, a seaside temple; Goa Lawah, famous for its cave filled with bats; or, whenever possible, Besakih, high on Mount Agung, the most important temple in Bali); lesser lords frequented lesser hilltop temples near the Karangasem border.[18]

To *nakti* entails overriding certain powerful cultural dispositions and thus already presupposes a potential for success. First of all, it must be done in the middle of the night, preferably beginning precisely at midnight, a magically dangerous time. For Balinese, night is a time to stay safely at home. Second, going to a temple to *nakti* is not like going to a temple during a ceremony. Rituals are noisy, crowded, full of color and activity—desirable experiences summed up by the term *ramé*. Solitude is something many people dread, and indeed Balinese are rarely alone; even to sleep people prefer to curl up with family members or friends. So to venture forth in the middle of the night by oneself, let alone to pass outside of the safe confines of the village to the isolated places where temples best suited for asking for boons are commonly located, takes courage. But power requires a willingness to master fear.

The supplicant brings with him a set of offerings, which he places before the shrine and dedicates to its divinity.[19] He sits cross-legged (women sit with legs folded to the side) facing the shrine from which he is seeking aid and lights incense. He must then try to focus all of his thoughts upon his goal and maintain this concentration in spite of whatever he experiences. Whatever deflects his attention must be resisted. Indeed, such resistance is crucial to achieving the desired goal, for the gods, while ultimately generous, test a supplicant's firmness of purpose by sending multitudinous trials, temptations (*gegodan*) to abandon the quest.

Some people, in fact, claim that the disturbances inevitably experienced are the divinity being supplicated temporarily manifesting itself in its negative aspect; if one remains calm and unruffled, they will pass as the divinity meta-morphoses back into its benevolent form. Ida Bagus Jagri told me that if one keeps one's thoughts entirely and completely focused upon what is desired, it will be quickly obtained—but such consistency is the most difficult of all things to achieve, since thoughts change constantly, as anyone who has ever tried to meditate can attest.

Temptations take various forms, ranging from frightening visions to wandering concentration to discouragement. Indeed, anything that potentially hinders a person in the attainment of a goal is interpretable as a form of temptation: if one's thoughts wander, that is a temptation. If one feels ants crawling over one's body or if mosquitoes continuously nip at one's skin, these are also temptations. If on the way to the temple a mischievous neighbor makes a loud noise to frighten you and you run in terror for home, that too is a temptation. Frustration, boredom, despair, hopelessness, and depression are also temptations—dangerous ones, since they may lead to the abandonment of the quest. But the temptation most relevant to this cultural practice is fear. The only solution is perseverance, and Balinese have faith that constancy is rewarded. Indeed, to be *pageh*, unwavering, is both the basis of power and its major behavioral sign.

While fundamentally all temptation is psychological (at least from a non-Balinese perspective; for a Balinese all psychology is at base spiritual since moods stem from the presence or absence of Divinity), the scenario of the quest commonly concretizes it, especially temptation on the brink of success, in the form of frightening visions. The one seeking power may suddenly be confronted with a ghoul of terrifying appearance, or a snake may coil over his lap. If, however, he manages to remain serene, to accept with tranquillity, or even to approach, whatever appears, success will finally be his: ghouls in fact are servants of the gods, and in such circumstances they may come bearing gifts.

Requests are never granted on the first try. Normally, success entails repeated visits, especially if the temple is one to which the supplicant has no prior ties. This too is a test of firmness of purpose. And the more significant and valuable the goal, the greater and more numerous the temptations. In fact, rather than concluding that apparently endless obstacles signify the inappropriateness or impossibility of a goal, Balinese interpret such obstacles as an especially subtle and pernicious form of temptation, which signifies that the goal itself is a particularly important one. In this respect, the practice of seeking a boon is a more formal (and more difficult) version of a generalized Balinese attitude: the need for steadfastness, and the idea that obstacles are tests, is not limited to those who *nakti;* rather, people often say that efforts to achieve any goal, especially a socially valued one, will be blocked by divinely sent tests (*miyasa gedé, gegodan gedé*). In effect the process of acquiring power is iconic of power, involving as it does a refinement of intent. But once achieved, power appears to others as uncanny effortlessness.

If the attainment of power, which entails a transformation of consciousness, is culturally modeled as a quest in which the seeker is confronted with numerous difficulties, success is stereotyped in similarly concrete ways. The fulfillment of the quest commonly takes the form of an object, which often seems a materialization of the vision through which self-mastery was achieved. The snake coiling over one's body, if grasped, turns into a piece of cloth; a small fire, when reached for, becomes a gemstone. Some argue that there is nothing miraculous about this: the object was there all the time, but the seeker's imagination (perhaps inspired by anecdotes about similar quests) transformed it into something frightening. Others claim that the vision is a glimpse of the nebulous invisible force embodied in the object.

The object itself is usually something that can be carried or worn upon the body. The most valued gift is a keris. Occasionally a supplicant will receive a palm-leaf text, which he must then study. Whatever its form—a piece of black and white checkered cloth, or solid yellow or white cloth; a gem or lesser stone; a Chinese coin with unusual markings, such as an incised representation of a shadow-play hero—the gift is brought home, ceremonially presented with offerings, and put in a special place, out of sight.[20] The object henceforth serves as the source of special abilities, acting as a conduit between the will of its owner and the efficacy of the invisible world. It is, in part, an embodiment of his new state of consciousness, his steadfastness, fearlessness, and will, and periodic offerings serve as reminders of this. The successful supplicant must also remember to bring offerings to the divinity who granted the gift, even if he is not a member of the group that supports the temple in which his quest has been fulfilled; and, if he plans to pass the object to his heirs, he must make sure that they know to do so as well.

Tests do not end with attainment: there is still a risk of loss. The person who has been successful may not speak of it, must not be tempted to augment his prestige by boasts about the gods' favor or his capacities: this is the fastest way to forefeit what has been won.

Objects obtained in such a fashion may become heirlooms; often, however, they only confer some limited form of power (such as invulnerability) upon the person who received them. It is as an individual that such bonds with divinities are formed, although powerful people occasionally pass on their power to a descendant of similar inclinations. Sensing that death is near (the powerful usually know such things), a man may call his heirs around his bed and inform them that whoever dares ingest the substance that emerges from his mouth at the moment of death will inherit his power. The revulsion that must be overcome to do so is, of course, a test. As with asking for gifts at temples, power is a product of self-control.

These various techniques to achieve power are by no means mutually exclusive. On the contrary, the biographies of powerful persons often encompass study, temple vigils, and unexpected and unsought gifts (stories concerning the ancestors of at least two ruling houses involve such incidents; see Worsley 1972 and Mahaudiana 1968). Study may also aid those who seek boons in temples, since certain texts contain mantras and information on what spirits take what forms. Ultimately all power comes from the gods. But all power is not equal. An object manufactured by a person who knew exactly which syllables and offerings would invoke which aspect of Divinity could prove superior to one with more mysterious origins. It is as if the more human activity is associated with seeking connections with the invisible world, the more reliable and enduring the power thus achieved.

KERIS

The material culture of power is most perfectly represented by an object famous throughout the Malay archipelago: the keris.[21] Keris instantiate particularly potent relations to the invisible world. They were, if anything, even more important in precolonial Bali.

Keris are long daggers, stabbing weapons suitable only for close combat. As objects, they are often spectacular. The longer edge of the upper part of the blade is frequently carved with curlicues, barbs, or even figures. Silver and black damascene patterns along the length of the blade are created by beating altogether alternating layers of iron and nickel (or nickelous iron); rubbing the blade with citrus blackens the iron to bring out the design, called *pamor*. Many keris also have wavy blades, resembling flames or the sinuous motion of a snake (see fig. 2). The curves of the blade (*luk*), like the roofs of Balinese shrines (*méru*), come in odd numbers. To compare keris blades and shrine roofs is not whimsical; the blade of a keris is in certain ways a portable shrine, and in both instances, the greater the number, the higher the spirit that inhabits them.

Like other objects with an aura of the numinous, powerful keris are kept in shrines or similarly consecrated spaces, and their comings and goings are accompanied by ritual acts. During the days Balinese smiths still manufactured keris, their skills involved more than a knowledge of forges and bellows; every step of the process required the recitation of mantras and the making of offerings, before the keris was finally brought to life by means of ritual. Through these processes each keris was shaped to have a distinct "personality"—a distinct form of efficacy. To maintain a keris's power requires a symbolic reproduction of its creation through a regular practice of making offerings. The day known as Tumpek Landep, Saturday-Kliwon in the week Landep (which means "sharp"), is sacred to metal objects and weapons, especially keris. On that day, keris are taken down from their shrines, lovingly cleaned and rubbed with oil, purified with holy water, and provided with offerings. The most important of these, the *tebasan pasupati*, the ingredients of which are entirely red (the meat of a red chicken, red rice, red fruits, red pastries, and a dab of chicken blood), recharges their *kasaktian*.

In precolonial Bali keris were in important ways agents of social reproduction, for the practices involved in keeping a powerful keris produced both gender and hierarchy, dividing male from female and aristocrat from commoner. First of all, they were and are markedly gendered objects. Gender was linked to keris throughout the life cycle. For a boy to receive a keris marked his attainment of adulthood. To wear a keris was to be or become a man, to be capable of fighting wars and spilling blood in animal sacrifices (and preparing their meat for ritual offerings). Girls, when they begin to menstruate, are even nowadays usually forbidden to touch keris. While menstruating women are regarded as dangerous to any object or person closely tied to the gods, that this danger is particularly marked for keris is indicated by the ban on contact at all times until a woman's menopause, a prohibition still strictly observed in Klungkung ruling class households.

The gender distinction extends even to offerings. A special kind of holy water made on Tumpek Landep may only be used by males. Moreover, women are prohibited from eating the leftovers of the central offering, the

Figure 2. Keris with fifteen curves taken from the royal house of Klungkung in 1908, currently in the collection of the Rijksmuseum voor Volkenkunde, Leiden (no. 1684/52).

tebasan pasupati; to do so, it is said, could cause menstrual irregularities or make a woman easily angered and hard of heart.

In precolonial Bali, all men owned at least one keris. This marked, in part, their status as warriors. Since all of a ruler's adult male subjects were expected to fight in his wars, as instruments of royal agency, keris defined manhood in relation to a certain kind of political order. Keris also marked distinctions of rank: high-status men *nyungklit* their keris, wore them on their backs, hilts peeking over their shoulders; others *nyelet* their keris, wore them at their waists. For a man to step outside the walls of his compound without a keris was once a social (and legal) offense, a kind of culturally defined indecent exposure. In particular, men were expected to wear keris to court and to temple rituals. Even in the 1930s, when the colonial government had eradicated warfare, men were still required (at least in some villages) to wear their keris to meetings and for all ritual or state occasions (Covarrubias 1937:198).

His keris could, in certain contexts, even represent a man: someone who could not attend a meeting could send his keris in his place; a man of rank could marry a low-ranking woman by proxy, using one of his lesser keris. Keris are rather obvious phallic symbols; in marriage rites, the groom still stabs a keris through a small bamboo mat to symbolize the sexual relation between husband and wife even though nowadays his wedding is the only occasion on which a man is still likely to wear a keris.[22]

For precolonial Balinese keris were artifacts that condensed beliefs and practices concerning power. They were associated with events that constituted power and rank, and thus with history. As both tokens of history and, as enspirited objects, sources and means of power, they were central to the representation and practice of precolonial political authority. The value of a keris was partly derived from the narrative of its relationship to a particular kin group. As we will see, the opening sections of chronicles concerning politically prominent Balinese clans invariably include accounts of the acquisition and characteristics (including proofs of its supernatural abilities) of one or more named, magical keris (or sometimes spears); indeed, in Balinese historiography the coming of such objects to a pivotal ancestor more often than not marked the beginning of a family's rise to power.[23] Keris are also, as we will see, central characters in Klungkung narratives concerning the conquest. Their role in making Klungkung history suggests that such objects were crucial to royal agency.

The keris inherited by a ruler upon his succession to the throne were known as *pajenengan*, which could be translated as "regalia." The phrase *nyeneng ratu*, "to reign as king," built around the active verbal form of the word, emphasizes the close connection between regalia and rule. Since *nyeneng* alone means "to live," another possible meaning of *pajenengan* might be "that which confers life," especially as for some Balinese *pajenengan* is almost synonymous

with *kawitan* (origin, source); heirloom keris are sometimes referred to as Betara Kawitan (Divine Origin) or Betara Pajenengan.[24] *Pajenengan* were historical individuals, with many of the attributes of persons. They were referred to
by proper names, preceded by the nominal particle *I* or *Ki*, which signified
that they were agents.[25] While not all *pajenengan* were keris (other weapons or
objects such as Klungkung's slit-gongs could also be regalia), keris were the
most common and important.

Such keris, however, did not function on what could be called the Excalibur principle: that "whoever bears this sword is henceforth king." Their
biographies, the narratives of their relationship to a particular descent group,
were inalienable. To anyone else their value would lie in their qualities, not
their history.

The role regalia played in maintaining the welfare of a realm will become
clearer through narratives recounted in later chapters. Here suffice it to say
that a ruler's heirloom keris provided protection against all kinds of enemies:
other rulers, testing their strength against his; rebellious lords in his own
realm; forces that threatened the welfare of his dependents. This is not to say
that they were commonly worn or wielded; they were only used to fight, for
example, under extreme circumstances.

Gifts of keris—from hierarchical superiors, which included nonhuman
agents—were grants of power. When a ruler established a lord or kinsman as
protector of a domain, he commonly gave him a keris to help him. Such a
keris became a sacred heirloom to the lord's descendants, belonging in turn
to each of his successors. Keris, then, indexed authority, and the durability
of the material from which they were made enabled them to serve as tangible
tokens of continuity that could suggest power's immutability. As heirlooms,
they formed a bridge between the great deeds of the past and those possible
in the future. They instantiated their owners' potential ability to draw upon
past relationships in the service of present interests.

The role keris played in constituting power hinged upon the fact that
keris were first and foremost weapons, meant to be used against external enemies in war or internal ones in executions. Power, in other words, had a fierce
aspect. This is still evident in representations of divinities: at temple festivals,
the space before shrines is festooned with spears and tridents; in cosmological
lore, the gods of each direction are associated with different weapons.

The power of whatever spirits "sat" in a keris at the time of its acquisition
could be augmented by offerings or by use. Several nineteenth-century European sources note that the older a keris, the more it was valued. But it was
not simply its ability to evoke memories of genealogical predecessors that
increased the reverence in which older keris were held. According to some
nineteenth-century sources, the value of a keris increased with the number
of deaths attributed to it, which both constituted proof of and added to its

potency (Anonymous [Medhurst] 1830; Helms 1969). In Bali I was told that keris that have tasted blood are dangerous to unsheathe—for the *kala* in them want more. Such a keris could cause a man to run amok. Thus whenever they are unsheathed there is a *tabuh rah*, a blood offering—as there is at Tumpek Landep.

Forging a keris brought into play the elemental forces of fire, water, and air, and thus the gods Brahma, Wisnu, and Siwa, but Brahma is the deity most relevant to discourse about keris. Keris, associated as they were with fighting and war, are still spoken of as "hot" things, and their power (sometimes power in general) is frequently represented as flames, a fire symbolically re-created in the red offerings made every Tumpek Landep. Many tests of keris evoke heat as well. A man who acquires a keris might test it by keeping it in the room where he sleeps or by submersing it in water. People told me that the heat powerful keris generate makes it difficult to sleep in the same room with them; friends of mine told me they once proved the power of a blade by immersing it in a tub of water: tiny bubbles demarcating its shape rose to the top. The blade of a powerful keris is said to feel to experts as if an electric current were running through it.

It is the blade that bears a keris's name and personality, that is the receptacle for the spiritual forces inhabiting the weapon. In fact, since hilts (see fig. 3) are detachable, in precolonial Bali different hilts might be worn by a blade on different occasions, for example, at audiences or in battle. But if not the source of a keris's potency, both sheath and hilt may enhance its capacities and value. Indeed, both hilts (*danganan* or *ulu*, "head") and sheaths (*sarung*) of keris belonging to rulers were frequently embellished in ways that imaged or added to the qualities of the blade to which they ordinarily belonged.

Many royal keris, for example, had golden statuettes for hilts, in the form of such figures as the god Kala or *raksasa* (ogres). According to the *Kidung Pamancangah* (Berg 1929), the hilts of three of Klungkung's most famous regalia were in the shape of the god Bayu, god of wind and breath, or more generally force or energy. This was, of course, extremely relevant to the way these objects served as instruments of power, for, as Ida Bagus Jagri noted, *bayu* is what enables a person to achieve his goals.

The navels (center of the life force) and sometimes foreheads (location of the invisible "third eye" that sees what is *niskala*) of these statuettes were set with *mirah*, precious and semiprecious translucent stones cut into cabochons, as was a golden ring set just below the hilt. In a particularly fine keris these stones would be carefully chosen for their abilities to supplement the powers of the blade itself.[26] Diamonds, for example, are "poison" and so counteract the poison of an enemy.

Sheaths are also important, for they protect blades, not only from damage but from substances that can pollute them. In addition they shield people

Figure 3. Keris hilt. Collection of the Tandjung Sari Foundation, Bali.
Photograph by Garrett Solyom.

from a blade's power. Many scabbards are made of special varieties of wood; some contain ivory, which has the power to repel enemies, including those who use magic. Scabbards are sometimes carved, occasionally with scenes from famous legends that further image the blade's qualities. Sheaths belonging to wealthy or important people may be trimmed in gold or silver and even encrusted with gems, but the precious metals and stones decorating both scabbards and hilts may be sold or pawned if necessary (Covarrubias 1937:199).

INVISIBLE AGENCY AND HISTORY

The ways Balinese speak and act in relation to keris and practices like "asking for a gift" raise more general questions concerning how such discourses are to be understood. Almost invariably, objects, tales, and activities like these have been interpreted by anthropologists as "symbolic" of other, human realities. Objects, when taken seriously by anthropologists, are regarded as symbols of identity, for example, or of social relations established by processes of exchange or production (see Thomas 1991 for a good critique). But objects like keris do not "stand for" power; the praxis associated with them creates it, and their value depends on more than the social relations in which they are or were embedded.

What matters most about keris is their effect on consciousness. It is not hard to imagine the effect of holding in one's hand an object about which extraordinary stories are told. But keris do not only affect the consciousness of their possessors; powerful ones are said to affect others as well. Here it is important to note that I am not saying that Balinese "believe" in keris, for I am reluctant to reduce what Balinese say about keris to a psychology of belief. Belief in and of itself has limited efficacy, as many religious people know all too well. Moreover, Balinese do not claim that all keris are effective, or effective in the same way. Powerful keris may work magic, which is a name we give to what surprises us into acknowledging that there is more to the way we act and perceive in the world than we normally agree to agree about. Such surprises are efficacious, for they allow people to step beyond the boundaries of what they normally can accomplish or sense. This may seem a mystification, but then Balinese do not claim to understand how these things work. Primarily they are allowed to operate without interpretation, without the active intervention of authoritative discourses.

An incident in which I was involved may prove illuminating here. Early in my stay in Klungkung, an offerings expert I knew named Dayu Biang Apuan informed me that in the last century Klungkung's rulers had held a great ritual to purify the souls of their ancestors. And so beloved were they by the gods, that a spirit had provided a rhinoceros, an animal only known through legends, to be sacrificed for the occasion.

My first reaction to this news was cynical. I knew that such a ritual had been held, and that a rhinoceros had indeed been sacrificed. A poem had been written by a Klungkung prince to commemorate the occasion; the rhinoceros was, moreover, mentioned in Dutch sources.[27] According to the latter, the animal had been brought to Klungkung at the Déwa Agung's own request, and at considerable expense and trouble, by Boele Schuurman, the agent for the Netherlands Trading Society, as part of the early diplomatic efforts of the Netherlands Indies government. It was hardly surprising that the rhinoceros had made a powerful impression; rhinoceri were known only from texts, and to actually come face to face with such a peculiar beast had no doubt been a memorable experience. The Déwa Agung's ability to carry off this amazing ritual coup on behalf of his ancestors probably added immeasurably to his prestige.

But spirits? This talk of spirits seemed an obvious confession of ignorance about "real" causalities; the myth that had developed seemed patently political in motivation, an attempt to bolster the reputation of Klungkung's rulers. I told Dayu Biang Apuan that I knew about the rhinoceros, but it had been no spirit, merely a Dutchman, who had given it to the court. She scoffed at me: that was no Dutchman, and that was no ordinary animal either—why, until mantras had been recited, no one had even been able to kill it.

Taken aback by this rejection of what I considered provable historical truth, I raised the matter with Ida Bagus Jagri. How could Dayu Biang be so unfazed by my information? He listened carefully, then proclaimed that the Dayu was clearly correct. Perhaps a Dutchman did deliver the beast, but what could have inspired him to do such a thing but a prompting from the invisible world, a manipulation of his will by the forces that supported the ruler of Klungkung? In short, the rhinoceros was a gift from the spirits, not from the Dutch, even if they had been the vehicle by which the gift had arrived at its destination.

To bring his point home, he brought up another gift, which I had brought back for Pedanda Gedé Kenitén from Singapore when I went to obtain my research visa. I had told Ida Bagus Jagri how, all my gift shopping done, I was headed to my hotel room to pack for my flight to Indonesia early the next morning when my eye was caught by the window of a shop that had already closed for the night. I had so wanted to see what was inside that I took a later flight. In the shop I found myself drawn to an old ivory bracelet made in India, with a large white stone in a heavy silver setting, and although it cost more than I intended to spend, I bought it for the Pedanda. On the flight back, I had second thoughts. Ida Bagus Jagri had once told me that ivory had protective powers, but the bracelet was not the sort of thing that I had ever seen anyone on Bali wear. But when I presented it to the Pedanda, he turned it over and over again in his hands, his eyes shining with pleasure. He remarked that for many years he had wanted something triply white (silver is a "white" metal) but had not be able to picture clearly what it would look like. And now, he laughed, here it was. This episode, said Ida Bagus Jagri, was just like the one with the rhinoceros. Like the Dutch, I had been a vehicle through which the invisible world had operated. It was the Pedanda's *kasaktian* that had brought the bracelet to him, just as more than a century ago the Déwa Agung's had brought him a rhinoceros. Dayu Biang Apuan's tale simply bypassed the irrelevant appearances.

I tell this tale because its implications are profound. Academics often think as I initially did, that anecdotes like Dayu Apuan's code "real" history in metaphoric form. To be sure, overlaps between European and indigenous sources are fascinating. But to use them to separate the historical wheat from the "mythical" chaff of non-European narratives is an exercise in ethnocentrism that seriously underestimates the intelligence of indigenous people— not to mention ignoring the mythical dimensions of European representations.

In general, when people being studied by anthropologists say or do something fantastic by the standards of Enlightenment rationality, anthropologists think it charitable to show that they are really talking about something else. To interpret away as metaphor or ideology whatever does not correspond to familiar canons of evidence and truth, to see such statements as disguised versions of what *is* familiar, takes far too much for granted concerning the nature of the real and of human motivations.

Discourses of magic are rarely taken seriously by Euro-American analysts. Their dismissals, however, ultimately derive from a political project that authorized certain discourses and relationships over others, justifying subordination both domestically (over the superstitious lower classes) and abroad (over the "heathen savages").

When Balinese talk of spirits, they are speaking of agencies understood to be the real processes at work behind events. Euro-American historians or anthropologists may congratulate themselves on their subtle grasp of the political and social nuances of magical anecdotes, on their ability to recognize such statements as strategic. But many Balinese intellectuals appreciate profundity of a different kind: to identify the invisible forces at work in events is to assess their significance.

KINGS AND THE INVISIBLE WORLD

I started this chapter by referring to the delight people in Klungkung took in the deceptiveness of appearances. It is now obvious that this is a general theme in Bali. As might be expected with people who think there is more to the world than meets the eye, many Balinese delight in tales that show what seems ordinary to really be wondrous (and often vice versa). Take, for example, a legend people tell concerning Danghyang Nirartha, ancestor of most of Bali's Brahmanas. One day, when he was taking a walk, a man came up to ask him for holy water. Taking the bamboo tube that the man extended, he dipped it into a nearby irrigation ditch and handed it back, much to the man's dismay. He smiled and thanked the priest but, as soon as he was out of sight, tossed the water out in disgust, feeling singularly cheated. As it fell, it hit the carcass of a dead dog, which was immediately restored to life.

Tales like this are extremely pertinent to Klungkung history, for what made Klungkung's rulers what they were was not visible grandeur or pomp but their relations to the invisible world. In later chapters I will argue that the Déwa Agung, ruler of Klungkung, was uniquely responsible not only for the people and land of Klungkung but for Bali as a whole. In texts he was sometimes referred to as Sang Aji Bali. In modern Balinese *aji* means "father," and "the Father of Bali," like all fathers, was ideally a protector and guide for those dependent upon him. This status rested upon his relationship to the deity of one particular temple: the temple of Besakih, on the slopes of Bali's highest volcanic mountain, Mount Agung. It was on the basis of this relationship that other rulers paid him allegiance or attempted to withhold it.

Such supremacy did not, however, mean that the Déwa Agung and/or his priests told other priests and other rulers what to do, let alone when, where, and how. Precolonial Bali was characterized by multiplicity—ritually, politically, cosmologically. Indeed, the value placed on such multiplicity is expressed by a phrase, *désa, kala, patra*, "place, time, and circumstance": the gods and spirits of one place have different requirements from the gods and spirits of another. Even if, as a consequence of war, a stretch of territory changed hands from one ruler to another, the ritual practices of the conquered region were left as they were. Authority in precolonial Bali was dispersed, and each ruler took care of the affairs of his own subjects in his own domain. Other rulers, however, did consult the Déwa Agung, and occasionally they asked permission for his priests to perform especially important rituals on their behalf. They were also expected to make an appearance and perform acts of ritual obeisance at his great works, and he would grace them with his presence or some symbolic token thereof at theirs in return.

It would be a mistake to conclude from the importance of ritual that the ideology of rule in Bali was "religious." Such characterizations obscure more than they clarify, since religion is presupposed as a distinct sphere of social action. But Balinese praxis and discourse blur the lines between sacred and secular, for almost everything Balinese do involves seeking the aid of auspicious forces or asking for protection against inauspicious ones. In precolonial

Bali there was no clearly demarcated domain of action that could be termed "religion," since all power was understood to derive from relationships to invisible forces.

This is not to say that all power was the same. While all power rested upon divine favor, the particular invisible forces involved were different, and the power such relationships created was directed to different ends.[28] It is important to emphasize that rulers' activities particularly involved them with inauspicious forces. The realm purifications that were the quintessential royal rites were thematically linked with the fearlessness needed to acquire power and with the military-magical uses of royal regalia.

The power of Balinese rulers—especially the kings of Klungkung—rested on their ability to mediate between the numinous and the ordinary. Their relationships to invisible agencies enabled them to affect the visible world. Proof of these relationships was manifested in events. Conversely, anyone who wished power would begin by seeking relationships with the invisible world and would seek some tangible sign of these in the form of objects.

This is not the same as saying that one who had managed by force of personality to gain power would then seek to "legitimate" that power symbolically. What Euro-Americans commonly regard as "real" power (influence over other persons) would only have been possible to one already favored by invisible forces. The real question was how long those forces would continue to confer their favor. Thus when Balinese say (as they do) that Klungkung is venerated as Bali's "eldest" kingdom, they are not only making a formal statement about the respect due to elders. The historical depth associated with the Klungkung royal house suggests the strength of its ties to the invisible world.

It was the hoped-for permanence of such relationships that was encoded in the form of heritable rights over objects like keris and spaces like temples. These objects and spaces indexed the kinds of invisible forces, and thus the nature of the power, at a person's disposal. There are therefore important nuances that accrue to the particular objects and particular spaces under a ruler's authority. Some of these will be explored for Klungkung in chapter 5.

Heirloom weapons, temples, and the practices associated with them constituted Balinese kingship. Heirloom weapons linked rulers of the same dynasty temporally, suggesting at the same time that they were potentially paradigms of one another. A ruler's presence at rituals in the temples of his realm similarly established a relationship between them, and between the groups, divinities, and activities associated with them, thus constituting the social whole of his realm.

It is hardly surprising, then, that attempts to fix Klungkung's authority as "political" or "spiritual" proved so difficult for colonial bureaucrats. There was a sharp disjunction between the presuppositions of colonial officials and those of Balinese lords. To the extent that scholarly accounts of Balinese history not only depend upon materials written by such officials but share their categories and assumptions about society and reality, they are bound to misread the actions and motivations of Balinese agents.

bave
theirs.

FOUR

Making History: Balinese and Colonial Practices of Knowing

According to a story people tell in Bali, there was once a time when divinities and spirits were knowable through ordinary human perception. In those days humans had completely black eyes, like those of dogs and other animals, and, like dogs, they could see spirits; more important, being superior to dogs, they could see divinities. The Balinese version of the expulsion from the garden is, characteristically, funny. One day, a fellow was shitting in the woods when a god (which one isn't mentioned) walked by. Without thinking, he called out cheerfully the usual friendly Balinese greeting: "Betara, where are you going?" Such impertinence could not be allowed to recur. By covering the larger part of human eyes with a white membrane, the gods made it impossible for people to see them, and so matters have remained to this day.[1]

This little fable does much to explain why according to Klungkung tales various rulers addressed colonial officials as "white eyes." Between the odd color of European eyes, reminiscent of the blue cast of the eyes of the elderly—who not uncommonly have poor vision—and European styles of speaking and acting, powerful Balinese concluded that the Dutch must be blind to invisible forces. That the Balinese word for blindness is *buta* is equally relevant, for Europeans appeared to be not only ignorant of Divinity but driven by the arrogance and greed typical of those possessed by such non-human agents.

Ironically, for Europeans vision was the primary trope for knowledge, and the ability to make things visible was a cornerstone of imperial power. Like metropolitan forms of what Foucault calls the regime of "disciplinary power" emerging in Europe, the colonial state attempted to impose on those it subjugated "a principle of compulsory visibility" (1979:187). The effect of various investigative procedures was to constitute a colonial subject of whom it could be said: "He is seen, but he does not see; he is the object of information, never a subject in communication" (Foucault 1979:200). But, as the epithet "white eyes" suggests, European epistemologies of empire also had their characteristic blindnesses.

76   "Visibility" and "invisibility" refer, then, not only to Balinese ontological

distinctions but also to the biases of two distinct regimes of knowledge and
power: that of the Dutch colonial state and its agents, and that of Klungkung's
ruling class and its descendants. Each of these regimes was characterized by
specific communicative practices and textual productions.

According to Richard Price, to write an ethnographic history requires
not only a continual attempt to tease out "the significance of experience and
actions to the actors," but also an awareness of the forces which shape the
sources on which one may draw in imagining a past (1990:xvii). Therefore,
understanding something of these practices is helpful in interpreting the
memories and material traces generated by relations between Klungkung and
the colonial government. Before proceeding to Balinese and Dutch accounts
of those relations, I want to attempt to make explicit some of the assumptions
that shape colonial documents and Balinese texts and narratives.

BALINESE ETHNOHISTORY

In chapter 1, Klungkung discourse about the colonial conquest was contrasted
to two more official forms of discourse: that of the colonial government and
that of the modern nation-state. In this section, I want to compare it to a
third, which in many ways it strongly resembles: that of *babad*, chronicles,
one of which will be the topic of the next chapter. What concerns me here
are both differences in the authority of such discourses and in the roles they
play in Balinese experience, and similarities in their rhetorical styles.

To call *babad* "chronicles" is somewhat misleading. *Babad* center on the
founding of (usually high-ranking) clans and the deeds of their most famous
members. Mainly they consist of genealogical notes, interspersed with narratives.[2] Generally those portions of the text concerned with earlier events con
tain more narrative; as the action of the text approaches the present, genealogies prevail and are more detailed.

In an important sense *babad* are Malinowskian charters. The paucity of
genealogy in the beginning of such texts is reminiscent of oral lineage histories and suggests that *babad* stress present social relations over past ones: as
such texts are transmitted over time, ancestors whose lines have become irrelevant to the living are no longer mentioned. But there is more to the structure of *babad* than this. The narrative richness of earlier sections implies that
more "happened" in the distant past, that events of long ago were not only
consequential but constitutive.

This in fact lies precisely at the heart of what Balinese mean by *babad*:
such texts deal with *kawitan*, origins. The term *kawitan* derives from an Old
Javanese root, *wit*, which means not only "origin" but also "cause," "foundation," and even "tree" (Zoetmulder 1982:2345). That the latter is relevant
here is suggested by the fact that *mabad*, a verbal form of *babad*, literally means

"to clear a forest." *Babad,* then, are texts concerned with the founding of a prominent family and the ties that link living persons to a single *kawitan* or family tree.[3]

Balinese generally consult *babad* to clarify identities, to locate themselves and others in social space in relation to their *kawitan.* Some study such texts for inspiration: an awareness of the accomplishments of one's ancestors can encourage belief in one's own potential abilities. More commonly, Balinese refer to such texts for aid in ritually "remembering" their ancestors, persons transformed through death rituals into nonvisible agents. Such remembering is crucial to well-being, for "forgetting"—an idiom that indicates a failure to make offerings to a spiritual patron—is often diagnosed through healers as the cause of illness, dissension, and other misfortunes. *Babad* indirectly organize certain forms of ritual practice: to know one's origins is to know at what shrines (also called *kawitan*) one should be making regular offerings. The texts themselves rarely mention temples, but they allow a person to deduce from what branch of what family tree his twig may have fallen, and therefore to locate the genealogical and spatial nodes marked by temples to his ancestors.

It is to such matters that most people refer when they speak of *sejarah,* "history,"[4] which explains why when I first arrived in Klungkung and described my project as historical I found myself directed to men with local reputations as experts in *babad.* In fact one folk etymology derived *sejarah,* an Indonesian term, from two (Balinese) words, *saja,* "truly," and *rah,* "blood."[5] Such a gloss fits perfectly the genealogical focus of *babad.* But then *sejarah* itself originally had similar connotations (Bottoms 1965:180).

Given these associations, it is not surprising that I elicited few accounts of Klungkung's relations with the Dutch when I inquired about "history." Narratives about such matters are referred to not as "history" but as *satua,* stories, or *orti,* news, and they enter into discourse as gossip, rumor, reminiscences, and anecdotes. In recounting such stories, people peppered their narratives with words like *kocap* or *reké,* "it is said," or "I have heard"; frequently, they would emphasize that they were simply passing along something they had been told, and that they could not vouch for its accuracy. The subjunctive voice in which such narratives were usually related was also highlighted when every now and again someone vehemently declared that *this* story—generally referring to something experienced by his or her father—was true.

Babad, it would seem, have an authority, a collective truth value, that mere stories lack. One reason may be that they are written: the letters of the Balinese alphabet are considered dwelling places of the goddess Saraswati. Probably more relevant is that "stories" or "news" appear to reflect ongoing efforts to assess the meaning of relatively recent events. That they are tentative shows that rival interpretations of the past still exist, that they make claims that have not yet been satisfactorily proven, in contrast to what is written in *babad*. Thus they only express "what is said."[6]

But the social power of "what is said" should not be underestimated. Nor should one take at face value disclaimers that these are "just" stories. Ida Bagus Jagri liked to provide folk etymologies of *satua*, the word for story. Once he noted that *satua* contained the words *satu*, "one," and *tua*, "old": hence, "an old one," words from long ago. On another occasion he derived it from *sa* (again, "one") and *tuara*, "nonexistent," an allusion to the invisible world that implied to him the profundity of many such "stories."

Some people were more willing to pass along these stories than others. Commoners, for example, were often chary of repeating stories concerning the conquest, at least to strangers such as myself or Dayu Alit; many would talk only of what they themselves had personally experienced. To be sure they had less stake in such tales, less motivation to ensure their transmission, and then again some of these stories involved unpleasant rumors about people who still had living descendants, descendants who were, moreover, very sensitive about their ancestors. But for the most part such reluctance reflected a pervasive cultural attitude toward speech.

Speech and Silence

One reason Klungkung's power was invisible to the Dutch—and has continued to be invisible to scholars—is that Balinese speech about power and the invisible world is subject to a number of constraints. Understanding the rhetorics and interpretive practices appropriate to such matters is essential to "reading" Klungkung words, written and spoken, past and present.

Several forms of speech are considered positively dangerous. Most dangerous are mantras, powerful syllables and Sanskrit words used to summon invisible forces; even to study certain mantras requires ritual consecration. Certain unfortunate people were pointed out to me as examples of the fate that befalls those who study mantras for which they are not qualified. Almost as risky, some people think, is to ignore the injunction "do not divulge" (*aja wéra*), which often appears in texts concerned with metaphysical speculations: this is a likely way to lose one's sources of spiritual protection.

But even matters not explicitly proscribed are not necessarily shared with just anyone. Those who speak wrongly or improperly, who are *pelih ban raos*, not only may risk human enmity but may anger ancestors or alienate the gods, with dire consequences. There are numerous forms of improper speech: to speak authoritatively of what cannot be known is one; to talk capriciously of what has not been proven is another. (Some people are consequently reluctant to express opinions, for one cannot "prove" one's thoughts.) Many errors of speech are evaluated as arrogance, perhaps the cardinal social sin.

Thus Balinese tend to modesty in their claims about themselves or the world. The gods particularly dislike braggarts, as the anecdote narrated in the last chapter demonstrates. On the whole, those who talk don't know, and those who know don't talk.

The gods do not hold the ignorant as responsible for their words as they do those who should know better, however. Elders—culturally defined as those entrusted with the ritual and material welfare of others—are under the most pressure to speak and act with prudence. Priests must be especially cautious; their consecration means that Divinity is close to them and will therefore respond to their errors of speech, including exaggerations and distortions, swiftly. Since women are less commonly elders (with the exception of priestesses), they are less burdened with the need to guard their words; indeed, both men and women sometimes say that women talk *too* much (*nglamis*), which explains (along with the fact that women are said to pay more attention to things) why in some ways *orti* is women's talk. But Divinity will protect true innocents, who simply state what they honestly know (*anak pasaja*), regardless of what they say.

Only the innocent, the ignorant, and the immature, therefore, speak without caution, saying whatever comes to mind. Those who "understand" use *raos mataled*, literally, "speech resting on a foundation." For example, rather than making promises, asserting that they can accomplish some deed, or boasting about their skills, the wise merely say they will try. Another example of *raos mataled* is to respond to praise with disclaimers, and even declare oneself ignorant. Thus people with reputations for power and knowledge will, if approached directly, deny they know anything, so they will not appear arrogant—which often clinches the matter. Phrases like *kocap*, "it is said," are further examples of *raos mataled*, which puts a rather different spin on the rhetoric of storytelling.

Such practices create a very nuanced social world, where people are adept at insinuation. For one, the ambitious cannot create reputations by self-assertion; abilities are intimated, rather than explicitly declared, and reputations spread outward in a ripple of rumor. These practices also explain why Balinese, when they speak of power or the invisible world, necessarily speak elliptically. As the saying goes, such speech comes "with a skin" (*makulit*) and requires listeners be skilled at "peeling" (*melutin*). Tales of power, therefore, tend to be elusive and oblique, to hint rather than declaim; but then the gods themselves communicate through signs.

Not all people, however, are equally adept at distinguishing peel from pith. It is understood that interlocutors will draw different conclusions from the same words or signs, depending on their level of understanding. The ideal interlocutor is *wayah di tengah*, literally, "mature inside." One who is mature understands things, knows what should and should not be said, appreciates consequences both visible and invisible. Those who are *wayah di tengah* also choose carefully to whom they may reveal their opinions.

This is particularly true regarding *niskala* matters. Even though one may in theory speak directly with those at one's own level of knowledge or higher, both the risks and the paradoxes of communicating about the invisible world usually mean that people who study such matters delight in witticisms, proverbs, and plays on words, especially folk etymologies and puns. Once a friend of Ida Bagus Jagri simply looked him in the eyes in my presence and pronounced *"alas, alis, alus"* (literally, forest, eyebrow, refined), to which he responded with an appreciative laugh. (Later, when I asked, Ida Bagus Jagri interpreted this for me as meaning that a forest is dense and dark; inside it is hard to see; but forests are inhabited by what is "refined" or invisible, that is, spirits.) On several occasions I heard him chuckle with friends over the phrase *ana tanana: ana* means "there is" or "there are"; *tanana*, apart from referring to a kind of spirit or the invisible world in general (so the phrase *ana tanana* could mean "there was a spirit" or "there is an invisible world"), can be broken into the two words *ana* and *tan*, a negation (hence the phrase could also be translated, "there is, there isn't").

There is, then, much reading between the lines. People grant much more responsibility to their interlocutors than Euro-Americans are accustomed to doing, and they expect people to understand things without having to have them said. Ida Bagus Jagri used to instruct me that one can know what people think from their eyes and their lips; indeed, those who "study" often recognize each other by their eyes. People are also very sensitive to body language. There are even texts concerning the interpretation of character from such things as how people hold themselves, or the expressions on their faces. In general, people rely much more on informal and implicit modes of knowledge of the kind we call empathy and intuition.[7]

Such rhetorics of innuendo clearly limit what an outsider can understand, and it was in no small part for this reason that Ida Bagus Jagri and Dayu Alit were such invaluable teachers, for they corrected many of my more blatant errors. For example, when I would attempt to elicit explicit explanations, and people murmured in response phrases like "one cannot speak of that," I initially assumed that they were rejecting my interpretations. But eventually Dayu Alit corrected this misapprehension and informed me that by using such phrases people were agreeing with me, while refusing to engage in continued discussion of a dangerous matter. Then there were occasions when I would spend hours looking over interview transcripts in a fruitless search for particular statements, to the baffled amusement of Dayu Alit who would say that of course the person in question had told me what I thought he or she had, regardless of whether the words were there—and when I would go back and ask directly, I would often indeed have my conclusions confirmed.

One effect of these styles of discourse was that if I wanted to know anything about the invisible world, I had to take seriously the responsibilities that such knowledge entails. This is a discourse in which, as Favret-Saada (1980) notes about speech about witchcraft in rural France, one must either take a position or be excluded completely. Since matters concerning power and the invisible world cannot be discussed with the ignorant, unless one shows one is not ignorant one will learn nothing.

It is also important to note that these rhetorical styles seem to have existed precolonially, and therefore affected what colonial officials could learn as well. One sees traces of them in Dutch accounts in remarks about "Eastern" indirection or excessive politeness, or in references to Balinese fear, prevarication, and intrigue. Van den Broek even complained that he found it difficult to accomplish his mission "on account of the extreme distrust of the Princes and of the timidity of their subjects in relation to everything that was asked of them, which they continually or totally evaded, or answered with the greatest obscurity or ambiguity" (van den Broek 1835:159).

Balinese Texts

Whatever caution people take in speaking, they are nonetheless more candid and less veiled than are many genres of texts. Wordplay, for example, is even more common in texts than in speech, especially those texts that provide clues about matters that cannot be known in ordinary ways. But before discussing such texts, it is important to note some more mundane features of Balinese textuality, which complicate their use as sources of insight into Balinese constructions of knowledge and power and into Balinese styles of making history.

First of all, not everyone in Bali can read texts. Precolonially, literacy was largely restricted to high-ranking persons and experts such as architects, healers, and performers who needed some mastery of esoteric textual knowledge in the practice of their art; nowadays, while children are taught to read Balinese characters in school, few develop an interest in texts until much later in life.

But textual literacy involves not only mastery of the Balinese script: it also requires an understanding of Kawi (also known as Old Javanese), the language in which most texts are written.[8] Kawi is iconic of the antiquity texts represent. Although Austronesian in syntax, a good 30 percent of Kawi's lexicon derives from Sanskrit. In the complex verbal world of performance, Balinese treat Kawi (which means "poetic") as the highest register of their language, a language in which different lexical items, coded high and low, are appropriate to distinct forms of social interaction: Kawi is the language of gods and heroes (Zurbuchen 1987). In fact, most people pick up their first Kawi from shadow-puppet plays or other performances.

Understanding texts is further complicated by the fact that there are few institutional arenas to hone or even develop the necessary interpretive skills, although some genres are more accessible than others. Literary texts, *kidung* and *kekawin*, are probably the most accessible of all, despite their difficulties. Considered sources of insight into living a moral life, they are studied in special associations known as translation or reading clubs, where they are sung aloud, glossed into Balinese, and discussed (Zurbuchen 1987; for a discussion of such texts, see Zoetmulder 1974). Even here comprehension is by no means easy. In addition to Kawi, the student of poetry must master the complex and intricate metrical rules according to which such texts are composed, and a more profound understanding of them requires appreciating the lessons they offer for living one's life. But such texts are intended to be sung aloud—and they are, at rituals during which reading clubs are asked to perform in public. Thus they exist in a relatively public arena; other types of texts are read only in private and enter public discourse in more elliptical ways. *Babad*, for example, may be read aloud on certain rare occasions but are usually either interpreted through dramatic performances or studied in private.[9]

Unlike narrative texts, there are no contexts in which speculative or "metaphysical" texts—texts recounting offerings and mantras to cure an illness, invoke a deity, or liberate the soul; those narrating mystical connections between divinities and categories of persons; or those concerning the structure and origins of the cosmos—are voiced; some say they cannot even be discussed, though clearly they concern extremely important matters. Although they are not as secret as priestly liturgies, which consist largely of mantras and which no one who has not undergone a consecration may even study, texts like these, often called *tutur* (lessons) are equally obscure. While these are the texts most likely to bear warnings not to reveal their contents, they are also the most difficult to understand. It would seem that the more a text is relevant to the most valued and empowering forms of knowledge—to heal or harm, to liberate and achieve release from human limitations—the less representational its language. Such matters are presented as profound puzzles, the solving of which involves more than intellectual capacities. A mere understanding of the words is not enough, for such texts are remarkably (and, in the opinion of some Balinese, deliberately) obscure. This is a function of what these texts are about, for since the invisible world is impossible to know in ordinary ways, all one can do is allude to it, hint, and so force a reader to think—and feel—his way to it. Measures of success are fairly pragmatic: as Ida Bagus Jagri once said, if after studying a text about healing you can heal, the text (and your interpretation of it) was true.

These texts in particular—but to some extent all texts—are written in an opaque, highly condensed style, filled with terse allusions and subtle wordplay. For example, a word is divided into component syllables, which are then treated as if they were morphemes and combined with others to form new words to reveal the secret meanings of the original. Such wordplay, finding in similarities of form identities of meaning, suggests hidden connections. Names also may appear in disguised forms, constructed on associations to the original.

Since many texts are means to power, they are not treated lightly; nor may just anyone have access to them. Pedanda Gedé Keniténnot, for example, would not lend me a manuscript on royal coronations, which he said might only be safely read by another priest. Such concerns affect the availability of texts from Klungkung more generally. The status of the Klungkung court probably explains why few texts identified as coming from Klungkung may be found in any public collection. Apart from the royal palace's own vast collection of texts, taken in the sacking of the capital and now in the National Museum in Jakarta, one rarely comes across even transcriptions of Klungkung manuscripts. There is certainly no lack of interest in texts, for there are extensive libraries in the regency, particularly in its priestly houses—and Klungkung has long had a reputation for having more priests than other, larger regions. Yet few of these houses are even mentioned on a list of private collections drawn up for the Dutch in the 1920s; for example, Pedanda Gedé Kenitén's father, who was then one of Klungkung's court priests, is credited with possessing only twelve manuscripts (Caron 1929). This was clearly not just an oversight; but neither was it accurate.

Variation and Interpretation

Having considered the dialogic nature of written and spoken discourse, there is yet another manifestation of this that affects Balinese textuality, which I want to discuss largely in relation to *babad*: variation.

Balinese texts are written on the dried leaves of the lontar palm, which are cut into long rectangles, incised with Balinese letters, and then inked. Since such leaves last at most for a century or so, to preserve a text it must be copied over by hand. Philologists assumed that all texts with the same name could be traced to some original, that over the course of time texts were "corrupted" by mistakes and misunderstandings through the process of copying. By comparing all extant versions, accretions and alterations could be cleared away, and something like the original text reconstructed. Much effort went into producing standard editions based on comparisons between multiple versions of a "single" text. Coming from a print-oriented culture where the reproduction of authorial intent was crucial, it was hard for European scholars not to see in Balinese texts mere technological incapacity.

To be sure, people make mistakes in copying texts. But Balinese texts vary in ways that cannot be accounted for by scribal errors alone. For example, it is common to find passages virtually identical in meaning but differing in linguistic shape. This suggests that rather than copying passages verbatim, scribes often substitute synonyms and synonymous phrases.[10] Texts may also differ in content: one manuscript, for example, may include episodes not found in others, or narrate an episode in greater detail.[11] Such divergences often stem from the use of multiple sources. Robson (1972), for example, found that copyists might consult two or three manuscripts in preparing a new one. This procedure brings into serious question the idea that texts are simply "copied." Indeed, such variations suggest that the process of inscribing a text may be a highly creative activity.

Balinese, of course, do produce texts that are more or less duplicates of others. For some Balinese, all written texts are sacred, heirlooms from revered predecessors. Ida Bagus Jagri, for example, claimed that since the texts in his possession had been composed by ancestors whose wisdom was superior to his own, their obscurities were clearly deliberate, and he had to learn to make sense of them exactly as written. Moreover, he argued that since Saraswati, goddess of learning, dwells in the letters of the Balinese script, whatever is written must be true. Copyists of this sort—motivated by culturally specific ideas about language and the past—are the conservatives philologists took for granted. In short, "copying" is by no means a simple and mechanical act of reproduction. Even when texts *are* copied virtually unchanged, such replication has significance for the agents involved.

For Balinese, texts are sources of knowledge and power, with eminently practical uses. People copy or seek texts in order to accomplish personal projects. It is not, therefore, uncommon to find palm-leaf booklets incorporating passages from many types of texts, blending together mantras, narrative episodes, speculative cosmologies, instructions concerning offerings the compiler did not want to forget. In the case of *babad*, copying is often motivated by a desire to chart someone's place in a wider social universe. Copyists of *babad* are frequently descendants of persons mentioned within the text or are copying the text for such a descendant. They often add accounts of more recent antecedents to the original, or they only copy it up to the point where the pertinent line branches off and then append additional material. But the knowledge contained in a *babad* is not only genealogical. At least the *Babad Dalem* contains a number of allusions to esoteric matters, and as with epics, the stories it narrates are regarded as rich in lessons for living.

Since texts are copied for specific persons for specific purposes, the values and interests of the copyist have a major role to play in determining the shape of the final product. And since manuscripts are produced for personal consumption, there is no reason not to change a word or phrase here and there in the interest of making the text more aesthetically pleasing or comprehensible.

This explains the prevalence of synonyms. A delight in verbal equivalence is pervasive among literate Balinese. Indeed, when I was learning Balinese I was frequently told that every concept has "ten names" (*dasa nama*). The same aesthetic informs the use of proper nouns in *babad*: persons and places are often referred to by several different epithets. In other words, some variation is inspired by the sheer pleasure people take in rhetorical skill.

The fact that texts are written in a highly condensed language also stimulates alterations. Additions and emendations may be made to clarify ambiguities or draw out the significance of a scene or phrase. Equally important to the process of variation are the episodic structure and sketchy narration of *babad*. *Babad* are in fact composed of kernels of narration, about each of which a longer story may always be told.

Mainly those longer stories are told in performances. Like most Balinese literature, *babad* are associated with a particular performance genre. What shadow-puppet theater is to *kekawin*, *topéng*, a masked dance-drama, is to *babad*. In these dramatic arts, texts provide an ancedotal core around which performers weave improvisations that demonstrate the relevance of the tale to more recent events, including the performance context itself (De Zoete and Spies 1938). Such performances frequently accompany rituals, where, as entertainment for the gods, they may attract only small human audiences, but even so they concern matters of collective significance.[12] Perhaps even more critical is that, by tying stories to present-day concerns, Balinese theater encourages Balinese to make history by literary precedent. Copyists who append references to current events as colophons to a text are doing much the same thing.[13]

Performances typically improvise upon a mere one or two episodes. Such elaborations are what makes it possible for the texts themselves to remain so lean. In turn, because performed versions of a tale, which have their own lines of transmission, are often more widely known than textual ones, over time they affect interpretations of the written tradition. Eventually some copyist makes more or less subtle changes to make a written episode correspond to his memories of its performance. A recent Balinese version of the *Babad Dalem* (Agung n.d.) exemplifies this process.

On the other hand, that texts are composed of episodes also encourages abridgment. A copyist may be uninterested in certain incidents, because (for example) they are already known to him from other texts; such passages may be telescoped, reduced to bare sketches that allude to stories more fully developed elsewhere. (Thus at the beginning of the *Babad Dalem* are very brief references to Mayadanawa, one of the main characters of a text known as the *Usana Bali*.) Indeed, in a sense Balinese texts have no boundaries; any particular text is part of a larger discourse including performances as well as other texts that recount some of the same incidents but are not necessarily known by the same titles.

Texts, then, often contain allusions to, or otherwise depend upon a knowledge of, other texts. Much is not explicitly stated in the text itself but only insinuated. Key themes may be merely sketched, to be filled out by interpretation, especially through recitation and performance. Similar attitudes are evident in the way Balinese tell stories orally, which is highly interactive and dialogic. As Bateson and Mead note:

> The Balinese story teller does not continue gaily along through a long tale, as the story tellers of most cultures do [*sic*], but he makes a simple statement, "There was once a princess," to which his auditors answer, "Where did she live?" or "What was her name?" and so on, until the narrative has been communicated in dialogue (1942:15).

In general Balinese texts are more mnemonic than propositional—more like handbooks than textbooks. The intelligibility of even narrative genres like chronicles depends much more overtly on the interpretive skills of their readers than European texts do. Much is meant to be filled in: by recitation, performance, or interpretation. They cannot, therefore, be read as self-contained, autonomous wholes. As Bakhtin notes, texts never are self-contained; Balinese do not pretend otherwise. In a sense *babad*, perhaps all texts, are part of a larger, only imagined, whole.

It is therefore not surprising that manuscripts of the "same" text differ from each other, for in a sense each copy of a text constitutes a distinct interpretation. Yet there are also constraints upon alteration. Taking the *Babad Dalem* as an example, the order of events remains fairly consistent between manuscripts, and each contains virtually identical passages describing the beauty and perfection of certain rulers and their courts. The latter are an example of the kind of "trunk narratives" common to Balinese narrative literature (Vickers 1986; Zurbuchen 1987).

DUTCH SOURCES ON BALINESE HISTORY

To appreciate the kinds of history colonialism made requires taking note of what its agents thought worth knowing about Balinese, the kinds of relationships that made that knowledge possible, and the kinds of persons sanctioned as experts. Dutch publications and archival documents reveal what was considered important to record about the Balinese and suggest some of the ways knowledge was authorized and reproduced.

There were basically three ways in which the Dutch learned about Bali: first and foremost, by observation in the course of official tours through

Balinese domains; second, through information provided by paid spies and others; third, by studying Balinese customs and texts.

Power

The structure and nature of the colonial administration help account for the forms of knowledge it generated and the ways in which these were used. Officials began their careers as low-ranking district officers (or assistant district officers) called controleurs. If they performed satisfactorily, they might hope to be promoted to Assistant Residents; a lucky few eventually were appointed Residents and placed in charge of entire regions at the pinnacle of a local hierarchy that included native rulers as well as lower officials. No matter what their rank, however, officials were responsible for filing regular reports. The novelist Multatuli, a former colonial officer and a caustic critic of the Netherlands Indies administration, has vividly described a regime in which officials were bowed under the weight of paperwork and distortions were commonplace (Multatuli 1967). According to him, officials tended to write reports that made them look competent and that validated, rather than challenged, colonial policies. With the development of rapid forms of transport and communication by the late nineteenth century (especially the telegram), the actions of agents in peripheral regions became increasingly easy to monitor and control. This habitus of authority made Balinese multiplicity look chaotic to Dutch officials.

Officials began their reports and letters with florid salutations acknowledging the chain of command: "I have the honor to tell Your Excellency" is summarized in copies of reports sent to the Netherlands as "the usual introduction." On special missions, diplomatic envoys and military chiefs of staff also kept running journals. At the conclusion of a tour of duty in a particular office, officials produced summary reports or memoranda for their successors, which were read by their superiors as well: the earliest *Memories* by Bali's Residents, for example, were forwarded to the Minister of Colonies.

As a rationalized bureaucracy, administration was organized as a strict hierarchy, in which information flowed from the bottom and policies were issued from the top. Controleurs reported to Assistant Residents, who reported to Residents, who reported to the Governor General in Batavia. Back down along the same ladder came the Governor General's Decisions (*Besluiten*), which he issued after taking into account correspondence with not only Residents but the directors of various administrative departments in the colonial capital (for example, the departments of finance, war, education, and so forth) and following consultation with his advisory body, the Council of the Indies. But the Governor General himself had to report to the Minister of Colonies in The Hague, who in turn reported to the Dutch king and, in later years, the legislature.

Colonial reports were implicated in a practice of precedents. As information moved up the chain of command it was preserved. Dossiers in the archives of the Ministry of Colonies consist of layers of reports and letters, ranging from those by officers in the field to the Advice of the Council of the Indies, topped by drafts of the Minister's response. But the layers are surprisingly repetitious: whole paragraphs from the reports of lower-ranking officials were repeated in the reports of their superiors. Pronouncements were treated less as the words of particular persons on particular occasions than as truths. During crises, officials turned to the archives for background information. It was common for material related in earlier correspondence to be incorporated as justification for particular courses of action.

Colonial policy was hardly, however, a direct reflex of information provided from the field. Rather, it was negotiated within a complicated field of political relationships, especially after 1848 (Furnivall 1944; van Niel 1963). The periods into which Ministry of Colonies archives are grouped— 1816–49, 1850–69, 1870–1900, after 1900—mark distinct phases in the history of Dutch colonialism, reflecting changing politics in the Netherlands and, therefore, changing relations between the Netherlands and its colonies and between the colonial state and indigenous polities.[14] Until 1849, the law gave the Dutch king exclusive control over the Netherlands' overseas dependencies, although in practice many important decisions were still made, as they had been in the days of the VOC, by the Governor General (Day 1904:318–19). Metropolitan interventions were mainly motivated by decreased profits or fears of potential threats to Dutch interests, particularly from the British. As a result, relatively limited information concerning local affairs reached the Netherlands during this period. However, since several colonial Ministers had previously served as Governor Generals—Jan Chrétien Baud, Minister from 1840 to 1848, for example, was Governor General from 1833 to 1836—they were not entirely ignorant of conditions in the Indies.

The political upheavals in Europe in 1848 altered this arrangement, giving the Chambers of the States General in the Netherlands greater rights over the colonies (Day 1904:323–33; van Niel 1963). While it took another decade for the practical effects to be fully felt, the shift in authority is marked by the fact that beginning in 1850 the Ministry began to record all incoming documents in enormous handwritten indices for each half year. Every document received from the colonies was dated, numbered, and classified by destination as either Public or Cabinet.[15] Cabinet documents, which were also labeled "secret," commonly concerned administrative matters, such as the transfers and appointments of colonial officials, and foreign affairs, particularly reports of relationships between archipelago rulers and members of other European or Asian nations. If a response was made to a public document, the dossier in which it was filed was thereafter referred to as "minutes" (*verbalen*), after the draft response on its cover.

By the 1860s decisions about colonial policy were increasingly made by the Dutch legislature, and the rise in the volume of correspondence probably reflects increased concern with affairs in the Indies. In 1869, for example, the Governor General's office began to send the Minister of Colonies "mail reports," numbered summaries of events occurring throughout the archipelago both in regions administered by the colonial state and in areas pertinent to Dutch interests. Extensive appendices were attached to the letter: copies of exchanges of letters between a Resident, his staff, indigenous rulers, government secretaries, and, when pertinent, higher-ups such as the commander of the colonial army, the Minister of Justice, etc.[16] If matters developed further, these appendices would be moved to a "minutes" or cabinet dossier.

Bali is only mentioned once during the first three years of the mail report system. This changed in 1872, after the Minister complained to the Governor General that he had read in the *Surabaiasch Handelsblad* (a colonial newspaper, which had a correspondent in North Bali) about an affair not reported through official channels: from then on Bali appears regularly.[17] The abundant flow of information about the island continued until the archipelago was firmly under Dutch control and administration was routinized.

Once Dutch rule was established in Bali, much less information was sent to the Ministry. Reports became formulaic, their concerns bureaucratic: instead of accounts of recent events, most were occupied with discussions of finance, agricultural production, construction, and public health. It was as if once a region was brought under colonial domination, nothing happened there any longer. There was some cultural truth to this; to the extent events had centered around the activities of rulers, kingless realms were by definition ones in which little could happen. But the shift in concern was also a function of bureaucracy: as a regime of disciplinary power, the colonial state produced knowledge mainly in the form of statistics and regularities.

The same shift led to a decline in the amount of information generated about Bali, and justified and reflected an administrative decentralization. A new printed form, "Decisions of the Resident," indicates that as time went on Residents no longer had to seek the approval of the Governor General for every action they took.[18] As more and more matters were handled locally, there was less and less to report to the Ministry of Colonies. By 1922 only short, semiannual summaries were sent to The Hague concerning Bali.

Knowledge

If the problem in interpreting Balinese stories and texts is that they are elusive and allusive, a different difficulty appears in interpreting Dutch accounts: their apparent common sense. Given the authoritative voice in which colonial documents are written, it is easy to fall under their spell and believe they do what they purport: simply report "facts."

But a glance at the categories and concerns of such documents shows precisely why they are not commonsensical, for these have little in common with those of Balinese. For colonial administrators, for example, the relevant units of analysis were territories, each of which was treated as a historical individual, easily detached from others. Character is another salient category, drawn upon to assess the predictability of Balinese lords. In addition, apart from routine accounts of meetings, and regular reports on conditions (such as an annual summary of the "political situation" on the island), letters were usually generated in response to events perceived as natural or civic disturbances, such as wars or epidemics. Events such as rituals, for example, were only mentioned when they had what officials could recognize as "political" implications, that is, when they potentially affected the colonizing process. In short, colonial reports had their own "mythic" components, not least of which was the superiority presumed by the cynical, worldly, and mildly contemptuous tone in which they were written.

Apart from accounts of visits to Balinese courts, it is important to note that much of what colonial officials reported came secondhand: from non-Balinese living in Bali, including Chinese and Arab merchants (who were probably paid); from Javanese envoys, traveling undercover; and from hired spies. Dutch intelligence-gathering also benefited from local conflicts, which motivated various interested Balinese parties, usually rulers, lords, or their spokesmen, to speak to them as well. Although officials rarely appreciated what was actually being contested, the information provided by such persons as Gusti Ngurah Kesiman of Badung in the 1840s and informants in Buléléng and Gianyar later in the century played a key role in shaping European interpretations of Balinese affairs.

Colonialism did not only produce official reports, however. The growing confidence of imperial agents in their ability to accurately represent archipelago peoples was both represented and reinforced by the role they played in the public domain as authors of journal articles and books, and as collectors of artifacts and texts. For some, activities like these gave them influence vastly beyond what they could hope to achieve through a letter or report, and as a consequence of their prominence in public forums the voices of certain officials have had greater historical resonance than the voices of others. Accounts that authorized and were authorized by interventionist colonial policies had particularly perduring effects.

Dutch scholarship on Bali began with and was subordinate to the pragmatic needs of colonial administration. There was an unusually intimate link between politics and science. Many of the experts on archipelago languages, cultures, and *adat* (customary law, a preoccupation of Dutch Orientalism) were or had been colonial officials. For example, G. F. de Bruyn Kops, the Resident who engineered Klungkung's conquest, was a contributor to the authoritative eight-volume *Encyclopedia of the Netherlands Indies* (among other things, he wrote the entry on the Balinese); he was also possibly the first person to plan a museum in Bali, devoted to Balinese handicrafts. F. A. Liefrinck, a member of the Council of the Indies sent to investigate the incident that led to Badung's conquest, also served as president of the Batavian Society of Arts and Sciences and published several collections of customary-law documents from Bali in translation. Officials were in any event avid contributors to the increasing number of scholarly journals founded in and concerning the Indies. By the twentieth century it was common for aspiring colonial officers to undertake training in Indonesian languages, literature, and ethnography, and quite a number of those stationed in Bali wrote on those subjects, basing their work on observations made in the course of performing their administrative duties (see Swellengrebel 1960 and 1969).

In contrast to official documents, publications concerning Bali follow a steadily escalating curve (see Lekkerkerker 1920). But the most influential writings about Bali were not necessarily produced by persons with much firsthand knowledge. For example, Jacobs, van Kol, and van Hoëvell, all of whom produced widely read books about Bali, spent very little time there. But van Kol and van Hoëvell both served in the Dutch Parliament, and their earlier careers in the Netherlands Indies (van Kol as an engineer, van Hoëvell as a minister of the church) lent them considerable authority in debates over colonial policy (Furnivall 1944). On the other hand, Schwartz, who was much admired for his fluency in Balinese and who spent twelve years in Bali, moving up the colonial hierarchy from controleur for land rent to controleur for native affairs to Assistant Resident of South Bali (Kats 1939:86), published virtually nothing about the island.

Not all of those who affected the way Bali was represented published, however. Several European expatriates had an enormous effect on what other Europeans thought or said about Bali, for every important European visitor to Bali inevitably found his or her way to them: the first, Mads Lange, the Danish trader who lived in Badung from 1839 until 1856, wrote about the island solely in the form of letters in appallingly spelled English; a German artist named Walter Spies had a similar impact during the colonial 1930s, as did the linguist Herman Neubronner van der Tuuk, who lived some twenty years in Singaraja (in the "native" style) during the late nineteenth century and was known to and admired by some of Bali's rulers (according to Jacobs [1883:10] one of Badung's rulers said of him, "There is on all Bali but one man who knows and understands the Balinese language, and that man is *van der Tuuk*").

Colonial officials were also intimately involved in Dutch Orientalism. The history of European collection and study of Balinese texts, for example, belongs quite directly to the history of imperial expansion. It begins in 1846, when R. Friederich, a German Sanskirt scholar and assistant librarian at the Batavian Society for Arts and Sciences, was sent with the First Bali Expedition to Singaraja in order to secure religious and literary manuscripts and other artifacts obtained as war booty. J. L. Brandes, another philologist associated with the Batavian Society, accompanied the expedition against Lombok in 1894, and when the Dutch destroyed the palaces of Badung and Klungkung their extensive libraries were among the booty sent back to Batavia (Wiener 1994).

The relationships enabled by colonialism allowed for less coercive forms of collection as well. After the First Bali Expedition, for example, Friederich spent two years living at Mads Lange's factory in Badung, researching Indian influences on Balinese literature and liturgy. Lange introduced him to Badung princes and priests, from whom, because of his knowledge of Sanskrit, a language Balinese associate with expertise in sacred matters, he was able to borrow texts only those consecrated as priests are usually permitted to read. Unusually for a philologist of this time, he was also interested in Balinese chronicles, and he published a translation of the *Usana Bali* (Friederich 1847). Later in the century the government funded van der Tuuk for nearly a quarter century while he collected poetic texts, *kekawin* and *kidung*, as sources for his posthumously published Kawi-Balinese-Dutch dictionary. In addition, texts considered pertinent to colonial administration were collected by a number of officials, particularly texts on customary law.

In the 1920s administrators and Orientalists became interested in more systematic forms of collection. The government initiated a survey of manuscripts in private libraries all over the island, and in 1928 established the Gedong Kirtya–Liefrinck–van der Tuuk in the colonial capital of Singaraja (Caron 1929). This institution made efforts to obtain copies of manuscripts from all over Bali and to make typed transliterations of them.

The Japanese occupation and the establishment of the Indonesian republic temporarily put a stop to European philological activity. The Balinese staff of the Kirtya, however, continued to copy texts, and its reading room became a center for Balinese excited by revolutionary ideas about universal literacy and education. Other Balinese institutions—the Museum Bali in Denpasar (again originally a colonial institution) and the library of the newly founded Udayana University—also began to collect manuscripts.

In 1972 Christiaan Hooykaas, a former colonial "language officer," started a new project to produce typed and transliterated manuscripts from collections all over Bali. Several university libraries provided funds, in return for which they received a copy of each manuscript (Hooykaas 1979a). Since Hooykaas's death in 1979 the project has continued (Hinzler 1983). While it covers an enormous breadth of topics and genres, texts have mainly come from a limited number of private libraries. Tabanan, the area from which

Hooykaas's Balinese collaborator came, is, not surprisingly, represented best. Key sources elsewhere probably reflect his social networks.

In the colonial period, Orientalist preoccupations shaped both the kinds of texts collected and their interpretation. Only certain texts were deemed interesting—mainly epics derived from Indian or Old Javanese originals, texts on customary law that could be used in administration, or religious texts that could be compared to Indian ones. It is no accident that the major catalogue of texts in the Kirtya and the Netherlands is entitled *The Literature of Java* (Pigeaud 1967–80) even though many of the texts described were collected in Bali. These are attributed to court poets from the Majapahit empire, whose work Balinese recopied over centuries because of their adherence to Hindu-Buddhist traditions. *Kekawin,* poems based on the great Hindu epics, were especially valued, as "survivals" of a "classical" Indian or Javanese past; the Balinese world in which they were discovered was of little interest in itself. As a result, apart from Friederich, there was minimal interest in texts like *babad.* As Said has made us aware, these are familiar claims and assumptions. But the biases at work were not entirely European; although it had a different significance, Balinese themselves emphasized their connection to Majapahit. And if *kekawin* and *kidung* are especially well represented in European collections, it is not only a consequence of antiquarianism; Balinese textual practices made these texts particularly accessible to outsiders.

Apart from scholars, travelers, and administrators, there was yet another source of knowledge about the people of the Indies: newspapers. Those who have written about the Netherlands Indies were struck by the fact that despite the enormous tolerance for which the Netherlands remains famed, Dutch administration in the Indies brooked no public criticism of the colonial state. Indeed, persistent troublemakers risked deportation to Europe. Like other purveyors of public discourse, journalists were subject to extensive censorship.

The style of both scholarly and administrative writings is detailed and empiricist, devoted to a minutiae of observations. Dayu Alit's response one day as I recounted to her several accounts by colonial officials of meetings with the rulers of Klungkung is worth reporting here. She remarked that they seemed to have had plenty of time on their hands, and she wondered what they were up to, writing down such things. If the Déwa Agung farted, she noted tartly, they wrote it down, and if he shat, they wrote that down too. They seemed to be looking for fault, looking for trivial offenses they could recall when angered and use as an excuse to bring in their guns. One is reminded of Foucault's observation that one might write a history "of the utilitarian rationalization of detail in moral accountability and political control" (1979:139). Painstaking attention to information was an intimate and important part of the power/knowledge configurations of colonizing: "A meticulous observation of detail, and at the same time a political awareness of these small things, for the control and use of men . . . [bear] with them a whole set of techniques, a whole corpus of methods and knowledge, descriptions, plans and data" (1979:141).

What is striking about this colonial empiricism is that the conclusions officials drew from their often keen observations were based upon preconceived notions and were saturated with cultural assumptions. Often the Dutch do appear blind, for they could not always see what they themselves observed. Such "blindness" is by means peculiar to colonialism or to Europeans; it is perhaps the most difficult of all things to learn something new. The problem with empiricist theories of knowledge is that they refuse to acknowledge that observations are laden with assumptions. But officials did not make things up, nor is there is nothing in what they say. Indeed, because the Dutch were so meticulous, it is possible to read what they wrote against the grain, from a different angle. This is helpful, particularly because, since interactions between Klungkung's rulers and colonial officials were of little interest in Balinese history making, certain aspects of Klungkung's past can only be traced through Dutch materials.

But from whose point of view should those materials be analyzed? Since nineteenth-century Balinese did not record the same incidents or chronicle their encounters with the Dutch, where may one stand to approximate their position? There is no easy answer to this. But one possibility is to consider the interpretations of Balinese in the 1990s. I commonly found, when I discussed incidents recorded in colonial archives with Ida Bagus Jagri and Dayu Alit, that their interpretations of what Balinese agents were up to were refreshingly different from colonial ones, or from what I might have inferred on my own. It is customary to warn against the dangers of reconstructing the past on the basis of ethnographic fieldwork. The risks are clearly real, and they appear even more problematic given critiques of ahistorical understandings of culture. But as Collingwood (1946) notes, all reconstructions of the past are ultimately shaped by present concerns and perspectives: why should they not be Balinese concerns and perspectives? Or at least the hybrid Balinese perspectives constructed in the course of collaborative ethnographic fieldwork.

Collaborations are all the more critical given that Balinese forms of communication involve presumptions and conventions that are all too easy to miss and all too hard to understand. During the colonial era the prevailing linguistic ideologies were such that officials thought all that was necessary to understand other modes of discourse was to master a semantic code, whether to read and understand Balinese texts or to listen to and understand their conversations. The styles in which important topics were communicated and the

vision

all,
seeing

cultural knowledge they presupposed were ignored. Under these circumstances it is not difficult to see why powerful Balinese might have thought
them blind.

Such blindness was further promoted by the politics of colonialism and
by the constant concern with colonizer prestige. By the time the Dutch colonized Bali, the mores of colonial culture made it unacceptable for officials to
adopt local customs or to live openly with native women. Social distance had
serious consequences, for even if an official learned the local language (most
officials mainly spoke Malay, the language now known as Indonesian), he was
in no position to learn to appreciate subtleties of communication. If one con-
siders the barriers to understanding in ethnographic fieldwork, which at least
offers the potential for intimacy, then the likelihood that colonial officials had
much insight into local concerns seems small. For them, Balinese were never
equal interlocutors. But then cross-cultural understanding was not the primary
goal of colonial administrations. And the difficulty of understanding worked
very much to Balinese advantage, for, to evoke Foucault yet again, "visibility
is a trap" (1979:200).

All of this is, of course, particularly pertinent to the kind of knowledge
colonialism could and did produce about Klungkung. Given Balinese practices connected with power, it is hardly surprising that discourse about Klungkung is filled with innuendo and images. It is to such images that I now want
to turn.

FIVE

The Babad Dalem: The Sources
of Klungkung's Power

T hus far we have looked at several images of Klungkung: both present
indigenous ones and past foreign ones. While the idioms in which these images are cast vary, they nonetheless give the impression of approaching the
same elephant from different directions. But the shape of the beast is still
murky. In this chapter yet a third set of images will be examined: the Babad
Dalem, a textual representation of Klungkung's royal house dating from the
precolonial era. In a sense this text is the elephant itself. Presenting the terms
in which the power of Klungkung's royal house was culturally constructed, it
lays the groundwork for the discourse concerning Klungkung both in the
nineteenth century and at present.

The Babad Dalem, like other texts of this kind, is in part used to identify
people as members of a particular agnatic clan, or semetonan.[1] Anthropologists
would regard aristocratic semetonan as conical clans, organized by a principle
of primogeniture that creates ranked lines. The senior, highest-ranking line in
the clan in theory traces descent through eldest sons of eldest sons back to
the pivotal ancestor. In practice the core line was constituted by the series of
persons who occupied the status position, regardless of genealogical relationships.[2] The ranking man of a royal core line is the clan's ulu, "head," or pengarep,
"foremost" or "most important," the person responsible for the clan's well-being
and therefore for the heirlooms, shrines, and lands that ensure it.

The subject of the text is the core line of the Ksatria Dalem clan, which
formed the ruling house of Klungkung. For ease of reference, I will call this
family the Kapakisans, after the name of its pivotal ancestor. The chronicle
begins with allusions to Bali's pre-Kapakisan rulers and with an account of the
origins of the Kapakisan line. It then traces the line's dominion over Bali to a
conquest by the Javanese empire of Majapahit and recounts the subsequent fortunes of the court, centered first in the town of Gélgél and later in Klungkung.

The Babad Dalem provides invaluable insight into the self-conceptions of
Klungkung's rulers and therefore into the way they made history, for it still
shapes the way members of Klungkung's royal clan think of themselves.
Knowledge of the text generates an awareness of the present and future potential of clan members, all the more so as Balinese believe that ancestors   97

reincarnate within the same family. The relationship between the past represented in the text and the present is paradigmatic as well as syntagmatic. Incidents from the *Babad Dalem* form a tacit background in speaking of more recent events. The text is sufficiently elaborate to allow different images of power to be highlighted at different points in time. In short, the text offers a complex set of significations upon which to draw to enact or narrate history.

The *Babad Dalem* was the Klungkung court's official representation of itself to itself and to the rest of Bali. A congeries of images of Balinese kingship seen from its center, the *Babad Dalem* also offers a culturally compelling representation of the bases of royal authority. The images found within this text form a set of prototypes for the theory and practice of royal power, not only in Klungkung but in Bali in general. Indeed, other Balinese princes asserted and expressed their claims to power in terms of the same discourse, often alluding to (or even copying passages from) Klungkung's dynastic chronicle in composing their own. The terms in which the text structures the power of the Kapakisan dynasty, therefore, formed a constraining paradigm for Balinese aspirants to political prominence.

THE *BABAD DALEM* AS A TEXT

As there is no authoritative version of the *Babad Dalem*, the first question is, what is the "text" that will be analyzed? Manuscripts with this name can be found all over Bali—a cursory survey of part of the Hooykaas Collection, for example, revealed at least twenty manuscripts entitled *Babad Dalem*—but since they range in length from 5 pages to 107 they are hardly identical.[3] Like most Balinese prose texts, these manuscripts are anonymous and undated.[4]

The episodes generally referred to as *Babad Dalem* appear to have been written in at least two segments. Because the first of these concludes with events that can be dated from colonial sources to the late seventeenth century, it could not have existed in its present form until shortly thereafter (Hinzler 1984; Stuart-Fox 1987:321),[5] though it is possible that before these incidents were inscribed they were recounted orally and in dramatic performance, as Vickers (1986) suggests for the *Malat*. The earliest extant manuscripts known, however, date from the first half of the nineteenth century. The identity of the original author/compiler is unknown, but a reasonable guess would be a member of the court's inner circle, possibly a priest.

The second segment of text was definitely composed by a priest, Pedanda Gedé Rai of Geria Cucukan in Klungkung. Written as a dialogue between the author and Klungkung's ruler, it narrates events from the seventeenth century through the nineteenth and was probably composed between 1854 and 1884.[6] Manuscripts of this portion of the text are sometimes found under the title *Babad Ksatria*. Since the beginning of the twentieth century, addenda have been made to the text, largely in the form of genealogical information, and it is difficult to say with any certainty where the late-nineteenth-century author stopped his narration and other hands picked it up. The history was continued through the Dutch conquest early in the colonial period, probably by Cokorda Anom, a branch-line prince (see Pidada 1983). The texts known as *Babad Dalem* may consist of episodes from only the Gélgél period, the later addenda, or both.

This chapter will focus on the best-known and most frequently reproduced portions of the text, from the founding of the dynasty up to the fall of Gélgél. That this text was widely known when colonial envoys first visited Bali in the early nineteenth century is indicated by what they report about Klungkung, which reflects textual images of the constitution of Klungkung authority. It is also from this portion of the text that episodes are selected for *topéng* performances or for copying over in the *babad* of other kin groups.

That manuscripts of this portion of the *Babad Dalem* are abundant makes excellent sense. According to Hinzler (1976:46), it is one of four charter texts of Balinese society, along with the *Usana Bali*, the *Usana Jawa*, and the *Calon Arang*. While the focus of the *Babad Dalem* is the Kapakisan dynasty, there is considerable narrative about members of other clans—the nobles and priests who composed the king's court. The text identifies, for example, all of the aristocrats who followed the first Kapakisan ruler to Bali. Such tales are important to many high-ranking Balinese, who trace their own descent from these figures; as already noted, passages from it are frequently reproduced in the *babad* of other clans (see, e.g., Worsley 1972).

Since one reason to study this text is to understand how Klungkung's nineteenth-century rulers constructed their power, the manuscript belonging to the precolonial court would be the ideal one to analyze. Unfortunately the whereabouts of this manuscript are unknown. When Klungkung was conquered in 1908, the royal palace was looted, and its "library" was removed to Batavia. After being sent to Leiden for cataloguing (which included a brief description of each palm-leaf manuscript, based upon the first few leaves), the texts were returned to Batavia. Curiously, not a single *babad* is listed in this catalogue (Juynboll 1912a), even though such texts were among the paraphernalia of any royal court (Korn 1932); indeed, postcolonial royal libraries even contain *babad* concerning commoner clans. Local rumors (and a comment about a Tabanan *babad* in Hinzler 1976) suggest that all of the *babad* from Klungkung's palace may have been given to I Gusti Putu Jelantik, who accompanied the expedition as interpreter and later became ruler of Buléléng. His library is unusually rich in texts of this sort (Berg 1929:4), and the Klungkung court's *Babad Dalem* may well be among them, although difficult to identify.

Under these circumstances a text from a branch line close to the core or from one of the priestly houses (*geria*) that served the court would seem a reasonable alternative. While few copies of any Klungkung *Babad Dalem* have been transcribed, it happens that one of these, H2935, comes from Geria Pidada, an important priestly house during the nineteenth and early twentieth centuries.[7] Cokorda Anom of Puri Anyar, a branch-line prince regarded as the family expert on genealogy during the 1930s,[8] apparently copied the text for the *geria* during the colonial era. Since the Cokorda was not exiled, and his puri was not destroyed, it is possible that he took as his original a text belonging to his own line.

I have compared H2935 with several other transliterated manuscripts of the *Babad Dalem*. While, as one would expect, no two manuscripts are exactly alike, the differences between H2935 and *Babad Dalem B* in Warna et al. 1986, *Babad Dalem* K1252, *Babad Dalem* H3574, and *Babad Dalem* H3837 are relatively minor except for one episode (noted in the commentary). Similarities between the Geria Pidada text and *Babad Dalem* H3837 and *Babad Dalem* K1252 give provisional cause to think it represents the text as it was known in the nineteenth century, since *Babad Dalem* H3837's colophon is dated 1826 and *Babad Dalem* K1252's is dated 1868.

Two other manuscripts I consulted are significantly different. *Babad Dalem A* (Warna et al. 1986) has many interpolations, possibly of recent origin as the colophon dates this manuscript to 1942. Although most of these concern the family that owns this manuscript, others provide interesting nuances on material found elsewhere.

A *Babad Dalem* composed by Cokorda Gedé Agung (n.d.) of a branch line of the Kapakisan clan in Sukawati is a more radically different version of the text, and also (since it was written in the 1970s, and in Balinese rather than Kawi) the most recent. The author's synthetic style is very modern; he draws numerous sources together into a very long narrative that begins (unlike other *Babad Dalem*) with the origins of the universe. What makes this text interesting is, first of all, the philosophical richness of some of the author's interpretations, and second, that his expansions upon many episodes appear to be based upon performance traditions. While textual precedents may yet be found for all of the narratives he includes, since several of them were told to me orally in Klungkung, often by people who were performers, it seems likely that his elaborations stem from ways of performing the incidents. This makes the text a useful indigenous commentary upon the more "basic" *babad*.

METHOD OF ANALYSIS

The sections that follow comment upon a series of episodes from the *Babad Dalem*, often translating passages from the text or closely paraphrasing them. My remarks are based upon contemporary claims and practices concerning *interpretations of text based on contemporary claims.*

Klungkung's royal house, thus showing how it resonates with other Klungkung representations. The episodes I have selected contribute to an understanding of royal power in general and to an appreciation of the powers attributed to Klungkung's rulers in particular. Certain themes are reiterated in
observations made by European visitors to precolonial Bali; others are developed further in the discourse examined in part 2.

Manuscripts give considerable narrative space to many events peripheral
to the Ksatria Dalem clan per se. There are numerous episodes concerning
nobles in attendance at the Kapakisan court, especially during the reigns of
Dalem Bekung and Dalem di Madé. Similarly, the account of events during
the reign of Dalem Watu Rénggong is interrupted by a long story about
Danghyang Nirartha, regarded as the first Brahmana priest to reside in Bali
and ancestor of all of Bali's Brahmana Siwa. There are also tales concerning
some of the priest's descendants later in the text.

Its inclusion of tales about other groups distinguishes the *Babad Dalem*
from other *babad*. By incorporating such accounts the *Babad Dalem* situates all
of Bali's major political actors in relation to the Kapakisan dynasty, affirming
that dynasty's centrality in constituting the order of society. Klungkung's role
in Bali, suggests the text, was encompassing; it defined the whole, the totality, of which others were mere parts. Such episodes are important to appreciating the role the text plays in social reproduction, but the particulars are
tangential to Klungkung's story, and so they have been left out.

In addition, I have omitted the long passages, found especially in accounts of the reigns of the first Kapakisan rulers, describing audiences. In such
passages narrative action freezes on a lengthy visual scene. The lords in attendance are carefully identified, and typically the king's clothing and his effect
on those assembled are the focus of attention. For example, when Dalem
Ketut goes to Majapahit to appear before the Majapahit emperor, every step
along his journey is described in detail, including the admiration with which
he is everywhere received; this is followed by panegyrics on the magnificence
of the Javanese court. Such events were obviously important to the political
culture of precolonial courts, but given my purposes in this chapter I offer
only one example, to illustrate the role attraction played in the ideology and
practice of Balinese kingship.

In several instances, I discuss episodes not narrated in the *Babad Dalem*.
The text alludes to quite a few other well-known tales, some of them com-
monly performed in *topéng* dramas. Most *Babad Dalem*, for example, begin with
short accounts of the fates of two early Balinese rulers—Mayadanawa and
Bédaulu—whose tales are narrated in detail in other texts (e.g., *Usana Bali,
Usana Jawa, Mayadanawatattwa*). There are even briefer allusions to the *Calo-
narang*; elsewhere, a phrase or name points to yet other tales. Since many
Balinese would catch these allusions, I have provided summaries of such

stories, where they are known to me. I should note, however, that my précis of the tales of Mayadanawa and Bédaulu differs from texts I have consulted. The *Babad Dalem's* resumé of Mayadanawa's story makes no reference to the cosmological events that elsewhere precede it. Since these are important for understanding the implications of both what is recounted concerning one of Klungkung's heirlooms and narratives about Klungkung's fall, I begin my summary with them. However, this cosmology is itself found in many versions in many different texts;[9] in order to avoid complicating matters unduly, my account is a composite. My version of the tale of Bédaulu, which is dealt with in only a few sentences in the *Babad Dalem*, is a summary of what was told to me by several persons.

PRE-MAJAPAHIT BALI: THE DEMONIC FACE OF KINGSHIP

In the distant past, the island of Bali was unstable, rocking on the waves, "like a boat upon the waters."[10] Then Betara Pasupati took the top of Mount Mahaméru (from either Java or India) and ordered it brought to Bali, where it became known as Mount Agung or Mount Tolangkir. The turtle Si Badawangnala was commanded to support the base of the mountain, while the serpents Sang Anantaboga, Naga Basuki, and (sometimes) Naga Taksaka were ordered to bind the mountain to the island. Pasupati instructed his son Putrajaya (also called Mahadéwa) to live on the mountain and be worshipped in the temple of Besakih. Putrajaya's younger sister/consort Déwi Danu, goddess of the lake, was sent to Mount Batur, and other gods, kinsmen of this pair, were placed in other mountain temples, notably Genijaya (Victorious Fire) on Mount Lempuyang.

Some time later, Mayadanawa (Illusion Demon), a kind of ogre (*danawa*), became ruler of Bali. He was extremely *sakti;* however, he was also greedy, violent, unable to control his passions, and disdainful of religious precepts (1a). Arrogantly proud of his great power, he forbade people to worship the gods at Besakih, ordering them to direct their offerings to him. Angered by his presumption, Betara Mahadéwa, god of Besakih, complained to his father, Betara Pasupati, on Mount Mahaméru. They asked the help of Indra, king of the gods, in waging a war against Mayadanawa. After a long and hard fight, the gods won and Mayadanawa was killed. Later the gods ordered Mayadanawa to be reborn as Bali's ruler. He appeared in a coconut as a pair of male and female twins, Masula Masuli, found by a temple priest in the precincts of Besakih. The twins married and reigned over Bali until they *moksa* (to unify with the *niskala* in body as well as soul, something only extremely powerful and knowledgeable people can do). Their children, also twins, married and reigned, and so things continued for several generations. Finally a son was born who married exogamously. His name was Tapaulung,[11] more generally known as King Bédaulu (Different Head) (2a).

Some claim that the name Bédaulu refers to his capital, the village of Bedulu; others, to the fact that he differed (*béda*) with his superior (another connotation of *ulu*, "head") in Majapahit. Most commonly people derive his name from his appearance, which is in turn a consequence of an event narrated more or less as follows:

Like Mayadanawa, he had great power. To show off, he took off his head and sent it to *sorga*, heaven, where the god Siwa saw it and became annoyed. Bédaulu, he declared, was too arrogant and greedy, behavior more fitting for an animal than a human being. And so the god exchanged Bédaulu's head with that of a pig. When Bédaulu returned to his body, he discovered what had happened. To live with the shame, he decreed that from that moment on no one was to look him in the face, and he built a high scaffold to sit upon to ensure this. Not long after, a servant with a wounded hand was preparing Bédaulu's dinner, and some blood fell into the food. When Bédaulu ate it, he demanded that the same delicious spicing be used ever after. All of his meals from then on contained human blood. At this point people sent word to Gajah Mada, prime minister of Majapahit on Java, asking for help. Gajah Mada dispatched an envoy to investigate whether it was true that the king had the head of a pig; if so, he said, he would depose him. He instructed his envoy in a ruse. When offered food, he requested *paku*, a stringy green vegetable eaten by lowering it into the upturned mouth, and therefore was able to see the king's head. In his shame the king decided to leave the world permanently (according to other versions, he was killed by Gajah Mada). Gajah Mada then declared war upon Bédaulu's lords. Arya Damar led the Majapahit forces, and Bali was subdued.

These two tales concerning indigenous Balinese kings exhibit striking similarities; indeed, some narrators confuse them with one another. Both recount tales of *sakti* kings who offend the gods, are deposed following a war, and are replaced.

His name identifies Mayadanawa as a *danawa*, a kind of *raksasa* or ogre, creatures commonly characterized by excessive greed. By setting himself up as equal to the god of Besakih, he oversteps the bounds allowed a king. Such excess renders him vulnerable to conquest despite his power, although only the gods can actually defeat him.

The same theme is replayed in the fall of Bédaulu. Bédaulu is, like Maya-danawa, arrogant. He even resembles Mayadanawa, as *raksasa* are commonly portrayed with fangs or tusks resembling those of Balinese boars (Forge 1980b). The pig's head that replaces his own not only indexes a demonic nature (which his taste for blood further proves) but is also a form of pollution, since the head is the purest part of the body.

In overthrowing such a scandalous ruler, Gajah Mada, chief minister of the Majapahit empire, acts as an agent of Divinity, for Bédaulu's behavior has cost him the gods' protection. According to some tales about him, Gajah Mada was even an incarnation of Divinity. Both Gajah Mada and the gods are also "foreigners," from India or Java. Indeed, all of the institutions most identified with Balinese culture are attributed to Javanese: according to other texts, Bali's most important temples, including Besakih, were founded by a Majapahit priest even before Gajah Mada's conquest (see, e.g., Soebandi 1981 and 1983). Note that while the *Usana Bali* identifies Mayadanawa as simply the successor, probably the son, of a previous king who was also a demon (since his name is Detya, "demon"), according to the *Mayadanawatattwa*, his mother was Déwi Danu, a deity associated in some contexts with autochthony and irrigation.[12]

We will see that the connection between Besakih and kings sounded in the legend of Mayadanawa reverberates through the *Babad Dalem*. Here, Mayadanawa brings about his downfall by prohibiting worship at Besakih, usurping the place of its god. That on his return to earthly existence he is discovered in a coconut in Besakih's courtyard suggests the restored Mayadanawa is now subordinate to the god by virtue of their identity, for in the *Usana Bali* Putrajaya and his sister/consort Déwi Danu first appear in Bali in the same way.

Another parallel between the tales of Mayadanawa and Bédaulu is important in Klungkung historiography: both tales contrast just kings with greedy ones in terms that resonate not only with cosmology (the just kings are in some manner divine or priestly, the greedy ones in some ways demonic) but also with the kind of alteration accomplished in key royal rituals. The victors in both cases reconstitute Bali as a polity, and the new rulers are affiliated with the positive aspects of divinity. The reincarnated Mayadanawa, born with a twin sister-wife, is, like a divinity, completely self-contained, the reverse of a voracious demon.[13] Moreover, his appearance in a coconut has priestly overtones, for coconuts are associated with offerings requesting the god Surya or his priestly surrogates to witness a human activity or intention. We will see shortly that Bédaulu's successor is in fact a (potential) priest. Mayadanawa's transformation is reminiscent of *buta-yadnya*, rituals to invoke or placate demons: a demon is turned into a divinity. The Bédaulu story involves a diluted version of the same process: a polluted ruler is re-placed by one with the capacity to purify.

THE ORIGINS OF THE KAPAKISAN DYNASTY: PRIESTS AS KINGS

It is against this background that the narrative now turns to the Kapakisans. The text begins by establishing the identity of the family's founding ancestor. Surprisingly, this ancestor turns out to be of priestly rather than royal descent:

> After the Javanese expedition, Bali was without a king, and the populace was disturbed. Gajah Mada decided to find someone in Majapahit to serve as Bali's ruler on behalf of Majapahit. He chose the youngest son of a Brahmana Buda priest, a young man named Sri Kresna Kapakisan (2b–3a).

Note that, unlike the previous demonic kings, the priestly Kapakisans are not Balinese. As in many tales concerning kings (cf. Hocart 1970, Sahlins 1985), they are foreigners.

At this point some *Babad Dalem* include a summary of the forebears of Sri Kresna Kapakisan. Here is a verbatim extract of the relevant passage:

> There was a brahmana named Mpu Bhajra-satwa, the son of Mpu Pa-nuhun, grandson of the god Brahma. He was Jina [the Buddha] in visible form. . . . Mpu Bhajra-satwa had a son, Mpu Baraddha, the one who killed the Widow of Jirah. He had a son, Mpu Bahula, who married the child of the Widow of Jirah, her name was Dyah Ratna Manggali. . . . There was a child, a boy, named Mpu Tantular, the one who is well known as the author of "Sutasoma," "Kaki-Twa." He had four sons . . . : Danghyang Asmaranatha, Danghyang Siddhi-mantra, Danghyang Pan-awasikan, and the youngest Danghyang Kresna Kapakisan (3a–3b).[14]

Danghyang Asmaranatha, the eldest brother, is the priest from whom all of Bali's Brahmanas claim descent. The youngest of the four brothers, Dangh-yang Kresna Kapakisan, is the ancestor of Bali's new kings: thus the text as-serts that the relationship between Brahmana priests and Kapakisan kings is that of elder to younger brothers.

> Danghyang Kresna Kapakisan produced a son by performing yogic meditations upon a stone. This son later similarly meditated in a garden, as a result of which a *widiadari*, a beautiful celestial nymph, appeared, whom he married. They had four children, whom Gajah Mada made rulers over conquered realms in the greater Majapahit empire: the eldest

became the ruler of Blambangan, the second eldest ruler of Pasuruan (both in East Java), the third, a daughter, wed the ruler of Sumbawa, and the fourth and youngest, Sri Kresna Kapakisan, was appointed ruler of Bali (3b).

This statement of sibling relationships is a charter of later politics. At various times in Balinese history, the realms of Blambangan and Pasuruan were subject to Kapakisan rulers or other Balinese princes, and they were a point of contestation between Bali and the Islamic Javanese kingdom of Mataram. Here the text lays ground for Bali's claims. Balinese rulers also competed with the Islamic kingdom of Makassar for control over Sumbawa, which they lost; but Sumbawa was, unlike the other realms, represented here as only affinally linked to Bali.

The text identifies the Kapakisans' apical ancestor as the god Brahma. Bali's smiths also claim Brahma as their progenitor (Guermonprez 1983), but so do probably all clans; Brahma is, after all, Divinity in its creative form. There are alternate versions of Klungkung's divine origins: a genealogy I was shown by a member of the royal family claims Pasupati as apical ancestor. Recall Pasupati (a name for Siwa) is identified as the god of Mahaméru and the father of Mahadéwa, god of Besakih. Sometimes Pasupati himself is said to reside on Agung. This would suggest a kinship between Kapakisan rulers and Besakih's god.

The difference between these alternatives is more apparent than actual. For example, in relation to the world outside of Bali, the god of Besakih is not supreme but a mere surrogate; on Bali itself he is Pasupati, principal deity. There is also no contradiction between claiming descent from Pasupati and from Brahma, since as a form of Siwa Pasupati is the more encompassing (i.e., "earlier") divinity. Both Pasupati and Brahma are also associated with powerful weapons. Pasupati is the name of a magic arrow Siwa gave the semidivine hero Arjuna in the *Barata Yuda* (see Zoetmulder 1982). The ingredients of the *pasupati* offering (probably named after this legendary weapon) that reempowers keris every Tumpek Landep are red, Brahma's color.

The most important claims made in this story of the origins of the Kapakisan dynasty, however, are that they are Brahmana, specifically Brahmana Buda, and that they are descended from a Brahmana Buda priest famed for his victory over a notorious witch.

POWER AND PRIESTLY TRANSFORMERS

The priestly origins of the Kapakisan dynasty have two implications. First, priests are obviously mediators between the visible and invisible worlds. Second, that the king is by birthright a potential priest implies a capacity to totalize: in theory, his power includes the power of priests. And indeed, since at this time there were no other Brahmanas in Bali (see below), Sri Kresna Kapakisan, though not consecrated as a priest, presumably drew upon that power.

Many Balinese, however, claim their ancestors were originally Brahmanas. The test of such claims is the willingness of others claiming the same ancestry to treat one as kin. This is marked by a number of practices, particularly by a willingness to address and be addressed by kin terms and to participate in something known as *sidikara* relations. These make their appearance during life-cycle rituals, particularly those for marriage and death, and involve the consumption of ritual leftovers and the performance of ritual obeisance.

In ritual, the essence (*sari*) of food offerings is consumed by the divinities, spirits, and ancestors to whom they are offered, and the "leftovers" (*lungsuran*) by their human worshippers. In general Balinese "eat up": to eat leftovers is to assert solidarity or inferiority, a kind of alimentary structure of kinship. This is especially true of *paridan*, offerings made to the spirits within the body of a person on the occasion of rites of passage. An even more important practice is to *nyumbah*, to offer obeisance at the body of a person just prior to the cremation rites that will transform him or her into an ancestor. One only offers such homage to hierarchical superiors or to genealogical (as opposed to merely chronological) elders.[15] To *nyumbah* or *maparid* a person of lower rank results in a permanent reduction to that rank and in being cast out (*makutang*) by one's kin—that is, one is no longer a member of the *sidikara* group. Such degradation is contagious: anyone eating the ritual leftovers of or performing an obeisance for such a diminished kinsman would suffer the same fate. High-ranking people are extremely protective of their exclusiveness.

This is what makes the actions of Brahmanas in and near Klungkung extraordinary. Not only do Brahmanas acknowledge their kinship with Ksatria Dalem based upon common descent, and not only do Brahmanas and members of the royal family in general address each other by kin terms, both of which are already extraordinary, but when there were still kings in Klungkung unconsecrated Brahmanas happily ate the leftovers (*paridan*) of offerings made during rituals that marked the ruler's life and death. Nothing like this occurred anywhere else in Bali.

Other marks of kinship were, however, forbidden: Ksatria Dalem and Brahmana did not marry one another, for example; more important, even unconsecrated Brahmanas could not *nyumbah* the ruler, perhaps the most important sign of a *sidikara* relation. This could be interpreted within the idiom of kinship as merely indicating relative "age." The first Kapakisan ancestor was, after all, the *youngest* brother of the ancestor of Balinese Brahmana.

But Sri Kresna Kapakisan was not only a Brahmana: he is explicitly identified as a Brahmana Buda. There are two kinds of Brahmana priests in Bali, identified as Siwa and Buda, and said to be elder and younger brothers. The differences between them, while hardly recognizable as the differences between Hindu and Buddhist priests elsewhere, are structurally significant. Siwa priests are renouncing ascetics who let their hair grow long (and wear it in a topknot) and must observe a variety of food taboos. Buda priests wear their hair short and may eat anything, even foods ordinary Balinese find disgusting. Not only may they come into contact with what would pollute a Siwa priest, they are said to be able to transform it. Buda priests need renounce nothing: they do not purify by exclusion but by encompassment. Because they may traffic with dangerous matters safely, it is said that Buda priests once played the primary role in rituals involving radical transformation: of demons to divinities in purificatory exorcisms (*buta-yadnya*) and of human flesh to ancestral spirit in cremations, the first of the death rituals. In contrast, Siwa priests were specialists in sacrifices to divinities and postcremation rituals for the purification of the soul. At present, no such specialization exists, although in major *buta-yadnya* one Buda priest is always present. Since rulers were particularly responsible for organizing rituals to placate negative forces, an emphasis on Kapakisan descent from powerful Brahmana Buda would obviously reinforce their faith (and that of their subjects) in their efficacy.

The capacity of the Buda priest to transform negative to positive is also, as even Brahmana Siwa say, a sign of their greater *kasaktian*, which legend traces to an incident in which the first Buda priest proved himself braver and more steadfast (*pageh*) than his elder brother.[16] Siwa priests may be purer, but Buda priests are more powerful. The difference between their powers is demonstrated in an incident later in the text (see below).

That Brahmana Buda are identified as younger brothers and Brahmana Siwa as elder is also of interest. Since Brahmanas in general are "elder brothers" to kings, it suggests again the royal identification with Brahmana Buda. The emphasis on younger brothers is, however, repeatedly reiterated in this text: Empu Kapakisan is the youngest of four brothers, just as his grandson, Sri Kresna Kapakisan, is the youngest of four siblings. Indeed, throughout the history of the dynasty younger brothers turn out to be more important than their elder brothers. Significantly, in speaking of a number of irregular successions, often people explained to me that the elder brother had abdicated because he preferred religious study—echoing the Brahmana/Satria distinction.

But there is more to be said about the Kapakisans' Brahmana ancestors. They specifically include a pair of figures—Empu Baradah and his son Empu Baula—who are central to another text, the *Calon Arang*. Their names are enough to evoke their story, since it is often performed (as dance-drama and shadow theater), commonly as a form of exorcism:

The widow of the king of Jirah in Java was a fantastically powerful witch, beloved of the goddess Durga. Enraged by the fact that Ratna Manggali, her beautiful daughter, remained unwed because no man dared to court the daughter of such a frightening mother, the witch received the goddess's aid in sending a fearful epidemic out over the land. The priest Empu Baradah resolved to find the means to defeat her. He sent his son, Empu Baula, to marry the princess and search out her mother's secrets. Empu Baula discovered that her power derived from two palm-leaf manuscripts, gifts from the goddess, one concerning magic of the left (*pengiwa*, "black magic") and one magic of the right (*penengen*, "white magic"). Empu Baula stole these texts and brought them to his father. After studying them, Empu Baradah was able to destroy the Widow of Jirah and restore prosperity to the land.

Not only *Babad Dalem* texts but also genealogies kept by members of the royal clan claim these two priests as ancestors of Klungkung's royal house: it is a vital part of royal self-consciousness. Indeed, occasionally a member of the royal house would make the point quite explicit by speculating about whether those famous palm-leaf texts might not have been one of the sources of the *kasaktian* of one or another Kapakisan king. There was little doubt in many minds that they must have been part of the royal library up to the fall of Klungkung; and, in fact, the catalogue of that library includes a text three palm leaves long, containing a mantra to destroy black magic and expose sorcerers, which the cataloger describes as deriving from Empu Baradah (no. 412 in Museum Nasional n.d.).

There are, furthermore, certain similarities between the power of Brahmana Buda and the power of sorcerers, since both traffic with the forces responsible for death, destruction, and pollution. But where the priest uses his power for collective ends, attracting negative forces in order to transform them, sorcerers use power for self-aggrandizement and revenge, employing negative forces to wreak social havoc.

If agnatically the rulers of Klungkung trace their origins to Brahmana Buda, their "female" antecedents (in addition, that is, to the witch) are rather more peculiar: a rock and an angel. The *widiadari* may be one source of the allure of later Kapakisan descendants, a theme that will be returned to later. About the rock, I can only speculate. On the one hand, it may simply stand for the female principle known as Ibu Pertiwi, "Mother Earth." But that the text specifies a stone must have some relevance. Ida Bagus suggested it was an allusion to Betara Wisnu, since stones are often sources for water. Or perhaps the stone was worn as a ring, which the priest used to focus his meditations, unifying the force of his will with the powers in the stone. Both tales in any event suggest the Kapakisan capacity to make manifest in the visible world what is ordinarily invisible, to bring into existence as objective reality their own desires. According to certain cosmological texts, the gods created the universe, including mankind, by means of similar yogic meditations (Hooykaas 1975).

I DURGA DINGKUL: THE TRANSFORMATION OF A PRIEST INTO A KING

So far the *Babad Dalem* has narrated two beginnings to the story of the Kapakisan dynasty: first, an account of how Bali came to be dominated by Java; second, an account of the ancestry of the first Kapakisan ruler. Now a different motif about origins is introduced as the reign of the new king gets underway: the potential priest must be transformed into an actual king. The agent of this transformation, which occurs in two stages, is a keris.

Sri Kresna Kapakisan, who was like the god Wisnu, established his capital in the town of Samprangan, southeast of the former capital of King Bédaulu. He was accompanied to Bali by an entourage of the Javanese nobles, many of them princes themselves, who had helped in the conquest of the island. These nobles are identified by name;[17] they included, among others, the ancestors of the later rulers of Tabanan and Badung and of Mengwi and Karangasem. He also brought with him the complete ceremonial accouterments of kingship, including a keris named Ki Ganja Dungkul, "with an ivory hilt, adorned with the pattern *tanjung kapatihan*, overlaid with jewels" (3b–4a).

But not all of the Balinese were willing to accept their new ruler. A large number of the malcontents retreated to mountain villages, where they fomented rebellion.[18] Sri Kresna Kapakisan felt unequal to the situation and sent word to Java, asking Gajah Mada to allow him to return home. Gajah Mada, however, refused this request. Instead he sent the king a new keris, his own weapon Ki Lobar, "which caused fear and dread in all evil-doers because it is a visible manifestation of Si Sangka Pancanjaniya [the Conch Shell Pancanjaniya]," one of Wisnu's weapons. By accepting this weapon the king "put on kingship [*rinangsuk ikang kadipatyan*]"; he had its presence (*bawa*) at his side whenever persons in a rage approached him. If he pulled it out of its sheath, Durga Dingkul [*dingkul* means "lying or falling crumpled"] was seen. The keris is said to be a manifestation of Gajah Mada himself. With this keris Sri Kresna Kapakisan brought the rebel villages under his domination. So successful was he that crop diseases and plagues kept far away from his domain, out of fear of the king (4b–7a).

The new king, with his priestly origins, cannot at first successfully exercise authority over his new subjects. It is only when he receives a keris as a gift from Gajah Mada that he "puts on kingship." Note that the weapon provides him with a way of being, *bawa*, which signifies "becoming, being; manner of being; character, temperament, state of mind or body, manner of acting, behavior, way of living, appearance, dress" (Zoetmulder 1982:226). Moreover, the character and appearance that the keris endows, the temperament and bearing of a ruler, involves the ability to inspire fear in wrongdoers—both those in the visible world (the rebel villagers in the mountains) and those in the invisible world (crop diseases and plagues are manifestations of the actions of malign spirits).

The keris can empower Sri Kresna Kapakisan in part because, the Balinese text notes, it is a surrogate of its giver, Gajah Mada: by possessing it the king is himself transformed into the conqueror of Bali. Aside from its connection to Gajah Mada, the keris has other properties in and of itself, marked first and foremost by the name by which it was most commonly known in Bali: Durga Dingkul, from the somewhat obscure passage in the text's description of its qualities. Many interpret this passage to mean that the keris had an image of the goddess Durga on its blade; others assert that the keris embodied and/or manifested the power of Durga, making her "visible."

Durga, the frightening aspect of Siwa's consort, is mistress over the *butakala* and, as already noted, patron of witches and epidemics. In Kawi *durga* also signifies "inaccessible, hard to overcome or approach" (Zoetmulder 1982); however, given the association between the Kapakisans and the goddess (in the tale of the Widow of Jirah, and there will be others), it seems more likely that it is the goddess who is relevant to the working of the keris rather than some general quality of rendering the king unapproachable—certainly Balinese in the 1990s think so. Agung's claim that the rebels in Bali's mountains used witchcraft to create havoc in the realm suggests a similar interpretation (n.d.:19–20).

Durga is a palpable presence in the Balinese landscape since virtually every Balinese village has at least one temple dedicated to her. Her temple, located next to the burial and cremation grounds, and generally surrounded by a patch of wild, uncultivated brush, is called the Pura Dalem. She herself is euphemistically referred to as *Betara ring Dalem*, "the goddess of the Pura Dalem" or "the goddess of the inside."

The name of her temple hints at a relationship between the goddess and Kapakisan rulers, who were known as Dalem. Most people I asked regarded the conjunction of names a mere coincidence. There are reasons to question this, however, and not only because of a few scattered remarks in the *Babad Dalem*. It is striking that in Klungkung, for example, members of royal and Brahmana clans did not traditionally support or worship in local village temples (Pura Desa) but did worship in their locality's Pura Dalem. Recall too the obligation of rulers to placate demonic forces that could or did harm their realms, forces ultimately subordinate to the goddess of the Pura Dalem. Rulers could only ensure prosperity with her aid. The royal title might have come from the goddess's, or perhaps at one time Pura Dalem meant "the king's temple"; in any event a connection is clear.

The text associates another divinity with this keris as well: Wisnu. As we shall see, Wisnu comes up repeatedly in the course of the narrative; already two Kapakisans have been named for that divinity, as Kresna was Wisnu's most famous incarnation, and Sri Kresna Kapakisan has been overtly likened to the god. Here I want to note the analogy drawn between the keris Durga Dingkul and Wisnu's weapon Si Sangka Pancajaniya, a conch shell. In his incarnation as Kresna, Wisnu took Pancajaniya from a demon (Zoetmulder 1982). Conch shells also form part of the ritual paraphernalia of Balinese demonic exorcism.[19] Conch shells, of course, come from the sea, which, like all water, is identified with one of the forms of Wisnu.

It is, then, a keris that establishes the new king's authority over Bali, a keris associated with negative aspects of Divinity and exorcism: to succeed as ruler, the priestly king must show himself to be fierce. On the one hand, the fierceness merely draws out his identity as a Buda priest's son; the weapon even appears to have some association with priestly paraphernalia. But if the weapon is likened to Kresna's conch shell, it nonetheless *is* a weapon and a keris, and thus differentiates king from priest.[20]

Sri Kresna Kapakisan, however, already possessed a keris when he arrived in Bali, Ki Ganja Dungkul. Why the need for another?

There is no indication that Ki Ganja Dungkul had great power. Its name appears to be purely descriptive: a *ganja* is the upper part of a keris blade, which widens into a triangle under the hilt; *dungkul*, literally, to "be in one's shell" or "pull in one's horns" (Zoetmulder 1982:434), suggests being closed in on oneself, or curled into a ball. The text does note its hilt was made of ivory, to which Balinese attribute protective power. However, *tanjung kapatihan*, the pattern carved upon it, may indicate why Ganja Dungkul was not equal to subduing the rebellious Balinese. *Kapatihan* derives from the root *patih*. A *patih* was a high court official, usually a ruler's primary advisor. The design, therefore, appears to be one appropriate to a subordinate, which was indeed the ruler of Bali's position in relation to the ruler of Majapahit. In obtaining a new keris suitable not merely to a minister (*patih*) but imparting qualities associated with kingship (*kadipatyan*), we see prefigured Bali's eventual equality with Majapahit.

In modern Klungkung, Ganja Dungkul and Durga Dingkul/Lobar tend to be conflated into one keris, known as Durga Dungkul. A later episode in the text seems to make a similar identification. Indeed, it seems more or less reasonable to think of Ganja Dungkul, Durga Dingkul, and Lobar as one and the same object. The name Durga Dungkul was explained to me by a folk etymology: when pulled from its sheath and held up, the power of the goddess Durga would cause people to *dungkul*, curl into a ball as if paralyzed. Moreover, if the keris did contain a representation of the goddess Durga on the blade, the most likely place for it would have been the *ganja*, the longer edge of which was often carved.[21] But if the keris are "really" one and the same, why talk of them as if they were two?

The duplication of keris reiterates the importance of keris in constituting Sri Kresna Kapakisan as a king, attributing a dual significance to such objects: in the first instance, as part of the paraphernalia of the court, expressive of the external appearance of authority; in the second instance, as embodying actual power, a power complexly delineated in terms of potentialities for action encoded by certain forms of Divinity.

More generally, however, reiteration is frequent in the text. There have been at least two examples thus far: the story of Bédaulu, which is a repetition of that of Mayadanawa; and the two meditations of Kapakisan priestly forebears, one of which produces a son and the second a wife. Moreover, in these instances, as in the case of the keris, Balinese often collapse the two stories into one when they tell them orally, which further proves their ultimate identity. The duplications may simply suggest alternate versions preserved in written form, which (since their "message" is the same) cannot be chosen between. But duplication also seems to be used to index a crucial theme. It may be relevant that Indonesian languages, including Balinese, use reduplication for emphasis.

THE FOUNDING OF GÉLGÉL

Dalem Sri Kresna Kapakisan had three sons: the eldest, Déwa Samprangan or Déwa Ilé, was a fop who spent his time dressing up in fine clothes; the next eldest, Déwa Taruk, was mad; and the youngest, Déwa Ketut Ngulesir, went from village to village gambling. The eldest and heir spent so much time fussing over his appearance that he neglected his duties. After waiting for hours one morning to meet with him, the chief minister, Gusti Kubon Tubuh, left in annoyance and went to find Déwa Ketut to ask him to become king. Déwa Ketut was reluctant, citing his inadequacies, but Gusti Kubon Tubuh persisted and offered him his own compound in Gélgél as his palace. The new king and his court moved to Gélgél; no more is heard of Samprangan or Dalem Ilé (11a–11b).[22]

Once again a youngest brother became king. Why, however, should a gambler be more suitable than a dandy?

If the text merely identifies Déwa Ketut as a gambler, Balinese read this in a more specific way: he is a devotee of cockfights. Geertz's famous article (1973a) explores certain cultural dimensions of cockfighting, in which reversals of hierarchical order may temporarily manifest themselves: whatever relationships of deference normally obtain, in the cockfighting ring a bird belonging to a commoner may demolish one belonging to a prince. This is a fitting image for an unorthodox succession, in which a youngest son is chosen by the court and implicitly favored by the gods. But this does not explain Déwa Ketut's suitability; it merely complicates it.

The willingness to put oneself at risk entailed by gambling is not necessarily negatively valued in Bali. Given Balinese ideas about the invisible world, gambling becomes particularly exciting, as a test of the strength of one's intent. (Unusual success, of course, would indicate an especially strong connection to the invisible world.) Judging by reminiscences about Klungkung's last king, gambling was also a mark of a generous and open-handed sovereign, one with the common touch. Moreover, a king's willingness to gamble implied that infinite resources were at his disposal, a sign of the favor of the invisible world. The theme of bounty is almost certainly relevant here, since the new king named his court Puri Suécapura, the place of graciousness, of generosity.

Cockfights also evoke themes pertinent to rule: they are sacrifices to demons. Kings received a tax on cockfights and sponsored an annual grand cockfight lasting two months (for which certain subjects had to provide two cocks apiece) in the cockfighting ring outside of the royal residence (van Bloemen Waanders 1870:232–33). While sources do not specify which two months these were, they were probably sometime between the sixth and ninth months of the Balinese year—roughly, between November and March—during the inauspicious rainy season. One avid gambler I knew in Klungkung recalled that in his younger days men were obsessed by cockfights during these months, a sign, he suggested, of their possession by the bloodthirsty demons who temporarily had the upper hand over the land. With the passing of the season (marked by the annual Taur Agung, which placated the demons and restored them to a benevolent form) their passion would quell. Such associations suggest that the new king, like his Brahmana Buda forefathers, was a kind of exorcist.

DALEM KETUT NGULESIR: THE PARADIGMATIC KING

Worsley (1972) notes that narratives concerning a clan's pivotal ancestors are among the richest and most elaborated parts of a *babad*. Although Dalem Ketut (known after his accession as Dalem Ketut Smara Kapakisan) was not the first Ksatria Dalem ruler, he did establish the court of Gélgél, which as the site of the dynasty's greatest fame forms a kind of origin-point. It is probably for this reason that stories about Dalem Ketut Ngulesir provide the strongest statement of Klungkung's particular relations to the *niskala*, the invisible world, and that the *Babad Dalem* devotes so much narrative space to his reign.

Dalem Ketut is identified with a plethora of divinities and heroes. The very first passage about his reign makes this evident, glorifying this exemplar of the good king:

> It had been a long time since the God of Love had arrived to reign in Gélgél, to be the protector of the kingdom of Bali. The entire realm was prosperous and tranquil, there were no arguments, all kinds of food were cheap and copious. For he was an incarnation of Sang Hyang Tolangkir, as handsome as Arjuna, without equal among men, completely capable, respected by all of his ministers and all of the lower officials. So it was with the one in Bali (12b, verbatim).

Arjuna, one of the five Pandawa brothers in the epic *Barata Yuda*, is famed for his great attractiveness, refinement, and skill. But more important, the king is identified as an incarnation of Betara Smara, the god of love, whose name he took, and of Sang Hyang Tolangkir, the divinity of Besakih. The text reiterates these identifications, both in its descriptions of the king and in its account of the major events of his reign.

The King as the God of Love

Several passages depict Dalem Ketut as Smara, in lyrical descriptions of his attire and impact. The following is typical:

> Let us now speak about the king of Bali, approached in the Red Pavilion on the tenth day of the full moon. He was wearing his hairknot becomingly, in the style called "shrimp claws." It was filled with nine jewels, and in the front on his forehead was a diamond like a star. His headdress was decorated with a Garuda image facing toward the back. His ear ornaments were shaped like leaves, and he had frangipani flowers behind his right and left ears. He was wearing a betel-nut-flower bracelet with precious jewels, and a ring with a red stone on his index finger. His fine fingers were very attractive; his fingernails flashed like butterflies when struck by the rays of the sun. His teeth were rubbed so they shone like pearls. He had chewed betel twice, and his lips had a trace of lime on them, like a drop of honey, and his gums were reddened. The hearts of all who saw him, looking like the god of love, were enchanted, and also all of the young women were disturbed. The god of love had come down to earth and was on everyone's lips. Their hearts

were destroyed and dissolved, like an incense burner made of tin melting from the heat, seeing his sweetness. That finished, he emerged, wearing a keris in his belt with a golden hilt adorned with precious jewels, and a sheath overlaid with an image of the death of the god of love, of extraordinary sweetness, pale yellow like a painting. He was wearing a red silk kampuh with an "illusion of clouds" pattern applied with gilt. The cloth around his hips had a "fine rain" pattern, on a foundation of gold. He was a wearing a golden collar studded with jewels. His wide arms were clearly visible through a thin shawl, wavy like the sands of the ocean. It is difficult to render it. Like the sun when the sun is glittering, his glances were like intertwined flashes of lightning. His eyebrows were shaped like *intaran* leaves, clearly vanquishing the hearts of all of the young women. He was wearing his keris Si Tanda Langlang, for it is like the weapon of the god Wisnu in slaying enemies. All was complete with rattan mats and parasols, like the shining disk of the moon, a dazzling pinnacle of radiance, with a treasure hoard of gems (13a–13b, verbatim).

An identification with Betara Smara, god of love, desire, and attraction, while expressly stated in the case of Dalem Ketut, is a central motif for successful kingship in general. According to Pedanda Gedé Kenitén, during coronation ceremonies a large offering was made to imbue a new king with Smara's qualities. Further connections with Smara were sought through study: Klungkung rulers had a great many texts on *pengasih*, the power to attach through attraction, in their library (see Juynboll 1912a). Smara's continuing importance to the Kapakisans is suggested by the fact that the Klungkung court was even named Smarapura, "Smara's Abode" (see below).

The appeal of the themes of seduction and desire to precolonial Balinese aristocrats is evidenced in the courtly fascination with the legendary adventures of the alluring prince Panji, which were commonly performed by and for royal audiences (Vickers 1986). Without underestimating the pleasures involved, royal seductions had pragmatic consequences in which many parties had a stake. Not only marriages but even lesser liaisons brought a ruler followers, in the kinsmen of his partners. It has commonly been observed that the strength of Southeast Asian rulers depended upon the size of their entourages. Since one acquired an entourage through feats of courtliness and prowess that led to widespread admiration, it is hardly surprising that one finds an emphasis on the attractiveness of rulers in literature and other artistic forms throughout the region (see Anderson 1972 and Milner 1982 for other parts of the Malay world). If in marrying a ruler could gain not only a wife but allies, the polygyny allowed to Balinese rulers was a decided political advantage.

But Smara's patronage did not only render rulers attractive to potential lovers or followers. Relationships with *niskala* forces are also commonly expressed in an idiom of attraction. Indeed, the aesthetic richness of Balinese ritual is a product of efforts to attract Divinity through the delicate fragrance of flowers and incense, the dazzling colors of clothing and offerings, and the performance of dance and music.[23] Since attraction is essential to the ritual process, Smara's presence is crucial. In Klungkung, when persons are purified to become temple priests or healers or to undertake the study of texts, a cloth with a drawing of Smara and his consort Ratih (goddess of the moon) is placed on their bodies, a symbolic act representing the hope that these divinities be permanently *em*-bodied. Thus a ruler's identification with Smara also implied a capacity to attract other *niskala* aid when needed.

It is obvious that the glittering and magnificent wealth so lovingly elaborated in passages like this one contributed to royal attractiveness. Wealth was both a sign of divine favors already conferred upon him and a means to display himself to best advantage.

The King as the Maintainer of the World

In the passage cited above, two of the king's accouterments—his keris Si Tanda Langlang, and his headdress, which is in the shape of a *garuda*, a legendary bird that is the vehicle of Wisnu—once again evoke that god.[24] Throughout the *babad*, Kapakisans are often likened to Wisnu.[25] Even more commonly their weapons are said to be reminiscent of Wisnu's.

In contemporary Bali, Wisnu is usually identified as Divinity as preserver or maintainer of the world. He is particularly associated with water and such desirable qualities as coolness and *darma*, correct and right (and, so I inferred from discussions and observations, calm and mild) behavior. Wisnu's consort, Sri, is the goddess of rice and thus a source of bounty. To liken a ruler to Wisnu, then, would seem to be to praise his benevolence and the harmony, prosperity, and productivity of his realm.

But Wisnu is not only a god of reproduction. To protect the world also requires a willingness and capacity to fight, to engage in battle. Hence powerful keris are likened to Wisnu's weapons, and iron is one of his elements. According to the *Purwa Tattwa*, for example, a glowing piece of iron found within a temple should be treated as an embodiment of the god Wisnu. (Iron, of course, is cool and dark, both qualities associated with the god.) Moreover, it is said that those who die in battle go directly to Wisnu's realm. And it was Kresna, the incarnation of Wisnu after whom several Kapakisans are named, who admonished the hero Arjuna in the epic *Barata Yuda* that fighting in the great war at Kuruksetra, even against his kinsmen and teachers, was his duty as a *ksatria*. Indeed, it is largely in praising a Kapakisan's military might that the text likens him to Wisnu.

Dalem Ketut's relationship to the god of Besakih will be discussed shortly.

Note that the origins of Si Tanda Langlang, the weapon likened to one of Wisnu's, are not mentioned. The text goes on, however, to recount his acquisition of another keris, which like Durga Dingkul was one of the famous heirlooms of the Kapakisan dynasty.

I BANGAWAN CANGGU

After some time Sri Hayam Wuruk, the Majapahit emperor, summoned the rulers under his overlordship to his capital, including Dalem Ketut. Everyone was delighted by Bali's king, who looked exactly like the god of love and demonstrated such perfect mastery of court etiquette. Sri Hayam Wuruk had heard that Dalem Ketut's body was marked by a curious sign and asked to see it. Dalem Ketut declared his person indeed had a defect and, apologizing for exposing his lower limb to his hierarchical superior, lifted his garments to reveal it: on his thigh was a birthmark resembling the head of Kala, "a sign he is valiant in war." The text comments: "He embodied the god Aswino." Hayam Wuruk, pleased, presented him with cloth and a keris decorated with a snake design (*nagapasa*), saying, "This is a sign of my love for you. A proof that we are one. We are permanently united." On the way back from Java, the keris dove into the water of the Canggu River. But when its sheath was held out, it jumped into it. The keris was henceforth known as Ki Bangawan Canggu, "the Great Canggu River" (21a–22a).

There is a dense network of allusions in the episode concerning Bangawan Canggu, much "skin," as Balinese say, "to peel." This in itself is a clue that the object was singularly important to the Kapakisan clan. Indeed, it both unifies multiple significations concerning royal power and marks the dynasty's future role.[26]

Although the keris is a gift from a king, it is also indirectly a divine gift: given because of a bodily blemish itself endowed by the gods. It is a token in recognition of the secret mark upon the ruler of Bali's leg: a mark that resembles the head of Kala, the frightening aspect of the god Siwa. That mark signifies victory in warfare, an activity over which Kala holds sway, and thus it is fitting that it be acknowledged by the gift of a keris.

But the mark on Dalem Ketut's leg also signifies his identification with Aswino, god of healers. Zoetmulder identifies this figure with twin Indian divinities, handsome celestial physicians who "avert sickness and misfortune" (1982:151). If Dalem Ketut is said to embody Aswino, Kala's mark must denote his abilities to exercise dominion over that which is brought by Kala, "sickness and misfortune." The birthmark is a sign that he is himself master over Kala's minions. If the birthmark is also a sign of victory in war, there must be a connection between warfare and healing.[27] As we shall see momentarily, the keris itself invokes both activities: warfare, because it is after all a weapon; healing, in part because it is ornamented with a snake.

An interpolation at this point in *Babad Dalem A* (Warna et al. 1986) suggests that the "healing" attributes of this keris may be interpreted in terms of exorcism. The author of this version writes that the original name of Bangawan Canggu (which he claims to be the Snake Basuki, an identification mentioned much later in other texts) was Ki Sudamala (Cleansed of Evil or Pollution) because it was capable of purifying the realm. *Sudamala* is the name of an offering used in exorcisms. It is also the name of a poem concerning the goddess Durga. According to the story, Siwa's consort Uma was cursed to live as a demon (i.e., in her terrible form, as the goddess Durga) in Gandamayu cemetery as a punishment for infidelity. She was accompanied by Kalantaka and Kalanjaya, two other divine beings similarly cursed. With the aid of Betara Guru (the Divine Teacher), Sahadéwa, one of the five Pandawa brothers (and a twin, like Aswino—indeed, Balinese identify Sahadéwa and his twin with Aswino), restores her to her benevolent form by performing a purification rite. Sahadéwa (now called Sudamala) then battles Kalantaka and Kalanjaya; when he defeats them, they too resume their divine forms. Shadow-puppet performances of *Sudamala* are said to be able to reverse curses, ward off disasters, and neutralize negative forces (Zoetmulder 1974:433–35). Although only this one text explicitly makes a connection between Bangawan Canggu and Sudamala, it is clearly not an arbitrary one. According to Agung (n.d.), for example, the mark on Dalem Ketut's thigh represented Durga rather than Kala. Thus the keris also reiterates certain themes associated with Durga Dingkul.

To return to the main text, the keris is symbolic of a dual objectification. On the one hand, it is iconic of the mark on the royal body, thus itself "a sign he is valiant in war," an objectification of the royal capacity to destroy and to heal. It is also, however, an index of the giver, "a sign of [his] love," an objectification of the unity of the power of the king of Bali with that of the emperor of Majapahit. This is certainly a significant statement: it suggests that the Kapakisans inherit the mantle of Majapahit. If the keris is a token of the unity of Bali and Majapahit it is not only, however, because of a Maussian principle by which gift unites donor and recipient. Significantly, the unity of Bali's ruler and Majapahit's emperor has been suggested even before this scene, for prior to Dalem Ketut's arrival in Majapahit, the text describes Sri Hayam Wuruk as Aswino as well. There is yet another way in which Bangawan Canggu unifies Bali and Majapahit, however, since this keris also serves as a sign of a capacity to unify, a motif that encompasses several levels of meaning and explains why the keris is adorned with a *nagapasa*.

Nagapasa first and foremost is a kind of *naga*, a crowned serpent. That Zoetmulder also identifies *nagaposa* as a magic noose used in battle (1982:

1168) not only reinforces the military theme but points to a major feature of *naga*: their capacity to bind. As noted above, the gods used the *naga* Ananta-boga and Basuki to bind Mount Agung and the island of Bali to an underwater turtle and thus stabilize it. (Later in the text, Bangawan Canggu is specifically identified with Naga Basuki.) Hence *naga* inhabit the waters beneath the earth. Given the *naga* that adorns it, it is not surprising that this keris has an affinity for watery depths; in Agung's version of the story, Dalem Ketut is even warned that the keris is attracted to water.

Naga, then, have cosmological associations. Some Balinese temples (and in Klungkung, nearly all temples) contain a shrine called a *sapta patala*, which represents the seven layers of the earth bound together by two *naga*.[28] Other shrines also represent the cosmos this way: shrines to the god of the sea commonly have images of a turtle and/or *naga* at their base (as at Klungkung's state temple Batu Klotok); *padmasana*, the tall seats for Divinity in its most inconceivable forms, always do. Returning to keris, the base of the main *méru* shrine in Klungkung's temple Taman Sari (see below), to which the royal keris were brought every Tumpek Landep for offerings, was encircled by a *naga*, and the entire shrine was surrounded by a moat: perhaps a reference to Ban-gawan Canggu itself.[29]

But the binding power of snakes need not refer to the cosmos. In the "little world" (*buana alit*) of the body, what may be bound is one's *kayun*, one's desires, feelings, and thoughts. For Ida Bagus Jagri snakes signify concentra-tion: the focusing of one's *kayun* on the invisible world to achieve particular ends. Hence snakes are associated in general with *kasaktian*, which is achieved by remaining *pageh*, firm and resolute. For this reason, there is also an associa-tion between snakes and healers: one who saw a snake, for example, in asking for a gift at a temple would probably be granted an object (say a length of checkered cloth) endowing the power to heal. Similarly, keris like Bangawan Canggu with snake motifs incised on the blades are also deemed appropriate for healers. Many healers wear a bracelet of a barklike coral, fashioned at one end in the shape of a serpent's head.

There is one further cultural association that expressly links *naga* and binding to kings. A major offering at royal cremations is an enormous repre-sentation of a *naga*, called the *nagabanda*, the "snake chain" or "binding snake." This *naga* is "killed" by the officiating priest with a flower-arrow. Killing the *naga*, I was told, liberates the ruler's soul. It also releases his hold on his realm and his subjects, and theirs on him.

Bangawan Canggu, with the snake on its blade, also had the capacity to bind people to the king, to inspire their devotion.[30] This is shown in Agung's *Babad Dalem*, in an episode in which the founder of the Sukawati branch line asks his elder brother for the keris Bangawan Canggu. When he is refused, the gods give the disappointed prince a palm-leaf text about *pangasih*, "inspiring love," as a substitute (Agung n.d.: 83–86; see also Sanggra 1971:2). Another Sukawati source, the *Babad Timbul Sukawati*, asserts that Bangawan Canggu was the "cord that bound the island of Bali" (Sanggra 1971:1).

The gift of Bangawan Canggu to Dalem Ketut Ngulesir foreshadows and perhaps even explains the next episode in the text: the fall of the Majapahit empire.

> Some time after Dalem Ketut's return to Bali, Majapahit was destroyed. Hayam Wuruk died, and Majapahit's lords fought with one another, quarreled as if possessed by malign forces, and were continuously drunk. Divinity appeared, in the form of Kala with one eye, and proclaimed, "Empty, Empty, Empty." Whoever heard this voice died. The city of Majapahit decayed, and the land returned to forest. All of the gold, jewels, and especially the keris of the Majapahit realm were dispersed to Majapahit's former dependencies, including Bali (22a–22b).

Majapahit's fall is attributed to the inadequacies of its leaders, and ultimately to fate; perpetual quarreling and drinking are also signs of being overmastered by malign forces. But, having already transferred his power to the ruler of Bali (through the gift of a keris that symbolized their identity), there was no further need for a ruler in Majapahit. At the final moment of destruction, the forces the leaders of the realm have allowed to dominate their actions are objectified as Kala—the destructive aspect of Siwa and also "time."

BESAKIH: THE "HEAD" OF GÉLGÉL

The *Babad Dalem* narrates one final episode concerning Dalem Ketut, which makes explicit at last his relationship to the god of Besakih:

> Dalem Ketut conceived a desire to undergo a ritual consecration and invited a Brahmana from Keling to Bali to conduct it. On his way to Gélgél, the priest noticed a glow emanating from Mount Agung and went to investigate. The source of the glow was found at the temple of Besakih: the god Mahadéwa. Mahadéwa asked the priest where he was going, and the priest explained that he was on his way to perform a purification ceremony for the king. At these words the god held up his hand, from which fire emerged, and asked the priest if he knew what it was. The priest said yes, it was the "five fires." The god then asked where on the priest's body he should throw it: On his heart [literally liver]? His neck? The priest fell silent, and Mahadéwa vanished. The priest then resumed his journey to Gélgél. Ushered into the king's presence, he was amazed, for the king looked exactly like the god. After performing the ceremony, the priest returned home (23b–24a).

This episode begins to distinguish priests from kings, for it shows there are goals kings cannot achieve without them. But since priests are still peripheral to the narrative—this one returns to Java—we will return to this theme later.

The most important detail in these episodes for present purposes is the reiteration, in dramatic form, of an identity between the god of Besakih and the ruler of Bali: they are physically indistinguishable.

Tolangkir is a different sort of god than Wisnu or Durga: a more specifically Balinese form of Divinity. He is also known as the god of Mount Agung, the island's highest mountain, and his temple is the most important meeting point between the visible and invisible worlds on Bali.

Besakih is both the largest and most encompassing of Bali's thousands upon thousands of temples. People speak of it as Bali's "highest" temple, which it is less by virtue of its physical location (which is also "highest") than by virtue of its ritual position. It is unique in being the one temple at which all Balinese may pray, and people seek holy water from the temple for rituals at other, lesser temples. Other important Balinese temples invariably contain a shrine for the god of Mount Agung.

Located midway up the slopes of Mount Agung, Besakih is really a multi-level complex of temples, which some claim has been a holy site for a thousand years.[31] There are an enormous variety of shrines, dedicated to many different forms of Divinity. Many of the gods who have shrines in the complex are no longer familiar to most Balinese, although temple priests continue to ensure that they receive the appropriate offerings. The temple also contains shrines consecrated to the ancestors of various Balinese clans, particularly those that exercised political authority during the Gélgél and early Klungkung periods. Klungkung's royal house itself has a set of six shrines at Besakih dedicated to its ancestors.

That various texts refer to Besakih as the "head" (*pengulu*) of Gélgél (*Usana Jawa* K1516; Friedrich 1847:267) shows how central it was to Kapakisan authority. Until quite recently Klungkung's royal house was responsible for Besakih. While early in the eighteenth century Klungkung's ruler appointed certain persons and their heirs to oversee the daily maintenance of the temple, and various lords were assigned responsibilities for rituals in portions of the enormous complex, the king retained for himself the duty to organize and witness major rituals in the Pura Penataran Agung, the central and most important part of the complex. This section of the temple contains shrines for Divinity in all of its most encompassing forms, from Tolangkir himself to the tripartite Hindu divinities Brahma, Wisnu, and Siwa. The dynasty also retained responsibility for Pura Gelap, a smaller temple in the complex dedicated to Divinity in the form of Siwa/Iswara (god of the east, whose color is white).[32] Pura Gelap's annual rite was known as *pangenteg gumi*, "so that the country be stable." Nowadays the regency of Klungkung is still responsible for Pura Gelap and continues to contribute offerings to the annual ritual at the Penataran, which members of the royal family attend as witnesses.

The link between Klungkung and Besakih was so important that when the road north to the temple was blocked during a war between Klungkung and Karangasem, a temple for Besakih's gods, called the Pura Penataran Agung, was built in the capital. To this day the gods of Besakih stop there to receive homage whenever they are brought to be purified by the sea at Klotok.

It was through their relationship to the god of Mount Agung that the Kapakisans protected Bali. The five fires on the hand of Besakih's god in this episode show him as the source from which power emanates to all points of the compass. If Tolangkir actually manifested himself physically in the royal form, it is small wonder that the realm prospered. Nor was Dalem Ketut the only Kapakisan on intimate terms with Besakih's god (see chapter 11). Possibly—though texts and oral traditions do not explicitly state this—all Kapakisan rulers had such a close relationship with the god.

DALEM WATU RÉNGGONG: ROYAL POWER CONSOLIDATED

Dalem Ketut was succeeded by his eldest son, Dalem Watu Rénggong. The text describes him as "accomplished in valor," like the god Wisnu when he manifests with four hands, in each of which he holds one of his weapons: discus (*cakra*), bludgeon (*gada*), conch shell (Si Sangka Pancajaniya), and sword/keris (Si Nandaka). The king's keris Lobar and Katitinggi (Bedbug) are likened to the bludgeon and discus; Tanda Langlang and Bangawan Canggu are likened to Nandaka and Pancajaniya. The kings' army was like the god Kala in eating the souls of men, and Ularan, the lord who led it, was a visible form of death personified. This army was deployed against the ruler of Blambangan, whose daughter refused to marry Watu Rénggong. The king of Blambangan also deserved death for his mistreatment of the priest Danghyang Nirartha, who fled Blambangan for Bali (24b–26a).

Once again a Kapakisan ruler is likened to Wisnu, and his regalia to the god's weapons. In addition to keris familiar from earlier episodes (Bangawan Canggu, Lobar, and Tanda Langlang) there is a new one, whose name, Bedbug (Katitinggi), marks its taste for human blood. Note that here Bangawan Canggu rather than Lobar is identified with Wisnu's conch shell.[33] The importance of war, and its associations with the fierce aspects of Divinity, are apparent from the description of Bali's army.

The text explains that Danghyang Nirartha, ancestor of all of Bali's Brahmana Siwa, came to the island to escape the wrath of Dalem Blambangan, who had previously liked him well enough to marry him to his sister. The priest's natural fragrance proved irresistible to the ladies of the court, and the king unjustly suspected him of using magic to achieve this effect. On the other hand, Dalem Watu Rénggong attacked Blambangan (thus serving as an instrument of divine justice, unwittingly avenging the priest he had not yet met) because of a failure to be irresistible: a portrait of the king sent to woo Dalem Blambangan's daughter misrepresented him as so unattractive that she vowed to kill herself rather than wed him.

After proving his power in a series of remarkable demonstrations, Danghyang Nirartha became the court priest. The rites he performed made Dalem Watu Rénggong even more *sakti*, as they rendered him even more attractive to *niskala* forces:

> Nirartha purified the king and his two hundred wives, after which the king became one with his teacher—equal to him in knowledge and power. The realm prospered. The king was also just. When one of his servants was discovered stealing he asked him why, and when told he was given very little to eat he not only fed him but punished the lord in charge of stocking the public kitchens. Such was the king's *kasaktian*, says the text, that even epidemics and pests feared him. Everything planted flourished, and prices were low (32b–33a).

The claim that after his purification the king's power was so great that epidemics and pests feared him, and therefore spared his realm, is virtually identical to what was said about Sri Kresna Kapakisan following his acquisition of Durga Dingkul. This suggests the equivalence of various paths to power.

Danghyang Nirartha (about whom the text has much to say) was not the only priest to come to Bali at this time. His nephew Sri Astapaka, a Brahmana Buda, arrived a short time later:

> Sri Astapaka asked Danghyang Nirartha why he had not yet performed a *homa* ritual, and the two priests then proceeded to do so.[34] The text notes that Danghyang Nirartha immersed himself in a raging fire but was unscathed. Sri Astapaka made a fire underneath a banyan tree, and not only was the tree unharmed but a spider even continued to weave its web safely above the flames. After the ritual all of the plant life in the kingdom flourished: coconut trees bore as many as two hundred nuts each. Both priests instructed the king in religious matters and purified him every full and new moon (33b).

The difference between Siwa and Buda is articulated in the *homa* ritual as a difference between a capacity to protect the self from harm and the capacity to affect the object world. The path of Saivite purity and study results in a transformation of the self; the path of the Buda priest, however, can transform the world (or one's perception of it). Agung's *Babad Dalem*, which substitutes another well-known tale for that of the *homa* ritual, clarifies this. When Sri Astapaka arrived in Gélgél, Dalem Watu Rénggong tested him by hiding a goose and asking him what animal he had hidden. The priest proclaimed it was a *naga*. When the king opened the hiding place to reveal the priest's error, he was astounded to indeed uncover a *naga* (Agung n.d.; see also Friederich 1959).[35] In the end, however, the difference between them is minor: they simply follow two paths to a single goal.

DISTINGUISHING KINGS AND PRIESTS

In Watu Rénggong the power of the Kapakisan dynasty is actualized in its totality. In the introductory passage of this section the king's power is the summation of the power of his various weapons. As the narrative concerning this king unfolds, various aspects of royal power are laid out, at one moment differentiated by their objectification into other figures, at the next reassimilated as these others are revealed to be extensions of the royal person.

This is especially true of the distinctions made between priest and king and between Siwa and Buda priests. Initially the text distinguishes the priestly and military aspects of power. Note that the king is initially described as fierce and terrible, and Dalem Watu Rénggong is the first king to be actively involved in conquest, a most unpriestly activity. At the same time, Brahmana priests finally settle on Bali and begin to serve the king. The first to arrive is a Brahmana Siwa, that is, a representative of that form of priesthood most distinct from Kapakisan kingship. But the king ultimately assimilates his power and knowledge. It is only after his consecration by Nirartha that the land is said to flourish and the king to be just. Unlike the power embodied in his keris, however, this power is not heritable. To reproduce it requires the continued presence of priests on Bali.

At that point a second priest arrives, a Brahmana Buda, re-creating the distinction between priest and king. When Sri Astapaka joins his Siwa uncle, the benefits deriving from the presence of priests are further clarified: they are able to perform ceremonies that augment the prosperity of the realm; they tutor the king in religion; they purify him every full and new moon.

The development of the story is almost Hegelian: within a unity exist opposed tendencies, which as they manifest become separate. Yet they may at any time resolve into their original unity. While the *Babad Dalem* plays with difference and identity between kings and priests, either may be emphasized in other texts or actual practice. For example, Agung both stresses and clarifies the distinction between king and priest. In his version Dalem Watu Rénggong does not undergo a purification ritual and become "one" with Danghyang Nirartha. Instead he asks the priest which path is better: that of *kadiatmikan* knowledge of inner, mystical matters; or *kawibawaan*, power and influence.[36] The priest declares they are equal, but if the king pursues the first—that is, if he acts as a priest—only he will benefit. If he chooses the second, he will be able to defeat enemies, which will aid his people. In order to achieve *kawibawaan* the king is advised to make offerings in all of the temples of Bali. He is also instructed to perform rituals to purify his ancestors and to placate demons (precisely the rituals for which Brahmana Buda are especially qualified), as well as to make offerings not only with flowers and incense but also with meat, which is attractive to lower forms of Divinity and demons (Agung n.d.: 37).

Dalem Watu Rénggong's superiority to his lords, however, is unquestioned. In one spectacular scene, he rides his chariot out to sea to confront an enemy, while his lords cower on the shore, unable to follow.

The final remarks in the *Babad Dalem* concerning Dalem Watu Rénggong summarize the nature of fully realized royal power in all of its multiplicity:

> The king was the epitome of *darma*, and all of Bali's enemies were still and quiet. No one could resist his *kasaktian*. He conquered not only Blambangan but also Sumbawa and Pasuruan. He instructed his subjects to hide their beautiful wives and daughters, as it was difficult for him to control his sexual desires. Watu Rénggong was master of all knowledge important to a king: the rules of governing, the proper conduct of war, the four means of destroying enemies, horse training, and the arts of sexual love (33b–35a).

Note that the areas he is said to have conquered are those that were once ruled by his grandfather's siblings.

STERILE AND FERTILE KINGSHIP

With the reign of Dalem Watu Rénggong, royal power is at its height and all of its elements have been brought into the open. Episodes narrated in the remainder of the text have a less foundational flavor. Indeed, the wheel begins to turn, and the realm is threatened by disorder and dissolution.

> Dalem Watu Rénggong had two sons, Déwa Pemayun and Déwa Anom Segening. Because both were young when their father died, a great-uncle was appointed regent. But it was the Kali-Yuga, a time of destruction. The chief minister, Gusti Batan Jeruk, student of a Brahmana Buda priest, was overcome by "greed, folly and blindness to what is correct, and unbridled violent passion." He and the regent planned a revolt in order to usurp the throne permanently. The conspirators were, however, defeated. Gusti Batan Jeruk fled east to Karangasem (35b–37b).
>
> The new king, Dalem Pemayun Bekung, had poor discrimination,

and his judgment was distorted, unlike his younger brother's. His infatuation with one of his wives, even after he had evidence of her adultery with one of his courtiers, led him to ignore his duties as well as to make improper decisions. His officials quarreled with one another and bred trouble. Certain territories conquered by his father were lost. Yet he still was *sakti*: he prevented an attack on the capital by causing a river to flood. He was replaced by his younger brother, Dalem Segening, though it is unclear if he abdicated or was simply succeeded by his brother. Dalem Segening was a good king, with many wives and children (37b–51b).

If the Watu Rénggong section of the text distinguished kings from their priests, here the unity of interest between kings and their ministers and kings and their branch-line kin begins to dissolve. Not only does the prime minister plan a revolt (in which a royal relative participates), but the text devotes considerable narrative space to recounting the exploits of various nobles.

As far as the royal line itself is concerned, a familiar theme is reiterated: the superiority of a younger brother. The contrast between elder and younger is here figured as a distinction between sterility and fecundity. Dalem Bekung apparently had no heirs; in fact, *bekung* means "infertile," though this may be a euphemism to refer to his reign in general. His successor, Dalem Segening, is by contrast famous for his fertility, and it is through him that the royal line perpetuates itself. Indeed, his fecundity, which is a form of efficacy, is also a sign of his *kasaktian*.

The story also suggests another reason why polygyny was important to the practice of kingship. Dalem Bekung's obsession with one woman, a wife who moreover was involved in an adulterous liaison with one of his own nobles, distorted his judgment and undermined his authority. The gaze of a ruler with many wives and offspring, which linked many subjects to him as kinsmen, was, in contrast, turned outward toward his realm.

Oddly, little else is said of Dalem Segening, although his memory was important to several nineteenth-century political leaders. There is, we will see, a royal temple dedicated to him in Klungkung, and he was claimed as a pivotal ancestor by at least two other Balinese royal clans through illegitimate (or at least not officially acknowledged) connections.[37]

THE FALL OF GÉLGÉL AND THE FOUNDING OF KLUNGKUNG

Dalem Segening was succeeded by his son, Dalem di Madé. His reign is initially characterized in glowing terms:

The land was prosperous from the sea to the mountains; goods were inexpensive and the people content. The king was like the god Siwa.

Conditions in Bali were reminiscent of Majapahit. The king was fortunate in having powerful keris: Titinggi, Kala Dangastra (Kala's Tusk), Lobar, Tanda Langlang, Si Naga Basuki, also known as Si Bangawan Canggu, and Ganja Dungkul. The king was the incarnation of Darma (60b–61a).

The reiteration of the royal keris (with another new addition, Kala's Tusk, the first and only reference to this weapon) at this point in the text is significant.[38] To list the regalia demonstrates their orderly transmission, showing the reproduction of power over time. Such recapitulations are typical of monarchs marked out in the text as especially important. However, the list may serve another purpose: Dalem di Madé was Gélgél's last ruler; after Gélgél's fall some texts indicate that certain regalia were dispersed outside of the core line.

It is in the midst of this inventory that Bangawan Canggu is identified with Si Naga Basuki. Basuki is also identified with the temple of Besakih, the name of which is commonly held to be a form of his name. Some cosmological texts assert that Mahadéwa, god of that temple, created serpents, and that he is the deity who takes the form of *naga* and other serpentine beings (Hooykaas 1975). Basuki himself has two small temples dedicated to him in the lower (*kelod,* or downstream) section of the Besakih complex. One of these, Pura Goa, is said to be linked by an underground tunnel to the cave by the sea at Pura Goa Lawah (Bat Cave Temple), one of Klungkung's state temples (Stuart-Fox 1987:125). Goa Lawah, a temple many Balinese visit in the course of performing death rites for their ancestors, is a meeting place between mountain and sea and has a number of divinized pythons living inside of its cave. In a sense Goa Lawah and Bangawan Canggu appear to be analogs of one another, one in the system of royal temples, the other in the system of royal keris.

The three *naga*—Anantaboga, Basuki, and Taksaka—are also said to be incarnations of Brahma, Wisnu, and Siwa respectively. Thus Basuki is another form of Wisnu, yet another reason to associate the keris identified with Basuki with water. Commonly the three *naga* are merged into one, also called Basuki.[39] Stuart-Fox notes that in mantras Basuki is sometimes referred to as Indragiri, Lord of the Mountain, imaged as lying with his tail at the summit of Agung and his head in the ocean, with the waters of Bali's rivers flowing on his body from tail to head to the sea (1987:465). Thus this keris is linked back to both Wisnu and Besakih.

Despite its auspicious beginning, Dalem Di Madé's reign ended in disaster. The text does not blame this on the king. Some versions assert that the *kali-yuga,* the age of misfortunes, had arrived, and people forgot what is right and proper (*Babad Dalem A* in Warna et al. 1986). Once again a chief minister,

Gusti Agung Maruti, rebelled against the king, but unlike Gusti Batan Jeruk he was successful. Dalem di Madé and three hundred followers fled to the village of Guliang, leaving the usurper in power in Gélgél. Most of Bali's lords also left the court for their own domains. From VOC sources Gusti Agung Maruti's reign as Bali's king can be dated from 1650 to 1686.

The dissolution of the Gélgél court is foreshadowed in the narration. Starting with Dalem Bekung's reign, increasing textual attention is paid to lords of the realm, members of other, noble clans—mainly those that became major political actors after the fall of Gélgél and remained prominent through the colonial period. During the reign of Dalem di Madé, the text includes episodes concerning the clan of the Gusti Jelantiks (associated with the rulers of Buléléng and the region of Blahbatuh), the origins of Déwa Den Bencingah (ancestor of the rulers of Bangli), and tales about the ancestors of Badung's royal house (69b–75a).

Dalem di Madé died in exile in Guliang. Déwa Agung Jambé, his son by a wife from Badung, went to Sidemen to stay with Kiyai Anglurah Singarsa, whose family had been given responsibility for Besakih by earlier rulers of Gélgél. With the help of Singarsa and other lords, Déwa Agung Jambé eventually attacked Gusti Agung Maruti. These included the lord of Badung (Déwa Agung Jambé's mother's brother), the lord of Buléléng (according to the *Babad Buleleng* a son of Dalem Segening), and Kiyai Déwa Pungakan (founder of the realm of Bangli). Gélgél was retaken and Gusti Agung Maruti killed. Déwa Agung Jambé built a new capital several kilometers north at Klungkung and named his puri Smarapura, "Abode of the God of Love" (75a–76a).

At this point in the story many manuscripts of the *Babad Dalem* come to a halt. This is probably the core of the text written sometime in the late seventeenth or early eighteenth century.

THE *BABAD DALEM* AND KLUNGKUNG ON THE EVE OF DUTCH INTERVENTION

The *Babad Dalem* forges a complex but highly specific picture of the bases and nature of Kapakisan power. First of all, Klungkung's dynasty is identified as a mediating point between two distinct constituting centers: Majapahit and Besakih. More generally, the text portrays royal power as suspended between two poles, between which the best rulers mediate. The contrast between those poles is at first extreme: an antithesis of demonic and divine. This is gradually mediated into a contrast between benevolent and fierce aspects of royal power. The Kapakisan identity as Brahmana Buda is a first statement of this mediation, which is reiterated in the various heirloom keris. Just as Brahmana

Buda have the power to transform destructive forces (demons) into benign ones (gods), so too, with keris like I Durga Dingkul and I Bangawan Canggu, Kapakisan kings are able to influence the agents (visible and invisible) that potentially threaten them or their realm so that rather than harming they help.

The dynasty's two most famous keris also draw together the various sources of Klungkung authority. They are, on the one hand, gifts from powerful hierarchical superiors in Majapahit. Their power derives, however, from their ability to represent, embody, or refer to three major invisible forces: the cosmic snake Basuki, Durga (and her minions), and Wisnu.

It should be noted that, despite their identifications with divinities, little or no reference is made to the responsibility of rulers for temples or rituals. Even Besakih is indicated only by extension; it is the royal identity with its god that is stressed, not the role rulers played in its ritual life. The absence of reference to temples is in stark contrast to recent versions of the *Babad Dalem*, such as *Babad Dalem A* (Warna et al. 1986) or the *Babad Dalem* from Sukawati (Agung n.d.), which piously interpolate passages in which Gajah Mada and Hayam Wuruk not only present Bali's kings with keris but also explain the importance of maintaining Bali's temples and honoring their gods.[40] This was in fact something kings did, and not just in the twentieth century, as other texts—more directly concerned with ritual matters—amply demonstrate;[41] however, it is not mentioned in older *babad*. The *Babad Ksatria*, written in the late nineteenth century, does refer to princes asking for aid at state temples (Goa Lawah in one instance; Pura Dasar, in Gélgél, in another) prior to commencing important activities, which might suggest that temples became more important to Klungkung's rulers in the nineteenth century. But here too, royal responsibilities for temples and their rituals are not at issue. The overt concern with ritual praxis in recent texts reflects the historical transformation that will be argued in part 2.

However, there are glancing allusions to temples even in older *Babad Dalem*, since some of the invisible forces with which the Kapakisans are repeatedly associated are connected to them, even if the text is not explicit about this. These include temples cared for by Klungkung's rulers—especially Besakih and Goa Lawah—and a temple type, associated with the goddess Durga, the Pura Dalem.

The *Babad Dalem* provides invaluable insight into the rhetorics and assumptions of Bali's precolonial ruling class. Given that Balinese cultural forms and ideologies have obviously not remained static since the nineteenth century, and given that colonial descriptions of Bali have their own premises and politics, it is crucial to have documentation of the theory and practice of power in precolonial Bali.

That the representation of Klungkung's power in the *Babad Dalem* was well known to Balinese aristocrats (and perhaps to Balinese in general) is actually confirmed by Dutch sources. A number of the earliest colonial descriptions of Bali refer to incidents from the text (albeit often in tangled form), as, for example, the citations from van den Broek and Dubois in chapter 2 show.

A later example comes from a book by Ludwig Helms, a man who served for a time in Badung as Mads Lange's assistant. Helms provides a somewhat different account of Klungkung's origins in that he identifies the ancestor of Klungkung's rulers as the son of the last Majapahit king. According to his version, the prince fled Majapahit after a priest predicted it would fall in forty days. When he arrived in Bali he took "the title of Supreme Sovereign, which title still continues hereditary in the Rajahs of Klongkong, who, proud of their pure descent, seek to maintain its purity by enforcing the rule that the Dewa Agong, the Rajah of Klongkong, shall marry his own sister" (Helms 1969:33).[42] That he traces Klungkung's descent to a Majapahit king rather than a Majapahit priest at first glance suggests that the identification of the Kapakisans with Brahmanas was a later interpolation, but he also notes that two title groups were identified by Balinese as Brahmanas at that time: the "Idas" (Brahmana proper) and "those who are descendants of Brahmins, but who do not act as priests, and are called Dewa, i.e., god" (1969:35).

Colonial accounts are not the only evidence that images from the text were important in nineteenth-century Bali. Additional evidence is written in stone, in the form of a complex of temples in the northeast corner of Klungkung's capital, which were probably built not long before the first colonial envoys appeared in Klungkung.

Two clusters make up the complex as a whole. The first consisted of the temples Pura Dalem Agung and Pura Manik Mas. Pura Dalem Agung, the Pura Dalem for the capital, stands northwest of Tegallingah, the broad and long field that is now Klungkung's cremation ground; Pura Manik Mas lay at the southern end of that field (see fig. 4).[43] The spatial relation between the two mimics (although it directionally inverts) the relationship between another Pura Manik Mas and another Pura Dalem (Pura Dalem Puri) at Besakih. This is not fortuitous: the entire area is called, after its Besakih counterpart, the "Field of Suffering," Tegal Penangsaran.[44]

The second cluster, south and east of Pura Manik Mas, consists of a row of three temples just behind the giant banyan tree where Klungkung's grandest cockfights were held. These three in particular encapsulate those images of Klungkung from the *Babad Dalem* most pertinent to nineteenth-century self-conceptions.

The first of them is the Pura Penataran Agung mentioned above, which now appears as only one of a larger set of references to Besakih. Located to its north is Pura Taman Sari, the temple at which royal weapons were given

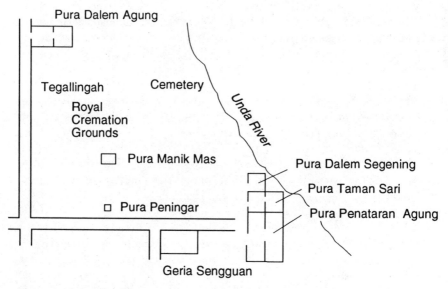

Figure 4. Temple complex in the capital.

offerings every Tumpek Landep. It consists of two eleven-roofed *méru* shrines, with a carved *naga* encircling the base of one of them (see fig. 5). Next to Taman Sari is a third, smaller temple, Pura Dalem Segening, a clan temple for all Ksatria Dalem, named for their most fertile ancestor. Taken together they recapitulate the themes of descent (with underlying nuances about reproductive power), keris (and implicitly warfare), and Besakih.[45]

CONCLUSION

For the most part, the text portrays Klungkung in ways congruent with colonial representations. The *Babad Dalem* highlights just those features of Klungkung's identity cited by colonial accounts as evidence of why Klungkung's court was held to be superior to others: the descent of Klungkung's rulers, and their associations with "religious" phenomena.

But colonial officials failed to appreciate an important dimension of Balinese kingship: keris and all they represented. Royal authority is portrayed in this text as dependent upon the possession of powerful keris. Gifts of keris, at decisive moments in history, establish Kapakisan rule over Bali, and the text attributes the success of subsequent kings to their continued possession of these same (and newer) keris, returning at various points in the narrative to list them. That keris were important to Klungkung royal practices in

Figure 5. Main shrine of Pura Taman Sari, c. 1920. Photograph by Theodor van Erp. Used with permission of the Rijksmuseum voor Volkenkunde, Leiden.

the nineteenth century is shown by the building of Pura Taman Sari. More-over, stories about the same and other weapons crop up in later narratives, both oral (as we will see) and written. In the late-nineteenth-century *Babad Ksatria*, for example, Bangawan Canggu plays a central role in a war between two royal brothers. The Dutch experienced some of the pragmatic conse-quences of this royal concern with keris in military engagements in Bali but never theorized them. Preoccupied as they were with the question of Klung-kung's power vis-à-vis the other realms, engrossed in their own distinctions between temporal and spiritual authority, they could not appreciate the con-cerns that consumed Balinese.

If the Dutch claimed that Klungkung's ruler was a kind of "spiritual over-lord," it would appear from the *Babad Dalem* that this implied something more complex than merely a preoccupation with Divinity. The Déwa Agung con-cerned himself with numerous spirits, gods, and demons, and, so this text declares, they concerned themselves with him as well. Thus, in contrast to Geertz (1980), the symbolic construction of royal authority was not based upon the premise that rulers mirrored an ideal cosmological harmony. Instead discourses about power, morally ambivalent and densely woven, locate Klung-kung's kings in an ideological space somewhere between demon and Brahmana priest.

PART TWO

The Colonial Encounter

At the end of the first section of the story of the
descendants of Sri Kresna Kapakisan from the
island of Jawa, which was told by Pedanda Gedé
Rai to the king Déwa Agung Putra, Déwa Agung
Putra inquired further. He spoke politely and
clearly, like the sound of thunder in the fourth
month which causes pleasure in all who hear it:
"Most revered and venerable one. My faith in
your wisdom is eternal. Tell me more about the
one who was my ancestor. After he settled in
Smarajaya, after the defeat of Gusti Agung Maruti
in Gélgél, what became of him? How many
descendants did he have? Teach me about that,
great priest. So that I will know."

Pedanda Gedé Rai answered, "Oh, is that my
lord's desire? You wish to understand the story as
clearly as possible. But it is difficult to speak of it.
The story of your majesty's ancestors is very
heavy. Be patient. To understand, to interpret its
meaning, feels the same as interpreting a *sloka*."

Babad Ksatria

SIX

Klungkung and the Dutch, 1840 – 1849: Encounter with Hegemony

I t is time to turn at last to Balinese-Dutch relations, beginning with the first diplomatic mission to Klungkung in 1840 and its political consequences. J. H. Huskus Koopman's embassy provides an ideal starting point to explore the complex interactions between the Dutch and Klungkung and Klungkung and the rest of Bali during the crucial decade of the 1840s, which culminated in the first military confrontation between Balinese and the Dutch. With Huskus Koopman, Klungkung finally begins to play a role in colonial descriptions of Bali and the formation of colonial policy. Not only was the mission important historically, but by great good fortune Huskus Koopman narrated his first visit to Klungkung in a journal, which unlike the usual colonial report describes his interactions with Balinese lords in detail. Those descriptions are particularly valuable because several practices that informed Dutch-Klungkung interactions up to the conquest were displayed here in their most overt form.

To contextualize that meeting, however, requires a reconstruction of the political relationships obtaining in Bali at that time and an analysis of the practices—ritual, architectural, linguistic, marital, and martial—that constituted Klungkung's ruler as supreme.

KLUNGKUNG AND THE REST OF BALI CIRCA 1840

Textual representations of the origins of Klungkung's power provide little guide to how such power was realized in practice. The Gélgél court was composed of nobles who bore the title of Gusti and claimed descent from the lords (Arya) who accompanied Sri Kresna Kapakisan to Bali. These Gusti led the Dalem's armies and advised him, although—at least as represented in the *babad*—much of the time they merely attended him at court. Few brothers or lower-ranking sons of the rulers of Gélgél are mentioned in the *Babad Dalem*, which suggests that they had little political influence.

By the nineteenth century the situation was reversed. Although still regarded as the king's *punggawa*, his lords and representatives, the Gustis spent less time at court; instead they were spread over the island in their domains, appearing at Klungkung only to pay homage or when summoned by their overlord. Royal brothers and lower-ranking sons replaced them in the inner ring, settling closer and closer to the king's residence as time when on, and constantly in attendance as his advisors.[1]

The Klungkung Succession to 1840

Déwa Agung Putra II, the ruler Huskus Koopman was to meet, was the fifth Klungkung ruler since the defeat of Gusti Agung Maruti in 1686. Both oral histories and the *Babad Ksatria,* the addendum to the *Babad Dalem,* bring dynastic history into the nineteenth century.

The *babad* suggests that after Klungkung was founded there was a certain ambiguity in deciding exactly which was the true core line. It was resolved through struggles over the major tokens of power: the palace and the regalia keris.

The ambiguities begin with Déwa Agung Jambé, who did not return to Gélgél or take the title of Dalem after Gusti Agung Maruti's defeat. Instead he built a new palace called Smarapura, "Abode of the God of Love," several kilometers up the road in Klungkung. Much has been made of these breaks with the past: they have been taken as evidence that there was no longer a single Balinese king or that Gélgél's fall implied a diminishment of the distinction of the house. Several people in Klungkung, however, simply observed that the new king had an elder high-ranking brother with a better claim to the title, and to mark his respect Déwa Agung Jambé did not appropriate it.[2] His heirs in turn dared not use a title higher than that of their progenitor. However, Klungkung rulers were still often referred to as Dalem by nonkinsmen. The *Babad Ksatria* identifies the first few generations of Klungkung rulers by name rather than title.

Déwa Agung Jambé's sons established themselves in three possibly rival houses: Klungkung itself, Sukawati (relations with which were broken off when its founder requested one of the heirloom keris), and Gélgél. Although Puri Gélgél is portrayed as a loyal subordinate, a move back to Gélgél so soon after Klungkung's founding quite likely had threatening connotations. (Friederich [1959:117] even claims that Gélgél was the center.) In any event the Gélgél house was disproportionately powerful through the nineteenth century: for example, its head was generally addressed as Déwa Agung by other members of the royal clan. Indeed, just as Déwa Agung Putra eventually became the standard title for Klungkung's ruler, the ruling lord of the Gélgél house was conventionally known as Déwa Agung Jambé. Gélgél's lord was also responsible for two of Klungkung's state temples (Pura Dasar, in Gélgél itself, and Pura Klotok, by the sea), and, according to both the *Babad Ksatria* and oral narratives, the invisible armies at the command of Klungkung's ruler served Gélgél's princes as well.

In the generation that followed, Déwa Agung Gedé and Déwa Agung Madé, sons of different high-ranking mothers, openly disputed the succession in Klungkung. Their claims were sufficiently equal that for a time they ruled jointly, and even the heirloom keris were divided between them: Déwa Agung Madé, the younger brother, kept Bangawan Canggu and remained in Puri Smarapura; while Déwa Agung Gedé, who took Durga Dingkul and Ganja Dungkul, built a new residence nearby.³ As this division foreshadowed, the younger eventually prevailed and his brother left; the keris he took with him were later returned to the core line in a war.⁴

Klungkung's authority probably reached its nadir with the next king, in the late eighteenth century. Déwa Agung Sakti, despite the power to which his name attests, was mad. While he was still officially king (he lived in the capital, in the decaying Puri Smarapura), the de facto ruler was his younger brother Déwa Agung Panji, who built a palace in the port town Kusamba. The mad king's highest-ranking son and heir apparent grew up under the protection of the ruler of Karangasem, where his mother had fled for fear of her husband's unpredictability, and married that ruler's daughter.

It is with this prince, Déwa Agung Putra I, that Klungkung's fortunes began to improve. At first glance he seems an unlikely person to have regenerated the realm. For one thing, his authority was ambiguous: his father, albeit mad, was still alive. For another, his reign was short: he was killed in a war with Bangli in 1809, still a relatively young man. Yet tales suggest a restoration of Klungkung prestige with this prince: the author of the *Babad Ksatria* even likens him to the god Wisnu, always a mark of great rulers. According to the same source, he returned to Klungkung to claim the position of Déwa Agung at the request of the rulers of Gianyar, Mengwi, Badung, and Tabanan, who encouraged him to declare war on his uncle and replace him in Kusamba. This proved to be the first of several military contests, which appear to have had as one of their goals the recovery of various regalia that had been lost to the core line. The war against Déwa Agung Gedé's descendants in Puri Satria Kanginan, through which (according to the *Babad Ksatria*) Durga Dingkul was repossessed, almost certainly involved such an intention, and a war against Déwa Gedé Tangkeban, a subordinate lord of Bangli ruling in Nyalian, may have as well.⁵ These activities suggest an attempt to augment his power. He was also the first Klungkung ruler referred to by the title Déwa Agung Putra, although in his case the title was probably descriptive: *putra*, high Balinese for "child," suggests a recognition of his father's superior claim.

Déwa Agung Putra I's death in 1809 left the succession unsettled. First of all, his indestructible father was still alive and so, officially, still in charge. Second, Déwa Agung Putra had not yet fathered a high-ranking son. His only offspring, both still quite young, were a daughter by the Karangasem princess and a son by a low-ranking wife. By rank the daughter's claim was superior, but her sex rendered a straightforward succession problematic. Women were by no means excluded from rule in nineteenth-century Bali; somewhat later there was a female ruler in Mengwi and another in Lombok (Schulte Nordholt 1988; Lekkerkerker 1923). But the Mengwi ruler succeeded her husband, and the Lombok one a brother, and both were undoubtedly older. Given gender roles, and the martial and marital conquests admired in young rulers, a young woman would have been politically disadvantaged.[6] At the very least, her gender would have provided grounds for those with other agendas to argue against her.

As the offspring of a woman of no consequence, however, Déwa Agung Putra's son was in no position to assert his claims in the face of his powerful stepmother from Karangasem. It might have been expected that one of Déwa Agung Putra's many brothers would step into the vacuum, but this did not happen. Instead, about 1815 (possibly after the death of Déwa Agung Sakti) a compromise was reached: the son was established as Déwa Agung Putra II, but he was to rule jointly with his sister.[7] He was the ruler van den Broek described as an "insignificant youth" in 1817 and Huskus Koopman identified as Bali's keizer.[8]

Interestingly, Balinese remember the sister, to whom Huskus Koopman makes no reference, much more vividly. A text written in Gianyar (Mahaudiana 1968) refers to the queen in glowing terms, never even mentioning her brother's existence. In Klungkung oral tradition Déwa Agung Isteri Kania, "the Virgin Queen," is renowned for both beauty and brilliance. A skilled poet in her own right (Kanta 1983), she was also a patron to other artists; the *Babad Ksatria* likens her to the goddess Saraswati, and she is said to have been the force behind Klungkung's literary efflorescence, the building of the temple complex in Sengguan, and the organization of the great *maligia* in which the infamous rhinoceros was sacrificed. Ironically, the sole reference to Huskus Koopman in Balinese historiography comes in a text generally attributed to her authorship: she notes that, although his manners were good and his clothing fine, his teeth were stained and his breath rank (Narayana et al. 1987:44).

The Structure of Klungkung

Precolonial Balinese realms were not conceived in territorial terms. Ultimately, a realm was a system of relationships—of descent, alliance, and patronage—encoded ritually and fueled by exchanges of goods, services, and persons. Its crucial spaces were marked by temples, courts, and priestly residences (fig. 6).

By 1840 there were some thirteen houses of the royal clan in the vicinity of Klungkung. All of them had branched off from the core line in the six generations following the establishment of Klungkung. Members of each of these houses were agnatically descended from a brother (usually, but not

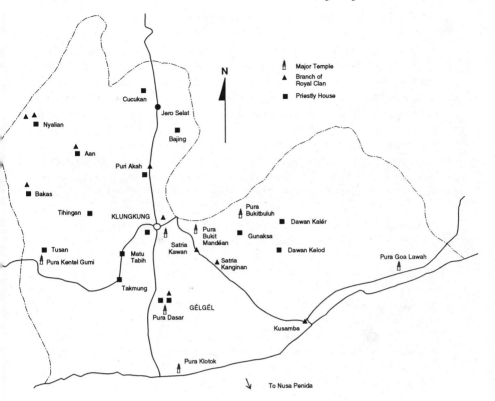

Figure 6. Map of the Region of Klungkung.

always, of a different mother) of a reigning king. Increasingly, the houses tended to cluster in the capital, making them far more dependent upon the core-line house: a total of eight of the branch houses were located in the immediate vicinity of the main puri.[9]

Each branch house had its own core and branch lines. Younger brothers, however, rarely moved out of branch-line compounds; instead their distinction from their local core line was marked spatially within it. The ranking man lived in a portion of the puri called the *saren*. The bulk of the political authority within the realm was vested in the hands of the lords in the various branch-house *saren*. Contrary to what appears to have been true in Tabanan (Geertz 1980:31–32, 58), the most recent branches were not always powerful, nor were older branches necessarily weak.

In 1840 none of these branch houses belonged to brothers or sons of the ruling king, as he had neither. The most influential houses included the *manca* houses (Akah, Satria, and Gélgél) and several houses that had been established by the king's father's brothers, particularly Puri Kalér-Kangin and Puri Kaléran (see Appendix).

Marriage and adoption played important roles in consolidating political relationships between core- and branch-line houses. Although women from the core line were rarely allowed to "go out," rulers could and did take wives from peripheral houses, and males could move in either direction. By adopting a branch-line boy (who might then spin off a new branch, higher in rank than that of his original line), a ruler ensured the loyalty of his kin. At the same time, a ruler could give one of his low-ranking sons to an important branch house for adoption, effectively raising the status and importance of that house, or even to a favored lord, a motif in the origin stories of several important Balinese clans though no longer practiced by the nineteenth century.[10] Such practices satisfied both the branch lines, which ran the risk of becoming more and more remote from the source of status and power as generations passed, and the ruler, since remote kinsmen could provide support without threat.[11]

As elsewhere in Bali, not all of the houses influential at court were royal. Persons from a number of noble and even commoner houses were instrumental in executing the business of the realm. Among the most important was Jero Lebah, a commoner house descended from a royal bastard. Priests in certain Brahmana houses, in addition to conducting royal rituals, also served as advisors to the king. Friederich (1959:107) confirms that in the 1840s two priestly houses were particularly important: Geria Gedé Kenitén in Dawan Kelod (an offshoot of Geria Jumpung in Kamasan, which had long served the Klungkung dynasty), and Geria Pidada in the capital (founded by a kinsman of Karangasem's court priest who came to Klungkung with the Karangasem princess). Finally, the ruler relied on various Islamic residents of his realm to serve as his interpreters for dealings with the Dutch, and they lived in special neighborhoods in Klungkung and Gélgél (see fig. 8).

In villages that had no branch of the royal family (which was most of them), there were other *jero* and *jeroan*. These mainly belonged to very distant kinsmen of the royal clan (with the title of Déwa, or, if they had declined in status, Pungakan),[12] nobles of lesser lineages (with the title of Gusti), and commoners who often claimed that they were fallen descendants of once noble or even royal houses. The most significant Gusti house was Jero Takmung, which had branches in Banda, Tihingan, and the capital itself. There were also Gusti houses in Selat, Sulang, and Dawan. The royal house, including the core line, frequently took wives from the prominent commoner houses in the realm; conversely, a commoner house from which the king had taken a wife could achieve prominence. The influence of certain commoner houses was also measured by the fact that the court appointed a number of them as hereditary providers of temple priests for various state temples: to give an example, the *jeroan* in the village of Pasinggahan, which was linked to the Gélgél branch house by ties of marriage, furnished both *perbekel* (local officials) for the village itself and *pamangku* (temple priests) for the nearby temple of Goa Lawah.

Bali's Other Realms and Their Relationship to Klungkung

The far-flung lords of Bali were in perpetual competition with one another for followers, territory, wealth, and prominence. Between the founding of the Klungkung court in 1686 and the arrival of the Dutch in 1817, various noble houses had their moments of glory and faded from view, becoming subordinate lords of semiautonomous domains under the authority of more successful competitors. Nineteenth-century realms were far from being the fixed, territorially bounded entities they became under colonial rule. They were rather loose coalitions of prominent clans, to which were attached commoner subjects. These coalitions were subject to constant reshuffling through the contingencies of kinship and death and the praxis of warfare, ritual, and marriage. The dominant houses of Bali in 1840 belonged to less than half a dozen clans.[13]

Only one of these clans was content to trace its descent simply and clearly to one of the noblemen who had accompanied Dalem Sri Kresna Kapakisan to Bali: a certain Arya Kenceng (according to the *Babad Dalem*) or Arya Damar.[14] The rulers of both Tabanan and Badung were members of this clan, and they affirmed their unity by frequent intermarriage. Tabanan was the older, wealthier, and more populous realm, but in the nineteenth century Badung was more influential, despite the fact that its rule was divided among three closely related houses: Pamecutan, Denpasar, and Kesiman, with the last the most vigorous and visible. While Badung and Tabanan had no Kapakisan ancestors, Klungkung's rulers periodically took wives from Badung, among them the mother of Déwa Agung Jambé, Klungkung's founder.

A second major clan was Badung's chief competitor, the one headed by the ruler of Karangasem. According to most accounts, this clan's pivotal ancestor was a certain Arya Kapakisan, commonly identified as one of the noblemen who came to Bali from Majapahit, but he is not mentioned in the *Babad Dalem*. The similarity between his name and the ruler's is notable. According to one explanation I was given, he, like his royal overlord, came from the Javanese village Kapakisan. There seems to be a second (Badung-derived) tradition, however, often repeated by nineteenth-century Dutch sources, which identifies the pivotal ancestor of this clan as Gajah Mada himself (Friederich 1959; Jacobs 1883). That version seems to play on the nineteenth-century competition between Karangasem and Badung, for it represents Arya Damar as conquering most of the island, while Gajah Mada dallied in the northeast.

This clan exercised considerable influence from the Gélgél period on. One line served as Gélgél's chief ministers, while others (such as the Arya Dauh and the Gusti Jelantiks) filled additional court functions. Gusti Batan Jeruk and Gusti Agung Maruti, the two chief ministers who turned rebel, were both members of this clan, and Karangasem's royal house regarded Gusti Batan Jeruk as its founder.[15] Around the middle of the eighteenth century Karangasem began a period of expansion that lasted until the turn of the nineteenth century: Lombok, Jembrana, and Buléléng were conquered, and younger kinsmen of Karangasem's ruler were placed in charge of each; the regions belonging to the lords of Sibetan and Sidemen to the west (which included the Besakih area) were annexed, as were areas belonging to the lord of Taman Bali; and for a time Mengwi was threatened.

Mengwi's ruler also traced his descent from Arya Kapakisan, although kin ties between the Mengwi and Karangasem branches of the family were quite distant by the mid-nineteenth century. Mengwi's royal house is sometimes said to be descended from Gusti Agung Maruti.[16] It was the Mengwi rather than the Karangasem branch of the clan that was periodically identified as the Déwa Agung's chief minister during the eighteenth and nineteenth centuries. During its eighteenth-century heyday, Mengwi controlled Blambangan in East Java, what became the territory of Badung, and areas to the north later taken by Tabanan, and it was allied by marriage to the Buléléng court.

Bali's other rulers made multiple, ideologically complicated claims about their ancestry, claims that connected them to a greater or lesser degree to Klungkung's royal clan.

The most clear-cut of these was that of the Déwa Manggis, ruler of Gianyar, who traced his descent from an unofficial liaison between Dalem Segening and one of his branch-line kinswomen. The woman's status entitled her illegitimate offspring to the Ksatria Dalem title of Déwa. Beginning as a minor noble house in the region of Beng, by the mid-eighteenth century the clan had managed to subdue other lords in the vicinity, and the Déwa Manggis is described by Dubois around 1830 as ruling over a federation of twelve smaller principalities.[17] Apart from branch houses of the Déwa Manggis's own clan, quite a few of these belonged to descendants of a former competitor, the Ksatria Dalem house of Sukawati. Others were noble houses, like the Gusti Jelantiks of Blahbatuh or Gusti Agungs of Kramas, whose prominence was on the decline.[18]

According to the *Babad Buleleng*, the founder of the realm of Buléléng was also a son of Dalem Segening, by a commoner woman from the North Bali village of Panji. However, the king gave the pregnant woman and the child she carried to the prominent lord Gusti Jelantik to raise as his own (Worsley 1972), rather complicating the question of the clan's origins.[19] By 1840 this house was no longer political overlord in Buléléng, which had been conquered in the late eighteenth century by Karangasem. Nonetheless, it retained importance in the Buléléng area and was intermittently restored to power later in the nineteenth and twentieth centuries by the colonial government.

Such claims to Ksatria Dalem ancestry could be interpreted as an assertion of a capacity to rule. And indeed they are, but not to rule Bali as a whole, only a portion thereof. By professing a kin tie to Klungkung, lords also acknowledged that they were part of a clan of which the Déwa Agung was the head, and so accepted the order of things.

The realm with the most anomalous—and in many ways most interesting—legends about its origins was Bangli. Some traditions assert that its ruler, who also used the title Déwa, was yet another descendant of the prolific Dalem Segening;[20] this may be an interpretation of the more extraordinary *Babad Ksatria Taman Bali* claim that the clan's pivotal ancestor was the son of Wisnu, since we have seen that Kapakisan rulers were commonly identified with that god. But the textual claim is sufficiently ambiguous to have been interpreted in various ways at various times. The *Babad Dalem* does concur in Bangli's claim that the clan's pivotal ancestor married a daughter of Dalem di Madé and was granted a keris and lands at the same time by his father-in-law, which is sufficiently remarkable given the rule of hypergamy. Bangli is in any event associated with the god Wisnu in other contexts as well, since at Besakih Bangli was responsible for the complex Pura Batu Madeg, "Temple of the Standing Stone," dedicated to that god.[21] Since Wisnu is the royal god, the association could be seen as a serious challenge to Klungkung hegemony; however, Klungkung's identifications at Besakih encompassed Bangli's, involving as they did the Penataran where all facets of Divinity in its most totalizing forms were located (e.g., the trinity Wisnu-Brahma-Siwa; deities associated with the netherworld and upperworld; Tolangkir). Bangli was also closely associated with Batur, a region heavily identified with both autochthony and the goddess of the lake, which suggests a truly alternative claim to royal legitimacy. But then Bangli was anomalous in other respects as well. It was Bali's only landlocked realm, and its ideological orientations in part reflect its geographical situation: upstream (and thus in a singularly advantageous position to control the supply of irrigation water, which Bangli rulers often did by cutting off water to downstream enemies); in the mountains (where many of the villages identifying themselves as Bali Aga, "indigenous Balinese," were located, including most of the villages listed in the *Babad Dalem* as resisting Majapahit domination); and in the center of the island (thus in an even more advantageous position than Klungkung from which to represent "divinity"). Bangli's royal house seems to have emphasized its relationships to water deities: the *babad* that traces the clan's ancestry to a divinity makes reference to various sacred springs. In addition, Bangli's ruler is the only one outside of Klungkung's whose ritual activities make their way into scattered remarks in Dutch reports.

By the 1840s such representations may have been politically significant, as Bangli's relationship with Klungkung was strained. The friction stemmed in part from the war in the early nineteenth century and in part from Bangli's ongoing enmity with its downstream neighbor Gianyar, at this time a Klungkung favorite. Further tensions ensued after 1844, when Klungkung took charge of the semiautonomous realm of Payangan, formerly under Bangli's authority. According to certain Dutch sources, Bangli's ruler, Déwa Gedé Tangkeban, was the only Balinese prince who had never taken an oath of allegiance to Déwa Agung Putra II (Weitzel 1859).

The two most powerful houses in Bali in 1840 were those of Badung and Karangasem. It is significant that neither of them represented itself as kin to the Déwa Agung. Rather, both claimed descent from Majapahit princes and generals. In competition with one another for the role of Klungkung's "chief minister"—Klungkung's exterior second—each had its allies and enemies.

In 1840 Klungkung was especially close to Karangasem, through Déwa Agung Isteri Kania's matrilateral connection to the Karangasem royal house, and consequently on troubled terms with Badung. Déwa Agung Putra I had, in fact, also married a princess from Badung, but the Karangasem princess had her poisoned shortly after the wedding, a matter that still aroused Badung ire (Friederich 1959 [1849–50] and Lekkerkerker 1923). It was in part to counter the Karangasem princess's influence that Badung had supported Déwa Agung Putra II's accession, but this did not affect Badung's status as had been hoped. While Badung's lords swore vows of loyalty to the Déwa Agung in 1829 and 1837 (Korn 1922), their growing friendship with the Dutch increasingly affected their relationship with Klungkung for the worse. For most of the nineteenth century, Tabanan's rulers largely followed Badung's lead, in relation both to Klungkung and to the Dutch.

Gianyar's rulers were, by contrast, on excellent terms with Klungkung. The Déwa Manggis was a loyal supporter of the Déwa Agung, frequently providing troops at his behest and even sending some of Gianyar's finest sculptors to Klungkung to execute the carvings in the new temple complex.[22] According to Huskus Koopman, the rulers of both Gianyar and Mengwi were Klungkung's "vassals." As we shall see, both actively supported Klungkung against the Dutch.

Karangasem's ambitions are the most difficult to decipher. By the turn of the nineteenth century, members of the Karangasem royal house were ruling Jembrana, Buléléng, and Lombok as well as Karangasem itself. Through Déwa Agung Putra I, who had been raised in the court of Gusti Ngurah Gedé Karangasem and had married his daughter, Karangasem also had strong ties to

Klungkung. According to Lekkerkerker (1926), that Karangasem ruler was as unreliable a guardian as his ancestor Gusti Batan Jeruk had been, since he wrote to the VOC to suggest that they support him in an attempt to become Bali's sole ruler. They did not, and he died in 1805 or 1806. However, Karangasem's ambitions may not have been as grandiose as the Dutch believed; it is noteworthy that even when he annexed the land north of Klungkung up to Besakih around 1775,[23] he did not usurp the Déwa Agung's prerogatives at the temple, as he presumably might have had he planned to replace Klungkung.

Representations of Karangasem's royal house suggest that certain perduring relationships inform the exploits of its members. Gusti Batan Jeruk is said in the *Babad Dalem* to have been an avid student of a Brahmana Buda priest, and in fact the core line of all of Bali's Brahmana Buda is located in Budakeling, a Karangasem dependency. The *Rajapurana Pura Besakih* allots Karangasem responsibility for that portion of the Besakih temple complex called Pura Kiduling Kreteg, "the Temple South of the Bridge." This temple, which is dedicated to the fiery god Brahma (hence south), is associated with control over pests—that is, exorcism. Also in Karangasem is the temple Lempuyang, where Betara Genijaya—"Victorious Fire"—dwells. When I first arrived in Bali, I heard from several persons in Gianyar that people in Karangasem were "hot": quick-tempered, fond of meat and *arak*, and quarrelsome. The history of the Karangasem royal family is full of accusations of incest and bloodthirsty behavior (see, e.g., Friederich 1959, although his Badung sources were biased). There were in any event various disagreements, often violent in nature, between the kinsmen ruling Buléléng, Karangasem, and Lombok. It was just such a quarrel that precipitated the Netherlands Indies government's first diplomatic overtures to Bali

By the 1830s, wars between the Karangasem princes on Lombok had resulted in the emergence of two principalities: Karangasem-Lombok (also called Singasari) and Mataram (see van der Kraan 1980 and Vickers 1986). The rulers of these realms were rivals, and each was aided and advised by European merchants: an Englishman, John Burd, and his Danish assistant Mads Lange in Karangasem-Lombok, and another Englishman, George King, in Mataram. In 1839 Mataram attacked Karangasem-Lombok, imprisoning its ruler, whose two small children were brought for safety to Klungkung. This displeased the Déwa Agung, who supported Karangasem-Lombok, as did the rulers of Buléléng and Karangasem-Bali. Burd and Lange had tried for years to solicit the Governor General's aid for Karangasem-Lombok's ruler, but by the time the Governor General, for reasons of his own, became interested in what was going on, the prince had been killed (Lekkerkerker 1923).

To sum up the political constellation around 1840, Klungkung was close to the rulers of Karangasem, Buléléng, Mengwi, and Gianyar, and with

Bangli, Badung, Tabanan, and Mataram (Lombok) relationships were either strained or unpredictable. Badung and Tabanan were hostile to Mengwi and to the Buléléng-Karangasem bloc. Bangli had a history of enmity with both Buléléng and Gianyar.

STRUCTURES OF POWER

In chapter 2 I touched on several reasons why colonial officials and scholars assumed that Klungkung's power was nominal. One major theme involved interpretations of the ruler of Klungkung as a fundamentally religious authority. The division of Bali into nine principalities was also grounds for claims about the limits of Klungkung's power, however: comparisons between Bali's realms, particularly of their wealth and potential military strength, and observations that Bali's other rulers did not consistently appear to obey the Déwa Agung's wishes suggested to officials that the Déwa Agung was merely a figurehead. I have already shown that the division between sacred and secular power was irrelevant to Balinese understandings, but merely explaining Balinese ideologies about power does not prove that Klungkung was politically effective, especially given the existence of nine purportedly autonomous realms. Balinese theories need to be more explicitly connected with observed practices. In this section, I would like to counter the presuppositions that inform colonial and academic interpretations with discussions of agency, hegemony, and the specific rhetorics and material practices through which Balinese political authority was constituted.

Basically, officials and academics have used two models to make sense of nineteenth-century Balinese political relations: either Bali was a centralized state, under the domination of a single sovereign, or it was a congeries of entirely independent petty states. Some recent discussions of agency based upon the work of the philosopher Collingwood provide grounds to contest these alternatives. It makes more sense of what the Dutch observed and what Balinese say about precolonial Bali to adopt Inden's notion of an "imperial formation" or "scale of kingships" (1990:215). Precolonial Bali could be described as a collection of agents ranked as greater and lesser, whose acts were "scaled in accord with the lordships or masteries they constituted" (1990:231). These agents included nonhuman ones (Hobart 1990:97), especially divinities, who were in fact the source of all agency. As Hobart observes, a person might be an agent in one situation and an instrument (a lesser agent through which a greater agent operates) or even a "patient" (a still lesser agent affected by the acts of greater agents) in another (1990:96).

This notion of a scale of lordships seems to conform to indigenous notions quite well, to judge both from the history recounted in the *Babad Dalem* and from Balinese cosmologies (e.g., Hooykaas 1975). Such lordship was articulated in terms of overlapping "ownerships." Ultimately the gods, as supreme agents, "owned" Bali (the Balinese term is *dué*). In the visible world, however, it was the Déwa Agung who "owned" Bali. Thus the ruler of Buléléng could write the following in response to a suggestion that he surrender Jembrana (which Buléléng then controlled) as compensation for expenses the Dutch had incurred during a recent expedition against him:

> I don't dare give the Government Djembrana, since even the ground on which I have my residence belongs entirely to the Tjokoerda [i.e., the Déwa Agung], I only have the rule over it—in fact the whole land Bali is the property of the Tjokoerda.[24]

This is another way of stating that the Déwa Agung served as Bali's steward and protector; in short, that he was the "father of Bali." Recall van den Broek's observation that, even when young, Déwa Agung Putra II was addressed by this term. Bali belonged to the Déwa Agung in the same sense that members of a family are said to "belong" to one another: he was responsible for its welfare.

Klungkung, then, was the head of a polity organized by a different understanding of supremacy than that envisaged by colonial authorities. Both Dutch officials and Euro-American academics have assumed that Bali's rulers were competing for overlordship and that the sign of such overlordship was a unitary state with a sovereign authority granted absolute obedience. From this perspective Klungkung's supremacy could only appear nominal, a token gesture of respect for the past. But from a Balinese point of view, multiple powers were normal. Just as in the invisible world Divinity became divinities (while retaining its unity), similar processes of emanation were at work sociopolitically.

Recall that the Balinese notion of Divinity is both hierarchical and multiple.[25] While the divinity sometimes called Sang Hyang Widhi is the ultimate source of all that exists, lesser gods have their own spheres of authority. Thus in ritual one never gives offerings only to Sang Hyang Widhi. Other gods, and even demons and lesser spirits, must also be "remembered," or they have the right to cause misery to those who have forgotten them. Dayu Alit once said that she thought Sang Hyang Widhi's job was really to serve as a witness: to approve or disapprove the independent actions of gods, demons, and spirits. But if someone conscientiously remembered Sang Hyang Widhi and ignored, for example, Betara Brahma (or even the *buta-kala*), Brahma would be absolutely within his rights to cause trouble for the negligence; at best Widhi could suggest limits. It is important that the highest divinity is *not* described as omnipotent. Sang Hyang Widhi Wasa is the *most* powerful, a rather different concept. Power is inherently divided and dispersed, although the original/highest god ultimately contains (as he is the source of) the rest.

In the same way, while in theory the Déwa Agung's power encompassed all the rest, his authority to intervene was as limited as Widhi's. Each lord had rights over what transpired in his own realm. But those rights originated in the fact that he or his ancestors had been granted authority (land, subjects, a keris) from a superior agent at some point in the past.

There is, then, no push in Balinese discourses, or for that matter in Balinese practice, toward totalities as there is in nineteenth-century Europe. Balinese appear quite comfortable with a world constituted by multiple powers rather than a single one, although they imagine these as ranked. Another way of saying this is that in Balinese historical memory and political practice there was no contradiction between the dominance of a center and the autonomy of multiple peripheries. At one time Majapahit was that center, and Bali one of many peripheries. With Majapahit's fall, however, Gélgél's rulers could attempt to make Bali itself a center, and the story told in the *Babad Dalem* about the acquisition of Bangawan Canggu suggests they did. Gélgél, however, had to compete with several new Islamic realms, mainly Mataram on Java and Makassar on Sulawesi, for dominion over former Majapahit dependencies such as Blambangan, Pasuruhan, Lombok, and Sumbawa. Gradually, as the VOC spread its control eastward across Java, the arena in which such contests could occur shrank. The realm of which first Gélgél and then Klungkung was the center was ultimately restricted to Bali and Lombok. But it was as a center that Klungkung was identified with Majapahit.

If the Déwa Agung was the supreme (visible) agent in Bali, lesser agents shared in his agency by acting as his instruments and patients, just as he was an instrument, patient, and lesser agent in relation to divinities. Hobart has made the interesting suggestion that agents are usually complex: that is, that "decisions and responsibility for action involve more than one party in deliberation or action" (Hobart 1990:96). The complex agent summarized by the name "Déwa Agung" was actually the Klungkung court, the acts of which, like those of other courts, were the outcome of deliberations between and execution by many agents, including nonhuman ones such as divinities, spirits, or even regalia.

I want to stress here that Klungkung's supremacy included the mobilization of armed force. From van den Broek to Geertz, foreigners have usually made the mistake of thinking that Klungkung's size implied military impotence. But Klungkung did not have to be populous, since the Déwa Agung could muster troops from other realms. Colonial officials noted this on numerous occasions (as we will see), but when letters reported, for example, such incidents as the time Tabanan and Badung took a Mengwi village and the Déwa Agung ordered troops to march from Klungkung, Payangan, and Gianyar to take it back,[26] it is striking that their authors and readers did not draw from this the obvious conclusion. (To speak to another possible confusion generated by colonial observations, the Déwa Agung's involvement with ritual did not preclude war; it was rather the very condition of its success.)

But Balinese realms were not always as compliant as Tabanan and Badung in this particular instance, and one of the grounds on which Klungkung's authority has been disputed hinges upon an assessment of relations of command and obedience. As Anderson notes, the modern European notion of power as theorized by political philosophers treats it as an abstraction from relationships in which people "appear to obey, willingly or unwillingly, the wishes of others" (1972:6).

Later in this chapter, and elsewhere in this book, a number of instances in which Balinese rulers did and did not obey the Déwa Agung will be described. Here I want to note that command and obedience no longer appear as compelling in understanding power as they once did. The writings of Gramsci and Foucault have significantly altered the ways in which we think about such matters. It would be interesting to clarify what historical conditions enable particular descriptions of power to arise and to be transformed; Foucault's analysis of discipline suggests that by the nineteenth century to think of power in these terms was to rely upon what were already residual concepts. For my purpose, however, what matters is that there are other ways to recognize power than through the terms deployed by nineteenth-century administrators.

Both Foucault and Gramsci suggest that power at its most effective operates less through obedience to the wishes of others than through internalized constraint and the domination of social convention. Comaroff and Comaroff have provided a particularly interesting reading of Gramsci's concept of hegemony as "forms of everyday life that direct perceptions and practices in conventional ways" (1992:28). It operates, they add, through "all signs and practices taken for granted as natural, universal and true." Thus much of what is commonly understood as culture involves hegemony, including aesthetic, ethical, and moral standards, not to mention the standards by which people judge things to be desirable, reasonable, and possible. In short, hegemony involves the power to define what people take as real.

Gramsci is more helpful than Foucault in evaluating Klungkung's position in Bali, for hegemony, as a concept developed in the context of a Marxist social theory, links cultural forms with the interests of a ruling class, in contrast to Foucault's more diffuse understanding of power.

There are many grounds on which one might conclude that Klungkung's position in Bali was hegemonic. Prime among these was the place occupied by Klungkung in key realms of cultural production, including those of history and art. The *Babad Dalem* articulated, as we have noted, the origin tale of the founding of the Balinese world known in the nineteenth century. The Klung-kung village Kamasan was the center of classical Balinese painting, which was commonly used to decorate temple and palace pavilions. Ritual objects were also produced by Klungkung artisans: thus craftsmen in Budaga made bells, incense burners, and other paraphernalia necessary to Brahmana priests.

Klungkung played a special role in legal codes as well. Friederich was told in Badung of a law book called *Swara* (which means "voice"), "issuing from the *Dewa Agung,* and in force for all princes and persons of rank" (Frie-derich 1959:33). Other reports indicate that the Déwa Agung could be ap-pealed to as the final arbiter of any dispute, and violators of the law anywhere in Bali could be exiled to Nusa Penida, in Klungkung's domain. As a corollary, transgressions were also treated more seriously in Klungkung than elsewhere: recall Dubois's description of Klungkung as a "land consecrated to virtue." Virtuous or not, the position of the Klungkung court meant that its rulers maintained distinctions of gender and hierarchy more strictly than other courts. Sasrowidjaya, a Javanese spy for the Dutch in the latter half of the nineteenth century, reported that in Klungkung men were not allowed to walk with women; nor could they enter Klungkung's market or make pur-chases from women there (1874:50). Even members of the royal family were not exempt from punishment for violations of order. Thus when a Déwa Agung's daughter-in-law was sentenced to drown for her adultery, the Dutch Resident commented on the sentence: "According to the pedandas the sever-ity is connected with the spiritual character that the position of the Dewa Agoeng bears."[27]

To understand other aspects of Klungkung hegemony, however, requires a short detour through some of the signifying practices through which rank in Bali was (and to some extent still is) constituted. (These are also important to understanding some of the tensions that emerged in face-to-face meetings between Klungkung's rulers and Dutch colonial officials, as we will see).

As already suggested, in precolonial Bali it was natural to think of both the cosmos and society in hierarchical terms. Discourse and practices, how-ever, elaborated hierarchy in spatial terms. Relations between various lords or between lords and their followers were iconically marked by practices differ-entiating them in terms of interiority and elevation. The symbolic significance of these spatial coordinates was experienced through the body and as part of the socio-natural landscape. Architecture and etiquette were particularly cen-tral to the technology of royal power, for both structured a Balinese habitus (Bourdieu 1977) by playing on contrasts between inner and outer, up and down, high and low, weighting spaces and bodies with moral values.

The two most important architectural structures were royal residences, *puri,* and temples, *pura.* The morphological similarity of the two words suggests to some Balinese a conceptual connection,[28] and indeed rulers, at least Klung-kung's rulers, were sometimes referred to as "visible gods." Architecturally, their similarities were equally striking: both, for example, were divided by gateways into inner and outer regions (*majaba-jero*, it is called in Bali).

The very appearance of these gateways marked a movement from more to less accessible. A "split gate," resembling a *méru* shrine cut cleanly in half and shoved apart, commonly led to the *jabaan*, forecourt. In palaces the outer walls running from such gates formed an openwork pattern (*mancak saji*), al-lowing visual access to the outer courtyard; *carangcang*, a green porcelain lat-tice tile, was, albeit expensive, a favorite material for that wall. At the far end of the outer yard, a much taller bricked wall was broken by an arched, closed gateway with wooden doors and steps, guarded on either side by stone ogres. Up the steps and past the door was the *jeroan*, "inside," where in temples the shrines themselves would be located and in palaces only important visitors or royal intimates could venture. In short, outer regions were architecturally more open (the split gate, the open walls), corresponding to their usage (most royal audiences, for example, took place in the palace forecourt); inner re-gions were closed, remote, and self-contained (the paneled and arched gate).

The regions separated by walls and doors were not only spatial but moral and political as well. Inside and out marked major categories of precolonial ethnosociology. Klungkung's Dalem was the ultimate "insider." Aristocrats were *anak jero*, inside people. Royal brothers "went out" from the puri to estab-lish branch-line houses—lesser "insides," *jeros*, to the wider social "outside." Commoner officeholders, whose homes were known as *jeroan* and who were addressed with the title Jero, were also "inside people," and the same position was extended to court retainers and servants (collapsed into one, for in rela-tion to his king a lord of the realm was also a "servant"): a female servant was a *penyeroan* (from the root *jero*); her male equivalent a *parekan* (from the Kawi root *parek*, "to come close"). Commoner women who married aristocrats (or Brahmanas) took new names with the honorific Jero; commoners of either sex who became temple priests or healers were also addressed as Jero. In short, *anak jero* were all of those persons close to the inner world of gods and rulers.[29] Everyone else was an outer person, an *anak jaba* (see also Geertz 1980: 107–8; Guermonprez 1985: 61–62; Vickers 1986: 135).

As in cosmology, an ideology of emanations pervaded social life. Many Balinese terms presume a perspective of "coming out" from some implied in-side: thus a doorway is a *pemedalan*, a place to come out, rather than as it is in English an "entranceway," and a clan is a *semetonan*, "people of one emergence," those who have emanated from a single ancestral source.

In moving from inside to outside, one moved as well from high to low, from up to down. In Balinese discourse "inner" commonly overlaps the range

of meanings associated with "upper," and "outer" the range of meanings associated with "lower." When a king emerged from his compound, or the gods
from their shrines, they not only "came out," *medal*, but also "came down,"
tedun. What was above, *duur* or *ka luan*, was superior to what was below, *betén*
or *ka tebén*. The habitus also had a temporal dimension: what was "first" and
"elder" was higher and more central.

Within the *jero*, the distinction between high (*singgih*) and low (*sor*) was
critical: between persons properly addressed in respectful language, full of
honorifics (*mabasa*), and those who could be addressed in ordinary language
(*nebah*), the language used for intimates, equals, and inferiors. Outside, high
and low were less important, but nonetheless learning the bodily and linguistic practices of rank was a crucial part of Balinese socialization.

Etiquette inscribed such distinctions onto people's bodies. In general anything associated with the head was superior to anything associated with the
feet; the head was, moreover, the pure part of the body in contrast to the
inauspicious feet. People did not dare to look at a king when addressing him;
certainly *anak jaba* lowered both eyes and head. When walking past the royal
residence, ordinary folk bent forward as a sign of respect, and a man on
horseback would dismount to preclude the possibility that his head might—
however momentarily—be above his lord's. People bent forward when passing
before a seated person of high rank for similar reasons. If a lord passed, peas-
ants squatted, and for a king even Brahmanas clasped their hands together.

The body also provided a source of metaphors to figure social hierarchy.
Kings were referred to as Sang Prabu, the "Head"; their lords and retainers,
as their *kaki tangan* (Indonesian), "feet and hands." Some lords were even the
tabeng dada, "breastplates," of the body politic. Rulers or priests could also be
referred to *sesuunan*, "borne on the head," like the seats of deities when carried
in processions.

These structures were inscribed on geography as well as the body, creating and created by the positive value associated with the mountains in the
interior of the island, where important temples were situated. Thus people of
rank stood or sat not only higher than others but (if possible) to the east and/
or *kaja* (high Balinese *kalér*), "toward the mountains" or "upstream," of the
lower ranked. *Kaja* is an auspicious direction; its opposite, *kelod*, "downstream," is inauspicious.[30] Ethnographies of Bali often identify *kelod* with the
sea, although Balinese I knew found this odd, especially since they do not
regard the sea's value as antithetical to the mountains'. The sea is a place for
ritual cleansing and healing, a place of power where negatives are reconsti-
tuted into positives, which is why it is the receptacle for such things as the
ashes from cremations, offerings to demonic spirits, and the bodies of violators of the law.

These were not, of course, the only ways that rank was constituted.

Clothing and living spaces were among other public signs of status. For example, only rulers could use golden parasols, wear gold ornaments on their heads, or dress in cloth embroidered with gold thread. And only persons of high rank could build certain gate and pavilion types in their compounds.

The bodily practices that marked *sidikara* relations, so far discussed as an index of relations of kinship and identity, also, and importantly, signified relations of hierarchy. A discourse of kinship permeated Balinese political relations. The consumption of ritual leftovers and performance of obeisance were powerful statements of relative ranking as well as the ranking of relatives. Kings treated inferior lords as if they were lower-ranked kin, using *sidikara* practices to demonstrate political hierarchy. To perform a *sumbab* during a lord's death rituals—a gesture involving placing the hands palms together, with the thumbs touching either forehead or nose, and head slightly lowered—was a declaration of dependency and inferiority.

Such ways of acting and speaking form a bridge between the discursive practices centering on gods, spirits, and other nonhuman agents so far described and the material practices that constituted Balinese political relations in the nineteenth century. For example, in theory at least, those who were inside and/or higher were closer to the *niskala* in its marked, positive sense. Those "outside" were subject to more dangerous and less predictable experiences of invisible forces—as spirits and demons, for example, rather than as gods. Like the gods, what was inside—shrines, heirlooms, god images, rulers—was hidden, and more potent. Just as gods, spirits, and demons were the invisible agents of ordinary human experience—the cause of not only events but even feelings—rulers too were hidden agents, ultimately responsible for events in their realms.

Klungkung's hegemony rested on its court's ability to generate and serve as a point of articulation for material practices and signs that articulated a Balinese social order. It was only in relation to Klungkung's court that a Balinese hierarchy could be enunciated. A variety of practices distinguished Klungkung as the most interior, highest, and eldest of Bali's realms. All of Bali's lords addressed the Déwa Agung in deferential language (*mabasa*) and were addressed by him in turn as intimate familiars (*nebab*). All made formal appearances at his court, or sent their sons and heirs to represent them, while it was rare (and theoretically an honor) for him to reciprocate: except on special occasions, usually involving rituals, the Déwa Agung did not go anywhere, others came to him.[31] While he took wives from other realms, he never gave wives in return: the daughters of the Déwa Agung either married close kinsmen or (more often) remained unwed.[32] Everyone could eat leftovers from his offerings to Divinity or from rituals centering on his own person, and at his death and cremation, all would make an obeisance. And everyone acknowledged his authority over Besakih and his close connections to the gods. These practices not only signified the Déwa Agung's place in a hierarchical order but served as some of the means by which his authority was generated and reproduced.

It is here that the entire discourse of *kasaktian* becomes relevant, for the spectacular array of heirloom weapons and key ritual spaces publicly associated with Klungkung's rulers had everything to do with their role in symbolic production and cultural reproduction. Through his relationships to the invisible world, the Déwa Agung was made responsible for securing the welfare of the island as a whole. Central to this function was the Déwa Agung's authority over key ritual spaces, including Nusa Penida's Pura Péd (home of the Fanged Lord), Pura Dasar, an origin temple for many commoner groups, and especially Besakih. It was the latter, I would argue, that ultimately served as the grounds of his authority. Consider this passage from a vow made by several Balinese rulers in 1829:

> If the Déwa Agung has the grace and will to insure the prosperity and
> well-being of the realm, we the undersigned realms will be loyal to him
> and hold up his position: Gianyar, Badung, Tabanan (Korn 1922:99).

The conditional nature of this vow would make it seem, however, that the major criterion by which the Dutch recognized authority—command and obedience—was operative. Could the Dutch, then, have been at least partly correct in their assessment of Klungkung's authority? Was it true that the Déwa Agung could not enforce his wishes? This would seem important insofar as *kasaktian* implies effective agency.

In the matter of obedience I find it instructive to consider what I learned through conversations with Dayu Alit and Ida Bagus Jagri: that even the most *sakti* of persons—or for that matter the most *sakti* of gods—might be ignored or disobeyed. The outcome of such defiance depended upon whether the commands of the one with power were based upon what was right. If they were, then whoever failed to carry them out would suffer the consequences of his or her neglect. But these consequences were not necessarily imposed by the agent defied; he or she might prefer to leave matters to fate. Balinese often explain misfortune as the effect of *karma pala*, the fruits of earlier actions by either the unfortunate one or his ancestors. One who broke a vow, for example, could expect the sufferings of his descendants to last for multiple generations. One might wonder, then, why anyone dared disobey. But Balinese observe practically that no one is always right or entirely faultless. Even the gods, Ida Bagus Jagri and Dayu Alit liked to say, are imperfect: Siwa has three eyes, and Mount Agung, Bali's most sacred site, is too cold. And when a person of power "forgot" Divinity, in his thoughts or acts, Divinity would not be present. It was at such moments that inferiors would dare defy even a person of great power—and would get away with it. Therefore, their independence did not mean that other Balinese rulers did not take Klungkung's power seriously or that Klungkung's claims concerning its relation to the gods were empty. That Klungkung's king was not always obeyed—and was sometimes even actively defied—does not necessarily imply impotence.

At the same time, the significance of obedience should not be overstated, which the colonial emphasis on it would seem to do. Even in those European institutions that served as a model for such definitions of power—absolute monarchies, the army, disciplinary bureaucracies such as those of the colonial state—no authority was *always* obeyed. It is important to remember that those who appear to be mere instruments or even patients are themselves agents, subjects rather than mindless objects. There is a difference between fulfilling a request or carrying out a command in full agreement, and expressing one's resistance through a host of noncompliant behaviors ranging from foot-dragging, pretending noncomprehension, and various forms of avoidance (see Scott 1985). At the same time, the extent to which noncompliance must be expressed in such symbolic and indirect forms is a good measure of the power of those in authority. The issue is less whether or not Bali's other rulers always obeyed Klungkung's, but of the limits of their acts of disobedience.

To appreciate the nature of Klungkung's relations to other Balinese courts, and any court's relation to its subjects, it is important to note that royal agency was symbolically structured by the spatial values already described. A ruler's responsibility was to think and decide; he was Sang Prabu, the "Head." He also remained inside the palace, while his helpers (*pengabih*), including his sons and younger brothers, moved to execute the court's will as his "hands and feet." As shown by both the *Babad Dalem* and colonial reports, priests and ministers also served as instruments of a court's agency by "finishing" (as Balinese say) its rituals, serving as its envoys, and conducting its negotiations.

By the nineteenth century, at least three categories of person performed executive functions in addition to priests and ministers. First, Dutch sources refer to a figure (no longer remembered by Balinese) they called the *rijksbestierder*: literally, "the governor of the realm" (Korn 1932:287–92).[33] In Klungkung the *rijksbestierder* was a near double of the king, his highest-ranking male kinsman. That he actually "governed" is unlikely, although he was undoubtedly a key royal advisor (cf. van Kol 1903:445). Rather, the *rijksbestierder* served as a kind of "secondary king," a mobile counterpart to the interior king "who carries out his wishes on the outside," as one such figure described himself.[34]

Other figures were royal instruments in still more exterior regions. These were the lords of the realm, *manca* or *punggawa*.[35] Klungkung's ruler was unique in having two categories of such lords, for Klungkung was the "inside" of Bali as a whole. Therefore, in addition to the lords within Klungkung (referred to as *manca*), the rulers of other domains were Klungkung's *punggawa* in relation to the larger world, fighting wars on his behalf and serving as his ambassadors to, for example, the colonial government.[36]

The same contrasts of inner and outer could be infinitely replicated. If in relation to the Déwa Agung Bali's other rulers were mere *punggawa*, in his own realm each was the local Déwa Agung (the title was even used for the kings of theater), with his own *punggawa*. In their turn the agency of seconds or *punggawa* could also (at least theoretically) be subdivided into more interior and more exterior. On the brink of the colonial conquest, for example, Klungkung's *rijksbestierder* concerned himself primarily with relations with other Balinese, while a lower-ranking royal brother took responsibility for dealing with the Dutch.

Thus the "independence" of other rulers did not make the Déwa Agung any less lord of Bali than the "independence" of local lords meant that there were no "realms" in Bali. From Klungkung's perspective, as top and center, Bali was a single polity. The Déwa Agung was Susuhunan of Bali and Lombok, and other rulers mere *punggawa*. But on another, local level, each lord, however insignificant from a global perspective, was the neighborhood "Déwa Agung." Thus just as other rulers consulted Klungkung's ruler about major rituals they were planning, their own subjects would seek their advice on similar occasions.

To say that the Déwa Agung was Bali's *sesuunan* is to emphasize that only he could represent Bali as a totality. After Gusti Agung Maruti, no Balinese lord tried to appropriate this role or usurp Klungkung's prerogatives. Balinese politics were characterized by continual contests between various lords, but such supremacy was not one of the prizes for which they contended.

ENCOUNTERS WITH EMPIRE

With this rather complex picture in mind, it is time to return to Huskus Koopman and his mission to Bali in 1840. According to his instructions, Huskus Koopman's goals were both diplomatic and investigative. If possible, he was to return to Batavia with signatures on the draft of a treaty by which Bali's princes would agree not to form any attachments to other European states; if this did not prove possible, he was to explain what obstacles stood in the way of such an agreement. He was also charged with making inquiries into the situation in Lombok and into British activity in the region.

After studying documents concerning Bali in government archives, and interviewing everyone he could find who had ever been to either Bali or Lombok, Huskus Koopman arrived in Kuta aboard a warship in April 1840, accompanied by Prince Sjarif Hamid of Pontianak, who was to serve as interpreter when necessary, and a navy lieutenant named Oosterwijk as his aide-de-camp (Agung 1991:39–41). Despite his preparations, from the moment he stepped off the ship he found himself caught up in a political world whose presuppositions and routines he found difficult to fathom, in part because his attention was not focused upon the practices that actually ordered it. His understanding of hierarchy and power was influenced both by his own prior experiences with archipelago rulers (his last posting had been in Pontianak, a realm in West Borneo, and one reason Huskus Koopman had been chosen for this mission was his poise and tact) and by the collective colonial experience of the princes of Central Java. If Huskus Koopman's diplomacy seems awkward, however, he can hardly be faulted. Fluent in Malay, he continually laments his ignorance of the Balinese language, which forced him to rely on interpreters he describes as "worthless." And so little was known about Bali's rulers and political structure that he could record at one point that Bali consisted of nine realms rather than the eight that had hitherto been mentioned.[37]

A Meeting with the Déwa Agung: J. H. Huskus Koopman, May 1840

Huskus Koopman began his Balinese sojourn in Badung, where he stayed with Boele Schuurman, the Netherlands Trading Company's new agent in Kuta.[38] His arrival was greeted, however, by envoys not only from Badung's rulers but from the Déwa Agung himself, who wished to know his reason for coming. Huskus Koopman notes this in his journal with satisfaction: the Déwa Agung's interest seemed to bode well for his mission. Sending the envoy off with assurances that he would come to Klungkung shortly, he turned his attention to settling in at Badung.

But the Déwa Agung was not to be put off so easily. His envoy, a certain Gusti Jong, returned to Badung to press Huskus Koopman for a definite date, and Huskus Koopman began to find himself in an awkward position. At first he palmed Gusti Jong off with gifts and vague expressions of goodwill, but when he returned yet again, Huskus Koopman promised to come to Klungkung as soon as possible. He then sought advice from Schuurman, who had already been in Bali about a year.

Huskus Koopman's affairs in Badung were going well. He had several visits from an envoy of Gusti Ngurah Kesiman, Badung's most powerful prince, and Schuurman had managed to arrange an audience with the prince of Pamecutan within his first week. The princes of both Pamecutan and Kesiman sent word that they would even honor him by calling at his quarters in Kuta. And almost daily he received other Badung notables: Kesiman's designated successor, local lords, a high priest, even prominent members of Badung's sizable Islamic community. With all of this activity Huskus Koopman wondered if he should not simply deal first with Badung's rulers, but the Déwa

Agung's importunity posed a problem. Schuurman advised deferring the decision to the Resident in Banyuwangi; in the meantime he could plan to go to Klungkung after accompanying Schuurman on a visit to Badung's rulers.

But only four days later Gusti Jong reappeared, to announce the Keizer was celebrating his birthday the following week, and requested Huskus Koopman's presence. Huskus Koopman immediately accepted the invitation, sending Gusti Jong off with a flask of *arak* and some copper coins. Shortly thereafter, he received word that the princes of Pamecutan and Kesiman were about to pay their promised visit, and he had to write to say he could not receive them, as he was leaving for Klungkung.

It was one thing to plan and promise, however, and another to act. First Huskus Koopman encountered enormous difficulties finding bearers to carry his supplies (which included an apparently inexhaustible supply of alcohol, flasks of which he continually disbursed as gifts). When at last he managed to set off, he got no further than the front of Gusti Ngurah Kesiman's puri, where he was left in the middle of the night. In vain he tried to gain access to the prince, hoping to procure his help and continue on his way. Alas, Kesiman was asleep and could not be disturbed, but as he always woke before dawn, so Huskus Koopman was informed, there would not be long to wait. Yet somehow that morning, the prince, contrary to habit, slept until 8:00 A.M. When he did emerge, rather than relieving Huskus Koopman's apprehensions and sending him merrily on his way, he informed him that he could not himself supply the number of men needed, so word would have to be sent to Pamecutan. In the meantime he invited Huskus Koopman to breakfast with him and to stroll around his gardens.

It was fairly evident that something was up, but Huskus Koopman, hoping to make the best of the situation, decided to turn the conversation to "matters of state." To his frustration Kesiman "diverted the conversation again and again to weapons, illness, and doctoring." (These were not uninteresting topics, as we will see in the next chapter; Kesiman may have been communicating, however allusively, far more than Huskus Koopman realized.) Finally Huskus Koopman broached the subject of his visit to Klungkung, at which Kesiman noticeably perked up. He explained that the Governor General had ordered him to go to Klungkung to discuss recent events on Lombok. The Balinese princes of Lombok had asked Batavia for help, and the Governor General wanted the Cokorda's advice before making any decisions. If the Dutch did get involved, Huskus Koopman explained, it would be purely out of neighborliness. Gusti Ngurah Kesiman heard all of this with a gleam in his eye, but to Huskus Koopman's disappointment he offered no comment. Matters continued in this fashion until 5:00 P.M. Just when Huskus Koopman had resigned himself to returning to Kuta—he no longer had any hope of arriving in Klungkung in time for the royal birthday—bearers suddenly materialized. Even then departure was delayed while each man was paid in advance.

It took the party until the middle of the night to reach Klungkung. Despite the hour, they were greeted by a gun salute, and a Brahmana showed them to their quarters—a small Balinese pavilion with woven bamboo walls. By then Huskus Koopman had proof that the business about bearers had been nonsense. Minutes after his party's departure they had been passed on the road by one of Gusti Ngurah Kesiman's own grandsons in the company of a large entourage, on their way to the very same ritual in Klungkung. Further evidence of Kesiman's neglect (or chicanery) appeared the following day, when Huskus Koopman's goods arrived: a box belonging to Oosterwijk had been stolen while the bearers and guards slept at Lépang, a Klungkung village.

Huskus Koopman's hosts in Klungkung were soothing and sympathetic. They told him that he had been the innocent victim of some difficulties between Badung and Klungkung: as Huskus Koopman put it, there was a "secret enmity existing between the usurper Kesiman and the Keizer of Klungkung." The Déwa Agung sent word that he had informed his lords to begin an immediate investigation to locate the missing goods and identify the thieves, and he sent the princes of Kesiman and Pamecutan home to inform their elders "of the behavior of their people." Such sympathy and alacrity pleased Huskus Koopman, and he looked forward to his audience with great optimism.

Huskus Koopman's treatment by Badung's rulers—very like something that might occur in contemporary Bali—suggests just how difficult it is to understand relations of patronage in terms of chains of command. First of all, the "enmity" to which Koopman refers needs to be placed in perspective. Both Molière and Schuurman reported that a kind of "rivalry" reigned between the Déwa Agung and Kesiman. Schuurman had found none of Badung's rulers very helpful in arranging the transport of Klungkung's rhinoceros, and Kesiman had openly expressed displeasure that a cannon that had been promised to him had been forgotten—a cannon still undelivered in 1840. The enmity that Kesiman's chicanery manifested seems directed not so much toward the Déwa Agung as toward the negligent and blundering Dutch.

From a Balinese perspective, Huskus Koopman's behavior toward both the rulers of Badung and Klungkung was problematic. The Déwa Agung had expressed a willingness to meet with him, and Koopman had responded with enthusiasm. Why, then, did he linger in Badung? By spending so much time in Badung, he seemed to be announcing himself a client of Badung's princes. Yet when he received an invitation to come to the Déwa Agung's ritual he responded at once in the affirmative, without seeking the advice or permission of his Badung patrons.

Badung's princes had good reason to feel that the Dutch "belonged" to them, given the length of their mutually beneficial commercial relations, and Huskus Koopman's initial behavior seemed to acknowledge the tie. As their patron, Kesiman had every reason to expect that should the Dutch need to deal with the Déwa Agung, he would serve as middleman. But Huskus Koopman had not only accepted an invitation to Klungkung without consulting his hosts, he had even rudely refused the honor of a visit from them on the same grounds. He intended to deal with the Déwa Agung directly, without any intermediaries, and therefore no one would benefit from the relationship. Here was Huskus Koopman, buttering up the powerful and forgetting those who had initially helped him. It was the rhinoceros and the cannon all over again—an arrogant snub, which needed to be answered.

By spoiling Huskus Koopman's travel plans and delaying his arrival (why, for example, was he not included in the party Badung's princes were already sending to Klungkung?) Kesiman attempted to make Huskus Koopman appear disrespectful of the Déwa Agung, thus alienating them. At the same time, the disappearance of goods belonging to Huskus Koopman's party took place on Klungkung territory—another potential source of trouble between Koopman and the Déwa Agung. But Gusti Ngurah Kesiman's strategy backfired; indeed, his scheming provided an initial bond between Huskus Koopman and the Déwa Agung. Kesiman need not have worried, however; Huskus Koopman managed to alienate Klungkung's ruler entirely on his own.

This is not to say that there were no tensions between Badung and Klungkung: by treating an invited guest of the Déwa Agung in this fashion, Kesiman was also sending a message to the king. Yet it is important that he communicated in an oblique fashion and that Huskus Koopman characterizes his enmity as "secret." The major marker of Badung-Klungkung relations is in fact something Koopman notes in passing: that the sons and grandsons of Badung's rulers attended the Déwa Agung's ritual. This was a statement of loyalty, as much so, according to custom, as appearing in person.

Huskus Koopman's first audience with the Déwa Agung took place the afternoon after his arrival. The meeting opened with an interaction that immediately challenged the Déwa Agung's goodwill. It involved the matter of seating, an issue that continually raised colonial hackles. In Bali, seating was iconic of rank: the higher the rank, the higher the seat. (Indeed, until recently in Bali to ask about someone's rank literally translated as an inquiry into where they "sat.") When Huskus Koopman was invited to settle on the floor at the ruler's feet, it showed that he was regarded as an "outsider" (*anak jaba*), a person without rank. This was nothing new. As Huskus Koopman noted in his journal, Granpré Molière had been forced to sit on the ground (and in the open air at that) when he visited Klungkung. But Huskus Koopman had no intention of losing the first round. He refused the place offered to him and had his interpreters tell the Déwa Agung that as he was there as a representative of the Governor General (whom Balinese rulers addressed in letters as the "King of Java, who holds court at Batavia"), he must be treated with the honors that gentleman would receive. The Déwa Agung absorbed this without comment and gestured Huskus Koopman to a place near his own person, much to Huskus Koopman's satisfaction.

While Huskus Koopman describes this event as if he had scored a moral victory, from a Balinese perspective he had done exactly the reverse. First of all, Huskus Koopman's reasoning was flawed. As the Governor General's representative he was *not* his equal; by definition an envoy is inferior, since he acts on another's behalf.[39] Second, where one "sat" was largely determined by birth. In assuming that their rank was subject to negotiation, the Dutch may have been affected by their experience of the somewhat more flexible Javanese courts, where different norms of politeness prevailed. Third, even if he had outranked his host, since Huskus Koopman hoped to gain something from the Déwa Agung, good Balinese etiquette demanded that he at least make the motions of taking an inferior place. Finally, openly refusing the place he was offered was tantamount to an act of aggression. Overall, Huskus Koopman's behavior would hardly have won him respect but rather signaled boorishness. The Balinese response to Dutch bad manners, however, was far milder than the Dutch response in similar circumstances, as we shall see.

The moderation of the Déwa Agung's reaction might, of course, have been due to the tact of his interpreter. Huskus Koopman and the Déwa Agung shared no common language, and the entire interaction was conducted through third parties, who translated Huskus Koopman's Malay into Balinese and the Déwa Agung's Balinese into Malay. Interpreters must have played an extraordinarily important role in early negotiations between the colonial government and indigenous rulers, although there is no way of gauging their contribution.

Once all were seated, the formalities began. Huskus Koopman read aloud the Governor General's letter and presented the Keizer with a "splendid saber, with silver hilt and chased sheath." Both letter and gift "were received by the king in a dignified manner." The Déwa Agung announced that he would have a written translation of the letter into Balinese prepared, "while the sword was considered by him with much attention and pleasure."

A brief exchange concerning this gift is worthy of note. Fondling the sword, the Déwa Agung remarked that it was not sharp. Huskus Koopman promptly responded with an impromptu moral lesson on symbolic value: the sword was not sharp because European princes had no need to defend themselves, as they were loved and thus protected by their subjects. (Balinese, of course, presumed that rulers loved and protected their subjects with their weapons.) For a prince, Huskus Koopman explained, weapons only served "as pomp." His explanation was received by the Déwa Agung "with an affable laugh of self-satisfaction," whereupon the audience was adjourned. Given the significance of regalia weapons in Bali, the Déwa Agung might well have been amused; if European notables really thought as Huskus Koopman did, they understood little about power. Moreover, for the Déwa Agung the sword might well have carried a rather different symbolic message. A blunt sword was hardly worthy of the dignity of the Déwa Agung's position. Might it not betray the real attitudes of the Dutch? They claimed friendship and made a show of generosity, but their gifts were useless; they did not actually trust the Déwa Agung with anything that might be used against them. The Dutch assumption that he could be easily duped and bribed provided more reason still for the Déwa Agung's "affable laugh."

As far as the Déwa Agung was concerned, his business with Huskus Koopman was now concluded: they had met, he had been given the Governor General's letter, and he had received a gift. Any subsequent contact was a mere formality, a gesture of esteem, since further discussion rested in the hands of the Déwa Agung's lords, especially his mobile counterpart, the secondary king. And indeed, the following day Huskus Koopman received an invitation from this very person, a man he identifies as Cokorda Ketut Rai.[40]

But for Huskus Koopman the invitation was tangential. In his journal he merely mentions it in passing, in contrast to the considerable space he devotes to his second audience with the king on the very same day, which he found as "fruitless" as the first. The large entourage of lords in attendance upon the Déwa Agung frustrated Huskus Koopman, who deemed it inadvisable to speak about important matters in public. As a result, he wrote, "the talk ran thus with the greatest difficulty along indifferent matters while [the Déwa Agung] said little or nothing." After a polite exchange of gifts—fruit from the Déwa Agung (almost assuredly ritual leftovers, the significance of which, being less obvious than that of seating, Huskus Koopman missed), reciprocated with two flasks of liquor from Huskus Koopman—the meeting was over.

Still focused upon the king, Huskus Koopman sought yet another audience the following day. This time he was rebuffed. The Déwa Agung, he was informed, was busy. Huskus Koopman received visitors of his own, however: a Cokorda Déwa Agung Gedé, identified as a cousin of the ruler and his heir apparent, came to see him, accompanied by a nephew of the ruler of Mengwi.[41] The crown prince was extremely warm and told Huskus Koopman that the Keizer loved him and would spare nothing to make his life agreeable. The Keizer would not only protect him from all harm but would guarantee any losses from the theft he had experienced—a firm pledge of patronage, which Huskus Koopman's subsequent behavior annulled. Huskus Koopman in turn smoothly declared that when (not, it should be noted, if) the Keizer sent an envoy to Batavia, his hospitality would be returned.

The following day he was granted a third audience—destined to be the last on this journey. Huskus Koopman was optimistic that this time he might get down to business. But to his chagrin everything was as before, and if anything worse. After returning his greetings the king "kept a deep silence." Huskus Koopman was finally driven to break it himself by asking if the Keizer did not wish to learn the reasons for his visit. The Keizer agreed.

Huskus Koopman began by summarizing for the Déwa Agung the colonial government's interest in Lombok as follows: in 1836 Gusti Ngurah Madé Karangasem, "usurper" of Karangasem/Lombok, had written to ask the government's aid against the ruler of Mataram, who was waging war against him. The Governor General had refused. But after repeated complaints (he does not specify from whom, but Lekkerkerker [1923] suggests Lange, Gusti Ngurah Madé Karangasem's supporter; Agung [1991] says John Burd), the Governor General had begun to reconsider his position. Before taking any action, however, he wanted to know the ins and outs of the whole affair from the Déwa Agung, "as Keizer of Bali and Lombok."

Whatever the Déwa Agung's thoughts about the course of events on Lombok, Huskus Koopman's request must have struck him as impertinent. The Governor General was not seeking instruction or permission from the Déwa Agung; instead he was treating the Déwa Agung as an inferior, who could and should supply him with information. This was not a part the Déwa Agung would play. Instead of answering, he suggested that Huskus Koopman speak to Lange, who was expected momentarily. But Huskus Koopman persisted, declaring that Lange was hardly a disinterested party. As the Keizer was the rightful judge of these matters, he wished to hear his opinion and to learn how the whole affair had started. The Déwa Agung then proceeded to ask a number of questions, which Huskus Koopman did not bother to record in his journal, dismissing them as "tangential." By now Huskus Koopman was convinced that the Déwa Agung was reluctant to speak frankly in the presence of his court. He requested a private audience, which was granted.

The presence of the lords of his realm would not have inhibited the Déwa Agung from speaking about these matters, but that Huskus Koopman thought it did reveals another difference in Dutch and Balinese presuppositions. It was not, after all, only in regard to audiences with the Déwa Agung that Huskus Koopman expressed such frustrations in his journal: even in conversations with lesser notables he often complains that there are always too many people about—including the necessary interpreters—to talk "safely." Huskus Koopman took for granted that political discussions should be shrouded in secrecy and were not for all ears. In Java private meetings between the Dutch Resident and the Susuhunan of Solo or Sultan of Jogja were long-established common practice. But such ideas about politics and privacy were not necessarily salient in Bali. It is matters involving the invisible rather than the visible world that

Balinese hesitate to discuss openly, in contrast to Europeans, who have few qualms about public discussions of metaphysics and think it their duty to spread word of their beliefs throughout the world. But it is not merely content that determines loquacity or its absence. As already noted, for Balinese, the closer one is to the *niskala* realm—whether in understanding or by virtue of hierarchical position—the more value is placed upon stillness in general. Royal silence on matters the Dutch considered crucial—and felt could only be properly discussed by the highest ranking—was precisely a major point of disjuncture between the Balinese and European understandings of power. Colonial officials seem never to have grasped this. Instead they interpreted each form in which such silence appeared—and there were many, as we will see—in terms of personalities rather than structurally. With such different presuppositions about what could and could not be said and by whom, the Déwa Agung and Huskus Koopman were bound to alarm one another.

If the Déwa Agung was willing to dismiss his lords from this meeting, it was not because he shared Huskus Koopman's desire to talk in private; on the contrary, his lords were his advisors, and thus it was essential that they know whatever he knew. More likely, he thought Huskus Koopman had something else to tell *him*, and he was waiting to hear what it was.

And so, at last alone with the Déwa Agung (except, that is, for the interpreters), Huskus Koopman found to his dismay that "the king kept up the most absolute silence." After a pause, Huskus Koopman finally declared that, given how important the matter was, the king might want time to reflect before responding. He would be available whenever the Keizer was ready to talk, Huskus Koopman stated magnanimously, continuing to patronize his host. But the Déwa Agung shook his head and said he knew nothing about it.

Now, such a disclaimer could have had any number of possible meanings. Huskus Koopman, however, was provoked by the Déwa Agung's coyness. He asked the king sharply "if the island of Lombok did not then stand under his orders and, if yes, if the prince ruling there at present was recognized as such by him, which question appeared to embarrass him." This outburst was followed by more silence. The king was more likely angered than embarrassed by such insolence, and his silence thus a sign of his efforts to remain courteous. But it only exasperated Huskus Koopman further, and his next remarks contained a direct threat. He writes that he "drew the king's attention to [the fact] that the Dutch and the Balinese had lived next to each other peacefully almost 250 years." The Déwa Agung certainly knew, he continued, that the Dutch dominated the whole of the Indies (it was, of course, because the Dutch did not control "the whole of the Indies" that he was there), and that it was only due to their benevolence that the Keizer continued to rule over his people. While the Governor General had every wish that harmonious relations between the Dutch and the Balinese might last another 250 years, "foreigners" must not be allowed to intrude between them, as had happened on Lombok. The Dutch were more than happy to respect Balinese manners and customs but not "novelties introduced by foreigners." The Governor General had sent him to Klungkung precisely to find a way to end such "irregularities" in the interests of general tranquility. At the conclusion of this speech, Huskus Koopman noted, the Keizer appeared to withdraw into a deep meditation; when (after what seemed a long time) he "awoke," he announced he wished to consult with his lords. With this the audience was at an end.

Huskus Koopman's remarks show that what was uppermost in the government's mind was George King and his potential English backers. Burd and Lange had encouraged the Governor General to think that King was responsible for the ferment on Lombok. Perhaps all that Huskus Koopman wanted was confirmation from the Déwa Agung and an assurance of his own royal disapproval. But the request to meet in private, and Huskus Koopman's arrogant and provocative remarks when they did—particularly his declaration that it was only by virtue of Dutch benevolence that the Déwa Agung maintained his position as Bali's ruler, implying the situation could change whenever the Dutch wished—was hardly likely to cement any bond of friendship. On the contrary, it was an assault on the Déwa Agung's dignity, and it is noteworthy that no colonial representative ever had another such private audience with a Déwa Agung for the remainder of the precolonial period.

Again, it is difficult to be certain whether the full brunt of Huskus Koopman's words was communicated, since interpreters might have had good reason to soften the message. But the Déwa Agung would not have attended solely to Huskus Koopman's mediated words. Instead, he would have been alert to the entire tenor of the conversation, including tone of voice and gesture.

Shortly thereafter Mads Lange arrived in Klungkung. Lange declared to Huskus Koopman that he had earned the trust of Bali's rulers over many years of residing in Bali and Lombok. The Déwa Agung, he boasted, consulted him about everything. As if to prove his point, in the middle of their conversation Lange received a summons from the puri.

According to Lange's report upon his return, the Déwa Agung told him what Huskus Koopman had said and asked what he thought. Lange, so he assured Huskus Koopman, had advised the Keizer that the time had come to establish his power with Dutch help. But the Déwa Agung did not seem very interested in hearing this. As Lange told Huskus Koopman,

the Keizer had explained to him that he dared act on no matters of importance as long as he had not fulfilled a promise he had made to the Great Spirit on Goenoeng Agong to establish a temple, for which he had sent for sandalwood from the Trading Society a long time ago,

while he certainly expected to apply for no blessing on all of his under-
takings before this.[42]

That the Déwa Agung fulfilled his promise to recover the goods stolen
from Huskus Koopman and deliver the men responsible, together with the
fact that Huskus Koopman continued to receive visits from the lords of the
realm, suggests, however, that the Déwa Agung had not yet made up his mind
about him. The very next evening the secondary king came by to question
Huskus Koopman about the power of the Dutch. All Huskus Koopman writes
about their conversation is that his questions "were answered properly by us,
while the talk ran further to indifferent matters."

Given later Dutch descriptions of Klungkung protocol, this was very
likely a more critical meeting than the one with the Déwa Agung himself. Yet
Huskus Koopman, still hoping for more face-to-face conversations with the
king, could not see this. Nor does he seem to have attached any weight to
the visits he received from other lords of the realm. A day later, Anak Agung
Madé Pemecutan of Satria stopped by, but although Huskus Koopman reports, like a bookkeeper dutifully maintaining his account book, the gifts he
received (a duck, a hen, and three coconuts), he says nothing of what was
discussed.

If Huskus Koopman, true to his name (*koopman* means "merchant"), be-
haved like a good Dutch burgher, noting down each exchange of goods (and
the journal was in part an account book, proof to his superiors of his expen-
ditures), the Balinese must have found his behavior in regard to gifts odd,
and perhaps further grounds to query his intentions. Every interaction with
any Balinese of note was followed by an immediate prestation, allowing no
time to develop the relationships that these gifts should have been meant to
cement. Moreover, since it was clear that Huskus Koopman wanted something, his gifts appeared for what they were—bribes. The few Balinese who
presented Huskus Koopman with gifts—apart from the Déwa Agung, these
included the crown prince and two lords of the realm—showed friendliness
by sending edibles (various animals and coconuts). Huskus Koopman gave
something to nearly everyone with whom he came into contact, generally a
flask of some alcoholic beverage, although he appears to have made distinctions by rank: thus Gusti Jong and Abdul Rahim (Muslim or no), as mere
representatives of the king, received *arak*; the two lords who made gifts to
him were rewarded with gin; the king, secondary king, crown prince, and
Brahmanas received liqueur; and finally, two flasks of red wine were sent to
the Déwa Agung in appreciation for his gift of cakes and fruit (again, ritual
leftovers).

Huskus Koopman soon heard discouraging news from Gusti Jong. He had
proposed better accommodations for Huskus Koopman, but the Keizer had

responded that this was not necessary, as he would soon be given an answer to his letter and could be on his way. At this point, a frustrated Huskus Koopman tried to take more aggressive action. He paid a visit to the crown prince, who of everyone in Klungkung seemed most favorably inclined toward him. The prince was friendly, introducing him to his wife and child, asking if he could eat goat meat (as Muslims did), and requesting advice on how to break his opium habit. Huskus Koopman presented him with his own gold cigar holder, which the prince had admired, and suggested that whenever he felt the urge for opium he take a nip of gin instead. Huskus Koopman's high hopes of this relationship were fueled when he learned from Gusti Jong that the prince had spoken positively to the Keizer on his behalf. The prince had supposedly declared that if Huskus Koopman were sincere, he wanted to "live with the Dutch as brothers." Huskus Koopman inferred that his major opposition came from Klungkung's priests, to whom the Déwa Agung paid close attention, and he noted, "It is to be deplored . . . that the priesthood here has so much influence."

Huskus Koopman was reassured by his meeting with the prince, especially when he was told that it was primarily illness that prevented the Déwa Agung from summoning him; the Keizer was also still waiting for responses to letters he had sent to all of Bali's princes. This may have been the first time—though it was hardly to be the last—that a Balinese lord claimed illness to avoid meeting with a Dutch official. Occasionally, of course, the excuse was true. But it was also a way of ensuring that meetings would be, from a Balinese point of view, productive. Audiences could not be held daily. According to the Balinese calendar, certain days were suitable for rituals (and different kinds of rituals) or going to war; others for conferences.[43] The "white-eyed" Dutchmen, of course, were ignorant of such matters. But Huskus Koopman, believing what he was told, asked after the Keizer's health daily, only to be informed that the Déwa Agung was still indisposed and no letters had yet arrived.

Huskus Koopman continued to do what he could. Since the crown prince and the secondary king had expressed interest in sampling European food, he sent them tins of salmon and vegetables, which were returned with the report that they were not to Balinese tastes: an omen or message, perhaps? The crown prince came by to ask him to obtain some saddles for him. After Huskus Koopman sent a gift to the secondary king, he was invited to visit and play his music box for the Cokorda's wife (but it broke). Of the one visit not initiated by himself, however—from Ida Wayan Sidemen, who belonged to an influential Brahmana house—he reports nothing other than its occurrence.

Ida Wayan Sidemen was apparently an important figure, since the following day he returned for a more formal meeting with Huskus Koopman, accompanied by Abdul Rahim, the Déwa Agung's "secretary," who served as interpreter. Huskus Koopman was again asked to explain the purpose of his mission to Bali. He writes that he explained the government's wishes "in detail," while trying to provide assurances that the Dutch had no desire to interfere with Bali's internal affairs. But the Balinese could hardly have missed the contradiction between the government's proclamations of friendship on the one hand and its detailed list of "wishes" on the other.

This was Huskus Koopman's last chance to plead his cause. Later the same day Abdul Rahim returned to prepare Huskus Koopman to receive the Keizer's response to the Governor General, along with the gift of a black horse. When these were brought—under the escort of eighteen Balinese bearing golden pikes—Huskus Koopman was informed that he was to leave Klungkung before sundown on the following day. Much taken aback, he requested a parting audience but was told that the Déwa Agung was still ill. He then asked after the crown prince but was informed he was staying overnight at one of his "country seats." Attempts to speak to other lords also came to naught. As for the letter, it informed the Dutch that the Déwa Agung wanted to have nothing to do with them.

Here Huskus Koopman's journal ends, but a report written some months later shows just how bad an impression he had made in Klungkung. The Déwa Agung sent letters to all of Bali's rulers forbidding them to have anything to do with Huskus Koopman and erected fortifications along Klungkung's beaches in the event of a Dutch attack. Nor was his distrust limited to Huskus Koopman; Schuurman too was no longer welcome in Klungkung (Lekkerkerker 1923).

But if Huskus Koopman failed miserably with the Déwa Agung, he achieved (by virtue of that failure) a fine rapport with Gusti Ngurah Kesiman. When Huskus Koopman returned to Bali six months later to attend the cremation of the ruler of Pamecutan, Gusti Ngurah Kesiman greeted him with warmth, explained he had learned Malay, and proceeded to chatter about family problems, about which Huskus Koopman offered advice. Kesiman was so delighted by this interaction that he swore his friendship; Huskus Koopman immediately suggested that as a token of it he should sign a treaty. Kesiman promised he would, eventually—and did, in June 1841, approximately one month after Badung's long-promised cannon was finally delivered. In the meantime he counseled Huskus Koopman to be patient and move slowly in the matter of Klungkung: sound Balinese wisdom. He would surely succeed in due course, Kesiman advised, but at that moment the Déwa Agung was adamantly opposed to the Dutch and there was nothing that could be done about it.

Kesiman's words proved prophetic; by December 1841 the Déwa Agung had signed a treaty, preceded by his allies in Buléléng and Karangasem. What induced the Déwa Agung to change his mind is, unfortunately, a mystery, since Huskus Koopman's subsequent negotiations are not documented. Within a few years, however, Klungkung's hostility toward the Dutch was back in full force.[44]

From Diplomacy to War

Even as Huskus Koopman was negotiating these treaties, they were being rendered obsolete by a series of other events: the stranding of a ship named the *Overijssel* off the coast of Badung; the appearance in an English journal of an article on the brisk trade at Lombok's ports; and Lange's reception of a friendly letter from George King on behalf of Mataram's ruler, hinting at a desire to be on good terms with the Dutch.

Ships frequently went aground off Bali's shores. Balinese regarded ship-wrecks and their cargo as gifts from Baruna, god of the sea, and by a custom called *tawan karang* they belonged to whoever managed to salvage them. In the bourgeois eyes of the Dutch, this was theft, an offense against the natural law of private property. A conflict between what amounted to two divine ordinances was inevitable, as increased trade led more and more ships to maneuver the treacherous reefs off Bali's coasts. The *Overijssel's* wreck precipitated that conflict because it was carrying Dutch passengers. While no one was harmed, the publicity led to calls for action. The Governor General decided that it was not enough for Balinese rulers to recognize Dutch sovereignty; they had to renounce their claim to shipwrecks and promise to restore what property survived to its rightful owner. While Huskus Koopman argued this goal would be easier to achieve through unofficial channels than by treaty, he was overruled.

The other two events led the colonial government to seek a treaty with Mataram. Huskus Koopman had returned to Batavia to recommend supporting a joint expedition by Klungkung, Karangasem, and Buléléng against Lombok, but he was too late. The discovery that Lombok was exporting fourteen thousand tons of rice annually, and that the trade was in the hands of Englishmen and Americans, made the island a focus of political concern: what if the British government made a move? While Huskus Koopman maintained that, since the Déwa Agung was Lombok's overlord, there was no need for concern, Batavia disagreed. The Déwa Agung might have rights, but could he enforce them? Lombok did not seem to pay much attention to his overlordship (Lekkerkerker 1923). Better to negotiate with Mataram directly, especially as George King's overtures boded well. This marked an important shift in policy. While Huskus Koopman had negotiated separate treaties with Buléléng, Karangasem, and Badung, these could be seen as strategic, a way of ensuring Klungkung's cooperation. Increasingly, however, the colonial government treated Bali's realms as separate polities.

In October 1842 Huskus Koopman concluded a treaty by which Mataram not only recognized Dutch sovereignty but renounced reef rights. Such a precedent left Bali's rulers with little choice but to accept this provision as well. Badung signed a revised treaty a month later; Karangasem, Buléléng, and Klungkung held out until May 1843. This time, Tabanan also signed a treaty.[45]

But all was not well, for when the Assistant Resident of Banyuwangi came to Buléléng in 1844 to deliver ratified copies of the treaties and began what he expected would be a routine review of their contents, he was received with astonishment: Buléléng's ruler denied he had ever signed such a thing.[46] Within a year Gusti Ketut Jelantik, Buléléng's chief minister, objected even more strenuously: as long as he lived, there would be no Dutch "sovereignty" over his land. Declaring that no mere piece of paper could make anyone master over another, he announced dramatically, "Let the keris decide!" Meanwhile, Balinese continued to salvage shipwrecks.

Beginning with van Hoëvell in 1854, Buléléng's reaction has been blamed on the hapless Huskus Koopman, who by 1844 had died. Lekkerkerker (1923), for example, claims that Huskus Koopman had verbally promised more than he could deliver, namely, aid against Lombok. When such aid was not forthcoming, the rulers of Klungkung, Karangasem, and Buléléng, who felt their trust had been betrayed, "pretended" they had not understood the treaties. Schulte Nordholt has more recently insisted in fact this was no pretense (1988). He claims that Huskus Koopman had explained the treaties as declarations of friendship. As friends, Balinese and Dutch could count on one another for aid, including military assistance. Since the treaties were written in Dutch, and translated not into Balinese but Malay, a language understood by almost no Balinese,[47] Bali's kings did not realize that the documents they signed in fact said something rather different. Gusti Ketut Jelantik's astonishment was genuine.

It is not necessary to postulate a deliberate intention to deceive, however. What the Dutch meant by "sovereignty" would hardly make sense to the rulers of polities where the same piece of land could be simultaneously "owned" by a farmer, the king, and the gods. If colonial officials believed that the rulers of Bali had ceded to them supreme rights over their realms, Bali's rulers would have understood the transaction differently. When a ruler granted land to one of his subjects, he did not abrogate his interests in it in perpetuity. Rather, he established a relationship, in which his superiority was acknowledged ever after by tokens of remembrance, in the form of labor, support, and ritual homage, just as all humans owed such tokens to the gods, to whom the land ultimately belonged. Surely it was such a relationship that they imagined themselves to be creating with the colonial government. As for relinquishing salvage rights, Lekkerkerker is probably correct in claiming that Bali's rulers believed that in exchange for this concession they would obtain something of equal value—although given that the colonial government had made a treaty with the ruler of Lombok, it seems implausible that they still had hopes of Dutch help against him. In any event the Balinese could hardly imagine that the Dutch were asking for something for nothing.

Quite apart from their content, one must wonder how the Balinese regarded the whole matter of treaties. Balinese princes did sometimes make written vows with one another regarding specific matters of mutual concern (such as the disposition of cows that wandered across borders; see Liefrinck 1915). But important vows would be made verbally, in ceremonies witnessed by Brahmana priests and gods, with supernatural sanctions lasting through generations should the oath taker prove false. Signing a piece of paper had little cultural significance; indeed, the Déwa Agung signed such documents with a stamp.

Colonial administrators, however, were rarely concerned with the interpretation of cultures, especially when what was at issue was the violation of a contract. But there is evidence that what led the Dutch to take military action was less the legal rationality of promises than the colonial logic of prestige. Whenever colonial officials came into face-to-face contact with Balinese rulers, they were treated as inferiors. In 1845, for example, Balinese ordered the Resident of Besuki (the East Javanese Residency responsible for Balinese and Lombok affairs) down from the palanquin on which he had been carried from his ship as he neared the residence of Buléléng's prince. Moreover, envoys of all ranks in the colonial service still found themselves seated below Balinese rulers. According to Schulte Nordholt, what finally precipitated a declaration of war was yet another affront: Gusti Ketut Jelantik spat on the passport of a merchant traveling under the Netherlands Indies flag. As the Governor General wrote to the Minister of Colonies, urging a military expedition: "Such insults must be avenged or it is over with our authority in India."[48] There was, of course, no recognition of any insults to the Balinese.

THE BALI EXPEDITIONS AND THE POWER OF KLUNGKUNG

The First Bali Expedition was intended to be a limited campaign, a "punitive" action, as colonial governments like to describe such affairs, against Buléléng alone. Buléléng's ruler agreed to come to terms after Dutch guns demolished his residence in Singaraja. So there could be no misunderstandings, the new treaties the Dutch drew up for Buléléng and Karangasem were written in Balinese as well as Malay and Dutch, and they included some new clauses: a pledge to send a delegation to the Governor General in Batavia immediately, and an agreement to abolish "slavery" in their realms (Arsip Nasional 1964: 87–96, 112–20).

Defeat, however, did not have the salutary effect the Dutch expected.

The treaties were not only ignored, but Buléléng's rulers began to stockpile weapons and build fortifications at Jagaraga, outside of Singaraja, in preparation for a renewed engagement.[49] Clearly, Buléléng's rulers did not share the colonial assumption that Dutch victory established their authority once and for all.

The expedition also forced the Dutch to take a closer look at Balinese political relations, especially the role played by the Déwa Agung. The Déwa Agung had mustered troops from his most reliable supporters to go to Buléléng's aid—three thousand from Gianyar; three thousand from Mengwi; five thousand from Karangasem; with another two thousand from Klungkung itself—and sent one of his own relatives to command them.[50] Noting this, a Dutch rear admiral wrote: "The influence of the Dewa Agong on the political affairs of Baly is greater than earlier reports led one to suppose, and . . . therefore negotiations will only be able to be conducted with the Dewa Agong." The advice was ignored, and an 1849 report by the commander of the Third Bali Expedition repeats almost exactly the same words: "The influence of the Dewa Agung in Bali is greater than was generally supposed."[51]

From the government's point of view, however, the Déwa Agung's authority was far too ambiguous. While he had rallied troops to fight in Buléléng, not all of Bali's realms contributed soldiers. That Gusti Ngurah Kesiman in Badung, the ruler best known to the Dutch, was among the dissenters tended to bias colonial administrators, who drew what seemed to them obvious conclusions about the limits of Klungkung's power. And the colonial government's major source at this point was Mads Lange, who had his own interests in Balinese affairs and colonial policy.

Lange had been appointed the official political agent of the Netherlands Indies government in 1843, at which time George King received the same position on Lombok. Lange performed those duties while simultaneously serving as Gusti Ngurah Kesiman's harbormaster. Although he had once boasted to Huskus Koopman of his intimacy with the Déwa Agung, their relationship had deteriorated. His reports to the colonial administration presented the Déwa Agung as, on the one hand, a dangerous and incorrigible enemy of the Dutch, to be subdued at all costs, and, on the other, as a figure whose authority within Bali was dubious and only maintained by a kind of reign of terror.[52] And of course the other colonial agent, George King, had long been harbormaster for the ruler of Mataram. King went so far as to advise the Dutch that

> with a people who use such a tortuous policy as the Balinese, and particularly the court of the present Dewah Agong, it is more than useless to attempt to do anything by negotiation. The only way is for Government as soon as they are able by force of arms to depose the present

Dewah Agong and Rajah of Buleleng and Karangasem and replace them by Rajahs who will come into the view of Government.[53]

But Lange was honest enough, and knew enough about Bali, that he could not help but report information that contradicted his own allegations. Thus while he claimed that Bangli, Badung, and Tabanan did not acknowledge the Déwa Agung's "power in the government of the island," when the Dutch were considering whether to make Klungkung a target of their second expedition, Lange noted that the rulers of those three realms "may not like to go against Klonkong" before hastening to assure them that "when Padang Cove [Karangasem] is taken, I do not think there will be much more fighting." He also reported that even the ruler of Mataram went so far as to warn the Déwa Agung in late 1846 that the Dutch were planning to attack Kusamba and that he should fortify.[54] One might call this group of rulers disobedient, perhaps, but not rebellious.

Indeed, it was not that they wanted to oppose the Déwa Agung but that Dutch actions against Buléléng and Karangasem stood to advance other interests. The problem was that the Déwa Agung's favorites were their enemies. If the Déwa Agung was the "father of Bali," he was contending with a bad case of sibling rivalry.

Badung, of course, had long held a grudge against the Karangasem bloc. But an additional issue was at stake: Badung's rulers were reluctant to forego the benefits deriving from their good relations with the Dutch when these conflicted with obedience to what they did not dare to deny was the power represented by Klungkung. Lange's report to the Resident of Banyuwangi on a series of exchanges between the Déwa Agung and Kesiman shows the terms in which their conflicts were aired. It began when the Déwa Agung wrote to Kesiman to enlist his support. In response, Lange wrote, Kesiman had said:

[If the Déwa Agung] would make all Bally one and establish peace among all the Rajahs and the Government of Java, he [Kesiman] then had no objection to be bound with Klonkong.

This was actually a rather ingenuous remark. The Déwa Agung had already tried to "make all Bally one." A month before, Lange reported that the Déwa Agung had made efforts to reconcile with the ruler of Bangli, but Kesiman had intervened. Then the Déwa Agung approached Tabanan; this time Lange blocked negotiations.[55] Clear at this point that the key to creating a united front against the Dutch was Badung, the Déwa Agung was going to the source. But Kesiman was no fool. As I read his remarks, he was challenging the Déwa Agung to prove his *kasaktian*. After all, if he could master the Dutch without fighting them outright, and establish complete harmony in

Bali besides, would this not show the Déwa Agung to be a king of peerless power, an absolute master of the forces of the cosmos?

The Déwa Agung's response was couched precisely in terms of his relationship to the invisible world, and—if we can take Lange at face value—it rather worried Kesiman:

> The next request from the Dewah Agong to the Rajah Caseeman was to drive me and all Europeans out of the Island, and that he would on his part exterminate you from Buleleng, that the gods of Bally demanded it.
>
> Raja Casseeman sent for me and explained this and I could perceive that they are confounded and do not know what to do.—He would not promise me protection but said he would wait for another letter from the Dewah Agong, and I really believe the old man is becoming so afraid that he will have to send us all away—.[56]

Kesiman had reason to be concerned. When he swore oaths to support the Déwa Agung and defend him against enemies in both 1829 and 1837, he invited the gods to shower him with catastrophes should he go back upon his word (Korn 1922:98–102). But eventually Kesiman found a way to respond to this threat; he told Lange that he wrote to the Déwa Agung:

> If the Dewah Agong wished to exterminate the Europeans from Balli; that when he had driven them away from Bleleling, he could easily get them away from Badong, as they would leave themselves—But Rajah Casseeman expressed a wish that the Dewah Agong would reconcile all Bally at first and afterwards with the Nederlands Government and that he and myself would assist him as much as lay in our power—
>
> Rajah Casseeman then told me, that if the Dewah Agong would not take his advice, he would not care for him or his orders. . . . Rajah Casseeman has heard from Klonkong that the Rajahs of Bleleling and Carang Assam have sent their contracts to the Dewah Agong to be kept by him; for they will not have anything to do with them, or the contents. It is likely the Dewah Agong letting Casseeman know this, wishes him to do the same with his Contract with Government.[57]

Kesiman's boldness should not be taken as agnosticism. The vows he signed had been conditional: he would revere and defend the Déwa Agung *if* he ensured the prosperity of the island. Buléléng's defeat suggested that at the moment the Déwa Agung's relations with Divinity were not, perhaps, so secure. It was even possible that their victory meant that the gods approved of the Dutch presence. Such defiance was a gamble, but there were reasons to risk it.

Lange notes that the Déwa Agung's only response to this missive was to order Kesiman to appear before him in Klungkung. Kesiman declined, excusing himself on the grounds that he was deaf and unable to hear—undoubtedly intended and understood allegorically. Lange claimed that he himself lived in fear of his life.[58] In the end Kesiman did go (Schulte Nordholt 1981:41), although there is no information on what transpired during his audience and what its immediate effects were.

The Resident, however, did not respond to Lange's reports as Lange expected. Instead he advised the Governor General to conquer Bali and then establish the Déwa Agung as supreme prince to administer it on behalf of the colonial government. But neither the Governor General nor the Minister of Colonies approved of such a costly plan.[59] Instead, they ordered a Second Bali Expedition, to "chastise" Buléléng and Karangasem. And to ensure that there was no further trouble, the Déwa Agung was included among their targets.

The Third Bali Expedition

It was not in fact until 1849 that Klungkung was attacked, for the Second Bali Expedition, launched in June 1848, was an unmitigated disaster for the colonial government. Forced to march inland to engage the Balinese at Jagaraga, the Dutch were bested by the unfamiliar terrain, a shortage of drinking water, and a well-organized defense. Many colonial soldiers collapsed from illness; others ran off in a panic.

The Dutch took this defeat as a terrible loss of face. As described by a later military historian, to be bested by an army of "natives" put their reputation at risk all over Indonesia (Arntzenius 1874:6). Preparations for a new expedition began almost immediately. It was the largest military expedition in the archipelago to date (van der Kraan, personal communication): twelve thousand men were dispatched to Bali, under the command of General Michiels, who had won the war against the Padris in Sumatra and, as civil commander of West Sumatra, became the first colonial official to lock horns with a young civil servant named Edouard Douwes Dekker, who immortalized him in a savage portrait in his novel *Max Havelaar*.

Michiels routed the Balinese at Jagaraga, although Buléléng's prince and chief minister fled to Karangasem, and various rulers quickly tried to turn the Dutch victory to their advantage, promising alliances to further their own political agendas: Gusti Ngurah Kesiman sent a request that he be allowed to conquer Mengwi, and a delegation from the ruler of Lombok promised eight thousand men for any action the Dutch might take against Karangasem. Déwa Gedé Tangkeban of Bangli came with a large entourage to offer his "submission" to Michiels, although Bangli had never been in any danger of attack; declaring himself a Dutch "ally," he told Michiels that he had already taken the liberty of occupying some Karangasem villages just over his border, and asked permission to reclaim several others that had once been under his authority. This was given in exchange for a promise of military aid against Karangasem and Klungkung, although in the event, he did not deliver (Arntzenius 1874:43–47).

Michiels was apparently much taken with Déwa Gedé Tangkeban, so much so that he proposed that once Klungkung was defeated, he appoint him as Déwa Agung. Interestingly Déwa Gedé Tangkeban refused the honor. Not only did he claim that Bali's other princes would never accept this, but he argued that Dutch interests would best be served by letting the present ruler of Klungkung retain his position (Weitzel 1859:128–29). News of this conversation reached the rulers of Badung and Tabanan, however, and alarmed them enough to shape their later actions.

Michiels then proceeded to move against Karangasem. He informed the ruler of Lombok that he would accept his aid, and four thousand soldiers were dispatched from Lombok immediately (with promises of more when necessary) to meet Michiels's forces at Padang Cove in Karangasem, just over Klungkung's border. Michiels's luck improved still further when Karangasem's chief minister and several other Karangasem lords volunteered their help against their ruler. Abandoned by his followers, Karangasem's ruler was killed by the advance guard of the Lombok troops, along with Gusti Ketut Jelantik and the ruler of Buléléng. All that remained was Klungkung.

The Campaign against Klungkung

The attack on Klungkung has been extensively narrativized by Dutch military historians, including a number of officers who took part in the Third Expedition. Michiels's army set off along the beach from Padang Cove. Not far into Klungkung, they reached the temple Goa Lawah (see fig. 6), which they found fortified and occupied by Balinese soldiers. After a heated battle, the Balinese withdrew west. With Goa Lawah secured, the Dutch marched to Kusamba, where they again engaged with Balinese troops. By the time the Balinese retreated, it was late in the day, and Michiels ordered a bivouac in the market place, next to Kusamba's puri, where his exhausted troops could quarter for a night's rest.

This they were not to have, for at 2:30 A.M. an outpost was attacked. Alarms went up throughout the bivouac, and soldiers awoke to noisy confusion and the glare of raging fires. Under cover of the chaos and darkness, a group of Balinese managed to penetrate to where Michiels stood with his staff, issuing orders. Shots suddenly rang out of the shadows, and Michiels fell to the ground, wounded in his right thigh by a large-caliber bullet. He was carried back to the ships at Padang, where his leg was amputated in an effort to save his life. But the wound proved fatal; by sundown Michiels was dead.

Michiels's death was a serious blow to the Dutch. The morale of the troops was already frayed by the length of the campaign (close to eight weeks), the relentless heat, and dysentery; new cases of illness were reported daily. Subtracting those who had been left to safeguard Buléléng or were incapacitated, only twenty-five hundred men of the original force were left at Kusamba. Under the circumstances van Swieten, Michiels's second in command, decided not to proceed with an attack on Klungkung, which would have entailed marching without guides across unknown terrain. The battles at Kusamba had also used up a considerable amount of ammunition. After sending word of Michiels's death to Java and asking for further instructions, he returned with the army to Padang (Arntzenius 1874:67–68).

So that the Déwa Agung would not think that the Dutch withdrawal from Kusamba was due to his night attack, however, van Swieten sent him a letter via Gusti Gedé Rai, the leader of the Lombok troops. He was informed that with the capture of Kusamba the Dutch had succeeded in punishing him for his "perfidious actions" (Weitzel 1859:177) and that the Dutch

> had also completely triumphed in the last attack. That, however, the Netherlands government, to prevent further bloodshed and to spare the Dewa Agong other disasters, still offered to him, as a noble enemy, a chance to submit. That he would then remain on the throne and enjoy the advantages of the peace, but in the opposite case, should satisfactory answer to this offer not be received within eight days, the army would march again toward Klongkong, united with the Lombok force, to dethrone the Prince and punish him terribly (Arntzenius 1874:78).

What the Déwa Agung made of this is hard to say. He responded by requesting a meeting between Gusti Gedé Rai and his own representatives— Cokorda Rai[60] and the rulers of Mengwi and Gianyar. At the meeting they seemed willing to make peace and agreed to attend a gathering of Balinese princes at Padang some days later. But van Swieten also learned that after the fall of Kusamba the Déwa Agung had ordered the rulers of Badung and Tabanan to assist him with troops. Furthermore, according to reports, Déwa Agung Isteri Kania opposed any peace with the Dutch and was supported by a certain Déwa Ketut Agung (identified as the *rijksbestierder*) and the ruler of Gianyar (Weitzel 1859:180–81).

Plans for the meeting, however, miscarried. On Gusti Gedé Rai's advice, van Swieten had sent the Déwa Agung a letter of safe conduct (written in Arabic letters and sewn into an envelope of yellow silk), only to receive on the following day a note signed by Déwa Ketut Agung declaring that neither the Déwa Agung nor any representatives would be coming to the meeting and that he found it highly improper that van Swieten had summoned him (Weitzel 1859:182). Accompanying it was a letter from the ruler of Gianyar, who announced he too would not attend the meeting. One of these notes (according to Weitzel, the *rijkbestierder's*; according to Arntzenius, the ruler of Gianyar's) added that if van Swieten wanted peace he should ask the Déwa Agung's forgiveness for attacking and destroying Kusamba (and, according to Arntzenius, pay for repairs to Goa Lawah). Clearly, the letter of safe conduct had been misinterpreted. Van Swieten's response, however, was to take up arms again.

The Dutch had retaken Goa Lawah and Kusamba and were about to set out for Klungkung when Mads Lange appeared to inform van Swieten that Gusti Ngurah Kesiman and the ruler of Tabanan had arrived in Klungkung the previous day with sixteen thousand men to urge the Déwa Agung to make peace and were prepared to fulfill their earlier promises by serving as mediators at the meeting at Padang. Lange warned van Swieten that with their arrival there were now thirty-three thousand men in Klungkung prepared to fight to the death to protect the Déwa Agung. Indeed, when van Swieten's representative accompanied Lange back to Klungkung he found the Déwa Agung and his priests preparing for "a great Amok":

> This Amok would have consisted, that all of his followers, armed with lances and kris would have thrown themselves on the enemy and sought death; a fanatical action, that on our side would also have cost a multitude of lives, leaving aside that, given the terribly superior power of the enemy the consequences could have been of an even more serious nature for our army (Arntzenius 1874:91).

Kesiman's involvement was motivated by concern over Dutch plans for Bali in the event Klungkung was conquered; he had no wish to see the ruler of Bangli appointed Susuhunan by the colonial government. The Déwa Agung's orders had made an impression on him too, but he had come to attempt to convince the Déwa Agung to make peace with the Dutch (Weitzel 1859:128–29); still he would hardly turn against him, in the event the Dutch attacked.

Fortunately the Déwa Agung was willing to be conciliatory. He even agreed to dispatch a legation to Batavia, to beg the Governor General's forgiveness for insulting the colonial government. With this, the war was over. The meeting at Padang was attended by Kesiman, the rulers of Gianyar and Mengwi, and a host of Klungkung and other Balinese notables. The Dutch were represented by Duke Bernhard van Saksen-Weimar-Eisenbach, who announced that the insult offered to the Dutch had been forgiven. As a reward for their aid, the colonial government appointed Bangli's ruler raja of Buléléng and placed Karangasem under a prince from Lombok. As for the rest, they were invited to Mads Lange's house in Kuta to sign new treaties. With the exception of the Déwa Agung, who sent Déwa Agung Ketut Agung (identified in the treaty as the probable heir to the throne),[61] all came, each with an enormous entourage, and were housed and fed at Lange's expense.

There are several things worth noting about the Kusamba War.

The first is the constitution of the legation that the Déwa Agung sent to Batavia. Like all Klungkung legations, including those to other Balinese rulers, it consisted mainly of Brahmanas, including a priest. In addition, like later Klungkung embassies to Batavia, these men were accompanied by high-ranking persons from outside of Klungkung itself. The members of this particular embassy are identified by Arntzenius as "Ida Noman Pedanda [a priest] and Ida Wayan Bagoes [an unconsecrated Brahmana] of Klonkong; Ida Noman Rai, Ida Noman Maas [both Brahmanas], and Pembukkel Toeban [a lower official] of Badong; Ida Made Jaksa of Tabanan ["Jaksa" indicates judicial functions]; and Dewa Noman Rai and Goetie Poetae Getassan of Gianjar [merely high-ranking nobles]" (Arntzenius 1874:91; explanations mine).

The second point is that even at the signing of the new treaty, the Déwa Agung did not appear himself but sent a representative. In this he is absolutely distinct from anyone else involved in these events. Indeed, his representatives include other rulers: thus the rulers of Mengwi and Gianyar met on his behalf with the leaders of the Lombok troops.

Third, for all of their purported enmity, the rulers of Badung and Tabanan did not take the Dutch side against Klungkung. Certain accounts of the Kusamba War make much of their arrival on the scene, even claiming that they forced the Déwa Agung to surrender (Schulte Nordholt 1981). In fact they helped protect the Déwa Agung, and had Lange been unsuccessful in convincing van Swieten to stop his attack, they would have joined in his defense, along with troops from Gianyar, Mengwi, and Klungkung itself. The sheer number of men massed in Klungkung is itself significant: it was probably the largest army ever assembled in Bali. And finally, the legation the Déwa Agung sent to Batavia to honor his promise to van Swieten included representatives not only from Klungkung and its ally Gianyar but also from Tabanan and Badung.

It is worth noting the role Goa Lawah played in Dutch representations of the war. Arntzenius identifies it as "the most revered sanctuary on Bali" (1874: 58), and Weitzel as "the oldest" (1859:150). Such rhetoric, of course, advertised their victory there as significant, especially if the Déwa Agung were Bali's "spiritual overlord."

Goa Lawah was certainly an important temple, arguably the most important in Klungkung. It was under the king's care, and a favorite place for powerful men to *nakti*. But Bali's "most revered sanctuary" was of course not Goa Lawah but Besakih, to which (to be sure) Goa Lawah had connections. At this time, however, colonial officers knew little about Balinese temples. While

Friederich (1959 [1849–50]) mentions Besakih as one of the great temples of Bali (the so-called Sad Kahyangan), the first outsider to visit it was a Javanese, in 1871 (Stuart-Fox 1987:339; Sasrowidjaya 1875:64).

Military historians were probably right, however, in thinking Goa Lawah was important to Klungkung's defense. According to stories told in Klungkung a century and a half later, the nearby border was defended by *bala samar*, spirit armies. That the Dutch managed to get past them suggested that something more was needed—a weapon named I Seliksik.

SEVEN

The Kusamba War

When they [General Michiels and the Dutch forces] arrived in the harbor [Padang Cove] he said: "We must also attack Klungkung. If Klungkung is not defeated, we cannot defeat Bali. Because it is said that Klungkung is the king of kings." Thus half of the army went to Padang Bai and from there to Klungkung. The other half went with the army from Lombok; Lombok joined in helping the Dutch crush Karangasem. Klungkung's strength was at Goa Lawah, Klungkung's army was at Goa Lawah. There was a furious fight there. It was late afternoon and the Dutch forces kept advancing, until they arrived at Kusamba. It is said that by late afternoon many Balinese had died, and the Balinese retreated. At night the Dutch made a bivouac, a place to sleep. The king of Klungkung then gave orders. That night they attacked Kusamba. Then Anak Agung—what was his name, from here, from Puri Kelodan, Anak Agung Sangging. He was the one who was ordered to investigate things in Kusamba. To attack Kusamba and look for the general. He went with someone from here, I Tagog was his name. That was the one who carried the rifle, the *pusaka* rifle of Klungkung. The rifle was named I Seliksik The southern portion of the bivouac was burned down. The rifles were firing—*dar, dar!*—like that. Anak Agung Sangging went to the north to see where . . . Probably the general wore epaulettes. He ordered Tagog to shoot. *Tak!* The general was hit. This was hit, his leg. His leg was hit. His thigh. He was immediately brought to the ship. "The bullet [wound] is here. How is it possible that . . . What is this? It's as if his whole body were wounded." As a result, on the ship he died. (Interview, Ida Bagus Rai Pidada, Geria Pidada Klungkung, 16 March 1985)

The elderly gentleman who told me this story got much of it from reading what was available to him of Dutch accounts of the Third Bali Expedition. A former civil servant, he preferred to speak Indonesian, considered himself "modern," and mainly trusted only written sources. His version of the events of the Kusamba War is thus not very different from colonial ones, and much of what he mentions is not generally part of Klungkung narratives.[1]

Yet despite his respect for books, he did not take them as his sole authority for reconstructing history. At first glance he seems to speak strictly within the canons of European historical practice, relying on local lore only to identify the major Balinese actors on the scene: the nobleman, Anak Agung Sangging, who led the Balinese forces, and the commoner, I Tagog, who actually fired the rifle that killed the Dutch general. It is in speaking of that rifle, however, that he diverges radically from European historiography.

As will be seen, the more common opinion in Klungkung is that it was actually the bullet that was named I Seliksik. In insisting upon the fact that a rifle was the puri heirloom (and he was quite insistent), Ida Bagus Rai was trying to reconcile Klungkung oral tradition with his colonial education, for some of the claims made about Klungkung's magic bullets—that they were alive, that they could return on their own—struck him as improbable.[2] But he nonetheless could not accept Dutch claims that the general was killed by an unfortunate mishap: accidentally hit by a stray bullet. Instead, Michiels's death—which is narrativized in Klungkung as a Klungkung victory—is attributed to the power of the court and its heirloom weapons.

In a sense the mere fact that the general was killed by a bullet wound implies that the ultimate cause of his death was Klungkung's ruler, since Balinese accounts suggest that all of the guns in the realm really "belonged" to the king, who gave the right to carry and use them to specified favorites. But Ida Bagus Rai's story goes further: it was not just any gun or any bullet that killed the general, but a named heirloom, a *pajenengan*, one of that limited class of objects that instantiated royal power. And here he no longer concerns himself with European criteria of plausibility. The damage inflicted by this weapon is extraordinary: European surgeons could not explain why with only one external wound the general's entire body appeared to have been traumatized. We are in the realm of the magical.

The mysterious weapon that killed the Dutch general—who is generally referred to as I Bintang Tujuh, a mixed Balinese and Malay phrase that translates as "Mr. Seven Stars"—is the focal point of Klungkung tales concerning the Third Bali Expedition, locally known as the Kusamba War. In some ways tales about the war are a mere footnote to stories about I Seliksik.

Before considering these narratives in detail, it is worth a brief look at another account. The narrator of this one, I Madé Regeg, was formerly head of the village in which Goa Lawah is located. His tale, spare and succinct, highlights just what struck people as worth remembering about those long-ago events:

> The Kusamba War, wasn't that the Dutch? Who started the war? I don't
> . . . I'll tell you [the story], I don't know it very well, but . . . At that time
> wasn't it I Déwa Agung . . . ? It was Déwa Agung Isteri Kania who was

the leader of that war. She was accepted as leader. I Déwa Agung Isteri
Kania. Now [Kusamba] had already been defeated by the Dutch. They
built temporary shelters there, the Dutch. She . . . who knows what she
was thinking/intending, she said to attack again, at night. At night. So
they went right there, to the middle [of the bivouac]. That's why he died,
the Dutch lieutenant [sic], Mr. Seven Stars. What was his name? That
one. There was an attack there. He was moved to . . . They moved to
Padang Bai, the Dutch. Didn't they already control Padang Bai? They had
surrendered in Karangasem. That's what I know, only that much. It was
[the weapon] I Seliksik that killed Mr. Seven Stars. At Kusamba. (Interview, Pasinggahan, 24 May 1986)

The first thing worth noticing is what is *not* mentioned: the presence of
troops from all over Bali ready to aid the besieged Déwa Agung. Yet their presence was a reflex of Klungkung's centrality. Why is it excluded from Klungkung history making?

It has been omitted for the same reason that other events—particularly
the death of General Michiels—have been highlighted. The Kusamba War is
important to Klungkung historiography as a demonstration of the *kasaktian* of
the royal dynasty. From such a perspective the troops were redundant: anyone
with the capacity to invoke invisible forces as spectacularly as Klungkung's
rulers did would naturally have no trouble attracting the loyalty of mere humans. Indeed, to talk of such troops would undermine the rhetorical force of
imagining Klungkung as a small and defenseless David miraculously capable
of defeating the apparently invincible Goliath of its enemies.

Moreover, from a Klungkung perspective, it was not the arrival of more
soldiers that won the war but the death of the general. To hierarchically
minded Balinese it is only common sense that to paralyze an enemy you need
only destroy his leader. This way of thinking was not, of course, so far from
that of similarly hierarchically minded European military men, and the loss of
Michiels was indeed demoralizing. And Michiels was killed by a bullet wound
delivered by Klungkung troops, not by the concerted action of companies of
extra-Klungkung soldiers, many of whom arrived on the scene after Michiels
was killed.

It is not, then, surprising that I Madé Regeg mentions the death of Mr.
Seven Stars (again crediting it to I Seliksik), or even the name of the ruler
responsible. But note that Madé Regeg emphasizes that Déwa Agung Isteri
Kania ordered an attack at night. Memories of such small details are never
arbitrary; the cultural motivations for this one are particularly significant.

According to Balinese rules of warfare, battles must be held in daylight,
with Betara Surya, the sun, as witness. To attack an enemy at night, then, was
highly unusual. There is, however, something Balinese call a "night war,"

usually with sinister connotations: magical battles between sorcerers or other persons of power to demonstrate which is the more *sakti*. The fact that Klungkung's victory over the Dutch came through a nighttime battle associates it with such events. And so does the focus of all of the stories: the weapon I Seliksik.

I SELIKSIK: NARRATIVES

The narratives I was told concerning I Seliksik make a series of culturally meaningful claims about Klungkung *kasaktian* and the Dutch. Presenting them all at once suggests how allusive and complex those claims are.

Anak Agung Jelantik, Puri Sunianegara in Klungkung:

> Before the realm was destroyed, how many times had the Dutch come here, planning to attack, and they couldn't. They couldn't. The head of the Dutch soldiers, one even died here.
>
> DAYU ALIT: What killed him?
>
> He was hit by one of those, a royal weapon, and he died. It was named Betara I Seliksik. It was a bullet, that one. Round.
>
> DAYU ALIT: Did you ever hear a story about the origins of I Seliksik?
>
> That one? It came from Above, that one. The graciousness of the gods came down. If there was a weapon made of metal, with a long shaft or handle [like a lance], it wasn't allowed to touch Mother Earth [Ibu Perthiwi]. If it touched Mother Earth, the land would sway. In those days.
>
> DAYU ALIT: Where did the king get such gifts?
>
> He would go at night to Besakih. Wherever there was a powerful [*tenget*] temple that was under his authority, Ida Betara Dalem would go there and pray. When Bali was still firm [i.e., before the Dutch conquest; see chapter 9]. (Interview, 20 November 1985)

Anak Agung Ngurah, Puri Nyalian (Aan),[3] a *topéng* performer:

> Wherever there was an enemy, it [i.e., I Seliksik] would just [go there], but you had to tell it . . . and it would just [go off].
>
> DAYU ALIT: What was its shape?
>
> Its shape? A bullet. There was a rifle, wasn't Seliksik the bullet? [It was] like I Tanda Langlang, the keris. But it would be red at the time that . . . when it had killed someone. That's why when the keris was seen by Ida Dalem Ilé, "I Tanda Langlang is red, did he kill someone? Go and look." (Interview, 28 February 1986)

Pak Morag, Klungkung, an elderly commoner, for a time chauffeur to the last king:

I Seliksik? It was a gun, it belonged to the lords here. This was told to me
by my fathers. The guns couldn't sound. Before the Dutch conquered
Klungkung, whenever they were going to come here to attack, the whole
shipload of Dutch soldiers could become ill. If they would make war,
none of their weapons would work. They would be silent. Dead. The Balinese guns could work. But then it was time for Klungkung to be defeated, right . . .

MW: So before that the puri's weapons were *sakti?*

Are you kidding? All of them were extremely *sakti*. Like the one named
I Seliksik, the gun Seliksik. It could look for the enemy. It would *nyeliksik*,
move about until it found what it was seeking.

MW: Oh, do you know that story?

Yes, I was told about that by my father when I was small. All the king
had to do was just look at the boat, and they didn't dare to land. They
would come down with all kinds of illness, they would vomit and have
diarrhea. (Interview, Banjar Meregan, 24 February 1986)

Anak Agung Oka, Puri Kanginan, Klungkung:

When Déwa Agung Isteri was informed the enemy was approaching, she
ordered Lobar and another *pajenengan* to be brought to the forecourt of
the puri. She sat in the palace and directed a *mantra pangastawa* [ritual in-
vocation]. A light emerged from the weapons of such force that the sky
turned orange-red as if in flames. There is a small river near Pura Goa
Lawah called the River Banges [Sharp Smell] that began to emit a stench
like a rotting corpse. The Dutch soldiers who tried to cross it couldn't.
They began to vomit and have diarrhea. Some died; others ran away.
(Fieldnotes, p. 837)

Gusti Lanang Mangku, Jero Selat. Member of a noble family whose ancestors
served as village headmen for several generations; the ancestor sent to Selat
was given a keris by the king as a token of his authority. Gusti Pekak himself
was a healer:

As for stories [*orti-orti*], there are lots of things I have heard. There was an
heirloom [*pajenengan*] named I Seliksik. It is said to have been the most
important one. That's why, at the time of the war . . . Now I will tell the
story, it's just a story. The *pajenengan* named I Seliksik, when it would go
about it made a noise like someone walking through mud.

IDA BAGUS JAGRI: What did it look like?

It was a dagger. A keris. If you told it to do something, it would obey.
"Go!" And it would go. It involved knowledge/power [*kaadnyanan*].

IDA BAGUS JAGRI: What kind of *kaadnyanan?*

Wasn't it a gift? A gift from Ida Sang Hyang Embang [Divine Emptiness].

It just came probably. The reason why it came, weren't there words from the old days [i.e., textual instructions concerning how to obtain such a thing]? God was gracious then, not like nowadays. Even nowadays s/he is gracious, but in a different way.

IDA BAGUS JAGRI: So it wasn't made by a person?

No.

IDA BAGUS JAGRI: Meaning . . . someone who can't be seen gave it to the king. But only he knew about it, that's your interpretation, right?

Yes, that's it. But no one knew. (Interview, 13 January 1986)

Ida Pedanda Gedé Kenitén, Geria Gedé Kenitén, Dawan Kelod. Court priest to the last king, from a line of court priests (his ancestor is mentioned by Friederich). He is famed for his own *kasaktian;* in addition to having initiated many priests, he is a renowned healer:

(a) My father here cleaned them and rubbed them with oil, the royal heirlooms. The one named . . . those bullets, the ones named I Seliksik . . . When the time came to clean them, he was the one who did it. The keris as well. There was no one else. They were cleaned with holy water. . . . The pouch in which I Seliksik was kept would often be partly empty. Then the next time [he took it down] there would be many. [But] in the rafters two of them would be discovered, covered with blood. That's what it was like.

DAYU ALIT: What was I Seliksik kept in?

A pouch, made of cloth. Moreover, the pouch was ripped, it wasn't whole. You would have expected what was in it to fall out. And you'd find some in the rafters. They had gone out. They would be bloody, and offerings would be made to purify them. (Interview, 10 March 1985)

(b) *Nah,* this is still "it is said." My father told me they were given to Betara Dalem [see chapter 8] at Pura Klotok by a *regék tunggék.* My father also told me about their container. It was full of holes, a pouch. It wasn't whole and intact. But nothing fell out of it. At the time . . . *nah,* wherever they were going to go, no one had to actually shoot them, they would take off by themselves. After they came [back], they would stay in the rafters,[4] covered with blood. That's why whenever he would clean and oil them my father would say: "*Béh,* there is this much blood, where could they have possibly gone?"

DAYU ALIT: Were there many, do you remember?

If I am not wrong in remembering his words, there were no more than a hundred bullets. They were round, he said. But after being cleaned and oiled, they would be yellow, like fine bronze.

DAYU ALIT: Where did they come from?

As I said earlier, they were a gift . . . a gift from . . . The one who gave them was from Klotok. That was the place. They were given to the king. He . . . *nah*, wasn't he *sakti?* He liked to *nyéwa seraya* [go to temples at night]. That's where he got them. He was told to take them from the [spirit's] back . . . from the hollow.

MW: Why were they known as I Seliksik?

The reason they were given such a name was because . . . This is a "probably," if you want an off-the-cuff conjecture. [Because] you didn't have to shoot them. Wherever [the enemy was] they would find them, they would look for the enemy. Then they would return, bloody. My father would then have offerings made to purify them. Like during, what's it called, the death of . . . Mr. Seven Stars. Isn't it said to have been I Seliksik who got him?

MW: I don't know.

That's right. I too am just telling you the story. Bringing stories. (Interview, 28 March 1985)

Anak Agung Anom, Puri Gélgél, a student of *babad:*

> I Seliksik was not obtained at a temple, it was manufactured. It was named after a court retainer who offered himself to be used for that purpose. The heart and liver of I Seliksik were mixed with gunpowder. The rifle used to shoot this bullet was I Kalantaka. Some say it was fired from the Kerta Gosa, others from the temple Bukitbuluh; the former is more likely. (Fieldnotes, p. 1036)

Cokorda Oka Lingsir, Puri Anyar, Klungkung:

> Cokorda Raka of Puri Kelodan led the forces at Kusamba. I Seliksik was fired off from the Kerta Gosa. It was brought to the puri by a Buginese, who told the king it needed the blood of a human being to be powerful. A servant [*kaula*] offered his life [*urip*]. After I Seliksik killed the general it returned to the puri, covered with blood. Sometimes there was only one bullet, sometimes as many as a hundred. (Fieldnotes, p. 822)

I Madé Kanta, Klungkung, a commoner whose family had close ties to the court and served as administrators. A *topéng* performer and student of *babad,* he helped write the book on Klungkung's history for the commemoration of the puputan:

> The general was hit in the thigh but the bullet went up to his stomach and he died. I Seliksik was made in Bali, not long before the Kusamba War. In addition to gunpowder it contained human blood, the blood of a temple priest named Grandfather Seliksik. During the reign of Betari Kania [i.e., Déwa Agung Isteri Kania], Grandfather Seliksik came to the court and requested an audience, at which he asked the rulers to take his

life. The queen was astonished, but the priest [*bagawanta*] from Geria Pidada explained that this man was a *patunang*.[5] The king asked what the
temple priest wanted: land, a woman, gold, what? He refused all and said
he only wanted to die, like an animal sacrifice to the demons [*caru*]. He
prayed and was given the offerings proper to a cremation ritual. Then he
was killed by the court executioner [*juru jenggot*].[6] His blood was mixed
with gunpowder and the bullet "lived," moving around all by itself. It was
kept in the storage shrine of the puri's house-temple.

Each time Klungkung was about to go to war there were signs, including the arrival of someone at the puri who would ask to be killed in this
way. When Mengwi was troubled by Balian Batur, its ruler asked Klungkung for a *patunang* and was thus able to defeat the enemy. Before the
puputan there was also such a volunteer, but the bullet that was made was
not *sakti* because the person wasn't pure—he was a thief. (Fieldnotes,
pp. 488–92)

Déwa Nyoman Pater, Klungkung. Member of a branch line of the branch
founded by Déwa Agung Anom in Sukawati. His father was a *punggawa* in the
colonial period. Déwa Aji himself was a student of literature, well known for
his mastery of the art of reciting poetry; he also wrote poems himself:

MW, after a discussion of the puputan: I've heard that Puri Klungkung
was the most *sakti* court in Bali.

It was the most *sakti*, in the old days. In the past. The story goes like
this. There was a *pajenengan* rifle here. Now this is again a lesson [*tutur*]
from my father, okay? Ida Déwa Agung wanted to make a rifle, a *pajenengan* it's called, that would have supernatural qualities [Indonesian, *keramat*],
right, that would be *sakti*. It is said that at that time an Arab came to
court: "There is such material. But it is very difficult."

"Even so, tell me, what is its basis?"

"A person's inner organs. Human innards are the raw material for such
a thing."

"*Bah*, in that case, forget it. Where could you find that?"

It is said there was a court retainer at the time named Grandfather
Mulu [Putrid, Rotten; alternatively, "to have a head"]. He spoke up:
"Why do you say that? I will serve. I will become that ammunition."

"Don't say such things." So, it is said, the Déwa Agung responded.
"Why would you do that?"

"No, allow me to serve. From the purity of my heart."

He was given rituals. He was cremated immediately. His death came
through having his throat cut. His inner organs were taken to be used as
ammunition, so it is said. His name was Grandfather Mulu. At that time,
so it is said, wasn't there a war at Kusamba? On the ship the general was

hit. Hit by that bullet. Afterwards, the bullet returned. At that time Widhi was gracious. That's how it was, it is said. (Interview, 22 April 1986)

Anak Agung Kalam, Puri Satria Kawan; a teacher and well-known performer, best known for his portrayals of wise royal advisors in *drama gong*:

The *pajenengan* I Seliksik, if I am not wrong . . . There was an old man named Grandfather Pulung [Shaped into a Ball] who had lived so long he was bored with living, and yet he couldn't die. He was from Kusamba, from Banjar Bias. No, that's wrong. It was Banjar Pandé [the neighborhood of smiths]. The one furthest west. Banjar Bias is east of Banjar Pandé. Because he had wanted to die for a long time and couldn't . . . I forget also the old man's name. I've heard a specific name. Later, when I have a chance, I will try to find out. This is what he did. He went to the palace in Klungkung and requested an audience with the Déwa Agung. "I ask of you, my lord, the following. I am bored with living. I present myself to you, and ask that you would be so kind as to kill me."

The Déwa Agung thought it over. There was a priest, the king's Brahmana, his helper from Geria Pidada. He was called to the palace. The Déwa Agung weighed things over with him.

"This is excellent, my lord, for something like this to happen. This is a superior person."

So they made a ritual for Grandfather Pulung, a sacrifice with offerings, and he cut his own throat. His blood was caught in a bowl. He cut his own throat, consciously, like this [gestures slitting throat and leaning over].

MW: In the way animals are killed for sacrifices?

Yes, like that. Only he cut his own throat, he wasn't killed by anyone else. Now, his inner organs were taken and mixed with water, and the combination was pounded together. If I am not wrong, it also contained *sendawa* [mushrooms, mold, fungus].

DAYU ALIT: Where did that come from?

Like the fungus that grows on cow dung, on pig dung. It was used as gunpowder. All of this was mixed together. It was pounded and then shaped into balls to be used as ammunition. The place was downstream, near where people are building the bridge, in Tapéan.

DAYU ALIT: On the Unda River?

Yes. There is a place there called Pengobatan [Ammunition]. The place where these bullets were made. It is said that one of them exploded in Lebah, west of the water channel. In approximately the place that I Linggih lives, west of Madé Serogog. That was the place where the bullets were mixed together. To become I Seliksik. After that, to move ahead in the story, they were shaped into balls. They took a *ngiu* [a round, flat bamboo basket], and put the balls into it and turned it in circles around and around like this [i.e., to dry them out]. They were alive, those bullets. They could move about.

MW: Didn't someone recite mantras?

They already contained *adnyanan* [knowledge/power].

DAYU ALIT: Wasn't it when they were mixed together that mantras were put in?

The power came from the thoughts/intentions, the good deeds of Grandfather Pulung, who was a superior person, where could you find someone else like that? Someone that brave, to present himself and cut his own throat. . . . Those bullets were a sign that there was a material realization of Divinity. A sign of Widhi's generosity. They lived. They were what brought victory to Klungkung. Because of them the Dutch couldn't enter. It was close to the time the Dutch were defeated at Kusamba. Governor General [*sic*] Michiels. It was someone from Sulang [a nearby village] who defeated the commander-in-chief. He was named, if I am not mistaken, I Jaya, together with Gusti Alit. This bullet is what they used.

DAYU ALIT: From Sulang?

Yes. It is said . . . The reason it was called I Seliksik is that the bullet was alive. Whoever was the leader of the enemy, whoever was their commander-in-chief, the bullet could remember and look for that person. It didn't kill people at random. It chose. Now that is the meaning of I Seliksik.

DAYU ALIT: It could choose, look purposefully.

Yes. After some time, it was gone, finished.

MW: Oh, finished.

Yes, the ammunition was finished. There was only as much as was necessary . . . the stomach of only one person. It was used up. They made another, using a prisoner. But there was an enormous difference, because the life of that person hadn't been freely given. Indeed, to find someone else like that would be difficult. This is what I have heard concerning the history of why there was I Seliksik, the puri's *pajenengan*. (Interview, 19 January 1986)

Cokorda Isteri Biang Sayang, Puri Anyar Klungkung; daughter of Cokorda Raka Pugog, an important figure in the immediate precolonial period, she was a student of poetry:

Now there were also bullets here, in the old days.

DAYU ALIT: There were bullets?

Bullets. They were made out of a human being. Out of the liver of a

person, his heart and his liver, his gall bladder. Those three. There was a
Daeng who offered the materials.

DAYU ALIT: Who?

A Daeng, from . . . what's it called now, Makassar, what is it now?
Sulawesi. Yes. A Daeng [a noble title among the Buginese] from Sulawesi
often came to audiences at the court. The Déwa Agung asked him about
making such a thing.

"I have the knowledge to make such a thing. However, my lord, you
must provide the main ingredients."

"What?"

"A liver, a heart, and a gall bladder."

"*Béh*, where could you find something like that?" Isn't that what the
Déwa Agung said? Then the king was quiet. "All right. I can do it."

"Déwa Agung, don't go and kill some prisoner. Someone in prison isn't
allowed. Such a person is as if already dead. It isn't allowed, my lord."

However, there was a person who said: "I am ready. To . . ." What's it
called? Lay a foundation for the world . . . "Déwa Agung, I offer my life
to you. I offer my heart, together with my liver and my gall bladder."

DAYU ALIT: Who was it?

The Déwa Agung "owned" him [i.e., he was one of his subjects]. And
then the Déwa Agung spoke: "Why would you want to do that? What's
the problem? What's more, you have a small child. Who is angry at you,
who is causing you trouble?"

"There is nothing like that. Everyone is fine to me. Cokoridewa, you
gave me life. Now I offer that life to you. Out of the purity of my feelings I will lay a foundation for the world."

He was going to . . . what do they call it nowadays, defend his
country.

"If that is really how you feel . . ."

"It is."

"You are not lying?"

"No."

He was made to swear a vow, it was called *macorin* in those days. To
swear an oath. All of the royal priests came to be witnesses . . . He was
to be cremated immediately. He was given a nine-roofed cremation
tower, just like me.[7] He had gone up, become a Satria. A nine-roofed
tower and a bull. He was just a farmer. A commoner, who served at the
puri. He had a child whose mother had died giving birth. He worked at
the puri with his child . . . That's how it was. The king felt sorry for him.

[The commoner said:] "I am giving my lord his slave. He is alive because of my lord. Now let's finish things off here. I will go with my lord."

He became ammunition. Now that's the end of that part of the story [*nyarik*; the active verbal form of *carik*, a mark in a palm-leaf text signaling the end of one topic and beginning of another]. That one, the Daeng, killed him. But the Déwa Agung ordered it. His teeth were brushed, his hair washed, he was ritually purified. He sat down. The Déwa Agung sat here, he sat there. He wasn't allowed to sit on a lower level. That means . . . he was like a kinsman. Even kinsmen weren't allowed to do that. But this one, he was allowed . . . He was killed in the Elephant Pavilion in the palace. He was given pillows to rest his head on, fine ones, all piled up. His throat was cut while he was dressed in fine clothing. His throat was cut with a keris, that's what was used to cut his throat. Whether it was Bangawan Canggu, or Arda Walika . . . in short, an heirloom [*kawitan*] keris, that's what was used to cut his throat.

And then the Daeng looked for his heart, together with his liver and gall bladder. The Daeng worked them up. They were buried at the split in the river for a month and seven days; in the Pura Dalem for a month and seven days; at the main crossroads for a month and seven days. Forty-two days; [to MW:] it's called a month and seven days . . .[8] After that they were taken and brought to the puri's house-temple. They weren't just taken just like that. There were offerings made, the priests recited sacred formulas [*weda*]. Wherever they were brought, from the Pura Dalem [for example], they were treated ceremonially. To bring them to the river. Each important day [the full moon, the new moon, the day known as Kajeng-Kliwon] they were greeted ceremonially, with offerings. A large group would go. Then it was all finished . . . My father said there were nine bullets. They knew how to bathe themselves. They would clean themselves with . . . with water, with fragrant oils. When they were finally clean, they would be still.

"Are you finished bathing? Okay, then come here." That's the way the priest would look for them. He was known as the *juru baru*. He took care of all the gods [i.e., powerful weapons].

A general died, he was cursed here. In Kusamba. [During the attack on the Dutch] Cokorda Gedé Sangging[9] was told to shoot off I Bangké Bai, along with these, the ones we were just talking about, those nine bullets. From here, from the Kerta Gosa. He fired. He was hit, the general. This was hit [patting her thigh], this, the one on the left. He fell down then, his friends came to him. They looked for the bullet, but it kept moving about [inside of him]. If it hadn't yet gotten these, the liver and the heart, [at least] one of them, it wouldn't leave. They were dizzy looking for the bullet. They'd feel it here, and it would vanish, here, all over the place, circling around the body . . . No wounds showed here or here [gesturing around her torso], only here [patting her thigh]. That's the way of those bullets . . . They had to keep going if they hadn't yet gotten the heart and the liver. Then it came home to the main puri once more. That's why it was *sakti*. Isn't that what is called *sakti?* His leg was hit, his left leg was hit, and they couldn't find [the bullet].

[Later] it returned. The priest [*pamangku*] was just about to go someplace, and he didn't get to go anywhere, it kept doing this: *ngueng, ngueng, ngueng* [gestures whirring around overhead]. "Okay, okay, [if you] are going to come down and bathe, okay, okay, come down." Like that. There was a small porcelain bowl . . . a white plate. That's what was used. It was filled with oil, it was very fragrant. I was told by my father. I know that truly, that the smell was very fragrant. (Interview, 14 March, 1985)

Ida Pedanda Gedé Tembau, Geria Aan. A priest with close ties to both the royal family and the government; also an expert on both poetic texts and *babad*:

(a) IDA BAGUS JAGRI: Have you ever heard about a *pajenengan* in the form of ammunition at the time of the Kusamba War?

Ammunition? It was named I Seliksik. It was like a nuclear weapon nowadays. It could be ordered to look for an enemy from your home. It was amazing.

IDA BAGUS JAGRI: What form did it take?

It was a bullet, a round one.

IDA BAGUS JAGRI: That is, that is the shape it took if seen by . . . for example, someone like me, a human.

It was made by a person, someone *sakti*.

PRIEST'S SON: An invisible force made it possible for it to act like that. There was also a gun, made of bamboo.

IDA BAGUS JAGRI: Was the bullet made by hand, or by . . . thought/ desire?

No, [it was made] by a smith. It was manufactured, made by hand, out of metal. However, the kernel . . .

IDA BAGUS JAGRI: The kernel was thought/desire, isn't that right?

Yes, that's it. Who knows what raw materials were used to make it capable of life . . .

IDA BAGUS JAGRI: It was probably similar to . . . excuse me, lord, I don't know. Like making a charm or amulet perhaps, was that it?

Yes, that's it, exactly, that's right. For example, black magic involving magical writing or drawings. Women [often] seek such things. If ordered or carried, one can take the shape of a monkey.

IDA BAGUS JAGRI: Is it true it was made from the liver of a person?

As far as the story goes, that's clear. Exactly like people at the base of a dam . . . It was like that, it is said, that bullet named I Seliksik. It's said that I Seliksik was the name of an old man.

PRIEST'S SON: It's only a story.

It's possible there wasn't such a person . . . *Nah*, whoever they were, all of the witches [*léyak*] in Kusamba. They were the ones who made it. (Interview, 29 November, 1985)

(b) The story of Kusamba. He had seven stars. He was felled by I Seliksik. Finally, they say, he died, being cut open. He died during an operation. Suddenly the bullet would be here. They would cut, and it would show up there. When they cut there, it would show up somewhere else. He passed away. Such was the magic of the bullet belonging to the ruler of Klungkung.

PRIESTESS: It was terrifying. It was a very *sakti* weapon.

DAYU ALIT: Didn't the king have many such weapons?

Yes, he was protected by Divinity. The god of Mount Agung also filled up his protective amulets, gave him *kasaktian* like a god. Like the last Déwa Agung, the one who died just recently, he was also a superior person [i.e., *sakti*]. He usually wouldn't admit he knew things. "No, I don't know anything." He was afraid [i.e., of being arrogant, of having the gods take away his power because he was boastful].

DAYU ALIT: Was I Seliksik obtained by asking for power in a temple?

No, it was made. Someone made the bullet, the ammunition. There was also a rifle. But in order to load that ammunition . . . Now, this is a story my father told me. It was kept in a small covered porcelain bowl, which was brought there to the *balé pengaruman* in the royal house-temple. The rifle was opened [i.e., to be loaded]; if you [ordered I Seliksik] it would go straight into the barrel of the gun. (Interview, 31 January 1986)

Anak Agung Kudar. Daughter of Cokorda Raka Jodog of Puri Kaléran, another important precolonial actor (his father and her grandfather was the secondary ruler during the reign of Déwa Agung Putra III); married to Anak Agung Gaci of Puri Bedulu Klungkung, who was a healer. He was present during many of our conversations and occasionally added comments:

(a) Oh, the ammunition that was named I Seliksik?

ANAK AGUNG GACI: Where could you ask about that now? Widhi sat there [literally, it embodied Widhi].

This is the way that it was, it is said, the reason why it was named I Seliksik. That person offered himself, his throat was cut, it is said. The words of my God [*Betara*], my father. His throat was cut. After his throat was cut . . . *Nah*, I'm going to say something bad. There were two people who were going to offer their breath to him [the king]. That one, it is said that I Seliksik couldn't . . . in short, his penis wasn't limp, that's why he was brave.

ANAK AGUNG GACI: One of them was Grandfather Mulu, Seliksik was earlier.

They took out the liver, the lungs were taken out. The liver and the lungs. They were mixed up together then, with the ingredients to make the ammunition.

DAYU ALIT: His penis wasn't weak, that's what you're saying?

Yes, he was still . . . If a man's penis is flaccid, isn't he afraid? That one, it is said, wasn't weak, that's why he was brave. He became that ammunition, that's how it was according to what my father said. That one, the other one, he was killed and it was weak, it is said . . . He offered himself . . . At the time they were going to be used . . . in short, at the time, it is said, before they were sprinkled with what wasn't what it seemed [see chapter 9] . . . that ammunition I Seliksik couldn't sit still, it is said. Wherever there was going to be a battle, they couldn't sit still, *kratak-krotok* they would mix together by themselves there, together with their friends. After that, *nah*, whatever was going to happen, wherever they were going to attack, whether to the west or to the east, wherever, there was no question they would go straight there. [Quickly lifting her hands, palms together, to her forehead, a prelude to mentioning an ancestor] I ask forgiveness, my Deified Grandfather was the priest [who took care of the bullets]. His grandfather, 'Gung 'Kak's [her husband]. He would clean them. If they had already gone off, if indeed they made a hit, right, they would come home bloody. That's how it was in those days. (Interview, 12 November 1985)

(b) The ammunition was named Pan Mulu, the ammunition. It was a person. The liver of a person together with the lungs of a person became that ammunition. Out of loyalty he offered himself . . . The liver of a person, the liver, together with the lungs, that was used as ammunition.

DAYU ALIT: Wasn't that I Seliksik?

That's just the point, that's what was called I Seliksik. That's what was named the ammunition I Seliksik. He became a *patunang* . . . *Nah*, at the time it was going to move, right, "Seliksik go now, at such-and-such place a war will be fought. They are going to strike, in short, the raja," isn't that right . . .

ANAK AGUNG GACI: At the time there were regalia [*pajenengan*], the lords [*Betara*, his deified royal ancestors] were very *sakti* then. At Kusamba the Dutch were hit by it. That's why it was canceled, their attack, the defeat of Kusamba. (Interview, 14 February 1986)

(c) The ammunition was named that, I Seliksik. The gun was called Bangké Bai.

MW: Why did it get such a name?

It makes the blood run cold [*serem*].

ANAK AGUNG GACI: It was a large gun, that had to be carried on the shoulders, by up to four people.

DAYU ALIT: Where did it get such a name?

The ammunition was made of a human liver, that's very sinister.

DAYU ALIT: Is it true it used a *bebai*, that one?

That's it, a *bebai* was probably what that one was called [i.e., the spirit that animated it?]. Which is why the gun was named Bangké Bai.

ANAK AGUNG GACI: A human liver was used . . .

DAYU ALIT: Meaning, to make such a thing, you'd have to know about black magic?

Yes. Someone who knew about things of the left made it. If that wasn't so, how could it be *sakti* . . .

DAYU ALIT: Was it made of metal?

Metal. The whatsis was metal, wasn't the barrel metal? The main part was wood, wood mixed with all kinds of things. If it truly made a hit, isn't that right, it would go away, vanish from there. When it returned it would be bloody . . . covered with blood. Another purification would be made, it would be given a *prascita* offering, cleansed . . .

ANAK AGUNG GACI: They were *sakti*, those regalia. Klungkung couldn't be defeated because of them. However many fought against [Klungkung], Gianyar, Karangasem . . . [see chapter 8]. (Interview, 16 February 1986)

DISCUSSION

In presenting these tales about I Seliksik, I have ordered them along a continuum, moving from stories in which I Seliksik appears to be a typical royal weapon, and is even identified as just another keris (implicitly by Anak Agung Oka; openly by Gusti Lanang Mangku), to stories that emphasize its peculiarity, and in so doing tacitly distinguish it from more familiar objects. It is this implicit contrast that I want to make explicit in the first part of my discussion. Those who stressed I Seliksik's singularity also offered the most elaborate accounts of its origins and characteristics, accounts that suggest there was something sinister about I Seliksik. And indeed, Pedanda Gedé Tembau even openly acknowledged a relationship between I Seliksik and sorcery: after speculating that it was manufactured in the same way as sorcery charms, he added: "*Nah*, whoever they were, all of the witches in Kusamba. They . . . made it."

Such remarks illuminate the terms in which the *kasaktian* of the Klungkung court was figured at the time Balinese first came into conflict with Dutch colonialism. Able to cause illness and death at a distance, Klungkung's rulers were in some respects like sorcerers. In this lay their capacity to protect Bali from the Dutch. So at least the stories about I Seliksik suggest, and in doing so suggest that Dutch power was conceptualized in similar terms.

Daggers and Bullets

The first thing worth noting about these tales is that the weapon used against the Dutch was not one of the *pajenengan* mentioned in the *Babad Dalem*. Indeed, I Seliksik belonged to a different genre of weapons, for according to almost all accounts the object referred to by that name was a bullet—or even bullets. At the very least, taking into account those who insisted it was a gun, the power that won the Kusamba War took the form of firearms. This theme receives further emphasis in a number of tales that pair I Seliksik with a gun, called either Kalantaka/Narantaka (God of Death) or I Bangké Bai (*bangké* means "corpse," and *bai* are a kind of spirit that, commanded by a sorcerer, can cause madness; hence, Corpse Animated by the Spirit of Madness).

Of course firearms were, after all, the weapons of the Dutch, and Euro-American common sense would argue that only firearms could be used to resist them. This is by no means so commonsensical to all Balinese, however; recall Pak Morag's tale (and there are others like it) and the devastating effects of royal power on the bodies and guns of Dutch soldiers. Nonetheless, it is significant that weapons like those of Europeans were used against them. As a general principle in Bali, to defeat an enemy one uses a superior form of his own power.

One striking fact about I Seliksik is that although firearms were also used in battles between Balinese, accounts of Klungkung victories against Balinese enemies rarely mention them, and even more rarely mention I Seliksik. Yet I Seliksik was still supposedly part of the royal arsenal in the early years of the twentieth century, since several people emphasized that their own fathers had seen or touched it. This suggests that I Seliksik was only deployed against certain kinds of enemies.

A reasonable hypothesis might be that I Seliksik was used against foreign or otherwise distant foes, whereas keris were effective against antagonists closer to home. In the nineteenth century an association of keris with nearness, and guns with distance, would have made good sense. Ordinary keris were manufactured by Balinese smiths, using nickel from South Sulawesi and iron salvaged from shipwrecks or purchased from Chinese traders who imported it from nearby Java. While some firearms were also manufactured locally, for the most part guns were purchased rather than made. In fact they constituted one of Bali's most important imports, particularly as the nineteenth century progressed; they were brought from Singapore, by both European and Indonesian traders (Anonymous [Medhurst] 1830; Helms 1969).[10] In addition, although nineteenth-century Balinese rulers were proud of their arsenals, they kept them apart from their heirloom keris. Guns, along with lances, were stacked in long rows in pavilions in the outer portion of palaces, where foreign visitors might be taken to see them, at least in the 1840s (Graves 1967; Helms 1969). Keris, on the other hand, were stored either in the sleeping quarters of their owner or in shrines in the royal house-temple, places off limits to non-Balinese.[11]

As weapons, keris and guns evoke similar distinctions. The keris is a thrusting weapon, and its use, for either offense or defense, requires physical proximity, in contrast with firearms. However, this difference was more potential than actual in the case of heirloom keris, since they also (even especially) operated over distances. According to many tales, an heirloom keris need only be displayed to incapacitate an enemy: when the king's keris were brought out during a battle, for example, enemy troops, overcome with fear, dropped their weapons and ran, or were frozen in place.

But such legends suggest that something other than propinquity might be at issue here. Heirloom keris implied continuity with the power and authority of extraordinary ancestors. The power of such keris instantiated the reproduction of a particular social order. Weapons like Bangawan Canggu and Durga Dingkul were gifts from hierarchical superiors, which, inherited over generations, evoked and reproduced their agency, affirming the immutability of particular relations of power. Such associations suggest why such objects should be prominent in narratives of indigenous warfare. The Dutch, on the other hand, indifferent to Balinese signs and significations, did not recognize the moral authority of Klungkung's heirloom keris. What was needed was a tangible demonstration of the Déwa Agung's power. And I Seliksik's effects were nothing if not tangible: unlike an heirloom keris, after use it is described as covered with its victim's blood.

Oral traditions concerning I Seliksik also emphasize a different relationship between power and history. I Seliksik was not inherited from the founders of the dynasty but acquired rather late, at the earliest in the eighteenth century (see below). Moreover, narratives show that not necessarily the *same* bullet was involved each time I Seliksik was used, and Madé Kanta and Anak Agung Kalam indicated that it could be depleted by use. This, of course, is only reasonable with an object made, as many insist this bullet was, of organic matter; it is also, of course, an empirical feature of nonmagical bullets that they can be used only once. I Seliksik, then, is ephemeral compared to the transgenerational life of a keris. Associated with temporality and impermanence, it is an appropriate symbol of the time of change ushered in by the first colonial wars.

Note here one further distinction between I Seliksik and other heirlooms.
Keris were primarily defensive weapons, which protected the realm against
(often) anonymous enemies. By contrast, I Seliksik acts with directed malevo-
lence, against specified individuals; indeed, several people emphasized that
seliksik means to look for something with precision. "It was," explained one
informant, "like a guided missile," a missile aimed at its victim's vital organs;
regardless of where it entered his body (Mr. Seven Stars was hit in the thigh),
it pursued that target relentlessly.

Origins of I Seliksik: The Magic of Islam

I Seliksik's suitability as a weapon against the Dutch must also, however,
have something to do with its origins, for this is a concern of many narratives.
Here too tales intimate a contrast with keris: I Seliksik's power does not derive
from relationships with hierarchical superiors (including gods and ancestors)
but from relationships with hierarchical inferiors and outsiders—with Arabs,
Buginese, commoners, and lower kinds of spirits.

According to most narrators, I Seliksik was manufactured, and in many
versions the expertise to make such a weapon is represented as non-Balinese,
as foreign. Since firearms were originally European weapons, this might not
seem surprising, but the foreigner who instructs the Déwa Agung in I Seliksik's
construction is described not as a European but as a Muslim.

It might be tempting to read references to Islam in these stories in the
light of Balinese experiences in postcolonial Indonesia, a nation-state whose
population is overwhelmingly Islamic. Undoubtedly such tales resonate with
contemporary images, reproduced through gossip and rumor. But that the
Muslims mentioned are specifically identified as Arabs or Buginese reflects
precolonial concerns and circumstances.

Alternatively, images of Islamic power might be traced to the religion's
arrival in the archipelago. It has been suggested that in response to the fall
of Majapahit, Balinese developed an identity centered around their Hindu-
Buddhist religion, which they protected by a deliberate policy of isolation
(Schulte Nordholt 1981:19; Forge 1980:221). Apart from the mounting evidence that Bali's isolation has been exaggerated, there is no indication that
Balinese considered Islam a threat. Islam is referred to briefly in the *Babad
Dalem*, in a passage shortly after the account of Majapahit's collapse, though it
is not represented as responsible for that event. The tale is instructive:

> During the reign of Dalem Watu Rénggong, an envoy came to Gélgél
> from Mecca, to convert the king to Islam. The king agreed to be cir-
> cumcised on one condition: that the razor first be used to cut off one of
> the hairs on his leg. The proselytizer accepted these terms. Not only

did he fail, however, in performing this apparently simple task, but his blade was blunted. When he tried to cut the nails on the king's hand with his scissors, the scissors broke. And so the king continued to follow the religion of his ancestors (35a–35b).

According to some stories told in Klungkung, the would-be proselytizer, too embarrassed by his failure to return home, became the first Islamic settler in Gélgél, which has the oldest Islamic quarter on the island.

By the nineteenth century, Muslims played a key role in mediating between Bali and the wider world. First of all, there was the matter of language. Since the days of the VOC, trade in the archipelago had been conducted in Malay, and Malay continued to be used as the language of diplomacy and colonial authority by the Netherlands Indies government. Because Balinese lords did not know Malay, at least in the 1840s, Arab traders or Muslims from other parts of the archipelago who settled in Bali were commonly employed by both Dutch officials and Balinese rulers as interpreters and scribes, as we have seen in Huskus Koopman's account of his audiences at Klungkung. Balinese did learn Malay as contacts with the colonial government increased, and in later years Balinese lords were responsible for housing and entertaining visiting Dutch envoys, but it is noteworthy that in Klungkung several of those who had the most to do with colonial officials had close ties with the Islamic quarter.

Their access to Balinese courts also put Muslim merchants in a position to make excellent spies, and on numerous occasions the colonial government either employed them as such or had native officials in the colonial service masquerade as traders to gather intelligence. Balinese were well aware of such possibilities: some stories of the 1908 conquest implicate local Muslims in the act of treachery that is said to have made Dutch victory possible. But if Muslims served as a means for the Europeans to penetrate Balinese secrets, they could in turn provide a way for Balinese to penetrate European ones—such as the secret of how to defeat Dutch firearms.

Interpretation and intelligence-gathering, however, were by-products of the role Muslims played in archipelago trade. Balinese apparently were never adventurous sailors, and they left matters of commerce in the hands of others. Non-Balinese harbormasters purchased rights from Balinese kings to serve as middlemen, selling Balinese goods and purchasing foreign commodities (Geertz 1980:87–97). The seaward sides of harbor villages were filled with foreigners engaged in some aspect of this commerce and with their countrymen (e.g., Grader 1960:192). Ports like Kuta, for example, were populated with exiles and fugitives from all over the archipelago.[12]

Most harbormasters were Chinese. Chinese also controlled commerce between Java and Bali and were middlemen in trade from Ceram, in eastern Indonesia. But most other trade was in the hands of Muslims, and of these the Buginese mentioned in several narratives were particularly important, for Buginese *prahu* carried most of the goods traded with the new British entrepôt of Singapore. This trade was considerable. A British visitor to Buléléng in 1830 noted that during his visit more than fifty *prahu* called at that port alone, twenty of them transporting goods from Singapore. Kuta and Padang Cove were even busier (Anonymous [Medhurst] 1830).

That rifles and ammunition were among the most important items imported from Singapore might be sufficient to motivate tales about I Seliksik, but Buginese were not merely associated with munitions as merchants. Several Balinese rulers employed companies of mercenary Buginese riflemen (van den Broek 1830; Vickers 1987). Their reputations probably originated during the VOC era, when Buginese helped the Company to defeat Makassar, which had earlier bested Bali in Sumbawa, and then to conquer East Java. More recently, in 1824 some Buginese had turned against the Dutch, attacking their garrisons; only after some fourteen years of resistance had they agreed to sign a new treaty with the colonial government.

There was more, however, involved in the reputation Muslims developed in Bali than proficiency as fighters and in the use of guns. More directly pertinent to narratives about I Seliksik, Muslims were regarded as experts in gun magic, that is, means to empower firearms. Balinese kings were as preoccupied by Muslim "mantras" as by munitions themselves. Take, for example, the Balinese rulers of largely Islamic Lombok, who successfully smuggled arms from Singapore even after the Dutch interdicted their sale to "natives" in the 1890s. The weapons alone were not enough. A considerable number of texts in their libraries (taken as booty after their conquest) were concerned with gun magic, and that magic was heavily weighted with Arabic phrases and names.[13]

Discourse about Islam and magic has wider ramifications, however, for Islamic spirits are not only linked to guns. Arabic phrases have woven their way extensively into the language of Balinese magic. Since rumors abound in contemporary Bali concerning the powerful "black magic" (Indonesian, *ilmu hitam*) worked by Muslims from neighboring Lombok and Java, it is perhaps unsurprising that such phrases are found especially in texts pertaining to sorcery, healing, and/or the "little world" (*buana alit*) of the body, but again these texts predate the postcolonial era.

Several texts known to me, for example, mention spirits with Arabic names such as I Jelahir or I Mokhair.[14] Another text, *Tingkahing Ngubuh Bebai*, links four spirits associated with the body (see below) with a variety of other spirits including Iblis (another name for the devil in Islam), I Amad, I Muhamad, I Brahim, and so forth (see also Vickers 1987). Tonjaya (1981) identifies one of those spirits of the body as belonging to the same class of potentially dangerous spirits as *tonya, jin,* and *sétan,* the latter two taken directly from Islamic demonology.

The kind of gun magic, then, in which the Déwa Agung was instructed by these Muslim visitors to Klungkung appears to have had links to sorcery.

Origins of I Seliksik II

Other stories attribute the acquisition of I Seliksik to more mysterious sources. According to Madé Kanta and Anak Agung Kalam, an *anak jaba,* a different kind of "outsider," unexpectedly offered his life as sacrifice to the Déwa Agung. The meaning of this extraordinary action is interpreted for the king by one of his priests. This story may not be as different as it appears. Geria Pidada, the house with which the priest is identified, was founded when a kinsman of Karangasem's court priest accompanied Déwa Agung Putra I and his Karangasem queen back to Klungkung in the beginning of the nineteenth century.[15] His descendant's familiarity with magical bullets might have derived in part from contact with Muslims, given Karangasem's conquest of Islamic Lombok. Moreover, Déwa Agung Putra I provided his priest with a compound just west of Klungkung's Islamic Quarter (see fig. 8).

Alternatively, narrators claim that I Seliksik was a gift to the Déwa Agung from the invisible world. This was, of course, a common way for powerful objects to come into royal hands, but two tales are unusually specific concerning the spirits involved. Here is what Pedanda Gedé Kenitén heard from his father:

> He said, my father, *nah,* [I Seliksik] was offered by a *regék tunggék* at Klotok to Ida Betara Dalem . . . By a *regék tunggék.*
>
> DAYU ALIT: What, lord, is that?
>
> IDA BAGUS JAGRI: It isn't allowed to speak of that . . .
>
> . . . That's the one who offered them.
>
> MW: Where did they come from?
>
> They were given by . . . at Klotok. That was the place. Offered to him. *Nah,* wasn't it like whatsis? He liked to go to temples at night, isn't that right? That's where they were given. He was told to take them from the back, from the wound, the hollow. (Interview, Geria Gedé Kenitén, 28 March 1985)

Betara Dalem, the hero of this tale, did not actually become king until two years after the Kusamba War. According to what Ida Bagus Jagri told me later, *regék tunggék* are the Balinese version of a famous kind of Indonesian spirit. From the front such spirits appear to be beautiful women; from the back they are horrific—all organs, bones, and blood. And it was from the back, said the Pedanda, that the Déwa Agung was told to extract a pouch filled with a hundred round yellow bullets, the size, the Pedanda had heard, of ball bearings.[16]

The spirit's form suggests a *buta,* and at least one text (Hooykaas 1975) refers to *buta raregék* who live at boundaries and are among the shapes taken by human spirit siblings (see below). Ida Bagus Jagri thought *regék tunggék* were servants (*rencang*) of the goddess of the Pura Dalem and usually inhabited cemeteries. But Klotok, the setting of this tale and one of Klungkung's four state temples, sits in splendid isolation by the sea: it even contains a shrine to Baruna, god of the sea. This is suggestive, considering the tales in which I Seliksik is provided by persons at home on the sea.

According to Cokorda Isteri Biang Sayang, the gun I Bangké Bai, used to "shoot" I Seliksik, had a similar origin:

Betara Balé Mas [Déwa Agung Putra II] went out one night to *nakti,* ask for magical power. Just beyond the puri he encountered a headless spirit named Tonya Mala Wayan, "Spirit of the Elder/Superior Impurity." The spirit grabbed him and whirled him around, flying with him in the air from about 8:00 P.M. to 1:00 A.M. A voice then ordered the Déwa Agung to reach down the neck of the headless torso and extract what he found there. He drew out of the spirit's body the weapon I Bangké Bai, a cannon or large gun. (Fieldnotes, pp. 531, 714)

The spirit's name is significant, for *mala,* which can be glossed as "impurity," refers as well to all kinds of substances (urine, feces, menstrual blood, and so forth) that cause impurity, as well as to experiences and emotions that lead persons to feel polluted. Recall here the text that grouped *tonya* with *jin* and *sétan;* again the flawed anthropomorphic form of this spirit marks it as a *buta.*

The frightful spirits of these two tales can be thought of as visible manifestations of the invisible forces that sat in these weapons. Both spirits evoke death (the *regék tunggék* as a sometime cemetery spirit; the *tonya* for providing an object named *bangké,* "corpse") and decay (the pouch in which I Seliksik is kept is threadbare; the *tonya*'s name includes the term *Impurity*), connecting them even more firmly with demons, and by association with sorcerers.

These tales have something else in common: the bullets in Pedanda Gedé Kenitén's story and the gun in Cokorda Isteri Biang Sayang's both come from *inside* a spirit's body. Here their stories begin to converge with those about Muslims, since the similarity between certain kinds of Balinese and Islamic spirits centers around their relation to the organs of the body. The recurring body motif is clearly integral to understanding I Seliksik, which is both made from vital organs and kills by seeking them.

Indeed, despite their apparent differences, those with whom I discussed tales of I Seliksik's origins thought that all of them really said the same thing.

In one sense, this is obvious, and rather like the affair of Klungkung's rhinoceros: if commoners volunteered their lives or Muslims their knowledge, or even if spirits presented these weapons as gifts, what prompted any of them to do such things if not the gods?

Even without reverting to ultimate agencies, however, the similarities between various stories are striking. To claim that the bullets were made from the organs of a human sacrifice is not so far from maintaining that they came from inside the body of a spirit whose form suggests a nonliving, perhaps decaying, human body. Even tales in which the bullets are ordinary ones made powerful by means of mantras are not as different as they first appear, since much Balinese magic involves the recitation or writing of syllables that are associated by a series of correspondences to the Kanda Mpat, spirits associated with the human body, including its internal organs.[17] In a sense all of them describe the same phenomenon. To speak of magical formulas is to represent matters in the most exoteric terms, whereas to identify the particular nonhuman agents responsible for the gift is to be daringly explicit. Accounts that refer to human sacrifice, on the other hand, illuminate correspondences between powerful words, spirits, and the human body.

Nonetheless, if from one perspective there is no distinction between these accounts, from another the distinction is crucial: as Anak Agung Kudar frankly observed, the idea that a weapon could be made of human organs is chilling. While the innards of animals are important components of offerings made to invoke or placate demons, only witches sacrifice human beings and use portions of their victims' bodies to further empower themselves.

Such allusions suggest that what was involved here was sorcery. But before discussing this possibility, I want to shift temporarily into a different ethnographic voice in order to talk about how Balinese talk about such things. For understanding what can and cannot be said on the subject of magic clarifies what is implied by certain of the narratives about the Kusamba War.

Interlude on Knowledge

The order in which I have presented texts and themes by no means recapitulates the order in which I heard them. Cokorda Isteri Biang Sayang's was one of the first stories I was told about I Seliksik and the Kusamba War, and it remained by far the most richly elaborated and detailed. It was in puzzling over just those details with Ida Bagus Jagri that I learned most of what I know about sorcery in Bali.

Ida Bagus Jagri's authority to speak about such things stemmed from the fact that he is a healer, though he prefers to speak of himself as a "student." His rejection of the title of healer (*balian*) has to do both with the high cultural value placed on modesty and with the dangers associated with such expertise. Healers are theoretically masters of knowledge of the "little world" (*buana alit*) of the body, knowledge that can be used either to help or to harm: if used for the former, such knowledge is spoken of as "of the right" (*penengen*); if used for the latter, as "of the left" (*pengiwa*).[18] All healers must know something about magic of the left, however, in the event that they are forced to engage in battle with those who have sent illness to their clients. Thus to claim the title of healer publicly is to make an assertion about one's knowledge and power—an assertion that will potentially attract the attention of persons concerned with similar affairs. Like a man with a prize fighting cock, many who seek esoteric knowledge of this sort are eager to test themselves against others of similar ability. Just as for the ardent follower of cockfights it is a matter of absorbing interest whether a cock with a particular set of characteristics (say, red feathers) fighting from a particular position (for example, the south) will prevail against another cock of differing qualities (say, a black and white speckled one, released from the north) so too the mystical combat between two *sakti* individuals, who have acquired their power from differing sources, is a test of the ultimate veracity of their knowledge. There are many texts: which one is superior?

Since the loser of such contests risks death, the prudent are reluctant to parade themselves as masters of magic. Only persons with enormous confidence encourage the development of a reputation, knowing that, as with the Western gunslinger, many eager newcomers will set out to challenge the pro. Such fear of inciting curiosity is one reason why Balinese tend to be cautious in discussing magic and sorcery. But there are others. To be a student of magical power is arduous, and it is not a path open to all. As already noted, it is risky to traffic with the spirit world: it requires, for one thing, a permanent modification of everyday behavior to ensure one's spirit protectors not turn against one, and, for another, that one be constantly vigilant in facing the seemingly endless tests the gods send to those who would seek their favor.

One reason these stories about I Seliksik are so interesting is that they are so elliptical, and the reason they are so elliptical has to do with Balinese understandings about magical things and the way they may be spoken of, or not spoken of. In general, matters pertaining to the *niskala* are esoteric, but when it comes to the kind of magic that is the province of sorcerers Balinese are more than usually reticent.

That I Seliksik has sinister associations is without question. There are multiple allusions to sorcerers and their activities in the way narrators construct their stories. But in drawing these out it is important to respect the style of these discourses. There are critical similarities in the ways people conceptualize the shadowy activities of sorcerers, but it is important not to overemphasize the systematicity of such representations.

Even where Balinese themselves systematize magical discourses—in constructing certain genres of texts, for example—the results are by no means identical. The systems presented in various texts belong to a common discourse: experts agree, for example, that there are correspondences between the four spirit siblings, the demons, the gods, the directions, body parts, and temples, and that knowledge of these correspondences and manipulation of them is the key to acquiring power over self and others, whether the power is to be used for good or ill. Yet the individual systems worked out in various texts may differ in almost every particular.[19]

A Balinese reader coming to such texts, and predisposed to find in them something of practical importance, will read them in the light of his or her own previous experience of the spirit world and will pick and choose, reconciling anything that appears contradictory with what that person knows. Systematicity is in a real sense a creative act.

Even if all texts were identical, however, to make sense of them would still require interpretation, a creative and inventive act of making sense rather than a passive reception of information. For the language of texts concerned with magic or cosmology is particularly obscure, even when compared to other types of Balinese text. It is typical of the genre, for example, to find sections in which a familiar phrase is deconstructed into its constituent syllables followed by a string of words using the same syllables, a complicated system of associations for which the reader must supply the connecting meaning. To speak of a correct interpretation in this circumstance is clearly nonsense.

In a sense, then, whatever I say about "Balinese beliefs concerning sorcery" is inherently as partial and yet as legitimate as any Balinese view. Indeed, I often found that when I would find patterns in things I was learning, and would tentatively present these to Ida Bagus Jagri and Dayu Alit, they would frequently beam in pleasure at the connections I discovered, less, I am sure, because I had come up with the "right answer" than because I had managed to make cultural sense of them. Ida Bagus Jagri told me several times that whenever he had asked his mother's brother, a Brahmana priest, questions about ritual practices, he would be told to think out the answers for himself. And when he returned, with some thoughtful analysis, his uncle would simply smile with satisfaction, no doubt beaming in the same pleased manner.

The reason I introduce witchcraft by means of this long digression is simply that had Ida Bagus Jagri not told me that he thought I Seliksik must be a kind of spirit called a *bebai*—an interpretation perhaps suggested by the gun I Bangké Bai, but also indicated by various details in Cokorda Isteri Biang Sayang's tale that happened to resonate with his particular areas of cultural knowledge—I would never have made certain kinds of connections between those stories and sorcery, even though it seemed that many of the stories alluded to the black arts. Eventually I did come right out and ask Anak Agung Niang Kudar, an outspoken and spirited friend with whom I had some of my best conversations, what was up, just to confirm that I was not placing too much faith in a cultural idiolect:

> DAYU ALIT: Is it true it used a *bebai*, that one?
> That's it, a *bebai* was probably what that one was called [i.e., the spirit that animated it]. Which is why the gun was named Bangké Bai.
> ANAK AGUNG GACI: A human liver was used . . .
> DAYU ALIT: Meaning, to make such a thing, you'd have to know about black magic?
> Yes. Someone who knew about things of the left made it. If that wasn't so, how could it be *sakti?*

But although she was amenable to this interpretation, it is impossible to say whether she secretly shared it but had not wanted to state it directly (given the perils of speaking of such things), or whether it conformed to a more inchoate understanding of which this articulation made sense.

I Seliksik and Witchcraft

Certain details concerning I Seliksik's manufacture particularly evoke its links to matters of the left. Consider Anak Agung Kalam's version:

> Now his inner organs were taken and mixed with water, and the combination was pounded together. If I am not wrong, it also contained *sendawa.*
> DAYU ALIT: Where did that come from?
> Like the fungus that grows on cow dung, on pig dung.

Mushrooms, molds, and fungi, especially the kinds that grow on dung, may be used in making magical materials either sinister or benign. *Sendawa* from pig dung was not something either Ida Bagus Jagri or Dayu Alit had ever heard of per se, but Dayu Alit had heard that pig dung itself is occasionally eaten by lesser sorcerers (their superiors eat human innards). Pigs are (relatively) impure animals in any event: pork, for example, is forbidden to Brahmana Siwa priests and sometimes others who have undergone ceremonies of purification. Thus they are appropriate material for sorcery.

Anak Agung Kalam's remarks on where the bullets were made also resonate with certain aspects of shared Balinese experience:

> The place was downstream, near where people are building the bridge, in the region of Tapéan.
> DAYU ALIT: On the Unda River?
> Yes. There is a place there called Pengobatan [Ammunition]. The place where these bullets were made.

Riverbanks are notorious haunts of *tanana*, and this is especially true of Klungkung's Unda River. Therefore, this is a suggestive location to be manufacturing a weapon.

Cokorda Isteri Biang Sayang's account is more elaborate:

> And then the Daeng looked for his heart, together with his liver and gall bladder. The Daeng worked them up. They were buried at the fork of the river for a month and seven days; in the Pura Dalem for a month and seven days; at the main crossroads for a month and seven days. Forty-two days: it's called a month and seven days . . . After that they were taken and brought to the puri's house-temple.

Each of the three places (three being a powerful number) where the bullets were buried is associated with invisible forces. The split of a river, once again, is a favorite abode of *tanana*. The Pura Dalem is of course the temple in the graveyard, where Durga, patron of witches, dwells. Crossroads belong to Sang Hyang Kala, the dangerous form of the god Siwa: according to texts, Kala has divine permission to "devour" anyone venturing into his space at midday and dusk—that is, to cause them misfortune or death (Hooykaas 1973). With each movement, the magic of the bullets is increasingly "domesticated" (each of these spaces is a bit closer to human habitation) and at the same time increasingly amplified. That the bullets are buried in each place for forty-two days resonates with another familiar experience: mothers and infants remain sequestered for forty-two days after childbirth. This suggests that the spirits that will animate the bullets are being subjected to a ritual process that replicates the creation of persons. And indeed, as Cokorda Isteri Biang Sayang reports, once this treatment was over, the bullets lived:

> [They] knew how to bathe themselves. They would clean themselves with . . . water, with fragrant oils. When they were finally clean, they would be still. "Are you finished bathing? Okay, then come here." That's the way the priest would look for them.

Nearly every detail Cokorda Isteri Biang Sayang specifies concerning these bullets has magico-ritual significance: there were nine of them, a number associated with *niskala* powers, and offerings were brought to them on powerful days of the Balinese calendar. It is in relation to Mr. Seven Stars's death, however, that she makes the most direct reference to sorcery:

> This was hit [patting her thigh], this, the one on the left. He fell down then, his friends came to him. They looked for the bullet, but it kept moving about. If it hadn't yet gotten these, the liver and the heart, [at least] one of them, it wouldn't leave. They were dizzy looking for the bullet. They'd feel it was here, and it would vanish, here, all over the

place, circling around the body . . . No wounds showed here or here [gesturing around her torso], only here [patting her left thigh]. That was the way of those bullets . . . They had to keep going if they hadn't yet gotten the heart and the liver. Then it came home to the main puri once more. That's why it was *sakti*. Isn't that what is called *sakti*? His leg was hit, his left leg was hit, and they couldn't find [the bullet].

Again and again she emphasizes that Michiels was shot in the *left* leg. Healers often diagnose illnesses caused by sorcery by the fact that the illness began on or only affects the left side of the victim's body.

As I have indicated, it was Cokorda Isteri Biang Sayang's profusion of explicit information on the procedures that empowered I Seliksik that led Ida Bagus Jagri to conclude that I Seliksik was a *bebai*, an interpretation about which he became increasingly confident the more stories he heard. *Bebai* are usually malignant spirits, who nourish themselves on human blood [20] and are used by sorcerers to cause a class of illnesses called *bebainan*. A sorcerer attracts a *bebai* to his or her service with ritual formulas and offerings. It then becomes the sorcerer's partner, responsive to his or her wishes. However, a *bebai* will only "eat" those persons who are both the enemies of its master and sufficiently in the wrong that the gods or their ancestors refuse their protection.

Ida Bagus Jagri had learned something of *bebai* from an uncle, a famous healer who had also dabbled in sorcery. *Bebai*, he was told, were attracted to what was *mala*, to such uncanny and/or foul substances as spiderwebs found on Kajeng-Kliwon, a day important to witches and those seeking *kasaktian;* the blood from childbirth, a physical embodiment of one of the Kanda Mpat; and human wastes, including such "cemetery garbage" as bones and decayed organic matter.

These materials would be buried for specified periods of time in places known to be *tenget*. During that time the sorcerer would make offerings and recite mantras to attract the appropriate sinister forces. At the conclusion of all of the ceremonial, the *bebai* (the term refers to both the spirit and its material representation) comes to "life": that is, it has energy or life-force (*bayu*) and thus the ability to move about on its own; a voice (*sabda*), which need not use sounds intelligible to humans (cf. Gusti Lanang Mangku's description of the noise I Seliksik made); and consciousness (*idep*).[21]

A *bebai* generally enters its victim's body through the feet. This is typical of sorcery—sorcerers often bury magical objects on pathways frequented by their intended victims—because feet are the part of the body most associated with *buta*. The *bebai* slowly moves up through the body until it reaches the vital organs. It is at this point that the victim of *bebainan* begins to manifest symptoms of illness, generally in the form of disturbed and disturbing behavior. Since, as we shall see in a moment, the liver is the seat of the emotions, and organs the dwelling places of the Kanda Mpat, which are aspects of the person, the *bebai*'s attack on these parts of the body produces the symptoms of mental illness. It is very difficult to dislodge a *bebai*; victims often die. The *bebai* will then return home to its master, its appetite temporarily sated.

Such is what I was told concerning *bebai*. There are, as always, other versions. Suryani (1984:95–96), for example, offers a somewhat different account of the manufacture of a *bebai*, which involves a mimesis of human reproduction:

> Belief in the powers of the newborn has inspired some Balinese who seek to practice sorcery or black magic (*ilmu pengiwa*) to capture those powers and transform them into those of a *bebai*. . . .
>
> . . . Bebai may be made of different raw materials such as an aborted fetus, a baby which has died before or during delivery, a placenta, a kind of banana (*pisang mas*) commonly used in ceremonies, which is still very small and unripe (*pusuh*), an egg of a black hen, the water which has been used for bathing a corpse, or the brain of a murdered person. The type of material used determines the power of the *bebai*. For instance, a *bebai* made from an aborted fetus of a female high priest (*pedanda isteri*) would be very much more powerful than another made of the fetus of an ordinary woman.
>
> Having found the material needed, the sorcerer then proceeds to treat the object as a baby. Like a real new baby, the *bebai* undergoes the normal series of ceremonies, performed for it immediately after "birth," after one (Balinese) month and seven days, at the age of three months, and finally at the end of six months. Unlike a human baby, after the last ceremony the *bebai* is taken to the cemetery where a special ceremony is performed. At this ceremony the sorcerer makes offerings to the gods, entreating them to bestow on the *bebai* the greatest powers possible. . . .
> Afterward, back at home, the sorcerer prepares rice and other dishes especially for the *bebai* which is now truly treated as a precious and precocious child. This next period lasts until it reaches the age when a normal child begins to talk. During this period, the *bebai* is not only fed regularly but is also given presents. . . . Finally now that the *bebai* can "talk" and "understand" it is regularly consulted by the sorcerer to ascertain its "maturity." Only when it is fully mature is it ready to be used. At this stage it is said to have acquired thirty powers or to have become thirty *bebai* in one. . . .
> Each of the thirty powers . . . has a particular name and produces a particular symptom through the person it possesses.

Suryani cites as an example the "king" of *bebai*, named I Rejek Gumi (Attack the Country), which "attacks its victim violently in the pit of the stomach, making the victim enraged before rendering him or her unconscious."

Apart from tales of its manufacture, I Seliksik has other things in common with *bebai*, including its responsiveness to orders and its manner of causing death (entering Michiels's body via his thigh—a lower limb—and then attacking his vital organs). What clinched things for Ida Bagus Jagri was that a text he owned on *bebainan* referred to a number of Islamic spirits.

There are still further indications that link the power deployed against the Dutch with the kind characterized as of the left. Pak Morag and Anak Agung Oka, for example, both mention that Dutch troops were afflicted with illness:[22]

> PAK MORAG: Before the Dutch conquered Klungkung, whenever they were going to come here to attack, the whole shipload of Dutch soldiers could become ill . . .
>
> MW: So before [the conquest] the puri's weapons were *sakti?*
>
> Are you kidding? All of them were extremely *sakti*. Like the one named I Seliksik, the gun Seliksik. It could look for the enemy. It would *nyeliksik*, move around until it found what it was seeking . . . All the king had to do was just look at the boat and they didn't dare to land. They would come down with all kinds of illness, they would vomit and have diarrhea.
>
> ANAK AGUNG OKA: A light emerged from the weapons of such force that the sky turned orange-red as if in flames. There is a small river near Pura Goa Lawah called the River Banges that began to emit a stench like a rotting corpse. The Dutch soldiers who tried to cross it couldn't. They began to vomit and have diarrhea. Some died; others ran away.

And last, but certainly not least, there was the human sacrifice that empowered I Seliksik, followed by the extraction of the victim's inner organs, which sought their counterparts in the enemy.

Inner Organs

A number of narratives insist on both I Seliksik's manufacture from human innards (Balinese *jajeron*, from the root *jero*, "inside") and its actions on the vital organs of its victims.

Balinese magical and ritual lore associates the organs of the body with four spirits known as the Kanda Mpat, who are referred to as the "siblings" of human beings. The four—best known by the names Anggapati, Mrajapati, Banaspati, and Banaspati Raja—nurture and protect every fetus from conception to birth, when they too are "born," temporarily taking material form as blood, amniotic fluid, umbilical cord, and placenta. They continue to serve as protectors as long as they are "remembered" with offerings, commonly during rites of passage. Outside of such ritual contexts in the early part of their lives, most Balinese ignore them, though some healers claim that neglect of one's spirit siblings leaves a person open to illness, particularly illness caused by sorcery. Healers and sorcerers pay great attention to their own spirit siblings, often offering the first portion of whatever they eat to them, so that they will defend and aid them. As a mark of respect, healers often do not eat inner organs, because of their close association with the siblings. Because every person has such spirit siblings, a healer can heal and a sorcerer afflict by deploying a person's own spirit siblings either to protect or to harm him or her. Such power depends upon understanding the role the siblings play in the body—an understanding that is not purely logical but involves sensory and emotional knowledge as well, which Ida Bagus Jagri referred to as "knowing oneself"—and using that knowledge to project one's will toward the appropriate spirit masters of the bodies of others.

Each of the siblings is said to dwell in a different portion of the body. As elsewhere, texts differ in their interpretations of precisely which sibling may be found where. The four take many forms and have many different names, including Islamic names, and healers and sorcerers must learn by what name to call them to achieve a particular end, and what offerings to make as well.

The Kanda Mpat are, then, identified with parts of the body, or perhaps to be more exact with the concept of the body, particularly with what is essential to, and symbolic of, life: the inner organs. Other Balinese discourses associate inner organs with strong emotions. Thus to be sad is literally "to have a sick liver" (*sakit ati*), the liver filling the same metaphoric space in Indonesian cultures that the heart does in European ones; to be angry is to have an "angry stomach" (*gedeg basangé*), at least in the expressive low Balinese. The Kanda Mpat appear to unite what Euro-Americans think of as most intimately part of the self—emotion—with something quite external, to be both "me" and "not-me" at one and the same time. The same duality is reflected in the way these most "indigenous" of spirits (as spirit siblings play no role in either Hinduism or Islam) are assimilated in texts to the same magical discourse as Islamic spirits and Hindu gods. They represent an objectification of self, with the potential either to help or to harm.

Inner organs are also associated with destructive forces in another way. Along with blood, they are important ingredients in offerings to *buta* and *kala*, who are attracted to them—as well they might be, for according to certain accounts the Kanda Mpat are themselves *buta*. Such offerings not only appease *buta-kala* but may be used to invoke them. They are so used in sorcery. And they once were in warfare.

Success in war required the aid of such forces. According to a text owned by Pedanda Gedé Tembau, Sang Hyang Kala, the destructive aspect of Siwa, was the patron of warriors. Another person I knew in Klungkung had heard that members of the king's special militia would not file their teeth—a rite of passage meant to reduce the grip of the *kala* responsible for antisocial human passions such as anger and greed.

Two Klungkung texts describe the offerings involved in preparing for battle in detail. They include the inner organs of a pig:

> Offerings on going to war, to be presented to Betara Pajenengan in the form of keris or spear: one set of *prascita* offerings; one set of *dadanan* offerings; three *takir* packets containing the fried innards of a pig, and minced cakes and bananas skewered and grilled; three sets of *saté* and *lawar* [ritual foods]; and a *segehan* offering made with entirely red ingredients. Mantra: Oh, honorable Kala Pernah, honorable Kala Suksema of the invisible night, honorable Kala Ebreh, here is your food. When you finish eating and are ready, call your followers and kinsmen to come to war. Take care. Take care. Take care (Text belonging to Cokorda Anom of Puri Akah).

A text belonging to Pedanda Gedé Tembau is even more detailed:

> This is the way, in going to war, to make the enemy afraid. Make a demon-offering (*caru*) using the head, meat, and innards of a pig costing 500 [Chinese coins]; cooked rice from the pointed tips of two bamboo steamers; a coconut shell of tuak; a jar (*guci*) of *arak*; a measure of cooked rice in the middle of which is white and red *lawar*; and a soup made from the joint bones fried with coconut cream and then placed in a container made of *kumbang* leaf. Offer [this] *caru* at the border. Furthermore, make a *caru* for those going to war, those who will face the enemy. Use rice cones in five colors [each set in the appropriate direction], a roasted five-colored chicken, the rice cakes called *geti-geti*, a large *segeh* offering with the innards of a pig, white and red *lawar*, and the offering called *peras panyeneng*; offer this on the forecourt of the royal compound. Furthermore, make a *caru* for the rifles: nine rice cones, each on its own platter, with fried liver as meat; *arak* and *tuak*; a *daksina* offering and a *peras panyeneng*. When leaving, departing from the forecourt after making these offerings, sprinkle holy water on all your clothes, sprinkle all the weapons with holy water. Finish everything with dance performances, and bring out all weapons. After wafting the essence of the offerings, leave to fight. Also [there is an] offering called "Submission of the Enemy," a *caru* using a pig costing 440, its raw innards, a container of blood, *a sega* offering, *tuak*, [and] water in a *kumbang* leaf container. Offer these at the enemy's fortifications. Also to repel the enemy, place a piece of copper, four fingers wide and the

length of a thumb, in a flag, after drawing on it a three-headed *buta* with two faces (the one on top has no face). On its chest draw one face; between its feet draw one face. After drawing, recite a warding-off mantra. It is a secret mantra of the right. . . . Also [there is an] offering (*sesayut*) called "ward off weapons" consisting only of a banana leaf container (*tékor*) of cooked rice; a collection of fruits and cakes; for meat, red nuts. This is the way to behave in battle. The proper way for all ministers [and] king's helpers to behave is to constantly pray to Widhi, to be devoted to the gods, in order to live long and win against the enemy. Make a *prascita* offering for all clothing worn in war, including your sarong if you fight. The way to go to war, again make a *caru* in the forecourt, using red cooked rice; five sets of white and red *lawar;* a container [*salimas*] of blood; fried liver; a coconut shell of *tuak*. Make a *segehan* offering, cutting off the head of a black chick. Waft the essence of the offering toward all the weapons. Ask for holy water from a *pedanda* and from the Pura Dalem, Pura Puseh, and all important temples, and request victory over the enemy.

I Seliksik resembles such offerings, except that human rather than porcine innards were used to attract demonic forces.[23] That I Seliksik's creation was a sacrifice to the *buta-kala* is also implied by references to the method of that human's death: animals used in sacrificial offerings always have their throats slit, and certain *caru* even require a *tabuh rah*, in which an animal's blood flows onto the ground.

But if, as stories insinuate, the forces that empowered I Seliksik were demonic, they were not those ordinarily invoked in warfare, precisely because they involved a human sacrifice. While one might make a case that those killed in battle were offerings to demons, this is not the way people talk, or at least not now.[24] Only sorcerers provide human victims for (and with the aid of) their demonic helpers and patrons, the same sorcerers who fight "night wars." That phrase itself distinguishes sorcery from warfare, glossing their difference as that between night and day.

The Kusamba War is represented as something midway between an ordinary war and sorcery. As in ordinary warfare, the weapon used had visible form. But its power came from a human sacrifice, the attack on the Dutch took place at night, and I Seliksik resembled a *bebai*.

Human Sacrifice

Legends and rumors attest to a good deal of uneasiness regarding the lengths to which rulers might go in their efforts to become powerful. Rumors concerning kings sacrificing their subjects appear to have been particularly rife in the years before Kusamba War. Friederich, for example, heard gossip in Badung concerning two failed attempts by Balinese princes to become powerful by human sacrifice, the first involving the ruler of Karangasem and the second the ruler of Gianyar (1959 [1849–50]:73). Such acts were represented to him as evil, as evidenced by the supernatural sanctions that befell those who had attempted them: the Karangasem prince was purportedly cursed by his priest, who discovered the body hidden among other offerings; the Gianyar prince sacrificed his own son by mistake.

Such rumors suggest that tales about I Seliksik date from this era, and some of the details narrators elaborate seem designed to carefully distinguish the Déwa Agung's activities from others of this kind, all the more since, unlike those others, the Déwa Agung's efforts are said to have been successful.

This is surely why narrators emphasize that I Seliksik's manufacture was both sanctioned and witnessed by Brahmana priests, and particularly why it matters that the victim was a volunteer. Indeed, the extremity of his subjects' loyalty evokes the Déwa Agung's identity with the god Smara.

Klungkung rulers certainly had knowledge of the left. A catalogue of the texts taken from Puri Klungkung in 1908 describes the contents of one as *mantra pangiwa kundagnimurti*, "formula for magic of the left, to take the form of sacrificial fire" (Juynboll 1912a). But what ultimately makes magic moral or immoral is its use. If used against power of the left, magic qualifies as of the right. And another story suggests that this was indeed the way I Seliksik was used.

Balian Batur

General Michiels was not the only victim of I Seliksik acknowledged by name. Another story, widely known outside of Klungkung, implicates I Seliksik in a different set of historical events.[25] Anak Agung Anom alluded to this story when he named Kalantaka as the gun used to "shoot" I Seliksik, and so did Madé Kanta when he casually mentioned a war against someone named Balian Batur.

This battle occurred more than a century before the Dutch became interested in Bali, not long after the court had moved to Klungkung:[26]

> In the beginning of the eighteenth century, the realm of Mengwi was ravaged by a terrible epidemic. People healthy and active during the day would become violently ill during the night and be dead by morning. It came to be known that the illness was being sent by Ki Balian Batur, a *sakti* man from the village of Rangkan. Mengwi's ruler sent his most powerful experts in "night wars" against him, but all were defeated. Finally Balian Batur informed one of them that he could only be vanquished by a weapon belonging to the ruler of Klungkung. Mengwi's ruler at once set off for Klungkung's court. After hearing his request,

Déwa Agung Jambé sent for Déwa Agung Anom, his youngest son. He gave the prince the weapons I Seliksik and I Narantaka and sent him west to Mengwi. Balian Batur was easily overcome, and the grateful ruler of Mengwi requested that Déwa Agung Anom be allowed to stay in his territories. Déwa Agung Anom built a royal residence in the eastern part of Mengwi's domain, which he called Sukawati.

In the eighteenth century, Mengwi became a realm of considerable power, and its ruler was sometimes identified as a descendant of Gusti Agung Maruti, the lord who had usurped Gélgél's throne a mere generation before.[27] Given those circumstances, the Balian Batur story appears to be a moral-cum-political lesson on Klungkung supremacy.

The terms in which that supremacy are asserted, however, are significant. Consider, for example, the name of the sorcerer responsible for the epidemic: Balian Batur. Some *balian* heal by interpreting their clients' misfortunes as a meaningful communication from the invisible world about the neglect of important, generally vertically oriented relationships: a person becomes vulnerable to adversity because he or those close to him have forgotten an agent who would normally be a protector, commonly a lineal ancestor. That Balian Batur reveals his own vulnerability suggests that he is an instrument of invisible forces, who are punishing Mengwi's ruler for attempting to create a realm independent of, and potentially even competitive with, Klungkung (see Agung n.d.). Indeed, one *Babad Mengwi* explicitly states that Balian Batur was told to make trouble to punish Mengwi's ruler for his neglect of the Déwa Agung.[28]

That the sorcerer, who lived in the village of Rangkan (Agung n.d.), was named Batur is equally suggestive. *Batur* means "foundation" or "base" (Zoetmulder 1982:225), but what seems to be foregrounded here is autochthony. That autochthony could be at odds with Klungkung authority. Batur was one of the mountain villages that, according to the *Babad Dalem*, resisted Majapahit supremacy. Batur is also generally associated with Déwi Danu, goddess of the crater lake from which the water that irrigates Bali's fields is said to flow. Her temple in Batur is nearly as large as Besakih; and her primary priest is always chosen from a commoner clan that identifies itself as indigenous in origin (Lansing 1991).

But if Batur suggests an enduring symbolic opposition to Klungkung hegemony, Klungkung (and Besakih) always emerge as superior.[29] Déwi Danu is, after all, also said to be Betara Tolangkir's younger sister or consort. Moreover, recall that when Mayadanawa, sometimes identified as Déwi Danu's son, attempted to usurp the place of Besakih's god, he was defeated, just as the rebels in Batur were subdued by Sri Kresna Kapakisan with the help of Durga Dingkul.

I Seliksik evokes themes, in fact, familiar from the legend of Durga Ding-kul, for here "Batur" is once again defeated by a Klungkung weapon associated with the destructive forces over which Durga is mistress. The Balian Batur story also evokes Empu Baradah's defeat of the Widow of Jirah, another person with the power to cause epidemics (see chapter 5). In fact, the *Babad Mengwi* to which I have already referred specifically compares Balian Batur's power to that of the Widow of Jirah. There seems to be a pattern in which earlier enemies become associated with subsequent challengers of Klungkung authority. Thus I Seliksik is also represented as an instrument of justice within Klungkung, finding and destroying would-be transgressors on its own initiative.

Colonial sources show that in the nineteenth century rulers could deal with sorcerers judicially, especially when it was politically advantageous. Gusti Ngurah Kesiman, for example, is reported to have had twenty persons put to death, including his nephew and several Brahmanas (among them a widowed priestess), for bewitching his daughter (van Bloemen Waanders 1859: 220). Bangli's ruler exiled a Brahmana priest who made the king's brother ill (van Kol 1903:456 and Schwartz 1901:128; Schwartz was put up in the priest's empty compound). In "more fanatical" Klungkung, a Javanese spy for the Dutch witnessed the Déwa Agung sentence a woman to be executed by keris as a witch after hearing testimony that she had caused the death of her neighbor's two-year-old daughter (Sasrowidjaya 1875). Balinese lords, of course, also protected their subjects by sponsoring rituals to placate the destructive forces sorcerers employed. But these recourses were not always enough.

Klungkung's rulers, heirs to Empu Baradah, had the knowledge and power to magically defeat powerful sorcerers. In Klungkung people like Déwa Mangku of Satra, whom I met during a ritual in one of Klungkung's state temples, still waxed nostalgic over the last Déwa Agung, stating that when he was alive Klungkung sorcerers were helpless; since his death in the mid-1960s, there has been a dramatic increase in local sorcery.[30] This power over sorcerers rested in part on relationships with the *niskala* forces sorcerers invoked. The spirits serving Durga, Kala, and the Fanged Lord of Nusa Penida both aided Klungkung rulers in their wars and obeyed them by not harming those they protected: in any event they obeyed their invisible masters, whose goodwill Klungkung's rulers had. The Déwa Agung could in part vanquish sorcerers because the spirits that carry out their commands put his desires first. The *Babad Dalem* showed the king was at once priest and warrior; stories about I Seliksik suggest he was also both sorcerer and healer.

The Balian Batur story, then, proclaims the superior *kasaktian* of the Klungkung court. Regardless of his military and other successes, Mengwi's ruler was unable to protect his realm against powerful sorcery. The only way to defeat an enemy like Balian Batur is to have more powerful invisible allies. And that, the story asserts, was uniquely true of the ruler of Klungkung.

The Night War against the Dutch

That certain Klungkung narrators who attributed General Michiels's death to I Seliksik invoked the more familiar Balian Batur legend suggests that the Dutch were thought to have had something in common with Balian Batur. It is unlikely that they similarly evoked autochthony, although since certain tales of the conquest identify the Dutch with pre-Majapahit Balinese, this may in fact be foreshadowed here. More probable, however, is a shared identification with sorcery.

The very first meeting with Huskus Koopman had suggested, and subsequent events had confirmed, that the Dutch were unpredictable, easily angered, apparently insatiable, and powerful. These stories frame the Kusamba War as the moment when the Déwa Agung practically enunciated the nature of Dutch power as of the left by deploying I Seliksik against them.

By insinuating that I Seliksik was a sorcery object, narrators implied that the Dutch (and their guns) used sorcery too. I Seliksik operated in the same way as a ward (*tetulak*, the Balinese one might translate as "ward," actually implies a return). I Seliksik worked on a principle used by Balinese healers: an illness caused by magic is cured by invisible forces the same as, or superior to, those responsible for it. In the same way, whatever the secret of Dutch bullets, I Seliksik as the *raja* of their magic could defeat them.

Hence the stress in these narratives on the age of the victim used to make I Seliksik. Recall that according to Suryani some sorcerers make *bebai* from fetuses or infants. By contrast, the person sacrificed to make I Seliksik is explicitly identified as old. His age is not, however, merely chronological. Madé Kanta, for example, claimed that "Grandfather Seliksik" was a temple priest, and Anak Agung Kalam that he was a person of great wisdom, one who "understood," both types of persons regarded in Bali as elders, *anak lingsir*. The power of the bullets stems in part from his virtues, however these are described; Anak Agung Niang Kudar, for example, thought that the victim's distinction lay in his virility.

The human sacrifice necessary to empower such a weapon can be read as a Balinese commentary on European power. After all, the keris indigenous to the region required no such violence against humans to be efficacious. It is striking that guns and bullets, commodities, were not regarded as powerful in and of themselves; to make them so required additional ritual work. Balinese recognized, even if Europeans did not, that the power of such things comes from human life-force.

It would be a mistake, however, to draw too strong a contrast between I Seliksik and other heirloom weapons. After all, the names of many keris and lances associate them with equally sinister forces. Two weapons belonging to a branch line of the Klungkung royal house, for example, were known as Old Ogre (Ki Raksasa Tua) and Witch (Ki Baru Léyak) (*Babad Dalem A* in Warna et al. 1986); one of Gianyar's heirloom keris was named Thirsty Ogre (Raksasa Bedak). Yet still the distinctions are there. Compared to most keris I Seliksik is relatively "left" rather than "right," relatively "below" rather than "above."

Historical Transformation and Narrative Variation

Earlier I attributed certain narrative variations to the circumspection of discourse concerning magic. I want to end this chapter by noting that representations of the Kusamba War also reflect a historical change, providing evidence of a complex transformation in Balinese subjectivities.

If some narrators were comfortable with the suggestion that Klungkung's *kasaktian* at its height was fearsome, those who simply described I Seliksik as a royal weapon indistinguishable from other such objects tended to represent precolonial kingship in entirely benign terms. There has already been plenty to suggest that matters were more complex. But that such representations have been forgotten is traceable to colonialism and the elimination of warfare. With Balinese princes denied the right to engage in battle, certain ideologies of kingly power were muted.

The eradication of warfare was a major transformation in the Balinese world. What is striking is how successful it was: warfare was abolished not only as a practice but even as a cultural value. Many Balinese now think of battle as something completely negative, associated with anger and fighting, which are not valued in contemporary Balinese life.

It is not that the current ideology is wrong; war *was* linked to anger and the spiritual forces associated with it. But this fierceness was actively sought in the offerings made before battle, and according to Dutch military historians, Balinese were opponents to be taken seriously. Indeed, precolonial Dutch travel writers invariably refer to Balinese bellicosity with a grudging admiration.

Some traces of a more positive evaluation of warfare remain, however, in the medical practices already described and in ritual and literature. At temple festivals, for example, shrines are festooned with lances and tridents, and metaphysical writings reveal that each god has a characteristic weapon. And after all, the central theme of the *Barata Yuda* (the local version of the Indian *Mahabharata*) is a war, a war its heroes are not permitted to avoid. From these stories Balinese know that those who die in battle are assured a place in Wisnu's heaven.

EIGHT

The Dutch and Klungkung
1849 – 1908: Relations of
Knowledge and Power

On the evening of 27 April 1908, the chief of staff of the Dutch army noted in the orders for the following day that "in the main poeri of Kloeng-koeng and surrounding poeris and Djeros, are gathered several thousand lance bearers under the command of their chiefs. At most are present 200 guns, of which four are repeating rifles and four small bronze cannons."[1] Spies had also reported that the villages surrounding the capital were heavily fortified and that two of the cannons had been placed at the southeast border of Sampalan and two on the eastern edge of Klungkung. If the Dutch managed to penetrate these defenses and reach the capital, the Balinese were prepared to fight to the death.

But when they attacked the next day the Dutch found fortifications aban-doned, and only the king, his close kin, and the most important lords of the realm fought against them. A reporter concluded that Klungkung's populace had felt no deep loyalty to the Déwa Agung. While they had been prepared to fight out of a "habit of obedience," that no longer sufficed when shells began to rain down on the capital from the warships stationed off the coast. This was comforting to the readers of colonial newspapers such as the *Java Bode* and the *Surabaya Handelsblad*, who wanted to believe that not only might but moral right was on their side. Journalists assured them that the people of Bali—described as industrious and honest—would be better off under colo-nial rule than subject to the whims of despots who showed little concern for their well-being.

The Dutch had expected a stronger resistance. That it did not materialize pleased them beyond their wildest hopes, since it made the politics of con-quest that much less problematic. Still it was striking enough that the com-mander of the expedition could write:

> Although the banner of resistance was now lifted up by the Dewa-
> Agoeng in his own person—the head of Balinese adat [custom or tra-
> dition] par excellence and the bearer of all old Balinese conceptions of
> power and royal grandeur—none of the Balinese princes followed his
> example. But still further, even the Kloengkoeng people, who as a rule

raise themselves above other Balinese on the grounds that Kloengkoeng
is the seat of Bali's Soesoehoenan, left their king in the lurch when the
troops marched against this seat, so that he perished surrounded only
by a few relatives.[2]

This was especially striking when compared with the thirty-three thousand
Balinese who had been ready to die defending the Déwa Agung when the
Netherlands Indies had last attacked Klungkung. One can hardly ignore the
impact that advances in European military technology made on the Balinese;[3]
still, even colonial officials did not attribute their victory simply to arms.

Something drastic had happened to Klungkung between 1849 and 1908;
that "something" was directly traceable to the Dutch. Following the Kusamba
War, the relationship between the Dutch and the Balinese underwent an
ineluctable alteration. While the Dutch exerted no force in South Bali until
close to the end, there is reason to think that their increasing presence
in North Bali generated a silent dialogue with Klungkung that affected all
of Bali.

IN THE WAKE OF THE THIRD BALI EXPEDITION

Colonialism in Bali had its start in the north, but it took some time to become
established. During the Third Bali Expedition the Dutch had conquered Buléléng, Jembrana, and Karangasem; however, at first the colonial government
wanted nothing to do with their administration. The territories were awarded
to Balinese allies: Lombok was granted Karangasem; Bangli, Buléléng.

Long-standing disputes between Bangli and Buléléng, which made that
arrangement untenable, led to the first stage of a more active colonial presence
in North Bali. Where the rulers of Lombok and Karangasem had been kinsmen, which made it relatively easy for Karangasem's lords to switch their
allegiance, Bangli's ruler had nothing but Dutch friendship to help him establish his authority over the lords of Buléléng. He soon gave up the attempt
altogether, and the colonial government appointed a Buléléng aristocrat as
regent. He was, however, to be advised by a Dutch controleur, as was the
usual policy in the administration of Java. This marked the beginning of colonial rule in North Bali. Moreover, the presence of colonial officials on the
island enabled an increased surveillance of other Balinese polities.

At this time colonial policy in the Netherlands discouraged interference
with indigenous states. Largely for financial reasons—what Multatuli called
the government's "heartbreaking thriftiness" (1967:194)—politicians in The
Hague wanted to avoid the direct control of political and economic affairs,
always backed by military force, of outright colonial rule in nonprofitable
regions such as Bali. Imperial agents in the colonial periphery, however,

tended to favor an expansion of colonial involvement, often motivated, especially after the publication of *Max Havelaar*, by idealism and moral conviction,
or simply the heady experience of power. In the long run, they won, but not
without resistance.

North Bali offers a perfect example of the seeming inevitability of the
expansion of colonial authority once the process had begun. On 1 January
1854, P. L. van Bloemen Waanders was appointed Controleur of Buléléng. By
1859 he had been promoted to Assistant Resident, with controleurs subordinate to him, and he was simultaneously appointed the Delegate in Charge of
Bali and Lombok Affairs, an office he held until 1863.[4] By 1866 the Resident
in East Java was urging the Governor General to establish a separate Residency
for Bali and Lombok, but the Minister of Colonies refused to authorize this.
The issue was again raised in 1872, following an investigation that led to the
exile of Buléléng's regent—the "abuses" and "cruelties" of Bali's ruling class
were said to require closer supervision—and once again rejected. A new regent, however, was not appointed; instead, Buléléng's administration was
placed under the Assistant Resident's direct authority. It was only a matter of
time before the government capitulated, and in 1882 a Residency for Bali and
Lombok was established in Singaraja, Buléléng's capital, with a concomitant
growth in staff.

The steady encroachments of the colonial government had to be dealt
with by a new cast of characters in Klungkung, for Déwa Agung Putra II died
without issue in 1850. He was succeeded by an adolescent cousin, who was
adopted by Déwa Agung Isteri Kania. The new king, Déwa Agung Putra III,
was the eldest son of Déwa Agung Ketut Agung, founder of Puri Kaléran, by
a princess from Puri Gélgél. Déwa Agung Ketut Agung had been the youngest
son (by a commoner) of Déwa Agung Sakti (see genealogy in Appendix) and
was born after the death of Déwa Agung Putra I. It was Déwa Agung Ketut
Agung who wrote the letter stating that Klungkung would not surrender in
1849 and who represented the king when the peace treaties were signed in
Kuta. At that time Déwa Agung Ketut Agung was probably still the designated
heir to the throne.[5] But when his son was stricken with smallpox, Déwa
Agung Ketut Agung vowed that if the gods would spare him, he would step
aside in his son's favor.

As we will see, the young Déwa Agung did not initially make much of an
impression on colonial officials. He was, however, in a propitious position to
become a strong ruler. In Klungkung, he had brothers willing and able to play
his seconds (brothers, moreover, who would have had no stature without
him), as well as a tie through his mother to the *manca* house of Gélgél. Outside of Klungkung, several powerful rulers had endorsed his accession, and he
cemented their support by a series of strategic marriages. One of his firmest
backers was Gusti Ngurah Kesiman; even after he died in the mid-1860s,

however, Badung's rulers continued to be dependable allies—but then the ruler of Karangasem was no longer a competitor.

The new Déwa Agung proved to be a serious opponent of Dutch colonialism. At times he impressed the Dutch, who praised him as "highly educated for a Balinese ruler"; at times he aroused their ire, for what they called his "intrigues." In any event, he was a force to be reckoned with until his death in 1903.

KNOWLEDGE, ETIQUETTE, AND DOMINATION

Colonial domination involved and depended upon an accelerating production of knowledge concerning Bali, its customs, and local politics. Prior to 1849 much of what the Dutch knew of Bali came from sporadic visits by men charged with specific purposes (apart from those like Dubois and Friederich, who spent several years in Bali, or Lange, who was a permanent resident) or from the casual visits of travelers in the archipelago. With the appointment of a controleur in the north, it became possible to monitor local affairs continually, and the trickle of information became a flow.

As his duties included "advising" the rulers of South Bali, the controleur made an annual tour of their courts, with additional visits whenever he deemed it necessary. Increasing access made it difficult to keep matters hidden from the colonial gaze—a gaze that saw things in a disconcertingly different way.

Colonial rule in the north also opened Bali to Dutch merchants, missionaries, Orientalists, and journalists (the *Surabaya Handelsblad*, for example, stationed a correspondent in Buléléng in the 1870s [T. 1874:439]). Their reports of events and accounts of Balinese manners and customs contributed in no small manner to knowledge about the island in Java and the Netherlands.

Domination by observation and representation was accompanied by a symbolic domination based upon etiquette. That the conviction of Europeans of their own superiority was not shared by Balinese sovereigns had been amply demonstrated in interactions over the previous thirty years: officials did not receive the deference they assumed was their due, and Balinese practices governing ranking were unacceptable to them. By using what they understood of those practices (filtered through their experiences in Central Java), the Dutch sought to impose their vision of proper political relations. The colonial government not only refused to accede to the place Balinese rulers assigned to its representatives—as low-ranking commoners—but established a protocol for official visits in a resolution passed in 1853:

REGULATIONS CONCERNING THE CEREMONIAL to be observed by the Delegate [*Gekommitteerde*] for Balinese and Lombok affairs[6] during visits to these islands, as well as the ceremonial that he can expect from the princes. Government Resolution 15 June 1853 lt. A.

ART. 1. The Delegate will inform the princes he wishes to visit at least two days before his approaching arrival in their realm, requesting them to hold quarters in readiness for him, and to dispatch someone to him at the borders who can point out those quarters to him. (This last is based upon the custom of the land in *Bali,* where high guests who are welcome are as a rule met at the border, in order that they be escorted safely through the land, and to point out the accommodations held ready for them.)

ART. 2. Upon arrival at the capital of the realm that he visits the Delegate will give notice of it to the prince.

ART. 3. He will acquaint the prince with the day and the hour on which he wishes to have fixed the official reception.

ART. 4. At the stated hour, the prince will send at least four lords of the realm to him, who will collect him and accompany him to the prince.

ART. 5. The Delegate will go to the prince in formal dress under golden parasols.

ART. 6. The prince will receive him at the door of the passebaan (main gateway of the poeri) and accompany him to the pandopo [i.e., the pavilion in the forecourt of the puri], where the conference must take place.

ART. 7. The Delegate will take a seat on the right side of the prince.

ART. 8. After the conference, the sending off will occur with the same ceremonial as ushered the Delegate in.

ART. 9. If the Delegate lodges in the kraton [i.e., the royal residence], the prince will receive him at the doorway of the pandopo, where the conference must take place.

ART. 10. The prince will make a return visit to the Delegate, the day and hour of which will be fixed by mutual agreement.

ART. 11. The Delegate will at the stated hour send his clerk to the prince in order to accompany him.

ART. 12. The Delegate will receive the prince at the door or gateway of his quarters.

ART. 13. He will be in formal dress under golden parasols.

ART. 14. He will escort the prince inside and make him sit down on his own right side.

ART. 15. He will not sit higher than the prince.

ART. 16. After the conference he will show the prince out in the same manner as he ushered him in.

ART. 17. The clerk of the Delegate will accompany the prince to the kraton. (Quoted in full in Jacobs 1883:245–46)

Certain provisions are worthy of comment. Note that one Dutch clerk is equivalent to four Balinese lords. And note as well that the rules seem as much intended to curb the excesses of colonial officials as the arrogance of Balinese rulers: thus article 15 admonishes that the Dutch delegate to Bali will not sit above a Balinese prince; that the reverse is forbidden is left implicit.

As this document demonstrates, in the early 1850s colonial administrators still regarded things Balinese through Central Javanese spectacles. *Passebaan, kraton,* and *pandopo,* for example, are all Javanese terms. Golden parasols—although they were also used in Bali (Arntzenius 1874)—were a Javanese royal prerogative, which the colonial government had abrogated for its officials for meetings with the rulers of Surakarta and Jogjakarta at the beginning of the nineteenth century (Day 1904:155). But if the Dutch initially relied upon Javanese terms and concepts in their efforts to control Balinese behavior, it was not long before they began to appropriate more local idioms.

By the mid-1870s, for example, even an official on a short-term assignment to Bali could write with authority about the implications of lexical choices in a letter addressed to him by the Déwa Agung. Indeed, Inspector Zoetelief, the official in question, paid as much attention to the language of the letter as he did to its contents:

> What attracted my attention at the first inspection of the letter was that it was written in low Balinese. I knew that in the estimation of the Balinese, speaking or writing in the low language to whomever is connected to the high position of the Dewa Agoeng. (N.B. A former Dewa Agoeng even wrote to the Governor-General in the low language. Later the Dewa Agoeng and some of the other princes gave preference to the Malay for correspondence with the European authorities, through which the question of which language they might use was avoided.) But I am of the opinion that in regard to a European official of the Netherlands-Indies Government he can be made to relinquish that prerogative, which I remarked to Intjik Hoesin [the Déwa Agung's envoy] in gentle but clear terms.[7]

When a second letter was brought, Zoetelief was pleased to note that it was written not only in high Balinese but in a conciliatory tone. After asking Zoetelief's forgiveness for his error, the Déwa Agung wrote that given his youth (the Déwa Agung was probably in his thirties at the time), Zoetelief should regard him as his "child,"

> while for the word "I" he used the respectful "titiang," which even the lesser princes dilute in their Balinese letters to European officials through the use of the Malay "saya" which the Dewa Agoeng also used in his first letter to me, but which is in fact just like the low Balinese word

"hitjang." Hoesin also said the Dewa Agoeng had instructed him to offer his excuses orally as well, and to explain that the fault had possibly been a mistake of the scribe.[8]

In the same letter, the Déwa Agung expressed his regrets that Zoetelief could not visit him in Klungkung, so that he might explain matters he was reluctant to put in writing. Such a remark should not, however, be taken to mean that Klungkung's ruler was now open to the kinds of private and frank conversation that Huskus Koopman had desired, for reports by colonial officials over the course of his reign make it clear that no such discussions ever occurred—at least not with the Déwa Agung himself. Instead this short exchange suggests one way in which the Déwa Agung tried to use Dutch proprieties—formally conceding their right to respectful terms of address, intimating openness—to create opportunities in which he could take their measure in brief formal encounters.

If, then, colonial officials used what they learned of Balinese practices in an effort to dominate, the Déwa Agung made use of what he learned of Dutch manners and customs to better resist that domination, while appearing to do the opposite. But because it was the Dutch who established the terms, they also had the advantage. Periodic descriptions of meetings between Déwa Agung Putra III and various representatives of the colonial government show a slow erosion in his capacity to parry Dutch interpretations of their relative power. The 1853 regulations were a form of symbolic domination, which had to be opposed in more and more subtle ways over the course of time.

A MEETING WITH THE DÉWA AGUNG: CONTROLEUR VAN BLOEMEN WAANDERS, JULY 1856

Van Bloemen Waanders introduces a distinctly different discourse concerning Klungkung and its rulers, one in which a cool and scientific objectivity establishes European standards as superior. Symptomatic of his attitude is an account of a visit to Klungkung in July 1856 (published in 1870), which is full of measurements: the thermometer registered seventy-four degrees at 4:00 P.M.; the breadth of the Unda River is 450 feet; Klungkung (like Gianyar) is 250 feet above sea level. His interest in "facts" is matched by a new and skeptical perspective on Klungkung, scornful of local significations and based entirely on readings that are unhesitatingly European:

> Kloengkoeng is a small, insignificant little state, with a population that one can estimate at 30,000 to 36,000 souls. The whole, even the royal residence not excepted, breathes poverty and decline. (1870:16)[9]

Everything is subjected to the same withering perspective. No longer is Klungkung represented as a "land consecrated to virtue." On the contrary, van

Bloemen Waanders notes that the slave trade continues there, albeit surreptitiously: people who cannot afford to pay fines are sold to Lombok, Sumbawa, and Java, often by Buginese middlemen (1870:16). On the other hand, he notes that Klungkung has nineteen Brahmana priests (Bangli, by contrast, had only six with a much larger population, 1870:24); fifteen years later van Eck was also to remark that Klungkung had more Brahmanas in residence than any other Balinese realm.

Van Bloemen Waanders was no more impressed with the young king than he was with anything else he encountered in Klungkung. But if the Controleur was determined to find nothing in Klungkung pleasing, some of his contempt may have been due to outraged dignity and to violations of protocol.

First of all, his party was housed with a local administrator (*perbekel*), who was a mere commoner.[10] While the Déwa Agung was informed of his arrival and of his intention to call at the puri late that afternoon, when van Bloemen Waanders reached the palace he was greeted by "only five musicians," and he had not yet been met by anyone of rank (1870:12). This was in marked contrast to the way he was treated when he continued his journey to Bangli: there the king's brother waited for him at the edge of the capital to escort him personally to the royal residence, from which the prince himself emerged to greet him (1870:19). His entry into the forecourt of Puri Klungkung was saluted "by a shot out of a mutilated lilla [small cannon], placed on a stone." And then he was forced to await the arrival of the king and his advisor, a priest named Pedanda Madé Rai. When these finally emerged from the inner reaches of the palace and the party moved to be seated in a pavilion, there was yet another insult: a place on the floor was indicated for the Controleur. Van Bloemen Waanders writes that, after thanking the king, he requested, "in a friendly manner," a stool.

Once seated, van Bloemen Waanders handed over the letters from the Governor General he was there to deliver. The reading and interpreting of these took a half hour, during which time no one spoke a word. When that was finished van Bloemen Waanders tried to break the "painful silence" and enter into a conversation with the Déwa Agung. But he did not succeed; the only answers he received to his questions were yes or no. Nor did the priest say anything.

Angry and humiliated by what he considered inhospitable behavior, van Bloemen Waanders not only cut the audience short but decided to depart the following day and sent word to the palace to have the necessary coolies readied. He then retired early to sleep, further disgruntled by the fact that no one had come that evening to speak to him.

The abrupt request for coolies had, however, signaled to his hosts that they had offended him, and after he retired he did, after all, have visitors: the king's younger brother (Déwa Agung Rai) and Pedanda Madé Rai. Finding him asleep, they returned the following morning to smooth his obviously ruffled feathers in a characteristically Balinese way. The priest apologized for any discourtesy he may have felt, explaining it was not unfriendliness but stupidity that was the cause; the king was very young and must be forgiven for his ignorance. They all hoped that van Bloemen Waanders would grant them the pleasure of his company several days longer. He agreed to stay one more day.

Van Bloemen Waanders spent most of that day seeing the sights: to wit, Kusamba and Goa Lawah, a fine demonstration of the continuing prominence of the Bali Expeditions in Dutch consciousness at that time. But Goa Lawah, with its eerie cave filled with bats, had begun to acquire a reputation on its own merits. Indeed, Van Bloemen Waanders notes that he had been told he could not possibly visit Klungkung without seeing it.

Van Bloemen Waanders, however, was not impressed. His reaction to the temple exemplifies his attitude in general:

> The temple lies on a small plain in front of the entrance to the grotto and is not at all remarkable. The grotto itself was unremarkable, and would be passed by anywhere outside of Bali. (1870:14)

He proceeds to prove his case by describing the cave, combining a tone of imperious scorn with a relentless recitation of measurements. He notes its length (seventy feet), breadth (twenty-five feet), height (twenty-five to thirty feet); the kind of stone deposits it contains; the absence of stalagmites—only losing his detachment to comment upon "the pestilent atmosphere generated by layers of bat excrement." His cool description of the cave not only subverts the enthusiasm of his fellow Europeans but simultaneously demonstrates that he had been inside it, thus proving his superiority to the Balinese about whom he comments: "Superstition and fear of Reksasas [sic] and Boetas keep the Balinese from going inside these caves; only the most courageous risk putting offerings for the evil spirits at the entrance" (1870:15).

When he returned in the evening for his second audience with the king, he found it far more agreeable. He was entertained by musicians and dancers, and the Déwa Agung was charming and loquacious. The king even took his guests on a tour of the inner quarters of the palace. Unbending a bit, van Bloemen Waanders notes that the king "speaks very good Malay, is vivacious, and appears to me to be a simple young man."[11] On the other hand, he showed no interest in discussing with his guest any affairs of state. Van Bloemen Waanders concluded that he left such important matters entirely in the domineering hands of the powerful Déwa Agung Isteri Kania and his priestly tutor and occupied himself instead with target-practice, hunting, and fishing (1870:15).[12] Thus even at his most positive, van Bloemen Waanders nonetheless manages to be condescending, dismissing Klungkung's ruler as a mere figurehead.

The priest whom van Bloemen Waanders believed so influential was, in fact, almost certainly the author of the *Babad Ksatria*, which is written in the form of a dialogue between priest and royal pupil. Huskus Koopman had also remarked on the great influence that priests had in Klungkung and, like van Bloemen Waanders, had deplored it. But it may be questioned whether van Bloemen Waanders was correct in his assessment of the Déwa Agung's lack of interest in anything other than the pursuits of a vigorous youth.

Indeed, one can see in the young king's gay talk a more acceptable (to the Dutch) version of the silence of the first audience. That first audience is strikingly reminiscent of those Huskus Koopman had with the previous Déwa Agung. A reluctance to discuss what the Dutch considered important matters was not only true of Klungkung rulers, since Huskus Koopman had a similarly frustrating exchange with Gusti Ngurah Kesiman, but it seems especially characteristic of them. Another kind of silence was achieved by avoiding meetings with colonial officials altogether: Déwa Agung Putra III sometimes excused himself from these on the grounds of illness, as his predecessor had with Huskus Koopman (a strategy adopted by many Balinese rulers); at other times he simply claimed to be too busy with ritual matters. But when meetings proved inevitable, colonial reports are remarkably consistent in the behavior they relate: the king says little, or little "of importance," and it is only at a visit from the secondary ruler (often on the following day) that the matters the Dutch have come to discuss are even broached. Silence, manifested in different ways, was a practice constitutive of the Déwa Agung's power.

In their meetings with van Bloemen Waanders, members of the Klungkung court discovered that some forms of silence were more acceptable to the Dutch than others, a lesson never forgotten by the astute young king. On their side, however, the Dutch never fully appreciated the political or cultural significance of royal silence although they did eventually come to read in certain of its forms precisely the evasion of their own supremacy that it implied.

ENDORSEMENTS AND REJECTIONS OF KLUNGKUNG'S AUTHORITY

Van Bloemen Waanders's 1856 visit to Klungkung had in part been intended to investigate recent conflicts between Klungkung and Gianyar. Their mutual enmity was indeed to prove a major factor in Klungkung's foreign and domestic relations over the next fifty years. It is referred to regularly in colonial reports. Klungkung was not often the source of what the Dutch recorded. But in 1873 the Déwa Agung initiated a correspondence with a representative of the colonial government, in which he addressed the origins of the dispute.

The Déwa Agung's correspondent was a special investigator named Zoetelief, who was temporarily stationed in Singaraja to settle affairs in Buléléng. Local complaints about the regent appointed to rule Buléléng had resulted in his exile in 1872. A provisional government was established while the administration evaluated the man who had been chosen as his replacement, but before any decision could be reached there were further "disturbances," and in 1873 the authorities decided to appoint a commission to conduct a full-scale inquiry. Zoetelief was charged with investigating both the misdeeds of the exiled regent and the qualifications of the candidates proposed by various factions in Buléléng. He was then to make recommendations to the colonial government concerning Buléléng's future governance (T. 1874:440–42).

That the Déwa Agung decided to initiate contact with Zoetelief, who had been given no authority to concern himself with South Bali, is significant. It meant that he deliberately bypassed the Assistant Resident and other officials stationed in North Bali in favor of a stranger. Perhaps he thought that Zoetelief was closer to the Resident in Java or even to the Governor General himself, to whom he urged Zoetelief to pass along his petition.

At this time, the Déwa Agung was probably well disposed toward the Dutch, for the Resident had recently managed to resolve a dispute between Klungkung and Karangasem in Klungkung's favor. A cargo of opium from Lombok had been seized at Kusamba, and the Déwa Agung had refused to consider requests for its return by the rulers of Lombok and Karangasem. After conducting his own investigation, the Resident had decided that Klungkung was in the right, and he had convinced the Lombok and Karangasem courts to accept his findings, thus averting a war (T. 1874:442–43).

Once matters of linguistic etiquette had been resolved to the Chief Inspector's satisfaction (see above), the Déwa Agung found an interested audience in Zoetelief. The Déwa Agung introduced himself through a short account of history ("I tell you how in the beginning the Betara, my ancestor, was Soesoehoenan of the islands Bali and Lombok. He was raised as prince there by the patih Gajamanda [sic] . . . of Madjapahit, and was accompanied by Satrias, Wesijas, and Soedras, to a total of exactly 100,000 men, not less") and noted that he possessed written oaths of fealty from all of Bali's lords to his late "father." Having established the grounds for his authority in Bali, the Déwa Agung then turned to an account of his protracted conflict with Gianyar, which according to his letter mainly concerned a territory called Nyalian.[13] Based upon his interpretation of what he wrote, Zoetelief wrote to his superiors that the Déwa Agung was seeking Dutch aid (presumably military) not only to have Nyalian returned to Klungkung but "to be returned to sole ruler" of Bali, with all of the other princes "again . . . under his government."[14] The Déwa Agung's letters make no reference to such issues; Zoetelief apparently reached this conclusion through conversations with Intjik Hoesin, the Déwa Agung's Muslim envoy, who was authorized to discuss matters the Déwa Agung was reluctant to commit to writing.

Zoetelief himself was entirely in favor of obliging the king. Indeed, he recommended that the best policy the government could adopt in regard to Bali would be to provide sufficient political and military support for the Déwa Agung to establish his authority indisputably on Dutch lines. Under this plan, Bali's other rulers would lose all autonomy. This would work to the advantage of the colonial government, which, he argued, would find it much easier to deal with one ruler than many. Inquiries in Buléléng suggested that the Déwa Agung was a man of "good character," and that he was tractable was proven by his alacrity in following Zoetelief's hints about the language suitable for addressing Dutch officials. As to how the Balinese would react, he noted that

> the influence of the Dewa Agoeng in the other principalities . . . may not be denied; the Bathara [sic] or Tjokorda was spoken about everywhere with respect and veneration, and everything that is arranged in harmony with him will require no further recommendation to be accepted by the people without any prejudice and respected as law.

If the populace was enthusiastic about the Déwa Agung, the other rulers "give him a more or less divine or sacred character." They also acknowledged his temporal authority, although, Zoetelief noted, mainly when his wishes did not conflict with some goal or interest of their own, or when they "consider it necessary to shelter behind him against the Government." Finally, he added that if the government adopted his recommendation, it need have no fear that the Déwa Agung might turn against them. Not only would he be indebted to them for their aid, but the Bali Expeditions had certainly taught the Balinese that they had no hope of successfully opposing Dutch military force.

This report was forwarded to the Ministry of Colonies in the Netherlands, along with the administration's unequivocal rejection of Zoetelief's plan as thoroughly contrary to Dutch interests.[15] In making its deliberations, it is worth noting, the government consulted van Bloemen Waanders, then Resident of Kedu in Central Java. His hand can be clearly seen in the following dismissal: "The Dewa Agoeng of Kloengkoeng—the smallest realm of Bali—has in reality no power or authority over the other states." This was neither the first nor last time that Klungkung's size was rhetorically used to underline its unimportance—a curious position for colonizers whose own nation occupied a mere corner of the European continent.

The government's reply demolishes Zoetelief's arguments point by point.

The character of Klungkung's ruler, for example, is said to be known to the Chief Inspector only by rumor. Various remarks in his own report suggested that even within Klungkung the Déwa Agung's authority was by no means indisputable. Surely any attempt to place him in absolute power over the whole island would be met with the strongest opposition; Bali's other rulers would never accept such subordination. The colonial government would, therefore, only be able to establish his domination by war, one that would be bloody, expensive, and possibly interminable. And to top it all off, if the government succeeded, it would create a situation potentially suicidal to colonial interests. For even if the Déwa Agung did prove loyal to the colonial government out of gratitude for their aid (which could by no means be taken for granted), nothing would guarantee that his successors would feel the same. A unified Bali under a powerful potentate was the last thing the Dutch wanted.

Was that, however, what the Déwa Agung had requested? His letters to Zoetelief refer only to Nyalian and Gianyar; the Inspector may have read more into them, and into his conversations with Intjik Hoesin, than was intended. The kind of absolute control that Zoetelief envisioned might have puzzled the Déwa Agung. Given how helpful the Dutch had been in settling the quarrel with Karangasem and Lombok, the Déwa Agung no doubt hoped he might have similar luck with Gianyar. He was not the first to think the Dutch might be used to accomplish a limited end. And the dispute with Gianyar had become undeniably annoying.

To return to his initial petition, what was Nyalian, and why was there a quarrel over it? Nowadays, Nyalian is simply a village in northwest Klungkung. In 1873, however, all of the land from Tohpati to the ocean, between the Bubuh and Melangit rivers, was under the dominion of Nyalian's lord. Nyalian had originally been granted by Dalem di Madé to Déwa Gedé Tangkeban, ancestor of the Bangli ruling house. Around the turn of the nineteenth century, however, a dispute broke out between the then Déwa Gedé Tangkeban and Déwa Agung Putra I over a keris in the former's possession. When Déwa Gedé Tangkeban refused to surrender it, the Déwa Agung ordered Gianyar and Buléléng to attack him (van Bloemen Waanders 1870).[16]

According to the Déwa Agung's letter, after Nyalian's defeat Gianyar was allowed to take charge of the region in return for paying a yearly tribute to Klungkung.[17] The arrangement continued after Déwa Agung Putra I's death, until a new king came to power in Gianyar who stopped paying the tribute. When Déwa Agung Putra III became ruler, he asked that either Nyalian be returned to Klungkung or that Gianyar resume payment on a regular basis. But the then Déwa Manggis refused to do either, arguing that the territory was Gianyar's by right of conquest. This, the Déwa Agung wrote, was the basis of the enmity between Gianyar and Klungkung, and Gianyar continued to persist in denying his request.[18]

Gianyar and Klungkung were not, however, the only ones involved. During van Bloemen Waanders's 1856 visit, Pedanda Madé Rai had informed him that hostilities had begun at the urging of Gusti Ngurah Kesiman (1870:16). Kesiman's interest in Gianyar's obedience stemmed from his desire to prevent further colonial annexations by unifying South Bali under a strong Déwa Agung. He had developed this ambition shortly after the Third Bali Expedition.[19] Even after Kesiman's death, Badung's rulers continued to try to convince their peers to support the Déwa Agung, often by exploiting fears of Dutch aggression (as we shall see later).[20]

The idea of a Bali unified under the Déwa Agung, then, was conceived by some of Bali's most powerful lords, rather than being the fantasy of either an ambitious Déwa Agung, attempting to use the Dutch to reestablish past glory (as Schulte Nordholt 1988 argues), or of an ingenuous colonial official. But acknowledgment of Klungkung's supremacy meant something rather different to the Balinese and the Dutch. Indeed, it goes to the root of the controversy with Gianyar.

The annoyance of both Gusti Ngurah Kesiman and the Déwa Agung over Gianyar's refusal to pay him tribute should not be assumed to have its basis in some natural human desire for wealth.[21] In claiming that Nyalian belonged to him by right of conquest, Gianyar's ruler was engaging in something akin to the sin of pride. The war in which Gianyar acquired this territory had occurred at the command of the ruler of Klungkung. He was, therefore, partly responsible for the outcome. In summoning other rulers to fight on his behalf, the Déwa Agung made them instruments of his agency. Gianyar's troops, then, were only one of the material means through which the Déwa Agung realized his intention.

In the eyes of the ruler of Klungkung (and Badung), then, Gianyar's "rights" over Nyalian did not stem from conquest. Instead rights to the products of land belonging to the Déwa Agung were granted to Gianyar's ruler as long as he continued to remember the true master of that land (in his turn a mere instrument of the divinities that ensured prosperity). In essence, the ruler of Gianyar's relationship to the Déwa Agung was like that of a favorite commoner to whom the court had granted rice land. The land could be used by the grantee and his heirs in perpetuity, but that it was never fully theirs was marked by gifts and services to the grantor.[22] In precisely the same way, these gifts and services—tokens of memory—were partially or totally used as offerings to the gods.

It is difficult to know what the Déwa Agung hoped the Dutch might do to help him with his recalcitrant neighbor. In any event, they were not interested. The next act in the dual dramas—the one involving the Dutch and the one involving Gianyar—opened some ten years later. Just on its brink there are accounts of another visit to Klungkung's court.

A MEETING WITH THE DÉWA AGUNG:
HEALTH OFFICER JACOBS, AUGUST 1881

In 1881 a certain Dr. Julius Jacobs, newly appointed officer of health in East Java, was responsible for arranging the administration of smallpox vaccinations in the Residency, duties that occasionally brought him to North Bali. There he became friends with Assistant Resident Vriesman and Dr. Herman Neubronner van der Tuuk, who was compiling materials for his great Kawi dictionary (Jacobs 1883:i–ii). In August Jacobs was invited to accompany the Resident to South Bali to try to persuade Bali's princes to support the vaccination of their subjects.[23]

Another member of the party (Lieutenant Bollaan, commander of the boat by which they traveled from East Java) was charged with making calculations that would allow the colonial government to construct an accurate map of Bali.[24] He took soundings, measured distances along the route with pedometers, and stopped to register the heights of mountains and the depths of ravines. Although he gently mocks Bollaan's dedication to duty in the face of scenes of great natural beauty, Jacobs himself demonstrates a similar passion for facts. His book is filled with lengthy lists of diseases, flora, and fauna, all supplied with their Latin names.

Klungkung was the third stop on this journey. From Singaraja, the party had traveled over the mountains to Bangli, then ridden to Gianyar. In Bangli, they had found virtually nothing satisfactory; in Gianyar, virtually everything. Klungkung fell somewhere in between.

An escort from Gianyar accompanied the party to neutral territory east of Lebih, where horses and coolies sent by the Déwa Agung awaited. After an hour's walk along the beach, they headed north through rice and tobacco fields and then through the villages of Tojan and Jelantik up a mild slope to Klungkung. Jacobs noted, "It struck me that so many *bedoegoel*'s (little temples for the goddess of the harvest) stood on the sawahs here" (1883:94).

After Gianyar's letter-perfect reception, Jacobs comments that not only were the horses sent by Klungkung not as fit, and the coolies not as responsive, but "there were no prominent chiefs to welcome the Delegate at the border [as regulations required], and above all the tidiness and order which had so taken us by surprise in Gianyar were wanting" (1893:94).

Jacobs, who cites van Bloemen Waanders as one of the two written sources he consulted in composing his book on Bali, reiterates that author's theme of decline in his first words about Klungkung:

Kloengkoeng, the once so powerful realm whose princes were the absolute monarchs of all *Bali*, is at present sharply in decay and the least populated of all Balinese realms. But a long time after the absolute monarchy of the prince of *Kloengkoeng* had ceased, the king of this realm was still considered as the most prominent prince of Bali and no other radja dared to carry out anything without the consent of the *Dèwa-agoeng* of *Kloengkoeng*. Even now . . . that his power is in large part clipped and his prosperity is on the wane, this prince still bears the title of *Dèwa-agoeng* while that of the remaining princes is *Anak-agoeng* and he always addresses the latter in the low language. But one realm after another renounced obedience to him, so that one can say that he still asserts himself at present only in the realms *Meng'wi* and *Bangli*. . . . [T]he word *Dèwa* indicates . . . the caste to which the person belongs. The prince of *Kloengkoeng* . . . belongs just as those of *Bangli* and *Gjanjar* to the second caste; the word *"agoeng"* behind his title means *"great," "elevated"*; the whole title, which he bears in distinction from the other princes, thus means *"the lofty Dèwa."* He is or rather was originally by way of being the pope of *Bali*, and still gives large public temple feasts (1883:95–96).

Jacobs attributes the decline of the Déwa Agung to his own generosity. The first Déwa Agung, he writes, was the prince of Majapahit, who came to Bali with various nobles after the conquest of Majapahit by converts to Islam and established himself in Gélgél. To his "vassals" he ceded "hereditary fiefs." And although he kept the largest amount of territory (not only Klungkung, but the regions of what later became Bangli, Gianyar, and Buléléng), he laid the grounds for his own undoing. It is worth noting that the regions Jacobs says were retained by the Déwa Agung are those whose rulers claimed descent from the royal clan.

After this introduction, Jacobs continues the narrative of his visit. The Dutch party was lodged in the *passangrahan* (guesthouse), where a Dutch flag had been set up, and their arrival was greeted by two of the king's brothers and a salute from "old rusty little cannons." Jacobs comments on their lodgings, which he describes as dirty, "We had not expected a *hôtel-Paulez* or *Amstel-hôtel*, but we had thought that the '*Soesoehoenan*' of *Bali* might receive the Netherlands Indies somewhat better." The Resident ordered the place whitewashed. That evening a gamelan and a dancer were sent to entertain them (1883:100–101).

The Delegate had sent word that he would visit the king at 10:00 A.M. on the following day, but the Balinese nobles who were to escort the Dutch party—with their paraphernalia of lance bearers, parasols, and gun salutes—did not appear until noon ("so that we had to wait for two full hours in full dress, until the '*Great Lord*' found it good to rise and receive us" [1883:105]). Their bad temper, however, was mollified by their reception by the Déwa

Agung. He greeted them with "utmost friendliness in a nicely decorated pen-
dopo; he was surrounded by a number of dignitaries, including a pair of his
brothers" (1883:106), one of them Déwa Agung Rai, the *rijksbestierder*. Jacobs
commented:

> The *Dèwa-agoeng* and his brothers make a very good impression. The
> first, with the name *Dèwa-agoeng Poetra*, is a man of between forty-five
> and fifty years and has a very attractive countenance. (1883:107)

The meeting was spent entirely in pleasantries. The Balinese made much
of the swords and sabers worn by the Dutch and went on to admire their
"watches, chains, uniform buttons, in a word everything that appeared of
gold." The Déwa Agung requested that the Delegate send him a cocked hat
like his own and gave him a sword to have regilded (he later asked Jacobs to
send him something from Java as well: a stronger pair of spectacles). And with
that the king "pressed us each to his breast in turn in a tender manner," announced he regarded them all as good friends who would always be welcome,
and sent them off (1883:106–8).

Later that afternoon they were regaled with another performance (this
time, significantly, a *barong*, which has exorcistic powers), and the *rijksbestierder*
sought some medical advice from Jacobs. The royal countervisit was sched-
uled for 6:30 P.M., but when the time came only the crown prince appeared.
His father, he explained, was ill with a stomachache—an ailment, Jacobs
wryly notes, endemic among Balinese rulers faced with meetings with colonial
officials (1883:111). This too was a perfunctory visit, involving a further
exchange of courtesies and gifts. Yet more gifts arrived later; the Déwa
Agung, hearing that Jacobs collected birds, sent him several valuable ones. In
the evening the Dutch were again entertained with a gamelan and beautiful
dancers, members, Jacob asserted, of the royal "harem" (1883:109–12).

With that the visit was finished, although the Dutch found one further
cause for complaint: they had planned to depart for Karangasem at 7:00 A.M.
the next morning, but nothing was ready until 10:00 A.M., and the Delegate
sent word of his displeasure at the delay to the Déwa Agung. On their way
east they passed through Kusamba, which Jacobs describes as "a place that
has obtained such a mournful fame in the Netherlands Indies history through
the landing and, following shortly thereafter, wounding of General *Michiels*"
(1883:116).

Obviously much had changed in the manner in which Dutch officials
were received since van Bloemen Waanders's visit. The Dutch were, for one,
greeted at the entrance to the capital not only by lords of the realm but by
the king's own brothers. What is *not* mentioned is as indicative of the change
as what is: the Dutch party were evidently not invited to sit on the floor, nor
was the king silent and distant. On the other hand, the Déwa Agung by no

means conformed entirely to colonial protocol: most important, he side-stepped the troublesome countervisit.

In contrast to van Bloemen Waanders, who found nothing in Klungkung worthy of his attention, Jacobs was an enthusiastic visitor. He was particularly impressed by the puri itself, which he describes as "a magnificent structure, as regards architecture as well as art." Among the extensive carvings he admired, certain sculptures especially struck his eye:

> On the forecourt of the *poeri* and above on the gateways stood various life-sized statues hewn out of stone which, judging from the costume, entitles the presumption that they are of European, probably indeed of Portuguese make, and perhaps once served as a gift from the Portuguese Government to one of the forefathers of the *Dèwa-Agoeng*. It is known that a couple of years before the first arrival of the Dutch on *Bali* the Portuguese tried to obtain a firm footing on this island. The statues, al-most all equipped with trousers, jackets with high collars, boots and a sort of hat, are in any case no product of Balinese industry. (1883:106)

Jacobs was wrong about the artisans who made these statues, and wrong too in believing that they represented sixteenth- or seventeenth-century Portu-guese. What caught his attention were in fact Balinese representations of Dutchmen (and, on the crown of the gateway itself, Chinese), which had been commissioned either by the Dèwa Agung himself or by Dèwa Agung Isteri Kania during renovations of the puri.[25] Had he been familiar with Bali-nese iconography, he might not have been so lavish with his praise. For the figures stood, guardians to the portal that led to the inner reaches of the palace, in a place normally reserved for *raksasa*.

THE DUTCH ESTABLISH A RESIDENCY

It was not long after Jacobs's visit that the Netherlands Indies government finally decided to establish a Residency for Bali and Lombok. In 1882 the Governor General sent letters informing Bali's rulers that the two islands had been elevated to a "special territory." The letters tried to reassure them by noting that although the Resident would now live in Singaraja rather than Banyuwangi, his duties, and therefore his relations with the courts of South Bali, would be basically unchanged.

The report of the emissary who delivered the letters deserves some atten-tion for what it reveals about colonial methods of gathering intelligence (and the kinds of intelligence the government sought), as well as for its interpreta-tions of political affairs in South Bali and reactions to the Governor General's news. The envoy was a Balinese *punggawa* named Ida Ketut Bagus, member of "one of the most prominent Brahmana families" in Buléléng. He was clearly selected for this mission because he was "well known in the independent realms, having many friends and kinsmen,"[26] from whom the government no doubt hoped he might hear news that would not have been told to a European.

Like other colonial envoys, Ida Ketut Bagus described for his superiors the reception of his message and his person (as a representative of the colonial government) in some detail. The letters themselves, he noted, were received with honors everywhere, "even in Klungkung." Nonetheless, there had been in Klungkung a departure from the "normal ceremonial," for only a golden platter shaded by a parasol had been sent to his quarters to collect the letter; the state lances and state gamelan orchestra did not appear until he entered the palace. (Apparently, not only envoys of the Governor General but even his missives were to be treated as sacred objects.) Moreover, no lodgings had been arranged for him; he had to find accommodations on his own with a Balinese "Mohammedan." Not only does this show that indigenous envoys were subject to different treatment than Europeans, but it is significant that he was extended so little courtesy in a realm well known for its respect for Brahmanas; it is hard not to conclude that in Klungkung eyes he had lowered himself in agreeing to serve as a Dutch messenger.

Only Gianyar's ruler read and answered the Governor General's letter at once. Both the Déwa Agung and the ruler of Bangli said they would send responses later; the ruler of Mengwi felt that none was called for; and the rulers of Tabanan and Badung did not even open the letters. Even so, Ida Ketut Bagus formed a reasonable impression of their reactions from conversations with his acquaintances.

Most important, a rumor had quickly spread that the colonial government would now declare war upon Bangli over certain territories along Buléléng's southern border. This had been the first thing that the Déwa Agung had mentioned, and there was a similar concern nearly everywhere else. Bangli's ruler had already armed his men, and was constructing fortifications at Bayung.

According to Ida Ketut Bagus, the source of these rumors was Badung. As he interpreted matters, by arousing anxieties over the possibility of another war Badung's rulers hoped to finally succeed in establishing a South Balinese coalition under Klungkung, in which they would serve as the Déwa Agung's chief advisor. A representative of the Denpasar court had informed Ida Ketut Bagus that his prince was trying "to reconcile all Radjas of Bali with one another" and ensure that they would "all place themselves again under the sovereignty of Klungkung, to which prince all of them would then pay a yearly tribute." To this end, Badung's rulers were busy trying to arbitrate various conflicts. They had already made headway in settling problems of some fifteen years' standing between Mengwi and Tabanan, and Gianyar's ruler had asked their aid in at last resolving his conflicts with Klungkung.

Despite such overtures, Gianyar still seemed to constitute the major obstacle to the coalition's success. Madé Pasek, Gianyar's chief minister and a man with great influence over the Déwa Manggis, distrusted the Déwa Agung and had seriously offended him, and the Déwa Agung insisted upon his extradition as a prelude to any negotiations. Moreover, Gianyar had recently attacked Mengwi.[27]

But Badung appears to have had some success, for not long afterwards Gianyar's ruler offered his realm to the Déwa Agung in exchange for protection.[28] Rather than establishing a solidary Balinese front against potential colonial aggression, however, this act was to eventually lead (through an extraordinarily complex concatenation of events) to the Dutch conquest of Lombok, the first step in the annexation of what remained of Balinese territory.

TROUBLE IN GIANYAR

In the 1880s the Déwa Manggis was beset with difficulties.[29] In addition to his dispute with Klungkung, he had hostile relations with Bangli, his neighbor to the north, originating in the same war early in the century over Nyalian, and compounded by other disagreements since. The dispute with Bangli was having particularly disastrous effects, since by destroying upstream dams Bangli could ruin the rice harvest in many portions of Gianyar. At the same time, the Déwa Manggis had instituted a series of new taxes, to be paid directly to him, thus exacerbating tensions within his realm that dated from the time of the first Déwa Manggis.

The realm of Gianyar came into existence in the late eighteenth century as a loose confederation of smaller semiautonomous provinces when the ruler of Sukawati, the paramount lord of the region, died, and his sons fought each other over the succession. Déwa Manggis, a minor lord, stepped into the breach, and the two sons, one in Sukawati and the other in Peliatan, became his subordinates.[30] Sukawati, the royal house founded by Déwa Agung Anom early in the eighteenth century, had several branch lines, not only in Peliatan but also in Singapadu, Negara, Mas, Tegallalang, and elsewhere. After Sukawati and its branch-line houses had acknowledged the Déwa Manggis, the Peliatan branch emerged as head of the clan.

The next Déwa Manggis extended his influence through war, marriage, and canny politics. He subordinated the powerful lord of Blahbatuh by a marriage to his daughter (the offer was initially refused, but after a battle Blahbatuh's lord became the Déwa Manggis's sworn ally). This same Déwa Manggis was the one who helped in the conquest of Nyalian. He also offered protection to Déwa Agung Putra I's uncle, Déwa Agung Panji, after he was ousted as regent in Klungkung, and it was Déwa Agung Panji's son whom

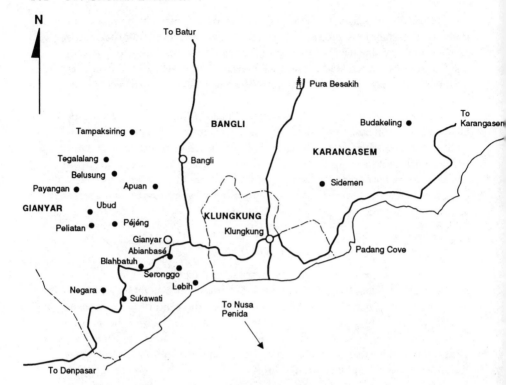

Figure 7. Klungkung and its neighbors.

the Déwa Manggis placed in charge of Nyalian. According to Mahaudiana (1968:34), the Déwa Manggis consolidated his power by destroying all rivals and placing his sons in villages throughout his realm; he also acquired some Mengwi villages from the queen of that realm, who was purportedly in love with him.

Under the next Déwa Manggis, however, this politics of expansion began to meet opposition from local Ksatria Dalem lords. It began when the new king sought to marry the daughter of Cokorda Pinatih, a descendant of Déwa Agung Mayun who ruled neighboring Péjéng. When he was refused, he declared war, and after Péjéng's conquest the Cokorda was exiled to Nusa Penida. Shortly thereafter he was faced by a series of rebellions: by Cokorda Pinatih's brother, who was responsible for Belusung; by Cokorda Anom Rembang of Tegallalang, one of the Sukawati branch-line lords; and by Cokorda Agung in Nyalian, Déwa Agung Panji's son. Unable to prevail, the three lords left and sought the protection of the ruler of Bangli, Gianyar's enemy (Mahaudiana 1968:35–36).

What was beginning to be at issue for Ksatria Dalem lords was the Déwa Manggis's attempt to assert his position through marriage and *sidikara* rituals. By descent they outranked him; to show their homage to him by making obeisance to the bodies or souls of a deceased Déwa Manggis or eating his ritual or other leftovers was therefore impossible, as was marriage to their sisters and daughters. Hence the refusals and rebellions.

It was such delicate matters of rank that appear to have fueled discontent. The war with Péjéng, after all, started with the Déwa Manggis's efforts to marry a daughter of that house; and Nyalian's lord may have been perturbed by the implications of a marriage between his father's sister and the previous Déwa Manggis. Tegallalang's lord had more complicated grounds for rebellion, although here too there was a sense that rights were being trespassed. The problem stemmed from the marriage between Peliatan's lord and the Déwa Manggis's sister, which produced a son. Because the lord of Peliatan died while his son was still a child, the Déwa Manggis temporarily took over affairs in Peliatan. But the Déwa Manggis did not relinquish control when his nephew had grown, claiming that he was incompetent. Since Peliatan was then the core house of the Sukawati clan, this met with considerable displeasure among branch lines, which Cokorda Anom Rembang saw fit to express in action (Agung n.d.: 137–43).

Given their family connections, it might have been expected that the rebel lords would have sought shelter in Klungkung, or that the Déwa Agung would have expressed concern over what was happening in Gianyar. But at this time the Déwa Manggis was very loyal to Klungkung, and Déwa Agung Isteri Kania supported the Déwa Manggis over her kinsmen (Mahaudiana 1968: 37–38). Friederich heard much criticism of this in Badung, where it was said that Gianyar sent the ruler of Klungkung many gifts "which cause him to forget that his nearest relatives are disgracefully oppressed" (Friederich 1959 [1849–50]:120), but since Friederich was in Badung after the First Bali Expedition, the Déwa Manggis's support of his policies toward the colonial government were probably of more immediate interest to the Déwa Agung than the welfare of his distant kin. This Déwa Manggis died in 1847.

His successor had trouble from the start. First of all, the lord of Seronggo, his kinsman and the former chief minister, wanted the throne for himself, and he was supported by kin in Bitera and Batubulan as well as by the princes of Badung.[31] But Klungkung supported the Déwa Manggis, and with canny political advice from a commoner named Madé Pasek (who was later appointed chief minister), the Déwa Manggis managed to oust his opponent, who fled to Badung.

Gianyar and Klungkung remained allies through the Kusamba War and the succeesion of Déwa Agung Putra III, but soon after relations deteriorated.

The roles played by the dispute over Nyalian and the interventions of Badung have already been mentioned, but the alliance may have been eroded by less momentous issues as well. So argues a Gianyar author, who under the name of Mahaudiana produced in the 1960s a history of Gianyar recapitulating late-nineteenth-century relations between Klungkung and Gianyar in detail.[32] His concern with justifying Gianyar policies and condemning Déwa Agung Putra III is in itself interesting, since it shows that enmity toward Klungkung was still felt to need justification nearly a century later. There are reasons to question many of his interpretations,[33] but a series of incidents occurring in 1854, which he takes as the basis for the development of hostilities between the two realms, do seem important, though not necessarily for the reasons he gives.

According to Mahaudiana, early in 1854 Gianyar took control of a number of territories which had belonged to Bangli, including Tampaksiring and Payangan.[34] To consolidate his position, the Déwa Manggis ritually adopted the sons of the lords of these realms, both of whom were Ksatria Dalem descendants of Déwa Agung Mayun (see genealogy in Appendix; Mahaudiana 1968:11). Adoption meant was that the two princes were now incorporated into the Déwa Manggis's clan and could therefore eat his *paridan* and *nyumbah* his body. This was a new attempt to solve the troubling matters of rank that had arisen earlier.

If earlier rulers of Klungkung had not shown much concern with their Gianyar kinsmen, this indifference was replaced by active interest during Déwa Agung Putra III's reign—for the *Babad Ksatria* written for him by Pedanda Gedé Rai is quite attentive to the branch lines founded by Déwa Agung Anom, Déwa Agung Mayun, and Déwa Agung Panji, all of which were now under Gianyar's authority. For their part, as Mahaudiana notes, various Cokordas in Gianyar were increasingly unhappy about their subordination to a ruler who was their inferior in rank; they may have reciprocated or even initiated the Déwa Agung's attention.

But while events in Tampaksiring and Payangan may have played a part in turning the Déwa Agung's attention toward his distant kinsmen, it was Bangli's ruler, who protested the loss of his territories strenuously, who sought to take action. He asked the Déwa Agung for permission to seek the aid of the Dutch (at this point still Bangli's allies) in having Tampaksiring and Payangan restored. When the Déwa Agung agreed, Bangli sent a message to Banyuwangi.

According to Mahaudiana, the Déwa Agung's decision showed remarkably poor judgment. He ignored what was in Bali's best interest in order to revenge a personal grievance. Not long before, the Déwa Agung had hoped to take a Gianyar princess named Déwa Ayu Muter as his wife. But before that could happen she was wed rather abruptly to her first cousin. Mahaudiana claims that the Déwa Manggis knew nothing of the Déwa Agung's intentions, but since a first-cousin marriage at this level would involve extensive ceremonies requiring much time to plan and execute, it is difficult to understand the haste unless either the young couple was in love and had heard rumors that the princess was desired by the Déwa Agung (in which case his intentions *were* known) or the Déwa Manggis did not want a marriage alliance with Klungkung.[35]

A different marriage alliance, however, did take place at around this same time. In August 1854 the Déwa Agung, already wed to a princess from Mengwi, went to Badung to marry Gusti Ayu Jambé, the adopted daughter of Gusti Ngurah Kesiman. The Déwa Agung planned to stop in Gianyar on his journey home, but (says Mahaudiana) in Badung he met Déwa Gedé Kepandaian, the man who had tried to claim the throne of Gianyar in 1847, who so fueled the Déwa Agung's resentment over the failed marriage to the Gianyar princess, that he changed his mind (1968:43–44). Regardless of how much influence Déwa Gedé Kepandaian may have had, it was likely on this occasion that Kesiman spoke to his new son-in-law about Nyalian. Not long after, hostilities broke out between Klungkung and Gianyar.

About a month after Bangli sent its request to the Dutch, a Javanese envoy from Banyuwangi, accompanied by troops, arrived to investigate the situation. He began by visiting the Déwa Manggis in Gianyar. Mahaudiana himself claims that by cleverly planting informants near his quarters Madé Pasek was able to convince him that the regions in question had voluntarily rejected Bangli overlordship in favor of Gianyar. Without even visiting these regions as he had planned, he informed the rulers of Bangli and Klungkung of his conclusions and left. Bangli and Klungkung began to move closer toward each other in mutual distrust of Gianyar.

This alliance was strengthened when in 1862 a prince in Tampaksiring[36] began to gather supporters to rebel against Gianyar. His plans were discovered, and he was exiled to Nusa Penida, where he was murdered on the Déwa Manggis's orders. When word came of his death, there were uprisings in both Tampaksiring and Payangan, which Gianyar subdued by force.

Meanwhile Gianyar was also involved in periodic battles with its neighbors. For example, in 1868 it was attacked by Bangli, Klungkung, Badung, and Mengwi; in 1874 Mengwi alone attacked. Although it managed to withstand these attacks, the realm clearly suffered under the continuous threat or reality of war.

The crisis came when the Déwa Manggis became obsessed with a beautiful dancer and turned the management of the realm over to her brother Ketut Sara, who proved utterly incompetent. Madé Pasek, the Déwa Agung's old enemy, resigned his position as chief minister in disgust, finally leaving the way open to make peace.

The form this peace took is somewhat surprising: in 1883 the Déwa Manggis agreed that Gianyar would henceforth be a part of Klungkung. So both rulers notified the colonial government, which sent its official recognition of the unification. The Déwa Manggis, however, did not intend to give up any authority by this action and even refused to come to Klungkung to make a formal oath of allegiance.[37]

Not long after this the village of Apuan denounced its allegiance to Gianyar in favor of nearby Bangli after the Déwa Manggis did not respond to a complaint against one of his sons and the latter's mother. The Déwa Manggis asked the Déwa Agung for help, but the latter pointed out that as the villagers had turned to Bangli voluntarily, he could not intervene, reminding the Déwa Manggis of the earlier affair of Tampaksiring and Payangan. Unwilling to accept this, the Déwa Manggis made a series of unsuccessful efforts to regain Apuan by force.

In early December 1885, Cokorda Oka, the lord of Negara, declared himself no longer a client of the Déwa Manggis and annexed several nearby villages. Other lords, including those of Peliatan and Tampaksiring, followed suit.

Casting about desperately for a way to salvage the situation and maintain his deteriorating position, the Déwa Manggis offered his realm to the Dutch, stipulating only that he remain its ruler. The Resident, however, who had only recently managed to persuade the rulers of South Bali that the colonial government had no designs on their territories, was not interested, especially since the Déwa Manggis had already voluntarily surrendered his realm to Klungkung. As he wrote to Batavia, if the Déwa Manggis could not retain power on his own it seemed rash to attempt "a political adventure" to support him.[38]

After being turned down by the Dutch, the Déwa Manggis decided to fight, and he ordered his lords to assemble their dependents. But by this time he had lost all support. Formally renouncing him, Gianyar's lords offered the Déwa Agung their homage and asked for his protection. He immediately sent one of his brothers to Mengwi to order that the regions on Gianyar's western border be placed under Mengwi protection. At the same time, Bangli appropriated several Gianyar villages in the north.[39]

At this point the Déwa Manggis capitulated. Although several of his kinsmen promised to fight with him to the death against the rebels, he decided instead to place himself under the Déwa Agung's protection. Accompanied by his wives, sons, and other followers, he went in procession to Klungkung, where he surrendered all of his regalia. He was then escorted to Satria in eastern Klungkung, where he lived until his death in 1891.[40] Both he and the Déwa Agung wrote to the Dutch to announce this change in Bali's political geography.[41]

So the matter of Nyalian appeared to have finally been settled. But the end of one dispute proved only to be the beginning of others.

NEW ALLIANCES

A number of unanticipated difficulties faced the Déwa Agung. The first began with a dispute over the Gianyar villages that Klungkung had asked Mengwi to place under its protection in 1885. Mengwi was reluctant to relinquish these villages to the Déwa Agung, thus re-creating the same problem that had initially caused difficulties between Klungkung and Gianyar over Nyalian.

Before the Déwa Agung could take any action in Mengwi, there was tumult in Gianyar. The Déwa Manggis's supporters and kinsmen had probably not been prepared for so radical a solution to the difficulties besetting the realm. The Déwa Agung had appointed his brothers as deputies, placing one in the puri in Gianyar and giving another control over Seronggo. Meanwhile, his major Gianyar ally, Cokorda Oka of Negara, pressed his authority over most of western Gianyar. Even lords who had desired direct subordination to the Déwa Agung did not find these arrangements to their taste.

Several kinsmen of the Déwa Manggis, the lords of Abianbasé, Sukawati, and Blahbatuh, finally decided in 1886 to restore him to Gianyar's throne. Their plans, however, were leaked, and they fled. By this time Peliatan, Ubud, and Tegallalang had also become disenchanted with the new order; the fugitives were sheltered in Peliatan before proceeding west to Mengwi, and from there headed to Karangasem.

By providing asylum for the rebels, Mengwi's chief minister exacerbated the deterioration of that realm's relations with Klungkung. Schulte Nordholt (1988) shows in detail that further actions by Mengwi's chief minister also conflicted with Klungkung interests, although his motivations are left unexplained.

Mengwi was in no position to stir up trouble. Incessant disputes with neighboring Tabanan and Badung periodically erupted into border incidents, and Badung was especially angered by the fact that for several years Mengwi had blocked the water supply to many of downstream Badung's rice fields; morevoer, substances were added to the water that was allowed through, so that anyone who touched it or drank it would be tormented by itching.[42] The chief minister had also alienated several important Mengwi lords, among them the lord of Sibang, who had ties to Klungkung through the Déwa Agung's Mengwi wife. Mengwi's fate was sealed when the chief minister meddled in a dispute between the lord of Negara and his kinsmen in Ubud and Peliatan.

Cokorda Oka of Negara was not only a loyal supporter of the Klungkung princes now in Gianyar but a direct beneficiary of the new order. He expanded the areas under his control in a widening circle around Negara, and in 1890 he attacked Ubud and Peliatan.[43] In the ensuring battle, both Cokorda Oka and several lords of Peliatan and Ubud were killed. A truce was called, and the survivors sat down to negotiate an end to the hostilities and to reaffirm their kinship. Their solution was marital: Cokorda Oka's daughter was promised to the lord of Ubud (Agung n.d.).

But before the marriage could occur, the princess eloped with another man. This was none other than a nephew of the Déwa Agung—a Cokorda Plonot of Puri Anyar. The Cokorda not only wed the princess but moved into the palace at Negara, completely destroying the possibility for a reconciliation between Negara and its northern kin.

Ubud and Peliatan decided to launch a retaliatory attack on Negara in January 1891. Because Ubud and Mengwi were united by ties of kinship (an Ubud prince had been adopted by a childless Mengwi ruler), Mengwi sent troops to help in the attack on Negara—and on Cokorda Plonot.

How these events were seen in Klungkung—or at least how Klungkung's court chose to present them to the colonial government—is clear from an 1891 report by Resident Dannenbergh. This was Dannenbergh's first official visit to Klungkung, and so he paid close attention to its circumstances and to his impressions.

A MEETING WITH THE DÉWA AGUNG: RESIDENT DANNENBERGH, MAY 1891

After traveling by sea from Singaraja to Padang Cove in Karangasem, Dannenbergh and his party, which included Controleur F. A. Liefrinck, were met by a Karangasem nobleman and escorted to the Klungkung border.[44] When they arrived, however, there were no horses and coolies waiting for them, and so the Karangasem party escorted them further, to the home of the lord of Kusamba. The Resident wrote in his report that he was told they had not been expected, and the lord of Kusamba immediately rode to Klungkung to inform the Déwa Agung of their arrival. He returned with horses and two other lords, who apologized on behalf of the Déwa Agung for the confusion over the date.

The party rode along the beach and over the rice fields to Gélgél, "where," so Dannenbergh notes, "there was a very interesting temple." At the southern approach to the capital they were met by an escort of men armed with lances, led by one of the king's kinsmen, who accompanied them to their quarters across from the puri.

Dannenbergh's remark about "the interesting temple" in Gélgél shows him to be a man whose sensibilities were closer to Jacobs's than to van Bloemen Waanders's, and this is confirmed by his remarks about the king. He describes him as "a man of 58 years with a favorable and energetic appearance. He gave the impression of being, for a Balinese prince, tolerably educated and very capable of leadership."

The first official visit to the king occurred on the following day. The Déwa Agung was at his most charming, telling Dannenbergh "with evident satisfaction" how he had given up opium on the advice of van Bloemen Waanders.[45] Among those present at the audience were Déwa Agung Rai, the king's brother and the acting secondary king, "to whom the Déwa Agung appears to leave the disposal of most affairs"; Déwa Agung Gedé, his eldest high-ranking son and thus heir to the throne (he had, adds Dannenbergh, "a stupid but good-natured appearance," an opinion later officials extended to his character); Déwa Agung Alit, a younger high-ranking son; two Brahmana priests, not identified by name; and various unidentified lords.

The following day, the Déwa Agung made a countervisit "in which even less was said than during the Resident's visit" about the main issue on the agenda: Mengwi. It was only on the third day, when the Dutch party received a visit from Déwa Agung Rai and other lords, that the Resident was told Klungkung's version of the origin and course of events concerning Klungkung and Mengwi "on behalf of the Dewa Agoeng."[46]

By 1891 visits to Klungkung's court by colonial officials had clearly become far more routinized. Of all the visits described so far, this one conformed most closely to the 1853 regulations. Persons of rank met the Dutch from their first arrival at the capital. The Déwa Agung visited his guests in person, even leaving his compound to do so. Where there were deviations from protocol—the failure to meet the Dutch at the border—apologies were made. (And however graciously Dannenbergh accepted them, he did make a point of noting their occurrence in his report). On the other hand, the Déwa Agung still did not directly address the business at hand himself.

As Déwa Agung Rai informed the Resident, reminding him that Mengwi had not signed a separate treaty with the Netherlands Indies in 1849 and that the government itself recognized Klungkung's supremacy over that realm, Klungkung regarded Mengwi as a dependent. But of late Mengwi's ruler paid little or no attention to their relationship, and some of his lords had participated in an attack upon Negara—which had once belonged to Gianyar but was at this point under Klungkung's authority. The attacking forces had surrounded and burned Negara's puri, knowing that the Déwa Agung's own nephew was inside. The Déwa Agung had summoned Mengwi's prince to Klungkung to ask forgiveness for this act of disrespect, but he had not come. Gusti Gedé Jelantik, prince of Karangasem, had also tried to mediate, but without success. At that point, so Déwa Agung Rai explained to the Resident, the Déwa Agung decided to teach Mengwi a lesson. He ordered Badung to take the territory of Sibang, on the Mengwi-Badung border. This too had no effect upon Mengwi's ruler. His patience at an end, the Déwa Agung and his lords had decided that the only thing to do was attack.

About a month after Dannenbergh's visit, letters were sent to all of Mengwi's lords informing them that the Déwa Agung was relieving their ruler of his authority and temporarily replacing him with the rulers of Badung and Tabanan. With that troops spilled over Mengwi's borders. The king fell; the chief minister and many of the lords of the realm fled for safekeeping to Ubud and Karangasem.[47]

BALINESE DOMINOES

By this time an alliance had coalesced between disaffected Gianyar lords (Ubud and its allies; the fugitive lords from Abianbasé, Blahbatuh, and Sukawati, who had been granted refuge in Karangasem; and the princes in captivity in Klungkung), Mengwi, and Karangasem, which was officially subordinate to the rulers of Lombok.[48]

When Mengwi was threatened, Karangasem activated several plans to distract Klungkung. First of all, the lords of Sukawati, Blahbatuh, and Abianbasé were sent back to Gianyar in mid-June of 1891. They immediately conferred with the lords of Tegallalang, Ubud, and Peliatan, and all of them sent word to their followers that they were now under the protection of Karangasem (Colonial Report 1892) and should prepare for war. On the eighteenth of June, Negara was attacked by the six allies and their armies, and its puri was destroyed. Cokorda Plonot managed to escape to Badung. His uncles immediately abandoned Blahbatuh and Seronggo and returned to Klungkung (Mahaudiana 1968:88–90).

In the meantime Badung and Tabanan had invaded Mengwi, and Karangasem resolved to send help. The Déwa Agung, as was expected, refused permission for Karangasem's armies to pass through his territory, but to Karangasem's surprise, all efforts to force their way through failed. As a colonial source reports it:

> Notwithstanding the considerably superior force which the rulers of Karang Asem had at their disposal—on June 24 they received reinforcements of auxiliary troops of plus or minus 500 men from the neighboring island of Lombok—all of their attacks on Kloengkoeng territory were repulsed with considerable losses. (Colonial Report of 1892:26)

The war with Klungkung proved more serious for Karangasem and Lombok than this, however. The conscripts from Lombok were recruited largely from the indigenous Sasak population, who were dismayed to find themselves called to war during the harvest season. Several East Sasak leaders (a Muslim region that had never been fully controlled by Lombok's Balinese rulers) rebelled, and by November Karangasem was sending troops to Lombok. But the insurrection was not easily crushed, especially as the rebels had written to Batavia complaining of oppression and asking for aid (van der Kraan 1980).

This letter could not have come at a more opportune moment. After years of ignoring suggestions by officials that more control be exerted over tyrannical indigenous rulers (including complaints by Dannenbergh specifically about the ruler of Lombok), the colonial government was beginning to change its policies. Officials sent to investigate produced a report detailing the unfortunate position of the Sasak under their Balinese overlords, and when a new interventionist Governor General was appointed in 1893 he took action. Violence erupted during a mission to mediate between the contending parties in 1894, and Lombok was conquered (van der Kraan 1980).

The very same report, however, also had repercussions for colonial policy concerning Klungkung. According to its author, despite Klungkung's claims to sovereignty over Gianyar and Mengwi, the Déwa Agung, who had a "chronic shortage of manpower," could hardly exercise any authority at all (Schulte Nordholt 1988 : 186). Moreover, it was suggested that the demonstrably despotic rulers of Lombok were on the brink of usurping Klungkung's position in Bali—for the rebellious lords of Gianyar and Mengwi, in allying themselves with Karangasem, had (it was argued) in effect become dependents of Lombok, Karangasem's superior.

Such claims had a major impact on colonial perceptions of Klungkung, largely as a result of their timing. The report tipped the balance permanently toward the view that Klungkung's power was nominal just as arguments for Dutch intervention in the affairs of indigenous states were becoming increasingly convincing to politicians in the Hague. Thus an image of Klungkung as impotent was established precisely at the moment it could most affect colonial policy in Bali.

In addition, although Lombok had been Klungkung's enemy, its fall did not in the end benefit the Déwa Agung, for the rearrangements it brought ultimately worked against his interests. By exercising extreme care, Karangasem's ruler had managed to distance himself from his kinsmen in Lombok when fighting broke out with the Dutch, thereby saving his realm from direct annexation and himself from exile or death. Still, as Lombok's dependent, the colonial government considered Karangasem a "Government Territory" once Lombok was taken. But so politic had its ruler been in dealing with the Dutch that he was allowed to retain power as their "viceroy" (*stedehouder*).

Here events come full circle. For Karangasem's new status created a precedent that secured Gianyar's position once and for all.

THE RESTORATION OF GIANYAR

In April 1891, shortly before events in Mengwi and Karangasem came to a head, the Déwa Manggis died in Satria, leaving two sons. They were in secret communication with supporters in Gianyar, and the ruler of Karangasem had hoped to free them when Karangasem went to war against Klungkung. But the attack had failed, and Karangasem was soon preoccupied with its own problems. Finally, in 1893, they were spirited away from Satria in the middle of the night by a group of supporters from Tegallalang. The elder of them, Déwa Ngurah Pahang, was established as the new ruler of Gianyar (Mahaudiana 1968:91–95).[49]

Gianyar was never again what it had been. Nyalian—now called Banjarangkan—remained under Klungkung authority, despite repeated efforts by Gianyar's new commander-in-chief (Cokorda Gedé Sukawati of Ubud) to retake the area (Mahaudiana 1968:95). On the whole, however, Déwa Ngurah Pahang was a successful if short-lived ruler. In 1896 he died suddenly and was succeeded by his younger brother and partner in exile, Déwa Gedé Raka. Déwa Gedé Raka soon found himself faced with the same difficulties that had defeated his father: renunciations of allegiance to his authority and wars with his neighbors (Mahaudiana 1968:95–99). He was saved only by his dependence upon Cokorda Gedé Sukawati, who was a brilliant warrior (some attributed his successes to his *kasaktian*),[50] but even so by the end of 1899 Gianyar's survival looked highly doubtful. Finally, the Cokorda advised the ruler to make another attempt to offer Gianyar to the colonial government. This time the Governor General was only too happy to comply. In March 1900 Déwa Gedé Raka was appointed Viceroy, and in 1903 the colonial government even financed a spectacular coronation ceremony for him.[51]

Not surprisingly, the Déwa Agung strenuously protested these arrangements and attempted to convince the government that Gianyar was not anyone's to give away. Not only were the Dutch there to stay, however, but their interest in extending their influence and the ruler of Gianyar's interest in opposing him undermined Klungkung's position to an unprecedented degree.

ETIQUETTE AND THE POWER OF THE DUTCH

The visits to Klungkung's court described so far provide glimpses of different stages of a transformation. Interactions between representatives of the colonial government and Balinese rulers mark a shift in relations of power.

When van den Broek visited Bali in 1817, he was struck by what he considered the lack of respect Balinese showed for Europeans. He indignantly noted that even ordinary people regarded themselves as his superior, citing examples of their behavior as evidence:

Our clothing, our customs, they find laughable. If one goes along the street it very often happens that one is seized familiarly by the hand by a common Balinese, and he asks to look at something or other, such as [one's] coat lining, or vest or watch chain. It also often happens that they stand in the road, right opposite one, with arms crossed over each other, and begin to laugh aloud or clap their hands. . . . At home one is also never free; everyone comes boldly inside, seizes hold of every-thing he sees, asks hundreds of boring questions, or stands with arms over each other looking impudently, and finally takes off with loud laughter. (1835:231–32)

But even more frustrating, van den Broek could find no way of ensuring treatment of a less offensive kind. For although he repeatedly complained to the prince of Badung, and was promised that something would be done, noth-ing changed. Indeed, the prince even told him on occasion that people meant no harm and that they showed him more respect than they had ever before shown to a European. He had even less luck when he went to Mengwi, where thousands of people lined up to see him:

They laughed, shouted, clapped their hands, and flourished white cloths to shy our horses. I told this to the Prince, whereupon he began to roar with laughter, saying that most of these people had never seen a European. When I departed the same scene occurred; the people even threw mud and stones after us, although the Princes stood looking at some distance and their bellies shook with laughter. (1835:233)

Indeed, on that occasion van den Broek became so enraged that he rushed the crowd, which scattered in alarm, and he told the prince that if he would do nothing to stop such behavior, he would order the four soldiers accompa-nying him to fire. In his report he apologized to the Governor General for losing control but said in his own defense that all of the humiliations he had undergone had finally pushed his patience to its limit. Had the prince not finally ordered his people inside their compounds, he would undoubtedly "never have returned to Java alive" (1835:233–34).

I have cited van den Broek at length to point out how dramatically things changed. Even by 1856 offended Dutch officials were no longer amusing but potentially dangerous: the king's brother and priest had to go and apologize for the king's ignorance.

What was at stake here was more than simply etiquette, since for many Balinese, especially as time went on, the Dutch were more than simply people. Even when the Balinese had little direct experience of them they believed them to be "monsters of cruelty" (van den Broek 1835:231). Inci-dents reported here and there in colonial reports show that by the latter half of the century the Dutch were popularly associated with the kinds of invisible forces that brought epidemics. In 1856, for example, the ruler of Bangli asked van Bloemen Waanders to cancel a proposed trip to Lake Batur. After a visit to Batur by C. J. Bosch (then delegate for Balinese affairs, who came to Bali on a tour of inspection), a "violent illness broke out in Bangli" and not only did many people die but the crops failed. When word had reached people of van Bloemen Waanders's plans they had petitioned their king, and he told the Dutchman that if the journey proceeded as planned "the prince would be accused of trespassing upon the interests and welfare of his subjects" (1870:25).[52] In 1898 Pura Tegeh Koripan, a temple in the Bangli region, was closed and enormous offerings were made (including animal sacrifices to the demons) on the command of the deity when, following a visit from the Resident and Controleur, a violent stomach illness broke out in the region (Schwartz 1901:125). The temple was still closed, at least to foreigners, in 1902 (van Kol 1903:457).[53]

A similar report comes from North Bali, the population of which was most familiar with the Dutch. Jacobs notes that the docking of his ship at the reef at Buléléng was regarded with some apprehension since the Balinese "have a firm belief that such events are followed by a cholera epidemic," a belief he thought likely to be reinforced "since cholera (*grubug*) again broke out on Bali after the *Watergeus'* arrival" (Jacobs 1883:4). Significantly, the two earlier occasions he cites marked moments when colonial control over Buléléng had been intensified: the end of an expedition against the rebellious district of Banjar in 1868, and the departure of the ship carrying Buléléng's regent into exile.

These reactions to the Dutch may explain the complex process of accommodation and resistance with which Bali's rulers attempted to deal with them. For the ritual response to dangerous forces is to give them just enough so that they will cease their predations. While the Déwa Agung seems to have had confidence in his ability to ultimately master the Dutch (the statues of Europeans standing guard like *raksasa* outside the door to his puri would appear to testify to that), ritual practice might explain the style of his dealings with representatives of the colonial government.

Within the framework of the 1853 regulations, both colonial officials and Klungkung's ruler acted upon their visions of each other. The Dutch attempted to treat the Déwa Agung as a native ruler, inherently inferior to European officials in the colonial service. The Déwa Agung in turn tried to prevent the Dutch, whose aggression and rudeness showed them clearly to be in the grip of demonic forces, from interfering with his goals and disturbing his poise, thus endangering his connection to the gods. He must have been sorely tempted.

Both Balinese and colonial officials negotiated their relationship through a symbolic language at its base Balinese. The Dutch had won the battle to determine who sat where and what form of language might be used by whom. Nonetheless the Déwa Agung could still restrict what was discussed and by whom when they met, and could to some extent control where colonial visitors were lodged.

We have already seen that van Bloemen Waanders was far from content with the accommodations offered him. By the time of Dannenbergh's visit, the Dutch had made some gains, for colonial envoys were no longer housed with commoners. By the 1890s official visitors to Klungkung were even lodged in a puri: Puri Anyar, just across the road from the royal compound itself (Schwartz 1901:121). On the other hand, they were never allowed to sleep in the royal compound itself as they were in Karangasem, where the Viceroy not only built the Dutch their own quarters but equipped them with European furnishings.[54] Puri Anyar was not even the residence of Déwa Agung Rai, the secondary king and the king's full brother. It belonged rather to his lower-ranking brothers, one of whom had adopted one of his sons. This son, Cokorda Raka Pugog, became the intermediary between the Dutch and the palace.

The fact that discussions *were* always conducted through intermediaries is another point worth noting. Although the protocol was clearly designed around the expectation of direct colloquy between Dutch envoys and Balinese rulers, in Klungkung this was successfully evaded.

But the Déwa Agung could resist only so far. Descriptions of various meetings show that officials noted every deviation from the rules and make it apparent that the Dutch were having an effect on the possibilities open to Bali's rulers. By the 1890s the Déwa Agung was making the countervisit that he could still avoid a decade before. As we will see, in the end their own violent abrogation of protocol signaled the end of this process; the Dutch no longer concerned themselves with the Déwa Agung's sensibilities.

And some of the accommodations by which Bali's rulers adapted to Dutch norms may well have undermined their followers' confidence in their spiritual power. Returning to van den Broek, I am especially struck by comments he made about the person of the ruler: "It is regarded as a great misdeed and sacrilege to touch the Prince's body above his hips" (1835:218). When the prince of Badung fell ill, he consulted the doctor in van den Broek's party. But when the latter moved to take the ruler's pulse, a member of the royal entourage sprang up in alarm and grabbed the doctor's hands. The prince graciously consented to let the doctor feel the pulse in his foot instead. What a contrast to Jacobs's account, in which no less than the Déwa Agung himself, obviously a canny observer of European mores, was willing to embrace each of the Dutchmen visiting his court.

INEFFECTIVE DESPOTS

By the turn of the century Klungkung's position was precarious. Two of its neighbors, Karangasem and Gianyar, were already under the authority of the Dutch colonial government. Some of the Mengwi exiles, who had managed to regain territory in Mengwi, also appealed to the Dutch for protection, restricting the sphere of Klungkung authority even further. Thus far, however, Dutch incursions into South Bali had still been more or less at the behest of Balinese. This was about to change. In 1901 the Netherlands government formally adopted an "Ethical Policy," in which it declared itself responsible for the welfare of the people of the Indies. Practices considered immoral by the Dutch—including slavery, smuggling, exploitation, and the "arbitrary" exercise of authority, all of which they themselves either were or had been guilty of—were to be eliminated, if possible by persuasion, if not by force.

In Bali the Déwa Agung soon became the epitome of all that the Dutch found wrong with native rulers. Gianyar's ruler played a role in this reimaging of Klungkung, by blaming the Déwa Agung for virtually all problems that arose in his realm, some of which colonial administrators later ascribed to his own inadequacies.[55]

While his status as a Viceroy of the colonial government protected Gianyar against attacks by Bangli and Klungkung, it could not alleviate friction within the realm or prevent rebellions by Gianyar lords and subjects. A bare two months after Gianyar was officially incorporated into the Netherlands Indies, a certain Déwa Putu Mekar of Batuyang, a village subordinate to Ubud, made an abortive attempt to place his village under the authority of Cokorda Plonot, who was then living in Badung. Around the same time, another Gianyar lord, a Déwa Gedor, stole gold and silver valuables from Puri Gianyar.[56] Gianyar's ruler told the Dutch that the theft had been committed at the instigation of the Déwa Agung, who denied it. However, the Déwa Agung did provide sanctuary for the thief, who was discovered by a delegation from Gianyar living in the market next to Klungkung's palace. When Gianyar's ruler requested his extradition, the Déwa Agung, after a long delay, replied that he would be happy to comply if Gianyar extradited in return persons guilty of crimes in Klungkung, especially a man who had committed adultery with the crown prince's wife. But since such a liaison was a capital crime, and the Dutch would not sanction the death penalty for what they regarded as a minor infraction of local custom, the exchange was forbidden.[57]

Disruptions to the irrigation system in the shared watershed of the Melangit River on the western border of Banjarangkan were also blamed on the Déwa Agung, although they probably had little to do with him. In general, officials took Gianyar's complaints at face value without further investigation—even though it later proved (when a particular case did precipitate further inquiry) that Gianyar's rulers were capable of significant misrepresentation.[58] In the eyes of colonial administrators, such incidents were interpreted as evidence of the Déwa Agung's refusal to recognize their authority.

What particularly irritated the colonial government was that not all Balinese appeared to share their appraisal of the Déwa Agung's inadequacies as a ruler. Several regions—among them Munggu, Sibang, Tampaksiring, and Payangan—even transferred their allegiance from Badung, Tabanan, and Bangli to come under Klungkung's direct authority. The Dutch (perhaps encouraged by Gianyar's ruler) could only attribute such events to Klungkung conniving. For example, when 54 villages (with a population of about twenty thousand) in the northern part of what had formerly been Mengwi became Klungkung dependencies in 1900, the Resident reported that they "were brought through the intrigues of the Dewa Agoeng under his own domination."

Such an analysis ignored the ties between Klungkung and Mengwi (whereas Mengwi and Badung/Tabanan had long been enemies) and the fact that the heir to Mengwi's throne (Gusti Gedé Agung) supported the move and was a loyal enough follower of the Déwa Agung to pay him tribute.[59] As for the other regions, the Déwa Agung's first wife was from Sibang, and the lords of Payangan and Tampaksiring were his kin.[60] Nor did such events cause any enmity between Klungkung and the remaining independent realms, as they might have had they really been due to Klungkung scheming. In fact the rulers of these realms continued to support the Déwa Agung. Thus, when the Déwa Agung sent an embassy to Batavia in 1902 to bring his concern over colonial encroachments directly to the attention of the Governor General, the group included representatives and gifts from the rulers of Badung and Tabanan as well.[61]

The government's negative view of the Déwa Agung is given most vivid expression by van Kol, one of the major spokesmen for the Ethical Policy, who visited Bali several times. His training as an engineer and allegiances as a Socialist would hardly have inclined him to enthusiasm over indigenous rulers in any event, but he is a useful weathervane for measuring the direction in which colonial policies were headed, and his works had an impact on public opinion. As he frequently lifted passages in their entirety from the writings of others, one may surmise that many of his remarks come equally unmodified from what he heard from local officials. Among other things, he reveals how some of the Déwa Agung's oldest strategies for dealing with colonial officials were now received:

He is pretentious enough to avoid as much as possible every contact with the Controleur of the Civil Service, as such an Official in his eyes is of too low rank to come into contact with him. (1903:478)

His pride makes the Dewa-Agoeng frequently impudent. When the Controleur wants to visit him, he mostly feigns illness, and he sends a subordinate person; if the Resident asks him something, he keeps [him] waiting for months for an answer. (1903:480)

A delegation sent to the Governor General, which ignored colonial hierarchies, particularly annoyed colonial officials:

Without the knowledge of the Resident, an embassy was sent to Buitenzorg . . . with the charge to ask back Gianjar. The Governor General promised to answer by letter, but in that time the embassy was the source of numerous false rumors. . . . After [their] return to Bali, the people of this embassy stayed many days in Boeleleng; some of them became sick and died there, but none of them took any notice of the representative of the Netherlands authority. (van Kol 1903:479–80)[62]

The condescension in van Kol's description is particularly noteworthy:

This old mischief-maker forges continual intrigues . . . and practices passive resistance as much as possible. . . . Mostly he knows [how] to push others in front in order to cover himself, and he pipes down if he is spoken to smartly. (1903:479)

From the Déwa Agung's point of view, of course, the intrigues were clearly all on the part of the Dutch. While colonial reports represent those who expressed an interest in coming under Dutch protection (such as Gianyar and various Mengwi villages) as seeking to escape oppression and tyranny, this would hardly have been the way it appeared to him. And the letter delivered to the Governor General by two Klungkung priests expressed his firm opinion that the territories in question were properly his.

In September of 1902 the colonial administration decided that the Déwa Agung needed a demonstration that it would not tolerate any opposition. With three warships stationed off the coast near Jumpai, the Resident demanded that the Déwa Agung agree to extradite Déwa Putu Mekar and Déwa Gedor; give his assurances that no damage would be done to irrigation works in watersheds shared with Gianyar; and leave the disposition of all territories under dispute to the colonial government, which would consult the people involved.[63]

A newspaper correspondent present on this occasion provides a final description of Déwa Agung Putra III:

An eyewitness writes . . . in the Java Bode of 27 September the following: "The old potentate, a vigorous, thick-set gentleman, graying, about fiftyish, did not say much but left the handling of affairs almost entirely to his brother. The latter, with the Princes, is like the King smart and stout, and a tireless talker." (van Kol 1903:481–482)

Even in what must have been an infuriating situation, note that the Déwa Agung maintained the silence appropriate to his position.

Matters were resolved to Dutch satisfaction; in any event the warships departed, and Resident Eschbach had few complaints about the Déwa Agung after this. But Balinese might have read in certain events that transpired immediately thereafter evidence of divine displeasure with Gianyar: heavy flooding destroyed or damaged dams, and a contingent of villagers from Samuan asked to be allowed to place themselves under the Déwa Agung's authority.[64] Perhaps the Déwa Agung had decided to focus his efforts entirely on the invisible world; it is suggestive that in February of 1903 he sent word to Karangasem's ruler that he wished to be friends and formally requested permission "to restore the temple at Besakih and visit other sacred temples in Karangasem."[65] In the event, however, he was unable to carry out these plans, for by the end of the year Déwa Agung Putra III was dead.

His cremation in 1904 demonstrates the corrosive effects of the colonial presence on Klungkung's authority. It was customary for all of Bali's rulers not only to attend such rites but to perform acts of obeisance. Neither Gianyar's ruler nor Karangasem's appeared themselves: Karangasem's ruler sent his nephew in his place (which, from a Balinese perspective, was in fact as good as coming himself, especially as he had no sons); Gianyar's, two unidentified lords.[66] Significantly, these representatives did not perform an obeisance. While their presence shows that the Déwa Agung could not be entirely ignored, it suggests that for some Balinese Klungkung had begun to become the "symbolic" overlord of modern ethnographic description.

At the same time, some customary forms of deference were now extended to the Dutch. Both Gianyar and Karangasem sent envoys to Singaraja on the Dutch queen's birthday—and for this occasion Karangasem's representative was the designated heir to the throne.[67]

KLUNGKUNG'S ROLE IN ISLAND POLITCS

There is little question that the Déwa Agung was at the center of the complex events that transpired in Bali in the latter half of the nineteenth century. The question is in what way. According to Schulte Nordholt, for example, colonial officials believed that Klungkung was rightfully and properly Bali's ruler, and their credulity inspired in the Déwa Agung a desire to restore his authority to what it was during the Gélgél era (Schulte Nordholt 1988:157). He was even willing to share power with the Dutch if they would help him achieve his ambitions. When this plan failed, he reversed his position and attempted to use the threat of Dutch control to unify other rulers under his control. This attempt also ended in failure; necessarily so, Schulte Nordholt argues, as the instability endemic to Balinese politics made such unification impossible (1988:159–66).

But such an analysis owes too much to colonial constructions and to the human motivations and political impotence they take for granted. Seen through colonial documents, Bali's rulers, the Déwa Agung in particular, appear preoccupied with political stratagem and maneuver. Language like "intrigues" and "cunning ways" suggests that the king was motivated by a natural desire for political supremacy. And the events the Dutch found worthy of reporting only reinforce this impression.

While the Déwa Agung's activities certainly had political goals and effects, the kinds of relationships they established cannot be understood merely in terms of European notions of domination. There seems little doubt that the Déwa Agung was attempting to forge a unity of some kind. That, for example, is how my Balinese friends interpreted his multiple marriages. Not only did he take wives from ruling houses in Badung and Mengwi, but he also married a sister of Bangli's ruler and a woman from a branch line of Gianyar's royal clan.[68] Within Klungkung itself he made a similar effort at unity. He already had a link with Gélgél through his mother; he forged one to Akah by taking a wife from a cadet line of the Akah house. Undoubtedly he had other wives from the royal clan; only those who bore children are still remembered.[69] Nor were marriages the only means by which he bound his kinsmen to himself. He adopted as a son a boy from a branch line and gave Cokorda Raka Pugog, his son by a low-ranking wife, to one of his lower-ranking brothers to serve as heir. The whole point is that these were kinship relationships, enveloped in expectations and sentiments that were not only culturally specific but utterly congruent with the Déwa Agung's role as "Father of Bali."

Schulte Nordholt's interpretation also presupposes the final colonial assessment of Klungkung's rulers: that they *were* only titular authorities without actual power, long before the Dutch appeared on the scene. I have already disputed this at length in chapter 6. As I read the evidence, what rendered Klungkung powerless was, in the final analysis, colonialism.

The Dutch posed a very real threat to Bali's ruling class. Some of them recognized this and attempted to resolve their disagreements and rally behind the Déwa Agung, whose spiritual resources made him best able to meet the threat. Balinese might say that such a great endeavor would naturally be filled with great tests. But its failure cannot be solely attributed to some fatal flaw in Balinese political structure. It was the Dutch themselves, a wild card in the shifting patterns of Balinese warfare and alliance, who made it impossible.

Gianyar's resistance to Klungkung authority and willingness to seek Dutch protection, however, need to be accounted for. Two factors seem to me to be pertinent here. First of all, there were cultural precedents for rejecting the suzerainty of supreme rulers. His enemies could tell themselves that the Déwa Agung's power had taken an ominous turn and that his actions suggested he was a Bédaulu or Mayadanawa—*sakti* but greedy. At the same time, the Dutch presence in the north made a rejection of Klungkung dominance thinkable, for the alternative was no longer rule by a peer. This entailed also rejecting Klungkung's interpretation of the Dutch as dangerous; indeed, it implied considering them saviors. And the very same legends provided precedents for that as well.

THE LATE NINETEENTH CENTURY: KLUNGKUNG ORAL TRADITION

Since the major sources on this period reflect the interpretations of Déwa Agung Putra III's enemies, it is illuminating to consider what people in Klungkung had to say about him. He is, first of all, recalled as a king of exemplary *kasaktian*, who was much given to night visits to the temples of his realm. Anak Agung Niang Bagus of Gélgél, for example, said he prayed in Gélgél every full and new moon, and Anak Agung Niang Mayun of Puri Kusamba claimed he had eyes like Bima, one of the five Pandawa brothers from the epic *Barata-Yuda*.

Déwa Agung Putra III's power is signaled by the name his descendants know him by: Betara Dalem. This epithet—literally, a deceased king whose soul has been purified and thus divinized, "Betara"; of Kapakisan descent, hence "Dalem"—is sometimes used for any Klungkung ruler or even Klungkung rulers as a group. To members of Klungkung's royal and priestly clans, however, it refers to only one man, the "Dalem" suggesting abilities equal to the dynasty's most famous ancestors.

What is striking about accounts of this period is that the Dutch are almost completely absent from them. However much it appears from colonial archives that Klungkung's ruler maintained as lively an interest in the doings of the government as it did in his, the Dutch are rendered nearly invisible by local concerns. The single exception to this silence is the 1902 confrontation, which was too direct a challenge to the Déwa Agung's power to be ignored. But Klungkung versions of that event hardly depict the Déwa Agung as cowed. Like tales about the Kusamba War, stories about this era are shaped by contrasts with the conquest just on the horizon. And so it is important to emphasize that while Betara Dalem lived Bali remained unconquered; any territory the Dutch acquired was not through military might. Narrators particularly stress that as long as Betara Dalem ruled, no one could defeat Klungkung—not Gianyar, not Karangasem, not the Dutch.

Of the long conflict with Gianyar very little is said. But Pedanda Gedé

Kenitén spoke of the last battle, in which Klungkung gained control over Nyalian for good: [70]

> My father told me this. Ida Betara Dalem was ruling in Klungkung. They came to the border at Banda [i.e., the Bubuh River: Banda lies just past its eastern banks, Banjarangkan on its west banks]. He took his regalia [*paje-nengan*] and hung them up, and held incense underneath, and fire came out [of them] . . . It was raining. After firing the guns, they would pour out the water, it would gush out. The enemy's guns couldn't fire; from [Klungkung], they fired continuously . . . Wasn't it because Ida Betara [Divinity] was sitting there?

Note that the power emerging from the royal keris took the form of fire, a theme of which we will see more. Mayun (n.d.) mentions a similar incident; in his version, Betara Dalem was present at the scene of the battle.

More spectacular events are recounted in Pedanda Gedé Kenitén's narrative of the war with Karangasem, but then Karangasem's attack on Klungkung may have been unprecedented, and the Dutch themselves could not understand how Karangasem could lose given the disparities in manpower:

> Even though it [the realm] is small, probably Ida Betara sits here. It's small but it can't [be defeated]. During the war with Karangasem . . . My father told me this. There was enmity with Karangasem, he [the king of Klungkung?] had closed off Karangasem, Klungkung was going to be attacked . . . My father recited mantras. To purify the fortifications . . . at the border with Karangasem. Together with his elder brother. They were still chanting when gunfire erupted. They [the Karangasem army] were shooting from the east. From here the firing was only sporadic. But probably the Great Emptiness was gracious. The one carrying the king of Karangasem was shot[71] . . . the one carrying the palanquin, he fell down. They boasted by noon they would attack Puri Klungkung . . . They were already outside of Goa Lawah, they were going to come here, and he ran away. Because there were . . . many at Goa Lawah. There were people with green shirts, green shirts. Umbrellas, umbrellas, umbrellas . . . where could they have come from? That's what it was like.
> DAYU ALIT: Not ordinary people?
> If you say they weren't ordinary people, they were ordinary people, but a moment before no one had seen them. There is a temple, Bukit Buluh.[72] At that one they had yellow shirts, they wore yellow shirts, they carried red umbrellas and had yellow shirts . . . But when it was over, and the troops were back home, there was no one.

I heard a similar report from I Madé Regeg, former headman of Pasinggahan:

Klungkung fought Karangasem. Klungkung was pressed hard, a fortification was made. Here at the promontory . . . It was already occupied [by Karangasem] . . . they'd already passed it and were coming here. My ancestor was in charge. He spoke to I Déwa Agung: "Déwa Agung, your Gélgél troops are at Kusamba, stopped there. They are waiting for news." My great-great-grandfather, I Macan Bongol [the Deaf Tiger], was told by I Déwa Agung . . . to go there. *Péh*. He was a brave one. Many people died, and plenty of the enemy were also killed. It reached all the way to the village, the war . . . Here, to the east, the Urusan River. The reason why it is called Urusan is because of what happened, it is said. It made a path for the blood. Then he spoke, my ancestor: "*Béh*, I Gedé Jambé, how do you come to be enjoying yourself here?" . . . He only had to say that and he got up, it is said, I Déwa Agung. The Gélgél troops carried lances . . .

DAYU ALIT: Who was called I Gedé Jambé?

I Déwa Agung from Gélgél [i.e., the lord of Gélgél] . . . He got up. *Bah* . . . The enemy fell all over themselves running away. They ran away, it is said. At the arrival of the Gélgél troops. They ran . . . That's why my river, the one to the south with the bridge on it now, is called the Banges River. Because the water was putrid and rotten. Because of the blood. There was so much of it.

DAYU ALIT: Gélgél had barely arrived, and the enemy just ran away, is that it?

They ran, right.

DAYU ALIT: Why?

I don't know. Probably, it was the power/knowledge [*adnyanan*] of the Déwa Agung of Gélgél. The *adnyanan* of the Déwa Agungs of Gélgél, doesn't it take the form of—[palms together at his forehead] I ask forgiveness—of *gamang*, of invisible armies? Invisible armies.[73]

What went on between the Déwa Agung and the Dutch in 1902 was described not in terms of materializations of invisible forces but as the effect of a display of royal temper. Consider, for example, this account by Anak Agung Pekak Gaci of Puri Bedulu:

When the Dutch first came to take the wealth of the land, I was already alive but I was still small. When they had a meeting. I was told about it by my father. I remember . . . what's it called? Only the Déwa Agungs. My Deified Grandfathers. The Dutch were going to exploit the land here. I remember that time. Then, who knows what he was thinking/feeling, [the king] became angry at the envoy, until, it is said, the Dutchman fell down unconscious. Now what he said was—I've been told, I am just telling what I've heard, isn't that so?—"What do you want, White Eyes?"

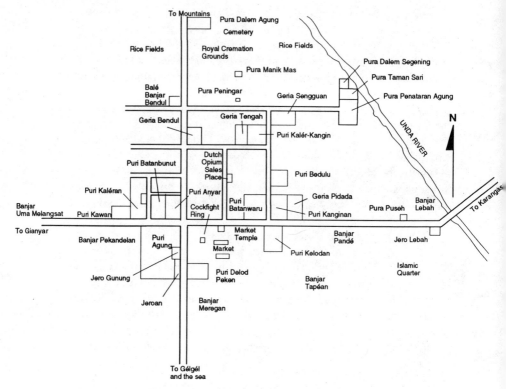

Figure 8. Royal houses, temples, and priestly houses in the capital in 1908.

He only said that much and the Dutchman fainted. And then his younger brother picked up the Dutchman, his brother from Jero Kajanan [a more intimate name for Puri Kaléran, where the narrator's wife was born; see fig. 8], and brought him there.

DAYU ALIT: What was the name of the one in Jero Kajanan?
Déwa Agung Rai.
DAYU ALIT: That one lifted up the Dutchman?
Yes, he brought him back there. It wasn't allowed. If an envoy died, wouldn't it have been bad? That's the way things were in those days. He was brought to Jero Kajanan. Jero Agung was his brother, Betara Dalem was his name. In Jero Kajanan was his full younger brother, I Déwa Agung Rai was his name.

It was not only through words that the Déwa Agung unleashed his anger, as a similar tale, told by Pedanda Gedé Kenitén in answer to a question I posed about a later event, shows:

MW: Did you ever hear about the time Déwa Agung Jambé went to Gianyar?

Yes, my father had already become a priest, at the time of the treaty. When there was only just a plan to sign it, it wasn't allowed by Ida Betara Dalem, right? It was going to be Betara Dalem, but he had already died.

DAYU ALIT: Did your father go to Gianyar?

No. No. It wasn't allowed by Betara Dalem. He said, "If there is such and such later, don't." That's what he said. That's the reason why he didn't follow, right? . . . He didn't dare disobey his command.[74] Betara Dalem had already died. At the time they signed it, he had already died. While he was still alive, they [the Dutch] didn't dare fight. If they were wrong, he only just looked at them, and they fell unconscious, because of his anger. The door was locked, and it would just open up.

DAYU ALIT: Oh, that's how things were in his time?

Yes, when he was still alive. This Déwa Agung [gesturing to photo of Déwa Agung Jambé] wasn't at all like that. He wasn't helped by Ida Betara Dalem. Because he disobeyed. From there [from that moment] there were the words "Bah, if that's the case, there is no way to prevent the realm from becoming the size of a *kelor* leaf" [about the size of a clover], that's what he [Betara Dalem] said. He didn't appear to be sick. But he was sick. He already felt . . . He had already been "tried" [i.e., his power had been tested] when they came here, south of Jumpai. If they faced inland, their guns wouldn't fire, if out to sea they would. It was still probably what's-it-called at that time, his *kaadnyanan*. Betara Dalem's.

MW: Didn't a Dutch ship come at that time?

That's what I've been talking about, ever since they experienced his anger, they didn't dare. That's my point, he was angered and they fell unconscious. That one [the Dutchman] fell unconscious . . .

DAYU ALIT: It was due to his *kaadnyanan*?

Yes, that's right.

MW: Why was he named Betara Dalem?

That's just it, since then there were no Dalems. They are all Déwa Agung Putra. He [Déwa Agung Jambé] hadn't yet been enthroned. Only he was crowned, Betara Dalem.

MW: I saw a photo . . .

However many times he was photographed, Betara Dalem, it wouldn't come out. That's why in the end they gave up. That's why there are no photographs of him.

The full impact of these narratives—and I heard them from others as well, though these are the only examples I recorded—is lost on a printed page. As narrators spoke, they often imitated the way that the Déwa Agung "looked" at the Dutchman: eyes widening and flashing with anger. And some accompanied this by a theatrical gesture: right arm extended with the index finger pointing and shaking in fury. Given how crucial a role body language played in the Déwa Agung's interactions with colonial officials, it seems a marvel of relevance and poetic brilliance that narrators focus on the king's body and his effect on the body of a Dutch envoy.

One might say that these narratives are insistently optimistic. That the colonial government coerced the Déwa Agung into signing a treaty does not signify—but the actual provisions of this treaty were not, in fact, especially important: what the Déwa Agung mainly lost was his hope of regaining Gianyar, and what the Dutch mainly gained was his "cooperation," just another form of the kind of placating at which he had long practice. What matters is that no guns were fired, and Klungkung remained undefeated. This was indeed no small victory given the outcome of events on Lombok not too many years before. These narratives assert, in a language of bodies and emotions reminiscent of tales about the Kusamba War, that Betara Dalem's power ensured the safety of his realm. But they make such claims in part to establish a dramatic contrast between this Déwa Agung and his successor.

What such tales say about Déwa Agung Putra III is that this was a man of power. And colonial accounts let us see something of how a man of power looked and acted and talked.

DÉWA AGUNG JAMBÉ: ACCOMMODATION AND DEFEAT

From the start Déwa Agung Jambé (see fig. 9) tried to cooperate with the Dutch, hoping to at least maintain things as they were.[75] He may even have believed, as Ketut Oka of Jero Lebah told me, that it was still possible for the Dutch to accord him honors similar to those given the Susuhunan of Surakarta or the Sultan of Jogja. But rather than placating the Dutch, each concession only led to escalated and more troubling demands. In the end his policy of appeasement lost him the respect and support of his lords and kinsmen, who rebelled against his efforts to play by Dutch rules.

On the one hand, the fall of Klungkung appears to depend upon a contingency: the existence of a weak king in Klungkung. But from a wider perspective, the weakness of the king only aggravated matters. Klungkung's position had already been eroded by colonial interventions in Balinese affairs. The problem was whether Klungkung could continue to accommodate the Dutch and still remain Klungkung. For Klungkung to accept colonial overlordship willingly—an option that was open to other rulers—would be to lose its very identity. But to refuse to do so was to run the risk of being destroyed.

Déwa Agung Jambé faced a very different kind of colonialism than his father had. By this time the Dutch were chafing to rid themselves of independent states throughout the archipelago. Already in direct or indirect control over half of Bali's principalities, they sought excuses to absorb the remaining four.

The death of Tabanan's ruler and his imminent cremation inspired colonial officials to take their first step toward improving Balinese morality: the abolition of the custom knows as *masatia*, the Balinese version of Hindu "suttee." In Bali *masatia* appears to have been restricted to royal wives. Nineteenth-century accounts of Bali invariably described such acts as evidence of barbarity (see, e.g., Geertz 1980; van der Kraan 1980).

Masatia, which means to be loyal or faithful, is understood to be inspired by love, although it appears that childless and low-ranking women were most likely to to elect such a fate. (High-ranking women or those with children had, for one thing, less to gain by such an action in the next world.) It was also a greater testimony to a king's attractiveness for younger women to demonstrate how bereft they felt at his loss. But although the loyalty of such wives was particularly exemplary, a ruler's subjects were also expected to demonstrate their devotion through an act of sacrifice. While the body of a king lay in state during the elaborate preparations for a royal cremation, his followers "sacrificed" their hair, *masatia rambut*, a symbolic participation in the king's death—and in Klungkung they did so even at the death of the last ruler, in the 1960s. By custom women cut off several locks of hair, while men (who wore their hair long in precolonial Bali) shaved their heads. Several times a month (minimally at the full and new moons) the royal body would be feted with entertainment and offerings, and new additions to the pile of human hair would be made. All of the hair was burned along with the body. In theory loyal subjects should die with their king; in lieu of that they offered their hair, rendering to Sang Prabu, the head of the social body, a sign of that same portion of their own anatomy.

Colonial officials had no quarrel with such symbolic acts, but, like the British in India, they found the idea of women leaping into flames to show their devotion to an old, polygynous husband repellent. But it was only now, when the government was prepared to take military action to enforce their point of view, that they pressured Bali's rulers to sign vows agreeing to prohibit such acts in the future.

Ironically the cremation of Déwa Agung Putra III provided the crucial test case. Given what they called Klungkung's "prestige," officials argued that the new Déwa Agung's compliance would make a strong impression on Bali's other rulers. While Déwa Agung Jambé obligingly forbade any of his father's widows from sacrificing themselves, the government showed little gratitude. During the negotiation of the *satia* treaty, the colonial government was also composing another document, by which the new ruler would guarantee to uphold all prior treaties in exchange for their formal recognition. It was on this occasion that the Resident raised the question of the Déwa Agung's title (see chapter 2). In the end the Déwa Agung was demoted from "Soesoehoenan of Bali and Lombok" to "Soesoehoenan of Kloengkoeng" without registering a word of protest.

Not long after, in late May of 1904, a ship wrecked off the coast of Badung, and its Chinese owner reported that its cargo had been stolen. The Governor General dispatched a special investigator, who adjudged that there had indeed been losses and demanded indemnities from Badung's rulers, invoking the 1849 treaty that renounced rights over shipwrecks. But having made his own inquiries, the prince of Puri Denpasar reported that no Badung subjects had taken anything from the ship. Therefore, he owed the Dutch nothing.

The Dutch responded by threatening to blockade Badung's harbors to all trade if they were not paid by January 1905. Still insisting that his people were innocent of any theft, the prince held firm to his refusal. The Dutch not only set up the blockade but announced that they would hold him responsible for the expense of maintaining it. Badung's rulers protested strenuously but continued to insist that, since no wrong had been committed, no payment should be made.

And so matters remained until January 1906, when the new Resident, de Bruyn Kops, began to increase the pressure on Bali's rulers. One of the first incidents he reported after his appointment involved the seizure of a group from Bangli who were bringing thatch to Badung. Since the thatch was for a temple, the ruler of Bangli requested that they be allowed to proceed; de Bruyn Kops coolly responded that *all* imports to Badung were prohibited.[76] This was not the way Balinese conducted political relations: when a Balinese ruler held a ritual even his most determined enemy would call a halt to hostilities, and might even engage in an exchange of gifts.

In April the blockade was extended to Tabanan, whose ruler had allowed goods to pass to and fro over his border on behalf of his kinsmen in Badung. As tensions escalated, officials monitored Bali's four independent rulers closely. De Bruyn Kops reported that they had sworn a vow of mutual aid and that Badung had sought a meeting with a representative of the British government.[77]

The Déwa Agung was placed in a difficult position: on the one hand, he needed to support his allies in Badung; on the other, he wanted to avoid a war with the Dutch. According to a Badung source, the Déwa Agung offered to help the lord of Denpasar pay in order to keep the peace (Alit Konta 1977:19–20). Colonial reports assert that he promised he would obey the provisions of the blockade and permit no Klungkung goods to be brought to Badung and Tabanan, or Badung and Tabanan goods to be sold in Klungkung. However, de Bruyn Kops noted that in Sibang and Abiansemal, areas near Badung that "belonged" to Klungkung, trade with Badung continued to be brisk. When the Déwa Agung was ordered to bring it to a halt, he assured the Resident that he would do everything he could. But the trade continued unabated, leading de Bruyn Kops to note in his next report that the Déwa Agung appeared to be utterly incapable of enforcing his commands.[78]

It was not long before the colonial government moved against Badung. Arguing that the government had not received any satisfaction from the blockade, the Resident urged more decisive action: such a long stalemate only undermined confidence in Dutch authority. War was declared in September 1906, and ships filled with troops, horses, howitzers, reporters, and a photographer set sail for Badung from Tandjung Priok in Batavia.

Despite de Bruyn Kops's reports of an alliance, Bangli and Klungkung remained carefully neutral when they were informed there would be a military expedition. Both rulers wrote to acknowledge the news, and both urged the Dutch to reconsider and seek a peaceful solution. Neither, however, sent troops to aid Badung. The Déwa Agung even wrote to de Bruyn Kops to explain that if people from Sibang and Abiansemal were pressured to take Badung's part, he hoped that he would understand that they had been coerced and not punish them. He even suggested that the colonial army be reminded that these lands were part of Klungkung, so that they would not inadvertently occupy them.

Although the Dutch military had anticipated a long and fierce resistance, Badung fell in a matter of days, with puputans at each of Badung's two courts. The ruler of Tabanan and his sister, brothers, and sons immediately surrendered, requesting that Tabanan be made a regency on the model of Gianyar and Karangasem, with its prince as Viceroy. This was refused, and the ruler, along with his sons and two of his brothers, was exiled to Lombok. On the first night of their captivity the ruler and the crown prince committed suicide.

Leaving troops and officials behind in Badung and Tabanan, the colonial expeditionary force set up headquarters in Gianyar. They were still spoiling for a fight. Later, colonial newspapers reported that only a direct order from The Hague stopped the army from moving against Bangli and Klungkung. Reports of the puputans in Badung had proved shocking to European sensibilities, and the government was adamant in insisting that no further massacres occur. The expeditionary leaders had to settle for new treaties and a show of force. Nonetheless, the treaties and the circumstances that surrounded their signing seem deliberately provocative.

The Déwa Agung raised no objections to the treaty itself (although, as we will see, it was a devastating document); he even agreed to surrender all weapons (which in fact he did not). But two demands he did his best to avoid fulfilling: that he come personally to Gianyar to sign the treaty, and that the colonial army be allowed to march through Klungkung. Cokorda Raka Pugog (the king's half-brother, who had become the emissary to the Dutch in the last years before his father's death) tried his best to find a way around the first and more problematic of these demands. He asked that the treaties be signed in Klungkung, on the grounds that the Déwa Agung was ailing. This was refused. The Déwa Agung then sent word that if it was unacceptable to the Dutch to sign the treaties in Klungkung, he could abdicate and let his younger brother (which one is not clear) go as king in his place to Gianyar.[79] That he even made such a suggestion shows how important the issue was: it was simply not in keeping with the Déwa Agung's position that he come to the Dutch, and to Gianyar of all places. But the Dutch refused this as well, since they could see no advantage to themselves in such a change. Several elderly persons in Klungkung could still recall how outraged many of Klungkung's lords were when the king decided to capitulate. But he was reluctant to precipitate a war, and decided he had little choice. Accompanied by a huge procession, he walked the entire way in the rain.

He had no better luck in dissuading the Dutch from marching their troops through his realm after he surrendered his weapons to them in accordance with their agreement. He humbly explained that his subjects would not know how to receive such a force, and he was concerned that through some inadvertent misunderstanding the soldiers might take offense. What he really feared were some of his kinsmen who were virulently opposed to the Dutch and could easily start a war. The Cokorda of Gélgél, who (according to some in Klungkung) had wanted to send troops to fight in Badung, was particularly hostile. But again the Dutch insisted.

The inspection came off without mishap, although trouble was clearly hovering in the air. The Dutch were feted and fussed over and then informed that, because of a temple ritual, access to Gélgél was closed. This was immediately challenged. Then the Déwa Agung sent Cokorda Raka Pugog to try a new tack to prevent the visit. He told the Resident that the *punggawa* of Gélgél was a heavy drinker, who had been dismissed from his office, and the king feared he might insult the troops. But the Resident said that the army would march through Gélgél regardless, and that he would be held responsible for any disturbances. He did, however, allow the Déwa Agung to send his own troops to keep the peace, and nothing untoward happened.[80]

The treaty itself (Arsip Nasional 1964:46–68) had thirty-one provisions and was written in Malay, although it was by now usual to provide a Balinese translation. The very first clause promised obedience to the directions and rules of the colonial government. Klungkung gave up Abiansemal and Sibang, a considerable symbolic blow to a ruler who was the adopted son of a Mengwi princess, and agreed to allow the colonial government to demarcate Klungkung's borders. The government claimed the right to dismiss the Déwa Agung from office, as well as the right to place colonial agents, if necessary, in Klungkung. Such agents (or the Resident) had the right to attend all meetings of Klungkung's lords. Klungkung, on the other hand, relinquished any rights to mingle in the affairs of any other realm. All fortifications had to be destroyed; if, however, the government wished to place soldiers or erect fortifications or offices in Klungkung, the king not only had to accept these but even had to pay the costs. The king agreed to rule "justly" (i.e., in accord with Dutch values) and protect all waterworks and roads (including those built by the colonial government). The Dutch were given the right to exploit any natural resources (tin, gold, oil, etc.). Klungkung belonged to the colonial empire in all but name. And that too was soon to change.

A MEETING WITH THE DÉWA AGUNG:
RESIDENT DE BRUYN KOPS, JANUARY 1908

From this time on, there was nothing to stop colonial meddling in all sorts of affairs. Information was requested on royal revenues and on "slavery," and the Déwa Agung responded with alacrity.

In 1907 the Resident produced yet another treaty for the Déwa Agung to sign. The colonial government had decided to extend its monopoly over the sale and distribution of opium, a highly lucrative import by this time, to include realms like Klungkung that were still nominally independent. The Déwa Agung, who leased the rights over imports to private merchants and received profits from the sales, was to be indemnified by fixed amounts of money for his loss of revenues.

The Déwa Agung had no objections to the treaty, nor is there any indication that the indemnifications were felt to be unfair. However, when de Bruyn Kops came to Klungkung to have the treaties signed, the Déwa Agung and his lords discovered just how much had been lost in 1906.

The Resident's party, which included the Assistant Resident and two controleurs, was as usual greeted by Cokorda Raka Pugog and lodged in Puri Anyar. And then de Bruyn Kops set off an explosion:

> Shortly after our arrival, Tjokorda Raka asked me when I thought to go to the great poeri to visit the Dewa Agoeng. I answered him that I expected the Dewa Agoeng to [come] to me first, and that I would thereupon reciprocate the visit.
>
> This was transmitted to the Dewa Agoeng, whereupon the great one [*die groote*] sent his spokesman to me to ask for further information in the matter of the visit. The Soesoehoenan asked me to take into consideration the following: that when at the time of the expedition the Government Commissioner and the General were at Kloengkoeng, he made the first visit to them because it was made clear at that time that the dignitaries occupied a higher rank than the Residents.

I gave thereupon to understand, that the Soesoehoenan must demonstrate homage to the Government and must do such by, among other
things, welcoming the highest present representative of the Government present in the region of Bali and Lombok on his arrival at Kloengkoeng. During the expedition the Government Commissioner was the
highest representative; at the moment of the discussion I was, and I
asked that it be made known to the Soesoehoenan that I expected him
quickly.

After some time came the news that the Dewa Agoeng, in compliance with the information given by me, would come to welcome me,
and inquired about 1:30 in the afternoon. Although he came at that
time, together with his brother Tjokorda Raka, the *rijksbestierder*, who on
account of illness could not come, was excused. After about half an hour
the visit was ended, and I made a return visit in the early evening, by
which opportunity at the same time the supplementary treaties concerning the taking over of the customs duties and the opium trade were
discussed and signed.

I had in the meantime let the *rijksbestierder* know, that I was a stickler
that he . . . also be present at this meeting to co-sign the treaty, to
which request the lord also complied. Outwardly he actually looked
more or less indisposed.

For the record he notes that after the 1906 expedition the Raja of Bangli
was zealous in treating Dutch officials courteously, "continually receiving me
at my arrival in his residency himself, standing on the main road before his
poeri."[81]

By so contemptuously and deliberately violating the protocol for visits to
Balinese courts, de Bruyn Kops sent a clear message that Klungkung's days
were numbered. The denouement came four months later.

THE CONQUEST OF KLUNGKUNG

Although the Déwa Agung had assured the Dutch that the *punggawa* of Gélgél
who had been so hostilely inclined toward them in 1906 was no longer in
office, this was not in fact the case. He was not only still master of his domain,
but he was if anything even more inclined to object to colonial intrusions.[82]
After Klungkung's conquest, Resident de Bruyn Kops wrote to the Governor
General that the Cokorda of Gélgél was only one of a group of disaffected
Klungkung lords, and this is how things are remembered in Klungkung as
well. Indeed, many of the most powerful lords of the realm—among them
the *mancas* of Akah and Satria, the secondary king Déwa Agung Smarabawa,
and Cokorda Raka Jodog, son of the deceased Déwa Agung Rai—belonged

to this party. Déwa Agung Smarabawa apparently even spoke to his maternal uncle, the ruler of Bangli, about supporting Klungkung in the event of some incident and on at least one occasion had broached the same possibility to Gusti Bagus, nephew and designated heir of the ruler of Karangasem. At least one Karangasem lord, the powerful *manca* of Selat, had also pledged his support to Klungkung in the event of a war with the Dutch.[83] Tensions were running high, and, according to de Bruyn Kops' report, the Cokorda of Gélgél had "let it out . . . that if a soldier so much as stepped across the border of his territory, he would begin the rebellion."[84]

Shortly after the opium treaties went into effect on the first of April, the Dutch decided to make a tour of inspection of Klungkung to ensure that all was proceeding smoothly and to double-check whether or not any nonmonopoly opium was being smuggled into the realm. A detachment of troops was sent from Gianyar and marched without incident to Klungkung's capital. When they conveyed their plans to continue south to Gélgél, however, the Déwa Agung was understandably concerned, but he could hardly explain to them why they should not go.

As the troops marched down from Klungkung, the king sent Cokorda Raka Pugog riding after them to preven any unfortunate incidents. He was, however, too late. On the command of Cokorda Jambé, Balinese marksmen fired upon the Dutch, and there were casualties. The small Dutch company, hopelessly outnumbered, immediately withdrew to Klungkung, but the atmosphere there was equally tense. The Déwa Agung even requested that they leave, as he could not guarantee their safety, but the captain refused. Throughout the night, Balinese men armed with lances crowded into the main puri.

Within days, von Schauroth, the military commander on Bali, ordered a punitive expedition against Gélgél. But although his puri was destroyed, the Cokorda escaped (with four hundred followers) to Klungkung. When the Dutch troops headed back to the capital, they found the road blocked. According to stories told in Klungkung, the Déwa Agung had the road blocked to prevent reinforcements from reaching the Cokorda of Gélgél from other Klungkung lords, but this was not the way it looked to von Schauroth. Furious, the commander ordered his men to raise a bivouac in the rice fields south of Klungkung. Not long after, envoys came from the Déwa Agung to assure von Schauroth that the king had no hostile intentions and to invite them to enter the capital, but he refused. He declared that the best proof of the Déwa Agung's intentions would be the delivery of the supplies that the Dutch had left behind in Klungkung before marching on Gélgél and the immediate surrender of all weapons. At this the envoy grew uncomfortable. The Dutch were informed that unfortunately their supplies had been ransacked. Moreover, the persons they had installed to sell opium had been attacked and killed, and the opium in their stock taken. With that von Schauroth marched back to Gianyar along the beach, where he ordered warships to bombard both Klungkung and Gélgél while he sent to Java for reinforcements.

Given the situation, the Dutch found a certain absurdity in the Déwa Agung's responses; for example, he requested them ("politely") to stop bombarding his capital, and on the whole he seemed to think that negotiation might still be possible. To the Dutch, however, it was obvious that the Cokorda of Gélgél either acted on the Déwa Agung's instigation (or with his approval), which proved his complicity, or independently, which proved his utter ineffectiveness. In either case, as paramount lord the Déwa Agung held paramount responsibility. It would not do to simply punish the rebel who had issued the actual command to fire. The king had to submit as well, and the kingdom, therefore, to fall.

The Déwa Agung's persistent efforts to make peace were hardly appreciated by the rebellious lords. Anak Agung Niang Kudar recalled having heard from her father that when the Cokorda of Gélgél found the road to Klungkung blocked he stormed up to the puri with his keris unsheathed, vowing to murder the king. While he was stopped, feelings ran high. Although it did not figure in any Klungkung narratives, a correspondent for one of the colonial newspapers reported as follows:

> Serving as a peculiar example of relations in Kloengkoeng and of the power of the dewa-agoeng, is that the leaders had already resolved, in case our troops suffered a possible rebuff, to depose and kill the dewa-agoeng, and to choose another as their leader in his place, as the dewa-agoeng in their opinion was too sympathetic to the Dutch.

He added to this the popular Dutch assessment of the situation after Klungkung's fall:

> The poor dewa-agoeng is a man to pity; by character good-natured and inclined to the Government, he was dragged along by the Tjokorda of Gelgel, from whose pernicious influence he did not know how to break himself (*De Locomotief,* 11 May 1908).

On the twenty-seventh of April, the Déwa Agung was sent an ultimatum: he had until noon the following day to surrender, with all of his male kinsmen. If he chose not to do so, he should at least send women and children to safety. The next day, it was all over.

With the fall of Klungkung, the last remaining ruler, in Bangli, immediately requested appointment to the same position as the rulers of Gianyar and Karangasem. The Dutch, in a show of magnanimity, granted the request: Bali was theirs. Or so they thought.

NINE

The Destruction of the World

Déwa Agung Jambé sigra	Déwa Agung Jambé quickly
nambut awinan	seized the regalia,
natang suweta rarawis,	a lance fringed with white
abubungkul mas,	with a gold knob
tinatah ya jajenggalan,	(ornately?) inlaid,
apamapag mirah adi	adorned with a red gem.
nuli angembat	Then he held it out;
norana guna umijil	no magic emerged.
Kroda sira winatang	Enraged, he pierced the ground
ikang lemah	with the lance;
nuli lumampah gelis,	then he quickly advanced.
keneng pelor dada,	His chest was hit by bullets
akrah sira ya kabranan,	in great numbers; he was
aniba nula wasyanti,	wounded; fell down.
kang brahmasara,	The guns,
luwir tabang-tabang umuni	like drums they sounded.

Buwana Winasa, canto 9, verse 20–21

The poem from which this verse is taken was completed in 1918 by Pedanda Ngurah of Abiansemal. The earliest Balinese description of the fall of Klungkung, it offers an image of defeat in which Klungkung's regalia are utterly impotent.

Earlier references to the same theme, however, are found in two Dutch sources. Van Kol, who visited Klungkung again in 1911, three years after its fall, offers the following vignette of Klungkung's conquest based on conversations he had there:

On the advice of the Cokorda of Gelgel, [the Déwa Agung] stabbed the sacred keris in the earth, by which a gaping chasm should open, and all enemies be swallowed up. Then a gunshot fell, and shattered his knee (1914:285).

275

Both van Kol and Pedanda Ngurah seem to be describing the same moment, although their accounts are differently nuanced. According to van Kol, the Déwa Agung intentionally thrust a keris into the ground in order to destroy his enemies, an act that (in Dutch eyes, "naturally") failed to have any effect. In Pedanda Ngurah's account, a lance was jabbed into the earth in frustration, *because* it was ineffective.

A third, even earlier, report also refers to a failure in the power of a royal weapon. Two weeks after the puputan, a correspondent for *De Locomotief* described the valuables found inside the puri and scattered among the bodies of the dead. Primary among these were a number of keris:

> Among the kris of the dewa-agoeng are also some which in the eyes of the Balinese possessed magical powers. To one of them is ascribed the power to cause earthquakes when the point is thrust into the ground; a second has the power to cause a person to immediately fall down to the earth dead, if its tip was pointed at him. It is said that the dewa-agoeng had this kris in his hand when he went to meet us, one knows with what result; the belief of the Balinese in magical force will be shaken in no slight measure. A third kris would make someone remain immobile in the position he had at the moment if spiral figures were described with it in the air (*De Locomotief*, 11 May 1908).

Except that they involve a keris instead of a lance, the rumors repeated by the reporter concerning the weapon carried by the Déwa Agung recall the *Buwana Winasa*. His summary of the powers of three royal keris is also clearly pertinent to the tale told by van Kol. In all of these accounts, powerful weapons prove impotent at the crucial moment of confrontation with the colonial army. Van Kol's version is the most dramatic; something akin to the image it presents is also preserved in Klungkung memories, in a slightly different form. Consider this extract of a conversation at Puri Kawan, Klungkung, in November 1985:

> COKORDA ISTERI DAYU: The regalia was stabbed into the [ground of] the yard and there wasn't anything. In the past, it would rain . . . At that time, it is said, nothing at all happened. They thrust it into the ground with great force, and still there was nothing . . .
> COKORDA ISTERI AGUNG (interrupting): As far as the heirlooms went, if they were even placed below, if they were put on the ground, and an enemy came, the enemy would seem to see many people. They wouldn't dare attack. If they came in bombers, the houses would be invisible. Such was the *kasaktian* of those keris.

That there should be similarities between a Klungkung oral tradition and the three accounts cited above is not surprising. All three must ultimately derive from Balinese sources in Klungkung soon after the conquest. Fragments of history, these accounts show that Klungkung's conquest was almost immediately figured in images centering on the royal regalia and the failure of their power. This failure is precisely what preoccupies Klungkung narratives.

But if the correspondent for *De Locomotief* thought that the conquest would provide empirical proof that belief in magical keris was superstition—that the conquest would be an intellectual as well as political one, in which Balinese would come to accept European common sense—he was wrong. For the people of Klungkung their defeat meant precisely the opposite: Europeans had finally learned something about power. Klungkung was conquered because the Dutch had penetrated its secrets.

I first heard what the Dutch were thought to have done with those secrets from someone with absolutely no stake in Klungkung's reputation: an elderly Chinese woman I met on a trip to Buléléng. When I explained in answer to her questions about what I was doing in Bali that I planned to study Klungkung's puputan, she told me the following story:

> In precolonial Bali, only the rulers of Karangasem and Klungkung
> counted, and Klungkung was the "highest" (*paling tinggi*). Klungkung
> owned a very *sakti* keris. This weapon was so powerful that the Dutch
> heard of it. They knew they couldn't conquer Klungkung as long as this
> keris was there. They hired a spy to find it and piss on it so it would lose
> its power. The king then knew he was lost since the weapon was useless,
> and so he decided to puputan. (Fieldnotes, pp. 223–24)

Klungkung's defeat, in short, was attributed to a deliberate desecration of the royal regalia.

Some version of this tale seemed to be known by just about everyone in Klungkung. Not everyone was satisfied that it truly explained anything and was not itself in need of explanation. For some the desecration of the weapons was only one of many signs of an unavoidable, even preordained, end to Klungkung's power; a few were even skeptical about the truth of the story. Nonetheless, everyone I asked had heard it.

Apart from its widespread circulation, however, the tale also vividly summarizes what was at stake in all Klungkung tales about the conquest. The desecration of the keris marks both an absolute break in historical continuity and a separation from the gods: indeed, it shows the two are much the same. In short, it epitomizes how the conquest was registered in Klungkung consciousness.

When people speak or write of the conquest they often use a phrase redolent with implications: *uug gumi*. *Gumi* (or sometimes *jagat*, the high Balinese equivalent) refers to both the natural world and the socially constituted realm; *uug* (*rusak* in high Balinese) means destroyed, damaged, broken, and defeated. Signs of a *gumi* that is *uug* include crops devastated by pests, epidemics, inflation, low-ranking men marrying high-ranking women, twins being born to commoners, and people running amok.[1] When the phrase *uug gumi* is used as an epithet for the colonial conquest, then, it suggests more than mere political defeat; it implies nearly every kind of disaster imaginable: a state of profound socio-natural turmoil and disorder. Indeed, the title of Pedanda Ngurah's poem, *Buwana Winasa*, is a slightly stronger way of saying the same thing in Kawi: it translates as "The World Destroyed." It was *that* which was at stake when Dutch shells began to explode on the quiet roads of Klungkung.

THE DESECRATION OF THE WEAPONS

The narratives below (and these are by no means all those I heard on the subject) exhibit a remarkable consensus as to the efficient cause of the loss of Klungkung's power.

I MADÉ REGEG: At the time Gélgél was defeated, Klungkung was defeated, that was the way it was. It is said someone brought holy water, brought holy water to sprinkle on the people who were going to go to war. They were told it was holy water from Above [*Luur*]. But later, after a long time, it was said to be Dutch urine . . . That "holy water" was from the Dutch ship. (Interview, Pasinggahan, 24 May 1986)

DAYU ALIT: Where was I Seliksik during the puputan?

COKORDA ISTERI BIANG SAYANG: They had all vanished, they had all been sprinkled with Dutch piss. What is there to say? They were all powerless.

MW: So I Seliksik still existed but was powerless.

Powerless. If it wasn't, the Dutch would have been defeated, that's certain. The Dutch wouldn't have been able to do anything. I Bangké Bai, if it was turned, it wouldn't go off.

DAYU ALIT: Who polluted the weapons?

. . . It is said [it] was someone from Besakih. He carried a bamboo cylinder on his head in the way one would carry . . .

DAYU ALIT: . . . holy water?

Yes, like that, singing poetry [*kidung*], with an umbrella [over the cylinder]. The people here, weren't they happy? Here was holy water from Besakih, sent by the temple priest. Didn't they all hold their hands up for the holy water [i.e., hold their hands out, palms up, the first step in receiving holy water]? Everyone was sprinkled. When that was done, they all slept like this, their heads falling to the side, again waking, again their heads lolling onto their chests, like . . .

DAYU ALIT: Oh, they all . . .

Fell asleep. Before that "holy water" came, all of them, as soon as there was the sound of gunfire from the south . . . well, all of them danced with joy, they ran after the bullets. That's how it was, beforehand.

DAYU ALIT: Yes, it was like that before they were sprinkled. Now, after being sprinkled with . . . urine, they were all sleepy.

They were sprinkled . . . and they all slept.

MW: They were no longer *sakti*.

Meaning they were defeated, yes. Piss was put on their *kasaktian* so that they would be frightened. So it's said, isn't that so? I only knew Bali after it was already broken. When I was grown I was told. [The temple priest] was given four hundred ringgits . . . Wasn't he happy? That was the way it was, he carried urine on his head, and got that much money for it. That was why Bali was defeated. (Interview, Puri Anyar, 14 March 1985)

DAYU ALIT: Did they pray before going out to meet the enemy?

ANAK AGUNG GACI: Pray? Hadn't they . . . starting probably a week before. I went there, to the house-shrines, the Great Shrines [Merajan Agung, the shrines in the royal residence] to worship at that time. There was a person who brought holy water, he said he was from Badég.

DAYU ALIT: And then?

That's what was used to sprinkle there, everyone instantly felt sleepy. Their weapons were left leaning against the base of the banyan tree. After using the holy water, everyone was put to sleep by it.

DAYU ALIT: Who brought that holy water?

A temple priest.

DAYU ALIT: From where?

From Badég. What kind of holy water can make people sleepy like that? No one suspected anything from that priest.

COKORDA ISTERI AGUNG: Meaning it was false. The reason the enemy knew to do such a thing, why they knew of it, doesn't it mean there were spies?

DAYU ALIT: Before the end, they were praying, the enemy was worried.

COKORDA ISTERI AGUNG: If they didn't do something, they probably wouldn't have been able to win.

DAYU ALIT: They kept praying. Now look for some bad holy water, so that, so that . . .

COKORDA ISTERI AGUNG: So there could be holy water, bring holy water from Besakih. The royal keris, if they were sprinkled with what was polluting, they would be powerless, they couldn't have any effect . . .

The one who would know that would be a Balinese. (Interview, Puri Bedulu, 8 November 1985)

ANAK AGUNG JELANTIK: The news . . . the reason why Klungkung was destroyed . . . There was a temple priest who gave notice to the puri. He spoke to let the puri know. [A court official] went to speak to the puri. He informed them about the holy water [*tirta*], about the temple priest from Besakih. The holy water was brought there, given to the puri. Then they sprinkled holy water there on all of the *prasasti* [i.e., all of the sacred objects of the puri], including . . . the weapons. Just after they finished cleaning everything with holy water, the heirlooms, the weapons, everything vanished suddenly [i.e., their power vanished, not the actual objects]. Fire came out. That's what was said by the elders.

MW: Was it before the puputan?

Before the puputan, yes.

DAYU ALIT: Long before?

There wasn't even a month. That's why the country [*jagat*] was destroyed [*uug*] . . . Before the country was destroyed, how many times already had the Dutch come here, planning to attack, and they couldn't . . . If there was a weapon made of metal, with a long shaft or handle, it wasn't allowed to touch Mother Earth. If it touched Mother Earth, the country would tremble. (Interview, Puri Sunianegara, 20 November 1985)

DAYU ALIT: From where did it come, that holy water?

ANAK AGUNG NIANG BAGUS of Puri Kawan Gélgél, a cadet line of Puri Gélgél: It came from the north.

DAYU ALIT: North.

From Besakih . . . There was someone who just came from Besakih, [so] he said. But the holy water, who knows what kind of holy water it was. People were just overcome with sleepiness, it is said. Everyone was drowsy as soon as they were sprinkled, all of them. They were suddenly tired. No one asked for it, it just came. Weren't people pleased? "Bah, this is said to be holy water from the God of Besakih." They weren't going to seek any and it just came. (Interview, 20 May 1986)

DAYU ALIT: When the country was still upright [*rajeg*], it is said that the lords at the Puri were *sakti* . . .

MANGKU KALER (former temple priest of Klungkung's Pura Penataran Agung): Yes, yes, *sakti*. They knew, they were *sakti*. That's why the regalia [*pajenengan*], if they were jarred just a little the country [*gumi*] would shake.

DAYU ALIT: The country. How could it disappear, that *kasaktian*?

Péh, I don't know. At the time that people whatsis, there was a person from Above who brought holy water [*pakuluh*] here. Perhaps it contained sulfur. It's true that afterwards it changed, that holy water. All of the decorations at the temple, everything was sprinkled. And then, at once, as if affected by a *sia mua* [literally, nine faces; a kind of *raksasa*], everyone just fell asleep. A *pengalah*, it contained a *pengalah* [literally, a means of defeat; countermagic].

DAYU ALIT: Where was it sprinkled? In the puri or where?

There [gesturing in its direction], at the Pura Penataran.

DAYU ALIT: Then didn't you get sprinkled with it?

I wasn't yet, you know [a priest], my fathers were still [serving as priests] . . . To go on, those who owned weapons, whatever was wound up, all were opened [i.e., their power was released].

DAYU ALIT: People here, they were sprinkled?

Yes.

DAYU ALIT: Oh, they were sprinkled in the Penataran, it affected ordinary people [too] . . . Weren't you frightened? Weren't you frightened when they attacked?

Béh, very. The guns sounded—*dar-dur!*—from the sea. From not being able to sound, they could sound. Bah, *gerang gerung!* Before there was that holy water, they couldn't go off, the cannons from the sea.

DAYU ALIT: There was still power/knowledge [*adnyanan*].

Power.

DAYU ALIT: The gods were still there, isn't that right? The Dutch cannons couldn't make a sound. Only after it vanished, the power, then— *dar-dur!*—they could. (Interview, Banjar Sengguan, 17 June 1986)

DADONG RIBEK (servant in the puri at the time of the conquest): The reason why the puri was destroyed, every day, daily, there was someone offering holy water, so it would be sprinkled in the royal house temple, in the puri. Sprinkled on the Regalia Gods [*Ida Betara Pajenengan*]. The country [*jagat*] was destroyed [*uug*] then, after he had finished offering what was bad [*kaon*]. So that they would go home, the Regalia Gods. Who knows what happened to all of the Gods in the Great Palace Shrines . . .

DAYU ALIT: Do you know who it was who brought holy water?

There were many retainers [*parekan*], male and female, who brought holy water there to the puri. From Puri Kaléran, Puri Kauh, the East Wing. That's what is said, I didn't see it, it is *orti*. I was little. Who paid attention to me? That [water was brought] so it would be sprinkled. So that the regalia of my Lords [*Betara*] would lose their effectiveness . . . That which was bad was given there. Holy water [*tirta*] from Above was carried on a head, holy water [*pakuluh*] from Above. Didn't they go home as a result, the Regalia Gods? To wherever. [If] their home was Above, in the Above, to Above they returned. Wasn't it very. . . ? There was just a country [*jagat*], there weren't any gods. (Interview, Losan, 15 February 1986)

All of these stories assert that the royal weapons were desecrated, rendered *punah* or ineffective, by physical contact with something described as *mala, cemer,* or *leteh. Leteh* and *cemer* can roughly be translated as "[spiritually] dirty"; *ala,* the root of *mala,* signifies what is bad.

In Bali purification is envisaged as a kind of cleansing; the ceremony that consecrates a Brahmana as a priest is called *mabersih,* to be cleansed, and since most purification involves the use of holy water, cleanliness is an obvious metaphor. People say it is always possible to know when a person has just used holy water: he will *look* different, light and radiant.

Mala covers a range of "bad" things: substances such as feces, urine, menstrual blood, and the blood from childbirth; undergarments; certain activities, depending upon one's rank; and even, at least in the interpretation of some Balinese, certain emotions or ways of relating to others, as when a Brahmana priest manifests greed or anger, forces others to follow his wishes, or quarrels. Both *mala* and *leteh* may also signify suffering and confused thinking, caused by emotions such as anger or despair.

Purity is also represented in terms of a spatio-temporal hierarchy: what is above (*luur*)—heads, ancestors, gods—is pure; what is below (*betén*)—feet, demons—is potentially polluting (i.e., prone to alienate the gods). Offerings to gods are placed on platforms or shrines, which are often above human heads; offerings to demons are commonly set on the ground, where human feet tread. The metaphor extends to the ranking of persons: those who truck with things above, such as priests, are "purer" than those who do not. Therefore certain reversals of hierarchical relationships, placing above things that belong below, can also affect persons with *mala,* such as hanging clothing belonging to the lower portion of the body—all clothes worn below the waist are *mala*—above the head of one's bed. A Brahmana priest, on the other hand, would be affected by even the shirt of a nonpriest. A priest who had sexual relations with someone unconsecrated would also be affected by *mala.*

Punah implies a loss of energy, a dulling.[2] Someone who was once *wibawa,* regarded with respect and dread, but is no longer, can also be described as *punah.* Powerful objects or persons may be rendered *punah* by breaking their connecting link to the *niskala,* which is the source of all efficacy. *Niskala* forces are repelled by *mala* substances, or by certain forms of improper behavior or violations of hierarchy; and of course certain spells can have the same effect. While the desecration of the royal weapons clearly involves the most blatant forms of *mala,* we shall see that the discourse of Klungkung's defeat also refers to more subtle contaminations.

Narrators, naturally, differed in their interpretation of both the nature and effect of the offensive "holy water." Some emphasized its effect on people: in the short run, making them drowsy; ultimately, literally dispiriting them. More important was its effect on regalia weapons, though there is considerable scope for interpretation as to when and how it was manifested. Several narrators whose accounts I will cite later maintained that fire emerged from the weapons when they lost their power, though not all agreed it was on this occasion. Dadong Ribek's claim that the gods who dwelt in the regalia "went home" was echoed by a number of other people—and in a moment I will comment upon her identification of "home" with "Above."

From what texts reveal concerning offerings made prior to war, those who polluted the water would know that it would be sprinkled in a variety of places. Thus it is not surprising that people refer to several different locations in narrating their tales: the house-shrines of the main puri; the temple Taman Sari, dedicated to royal weapons; the Pura Penataran Agung, associated with Besakih, as in Mangku Kalér's account.[3]

The actual content of the "holy water" was a matter for speculation. Most thought that it contained urine—usually Dutch urine. (Now and again someone would leave out the holy water altogether and simply claim that someone had pissed on the regalia.) A number of narrators merely noted that the holy water was somehow "false" or "bad": as Anak Agung Niang Bagus remarked, "Who knows what kind of holy water it was"; Anak Agung Gaci's query, "What kind of holy water can make people sleepy like that?" implies it was a very powerful sort of unholy water. Dayu Alit explained Mangku Kalér's reference to *sia mua* as a kind of *papetengan*, a magical substance to blur and befuddle, so people would forget the important things they knew and understood. Mangku Kalér also identified the substance as a *pengalah*, which again suggests magic, of sufficient power to destroy the power of the court. Pak Darma, a man from the village of Akah, was also certain that magic had been involved;[4] given Klungkung's power, the way he characterized it should come as no surprise:

> It is said, isn't that so? Who knows what the reason was why [Klungkung] was finished being, you know. What it was that was used as a means of defeat [*pengalah-alah*] against the knowledge [*kawikanan*] of the puri. It was the King of Black Magic, isn't that so? If that hadn't happened . . . It was fate. Fate, preordained. (Interview, 23 June 1986)

The substitution of urine for holy water is an especially forceful image. The two substances, absolute opposites, nonetheless have similarities: there is a bilabial likeness between an ordinary word for urine, *panyuh*, and a word for a certain form of holy water, *banyu*. Both in fact signify waste water (in high Balinese *banyu* can even be used to refer to the urine of high-ranking persons). *Banyun cokor* (implying water left over after washing the feet of the gods) is holy water "asked for" in temples as opposed to that made by Brahmana priests. This kind of "waste" water is properly carried on the head, since hierarchically gods' feet belong above human heads. Not so *panyuh belanda*, Dutch urine.

There is a perturbing irony in the claim of the false priest to be carrying not only holy water but holy water from *Luur*, "Above." *Luur* is a charged term, simultaneously signaling what is above metaphysically—the gods and the ancestors who are merged with them, who are sometimes associated with the *langit*, sky or heavens, and are also above by virtue of being earlier in time—and socially (hierarchical superiors). Here *Luur* is understood to refer to the temple of Besakih, which is doubly Above, by virtue of its location on Mount Agung and its supremacy over all other temples. The Judas of the tale, whether a real temple priest or not, is in any event asserted by several accounts (represented here by Anak Agung Gaci) to have come from Badég, one of several villages in the vicinity of Besakih that have obligations to the temple, derived from edicts promulgated by one of the Gélgél rulers (Stuart-Fox 1987:66). But in fact the "holy water" is sent by the Dutch, who indeed felt themselves to be "above" the rulers of Bali.

Klungkung's defeat is built around a number of powerfully evocative inversions; what should purify instead pollutes: holy water, priests, and even Besakih itself are used to destroy Klungkung's rulers. A temple priest (or at least someone claiming to be a temple priest) is even willing to carry an offensive substance on his own head, a head that should only bear objects embodying the gods of Besakih, thus polluting himself as well.

An attack on the regalia is a potent expression of the annihilation of Klungkung's power, for they are the exemplary signs of an originary divine favor. Through them all of the relationships constituting royal power, encoded by regalia keris, are severed: relationships to ancestors and the past; to the gods; and to those dependent upon the Déwa Agung's protection. And the weapon used—false holy water—hides itself under a discourse of sacrality.

Like the "holy water," Klungkung's regalia keris were also "from Above": from ancestors, and from Majapahit. Tales particularly emphasize, however, connections between the regalia and Besakih. Rather than being derived from social superiors across the sea, their power is linked to divine superiors high in the mountains: Majapahit and Besakih are conflated. But then, precedents abound: the stories of Mayadanawa and Bédaulu already suggested a paradigmatic relationship between them. Moreover, Besakih is commonly said to have been established by a Javanese priest, and Besakih's god is identified as a son of the god of the Javanese Mount Suméru (see chapter 5). The emphasis on Besakih may have further significance, for in the present era Besakih has replaced Majapahit as the symbolic focus of a specifically Balinese identity.

The false holy water is also sprinkled on the collective heads of members of the court. The lethargy that consequently overtakes them contrasts dramatically with the heightened perceptiveness and alertness that should ensue from a link to the invisible world. Instead, there is confusion, a blurring of awareness expressed in both words and deeds. Anak Agung Biang Raka, a widow of Klungkung's last king who was born in Puri Satria Kawan, heard the following tale from kinsmen:

> After everyone had used that holy water and felt sleepy, all of the wives prayed. They should have been asking for victory but what emerged from their mouths [in those days prayers were spoken out loud] was a request to be defeated in war. A servant overheard and said, "Déwa Agung, don't you mean to ask for success? Why are you asking for defeat?" But she didn't even know she had said such a thing. (Fieldnotes, p. 1266)

The Dutch did not destroy all power in Klungkung. Cokorda Anom of Puri Akah's core line had this to report about his own ancestor and the lord of Puri Satria:

> Anak Agung Madé Tangkas was sent to report to the king that Puri Akah and Puri Satria couldn't hold out against the Dutch. Then Déwa Agung Smarabawa decided that there had to be a puputan. Cokorda Gedé Rai (the *manca* of Akah) went with his followers to fight. Kaki Keseng, one of his followers, carried his betel-nut container, and he was borne in a palanquin. Several times those carrying it were shot down and fell dead, but at his touch they returned to life. He wanted to live long enough to reach Klungkung and die with his kinsmen. He was protected by two amulets (*sikepan*) he had received at temples at night: a belt from Pura Dalem Agung, and a neck piece from Mount Agung. The lord of Puri Satria also had amulets, from the temples Bukit Mandéan and Segening. When both of these lords arrived at Klungkung's crossroads they tossed aside these amulets, which immediately disappeared, returning to their sources. Even then the lord of Akah couldn't die easily because he was invulnerable. His body continued to twitch with convulsions among the corpses for a long time. (Fieldnotes, pp. 1572–73)

In the *Buwana Winasa* (canto 9, verse 17) Pedanda Ngurah recounts a similar incident: Déwa Agung Smarabawa, the king's brother, and the Cokorda of Gélgél cannot be killed by Dutch bullets until they toss aside their amulets:

Dewagung kalih nora ana kabranan	The two Déwa Agung were unwounded.
dadi aptiniya wasayanti	Angry,
busana binuncal	they threw their amulets
tekeng pamargané ika	down on the road.
angunus narana gelis	Drawing their keris, they were immediately struck
keneng pelor dada	by bullets in the chest.
karo pejah ngungsi luwih	The two died and went to paradise.

These objects, however, were personal amulets, not heirlooms. According to Anak Agung Niang Kudar, Déwa Agung Jambé had collected the entire clan's *pajenengan* in the core-line house-temple; hence all were rendered impotent at the same time as the core line's regalia.

DESECRATION AS AN ALLEGORY OF ROYAL WEAKNESS

For many it sufficed to say simply that the objects embodying Klungkung's power had been contaminated. Others in Klungkung, however, found this an unsatisfactory explanation, for it seemed to beg the question of how such a deception had been possible.

A cultural model of how sorcery works clarifies the problem. A person jealous of another's good fortune, Dayu Alit explained to me, might place something *mala* in the latter's house-shrines so that his ancestors would no longer be willing to "sit" there. However, for anyone contemplating harm to even be able to enter the shrine area undetected would already indicate that the area was unprotected. That is, the victim's relations to some invisible force—not necessarily his ancestors—would already have to be problematic for him to be vulnerable at all. So too, if the Déwa Agung could be deceived by false holy water he must already have lacked invisible protection.

A series of stories accreting around the theme of impotent weapons asserts that divine protection had been withdrawn from Klungkung's king before the arrival of the false holy water, as a consequence of his own inappropriate actions. Pedanda Gedé Kenitén, for example, was told the following tale by his father:

There were already signs, ravens were possessed, [and there were signs] concerning whatever people had that contained their power. The regalia. My father purified them. The ones named, those bullets, the ones named I Seliksik, he purified them. Even the keris, whether Bangawan Canggu or whoever. There was no one else.

IDA BAGUS JAGRI: The keris or the bullets I Seliksik, isn't that right? He was the one who purified them, yes?

Yes. Didn't he purify them on special days [*rarainan*], clean them? That's why . . . I Seliksik, in the past, sometimes there would be few [bullets] in the pouch, sometimes there would be many. Sometimes there would be two in the rafters, covered with blood . . . They'd be in the rafters. If they had gone somewhere. Covered with blood. And so a purificatory offering [*prascita*] would be made for them.

IDA BAGUS JAGRI: A *prascita*.

When everyone was preparing for the disaster it wasn't like that any more. They would just stay in place, the bullets [i.e., none of them ever went anywhere, none of them were bloody, etc.]. That's why [my father] felt, "*Bah*, what is going to happen? This is the first time it's ever been like this," isn't that so? "But when exactly is [the realm] going to be defeated?" There was already a sign when Ida Déwa Agung Rai was told to go to Gianyar. All of his "sons" [sons, nephews, younger men in general] told him not to. [But] he still wanted to go, to Gianyar. It was dark, it was raining. That was when there were fires from the Merajan Agung [the shrines in the puri]. As if they were headed northeast, who knows how many fires. It was a sign . . . In the Merajan Agung. That was the sign He who properly sat in them [the weapons] had probably gone home, isn't that so? . . . That's where they were stored, all of the daggers [*kadutan*], right? Lances, whatever there was that was . . . That's why during the defeat, it was the most . . . When [Klungkung's] enemies were still Balinese, they were flawless. I Bangawan Canggu and I Durga Dungkul, if they were just held at an angle, if you slanted them to the east, as far east as the enemy was they would be paralyzed. That's just it. That's just it, there were no signs at all. "*Bah*, this is how it is, the *gumi* is going to be defeated," right? (Interview, 10 March 1985)[5]

Here signs—or their absence—indicate impending defeat. When the regalia were cleansed and given offerings on Tumpek Landep, blood-stained bullets normally indicated I Seliksik's vigilance in protecting king and realm; I Seliksik's quiescence was, like the dog that did not bark in the night in the Sherlock Holmes story, a sign of trouble. Moreover, ravens hovered in the vicinity, "possessed." In Balinese visual and narrative arts, ravens vomiting blood are a sign of impending defeat in battle.

The Pedanda was not the only one to mention omens. Madé Kanta remarked that all of the bullets manufactured before the Kusamba War had been used up by 1908, and an attempt to make new ones failed because the person sacrificed was a thief. There were also other portents. One narrator, for example, recalled hearing that the banyan tree in front of Pura Taman Sari (another thought it was the one in Banjar Uma Melangsat) burst out in odd golden flowers. Pedanda Ngurah in the *Buwana Winasa* records a comet, a beached whale, and a mudslide (canto 8, verse 11). Some of these signs—the ravens, the comet—are literary conventions, often found in poetry. But people do not think that such events appear in poems because they are stereotypes; they are stereotyped because they have been repeatedly experienced.

Pedanda Gedé Kenitén, however, had heard that the source of the trouble lay in an earlier event, which he also calls a "sign." Here the "sign" is the consequence of poor judgment. The reason for the ill-omened journey to Gianyar is unexplained, but there may be a temporal confusion. The disastrous journey to Gianyar was surely the one made by Déwa Agung Jambé in 1906, when he was forced to sign the treaty that effectively rendered him impotent.[6] It seems likely that this is the event to which the Pedanda's father referred, especially as several elderly members of the royal clan linked a sign involving the royal regalia to that very journey to Gianyar, rain and all. Anak Agung Gaci of Puri Bedulu was one such person:

> DAYU ALIT: Do you remember any of the *pajenengan* keris?
>
> The *pajenengan* that lived in the Jero Agung? My grandfather was the priest [*pamangku*] there, in the Merajan Agung. My grandfather. When they went as witnesses to Gianyar, he said . . . they were all turned around, the keris [*para lingga*, all of the dwelling places for the spirits]. He [the king] went to Gianyar. It was raining violently, the raindrops were as big as large Chinese coins, it is said.
>
> DAYU ALIT: Why did anyone go to Gianyar?
>
> To testify they were going to be allies with the Dutch.[7] I Déwa Agung of the East Wing; the West Wing [Déwa Agung Smarabawa] didn't want to. They fought. They all, it is said, faced northeast, they were in the wrong places, the things he revered [*sungsung*], the god images [*rambut sedana* and *pratima*]. It was like that, "*geg, ged, ded, ded*" [i.e., the noise they made], it is said. My grandfather said, "Well, the *gumi* is going to experience a disaster, is going to be defeated." And then . . . it wasn't even another year, there wasn't even five months. (Interview, 8 November 1985)

Dewa Agung Jambé's concession to Dutch demands on this occasion suggested to Dayu Alit that he was insufficiently *pageb*, that he lacked faith in the gods: only if it was divinely ordained would Klungkung fall; unless the gods permitted it, regardless of what the Dutch threatened, it would not.

Capitulation to Dutch demands may itself be imaged as a kind of desecration: the ruler who belonged above allowed himself to be placed below. And in consequence the power of his regalia dramatically shot off into the sky in blazes of fire (despite the rain), returning "home." What remained behind was lifeless and inert metal, daggers absurdly unequal to repeating rifles.

Note that here, once again, power takes the form of fire. This image recalls not only the fire used to forge a keris but the symbolic fire (the red offerings made every Tumpek Landep) that reproduces it as a powerful object over time. As Brahma's element, fire is moreover a symbol of constituting origins, and thus of the role regalia play in establishing political prominence. Finally, as a source of heat, fire is associated with anger and fighting.

According to Pedanda Gedé Kenitén, the "home" to which the spirits of the keris returned was upstream and to the east [*kaja-kangin*], conventionally (and, in Klungkung, actually) the location of Besakih and Divinity in general. Dadong Ribek, a commoner less blithe about the place of origin of the spirits of royal regalia, suggested the same thing by her remarks that they might have returned to *Luur*, Above.

The fires leaving the keris signified that the realm was no longer protected. Signs, however, had a dual import in precolonial Bali. On the one hand, negative omens were indices to a ruler and his priests that the country had become "hot." Texts like the *Rogha Sangara Bumi* explained whether an earthquake was a good or bad sign (which depended upon the month in which it occurred and the direction from which it originated), the significance of the birth of twins of the opposite sex (ominous if to a commoner; auspicious if to a king; see Belo 1970), and additional disasters, social and natural. All of these were symptoms signaling distress in the *buana agung*, the socio-natural domain, and, like symptoms in the "little world" of the body, they could be treated, in this case by offerings and rituals to placate the *buta-kala*.[8] But just as illness is not always curable—if it is one's time, healers say philosophically, there is nothing to be done—the same is true of the body politic. Dynasties too have a life span. Signs may indicate a ruler is so much in the wrong with the invisible world that its protection is permanently withdrawn or that, unfortunately, his allotted time is over. And Klungkung's time was indeed up.

TANDA LANGLANG: THE TELL-TALE KERIS

Another tale about royal weapons insinuates that the Dutch played no role at all in severing Klungkung's connections to the invisible world. This tale implies that Klungkung lost divine protection because its ruler lacked self-control and was unable to maintain harmonious social relationships in his court. The story centers around a particular regalia: the keris I Tanda Langlang. Here is what I Madé Regeg had to say about it:

DAYU ALIT: Why couldn't they oppose the Dutch? Had their power disappeared?

It disappeared . . .

DAYU ALIT: How?

This is *orti*, okay? The Déwa Agung had a "servant" [*parekan*] he loved. He was beloved. Now, who knows what he did there, what kind of mistake he made at court, right? Involving one of the princes, or a royal kinsman, one of the king's kinsman. He died. The servant died.

DAYU ALIT: Where was he from?

He was a servant from Klungkung . . . I don't know exactly what village. If . . . he was from Takmung, or from [he shrugs] . . . Okay. He died. Then . . . the Déwa Agung became angry. Because this was one of his favorites. [The king said:] "Who was it?" Okay. "Whoever killed my servant, for as long as I live I will have no use for him here. Whoever did this to my servant, I will have no use for him."

As soon as he had spoken thus, it is said that there was a voice. In the air. "So, I Barak [the voice here addresses the Déwa Agung in very familiar terms; I Barak, literally, "Red One," is an affectionate term for a small child with a reddish complexion]. [That's how you treat] those who serve you. You don't know me [i.e., recognize or believe in me]. Okay. If this is your way, I Barak, if you won't be firm in ruling the land [*gumi*], I Tanda Langlang will leave. May you have enemies without end."

It's said it happened like that. This is just "what is said." All of a sudden, then, I Tanda Langlang vanished. Right after that [the Déwa Agung went] to its shrine and [found] blood. In the place where the weapon was kept.

DAYU ALIT: Meaning it was I Tanda Langlang who had killed . . .

Tanda Langlang, yes. How it all happened, probably . . . because he [the *parekan*] knew himself to be a favorite, right? He acted like he owned the place, he was too whatever, right? Isn't it like . . . the story of I Capung? Ngurah Telabah deliberately looked for some fault to have an excuse to kill him. Right? [This is a story from the *Babad Dalem*.]

DAYU ALIT: I Tanda Langlang knew what he'd done wrong, the Déwa Agung didn't. Because the Déwa Agung loved him too much . . .

It was fate [*gantos jagat*]. Nowadays aren't people cautious? "How did he die? Who dared to kill him?"

DAYU ALIT: Yes. Don't just speak [*mesuang baos*, literally, "make speech come out"].

Yes, investigate first, isn't that right? Investigate. Here he just . . . Truly it was so that the land . . .

DAYU ALIT: Yes, it was fate . . .

Yes, fate. (Interview, Pasinggahan, 24 May 1986)

Anak Agung Niang Mayun of Puri Kusamba heard about Tanda Langlang from her father, who served at court as a royal advisor during Betara Dalem's reign:

The Déwa Agung lost his power because he threw away his most important regalia [*pajenengan*], which were named I Langlang, I Baru Gedeg, and I Kelik Tanem. The reason why he did so was that these weapons killed a beloved lord of the realm [*manca*] without the Déwa Agung's knowledge, and he was very angry. He threw I Langlang and Kelik Tanem into the sea near Pura Klotok. They were carried out to sea by a small boat. As they vanished into the sea, a blaze of fire shot up and rose into the sky and a voice was heard, cursing the Déwa Agung, "May Klungkung not cease to have enemies." This was the reason why someone was able to piss on the royal lances later. Before then no one would have dared try such a thing. (Fieldnotes, pp. 1587–88)

Ida Bagus Gedé of Geria Sengguan had also heard of Tanda Langlang. He connected the tale to the affair of the foul holy water, which he said was witnessed by his great-grandfather Pedanda Ketut Jelantik, a royal judge:

The puri used to own a keris named I Tanda Langlang. If anyone at court or otherwise close to the Déwa Agung felt angry at him, or had any negative thoughts about him (even if there was no intention to act on these thoughts), the keris would immediately seek out and kill that person. This upset the Déwa Agung, since people of whom he was fond were dying. Believing that Tanda Langlang was killing people who had done no wrong, he threw it into the sea. As a result he was vulnerable, unprotected. Later a temple priest brought "holy water" from Besakih, supposedly to strengthen the power of the puri's *pajenengan*. The Déwa Agung told him to give it to the temple priest in the puri's house-temple. But it wasn't holy water; it was urine. The keris were sprinkled with it. That night, around midnight, the Déwa Agung woke to a terrific racket in the house-temple, a sound like many people running or like a cat makes chasing mice in the rafters. These were the weapons. They were upset; the noise was their power [*adnyanan*]. The next morning the Déwa Agung went to the shrines where the regalia were kept. All were in disarray. Those that normally faced east faced west, and those that normally faced west faced east.[9] The Déwa Agung instantly understood this was a bad sign. Formerly if one of the keris were poked into the ground it would cause the earth to rumble and shake. So he took it and tried, but nothing happened. The power was gone. This was why he didn't want to fight the Dutch; he knew he couldn't win. (Fieldnotes, pp. 984–86)

Tanda Langlang is the only keris identified by name in narratives about the conquest, and that name is the first thing worthy of note in fathoming this set of tales: *tanda* means "sign"; *langlang*, "wandering." Tanda Langlang is a wandering sign in many senses. Not only does the name capture its most characteristic feature, but it also describes its narrative function, as a symbolic operator agglutinating several stories and themes. For one, references to it are sprinkled throughout the *Babad Dalem*, yet that text offers no account of its origins or capacities; it mysteriously appears in one scene after another, weaving its way through the narrative. Second, Tanda Langlang narratives link together those that speak of portents preceding the conquest with those about the desecration of the keris. It was because the Déwa Agung was no longer protected by Tanda Langlang that his other regalia were vulnerable to desecration. At the same time, its disappearance is a sign that the king and his realm have already been polluted.

The Tanda Langlang stories depict the Déwa Agung as at least partly responsible for losing the protection of the invisible world. Rather than trusting in the loyalty and acuity of his keris—an agent whose perceptions were impeccable—he cast it away when it challenged his own assessment of those close to him. His angry and impetuous act again betrays a lack of faith in the invisible world: self-control is not only necessary to acquire power but essential to retaining it. In a ruler, who must be firm and dispassionate not only to maintain his connection to gods but to rule over people, such behavior is disastrous. The Déwa Agung, blinded by anger, is incapable of judging things correctly. As in tales about the journey to Gianyar, the Déwa Agung chooses unwisely, and the result is the same: the power that protects him leaves in a blaze of fire. Even more than in undertaking the journey to Gianyar, however, what is involved here is a kind of metaphorical pollution. As the king's *kawitan*, "origin," his heirloom keris are his hierarchical superiors. By his treatment of I Tanda Langlang, the Déwa Agung fails to respect what is above him.

The names of the weapons Anak Agung Niang Mayun associated with Tanda Langlang, I Kelik Tanem and I Baru Gedeg, reiterate the lesson. Telik Tanem were a category of persons, who functioned as the king's spies (Geertz 1980 says "scouts"), just as the weapon Tanda Langlang spied out miscreants. Baru is a common name for royal lances;[10] other sources claim that Klungkung had a regalia lance named Baru Gudug (see Goris 1937). *Gedeg*, however, is a forceful term in ordinary Balinese for anger—and it was anger that cost the Déwa Agung, and thus his realm, the weapon's protection. Having broken his connection to the gods, he could not later distinguish urine from holy water, *panyuh* from *banyu*. If the Déwa Agung's display of anger endangered his realm, it also showed in turn that he had already been abandoned by Widhi.

Some version of this story also seemed to be known to persons outside of Klungkung. I heard the following from a Badung narrator:

> Klungkung had two very powerful heirloom weapons: a whip and a dog with black and white markings. They protected Klungkung's rulers, and as long as they existed Klungkung could never be defeated. Then one day

something passed over the king's head and the dog leapt for it; in so doing, however, he too passed over the king's head. The whip, responding immediately to the breach of etiquette, killed the dog. The king grieved his dog's loss and in anger tossed the whip into the sea, which caused a tidal wave. After this Klungkung was vulnerable, and so the Dutch were able to conquer it. (Fieldnotes, p. 380)[11]

This too is a tale of both desecration and poor judgment, albeit in a different metaphoric register. Here the head of the Head is desecrated. When something threatens the realm (symbolized by the royal head), the king's protector acts immediately to redress the offense. A dog is an apt if homely expression of the protective function of regalia; recall that, like keris, dogs can see past the illusions of the visible world, and most Balinese keep dogs to "guard" their compounds, particularly against potential attacks by sorcerers. Dogs, however, are considered creatures low on the hierarchical scale, by virtue of both their ferocity and their gluttony. They bark at passersby, may bite without warning, and are perpetually hungry. Since they eagerly devour the leftovers of offerings made on the ground to *buta-kala*, they are implicitly both akin to them and even (since Balinese "eat up") beneath them. If they are effective guardians against the forces sent by sorcerers, it is because they recognize creatures like themselves.

For a dog to pass over a ruler's head, even in a just cause, is an unacceptable breach of a "natural" hierarchy, and the whip quickly punishes such audacity. But the king's excessive attachment to his dog blinds him to propriety: by casting away the whip that would protect him, he leaves himself open to calamity. Note the effect of this action is to cause a tidal wave: the land is inundated by the sea. This is an image that will come up again.

But there is more to be said about attachment and ruling. These stories about I Tanda Langlang, particularly Anak Agung Niang Mayun's, have a curious relationship to two deaths that occurred not many years before the conquest: one of Klungkung's *manca*, the lord of Aan (Cokorda Rai Grenyeng); and Déwa Agung Isteri, Déwa Agung Jambé's sister. Since people sometimes referred to these events spontaneously when talking about Klungkung's fall, it is safe to assume that they believed there to be a connection between them.

The lord of Aan, so people say, was extremely *sakti*—the result of a dedicated practice of meditation in temples at night. In fact, wherever Betara Dalem went to *nakti*, he found the lord of Aan already there. As a result the Cokorda became his favorite; he was known as the "breastplate" (*tabeng dada*) of the realm, its shield and protector. But such success brought danger, namely the envy of those less favored. Finally the Cokorda's enemies found an opportunity to bring about his downfall. His descendants claim he was slandered, and exactly what he was accused of is no longer clear. One person told me that when the Cokorda's only son and heir died, he was so overcome with grief that he refused to allow the body to be buried but slept beside the corpse, endangering the spiritual well-being of the realm. Most narrators and a colonial report merely say that he was insubordinate (thus "going over the king's head" as the dog did in the tale from Badung).[12] Cokorda Raka Pugog of Puri Anyar led a militia against him, but they were forced to retreat. A second force came, this time from Gélgél. Informed that the Déwa Agung had ordered him punished, the Cokorda no longer resisted. He asked time to return his power to its source, since otherwise he could not be killed, and he would suffer needlessly. This granted, he went to a nearby temple; when he returned he was easily overcome. (According to his descendants he was allowed an honorable death, to be stabbed by a close kinsman.) The troops then returned to Klungkung, carrying his keris to show the Déwa Agung as proof of his death. According to the Cokorda's descendants, the Déwa Agung had known nothing of the attack and was stunned at the news of the Cokorda's death. He died himself shortly thereafter, fulfilling a promise he had made to Aan's lord.

Was Cokorda Rai Grenyeng the "beloved *parekan*" of Madé Regeg's tale? *Parekan* may refer to anyone who served the king, from a lowly sweeper to his chief minister. Could the Déwa Agung have been so fond of his friend that he refused to condemn him even when his actions endangered the realm? Or perhaps the king so favored the lord that he failed to consider the effect on the rest of his court. Could the "keris" that sought him out and killed him be an image of one of the king's own vigilant lords? One intriguing point: the keris I Tanda Langlang had distant connections to the cadet house of which Aan was a member. According to some *Babad Dalem* manuscripts (e.g., K1252, H2935:75b), Déwa Agung Mayun, elder son of Dalem Di Madé, kept this keris when his brother became ruler at Klungkung; the lord of Aan was his lineal descendant.[13]

The relationship between the princess and Tanda Langlang is even more ambiguous but seems to center on the Déwa Agung's throwing a protector into the sea. Déwa Agung Isteri, elder full sister to Déwa Agung Jambé, was reputed to be not only exceedingly lovely but brilliant, especially at literature—rather like Déwa Agung Isteri Kania. It was said that she knew all the stars in the sky; one elderly woman even insisted that she was Klungkung's ruler. The princess fell in love with Déwa Agung Ketut Agung, Déwa Agung Rai's son, who as her father's brother's son was the only man of sufficiently high status to potentially be her spouse. But the marriage was forbidden, according to one source by her brother, who swore he would *amok* if his cousin tried to wed her. One can only speculate about why Déwa Agung Jambé might have so vehemently opposed the marriage. Déwa Agung Jambé was himself married to this man's sister, and high-ranking Balinese claim such direct reciprocity is inauspicious; perhaps he opposed a union that might produce a son nearly equal in rank to his own. Or perhaps he simply wished to keep his sister's talents and powers for himself: an echo of the endogamy of Masula-Masuli.

As Balinese expect with thwarted love, the consequences were dire.[14] Déwa Agung Ketut Agung sickened and died. The heartbroken princess kept vigil by his corpse until his cremation, praying daily for a way for them to be together. The path she eventually found seems a calculated reproach to her kinsmen for refusing to give her to an appropriate man. She indicated to the low-ranking kinsman who had served as her go-between with her beloved that he could claim a "reward" for his services. As she had hoped (perhaps planned?) they were discovered together. Such a hypogamous sexual union was more than a crime; according to texts, it was simultaneously cause and omen that the land was "hot." Only the death of both parties could restore the proper balance. The man was kerissed in the cemetery; Déwa Agung Isteri was carried out to sea and drowned. Stories have it that the ocean parted to reveal a path and that, as the waves closed above her head, the sky lit up with a yellow glow.[15]

As in the one story about the lord of Aan, the princess was killed for polluting the realm. Her sexual relations with a lower-ranking man reversed the proper relationship between above and below. Yet while her death was necessary, there is a suggestion—as there is in tales about the death of the lord of Aan—of something amiss.

Two persons who should have been mainstays of the realm—its most powerful lord and a brilliant high princess—violated the law. And tales imply that the Déwa Agung was somehow responsible, for many narrators seemed to excuse the guilty ones. Even if, as the lord of Aan's descendants claim, Cokorda Rai Grenyeng was slandered by envious enemies, this in itself suggests that the realm was divided at its very core. No one claimed that Déwa Agung Isteri was slandered, but her actions were so deliberate (and showed her to be so *pageh*) that little blame attaches to her. Certainly the signs attending her execution boded ill for the realm. (An elderly woman claimed that after her death flowers had no scent.) She and Tanda Langlang appear to be analogs of one another—divine gifts to the realm, thrown into the sea.

The equivalence between a princess and a regalia keris is not completely comprehensible. Perhaps her resemblance to Déwa Agung Isteri Kania is what is relevant here: certainly in the last confrontation with the Dutch the king's sister had been a "powerful weapon" who had helped to protect the realm. In any event, the tale of the princess and that of I Tanda Langlang do appear to be connected, since both I Tanda Langlang and another princess figure in a second story. This tale is set much earlier in time, in the Samprangan period of the Kapakisan dynasty:

Dalem Ilé married a *widiadari*, daughter of the god of Pusering Tasik at Besakih. They had a daughter, Sri Déwi, who was extremely beautiful, so lovely that Dalem Ilé couldn't bear to be apart from either wife or daughter, and thus ignored affairs of state.

Dalem Ilé's brother, Déwa Tarukan, had no children, and adopted a son of the ruler of Blambangan (thus his first cousin or first cousin once removed). The boy, Rakryan Kuda Penandangkajar, was handsome and smart. His new father gave him a dancing horse named I Gagak [Raven]. The prince, however, became ill; he fell and lay close to death. Déwa Tarukan vowed that if the youth's health were restored, he would marry him to Sri Déwi. The prince recovered, and Déwa Tarukan, true to his word, brought Sri Déwi to her cousin's bed.

Now the god of Pusering Tasik had also given Dalem Ilé a keris, Ki Tanda Langlang. If anyone dared to threaten the king, even in thought, it emerged from its sheath to kill him. While the young couple were having intercourse, Ki Tanda Langlang came and stabbed the prince, penetrating his body and impaling Sri Déwi as well. Both died at once. When Sri Déwi's attendant informed Dalem Ilé he refused to believe her. Then he went to the place Tanda Langlang was stored and found blood on its blade. Furious, he threw the keris into the sea, and ordered a search for his brother, who had run away. Dalem Ilé died, his heart broken. (See Agung n.d.: 22–23)

This story does not usually appear in *Babad Dalem* texts, which have little to say about Sri Kresna Kapakisan's elder sons. Like the tale about Balian Batur, it probably belongs to the performance tradition; during interviews two former *topéng* performers in Klungkung alluded to it.

I Tanda Langlang is strikingly reminiscent of I Seliksik, another wandering sign. Indeed, Cokorda Ngurah of Nyalian explicitly likened I Seliksik to this keris:

Wherever there was an enemy, [I Seliksik] would just [go there], but you had to tell it . . . and it would just [go off]. Like I Tanda Langlang, the keris. But it would be red at the time that . . . when it had killed someone. That's why when the keris was seen by Ida Dalem Ilé, "I Tanda Langlang is red, did it kill someone? Go and look." (Interview, Puri Nyalian Kelod, 28 February 1986)

The two resemble one another not only in their role as the ruler's spies and protectors, who execute the insubordinate, but also in the narrative part both play in signifying the danger in which Klungkung stood (cf. Pedanda Gedé Keniténs story).

The tale of Dalem Ilé provides the only account of Tanda Langlang's origins I have encountered. Unlike Klungkung's more famous regalia, this keris is identified as a gift from a god, which suggests that it was obtained during a night vigil. Moreover, Pura Pusering Tasik—literally, "Temple at the Navel of Salt" or "Temple of the Navel of the Sea" (Goris 1960b: 109)[16]—is linked to Besakih; indeed, it is a name for the crater at Agung's summit (Stuart-Fox 1987: 321). This would appear to be a puzzling name for a shrine at a mountain temple, unless one recalls the cosmologies that identify Mount Agung as a pillar keeping Bali fixed; the sea is beneath it. If it is to this sea that the keris returns, one is reminded of Pedanda Gedé Kenitén's tale, where the power of Klungkung's regalia heads northeast, toward Mount Agung.

The story set during Dalem Ilé's reign is not only similar to the one told about Tanda Langlang prior to the colonial conquest—in both cases Tanda Langlang is thrown into the sea by an angry ruler after it kills someone he loves—but uncannily recalls the events surrounding Déwa Agung Isteri's death. In the legend Dalem Ilé's daughter is killed for participating in a sexual relationship, and her lover is her father's brother's son—precisely the same kinship category as the man loved by the twentieth-century princess.

It is tempting to think that oral tradition confuses an event in the early history of the dynasty with an event (or set of events) occurring shortly before the Dutch conquest, or that the tale about Dalem Ilé was the paradigm for ones told about Déwa Agung Jambé. But as with I Seliksik and the Balian Batur tale, there is no way to demonstrate which came first: the oral tradition concerned with a relatively recent event, or the story about the distant past. Chronology is in fact less important than the implications of the parallelism: the story evokes a set of associations between a particular historical circumstance and the less illustrious rulers of the Kapakisan dynasty.

Dalem Ilé's excessive attachment to wife and daughter was certainly wrong, as it led him to ignore his realm. In most *Babad Dalem* such overattachment is attributed not to Dalem Ilé but to Dalem Bekung, another discredited ruler. What is significant about these stories is that although both the lord of Aan and Déwa Agung Isteri died during Betara Dalem's reign (albeit near its end), narrators speak as if Déwa Agung Jambé were already in charge of the realm.

All these stories—Dalem Ilé, the princess, the lord of Aan, and the original tale of Tanda Langlang—share a common theme about the dangers to ruler and realm of too much attachment, or attachments of the wrong kind. Is it fortuitous that Tanda Langlang, one of the only keris described in the *Babad Dalem*, has a representation of *smarantaka*, the "death of the god of love," on its ivory sheath? This is a poem in which Siwa kills Smara, the god of love, for disturbing his meditations (Zoetmulder 1974: 295). In these stories the god of love disturbs the resolute firmness, associated with meditation, that empowers rulers. Or perhaps the ruler, who lived in Smarapura, *was* the god of love, destroyed because instead of inspiring fidelity he was at one and the same time excessively attached and incapable of attaching.

THE UNBINDING OF SMARAPURA

Déwa Agung Jambé's inability to inspire love and devotion is suggested by memories of the adultery of several of his wives. First there was the local nobleman who fled to Gianyar when his crime was discovered; he was the man whose extradition was demanded by Déwa Agung Putra III in exchange for the thief who stole from Puri Gianyar. Second, Déwa Agung Smarabawa had illicit relations with as many as six of his half-brother's wives. He was not killed but spent some time with his mother's kin at the Bangli court when discovered.[17]

Déwa Agung Jambé was hardly the only prince ever to be made a cuckold. Déwa Agung Smarabawa himself later killed the mother of his eldest son in a rage when he discovered another man in her sleeping pavilion. Moreover, the incidents all seem to have occurred before Déwa Agung Jambé became king, which should render them less important. What prompts me to mention them is that they were generally enough known to have reached Dutch ears and, more important, that some people still spoke of them.[18] They are, therefore, relevant to Déwa Agung Jambé's reputation as a ruler.

Recall the role that love plays in representations of kingship. Royal power was based upon an ability to bind both persons and divinities to the king. Such extravagant adulteries demonstrate a failure at the first, which suggests a deficiency in the second.

A king himself should primarily "love"—that is, seek unity with—the invisible world; secondarily, he should promote and be the center of the unity of his kin group. It is significant that some narrators spoke of the Déwa Agung's desire to "love" (*asih*) the Dutch (e.g., Anak Agung Gaci, above); he certainly made repeated efforts to placate them, the very first of which rejected a duty of filial love: forbidding any of his father's wives from committing *masatia* at his cremation. Another narrator suggested that in general Déwa Agung Jambé was attached to all the wrong things—including wealth, and even opium.

Kings should inspire love without being mastered by it. There were those who expressed a conviction that Klungkung might have withstood a Dutch attack—or avoided one altogether—had someone else been king. But this merely creates a new question: why this man at this time? Before considering tales that view Klungkung's situation from a wider perspective, I would like to explore other intertextual relations of narratives of conquest: with tales about the Kusamba War and with the *Babad Dalem*.

INSIDERS, OUTSIDERS, AND THE MEDIATION OF DEFEAT

The Dutch victory in 1908 is intimately linked by Klungkung narrators with their defeat at Kusamba in 1849. This defeat "taught" the Dutch just how powerful Klungkung was; if the Dutch wished to overcome the power of its rulers, they had to sever it at its source.

That the Dutch used treachery to overcome Klungkung is a theme that even structured accounts by people familiar with the regency's book on the history of Klungkung (Sidemen et al. 1983): Cokorda Anom, Klungkung's first *bupati* and a former revolutionary, for example, told me that after the Kusamba War there were meetings in Holland to plan strategy. The Dutch decided that to defeat Klungkung they would first have to isolate its ruler by gaining control over Bali's other principalities. The point of view is entirely Klungkung-centered: it is only in order to defeat Klungkung that the Dutch carefully plot to seize the other realms.

Tales about the false holy water play the same Klungkung-centered theme but locate the source of Klungkung's power (and thus the means of destroying it) in its ruler's relation to *niskala* forces. But the strategy is the same: Klungkung and its rulers must be isolated, either from allies in the visible world or from protectors in the invisible one. The latter, however, is more difficult, as it necessitates intimate contact; to succeed in their plan, they must recruit Balinese aid.

In some Kusamba War tales, the Déwa Agung required the help of outsiders to defeat the Dutch; here outsiders help the Dutch defeat Klungkung. Many claim that certain Muslims contributed (in some unspecified way) to the puri's fall. But these were not anonymous overseas merchants as in the Kusamba War tales; rather they were local residents, whose families had lived in Bali for generations, and who were known by name.

But if, as one person said, "there was a traitor on the outside [*ring jaba*]," the "outside" referred in part to persons just beyond the puri's walls. Indeed, like the temple priest from Besakih, the majority of those identified as traitors were in Balinese terms insiders. Unlike their versions of Kusamba War tales, in telling these stories narrators name names, identify real persons. Particularly disturbing is that those named were persons of influence, the king's closest advisors: a Brahmana priest, descendant of the priest mentioned in tales about I Seliksik and a principal royal advisor; a commoner living by the Islamic Quarter, who served as minister and was acknowledged to be a descendant of a royal bastard; and (according to some) the king's brother by a commoner mother, who had been adopted into a branch puri that had only recently "gone out" from the center.

Those who accused these persons pointed to both opportunity and motive, namely, what they had to gain from a Dutch administration. All three had been envoys to the Dutch, speakers of excellent Malay who were responsible for entertaining and housing the Dutch when they came to the capital. After the conquest, the families of two of them obtained positions as native administrators for the colonial government. Their command of Malay and intimacy with colonial officials, their attempts to prevent a war, and their failure to participate in the puputan, all of which led the Dutch to trust them with important posts, were taken as evidence in Klungkung gossip of active treachery. Some claimed that they were responsible for betraying Klungkung, either by telling the Dutch how to pollute the regalia or by executing the act themselves. It was these persons, so it is believed, who arranged to bribe the temple priest (or someone dressed as one) to bring urine in place of holy water to the capital.

But—ultimate paradox—the king himself was said to be of the same faction as these supposed "traitors." Indeed, the truth of these accusations of betrayal is less relevant than the divisions that they evidence. Such factionalism was a sign that the realm was already broken.

Other narrators placed the blame further afield, on the rulers of Gianyar or Karangasem. Narrators noted, for example, not only that the "temple priest" mentioned above came from Badég but that Klungkung's major "villains" had family ties to important Karangasem clans. Gianyar's role was explained by Guru Ketut Lot, a former headman from the village of Pikat, in a more complex way:

> It is said they were close friends, the Dutch and Klungkung. But Gianyar became the means [*serana*]. The one that was the basis, the reason why they were close friends. They went to Besakih together, prayed, worshipped, made offerings, had photographs taken. It is said that the Dutch put urine in the holy water there. That's what is spoken, urine was put there, and it was used to sprinkle the regalia, to sprinkle whatever, that's why their efficacy was lost. That is the story. (Interview, Jeroan Pikat, 12 June 1986)

This claim that Gianyar provided the "means" or "basis" for a friendship between Klungkung and the Dutch is, perhaps, another reference to the 1906 treaty signed at Gianyar. This treaty was certainly both an indication and a cause of Klungkung's defeat. It also allowed the Dutch to destroy Klungkung in a very direct way, by affording through their "friendship" an opportunity to desecrate Klungkung's regalia, in this version at Besakih itself.[19] Gianyar's complicity is suggested by Guru Ketut Lot's use of the word *serana*, "ingredients," which commonly refers to the material content of a sorcery object—and since Guru Ketut Lot was a healer it is likely that he intended these magical allusions. If in 1849 the ruler of Klungkung was a master of sorcerers, including foreign ones, this ruler is represented as their victim.

In contrast to the Kusamba War stories, in which Klungkung seemed to exist in isolation, stories like this one demonstrate an acute awareness of political differences. Conflicts both between Klungkung and other realms and within Klungkung's own ruling class are obvious and overt, and they leave Klungkung open to treachery. The situation described in colonial reports and Klungkung oral traditions recognizably overlaps even if the dominant idioms differ. Dutch victory is implicitly or explicitly facilitated by the rulers of either Gianyar or Karangasem, Klungkung's enemies and regents of the colonial government. And these divisions within Bali are multiplied within Klungkung: there are factions, disagreements, controversies, not only at the time of the conquest but leaving a legacy in the present as well, yet another indication that the world is *uug*.

THE DUTCH CONQUEST AND THE MAJAPAHIT CONQUEST

The rumors, interpretations, cultural contents, and narrative allusions out of which all of the tales thus far considered are constructed have been patched together into a familiar structure. Klungkung's conquest by the Netherlands Indies government conforms to a cultural/literary pattern concerning the defeat of powerful persons.

In fact, tales about the Dutch conquest of Klungkung are reminiscent of stories told about Majapahit's conquest of Bali: an exogenous power from Java defeats a powerful indigenous ruler by means of trickery; the indigenous ruler is vulnerable because he has offended the gods.[20] The two rulers even respond in similar ways: Bédaulu decides to *moksa*, to permanently leave this world for the invisible one. According to some Brahmanas the puputan was also a kind of *moksa*, a union with the invisible world.

These parallels, however, would imply that the Dutch, once thought to bring illness to their wake and to be as greedy as *raksasa*, were now seen, at least by some, as instruments of Divinity, as Gajah Mada was. I have suggested in chapter 8 that this might indeed have been the case. Such a notion might have been a compelling reason to adopt Dutch styles of dress and furniture, as the Balinese who helped administer colonial Bali frequently did. But most Balinese seem to have regarded their conquerors more negatively, victors from Java or not.[21] However much narratives about the Dutch conquest parallel narratives about the Majapahit one, they are hardly determined by those parallels.

People do, however, often turn to the past to explain the colonial conquest. But they do not identify the Dutch with Gajah Mada or Klungkung's ruler with Bédaulu. Instead the Dutch are identified with a legendary figure named Kebo Iwa.

Most Balinese know Kebo Iwa's tale. Here is a summary of what I heard from various people on a number of occasions:

A wealthy woman was pregnant for a long, long time, years even, but could not give birth. She was miserably uncomfortable and finally vowed that if the child would only emerge she would give it everything it asked for, barring only the sun, the moon, and the stars. Kebo Iwa was born the next day, and as soon as he took breath he demanded rice. He ate a whole steamer full, and the next day ate two, and the day after three. His parents were soon reduced to poverty as they sold everything to buy him food. And still he demanded more. The neighbors were drawn into feeding him, and then the village, the kingdom, and finally all of Bali. He grew enormously large and incredibly strong. According to some accounts, he became Bédaulu's general, and as he continued to resist Majapahit after Bédaulu's death, Gajah Mada had to devise a ruse to defeat him. According to others, people were "hot," their lives made difficult by his constant demands, and various attempts to kill him failed; in desperation the Balinese asked help from Gajah Mada. In any case Gajah Mada convinced Kebo Iwa to come to Java, by praising his strength and promising him a wife. Gajah Mada led him to a large pit and told him that the princess waited below. But after he entered the pit, he was surrounded by the Javanese army and bombarded with arrows and lances. Bitter at being duped, he warned them they would never succeed in killing him that way, as he was impervious to ordinary weapons. But since he no longer desired to live, he would reveal the secret of how to kill him: they should shower him with lime, *pamor*. Before he died, however, he vowed to one day return, to reclaim Bali and get his revenge.

Covered with lime—a substance Balinese commonly use, to highlight the damascening on keris blades, as the catalytic agent in chewing betel-nut, and as whitewash—Kebo Iwa would appear white. And this, I was told (and not only in Klungkung), explained who the Dutch (who were not only white, but large in stature and clearly insatiable) really were: Kebo Iwa returning to claim his own.

ANAK AGUNG GACI: According to the lesson [*tutur*] I heard, the Dutch, it is said, were from the beginning [*kawitné*]. This is a story [*tutur*], another story. Together with Mayadanawa, who had many subjects, they brought him to Java. Once they were there he was tricked so he could be killed. And then this happened: "Yé, if this is the way you would kill me, it can't be done. Sprinkle lime on my eyes, that's the way."[22] So they took some lime. But after eleven generations, it is said, it would be asked for, the country. Like that.

COKORDA ISTERI AGUNG: That was I Kebo Iwa. That's why we were colonized by the Dutch. According to the opinion of Balinese, the Dutch were reincarnations of I Kebo Iwa. (Interview, Puri Bedulu, 8 November 1985)

Although Balinese legend speaks of the pre-Majapahit rulers of Bali as *"raksasa"* or "evil spirits" (Friederich 1959 [1849–50]:112; and see quotes from van den Broek in chapter 2), Kebo Iwa still had a legitimate claim to Bali because Gajah Mada, even if he represented the right side, used deceit and treachery to conquer him. While the gods favored Gajah Mada, they placed a limit on their grace and owed the losers (who were, after all, *sakti*, which is to say also recipients of divine favor) something as well.

This motif figures the conquest as a return to a prior situation rather than as something startlingly new. Moreover, it postulates that the Dutch, foreigners, are really the indigenous owners of the land and that the conquest is justified.

Kebo Iwa's fate, like Bédaulu's, shows that *sakti* persons are commonly defeated by treachery. Kebo Iwa's enemies must even be told how to kill him, since he cannot be defeated by ordinary weapons. Like Bédaulu's, Kebo Iwa's death also in some ways echoes the puputan, for the white lime that foreshadows his Dutch incarnation is the color of purity, signaling union with Divinity.

UNBINDING THE WORLD

Apart from keris another culturally significant artifact also receives mention in the discourse of the conquest: the closed, arched doorway of the royal residence, which like all such doors was an icon of Mount Agung. Compared to the keris, it is a supporting actor: an instrument that plays familiar themes, but in a minor key.

Only three narrators mentioned the door to me at all. The first of these referred to polluted holy water, but this time a door, rather than a keris, was the object desacralized. The door is not the Great Door of Puri Klungkung but its equivalent in the residence of the lord of Gélgél. This door no longer exists, and perhaps Anak Agung Niang Bagus's story explains why:

> DAYU ALIT: It is said that they were given holy water . . .
> That holy water . . . what was it that was said by people? It was dirty [*leteh*]. It was lifted up there, at the old Great Door, the one that was here [i.e., Gélgél], here at the forecourt [*bencingah*]. They looked for a way they could pass through the door. The holy water was going to be used so it would be destroyed . . .
> DAYU ALIT: It came here? There was that kind of holy water here too?

Here. [It; They] came to Gélgél first. Gélgél first, then Klungkung. Gélgél was first. They really were enemies with Gélgél. As for Klung-kung, weren't people already weak there? Here.

DAYU ALIT: It's said it wasn't possible to sneak past that door [before that]?

One can't sneak past the Kori in Klungkung . . . This is a *pamedalé* [a slightly less exalted doorway].

DAYU ALIT: [The water was used] so that it would be possible to pass through the door.

To look for a way to pass through, to be able to go to the inside [*jero*]. (Interview, Jero Kawan Gélgél, 20 May 1986)

The second tale was unequivocally about the Great Door of the main puri, and the narrator was Pedanda Gedé Kenitén:

There was already turmoil . . . but if it would be this day or that, when was not yet certain . . . That's why there were meetings, of all the priests [*sulinggih*]. Betara Dalem said, isn't it so? "*Nah*, if sometime in the future the land is in trouble. There is a finial on the Great Door. Just open that." They were told to open it. At the time there was going to be a treaty all of the elders, and the younger people too, forgot to open it . . . Be-cause of that, that's why Klungkung was going to be defeated. There were signs . . . There had been meetings of all the elders. That's just it. When it was proper that it was going to—what do you call it? Everyone forgot, didn't remember. Isn't that so? They didn't remember it . . . After that there was a what-do-you-call-it. From the Dutch, they were going to de-stroy it, the Door, isn't that so? As soon as they climbed up they saw the sea below. (Interview, Geria Gedé Kenitén, 10 March 1985)

What the effects might have been had the finial been "opened," he could not say. But the door was clearly intended to play a part in the magical defense of the realm.

A third account suggests that if the finial was forgotten, someone did recall that the door was in some way capable of being harnessed as a weapon. It also suggests what opening the finial might have accomplished. For Dadong Ribek, the former palace servant, remembered some interesting activities in-volving the Great Door before the final confrontation with the Dutch:

They opened the bottom step of the Great Door. The water couldn't come up. Its [i.e., the Door's] foundation is the sea, it is said. . . . If the water had been able to come up, wouldn't all of the world here, under the heavens/sky have become sea? But it couldn't. They were finished, dead, my Lords [*Betara*]. (Interview, Losan, 15 February 1986)

This effort to inundate the land harkens back to the tale told to van Kol: to the chasm that should have opened up, but did not, when one of the royal keris was thrust into the ground. It is striking how often people reiterate that image of keris coming in contact with the earth. (That anything *should* happen is something that is not, as far as I know, mentioned anywhere but in the context of these very same stories.) After all, the reporter for the *Locomotief* noted that three of the keris found after the bloody death of Klungkung's royal family had magical powers ascribed to them, and suggested that the Déwa Agung had a different one in his hand when he was killed.

The reference to three keris is itself suggestive since the *Babad Dalem*, while mentioning perhaps six keris by name, only provides accounts of the origins of the three most important. Are the two pairs of three one and the same? It is impossible to know; what is recorded about the keris in the *babad* and what people knew about them in 1908 are incommensurate. Some people with whom I spoke had ideas about the powers of Klungkung's famous keris, but whether they were reporting something they were told or piecing together what they had heard with what is written in the *Babad Dalem* I do not know.

Narratives concerning the conquest, however, provide suggestive hints concerning the identity of one of these keris: the one that caused earth tremors. Indeed, the more I thought through the stories, the more I was convinced I knew which keris this was. It was not only that it made sense of the earth tremors. It also tied together all of the multiple, disparate images concerning the conquest in general. Still, it was only an idea; perhaps I was overinterpreting, or wrong. But when I was next in Bali, I asked Anak Agung Niang Kudar, not even realizing at the time that she had never, in fact, mentioned the business, "Which keris was it that made the ground shake if it came into contact with the earth?" Without a moment of hesitation, she named the very one I had so painstakingly inferred: Bangawan Canggu.

If narrators remember the impotence reported by van Kol, it is perhaps because narratives about Klungkung's conquest form a kind of photographic negative of Bangawan Canggu's powers: as a force that binds the earth and keeps it steady and that binds hearts to a single center. Bangawan Canggu is an icon of the cosmic *naga* that maintain the stability of the world.

It is no accident that Balinese refer to the precolonial period as the time when Bali was "still firm or steady," *duges kari entegé* or *duges enteg guminé*. The same phrase was used in the colonial 1930s (see Bateson 1970:395). *Enteg*, "firm, stable, erect," belongs to a paradigm of terms representing culturally desirable firmness ending with the sound *eg*—*rajeg*, "upright, standing, a support"; *tegteg*, "immutable, fixed, strong, firm," *degdeg*, "calm, quiet, still," and *jegjeg*, "upright, erect" (*jegjeg ai* is high noon, when the sun is standing directly overhead). Such unwavering verticality—like a well-rooted tree—is a general value, and there are rituals to achieve this state or restore it. Certain offerings, for example, may be made for individuals on their birthdays to make their life-force *enteg*, to give them vitality and animation. And once a year, at Besakih's Pura Gelap, Klungkung's ruler (nowadays the Klungkung regency) sponsors a rite called *ngenteg guminé*, to make the country or land *enteg*. Such anchoring is the cosmological equivalent of the steadfastness integral to the acquisition of power itself. Indeed, several terms used for reigning derive from the same metaphor: *ngadeg* (which is part of the same *-eg* paradigm), which also signifies "to stand upright, to rise, to stand still, be vertical"; *ngrajeg* and even the Kawi *andiri* have similar meanings. Texts often note that kings *macekin gumi*, "nail down" the country. It is kings who keep the world steady with their own unbending intent and thus keep their subjects safe and prosperous.

That ability to keep things steady was also realized through objects like Bangawan Canggu and, tales about the Door suggest, the Great Door of Klungkung's puri. And therefore the Déwa Agung could potentially use that power to destroy as well, as he appears to have tried to do in his confrontation with the Dutch. But those efforts failed.

Only a short time before, Déwa Agung Putra III could strike a Dutch envoy down in a faint merely by pointing at him, or incapacitate an entire ship's crew with dysentery just by looking in their direction. A few short years later his son attempted the desperate measure of destroying the world, and he even failed at this. Or rather the world *was* destroyed, but not by royal command.

Perhaps, though, it was the gods who did not allow Bali's complete destruction, who caused the great men of the realm to forget about the finial, who prevented the sea from pouring out when the bottom step of Klungkung's Great Door was opened. For the gods are thought by some to have played more than a merely passive role in the events of 1908.

THE CONQUEST AS FATED

At one level, talk about Klungkung's defeat is talk about objects; at another, it is talk about the Déwa Agung's incompetence. But this explanation of the Dutch victory is equally unsatisfying, for it opens the question of why someone like this happened to be Klungkung's king at this time. Déwa Agung Jambé's deficiencies should be seen less as an explanation than as yet another sign. All of the contention that surrounds his memory only further suggests the predominance of negative forces.

The Déwa Agung and his counselors were not oblivious to such signs, for they made several ritual efforts to restore harmony to the land. First, although no one in Klungkung mentioned it (perhaps no one recalled it), Déwa Agung Jambé completed the ritual work that his father had initiated at Besakih: the restoration of several shrines. It is quite possible that some of his difficulties were attributed to the fact that this work had been left so long. The shrines were dedicated in November 1907 by the Déwa Agung and his brothers Déwa Agung Smarabawa and Cokorda Raka Pugog, at ceremonies attended by Gusti Bagus Jelantik (nephew and heir of the ruler of Karangasem) and four lords from Bangli. The Déwa Agung prayed that the gods would spare him the fate of Badung's lords—at least so it would seem from the report of the Resident, who had spies there:

> Nothing special was discussed by them. The only more or less striking [thing] was that the Déwa Agung directed a special prayer to the Divinity, to protect him from destruction—as prince.[23]

Only seven months earlier yet another major ritual had been held by the Déwa Agung: a realm purification at Goa Lawah to placate malign forces, at which seven water buffaloes were thrown alive into the sea.[24] Anak Agung Gaci remembered attending the ritual as a boy, and he recalled that its purpose was to purify the temple of Besakih, to which Goa Lawah has important connections:

> Here is what I heard. There was a Work [*karya*], people made a ritual. They went to worship there, to Above [*Luur*], to Mount Agung. They were from here, from Paksabali. There were seven of them. All of them wore gold to go there. When they arrived at the lower slopes [*bongkol*] of Mount Agung, the temple priest stopped them. They weren't allowed to wear gold to go up [to the peak].[25] That's the tale. They were ordered to leave it there. Who knows what they were thinking of, those wearing gold; they refused. They thought that there was some kind of trickery planned. "*Nah*, if that's the case I can't deliver you up there."
> DAYU ALIT: The temple priest said that?
> Yes. So the seven of them went [up] there [anyway], it is said. The story is that a monkey came, carrying a boulder, and all seven of them were covered over by it. They died. After they died, didn't people look for them there? Who knows how many days later, maybe seven, people looked for them there. They were taken down and brought here. The Déwa Agung was troubled, because there was pollution Above. He was going to offer a *pakelem* [a kind of ritual]. There, at Goa Lawah, that's where the ritual was held. Seven water buffalo were thrown into the sea . . .
> ANAK AGUNG NIANG KUDAR: Because there were seven people who brought pollution there. In short, there were corpses on Mount Agung.
> It was the Déwa Agung's Great Work. Seven water buffaloes with gold decorating their horns were thrown into the sea. I came to watch.

I stayed in Kusamba, spent the night, and I went there [to Goa Lawah] to pray. The day after the ritual, didn't I go home? I had just arrived home, and suddenly the wood gong sounded in Gélgél. Gélgél had been attacked. It started there, the war, the first battles were in Gélgél. My Deified Ancestor, Lord Grandfather [i.e., the Cokorda of Gélgél], sounded the wood gong so it was sharp and loud and clear, *téng, téng*. It could be heard all the way up here [about three kilometers]. I had just that moment arrived here, arrived home. Earlier in the day I had prayed at Goa Lawah. Suddenly the wood gong [sounded] there. *Pah*. (Interview, Puri Bedulu, 8 November 1985)

That Anak Agung Gaci's memory collapsed the time between the ritual at Goa Lawah and the outbreak of hostilities is significant, for the ritual was intended to protect Klungkung. Anak Agung Niang Bagus of Gélgél, who also remembered the Work, recalled hearing that its purpose was to "lock up" [*kancing*] the realm—to make it, in short, impenetrable. Some of the ways that this was to be accomplished were *sekala* as opposed to *niskala*. After the conquest, a *pedanda* from Takmung who was present at the occasion informed the Dutch that there had been a discussion at the temple between Déwa Agung Smarabawa, Gusti Bagus of Karangasem, and the ruler of Bangli, in which the latter two promised to help in the event anything happened in Klungkung.[26] Some years later, Gusti Bagus, by then regent of Karangasem, told van Kol that they even discussed strategy, although he assured van Kol he had warned Déwa Agung Smarabawa that it was impossible to resist the Dutch and that war with them should be avoided at all costs (van Kol 1914:268). But the ritual itself was also a strategy; had it succeeded in winning back the aid of the invisible world, Klungkung would have been spared.

That these ritual efforts were so ineffective, however, could only indicate that there were larger forces at work. Those who thought it through long enough could reach only one conclusion: that Klungkung's time had passed. Pedanda Gedé Tembau of Aan and Pedanda Lingsir of Bajing were quite clear about this and scoffed at the notion that the Déwa Agung was in any way responsible for the destruction of his realm:

> DAYU ALIT: Did you ever hear that during the "finishing" the power of the weapons of the puri was lost?
> PEDANDA GEDÉ TEMBAU: *Nah*, that's the story, it's true.
> DAYU ALIT: Why?
> Why were they ineffective [*punah*]? It had already come full circle, like the moon. It was time. The will of God. Sang Hyang Widhi canceled it. It was now time for the Dutch to own things. Their "turn" [*giliran*], according to Balinese ideas.

DAYU ALIT: Was there perhaps any wrong on the part of the Déwa Agung?

There wasn't any kind of wrong.

DAYU ALIT: Wasn't there some material to render them powerless?

[Their power] was indeed dulled, as a tool might be. Twice it happened. Earlier wasn't it decreased in Gélgél, when it was attacked, defeated by Gusti Agung Maruti? When that was over, it flared up again, which is why there is a story told about Kusamba. (Interview, Geria Aan, 31 January 1986)

DAYU ALIT: How was it Klungkung was defeated?

PEDANDA LINGSIR: *Nah*, it was only for that long that he could control the country. He had already had more than his time. The time was already up. There is a limit. For example . . . ten generations.

DAYU ALIT: So he didn't do anything wrong?

No. How could he? Whatever the Déwa Agung wants is allowed. (Interview, Geria Bajing, 19 October 1985)[27]

Balinese speak of fortune—whether good or bad—as inherently unstable, and acceptance of this is the cornerstone of wisdom. Contemplating the vagaries of fate, people often nod sagely and refer to *rwa bineda*, a Kawi expression that loosely translates as "everything has its opposite." If there is black, there is white; if there is day, there is night. Good follows from evil, and happiness from unhappiness. And success is eventually followed by failure. All glory, like all sorrow, eventually comes to an end. And so it is with power:

DÉWA PEKAK MANGKU, from the village Satra: The Dutch came to ask for income [*merta*] from Bali. They wanted the Déwa Agung to divide the wealth of the land with them, but he refused. He took up his keris and they didn't dare attack. He had no desire to be on good terms with the Dutch. The Dutch said they would attack if he didn't give in, and he still refused. They said they would come at twelve or one in the afternoon, and he should prepare to die by bathing, praying, and doing whatever else was right. Then the Dutch went to see their friends. They returned when they said they would, and all the people from the puri were waiting for them outside. They all died. The time for the puri's power was over. Gifts from the gods don't last forever. They have a limit. Klungkung's time had passed (fieldnotes p. 980).

DAYU ALIT, after talk about I Seliksik: What happened to this power, wasn't Widhi still generous?

DÉWA NYOMAN PATER: No. Even if the *pajenengan* were taken, thrust into the ground . . . [a gesture of futility]. It was finished, the grace of

Widhi. The power, wasn't it a gift from Widhi? It wasn't from cleverness [i.e., from studying texts].

DAYU ALIT: Was there some fault?

No. It had stopped, the grace of Widhi . . . it was finished. He didn't do anything. It just wasn't strong enough. (Interview, 22 March 1986)

NARRATIVES ABOUT THE CONQUEST AND THE POWER OF KLUNGKUNG

When both Balinese and foreigners speak of the puputan, they usually mean the puputans that took place in Badung, in 1906. Given that they received greater publicity, and given Badung's accessibility to colonial visitors and tourists as well as its present-day preeminence, the reasons are not difficult to find.

But in the early twentieth century, Klungkung's conquest was by far the more significant event. There is even evidence for this in a report written by de Bruyn Kops about ten days after Klungkung was taken. Pleased that Bali was so tranquil, he noted that matters might have been quite otherwise had the Dutch "suffered a smart check in Kloengkoeng":

> It can be accepted as certain that by such a check it would have become very lively in different parts of South Bali. Some lords had perhaps had some hope that Kloengkoeng, as in 1849—this is namely the Balinese reading—would call to the "Company" [i.e., a common Balinese term for the Dutch, a holdover from the days of the VOC] "to here and no further," and therefore it is good that the battle for this once [was] so quickly over—and that the fall of the Kloengkoeng royal house was so complete, while on the side of the Government only small, and in the actual battle with the Dewa Agoeng on the whole no, losses were suffered.
>
> The impression which this outcome must have made on all of Bali cannot be other than powerful. Everywhere, also in the other realms, people do their utmost to show their good intentions toward the Government, and it is not too hazardous to advance the supposition that with the Kloengkoeng realm a great obstacle for the consolidation and maintenance of our authority in Bali has disappeared.[28]

Pedanda Ngurah's poem also shows the impression Klungkung's defeat made elsewhere in Bali. The Pedanda devotes an entire canto (canto 10, verses 1–4) to the subject, choosing an especially mournful meter to fit his theme. In keeping with the notion that a *gumi* was more than a political entity, the Pedanda describes how the birds, trees, and flowers wept in sorrow; even the crimson of the setting sun is an expression of grief. There is nothing of this sort in passages concerning Badung's or Tabanan's fall, although the events themselves are described in far greater detail. Even the omens presaging defeat largely affect the natural world in the case of Klungkung: mudslides, a comet, and a beached whale (canto 8, verse 11). Most of the omens auguring the destruction of Badung and Tabanan involve structures belonging to the rulers: shrines in one of Badung's state temples, a pavilion in the Pamecutan puri, Tabanan's puri and the banyan tree that stands outside of it (canto 8, verses 5–6).

Precolonial differences between Badung and Klungkung also explain why there is nothing in Badung to compare with Klungkung's rich oral tradition concerning the conquest. Badung's defeat is not usually imaged in terms of the discourse of *kasaktian*. People I knew in Badung, even members of royal and priestly families who were more likely to speak of such things, had never heard anything of the sort. One Denpasar Brahmana was amused by my questions about *kasaktian* and told me that the superior military power of the Dutch superseded any "*kasaktian*" that the Balinese may have had.

It is tempting to rely on social science orthodoxies about "modernization" to account for these differences. Living in an urbanized capital, working in hotels and businesses, associating with many non-Balinese, Badung inhabitants tend to be more cosmopolitan than other Balinese. Euro-American academics expect such persons to scoff at tales of powerful weapons.

But people in Badung have hardly abandoned discourse about the invisible world. Sanur, despite miles of expensive tourist hotels, is still famed throughout the island for its powerful sorcerers and healers. And in much of Badung no ritual is felt to be complete until someone (preferably several people) has gone into trance, possessed by spirits. Pura Pengrebongan in Kesiman, one of Badung's state temples, to this day celebrates a rite that once had the goal of invoking *buta-kala* to possess Badung soldiers (see Grader 1960a:176; Belo 1949). If Badung has no stories similar to Klungkung's regarding the conquest this cannot be explained by glib Weberian allusions to rationalization or even (at least not completely) by more recent and more political notions, such as the colonization of consciousness (Comaroff and Comaroff 1992).

The kinds of invisible forces typically invoked in Badung, however, do suggest one reason why people in Badung may be content to attribute their conquest to Dutch superiority. From a Klungkung perspective, the trance so prominent in Badung more often than not involves *buta-kala* (although some, including Ida Bagus Jagri, say they often pretend to be divinities and ancestors), when it is not faked altogether. If these were the primary invisible forces upon which Badung could rely for its defense they were well matched to their Dutch opponents, who were after all clearly in league with, or possessed by, similar beings. On the other hand, discourse about Klungkung stresses the Déwa Agung's connection to gods such as Tolangkir and Wisnu. Its conquest can only be explained if these connections no longer existed: thus, by an act or acts of desecration.

To state that Klungkung's regalia were desecrated and made impotent is not to "explain" the conquest but to characterize it. Pollution reveals the meaning of Klungkung's fall: what is superior and belongs above has been violated by what is inferior and belongs below, a perfect expression of a world turned upside down, a world no longer "steady."

At one level, all of these stories could be read as metaphors of the political situation in 1908. With nearly all of Bali already under colonial control, Klungkung's authority had in a real sense been broken. By the time hostilities erupted, Klungkung's power had been even further eroded, since during their march through Klungkung in 1906 the Dutch confiscated a goodly number of firearms. To speak of the desecration of royal regalia weapons seems in this context an ideal metaphor summarizing these events: weaponless, no longer in any sense an encompassing authority, Klungkung was already defeated.

It is easy to see Klungkung oral tradition as a bricolage of historical fragments and cultural significations: going to Gianyar to sign a treaty indeed cost the king his power; the king allowed the Dutch to go over his head, to "piss on" his power. Repeatedly stories appear to transpose subjects into objects, especially into regalia keris, and to suggest their equivalence. The powerful weapon tossed into the sea is in a sense the Déwa Agung's sister; the loyal weapon, misunderstood by the king, is perhaps responsible for the death of the lord of Aan; the keris are polluted by false or magical holy water, or the king's followers are. But these tales are not merely mythical metaphors of a historical reality. Rather, they reveal the significance of historical events.

Badung discourse could represent colonial conquest as a matter of superior Dutch military might that had no moral implications. But Klungkung was not Badung. Klungkung's power was constituted by its rulers' special and unique relationship with the invisible world. Klungkung's conquest was problematic in a way no other conquest could be, for it had the potential to bring into question the very foundation of reality.

Both at the time they occurred and in retrospect Badung's puputan differed from Klungkung's. The defiant tone in celebrations and representations of the puputan in Badung reflect that difference. In Badung, to meet death bravely, in a manner befitting a *ksatria*, sufficed. The defeat of Klungkung had graver consequences and requires more explanation.

What the stories told in Klungkung do in fact is to deny that "conquest" was an issue at all. If the country is *uug*, it is not due to the superiority of Dutch power. It is rather because the Dutch were able to use the internal divisiveness of Bali at the time (itself a sign of the absence of divine favor) to learn at last how to defeat Klungkung. Klungkung was vulnerable because of inadequate royal resolution, or because of a debt to the gods dating from the

Majapahit conquest, or even because, in the erratic and unpredictable way that it does, the wheel of fortune had turned. The defeat of Klungkung had little to do with the Dutch. If they nonetheless benefited from Klungkung's fall, it was only because, ogres or not, they had certain claims that had to be given their due, if only for a short time.

Narratives about the conquest develop different themes from the *Babad Dalem* than do those about the Kusamba War. If one were to characterize the two periods by regalia, stories about I Seliksik recall I Durga Dingkul, while stories about the conquest evoke Bangawan Canggu: the king as healer, interpreting signs of his realm's ill health; the king as lover, trying to bind the hearts of his subjects; the king as the "snake" who binds the world and keeps it steady. The crisis facing Klungkung touched on everything it stood for, and narratives reflect this.

In tales of Klungkung's conquest images, fragments of discourse, are combined and recombined in seemingly endless ways by different narrators. Still, for most people in Klungkung the desecrated keris remain the central image of the problem faced by Klungkung's rulers. The solution was a puputan.

TEN

"Finishing"

If tales about desecrated keris capture the way Klungkung's defeat was experienced, they also constitute an interpretation of the situation faced by Klungkung's ruling class in 1908; such stories therefore help to clarify why Klungkung's lords chose to respond to the Dutch with a puputan. *Puputan* literally means "finishing" or "ending." It is a nominalization of the root *puput*, usually referring to some activity or work; when a Brahmana priest recites mantra during a ritual, for example, he is "finishing" (*muputang*) a sequence of actions that began with the manufacture of offerings. People in Klungkung rarely use this term, however; they speak instead of "when people finished" (*ugas anak matelasang*), employing an active verbal form of *telas*, a root which implies finishing off or using up. When I wondered to Dayu Alit just what had been finished off in 1908, she responded without hesitation: people's *kayun*, simultaneously their desires, feelings, and intentions. Those who "finished" poured all of themselves into a single goal.

But what was that goal? Was the puputan, as colonial accounts propose, simply a courageous and useless exercise in defiance? Or, given that power was tied to a praxis of sacrifice, was it intended to be somehow efficacious?

There are no obvious answers to these questions, but clues may be found in accounts of the event itself. Since no Balinese recorded their impressions at the time of the conquest, we must begin to search for those clues in the earliest written descriptions of what transpired in Klungkung: reports by the newspaper correspondents who accompanied the colonial army.[1]

DUTCH ACCOUNTS OF THE PUPUTAN

Almost all of the reporters begin with the morning bombardment of the capital from the sea and with the three companies of soldiers who marched up from Gélgél, where engineers systematically exploded the walls of every compound along the road to protect troops from possible surprise attacks. But they met no opposition and saw no armed men until they reached the capital:

> At 2:00 the great poeri came into view. The road close by the entrance was blocked by a barricade of bamboo and sharpened branches, which

3 I 4

barricade was destroyed with the help of explosives. . . . Before long appeared before us various Balinese armed with lances, who began dancing themselves to the front to meet the troops. Then followed round upon round, until finally the ground was covered with corpses and heavily wounded. (*Surabaiasch Handelsblad*, 29 April 1908)

Without meeting resistance, Klungkung was marched into at 1:00 P.M., and after some barricades had been removed, [we] marched to the poeri of the king . . . [The] 3.7 cM gun and the first platoon of the company . . . took position. Shortly thereafter little groups of five to six lance bearers, already threatening with their weapons, made for the troops. They were immediately shot down. This maneuver repeated itself several times, then women and children also armed with lances and kris came out of the poeri and the wounded began to kris themselves. . . . The company left of the road, which in the meantime had reached the poeri, exploded a wall and penetrated the already abandoned poeri. It was now obvious that the prince and all the realm's lords and most prominent people had sacrificed themselves, and that during the advance of the main force all of the supporters of the king had abandoned him. . . . Men still clothed in their battle uniform, with a white headcloth and a sort of white slendang came to offer their submission. (*Java Bode*, 4 May 1908)

Opposition was not encountered. Arrived at the poeri, the dewa agoeng, armed with lances, with the chiefs who remained loyal, behind whom were women and children, made a lance attack. A murderous fire from artillery and infantry felled the madmen. A few uninjured women were seen to go to the front and keris first the wounded and after that themselves. . . . Wounded women were seen, prior to sinking down for good, to give the deathblow to their children; the scenes which were enacted 100 meters distance before our eyes were heartrending. (*Java Bode*, 8 May 1908)

At 2:15 we entered Kloengkoeng; we knew then that the dewa-agoeng and Tjokarda Gelgel were in the poeri, but the reports concerning the number of followers were more and more favorable. At about 2:30 we saw a Native armed with a lance approach from around the corner of the poeri. It was the Tjokarda Gelgel, who had consecrated himself to death; he was shot down. After that the dewa-agoeng followed and again and again such single groups of poeri inhabitants armed with lances . . . approached the companies; all were shot down. . . . The artillery and the infantry on the road had before long mowed down all enemies, and 108 dead and severely wounded covered the road. . . . Holes were struck in the side walls of the poeri, or the walls were pulled down, and without any resistance Kloengkoeng had been conquered. (*De Locomotief*, 4 May 1908)

The overwhelming impression conveyed by these accounts is of irrationality and confusion. In one description the Balinese "dance" forward; another characterizes them as "madmen." Their best "maneuver" is for "little groups" to "threaten" with their weapons. Women slaughter their own children. None of this counts as serious opposition or resistance. Only the *Java Bode* mentions, off-handedly, that the Balinese were dressed for battle, white cloth around their heads and bodies. As for details, no two of the reporters agree precisely on what happened. According to one, Balinese men emerged in small groups of five or six at a time; according to another (in the same newspaper, four days later), the Déwa Agung led his followers forward in a single charge. The *Locomotief*'s correspondent asserts the attack was begun by a single solitary "native," who is identified, with complete assurance, as Cokorda Gélgél, the man responsible for all of the trouble; he claims with equal authority that the Déwa Agung followed immediately thereafter. In this version the Balinese continue to emerge one at a time, as if playing some peculiar game: did the women and children also come out singly?

Such chaos is very different from the drama recorded in an official report of one of the puputan in Denpasar:

> About 11 o'clock A.M., a great crowd passed the crossroads, clothed in white and armed, and marched in an eastern direction. . . . [The artillery fired] and although the effect of the fire in the densely packed crowd was appalling, no hesitation by the enemy was perceived. . . . Women with weapons in hand, lances or kris, and children in their arms, leapt fearlessly on the troops and sought death. Where we tried to disarm them, this only led to an increase of our losses. The survivors were repeatedly called upon to put down their weapons and surrender, but in vain. The uninjured made use of each pause in the fire to kris the wounded, and then rushed anew with naked weapons on the troops.[2]

Compare Badung's unhesitating and "densely packed crowd" with accounts of the confrontation in Klungkung. These Balinese managed to harm their enemies, even with lances and keris, and turned weapons on their fellows only to relieve them of suffering before once again charging into the fray.

Was the puputan in Klungkung really so different from the one in Badung, or does the difference lie in their representation? It is unclear from what vantage reporters could have witnessed the attack. Small groups or even solitary persons dispatched by reluctant marksmen one by one might have evoked images less disturbing to colonial sensibilities than disciplined troops firing into a determined crowd: it suggests less opposition. If the Dutch had to contend with only a few "madmen," then, however tragic their fates, what could be done? On the other hand, some differences in accounts of events in Badung and Klungkung no doubt stem from the fact that Klungkung's was a repeat performance: everyone already knew that participants in a puputan wear white and show determination and that the grim business cannot be stopped once it has started. But it is equally plausible, given historical circumstances and the differences between Klungkung's position and Badung's, that people went to meet the Dutch in a different style and a different mood in 1906 Badung and 1908 Klungkung. I see no way of resolving these questions, of determining "what really happened." Balinese accounts resemble neither of these descriptions; indeed, in certain ways they contradict them. They give, however, a clearer sense of what was at stake.

A KLUNGKUNG ACCOUNT OF THE PUPUTAN

The richest and most detailed Balinese account I heard came from a man who claimed to have been an eyewitness: the late Pedanda Madé Gélgél of Geria Sengguan. As a boy of about twelve, he had watched events unfold from a perch in the crook of a frangipani tree in the corner of a kinsman's courtyard at Geria Bendul, about two hundred meters north of the main Klungkung crossroads. The Gusti Putu Jelantik to whom he repeatedly refers was a nobleman from Buléléng, who held the position of *punggawa keliling* (a native official who accompanied colonial officers on their tours) and served as an interpreter during the 1906 and 1908 expeditions; many years later he became regent of Buléléng.

> I will recount [*nuturin*] as much as I remember. The guns were already lined up. So this is what happened. I arrived there, and I heard. . . . At that moment they were already preparing to finish there. . . . They all came out, wearing white clothing. Male and female. They were ordered by I Gusti Putu Jelantik to come out. They came out, male and female, including many court retainers [*parekan*]. When they came out weren't they there, then, on the road? . . . They were told to all wear white, that's how it was. They wore white, male and female, wore whatever they had, rings, rings . . . ah, all kinds of things, as much as they owned. They wore gold. Wore it in order to finish . . .
>
> They faced south, at the crossroads, the great crossroads.
>
> MW: In front of the Kerta Gosa?
>
> That's the place, that's where they stood. I Gusti Putu Jelantik had told the Dutch. Because the will of the Déwa Agung was to keep faith [*nyatiain*]

[with] the realm [*jagat*]. He prepared to die, to be true to the country.
The Dutch didn't agree. They said, "Why do you want to do that? Think
it over" [*mecikang kayun*, literally, "make your thoughts right"]. But he still
[held to his] words. In order to keep faith with the country. He didn't
want to fight. He had committed himself, surrendered [*nyerahang*, i.e., to
fate, the gods]. Together with all he had.

From here the Pedanda moved into an almost dreamy account of the sequence
of events:

They wore gold. Whatever belonged to the puri, the women put it on
and then came out. They came out from the jero. They came out there,
north of . . . There was a banyan tree, but it's gone now. That banyan
tree was a large one. They came there and adjusted their clothing. All
of them, the women, men, children as small as this [gesturing to one of
the children present, who was perhaps seven years old]. Lots of them.
They were the tip of the leaf, the children, in white all of them. They
were wearing keris at their waists, the children carried keris . . . They
came out, the little ones, and shouted loudly. It brought joy to the hearts
of their parents. They shouted and laughed angrily while drawing their
keris, all of them. You see, if they acted like that, the Dutch would understand it would really happen. They were fired upon then. *Béh*, there
was one whose hand was like this [dangling his hand loosely from the
wrist]. They all died there, the little ones.
    After they were finished, dead, the children, I Gusti Putu Jelantik
[called out], "If the king wishes to finish, tell him to come out." [But]
the women [came out] first, that's how it was, women first. They all wore
white, wore gold . . . they came out in rows. They were immediately
shot by the Dutch. That is, it wasn't the Dutch who fired, it was . . .
Javanese, Javanese soldiers. Yes, Javanese soldiers, those were the ones
who fired.
    The children were finished, scattered and dead. There was one
whose hand was cut off. He stuffed it into his waistcloth. When the
young people were finished and dead, the women emerged in rows . . .
wearing white all of them, wearing gold, whatever they owned . . . There
wasn't anything left in the jero. They came out in rows, from the west
they came, that's how it was.
    MW: Did they carry weapons?
    No. The women did not. Not the women. The children. They were in
white, all of them, like—what could you compare it to? Very white. After they emerged in rows, Gusti Putu Jelantik spoke to the . . . Dutch, so
they [the Balinese] would have a safe and tranquil path, so they would
shoot true. In rows from the west they came, in white. There were more

Figure 9. (From left): Déwa Agung Gedé Agung, the crown prince; Cokorda Raka Jodog of Puri Kaléran; Déwa Agung Jambé; Cokorda Putu Plodot (holding a betel-nut container named I Kawotan).

than a hundred who came out. Then the guns were fired until the ammunition was used up. They weren't Dutch, they were Javanese soldiers, soldiers who'd come from Ambon. Then they launched a shell. Toward the banyan tree. When it exploded it was dark, darkness poured out, no one was visible, you couldn't see anything. They fired into the smoke, the smoke that rose in an enormous cloud, that's what they fired at. After that was finished—one layer, three layers—the smoke cleared, it was over.

DAYU ALIT: They were dead?

The women had died. But there were still the men, another row's worth still. It was like that again, another grenade was thrown. A grenade was set off so that they wouldn't see the bodies probably.

PRIEST'S SON: They felt pity!

Smoke was used to wrap it up, and then they could shoot at that. It was done, they had all died. The men and the women, and the children.

I Gusti Putu Jelantik then spoke to the soldiers, who knows what he said. They were silent, then, the rifles. It was over. Then, those came out . . . the prisoners. Convicts from Java.[3] They all wore red shirts. They lifted the bodies. They were gathered together, piled up there below the banyan tree, all of them. "This one should be here, this one . . . here," like that. "That one there . . ." There was someone to direct it . . . There were those who were properly first, in the front. Those that should be further back, were further back. They were in rows, the bodies. *Béh,* the blood flowed in streams. I was there, watching. It flowed, that blood. Below the banyan tree, blood was scattered all the way south . . .

The convicts, the ones who lifted the bodies, got hundreds of rings, along with the soldiers. The ones with the red shirts, wearing red pants, they were convicts. From Java . . . Those rings, they were all gone, those were the ones who got them, the convicts. What could be done? They had all died. The country was destroyed [*gumi uug*].

IDA BAGUS JAGRI: Because he was true to his word.

Yes, yes. That was what he said, he would keep faith with the country. He didn't fight, no. He just readied himself. "If the Dutch wish to [attack], let them. I will be true to the realm. I don't want to make war. I don't have any weapons. I will share the fate of the land," that's what he said.

When it was all over, the bodies of those who had died were cremated. Pedanda Madé Gélgél recalled that the bodies were separated by rank: members of the royal family under the banyan tree, lesser folk near the Balé Banjar in Bendul ("They were piled up there. As if they weren't people . . ."). His own aunt, a court functionary (*sedahan*) who kept inventory of palace goods, provided a length of new white cloth to wrap the bodies of each person of high rank, and priests from Geria Sengguan and Geria Tengah organized the manufacture of a few offerings—the "named ones," Pedanda Madé Gélgél noted, the ones indexical of cremation.[4] There were so many bodies that there was no place to lay them out. Someone (it is unclear who) recalled that Pura Manik Mas had an unusually long *balé pawédan*, the platform on which Brahmana priests sit to "finish" temple rituals. (It was, recalled Pedanda Madé Gélgél, "decorated with gold leaf, full of gold leaf decorations. *Ratu*, it was amazing there.") This was used for the cremations.

After the bodies were burned, the ashes were sifted as is customary to gather bone fragments for a second ritual, in which they would be washed away to the sea. But as Pedanda Madé Gélgél recalled, not all of the bones ended up receiving this ritual treatment:

> The commoners were allowed to look for bones. Some of them asked for this, asked for that. They wrapped them up in cloth and carried them away on their heads. They brought them to their homes.
>
> IDA BAGUS JAGRI: To use as sacred relics?
>
> Yes, relics. The burnt bones . . . The people [*panjak*] fought over them so they [all] might get a piece. They put them in bottles, [in] whatever they had brought.
>
> PRIEST'S SON: They were that loyal. (Interview, Geria Sengguan, 27 April 1985)

COMMENTARY

In contrast to the chaos of the newspaper accounts, what is most striking in Pedanda Madé Gélgél's account is the tone of collective purpose, of methodical and deliberate intention. Rather than suddenly appearing out of nowhere, in spurts, the Balinese calmly prepare and then advance in orderly rows. Again, there is no question of determining "what really happened." Whether or not matters were as organized as his narrative indicates is irrelevant; what counts is that people think they were. And Pedanda Madé Gélgél remembers seeing it so.

The stateliness of this description is particularly striking. It is as if people were participating in a procession rather than a battle. And indeed, even the sequence in which, according to the Pedanda, the participants emerged echoes that of ritual processions—when deities are carried to the sea for purification, or bodies to the cemetery for cremation, to be unified with Divinity. On those occasions too children and youths lead, to be followed by women, and then the focus of the processional march: the objects in which deities sit in the case of processions to the sea, the body of the deceased on the occasion of a cremation. If during the puputan the king brings up the rear, analogy would suggest that the point of that procession, like others, might have been to effect a purification of its principal participant.

Other narrators could not imagine that the king was preceded rather than followed by women and children, however. In the *Buwana Winasa*, for example, Pedanda Ngurah claims the Cokorda of Gélgél and Déwa Agung Smarabawa were among the first to die, although they were immediately followed by the most important "little one" on the scene: Déwa Agung Gedé Agung, the crown prince, Déwa Agung Jambé's son by his first cousin (see ·fig. 9). Others regarded the participation of women as an act of *masatia*, in which case they should have followed, rather than preceded, the Déwa Agung (see, e.g., Helms 1969).

Yet the Pedanda was not alone in claiming that the king was among the last to die. It was the general consensus in Klungkung. Pedanda Gedé Tembau thought this was only right, for texts suggested that a ruler should not "come down" to the battlefield until all his defenders—foot-soldiers, lords, seconds—had been defeated. As in a game of chess, he came into play only during the endgame.

But others still found it peculiar that women should have been among those "defenders," and tried to explain why. One or two suggested that the women were following Déwa Agung Gedé Agung rather than his father Déwa Agung Jambé. (In a different context, Cokorda Isteri Biang Sayang asserted that during the puputan the crown prince carried Bangawan Canggu, the keris that binds and inspires love.) Then there were those who claimed that it proved that up to the very end Déwa Agung Jambé did not want to fight the Dutch. Only shame or grief at his son's death finally drove him forward.

Déwa Agung Gedé Agung—who could not have been more than twelve at the time—emerges in many accounts as particularly heroic, as do his lower-ranking elder brothers. Pedanda Ngurah's poem and a number of oral narratives mention that in meetings held in the puri to decide how to respond to the Dutch ultimatum he was among those who urged the Déwa Agung to take up arms. His cousin and former playmate Anak Agung Kudar was told by her father that he had declared before the assembled lords that there was no point in living only to become "food for worms." Cokorda Batu, the prince some identified as the one who calmly stuffed his hand (or arm) into his waistband after it was shot off, was Déwa Agung Gedé Agung's elder brother by a lower-ranking mother and already an adult. His indifference to pain and singleness of purpose figure in many Klungkung descriptions of the puputan:

DADONG RIBEK: Ida Cokorda Batu, his arm was severed. Severed. He took it, put it in his waistband, his arm. He was incredibly brave. There was a pregnant woman carrying a child on her back.

"Mother, my foot is severed, mother."

"Ah, quiet yourself, be quiet, be quiet."

It was true his foot was cut off. A small child, probably no more than five. His mother was pregnant. I don't know if he was a prince or a commoner. (Losan, 12 February 1986)

Historical contingencies, however, play no part in Pedanda Madé Gél-gél's narrative. There is too much intentionality in his description of three rows of participants. A Dutch source provides another reason why the Déwa Agung's wives and children might have died before him, which has nothing to do with royal hesitation. An assessment of the Balinese in a Dutch military history, written twelve years before the Netherlands Indies army had any direct experience of a puputan, describes precisely what such a practice entailed:

How much they are to be feared as enemies, is evident from the willing-ness to make sacrifices mentioned of them, which makes them ready to consecrate themselves to death with their king. In such a "popotan" sometimes 200 to 300 men, clad in white [and] armed with short cut-off lances, follow their beloved chief and, after having killed their wives and children, run with rage against the enemy, to conquer or be killed to the last man (Hooyer 1894:312).[5]

Note that Pedanda Madé Gélgél makes no mention of women stabbing children or the wounded; indeed, he insists—contrary to the journalists—that the women were unarmed. Others, such as the Pedanda of Geria Bajing and Ida Bagus Kakiang of Geria Bendul, heard that the women carried the shuttles from their looms. Some people suggested that not only the death of women and children but all of the violence that transpired was initiated by the Dutch:

COKORDA ISTERI BIANG SAYANG: People say this, they say that, there are all kinds of stories. This is what I heard here. The Lords [*Betara*], all of them, these ones, the most important Déwa Agungs. All of them sat like this [she demonstrates, cupping her right hand in her left at chest level, with the thumb and forefinger of the right hand and the thumb of the left meeting and pointing up. Ida Bagus Jagri said the gesture symbol-izes making one's thoughts "one"]. Wearing white, they sat like this. In the *musti* position. But their keris were opened, the keris, the daggers. All of them sat with their hands in a *musti* position. The keris were in front of them. All of them, male and female, exactly alike. Yes. What that means is to look for . . . a good road to Emptiness. That was what they did, they carried weapons in order to fight. If the enemy came to fight, they would resist with them. If not, they would remain still. Like this. To look for a road . . .

DAYU ALIT: Oh, if the enemy came here they would use the weapons, and if not just sit still?

Just remain there. Even if the enemy came, if they didn't attack, they wouldn't resist. But they already had their weapons by their sides. That is what is called bravery. (Puri Anyar, 14 March 1985)

Even Pedanda Madé Gélgél, who describes the Balinese as making the first move, suggests it was a feint. Others, however, were adamant that the puputan involved aggression:

PEDANDA GEDÉ TEMBAU: They drew their keris. They attacked. Probably if they had had guns, they would have opposed them. They still carried keris, but [the enemy would have to] be close for them to stab them, right, they were opposing guns. (Geria Aan, 31 January 1986)

But this reference to guns shows that the puputan was not an ordinary act of war. For in fact they *did* have guns. Although all of Klungkung's arsenal had supposedly been surrendered to the Dutch after Badung's conquest, the Dutch ultimately collected 357 guns in the realm of Klungkung; 24 of them were found in the puri itself.[6] Even though none was as sophisticated as the artillery wielded by the colonial army, they might at least have caused some enemy casualties had they been deployed. Thus the decision to use only lances and keris must have been deliberate. Indeed, such weaponry was typical of a puputan; Hooyer writes that participants even trimmed their lance shafts, making them suitable only for close combat. Ordinarily, of course, there was more to keris and lances than the sharpness of their blades or the skill of those who wielded them. Just when Klungkung's lords discovered what had happened to their heirloom weapons is unclear, but the impression conveyed by most of the stories I heard in Klungkung was that, contrary to what van Kol or the correspondent for *De Locomotief* reported, they knew before preparing to meet the Dutch that April afternoon.

The white clothing to which Pedanda Madé Gélgél repeatedly returned is also something mentioned by Hooyer. And many others recalled it too. When I asked Anak Agung Gaci, for example, if everyone had really worn white he commented, "All white? They did. All of them. Who knows how many measures of white cloth [*kasa*] were used."

Balinese associate *kasa*, white cloth, with very particular experiences. Temple priests wear white at all times; Brahmana priests dress in white to prepare holy water every morning by unification with the god Siwa, or when they finish (*muputang*) a ritual. And all Balinese are dressed in white when they die: their bodies are wrapped entirely in white cloth, both for burial and again (whatever is left of them) for their cremation.[7]

White is appropriate for both priests and the dead because it is the color
of purification, of an intention to be unified with the invisible world. The
rituals after death are meant to progressively dissolve a person into his constituent elements, to free his *niskala* soul (*atma*). Brahmana priests in fact symbolically die in the ceremonies that consecrate them, ceremonies often referred to as "cleansing" (*mabersih*). And white was the color worn by those who
participated in a puputan because they were undergoing a similarly transfor-
mative experience, one that, regardless of its outcome, required that they free
their minds and hearts of all that normally occupied them.

When people prepared to meet the Dutch by dressing themselves all in
white, therefore, they situated their action in the midst of a structure of meanings echoing around the theme of purity and death. Consecrating themselves
to the invisible world of the gods, they wore white garments to signify their
detachment, their indifference to the outcome of their act or to everyday self-
interest. Those who participated in the puputan had surrendered the situation
to the gods.

SUICIDE AND SACRIFICE

That those who joined in the puputan did so knowing that they might well
die is what has led Euro-Americans to characterize the puputan as suicide,
ritual, or some combination of both. The Dutch legal scholar Resink, for
example, describes puputan as "an act of ritual suicide" (1968:433). Geertz,
recall, refers to puputan as a "strange ritual"; Boon simply glosses it as "mass
suicide" (1977:29). But terms like these obscure Balinese intentionalities,
making us think we already understand them. Suicide is bound up in a Euro-
American discourse of emotion, irrationality, and impotence; ritual, commonly analyzed as a form of purely symbolic action, has some of the same
connotations.

For Balinese, puputan and suicide could not be less alike. There are two
ways in particular that they differ. First, the inner states they entail are mirror
opposites. The suicide gives in to temptation, to the presence of the *buta-kala*
who cause despair; one who chooses a puputan does not. Suicide is a reaction
to thwarted will rather than a perseverance of the will in the face of all obstacles. At base puputan is the ultimate example of the calm, fearless steadfastness Balinese refer to as being *pageh*. This is what makes such a death the
perfect one for lords whose power is thought to derive from just this quality.
As Pedanda Gedé Tembau of Aan noted, "A *satria* who surrenders is very low.
He is not brave, he doesn't have the blood of a *satria*."

Second, suicide is the worst kind of "bad death," specifically an *ulah pati*,
"cursed death". One who dies in such a manner is condemned to live as a
tanana, betwixt and between the visible and invisible worlds, a servant of the

gods and of powerful humans. By contrast, those who die in battle go to the highest levels of the invisible world (see below), where they live like gods, receiving offerings and homage from the living.

If the puputan was not a suicide, was it a ritual? People occasionally used the phrase *rana-yadnya*, "the sacrifice of battle," to refer to these events. Balinese rituals are commonly divided into five types: sacrifices to gods (*dewa-yadnya*, mainly temple rituals), sacrifices to demons (*buta-yadnya*), sacrifices to holy men (*rsi-yadnya*, which include priestly consecrations), sacrifices to humans (*manusa-yadnya*, the life-cycle rituals) and sacrifices to the dead (*pitra-yadnya*, death rituals). When I first heard the expression *rana-yadnya*, I wondered where it fit: was it a kind of *buta-yadnya*, as in some ways any act of war was? Geertz refers to a remark the ruler of Tabanan was said to have made, describing the war against Mengwi as a *caru*, like those made to demons (1980:254). There seems something Frazerian about royal deaths such as these. The sacrifice of the ruler might be a logical potentiality in a ritual system where rulers were responsible for placating and transforming demons through sacrifice. After all, in 1908 all signs showed that negative forces were in the ascension, and other rituals had not worked. Could the king's death cool down his "hot" realm where lesser sacrifices had failed?

No one volunteered such interpretations, but when I proposed them, usually to Brahmana priests, they more or less agreed, though they did not feel comfortable assimilating such matters to the current classification of ritual acts. Pedanda Gedé Tembau, for example, had this to say:

> IDA BAGUS JAGRI: If someone dies by "finishing," is it like a sacrifice [*yadnya*]?
>
> A sacrifice, but a sacrifice of bravery. Now this one doesn't enter the five *yadnya*. The sacrifice of the satria, it's indeed that. It's the highest form of death.
>
> PRIEST'S SON: It is said to be a sacrifice of bravery.
>
> MW: Yes, there are those who say *rana-yadnya*.
>
> . . . It's like incense, the great smoke (of the guns), isn't that so? Like a bell, the sound of the bullets, isn't that so?
>
> DAYU ALIT: It's like this: as far as deaths go, that's the highest, lord, is that it?
>
> Yes. That's why there's no need to start again, to perform death rituals. He's just burned. He who dies in battle is just burned. At a later date, a *maligia* or *mukur* [rituals to further purify the soul].
>
> MW: So it is like the body is an offering already?
>
> Yes, that's exactly it. The contents of the body are like an offering. (Interview, Geria Aan, 29 November 1985)

Given such responses I wondered if *rana-yadnya* might refer to some forgotten category of rite. Pedanda Gedé Kenitén merely said that *rana-yadnya* was the theme of the legendary Barata war and referred me to literature. But there are, I later discovered, texts entitled *rana-yadnya*, concerning the fate of those who die in battle. Pedanda Gedé Tembau told me something about this too:

> According to texts, he who is brave dies in battle, returns to the god Wisnu in Wisnu's realm. Wisnu also loves, cares for, what do you call it . . .
>
> DAYU ALIT: He is loved by Sang Hyang Wisnu.
>
> When he is eventually reincarnated, he will be reincarnated as a king again, that's what will happen. (29 November 1985)

This is, then, a king's death par excellence. In using his will to surrender himself completely to the invisible world, he is transported to Wisnu's realm. Recall Pedanda Madé Gélgél's interpretation, that the Déwa Agung "surrendered himself"—to Divinity—and went without hesitation to meet the Dutch gunfire. In this way, the Pedanda claims, he "kept faith" with his realm.

In making such a claim the Pedanda alluded to the effects of such a death on a ruler's subjects. When I asked people about whether a king who died that way could bring prosperity to his realm, they invariably agreed: "Isn't that the case?" said Pedanda Gedé Tembau. Dayu Alit pursued this further: "His spirit could protect [*ngerahayuang*] the realm, isn't that so?" "Protect the world," concurred the Pedanda. *Rahayu*, the root of the term used, means safe, prosperous, and tranquil.

It is striking that Klungkung priests consistently associated royal death in battle with the god Wisnu;[8] texts on *rana-yadnya* (see, e.g., H3941 and K370/7) offer a much more elaborate scheme of the destination of the souls of those who die in war, based upon just how and where their death occurs. For example, only those who die with their heads facing north go to Wisnu's realm. The stress on Wisnu in Klungkung emphasizes the king's role as warrior and protector. But some of Wisnu's other associations—to coolness, wellbeing, and water—are also relevant. From Wisnu's realm (and merged with the deity) the Déwa Agung could continue to exercise benevolent care for his former domain; he could, as Pedanda Gedé Kenitén put it, *ngetisang gumi*, "cool down," literally "sprinkle holy water on," the country.

Dayu Alit and Ida Bagus Jagri interpreted all of these remarks as suggesting that the Déwa Agung realized it was impossible to help his people from "here"; by dying he could go where he could do the most good. In so dying, Klungkung's rulers paradoxically asserted their power to make the world, for such death in battle ensured that they would become invisible agents in their own right. So the case could be made that the puputan was a sacrifice, intended to have tangible effects. And some thought that subsequent Klung-kung history proved the sacrifice had "worked."

But as my accounts of these conversations might suggest, these were not matters people were likely to volunteer. For where was the proof? These are precisely the kinds of things one knows through a *kleteg ring kayun*, a feeling, and are communicable only to those who are *wayah di tengah*, capable of un-derstanding without the need for words.

INTERPRETATION AND ITS LIMITS

There are several ways to evaluate the cultural and historical significance of the puputan: by looking backward at what preceded it, or by looking forward, to what followed it.

Looking back, for example, there are striking connections linking stories about events preceding and responsible for the conquest with the themes gathered together by the puputan. It is as if through this act every loss sym-bolized by the desecration of the regalia was recouped: wearing white signi-fied purity and purification, negating prior pollution; and his willingness to die in battle proved the Déwa Agung *pageh*, firm and resolute, thus worthy of power.

Or one could look back in another way: to the relationship between the way tales represent the puputan and the impositions of the colonial govern-ment. Recall that the primary theme sounded by colonial discourse at this time was the tyranny of the Balinese ruling class; colonial rule, it was argued, would liberate the Balinese people. Since one form that "liberation" had taken was a prohibition on *masatia*, it is significant that several of Betara Dalem's wives were among those who died in the puputan. Their participation was an expression of contempt for colonial authority, at once a violation and a rejec-tion of colonial values.

It is also striking that people in Klungkung sometimes refer to the pupu-tan as "the time of the loyalty of the country" (*uges satian gumi*). The Dutch, of course, made much of the fact that ordinary citizens did not defend their king. This claim is not accepted in Klungkung; after all, even accepting the Dutch count of those who died, some had to have been royal retainers. Sev-eral people emphasized the king's pity for his people, however, his desire to spare them. In the villages, there were those like Kaki Merta of Dawan, who recalled that the king told people to use arms only if their own villages were endangered. Others recalled running for cover, terrified by the morning of shelling. But loyalty is not only demonstrated by a willingness to die. Pedanda Madé Gélgél's tale of commoners bringing home fragments of burnt bone to keep as relics also denotes loyalty. And several elderly commoners to whom I spoke, in Pikat, Gélgél, and Losan, remembered how following the puputan people had "sacrificed hair":

> DAYU ALIT: At the time the realm was destroyed, how did the
> people feel?
> What can you say? They were sad, they all shaved their heads.
> DAYU ALIT: Shaved?
> Shaved. Those like myself, girls or women with long hair, cut it. To
> follow the Betara, who had died. All of the men and boys shaved their
> heads, near and far they shaved. That, it is said, is a sign of following
> him home. (Dadong Ribek, Losan, 15 February 1986)

Looking forward, the puputan takes on other significations, for it marks a historical transition. I will argue in the next chapter that after the puputan what kingship could mean in Bali was transformed. With the puputan certain descriptions of kings begin to be replaced by others, for among the things "finished" in the puputan was the identification of royal power with keris and all that this entailed. That the puputan as an event was ambiguously both battle and sacrifice only underlines the point. From this moment on descendants of Klungkung's royal clan ceased to protect their realms by magical-military means and, limited to ritual, began to take on certain attributes of Brahmana priests. Such priestliness is even in a way foreshadowed in these accounts, by the white clothing. The same liminality informs the narratives accounting for Klungkung's vulnerability to conquest, for the keris that are at the center of such narratives are spoken of mainly as sacred objects, subject to desecration, rather than as weapons.

But looking either backward or forward the puputan is almost unbearably moving. This has much to do with what people say—and do not say—about it. Pedanda Madé Gélgél, for example, though describing what had happened in great detail, offered few interpretations. What happened already said it all. In the same way, when I came to write about the event, I found it resisted too much analysis. Wittgenstein's comments on Frazer's *Golden Bough* sum up the matter beautifully:

> I think one reason why the attempt to find an explanation is wrong is
> that we have only to put together in the right way what we *know*, with-
> out adding anything, and the satisfaction we are trying to get from the
> explanation comes of itself.
> And here the explanation is not what satisfies us anyway. When Fra-
> zer begins by telling the story of the King of the Wood at Nemi, he
> does this in a tone which shows that something strange and terrible is
> happening here. And that is the answer to the question "why is this

happening?": Because it is terrible. In other words, what strikes us in this course of events as terrible, impressive, horrible, tragic, &c., anything but trivial and insignificant, *that* is what gave birth to them. Compared with the impression that what is described here makes on us, the explanation is too uncertain. (Wittgenstein 1979:2e–3e)

ELEVEN

The Empty Land

When people in Klungkung spoke of the conquest, they not only referred back to the Kusamba War but foreshadowed later events. Narratives
frequently foreground a young prince, knee shattered by bullets, found alive
under a pile of bloody corpses, still calling for the "White Eyes" to kill him.
The scene is almost a mirror image of the death of General Michiels, the
central symbol of the Kusamba War. There a Dutchman, shot in the leg with
a Balinese bullet, died when he should not have; here a Balinese, also shot in
the leg, but by Dutch bullets, lived when he had every intention of dying.

The prince in question was someone everyone knew: Cokorda Oka Geg,
eldest son of Déwa Agung Smarabawa. He was to be Klungkung's last ruler,
for the puputan did not mark the end of kingship in Klungkung after all. In
1929 the colonial government appointed the Cokorda as Klungkung's regent,
under the title of Déwa Agung, and it is their memories of his re-creation of
royal power that shaped the way many people spoke of precolonial Bali.

Given that arguments concerning the detrimental effects of Balinese rulers
on the welfare of their people had justified their conquest, a colonial revival
of kingship comes as some surprise. During the years of the Ethical Policy,
the colonial government was in general hostile to local forms of power, or
even emblematic signs of it. But by the 1920s colonial policy toward indigenous rulers had undergone an about-face. The Ethical Policy had lost support
in the Netherlands, in part as a result of the growth of nationalist movements
and political activism in Java and Sumatra. Such movements were stimulated
both by the extension of public education under the Ethical Policy and by the
increasing number of Indonesians making the haj to Mecca, where they were
exposed to Pan-Islamic and nationalist ideas. In reaction, a new, more conser-
vative colonial policy focused on *rust en orde*, peace and order. Throughout the
archipelago the colonial government sought to revive traditions, including the
prestige of indigenous aristocrats, for it appeared that rulers and their emblems of power—carefully monitored by colonial officials—might be useful
to the administration's efforts to maintain order.

On Bali, arguments for a restoration of kingship arose in the context of a
series of natural disasters, which began when a major earthquake shook the

331

island in 1917, destroying in its wake an enormous number of temple shrines, including the main shrine at Besakih. The earthquake was followed by epidemics and crop failures. It was at this time that Pedanda Ngurah composed his poem on the destruction of the world. Some Balinese took the occasion to argue that these misfortunes were signs of divine anger, due to the neglect of important sanctuaries formerly the responsibility of Balinese kings, especially Besakih (Stuart-Fox 1987). The Viceroys of Gianyar and Karangasem organized labor for repairs, which the colonial government was persuaded to fund. While the Dutch had little interest in Balinese ritual, Karangasem's ruler was able to insinuate that ignoring the situation could lead to disorder. Since much archipelago nationalism was organized under the banner of Islam, colonial officials began to think that support for Bali's Hindu religion might help prevent the nationalist movement from gaining ground on the island—and, Karangasem's shrewd viceroy urged, Bali's rulers had traditionally played a major role in religious leadership (Schulte Nordholt 1986:2, 1988:290).

By the mid-1920s the Dutch had decided to institute a system of indirect rule throughout Bali. Regents descended from the former royal families were appointed in areas that had been administered by European district heads since their incorporation into the colonial state. Klungkung was the last, in 1929. Nine years later all of Bali's regents, who already met regularly in a Council of Rulers, were granted a certain degree of independence when they were vested with the title "autonomous ruler" (*zelfbestuurder*) in a ceremony at Besakih, attended by colonial officials and celebrated with champagne (van der Kaaden 1938; Stuart-Fox 1987:354–56).

Colonial kingship, however, was a different business than kingship prior to Bali's fall. First of all, like colonial governments everywhere, a major element of colonial "peace and order" was a *Pax Neerlandica*. War was prohibited. There were also other limits to royal autonomy. The administration disapproved of customs that treated violations of hierarchy severely, as signs of cosmic danger. Sexual relationships between high-ranking women and lower-ranking men, for example, did not strike the Dutch as a legitimate capital offense. In a concession to local sensibilities the colonial government continued to condemn such relationships as criminal, but perpetrators were sentenced to permanent exile rather than death. Similarly, the Dutch forbade the execution of sorcerers. Rulers were to maintain order by becoming administrators. With other forms of agency so circumscribed, they became more and more involved with temples and rituals, trying to both achieve and demonstrate their power through increasingly spectacular rites. Under the circumstances, it is easy to see how they might appear mere impresarios of "theater-states."

The transformation was especially consequential for Klungkung. While Klungkung's new ruler was allowed to use the title Déwa Agung, the Dutch granted him no special privileges or powers. He was only one of eight equal "rajas" in what the Dutch called the *asta negara*, eight realms, their use of Kawi legitimizing the new order by making it appear to belong to the autonomous past. The other "rajas" did defer to him, however, as far as Besakih was concerned. The Déwa Agung increasingly emphasized his role as head of Bali's temple and ritual system. What had been implicit (temples) became overt, and what had been overt (keris) became memory. In short, the Dutch succeeded in making the Déwa Agung precisely what they had once thought he might be: Bali's "spiritual overlord."

These changes register both in stories about Klungkung's past and in the material forms that witness the history made by Klungkung's last ruler. Overtly, however, narrators deny change, stressing continuities and the similarities between this Déwa Agung and his ancestors. And, like the tales about the Kusamba War and the conquest, stories of this period continue to treat the Dutch as peripheral.

THE SUCCESSION

Cokorda Oka Geg (fig. 10) was marked out from the start as special.[1] Not only had he survived the puputan, but he was, by an odd set of circumstances, exempted from the exile that fell upon all of his close kinsmen.[2] Severely wounded, he was treated by Dutch doctors, who doubted he would recover. But recover he did. By the time he was well enough to be sent to Lombok a year had passed, and the government's mood had changed. When the new Resident wrote what he clearly expected would be a routine report of the action he had taken in regard to the young prince, he received a letter back inquiring why a mere child posed a risk: were conditions in Klungkung perhaps worse than the Governor General had been led to believe? The Resident hastened to assure his superiors that, on the contrary, Klungkung was thoroughly pacified, and not a trace of affection or nostalgia for their former rulers could be found among its populace. But the boy was, after all, a prince of high rank, and since his kinsmen of equal rank had been exiled as potentially subversive, so should he. The Governor General was not persuaded, and in the end the Resident sent a boat to Lombok to fetch the boy back.[3] The prince asked to remain with his kinsmen.[4] However, since he was in Lombok by choice rather than law, he was, unlike his "fathers," free to return to Bali.

Story has it that he did so a few years before the 1917 earthquake. On his way to Java for secondary schooling, he stopped off in Klungkung to visit his younger siblings. According to Cokorda Oka of Puri Anyar, he happened to arrive just as the new bridge on the Unda River was being dedicated, in conjunction with which cockfights were held for an entire week. The Cokorda was so enthralled by the excitement that he decided to stay. Cokorda Mayun

(n.d.) has a slightly different version: deciding he could not be that far from his siblings again, he declared he would forego Java and continue his education once a new school was completed in Buléléng. But when telegrams arrived to call him north, he had already married and had a son.

The selection and grooming of Cokorda Oka Geg as Klungkung's regent is described in the *Memorie van Overgave* of Controleur Haar, who was responsible for it. There were two major requirements for candidates for office: they had to be lineal descendants of former rulers, and they had to be educated. Haar's biography of the prince was therefore replete with details likely to be of interest to administrators, such as the fact that in Lombok the Cokorda had finished the course of studies in a "Second Class School." Haar does not describe his first meetings with the prince but merely notes that in 1927 he informed the Assistant Resident of South Bali and the Resident "that here was a pretender for the function of Regent of Klungkung." At the same time, he took the prince into his office in the capacity of clerk (*magang*). Pleased with the young man's progress, Haar encouraged him to try his hand at new things. Word then came to "keep an eye on this young man . . . and to train him to proficiency for an eventual higher function." In accord with a colonial bureaucrat's idea of how to school a king, the prince was immediately promoted and given charge of arranging the transport of trucks through Klungkung. As Haar explains, without a trace of irony:

> By this he got a look at the practical side of administrative involvements. Moreover I had him take lessons in Dutch. . . . Still later I appointed him to Head Mantri-Jalan [Overseer of Roads]. By so doing he had the legal management in Kloengkoeng and Bangli entirely under his supervision. At the same time he came into direct contact with the poenggawas and other heads.

By early 1929 the government had already made Cokorda Geg their nominee for Déwa Agung in Klungkung. When the position of *punggawa keliling* fell vacant, Haar proposed him for it on the grounds that it would allow him to become familiar with and well known to his future subjects. In that capacity he accompanied the Controleur on tours of Klungkung, often spending the night with the headmen of various villages. Finally, on 25 July 1929,

> he was ceremoniously sworn in at the Pura Dasar at Gelgel by the Resident of Bali and Lombok, in the presence of many authorities, as Dewa Agoeng of Penegara Kloengkoeng. (Haar n.d.:42)

Haar advised his successor that while "he has little experience yet, and still needs continual management with a firm hand . . . his prestige with and influence over the population are . . . of great importance in matters in which the Government must seek contact with the people." Perhaps most ironic is

Haar's conclusion, which reiterated an old colonial analogy: that the relationship between controleur and Déwa Agung should be like that between an elder and younger brother (Haar n.d.:43). Such images of the relationship between colonial officials and indigenous regents dated from the early years of colonial rule in Java. From a Balinese perspective, however, Dutch bureaucrats were claiming the place of Brahmana priests.

In Klungkung itself, Cokorda Oka Geg's rise to power is narrativized in much more remarkable terms. Emphasis is placed upon his discovery by the Dutch, efforts by enemies to prevent his accession, and signs that he was not only suitable by virtue of his descent but also favored by the invisible world. The Dutch controleur, while he does not quite vanish from the scene, becomes a minor supporting character, whose name is only sometimes remembered. Still, it *is* remembered, which distinguishes him from most other Dutch officials who served a turn of duty in Klungkung.

Stories present the Cokorda's accession to office as an overcoming of a variety of obstacles, a subtle evocation of the cultural plot concerning the acquisition of *kasaktian*. The first obstacle was his invisibility to the Dutch. The colonial government apparently had a difficult time finding a suitable candidate for regent in Klungkung. Many more members of the Klungkung royal house had been banished to Lombok than had been the case in either Badung or Tabanan, and they remained in exile long after the others were allowed to return to Bali. As far as the Dutch knew, all of the princes closest to Klungkung's core line were still in Lombok and could not therefore be considered; no one in the colonial administration recollected offhand the curious case of the young prince. And while people in Klungkung were reluctant to stoke old controversies, several hinted darkly that those who might have reminded them, Balinese who served in Klungkung's colonial administration, did not do so. There were, it seems, others who hoped to become king in Klungkung, though people were deliberately vague about who they were.[5]

Members of the royal clan generally tell two stories about how Cokorda Geg came to the attention of the Dutch. In the first and more colorful, a sow belonging to one of his female relations was found wandering loose in the streets of Klungkung (see, e.g., Mayun n d) Under new ordinances aimed at protecting public health, its owner was summoned to court so the case could be heard by the Controleur. As ranking head of the clan, Cokorda Oka Geg, then in his twenties, went to represent his "mother." It was a routine administrative matter; a bored Haar heard the evidence and ordered the pig's owner to pay a fine. But rather than complying without a murmur, the Cokorda declared that since the government had already taken everything that he owned this was impossible. The outspoken young man was identified to Haar as the son of Déwa Agung Smarabawa and the nephew of Déwa Agung Jambé. Impressed by his boldness, Haar took him under his wing.

A second story tells how the Dutch, continually frustrated in their efforts to find a potential regent by the uncooperative attitude of local native administrators, decided to go directly to the people. A carload of officials stopped a man at random and asked if there might still be any members of the royal family left. The man said there were indeed, and directed them to the young Cokorda, who was (contrary to Haar's narrative) very well known as he was a fixture at local cockfights. In fact, a popular story has it that the prince was gambling in far-off Buléléng when officials came to find him to persuade him to take a position in the colonial service—shades of Dalem Ketut Ngulesir, and not the last such hint to be detected in narratives of this king's life.

But while such mundane events may have brought him to the attention of colonial officials, a rather more remarkable occurrence is said to have convinced them to make him king. In 1926 Mount Batur erupted for the second time in less than a quarter-century. Despite continual supplications to the gods, the volcano continued to rumble and smoke ominously until someone thought to have Cokorda Oka Geg go there (literally, "go down") to pray. As soon as he arrived, the volcano quieted down. Or, as a more theatrical version has it, Haar, who brought the prince to Batur, berated him by asking, "How can you allow such a disturbance to your subjects in Bali?"[6] With that the prince walked to the crater's edge and spoke a few words, and the rumbling stopped. There was no question any longer in Haar's mind that this man should become Déwa Agung. According to Pak Morag, at that time a chauffeur for the civil service, who insisted he was there, Haar was absolutely passionate on the subject, striking a table with his fist when objections were raised, and announcing that "Cokorda Gedé Oka Geg must become the Regent in Klungkung. If he does not, I ask permission to resign my position as controleur here."

And, so the story goes, objections *were* raised. The Dutch were reminded that the prince's father had been a vehement opponent of the colonial government and that the prince himself had participated in the puputan. When this failed to make the necessary impression (it was all so long ago for a colonial administration now secure in its control over Bali), the opposition changed tactics: if the government found the Cokorda acceptable, there were reasons to think the gods would not. They argued that only someone who could be a vehicle for Divinity could become Déwa Agung; this prince was disfigured, for he walked with a limp. Memories of this accusation still rankle with many members of the royal clan, who note with some passion that the limp was the result of wounds honorably received in the puputan.

The debate—which did not in any event carry weight with the colonial civil service—is interesting, for it implied that the office of Déwa Agung had the same requirements as that of Brahmana priest. A candidate for priesthood may have no serious bodily defect; extremely poor eyesight or hearing, lameness, facial disfigurements, whether present from birth or the results of accident or age, are all grounds for refusing priestly consecration. It is equally significant that the prince's sympathizers did not reject the requirement but argued that what mattered was that the defect was not congenital; moreover, given that his wound was acquired in battle, it proved he was a true *ksatria*.

In any event, the gods clearly had no objections to this particular prince. Even his mercurial rise through the civil service from clerk to inspector of roads to *punggawa keliling*—a rise that must make a strong impression in modern Bali, where civil service jobs are coveted, and young men and women may work for years without pay in an office to be considered for one of the rare positions that open up—is spoken of with amazement, as if it were another manifestation of divine favor rather than the workings of the hand of a conscientious controleur.

That the gods had demonstrated their goodwill at Batur also retrospectively legitimated his line over that of other possible contenders. It was Bangli's royal house rather than Klungkung's that was primarily responsible for Batur. While in theory the Déwa Agung could call upon any of Bali's gods (and especially that of Batur, whose deity was younger sister/consort to Besakih's) Cokorda Oka Geg was not yet the Déwa Agung. The miracle at Batur, of course, is narrated precisely to demonstrate that he was the appropriate person to become so. But it is also noteworthy that the prince was related to the Bangli royal house: his father's mother had been the sister of Bangli's ruler. Implicitly, his success may have even suggested his father's superiority to Déwa Agung Jambé. As people constantly pointed out, it was Déwa Agung Smarabawa whose descendants survived. Not only Cokorda Oka Geg but two younger brothers and a younger sister lived "to continue the story"; the senior line in the East Wing perished completely. And as we have already seen narrators often contrast Déwa Agung Smarabawa with his brother as more virile, more powerful (he could not die till he threw his amulet away), and as an opponent of colonialism.

That Klungkung accounts of the prince's accession emphasize invisible forces is only to be expected. Colonial officials drop out of the story, except as ignorant agents of forces beyond their ken. Even in talking of the 1929 coronation Balinese narrators portray the Dutch as instruments whose control over events was far less than they themselves believed. The coronation itself was an odd affair, orchestrated and paid for by the colonial government, which also was responsible for deciding that the ceremony should be held in Pura Dasar in Gélgél, one of Klungkung's state temples. No doubt holding a coronation in a temple fit Dutch interpretations at this period of the religious nature of Balinese kingship; Balinese are quite sure that traditionally Klungkung's

Figure 10. Déwa Agung Oka Geg, dressed for his
coronation in 1929.

kings were never invested in a temple. There was certainly a Balinese ceremony at Pura Dasar in addition to the official swearing-in—full of extravagant offerings, ornamented by rows of beautiful young women from throughout the realm dressed uniformly in the most ornate fashion, and duly attended by colonial officials. But Pedanda Gedé Kenitén insisted vehemently that the ceremony in Pura Dasar was not the important one. The rites that really transformed the Cokorda into the new Déwa Agung took place beforehand in the house-shrines of the royal residence.[7] Afterwards, so said the Pedanda (whose father did the honors in the royal shrines), it was proper for the Déwa Agung to go to each of his state temples to inform the gods of the change in his status and beseech their blessings, and what transpired in Pura Dasar was only a much grander version of this. Whatever the Dutch may have thought, in Balinese eyes, power did not emanate from them, even indirectly; it came into being out of their sight.

But it was nonetheless at the ceremony in Gélgél that, according to at least one tale, the new Déwa Agung was confirmed in his office by the god of Mount Agung. At the climax of the ceremony a blaze of fire shot down from the sky from the direction of Besakih to enter the head of the praying king at the fontanel. It is hard not to see in this "fire" the same fire that went shooting off into the night sky before Klungkung's defeat in 1908, or the fire emanating from the hand of the god of Besakih in the story about Dalem Ketut told in the *Babad Dalem*. Although the story was not widely known (I heard it from my neighbor Ida Bagus Gedé, who probably heard it from I Cetig, the late king's chauffeur), its import was generally accepted: Klungkung's power had returned, and the young king had an extraordinary relationship with the god of Besakih. In fact, like Dalem Ketut, first king to rule at Gélgél, he and the god of Besakih were at one level "one"; the fire appears to have been in retrospect the god of Besakih entering the king's body.

THE KING'S TWO SPIRITS

I learned about Déwa Agung Oka Geg's connection with the god of Besakih quite by accident. Dayu Alit and Ida Bagus Jagri returned home to Peliatan periodically to attend rituals in Gianyar or Badung. After one of these visits, Dayu Alit asked me when the Déwa Agung had died. Surprised, I said that as far as I could figure it was in 1964, midway between two terrible events that everyone remembered well: the eruption of Mount Agung in 1963 and the anti-Communist massacres in 1965. At that she nodded triumphantly and said, "That's what I thought. I knew my elder sister was wrong. She couldn't possibly have met him!"

The sister in question was a priestess. She had been curious about our adventures in Klungkung and had asked her sibling all about them. Dayu Alit talked of this and that, mentioning our frequent visits to the royal palaces. At that her sister nodded sagely and noted that she had once been to the palace in Klungkung herself, before her consecration. She and her husband had asked Pedanda Gedé Kenitén, their "grandfather," to serve as their priestly initiator. Telling them that he could only do so with the permission of the king, he had arranged an audience. She remembered that the Déwa Agung, who was wearing a keris, sat on a chair in the Puri Agung, with two retainers on the floor below him. He spread a carpet for them to sit on, asked them many questions, and even promised to attend their consecration until the village headman, who had accompanied them, objected that the road was much too bad and he would be too embarrassed to have the Déwa Agung come there. The king then said that, in that case, after the ceremonies they should come to see him again in Klungkung. But as her sister reminisced, Dayu Alit was increasingly bothered by how little sense the story made. The Pedanda Isteri could not possibly have met the Déwa Agung, since she had not been consecrated until well after 1965, when the king had been long dead. But her sister insisted that the meeting had taken place, and they had bickered back and forth for some time. Hence her insistent question as soon as she saw me, to find confirmation for her own position.

Nonetheless we were both puzzled by her sister's story and decided she must have met one of the king's sons. Not long after, while we were chatting with Jero Ketut, one of Ratu Dalem Pemayun's wives, Dayu Alit remembered her sister and inquired who might have held such an audience with an aspirant priest in the main royal residence after the king's death. "Why," Jero Ketut said, "no one. Why do you ask?" Dayu Alit then told her the story. Jero Ketut shook her head and said that not only would no one have done such a thing after the king's death, but it was just as unlikely to have happened had he still been alive. In the 1960s he was rarely in the main palace, spending almost all of his time in his other two residences, where his younger wives lived. Moreover, once the colonial era ended, he never sat in a chair to greet people, and he never ever wore a keris. Besides, he had much too much respect for Brahmanas to have ever sat above one, let alone above his own priest. The whole thing was impossible.

And then Cokorda Isteri Agung, who was with us, said it was quite clear to her what must have happened: Dayu Alit's sister must have met the god of Mount Agung. This took Dayu Alit and myself by surprise, but Jero Ketut nodded and said that was probably it. They explained to us that Betara Tolangkir liked to do that, to take the Déwa Agung's form. It used to happen all the time. People would see the Déwa Agung somewhere and later discover that at the time in question he had in fact been at home. It was the god, dressed in his shape, they had seen. And they both settled back, smiling in a pleased way at the obviousness of the answer.

Needless to say, Dayu Alit and I were less sanguine. I dutifully wrote it all down, jotting a note to myself about how self-aggrandizing a claim it was. But Dayu Alit did not take it this way. While skeptical, she also was open-minded. And the more we heard about the Déwa Agung in the months that followed, the more convinced she became it was true.

Some people indeed told anecdotes about how the king had been seen in various preposterous (given the time and place) circumstances—riding a horse as the bridge over the Unda collapsed beneath a stream of lava, or on a palanquin during the Japanese occupation on his way to do battle with the ruler of Bangli; in fact, in such cases he was often seen on a palanquin—sightings that proved later to have been visions of normally unseen forces rather than of the king himself, although no one else saw fit to enlighten us about exactly Who it was who had taken the Déwa Agung's form. All the stories we heard about the Déwa Agung's power, however, proved to Dayu Alit's satisfaction that they were at the very least positive forces, and when we later heard about the blaze at the coronation she no longer had any doubts about the relationship between king and god. And although few were bold enough to come right out and say it explicitly, this did seem to be a common opinion in Klungkung. It was not unusual for someone to lean forward with a significant gleam in his or her eye and note that whenever the Déwa Agung prayed at Besakih he addressed someone there—and who knew who *that* was—as *mbok*, an ordinary Balinese term for "elder sister" that also, in the Klungkung royal family, is used for a high-ranking "mother."

Since texts identify Tolangkir, Besakih's divinity, as male, the *mbok* puzzled me. The divinities of all temples, however, are conventionally represented in images as a male and female pair, a sign of completeness. Was the king Divinity embodied as a human male addressing his other half as female, but marking his respect by calling her "elder"? Ida Bagus Jagri found this plausible, though uninteresting. In fact people were not concerned with such issues. What awed them was rather the use of a kin term. To use such language so casually and publicly and not be struck by divine wrath, in fact to prosper and perform wonders as this king was commonly said to do, was proof that he was no ordinary man. As for the gender implications of "elder sister," what mattered was mainly that his language showed he *knew* the form that the divinity took when it manifested itself.

It was commonly known that the Déwa Agung spent many nights at various of his temples, including Besakih. Like any sensible seeker after power he did not speak of these visits, let alone boast of his successes. But he was driven there by his chauffeur Cetig (who Pedanda Gedé Kenitén affectionately called his "Malén," after one of the loyal companions of the Pandawa brothers in shadow plays based upon the Mahabharata), and Cetig would occasionally peek or listen at the wall of the temple. He reported to a select group of friends (my neighbor Ida Bagus Gedé was one) some of the strange things he witnessed: a glow emanating from an open shrine, the murmuring of many voices. On occasion the Déwa Agung would take along a companion of a sort known to be on good terms with the invisible world—such as a local Brahmana woman who was slightly daft (*nyem*). She talked in turn as well, telling her kinsmen solemnly that while the king was deep in meditation at Besakih a snake crawled across his lap. Such stories, however, only confirmed what was already obvious. After all, the Déwa Agung addressed the god of Besakih in kin terms and was not harmed; on the contrary, it was clear that the invisible world favored him in ways both large and small.

For one thing, Pedanda Gedé Kenitén recalled in delight, although the Déwa Agung had little patience for the study of texts, he seemed to know their contents anyway. Often the Pedanda would discover in a manuscript something that he had heard the Déwa Agung say months or years before. The Pedanda Isteri of Gunaksa recounted an event that demonstrated the Déwa Agung's extraordinary knowledge and efficacy in another manner. The Déwa Agung requested her services at Besakih at a time when she expected to be menstruating and thus impure; when she attempted to excuse herself he told her not to worry about it, and indeed her menstrual flow not only did not come during the ritual, but it was days after her return home before it did.

More generally, the king was known to be accompanied everywhere by an entourage of spirits. These sometimes led to amusing inconveniences. Once, for example, as the king was being driven on the road north of Klungkung, he suddenly he ordered Cetig to stop. When the car halted, he announced firmly, "You can't all come along. The car is too heavy. Out with some of you!" A moment later the back end of the car visibly lifted several inches, and he calmly informed Cetig he could now proceed. On another occasion, the morning after the Déwa Agung spent a night alone in meditation at Puri Gélgél's house-shrines, the yard was strewn with cigarette butts, wads of tobacco, and betel juice, remnants of a large gathering.

Since everyone knew about the spirits, royal arrivals and departures were accompanied by small offerings (*segehan*) for members of his invisible guard—the same type of offering made whenever a powerful keris was taken down from its storage place. Despite the fact that he was poor, he always managed to find money for cockfighting—often conveniently left for him on tabletops by his spirit friends—and generally won. One particular spirit helper, who lived by a ravine at the western edge of the capital and was known to the Déwa Agung by name, had power over rain. Subjects planning large rituals would frequently ask him to intercede with her, which he usually did, addressing her in low Balinese.

Other well-known incidents were even more remarkable. When certain of his subjects had difficulty in getting a dam to withstand the force of the water flowing downstream, they asked for his help. He instructed each member of the irrigation society involved to bring a length of bamboo to the site of the dam. In ordinary language he asked the help of the appropriate divinities and spirits, then threw his stick toward the spot where the dam was to be. He then ordered everyone else to follow his example. The dam held; and the piece of bamboo that he himself had tossed into the water rooted and sprouted leaves. A similar maneuver diverted a stream of lava from Mount Agung from destroying Gélgél when the mountain erupted in 1963; it flowed around the town rather than through it, as its course seemed to suggest.

What was particularly striking about all of these stories was their emphasis on his benevolence. There are no stories of this Déwa Agung making anyone ill with a glance or inspiring fear. Instead, everyone stressed that he had been the epitome of *darma*, usually a priestly attribute: he acted without self-interest, for the good of all, and refused to see his subjects suffer. I heard repeatedly about a crowd of Klungkung dependents from Nusa Penida whom, when they turned up in desperation during a famine, the Déwa Agung managed to feed and house at the royal residence for months. And nearly everyone I met, even the most casual acquaintances, recalled the series of cremations he organized in the 1950s for the entire Klungkung region, in which he insisted every one of his subjects participate even if they could not afford to contribute anything toward the costs—and, people emphasized, he still managed to have food and provisions left over to redistribute, a sign of a ritual work blessed by invisible forces. It was hardly to be wondered that he was frequently asked to manufacture magically powerful masks to serve as protective guardians for villages in his realm. Such positive sentiments were expressed even by persons whose politics (so I was told) had been radically opposed to his. It seemed to be everyone's vehement opinion that had the Déwa Agung not died when he did no one in Klungkung would have died in the 1965 massacre of purported communists: he simply would not have allowed it.

Such wonders were not known only in Klungkung. Priests in other realms reported similar incidents, and priests were very familiar with the Déwa Agung for he was involved in organizing and witnessing rituals all over Bali. One of the prime responsibilities the restored kings of Bali abrogated to themselves when they established their council was the temple of Besakih, but the Déwa Agung took charge of several major *buta-yadnya* for Bali as a whole there, as well as overseeing the general maintenance of its ritual life (Stuart-Fox 1987:362; Goris 1969). He also made an appearance at large rituals elsewhere in Bali, generally at the behest of the organizers (see, e.g., Franken 1960:253—54).

These memories span both the colonial and postcolonial eras. What they track is a major transmutation in what it meant to be a "protector of the realm" as the spheres in which rulers could act publicly were increasingly constricted. This transformation occurred in two stages. The first was largely colonial and was marked by the loss of the regalia: for reasons to be discussed momentarily, the Déwa Agung had neither keris nor the ability to enact the practices they most exemplified. Second, when Bali finally became part of the Republic of Indonesia in 1950 after four years of war between republican and Dutch forces, and Bali's Council of Rulers was disbanded, the Déwa Agung had no longer even a nominal role to play in political administration. As ritual remained a prerogative of postcolonial rulers, the Déwa Agung reinterpreted his role as protector and father of the Balinese to become the spiritual leader colonial administrators had once imagined his ancestors were.

What was new was less Déwa Agung Oka Geg's involvement in ritual (and this was not, as we will see, all that being Bali's "spiritual overlord" entailed) than its place in representations of his reign. The only precolonial rituals anyone recalled were the Work at Goa Lawah just prior to the conquest and the nineteenth-century *maligia* in which the rhinoceros was sacrificed. I have already commented upon how rarely the *Babad Dalem* refers to royal rituals, and when it does they are usually rituals for the king himself rather than realm purifications or temple festivals. Therefore while stories about his reign claim a comfortable continuity with the past, they indirectly witness a transformation of consciousness. In contemporary Klungkung kingship is primarily discussed in terms of rituals and temples; moreover, with the military aspects of their power muted, kings seem more and more priestly.

To be sure, to some extent there were more prosaic reasons for these changes. With access to Besakih simplified by new roads and the chauffeured automobile that was a perquisite of his office, it was much easier for Déwa Agung Oka Geg to get there than it had been for his predecessors. For the same reason, it was easier for Brahmana priests to go there too, and therefore Besakih rituals were increasingly performed by court priests rather than temple priests, a shift that had already begun in the nineteenth century (Stuart-Fox 1987:246, 250–51).

In Klungkung there were textual precedents for a revaluation of kingship in the direction of priestliness. The *Babad Dalem* already proposed that the Kapakisans were "really" priests. The legends of Bédaulu and Mayadanawa also suggested that kings problematic enough to be conquered were followed by successors who exhibited marks of priestliness.

KERIS AND COLONIAL POWER RELATIONS

When Klungkung was conquered in 1908, its *pajenengan* keris acquired decidedly different values for surviving members of the royal clan and for the Dutch colonial government. The keris, of course, had been proved *punah*, although it would have been possible to restore their power under appropriate ritual conditions if the gods had been willing. But given the political circumstances, to do such a thing would have had little meaning. Perhaps this is why when Resident de Bruyn Kops offered two of the king's brothers, in exile in Lombok, a keris that had belonged to the Déwa Agung as a kind of keepsake, they refused it.[8]

Ironically, it was the colonial government who regarded the keris as powerful immediately after the conquest. In a report to the Governor General, Resident de Bruyn Kops declared that the continued presence of Klungkung's royal keris in Bali was dangerous to the stability of their new administration:

> Among [the keris seized on the battlefield] are various "sacred," to which the people attribute the possession of supernatural forces. To bring these again in the possession of Balinese lords would not thus be defensible.[9]

By 1938 the Dutch had reversed their position, precisely because they regarded colonial kingship as sufficiently domesticated. Perhaps the keris had been equally domesticated by thirty years on display in colonial museums.

In a secret letter written in May 1938, Resident Moll argued that it would be a good idea to return several of their "sacred heirlooms" to certain of the Balinese rulers about to be installed as autonomous rulers (*zelfbestuurders*) under the authority of the colonial government.[10] The rulers concerned were the Déwa Agung of Klungkung, the Cokorda of Badung, and the Anak Agungs of Tabanan and Gianyar.[11] The weapons of the first three had been appropriated by the government during the "pacification" of their realms. Gianyar, of course, had never been conquered, but its regalia had come into the government's possession upon the conquest of Klungkung, whose ruler still had the objects surrendered by the Déwa Manggis in the 1880s.[12]

In formulating his proposal, the Resident had asked Roeloef Goris, the administration's "language officer," who was considered an authority on Balinese religion and culture, for his recommendations.[13] Goris wrote a lengthy report, in which he argued that if the Resident decided to return the heirlooms to the rulers in question, he needed to be clear on precisely what grounds. There were, according to Goris, two possibilities: if they constituted an essential element in the "legal existence" of the ruler, they must, of course, be returned; if not, their return would be merely an act of goodwill, motivated by the value they held for their former owners and their heirs. According to Goris, only the latter was relevant. To prove his point, he discussed three categories of Indonesian artifacts that he said could be regarded as consecrated, sacred, or charmed.

The first category were *pusaka*, "consecrated family possessions," which could be found throughout the archipelago. According to Goris, *pusaka* were inherited along the lines of descent and "could be described as a kind of family fetish." Almost anything could become a *pusaka*: not only weapons but lengths of cloth, household goods, writings, stones, body parts of deceased persons, locks of hair, and so on. But such objects were significant only for the particular family in question.

Goris's second category consisted of "state objects," which he claimed symbolized political office and enhanced the prestige of their possessor. In Bali these consisted of various objects made of gold and silver—platters, containers for betel nut, dippers—carried in processions or during audiences by members of a ruler's entourage. He noted that in Bali gods as well as rulers owned such paraphernalia. These objects were very different, he claimed, than what he termed "realm ornaments," objects whose possession established a ruler's legitimacy: that is, whoever held them was recognized as rightful lord. Such realm ornaments were regarded as sacred or auspicious by the populace as a whole (here he cited Luwu, in Sulawesi, as an example). Offerings were brought to them during epidemics or other catastrophes; the objects even owned their own lands and servants.

The keris and lances so eagerly sought by the Balinese, he concluded, belonged somewhere between the first and second of these categories but were not essential for royal legitimacy or sacred to persons outside of the families in question. As proof he noted that they had been kept in the house-shrines of the royal line rather than in public temples.

Goris was quite right in observing that the possession of certain keris did not ensure the kingship—what I have referred to as the Excalibur Principle—but his argument is based on distinctions which had little to do with indigenous practice. To reduce regalia weapons to symbols of office and family good luck charms is a "Protestant" reading that ignores the role they played in constituting power. While people did not bring them offerings, they were nonetheless a means by which rulers ensured the prosperity of their realms,[14] as the *Babad Dalem*, a text with which Goris was familiar, states. But Goris could not take seriously claims that regalia keris gave their possessors access to potent forces they could use in the service of their office. Therefore, he implicitly reiterates the colonial ideology that held that Bali's kings were fundamentally peripheral to the lives of their subjects, a theme repeated constantly in popular representations of Bali in the colonial 1930s.

Resident Moll, however, did not entirely accept all of Goris's distinctions. In his letter he argued that while on the one hand returning the objects would be beneficial to the administration because the rulers in question were keen to have them back, accompanying their installation into their new positions with some tangible symbol would also be in keeping with "Eastern" thought. To return their "holy weapons" would be a token not only of friendship but also of trust, since the rulers involved were those whose realms had been "pacified" by war. What would make the gift especially appropriate to the occasion, he noted, was the fact that the objects traditionally served as symbols of political office.

The objects in question were all, the Resident explained, a type of *pusaka*, "sacred family possessions of a dynasty," called *pajenengan*, "objects which belong to the ruling prince in his quality as ruler (*djoemeneng ratoe*)." Unlike other heirlooms, they were not passed from father to son but from officeholder to successor. To ensure that this custom continued, the Resident would make it clear to the rulers involved that the weapons were not to be considered personal property. They could not be pawned, sold, or given away but only passed on to whoever held the position of "autonomous ruler." The Resident noted that these weapons would establish a relationship between these Balinese rulers and the colonial government not unlike that of European vassals to their feudal lords. In fact, the Resident added, that was precisely what the objects originally were: gifts from Majapahit rulers to their vassal kings in Bali, serving as signs of their authority over Bali.

The four rulers already had been asked which objects they wished to have returned, and almost all chose keris about which there were written legends. (The Resident noted about this: "They are like persons, with their own individual lives, full of very important events.") The names of the weapons were provided: the Déwa Agung requested I Durga Dingkul, but with the sheath and hilt of a keris called I Arda Walika, as well as two lances, Si Baru Ngit (Gnat) and Si Baru Gudug. Badung's ruler selected the keris Singa Paraga; Tabanan's, I Ganja Iras; and Gianyar's the keris I Baru Kama (or, if that proved difficult, I Raksasa Bedak) as well as the lance I Baru Alis. Descriptions, information on the relevant legends, and other lore associated with them had been collected by Goris and a controleur named Grader, and their report was also appended to aid the Batavian Society's museum curators in identifying the objects.[15]

The Déwa Agung's request was made in consultation with Cokorda Anom of Puri Anyar, a cousin some twenty years his senior who was the member of the royal family most familiar with the *Babad Dalem*. Cokorda Anom was also dispatched to Java to identify the objects selected for Goris. In choosing the keris that he did, the king was requesting more than a symbol of status and a family heirloom. He was seeking to restore the dynasty's access to very particular invisible beings.

That his choice fell on Durga Dingkul is in many ways surprising. Members of the royal clan and Pedanda Gedé Kenitén knew that the return of a keris had been an issue in the 1930s, but they did not remember which one it had been. The Pedanda was convinced that the king had asked for Bangawan Canggu, which I also thought the logical choice. Some of the powers attributed to it—stability, attachment—seemed suited to the limited possibilities available under colonialism. Moreover, there were parallels between the new king and his ancestor Dalem Ketut Ngulesir, to whom Bangawan Canggu was given: both were avid cockfighters reluctantly convinced to establish a new court; both were closely identified with the god of Besakih; both appear to have been skilled in evoking the devotion of their subjects.

I can only guess why Durga Dingkul rather than Bangawan Canggu was requested, and why it mattered that the keris be dressed in the hilt and sheath of a hitherto unknown keris named Arda Walika. Circumstances probably had much to do with it, since the choice was restricted to those objects that happened to have ended up in the museum of the Batavian Society as opposed to being shipped to the Netherlands (see Wiener 1994). But there may have been ways in which Durga Dingkul struck the Déwa Agung and Cokorda Anom as appropriate. The Déwa Agung was in certain respects in a situation similar to that of Sri Kresna Kapakisan. Although he held the office of king, he could not act as one; especially he could not enact the fierce aspects of power. Then too, Durga Dingkul had been a gift from Bali's conqueror Gajah Mada, which perhaps made it fitting that Bali's new conquerors, in whose name the Déwa Agung reigned just as his ancestor reigned on behalf of Majapahit, would give it again. And Durga Dingkul, as the earlier gift, was closer to ancestral origins.

That he requested the keris be accompanied with the sheath and hilt of Arda Walika is equally suggestive. An account of these events written by the late Cokorda Mayun (n.d.) of Puri Anyar mentions that Arda Walika's hilt was decorated with a *naga*, which suggests that the Déwa Agung was not entirely willing to relinquish the significations of Bangawan Canggu.[16]

But despite the Resident's recommendation, the keris were never returned. According to people in Klungkung, what sabotaged the plan was a controversy over the identification of the keris motivated by the envy and hostility of Gianyar's ruler.[17] I was told that a clerk from Gianyar working in the Residency office in Singaraja reported to Gianyar's regent that Cokorda Anom was on his way to Batavia; the regent immediately followed. He claimed that the keris Cokorda Anom identified as I Durga Dingkul was really his keris, I Raksasa Bedak.[18]

While it would seem from the descriptions in Grader and Goris's report that it would be hard to mistake any other keris for Durga Dingkul (Cokorda Anom said that there was a carving of Durga in the upper portion of the blade), Gianyar's ruler was adamant about his identification. There was no easy way to settle the dispute, because *babad* had little to say about the physical appearance of regalia, and few people had actually seen these keris unsheathed.[19] Even Cokorda Anom did not know if the blade of Durga Dingkul was or was not wavy. It was a matter of the Cokorda's word against that of the ruler of Gianyar, for the kind of tests Balinese might use to establish the identity of such things would have made no sense to colonial administrators.

Discord was not at all what Moll had envisioned when he advised the return of the objects—although since these were after all weapons, it might not be so surprising that they aroused aggressive emotions. And so the installation of the eight "autonomous" rulers was carried out without any tokens of feudal fealty.

There is one final twist on the tale. According to a story sometimes told in Klungkung, the keris had already been sent to Singaraja before it was decided they would not be returned to the rulers, and they had to be packed up and shipped back to Batavia. En route the ship was hit by a Japanese bomb and sank to the bottom of the sea—taking Klungkung's *pajenengan* with it.[20] This tale cannot be "true," for none of the thirteen keris donated to the Batavian Society after Klungkung's conquest in 1908 is missing. But it is suggestive, for once again it removes responsibility for important events from colonial hands.

THE RECONSTRUCTION OF THE ROYAL HOUSE OF KLUNGKUNG

When plans to return Durga Dingkul fell through, any hope of returning to the way things had been—if any such hope still existed—was forever dashed. Déwa Agung Oka Geg was forced to reinvent royal power, re-creating it through public acts. Many of these were ritual acts. I have already referred to the massive cremations the king organized for the benefit of his subjects in Klungkung and to the great works he supervised at Besakih for Bali as a whole. One of his greatest ritual works was only completed after his death: a *maligia* for all Klungkung ancestors from Déwa Agung Putra II through (as it turned out) Déwa Agung Oka Geg, including all who had died in the puputan.

Some of his involvement with the emerging sphere of "religion," however, had more political overtones. Indonesia was not a secular state. As a compromise with the Islamic organizations that had helped fight for independence, one of the five founding principles (*Pancasila*) of the new nation was that all citizens shared a belief in "one God." In practice, the Ministry of Religion regarded only practitioners of world religions as eligible for state financial assistance for such activities as rituals, the repair and construction of religious institutions, and programs of religious education. Bali's "religion of holy water" looked suspiciously like the "animism" practiced by groups targeted for religious conversion. In addition to the loss of financial support for the upkeep of temples and performance of rituals once financed by rulers and then to a modest degree by the Dutch, Bali faced the prospect of missionization. The

Déwa Agung belonged to a coalition of aristocrats, Balinese priests, and civil servants who pressed the Ministry to accept Bali's complex system of ritual practice as a form of Hinduism (Forge 1980; Geertz 1973; Stuart-Fox 1987). They were successful: when recognition came, Sang Hyang Widhi Wasa was proclaimed the Hindu Balinese version of the supreme deity, and Besakih designated its most holy place; and the same coalition continued to meet regularly to discuss the principles of the religion. Finally, during the tense years of the late 1950s and early 1960s, when Bali was torn apart by political factions, he founded his own, the Hindu Bali party, which he hoped might unite Balinese on religious grounds: its color was white, in contrast to the Communist party's red and the Nationalist party's black, and in Klungkung it was quite popular, at least until his death.

The Déwa Agung's construction of power also took a more literal and tangible form: he did a fair amount of building. Like the rituals, the structures he erected demonstrate shifts in emphasis from the precolonial period. They also show the ambiguity of power in the absence of keris.

The power that returned to Klungkung at the Déwa Agung's coronation was no longer incarnate in regalia keris but literally embodied in the king. This meant that it was inherently impermanent, no longer heritable by his descendants. Certain of the Déwa Agung's projects seem like efforts to secure new forms of power for his heirs. At the same time, they suggest that there *was* no way to transmit power without heirloom keris: any other symbol dissolves royal power into something else.

Two projects seem particularly revealing: the construction of new palaces and, within one of these, the erection of a shrine to the gods of Besakih.

The shrine, a stopping-off place for Besakih's gods, seems curiously redundant given the existence of Klungkung's Pura Penataran Agung, built by the king's ancestors. However, the new shrine differs from the older temple in several ways. While both its name and Klungkung public opinion proclaim the Pura Penataran Agung a way-station for Besakih—and the gods of Besakih always stop at this temple when they are carried in procession for ritual purification at the sea at Klotok—it does not in the least resemble the original. The Penataran at Besakih is Bali's largest temple: a complex of six courtyards terraced along the spine of Agung, so that as one moves from the outer portions of the temple to the inner reaches one also ascends. The six enclosures contain some fifty-seven shrines (Stuart-Fox 1987:93), each with a striking black stone base. There are pagoda-like *méru* with multiple roofs in almost every courtyard, four of which have eleven roofs. The most important courtyard is not the highest and most interior, however, but the second one, which contains the temple's *padmasana*. This *padmasana* is the most important shrine in the entire Besakih temple complex. It is the focus of all major rituals performed at the temple, and all worshippers at Besakih pray at it, regardless of what other shrines they also visit. This is contrary to usual practice: at most temples the principle shrine is the *méru* with the greatest number of roofs, and only Brahmanas do obeisance at the *padmasana* (and not at the *méru*). Moreover, Besakih's *padmasana* is of a unique form, a *lilajñana*; in the *Raja-purana Besakih* this term is used as a metonym for the entire Besakih complex (Stuart-Fox 1987:326–27). As Stuart-Fox describes it, Besakih's *padmasana* consists of "a common base from which rise three separate plinths bearing lotus-seats with high backs, each plinth resting on the representation of the cosmic turtle Bedawang Nala, around which twine the two cosmic nagas, Basuki and Anantaboga" (1987:97–98). The three seats are for Divinity in its tripartite form—understood as either Siwa, Sadasiwa, and Paramasiwa, or Brahma, Wisnu, and Siwa/Iswara.

In marked contrast, Klungkung's Pura Penataran Agung is an ordinary temple, with one inner courtyard containing a number of brick-based shrines. The temple's *padmasana*, as such shrines usually are, is a single high open seat, a place of worship only for Brahmana members of the temple. Most people make their offerings at the set of five *méru* along the eastern wall, which form an orderly progression from the eleven-roofed one in the north down to the three-roofed one to the south. These shrines resemble nothing in Besakih's Penataran; if they look like anything at Besakih it is a similar set of shrines outside of the Penataran, dedicated to the founding ancestors of the Ksatria Dalem clan. In fact, the Pura Penataran Agung even celebrates its 210-day anniversary on the same date as those ancestral shrines (as does the temple Pura Dalem Segening, the way-station for those shrines); on the dates on which there are rituals at Besakih's Penataran, no offerings are made at Klung-kung's. Aside from its name and the fact that Besakih's gods visit there when they process through Klungkung, the Pura Penataran Agung is really Klung-kung's equivalent of a village temple (*pura desa*).[21]

The shrine built by Déwa Agung Oka Geg is a different matter alto-gether. It is an exact replica of Besakih's *padmasana*. Not only does it resemble Besakih's shrine in appearance, but it even receives offerings on the full moon of the tenth month, the date of All the Gods Descend, Besakih's most impor-tant ritual.

But what is especially striking about this extraordinary shrine is its loca-tion. Although purportedly a place of veneration for anyone who wishes to pay respects to the gods of Besakih but cannot manage a trip to Mount Agung, it is not a public sanctuary in any ordinary sense. Nor is it anywhere in or near Klungkung's Pura Penataran Agung, the apparently appropriate site for it. Instead it stands alone in the northeast corner of a third courtyard in the house-temple of the royal clan. This house-temple (which is in Puri Saraswati) was built to replace the house-temple of the old Puri Agung. But the preco-lonial temple contained no such replica of the shrine at Besakih.[22]

To build such a shrine was a most public declaration of the intimate connection between king and god. It is not that no other shrines exist in Bali for the gods of Mount Agung; on the contrary, such shrines may be found in nearly every temple of importance. But these generally take the form of *méru* with nine or eleven roofs and are usually found in public sanctuaries, often those associated closely with the welfare of the realm.[23] This shrine not only mimics the form of Besakih's current *padmasana* but is located in a space associated with royal ancestors and origins.

Its location is one reason to think the shrine in part a substitute for the royal keris. In the absence of the heirloom keris that would once have held a place of honor in his private temple, the Déwa Agung represented the sole remaining source of his power: Besakih. By so doing, perhaps he was attempting to "capture" that power for his descendants: to locate the relationship between himself and its divinity in a more permanent receptacle than his own body. But for a shrine to serve as surrogate for keris is itself a sign of the priestly turn of royal power.

Placing Besakih within the inner recesses of the royal residence is also iconic of a privatization of the relationship between Klungkung's royal house and Bali's most important temple. In the years since Déwa Agung Oka Geg's death, the primary responsibility for Besakih and its rituals has been transferred out of the hands of Bali's former ruling class. A government-sponsored organization, Parisada Hindu Dharma, now supervises Besakih affairs. While Klungkung's royal family still contributes offerings for the annual rite in the Penataran, and the presence of the ranking men of the family as witnesses there is deemed desirable (it is said, in fact, that the gods refuse to descend if no representative of Klungkung's core line is present), the relationship between the court and the temple is now relatively hidden, just as the shrine is hidden. In a way, then, the shrine suggests the failure of power to endure in the absence of regalia as much as its postcolonial transformation.

A similar range of ambiguities is expressed by a second project: the two new puris Déwa Agung Oka Geg built in the 1950s. The mere fact that he needed three residences is itself an innovation; but the more radical departures from the past show in their architecture and names.

Most of the old palace was destroyed by the Dutch after the conquest. According to the Déwa Agung's kin, when he was installed as a regent the government offered him the use of what little remained of it: the plain leading up to the entranceway (the Kori Agung, or Great Door); two high pavilions, Taman Gili, surrounded by a moat and the Kerta Gosa, used by the colonial administration as a court of law; and those portions of its grounds not occupied by offices or homes. This he declined, though why is difficult to say: one member of the royal family claimed it was because he would have had to build a new entranceway, as the Great Door had sealed itself shut on the day of the conquest; the *Babad Dalem* suggests that to establish or revive a dynasty required a new court. In any event, he continued to live in Puri Kaléran, the house built by his great-grandfather and the highest-ranking branch puri before the conquest, merely renaming it Puri Agung (the Great Royal Residence) to indicate that it was now the dwelling place of the ruler. This still remains the core-line house. But after the establishment of the Indonesian republic, he built two additional residences: Puri Sunianegara, located in the west of the capital; and Puri Saraswati, southwest of the former royal palace.

People explained the building of these additional puris as a need for more space: the Puri Agung could simply not accommodate his forty wives and thirty-four children, even with the addition of new wings. Insufficient space is certainly a reason why people commonly build new compounds, but it is a peculiar explanation in this case. For one, new residences are normally built by younger or lower-ranking brothers or sons, not the head of a clan. For another, precolonial royal residences housed many times that number of people; when Assistant Resident Schwartz visited Klungkung in 1898, he estimated that some three thousand people resided in the three most important puris—not only wives and children but servants and retainers as well. The building of additional compounds for the royal family rather suggests a transformation of subjectivities, and a decentering of power.

All three residences were also unusual in layout. The architecture of traditional royal compounds was quite distinctive. Apart from the division into inner and outer areas (*majaba-jero*), royal residences contained sections and pavilion types not found anywhere else. As a branch-line house, Puri Kaléran would not have looked exactly like the core-line palace but would have been basically similar in form.[24] During Déwa Agung Oka Geg's lifetime it underwent several renovations, but these did not, as one might expect, have the effect of rendering it into a closer approximation of a ruler's puri. Instead they obliterated many of the features that would have marked it as a puri at all. For example, recall that the exterior wall of a puri's outer courtyard was ideally constructed of latticework, broken by a "split-gate" that afforded access to the puri, whereas its interior wall was bricked and interrupted by a closed gateway. In the Puri Agung this gradual transition between inside and out is obscured, as the exterior wall is entirely bricked and the closed gateway fronts the road. Just beyond it, as is proper, is a wide, open courtyard, but its central portion is covered by an enormous tin roof and ends in a high platform, on the walls of which hang photographs of the king, and there even used to be a broad road so cars could drive up. Within the palace, signs of a royal residence are even more meager. There are only a few of the individual pavilions that graced a traditional compound, and these are rather plain. One of these is, in fact, a colonial innovation referred to as a Gedong Amsterdam, a multi-room structure that houses the Déwa Agung's highest-ranking wife, accessible from the very same high platform that fronts the forecourt. Mostly people live in what Balinese call *kantor-kantoran*, "offices," square, ceilinged, and doored rooms on a Western model, clearly inspired by colonial architecture; *kantoor* is Dutch for "office." While the majority of these are of recent construction, some date from the king's lifetime.

The outer courtyard of Puri Kaléran at least contains some kind of public space, however unconventional; the two newer puris adhere even less to the conventions of royal architecture. Puri Sunianegara is an odd sprawl of courtyards with living quarters, its boundaries not even delineated by an outer wall and entranceway. Puri Saraswati is somewhat less erratic since it is clearly bounded by high brick walls and tall doorways, one to the west and one to the south, and entrance through the latter leads to a large, virtually empty courtyard. Puri Saraswati was meant to be the new Puri Agung, since it is there that the king built his new house-temple (the one containing the shrine for Besakih), and Klungkung's annual Taur Agung is held on the empty field to its north. Still, it lacks the detailed and differentiated spatial organization of precolonial palaces, especially the division between inner and outer, and again living quarters are mainly *kantor-kantoran*.

Klungkung was hardly the only place where architecture was "modernized," nor was the Déwa Agung the only colonial-era ruler to build himself several residences. However, given Klungkung conservatism in, for example, ritual practices or painting, such a rejection of meaningful forms is at the very least unexpected. The effect, however, is to create a frame around what remains of the former palace, turning its fragments of the past into tokens of something lost. In constructing his dwelling places the Déwa Agung made an implicit statement about the position of the old ruling class in colonial and postcolonial Bali. If aristocrats were expected to function as bureaucrats, why not live in "offices"? And with independence making the distinction between ordinary people and aristocrats increasingly murky, why mark it with forecourts and inner sanctums? Since it was no longer possible to enact the significations embedded in a traditional royal compound, to build one would have been to alter those significations. By not attempting to re-create a traditional palace, the Déwa Agung in a sense preserved the meanings associated with traditional forms.

But it is not just the appearance of these structures that is worth noting. The names of the new residences index an already familiar thematic transformation of royal power. To appreciate how requires a brief discussion of precolonial practices.

Core-line royal residences all over Bali are generally referred to as Puri Agung (Big or Great Puri) or, more modestly, Jero Agung (*jero* being a lower, and hence more polite, term). In Klungkung, branch-line puris were named according to one of two principles (which usually coincided), by reference to either the core-line house or their location: thus Puri Kanginan, "the puri east of it"; Puri Kaléran, "the puri north of it"; Puri Kalér-Kangin, "the northeast puri"; but also Puri Anyar, "the new puri," where what is marked is a temporal rather than a spatial relation to the core line. Another branch house was Puri Batan Waru, "the puri at the foot of the *waru* tree."[25] Earlier branch houses, built not in the capital but in outlying villages and towns, are generally named for those villages (hence Puri Akah or Puri Satria), just as the Puri Agung was sometimes referred to as Puri Klungkung, after the realm.

The core-line royal compound also had another, more elegant name, however. The Gélgél court was known as Suécapura, the place of graciousness, the fount of generosity, implying royal benevolence toward subjects and realm. The court established by Déwa Agung Jambé I in Klungkung in the late seventeenth or early eighteenth century was Smarapura, "Abode of the God of Love." The names Suécapura and Smarapura both emphasize the royal capacity to attract and please. In texts the realm was often referred to as Smarajaya, "the Victorious God of Love."

This is why the names of the residences built by the late Déwa Agung are of interest. Despite the fact that it is not the location of the core-line temple, the old Puri Kaléran remains the Puri Agung, and it has no other name. In contrast, the other two royal compounds *are* named, but not, as branch houses were, by reference to their locality or in relation to the Puri Agung. Rather they are named as core-line residences once were, by unique and highly specific epithets. And these epithets are rather different than those of former Kapakisan courts.

Puri Saraswati is named for the goddess of learning who "lives" in the letters of Balinese texts. Saraswati is not only a "textual" divinity, though; she is the quintessential Brahmana divinity. While her day is commemorated by all who have anything to do with texts and learning, it is particularly associated with priestly houses, and it is to the compounds of their priestly patrons that most Balinese bring offerings on that day. For the heir to the throne of Smarajaya, a name that connotes masculine attractiveness, battle, and virility, to have named his new residence after the feminine Saraswati demonstrates once again the changed nature of kingship, pointing to the turn to texts and priestly mildness.

It is Puri Sunianegara, however, whose name is most evocative of the paradoxes of power in postcolonial Klungkung. Sunianegara literally means "empty realm or land." Since this puri was built on wasteland, a tangle of trees and vegetation on the edge of a ravine, on one level its name is simply descriptive. But as a realm postcolonial Klungkung is empty in other ways. Sunianegara evokes loss and barrenness, the loss of Klungkung's wealth and stature under colonialism, and of its final vestiges of power in the postcolonial state. Members of the royal family repeatedly told me how "poor" they were, that they had nothing. They were referring in part to the sumptuous objects Goris mentioned in his report, which marked the splendor and authority of a court: the gold beakers and trays, the jewelry, the instruments encrusted with gems. But their poverty, and the realm's emptiness, were marked by one absence in particular: that of the heirloom keris, which still haunt Klungkung imaginations.

One hears, for example, periodic whispers, tantalizing hints, that the keris might not be gone forever. Someone told me in great earnest that in fact Bangawan Canggu has been in the village of Sidemen since the seventeenth century: it says so in a *Babad Dalem* belonging to a family there, who claim descent from an elder brother of Dalem Di Madé (see Warna et al. 1986). On the other hand, several people I knew opined that if Déwa Agung Oka Geg's highest-ranking son, who is currently Klungkung's *bupati*, head of the regional government, asked at Klungkung's state temples at night, the gods would surely return the keris. Perhaps he does and perhaps they will, for during the annual rite at Besakih's Penataran in 1991 someone fell into trance and announced that Klungkung's *pajenengan* would return, if not their physical form at least their *adnyanan*, power, although where that power will "sit" was not stated.

But this brings us to another meaning for *Sunianegara*, one that returns us to Klungkung discourse in the 1990s. As Ida Bagus Jagri often noted, "full places may be empty and empty ones full." If no people lived on the land on which the puri was built, it was and is bustling with invisible spirits. Indeed, Jero Nyoman, the spirit with power over the weather, lives beside the puri at the edge of a ravine, where the Déwa Agung erected a shrine for her. Moreover, *sunianegara*, like *niskala* or *tanana* can signify the whole invisible realm: recall that Sunia is a name for Divinity. In many ways Klungkung's "emptiness" is only a matter of what meets the eye. Power still exists, hidden as always, and potentially accessible to those with the courage to seek it.

Epilogue:
A Reinvented Klungkung

Klungkung remains as invisible to outsiders in the 1990s as it was in the first half of the nineteenth century. In those days, Europeans who came to Bali stayed in Kuta, to be entertained by Mads Lange in his factory, and Kuta's accessibility, like Klungkung's invisibility, persists.

Like the Dutch in the nineteenth century, the tourists who sun themselves on Kuta's beaches, and drink beer and eat pasta in Kuta's restaurants, know little or nothing of Klungkung. It is merely a place to pass through on the way to the beaches of Candi Dasa in the east or en route to the temple of Besakih to the north. At Klungkung there are no spectacular dance performances, only one or two dingy "hotels." The absence of trees along the roads makes it hot and dusty; the houses are cement, painted in pale institutional greens, with inexpensive tiled roofs rather than the quainter and cooler thatch that tourists expect to find in a tropical paradise. Those who consult their guidebooks may stop in the center of the town of Klungkung to see one of the regency's two tourist attractions (the other being Goa Lawah): the so-called Palace of Justice or Kerta Gosa, the ceilings of which are painted with dire warnings of what will happen in the afterlife to violators of the laws of this one. Klungkung appears a not very interesting, not quite bustling little town, something of a backwater.

Yet even within the tourist's itinerary one can begin to glimpse something of the hidden significance of Klungkung. It is no accident that the road to Besakih, to which tourists flock, passes through Klungkung. Nor is it coincidence that Klungkung's major tourist attraction is connected with royalty: the Palace of Justice is in fact the northeast corner of what remains of Puri Smarapura.

Oddly, the tour books do not mention the looming, moss-covered brick structure set back from the main road in a large empty courtyard slightly southwest of the Kerta Gosa (see fig. 11): this is the Great Door (Pamedal Agung), once the point of transition between the "outer" world of commoners and the mysterious "inner" world of the king whose very title was Dalem ("inside"). An observant tourist might notice that on the WELCOME TO KLUNG-KUNG sign visible just over the bridge on the Melangit River, which forms

Figure 11. The Great Door of Puri Smarapura. Photograph by Koes Karnadi.

Klungkung's border with Gianyar (or, coming the other way, on the stretch of empty sand that marks the border with Karangasem), there is a large plastic depiction of this Great Door, an iconic duplication that suggests that to cross that border is to enter the inner world of Balinese kingship. And in the center of this icon of the Great Door is a stylized keris, five curves in the blade, pointing upwards.

IF THE KERTA GOSA represents Klungkung to the tourist, it is the Great Door and the keris that have been chosen by Klungkung to represent itself to itself, as well as to other Balinese.

There is something paradoxical, however, in this choice of emblems.

What they invoke no longer exists, indeed quite literally ended with Klungkung's conquest. From the day of the puputan to the present, or so I was told, the wooden panels of the Great Door have been sealed shut and no one has been able to open it. But this is only fitting, for beyond the Great Door, which once led to the inner reaches of the royal compound, there are now only stairs leading nowhere. The interior of the compound, the myriad courtyards filled with pavilions decorated with carvings and gold leaf, was demolished after Klungkung's conquest. The grounds were used by the Dutch first as a prison, later as office space; nowadays ordinary houses stand upon the ground where once the king's wives and concubines came, perfumed and dressed in trailing brocaded cloth, to serve their lord. And on precisely the spot where the gods and royal ancestors came to sit and be ritually honored by their descendants, drawn by incense, the glimmering sounds of the Balinese gamelan, and a profusion of flowers, is the regional tax office.

As for the keris, emblems of both potency and fall, they have vanished too. In museums they have become signs in a different discourse; no longer identified as I Lobar or I Bangawan Canggu, but as "keris, Klungkung, gold hilt, wooden sheath . . .". Some have even been lost altogether. Over half of the Klungkung "state keris" donated by the colonial government to Leiden's Museum of Ethnology after the conquest were stolen in the 1960s. As there are no photographs of the missing objects, not even an image remains that might pick them out of the myriad keris circulating through the international art market.

WHILE THE COURT no longer exists, the Door remains a potent reminder of the power of Klungkung's kings. The area just outside of the Door, the outer courtyard of the palace, is to this day considered very *tenget*, enchanted, an area of apparent emptiness but in fact teeming with invisible (at least usually) spirits. It is a place to be avoided at night, unless one is deliberately seeking an encounter with the invisible world, upon some quest for power. But then, it was precisely because the whole area was so attractive to the forces of the invisible world that it glowed that Déwa Agung Jambé I built Puri Smarapura there at the end of the seventeenth century: no more appropriate site for the residence of a powerful king could be imagined.

While Smarapura was supposedly modeled upon the palace in Majapahit, the design for the Door itself came in a vision. Two artisans went one night to meditate by the sea. The first spent the night in Pura Klotok, the state temple perched above the black sands of the beach to which the gods of Besakih are brought for ritual purifications. The second prayed at Pura Ketapang Kembar, another seaside temple to Klotok's east, the outer wall of which is formed by a remarkable circle of twinned trees. When they rejoined each other at dawn they discovered that each of them had dreamed half a door:

placed side by side, the halves were a perfect fit. And so it was built, a towering brick and stone ziggurat.

During the colonial period the Dutch decided to have the Great Door razed, and they sent a crew of Balinese to chisel off the stone carvings of foreigners and mythical beasts that climb up and down its crown. But when they reached the top to begin work, they found themselves petrified by the view they beheld from the Door's heights: below them the ocean stretched out in every direction as far as the eye could see. Quickly scrambling down, they refused to have anything more to do with such efforts, and the Dutch abandoned the idea. Indeed, according to Klungkung legend the Door is the foundation of the world. Several elderly people recalled that their first act during the Great Earthquake of 1917 was to run to the center of town to see if the Door still stood. Their parents had informed them that if the Great Door were to collapse the ocean would come rushing up to inundate the entire island of Bali. Fortunately, despite the fact that lower walls had tumbled down and debris was everywhere, the Door was intact, a clear indication that the earthquake was not after all to be the end of the world.

But if the Door, like the interior mountains its shape mimics, is the fixed presence that perpetuates Balinese existence, it failed to prevent an inundation of a different sort. The wavy keris on the plastic icon seems to point to the stone finial that crowns the Door, which is reiterated not far below on the Door itself in a brick niche. When Betara Dalem summoned his sons and lords to tell them that if Klungkung were ever threatened they must open the top of the Great Door, did he mean the finial itself? The replica in the niche? No one will ever know. For, as we have seen, when the Dutch attacked in 1908, the warning was forgotten, even though the bottom step that leads to the Door was pushed out of the way in an effort to free the sea to rush up from below. The Door remained; but Klungkung fell.

THAT THE DOOR *did* remain has allowed it to become the key image of a reimagined Klungkung. It was as part of a series of activities to commemorate the heroism of the puputan that the office of the *bupati* held a competition to select a design to represent the regency. The winner was a princess from the Gélgél puri responsible for precipitating hostilities with the Dutch in 1908. A photograph of the Door was also chosen as the cover for the *History of Klungkung* book, written amid such local controversy by a government-appointed committee for the same event.

In a less obvious and more hauntingly evocative sense, the keris featured on the princess's winning design played its part in the proceedings as well. As we have seen, the destruction of the power of the royal heirloom keris is the central motif of Klungkung narratives about the colonial conquest. What, then, is one to make of the fact that in the very first year Puputan Day was celebrated, it "happened" to coincide with another celebration as a result of a calendrical conjunction? For in 1984, 28 April fell on the day known as Tumpek Landep: Saturday-Kliwon in the week Landep according to the 210-day Balinese *uku* calendar. This is not the case every year; indeed, the puputan actually occurred on Tuesday-Manis of the *uku* week Wayang. Tumpek Landep, recall, is the day sacred to metal objects and weapons, in particular keris—the day they are purified with holy water and offerings are made to recharge their power.

Precolonially the royal heirloom keris, along with similar objects belonging to the lords of the realm, were usually brought for these rites to the tall shrine, its base encircled with a large *naga*, in the temple Pura Taman Sari in the northeast corner of the capital. After Klungkung's conquest, Taman Sari was neglected and lapsed into disrepair, and in 1917 it suffered extensive damage during the earthquake. When the colonial government decided in the wake of that disaster to finance renovations of selected Balinese temples, Moojen, the official in charge, urged on aesthetic grounds that Taman Sari be one of these, but the government rejected his advice (Moojen 1920). The shrines were left to dilapidate further, although the statues of *raksasa*, demons, that had contributed to its local reputation (it was said that at midday they came to life and marched around) were moved to embellish the area around the Kerta Gosa (where they did the same). Even after 1929, nothing much was done there. The Déwa Agung's resources were too limited, and without the keris for which the temple had originally been built there may no longer have seemed much reason to maintain it.

It was only in the 1980s, at the request of the office of the *bupati*, that the temple was finally restored by Bali's Archaeological Service. Auspicious signs attended the work. while clearing the moat that surrounds the main shrine, workers were splattered by a sudden spurt of water from an underground spring. After an inspection by officials from the local Department of Religion, this was declared to be holy water. The reconstruction itself was completed just in time to reconsecrate the temple precisely on Tumpek Landep in 1984—Puputan Day.

There were, of course, no longer any keris to bring in procession to the temple. Yet keris and everything associated with them in Klungkung memory were the "absent presence" behind this conjuncture. For it was surely no accident that the first commemoration of the puputan was held on the day and in the place associated with keris, the embodiment of royal power.

Most of the events planned for the annual Puputan Day are informed with meanings that derive from contemporary Indonesian political discourse. Banners strung across the roads, and assemblies attended by civil servants and students, exhort the people of Klungkung to "use the spirit of the puputan" to develop Indonesia, economically, socially, and culturally. Public events, parades, and speeches are saturated with references to anticolonialism, national unity, the five principles on which the Indonesian state is founded, and the need for progress.

Yet the Great Door and the keris and the power they represent repeatedly, albeit subtly, weave their way into the annual proceedings. A ritual to ask the gods for continued good fortune for the Klungkung district in 1986, for example, attendance at which was mandatory for all civil servants in the capital, was held not in any of the local temples but in the forecourt of the old puri, just outside the Great Door. The absent keris have also been evoked in later Puputan Day celebrations. In the three-room museum, opened on another Puputan Day in an erstwhile school on former palace grounds west of the Great Door, one room, dedicated to "history," contains photographs of the Klungkung keris, booty of conquest, now in Jakarta's National Museum. Two people I know in Klungkung also thought that the Puputan Monument erected north of the Kerta Gosa and dedicated on Puputan Day 1992 was meant to resemble a keris handle—that was, at least, what it looked like to them. In the same year, the name of the capital was officially changed to Smarapura, after the precolonial palace.

Nothing in the book produced concerning Klungkung's history accounts for the photograph of the Great Door on its cover, nor is there any public statement to explain why the sign that greets drivers entering Klungkung reiterates the image of the Door and adds to it a keris. The Door *might* simply stand for the palace, the political history of Klungkung of necessity being a history of its kings; the keris *might* merely represent the weapons of the precolonial period, and thus serve as a reminder of brave, albeit futile, resistance. But then again they might not. During these annual celebrations no one mentions the stories I was told about colonial conquest, but the Door and the keris and the activities that surround them seem to bear witness to this suppressed discourse, visually and practically acknowledging what is verbally ignored.

THOSE NEGLECTED STORIES have formed the nucleus of this book. Like the Door and the keris in Klungkung's emblem, they center on potent but enigmatic images. Like all discourse about power, these tales are oblique, for in Bali power must be inferred: as a line from a well-known poem instructs, "Don't claim you can do things; let others say it for you." Insinuations, however, are lost on the ignorant, and elucidating them is necessarily problematic. An explanatory voice is not suited to such tasks, for it makes it seem possible to imagine that matters might be otherwise expressed, and risks reducing allusions to codes.

But if, as Wittgenstein remarked, "whereof one cannot speak one must be silent," one may still trace around such silence the contours of what remains unvoiced. And so I have presented a set of images of Klungkung at different times and from different perspectives, many centering, like the road sign at Klungkung's borders, around regalia.

It should be clear that Balinese images are intertwined with Dutch ones, for they mutually affected one another, and thus affected "reality." What happened between them changed the arena in which Balinese could act, and these changes register in stories about different historical periods. At the same time, narratives are a way not merely of talking about the world but of constituting it: stories are a form of praxis. With these stories the changes initiated by colonialism are resisted, even denied. Focusing on an entirely Balinese drama, they refuse the Dutch any agency in the making of the present.

There is a certain irony here. For it is commemorations of the puputan that purportedly enunciate anticolonial messages, while local legends are dismissed as "old-fashioned." One might say that in the narrative of progress such judgments imply (not to mention in nationalist rituals) lies another type of colonialism. Yet, as already noted, the legends are not entirely ignored. For what was the rededication of Taman Sari, or the sign erected at the borders of the realm, or the photograph of the Great Door on the cover of the committee's book, if not ways of *not* ignoring them, of pointing beyond what is explicitly said? Indeed, some activities sponsored by the government are even bolder than the stories in characterizing the invisible agencies responsible for Klungkung's fall. Thus when the well-known artist Mangku Mura was commissioned by the *bupati* to execute a painting of the puputan in traditional Kamasan style, he was instructed to design it exactly as he pleased, with only a single stipulation: the Dutch were to be portrayed as ogres.

But what is going on here? An effort to usurp familiar symbols of power to legitimate a new order? No doubt. A subtle subversion of the overt nationalist message, rallying Klungkung's population around images of the past? Possibly. Or perhaps merely the last gasp of a dying ruling class, attempting by such allusions to tradition to maintain its power? This too is conceivable, for after all, celebrations of the puputan began during the term of a *bupati* named Déwa Agung Gedé Agung, the son of Déwa Agung Oka Geg by a daughter of the ruler of neighboring Karangasem, and heir apparent to the no longer existing Klungkung throne. And his two predecessors as *bupati* were also members of the royal family: the first, his elder brother; the second, his cousin.

But such explanations again revert to familiar understandings of power. And they ignore the role of memory in Balinese praxis. For one factor that cannot be forgotten is that Klungkung's former rulers still potentially affect Klungkung life, as agents in the invisible world.

In short, stories and acts centered around the palace and other images of royal authority do more than merely resist colonialism, whether that of former Dutch domination or present Jakarta hegemony. Nor do they simply reinforce residual power relations. They also assert that Klungkung continues, despite the shifting ground of a no longer steady world, to be a place of power.

It is the keris and the Great Door that are most suggestive of how. Like all signs, they may be interpreted in multiple ways. For Balinese not themselves from Klungkung, the keris and the Door might evoke not only royal authority but history and the past in general, images most would find appropriate to Klungkung. For inhabitants of Klungkung, however, such images have more local and potent associations: to the events recounted in oral tradition, for example, or to the invisible forces to which they allude.

The keris and the Door have the potential to remind people that Klungkung is more than a typical town in modern Indonesia—with its government offices, night markets, and uniformed schoolchildren. It is also the center of a tiny land filled to bursting with an invisible population of spirits, who busily patrol the borders and sound the wooden gongs of the palace to warn people of epidemics. Both keris and Door are reminders of nonvisible realities, suggesting that there is still power in Klungkung, and even intimating that from the spirit world Klungkung's kings continue to protect their realm.

The keris and the Great Door that mark Klungkung's borders and feature in the stories of the elderly represent a world that, on the one hand, is irrevocably gone. They keep before consciousness realities that no longer exist. Yet both keris and Door symbolize sources of power that may always become reembodied. The realities they point to are not, then, entirely vanished. If they are tokens of the past, they are also figures of the present and images of a possible future.

In public celebrations emphasizing modernity and development, it is now Klungkung narratives that have become invisible. But subjectivities are not so easily shaped by national projects. As "what is said," the stories circulating in Klungkung continue to construct an alternative image of power. It is that image rather than nationalist hegemonies that constitutes a contemporary Klungkung public culture that restores to Klungkung some measure of its former prominence.

Appendix: Genealogies

THE FOUNDING OF THE DYNASTY

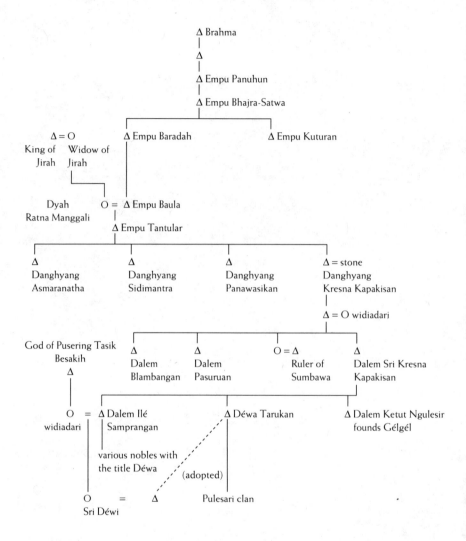

THE GÉLGÉL PERIOD

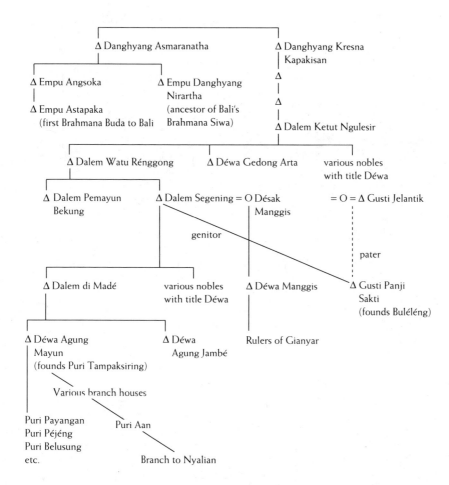

PRIESTS

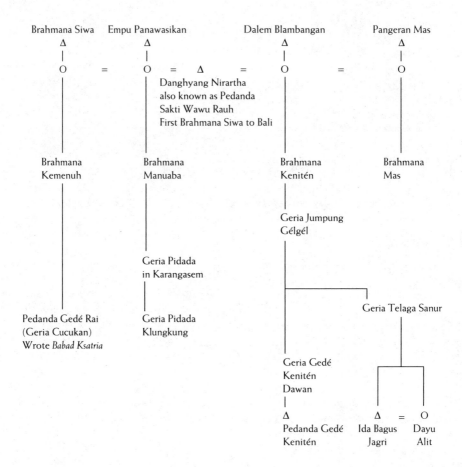

Brahmana Siwa   Empu Panawasikan   Dalem Blambangan   Pangeran Mas

Danghyang Nirartha
also known as Pedanda
Sakti Wawu Rauh
First Brahmana Siwa to Bali

Brahmana
Kemenuh

Brahmana
Manuaba

Brahmana
Kenitén

Brahmana
Mas

Geria Jumpung
Gélgél

Geria Pidada
in Karangasem

Geria Telaga Sanur

Pedanda Gedé Rai
(Geria Cucukan)
Wrote *Babad Ksatria*

Geria Pidada
Klungkung

Geria Gedé
Kenitén
Dawan

Pedanda Gedé
Kenitén

Ida Bagus
Jagri

Dayu
Alit

KLUNGKUNG PERIOD: CORE AND BRANCH LINES TO 1840

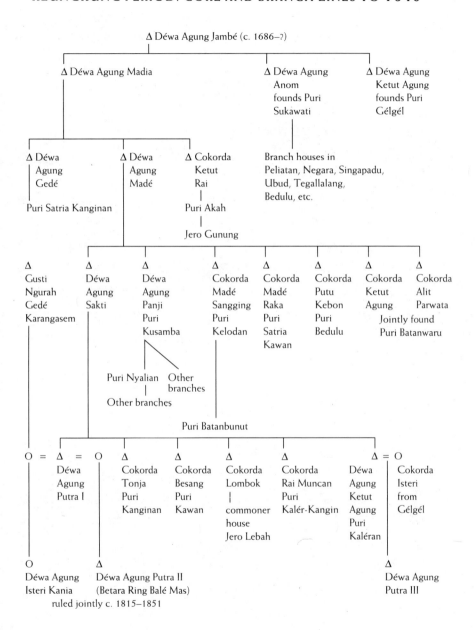

Δ Déwa Agung Jambé (c. 1686–?)

Δ Déwa Agung Madia

Δ Déwa Agung Anom
founds Puri Sukawati

Δ Déwa Agung Ketut Agung
founds Puri Gélgél

Δ Déwa Agung Gedé

Puri Satria Kanginan

Δ Déwa Agung Madé

Δ Cokorda Ketut Rai

Puri Akah

Jero Gunung

Branch houses in
Peliatan, Negara, Singapadu,
Ubud, Tegallalang,
Bedulu, etc.

Δ Gusti Ngurah Gedé Karangasem

Δ Déwa Agung Sakti

Δ Déwa Agung Panji
Puri Kusamba

Δ Cokorda Madé Sangging
Puri Kelodan

Δ Cokorda Madé Raka
Puri Satria Kawan

Δ Cokorda Putu Kebon
Puri Bedulu

Δ Cokorda Ketut Agung
Jointly found
Puri Batanwaru

Δ Cokorda Alit Parwata

Puri Nyalian   Other branches
Other branches

Puri Batanbunut

O = Δ = O   Déwa Agung Putra I

Δ Cokorda Tonja Puri Kanginan

Δ Cokorda Besang Puri Kawan

Δ Cokorda Lombok
commoner house
Jero Lebah

Δ Cokorda Rai Muncan Puri Kalér-Kangin

Δ = O   Déwa Agung Ketut Agung Puri Kaléran

Cokorda Isteri from Gélgél

O
Déwa Agung Isteri Kania

Δ
Déwa Agung Putra II
(Betara Ring Balé Mas)
ruled jointly c. 1815–1851

Δ
Déwa Agung Putra III

KLUNGKUNG PERIOD: 1840–1990S

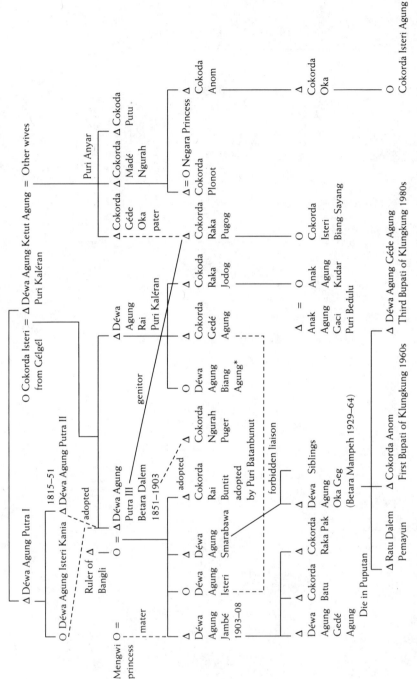

*Married to Déwa Agung Jambé.

KARANGASEM HOUSE

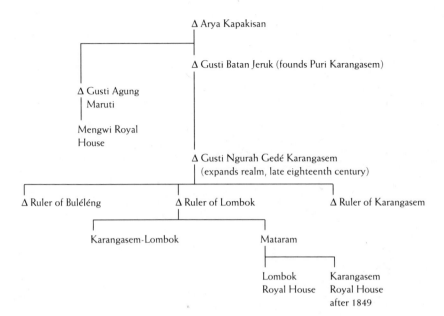

Glossary

alus Refined, ethereal.

anak Person.

Anak Agung Literally, Big Person; title for a member of the ruling class; in Klungkung, a notch down from Cokorda; elsewhere in Bali, a ruler's title.

Arya Title for nobles who came to Bali during the Majapahit era.

asih Love.

balé Pavilion.

Bali Aga Balinese who claim descent from the indigenous population conquered by Majapahit.

bebai A malevolent spirit.

betén Below.

Betara Divinity.

Brahmana Highest of the four *warna*; priestly caste.

buana agung. The "great world."

buana alit The "little world" of the body.

buta Demons; negative supernatural forces; blind.

buta-yadnya Rituals to placate the demons.

cacad Imperfect, damaged in some manner.

carikan Leftovers.

Cokorda A ruling-class title; in Klungkung, one notch down from Déwa Agung.

Dalem Literally, inside; the royal title for the Kapakisan clan, especially prior to the Klungkung period.

darma Mild and calm in relation to others; behavior appropriate to one's status.

enteg Firm, upright.

gegodan Test, temptation.

gumi Land, country, realm.

Gusti A title for nobles tracing descent to one of the Arya who came from Majapahit; sometimes considered wesia.

geria A compound belonging to a Brahmana.

jaba Outside or outsider; a commoner.

jagat Land, country, realm (high Balinese).

jero Inside; a title for commoner women who marry aristocrats or Brahmanas; a title for commoner holders of political office or temple priests; a royal or noble compound.

jeroan The house of a commoner who has attained higher status by virtue of political or religious office.

kaadnyanan Power; knowledge.

kabupaten Regency; an administrative division in the Indonesian nation-state.

kadutan A keris.

kaja Towards the mountain; upstream or upridge; in Klungkung, north.

kala A kind of demon, characterized by excessive appetites and passions; the terrible aspect of Siwa.

kanda mpat The four spirit siblings.

karya Literally, work; a major and expensive ritual.

kasaktian Power, efficacy, usually extraordinary.

kawitan Origin point; a place or object associated with a clan's history.

kayun Mind; heart; desire; intention.

kekawin Poem in specified meters.

kelod Downstream or downridge; towards the sea; in Klungkung, south.

keris A long dagger of iron and nickel hammered into a damascene pattern, often with an odd number of curves in the blade.

kleteg A knock; a feeling or thought; intuition.

ksatria Person of royal descent; persons related to the Klungkung royal clan; also **satria**

leteh Dirty, polluted.

lontar A kind of palm; manuscript made from the leaves of this palm.

luk Curves in a keris blade.

lungsuran Leftovers of a person of higher rank; specifically refers to food offerings made to ancestors or divinities.

luur Above; ancestors; Mount Agung or the temple of Besakih; the gods.

mala Bad, polluting.

manca A lord of the realm.

mantra An incantation using Sanskrit words and powerful syllables.

matelasan To "finish"; to commit a puputan.

merajan That portion of the compound of a high-ranking family in which shrines to ancestors and gods are located.

méru A shrine with an odd number of roofs, stacked pagoda-fashion.

moksa To merge with the invisible world; vanish into nothingness.

naga A cosmological serpent, usually represented wearing a crown.

nakti Visit a temple in the middle of the night to ask for a divine boon.

niskala The invisible world; unmanifested.

nunas ica To ask for a gift; beg forgiveness.

nyéwa seraya Meditation in a temple in the middle of the night.

padmasana A type of shrine, generally a very tall throne, with iconography representing the complete cosmos.

pageh Steadfast, constant, unwavering, resolute.

pakuluh Holy water, asked for directly from temple gods.

pangiwa Black magic; literally, of the left.

pajenengan An heirloom or regalia object, usually a weapon.

pamangku A temple priest.

parekan A servant; courtier.

paridan Ritual leftovers; usually refers to food offerings made during rites of passage, and wafted towards the body of the person undergoing the rite.

Pasupati A form of Siwa; the name for the divine energy that is invited to "sit" in a power object or in ritual paraphernalia, especially keris, shrines, sacred texts; an offering given to invite such divine energy to enter an object or to recharge a magical object with power, which could also be thought of as "feeding" the object.

patih Prime minister.

pedanda A Brahmana priest.

penengen White magic; literally, of the right.

perbekel Lower-level official.

polih nyambut To find (or have come to one) an object with potential power.

Prabu King; literally, head.

prasasti A text (inscribed on either palm leaves or copper plates) from the past, which is treated as a sacred object.

punah No longer effective; lifeless.

punggawa A lord of the realm.

puputan A fight to the finish.

puri Palace.

pura Temple.

pusaka An heirloom object.

ramé Noisy, busy, full of excitement.

raksasa Ogres with bulging eyes and fangs.

rana-yadnya The sacrifice of battle.

sakti Powerful.

salah pati A wrong death, as in an accident.

samar A kind of spirit.

Sang Hyang Widhi A name for the highest manifestation of divinity.

satia Loyalty, faithfulness.

sekala The everyday world.

semetonan A kinship group, defined as all persons agnatically descended from a common ancestor.

sesuunan Something revered; literally, carried on the head.

sidikara A kinship group, defined by the mutual performance of certain ritual acts.

sikepan Amulet.

Smara The god of love and pleasure.

sukla Pure; new or never used.

sumbah A ritual obeisance, made by placing hands palms together, with thumbs meeting at forehead or nose.

tanana Nonexistent; a class of spirit beings.

tenget Enchanted; a place favored by invisible beings.

tirta Holy water made by a Brahmana priest.

tonya A kind of spirit inhabiting ravines and large trees.

topéng A form of dance-drama, in which performers wear masks and use as subject matter stories from chronicles.

Tumpek Landep The day Saturday-Kliwon in the week Landep; day on which metal weapons are recharged with power.

uku A week in the Balinese 210-day cycle.

ulah pati A bad or cursed death, as in a suicide.

uug Destroyed, defeated, broken.

warna One of four types of person, determined by birth: Brahmana, Ksatria, Wesia, and all others.

wayah di tengah Mature; one who understands things.

wibawa An authoritative bearing; inspiring respect.

widiadari Celestial nymph.

Notes

1. INTRODUCTION

1. According to Balinese, the number of deaths was grossly underreported by the Dutch. Since the puputan has become a symbol of anticolonial resistance, they might have reason to exaggerate the numbers, but colonial officials had just as much reason, given the politics of their day, to understate them. Indeed, Day (1904) suggests that it was fairly common for the colonial government to manipulate the information sent back to the Netherlands.

2. Letter from Resident Veenhuizen to the Governor General, 15 March 1910, Mail Report #362 in V. 10 August 1911 No. 19/8, MvK Bali/Lombok Series IIIC7, ARA.

3. The Chinese, whom Balinese knew as merchants rather than conquerors, were also, however, regarded as fearful and dangerous.

4. Balinese names with their titles index social ranks, gender, and generation. An Ida Bagus is an unconsecrated Brahmana male, a Dayu (Ida Ayu) his female counterpart. A Pedanda is a Brahmana priest, and a Pedanda Isteri a Brahmana priestess; Déwa Agung, Cokorda, and Anak Agung (commonly shortened to 'Gung in speech) are all titles for members of the royal clan of Klungkung in descending rank order, with Isteri signifying a female; Gusti are lower-ranking lords. To these titles are added generation signifiers such as Niang (high-ranking grandmother), 'Kak (short for Pekak, high-ranking grandfather), Biang (high-ranking mother), and Aji (high-ranking father).

5. *Ratu*, which means something like "lord," is a respectful term of address for priests, Brahmanas, and members of royal families. Conversations with such persons are, in fact, peppered with continuous interjections of *'tu*, the shortened form. In Dalem Pemayun's case, *Ratu* is used in speaking of the prince, as well as to him. When he was consecrated as a priest, his kinsmen held long, involved discussions regarding the name he should take. Consecrated princes are usually called *bagawan*, but some family members felt this was too low a title for a member of the core line of Klungkung's royal clan. It was then suggested that since such consecrations had been common among the earliest royal ancestors, he should be known by the same title they used: Dalem. The fact that this prince had not previously undergone a coronation was ignored, and he has been Ratu Dalem ever since.

6. That I was taping our conversations occasionally inhibited people, but most told me far more than I was capable of understanding, and I am still discovering just how rich and subtle most of those conversations were. When it did not seem advisable to turn on my tape recorder, I jotted notes in a small notebook, especially of unfamiliar terms or particularly felicitous turns of phrase.

7. Balinese regard themselves as more or less divided into four social types or *warna* (from the Sanskrit *varna*) familiar from Indian texts—Brahmana, Ksatria, Wesia, and everyone else.

8. In theory, all Balinese Brahmanas have a common ancestor; they are, however, represented as divided into two clans, Brahmana Siwa and Brahmana Buda (see chapter 5). Danghyang Nirartha, identified as the ancestor of all Brahmana Siwa, had (at least) four wives, and they produced the four major subclans into which Bali's abundant Brahmana Siwa are further divided (see Appendix; Rubinstein 1991).

9. Other than specifically "historical" genres, many Balinese texts (including texts on ritual, curing, and cosmology) address matters of historical interest. People say that to understand kingship one should study the *Barata Yuda* and *Ramayana*, epic poems based on Indian originals, and various texts (such as *Rajaniti, Nitipraya, Kamendaka Niti*) concerning the behavior appropriate to kings; the same texts were mentioned to Friederich in the 1840s (1959 [1849–50]: 17–29). I focus on the *Babad Dalem*, because of its relevance to both oral narratives and Dutch accounts of Klungkung; I have made use of other texts where they seemed relevant, especially (in chapter 9) the *Buwana Winasa*.

2. COLONIAL REPRESENTATIONS OF KLUNGKUNG

1. Mengwi, defeated by its neighbors in a war in the 1890s, was not part of the federation.

2. Dubois wrote what might be considered the first "ethnography" of Bali in the form of a series of letters to an anonymous correspondent. The work, entitled *Légère idée de Balie en 1830*, was never published. A copy of the manuscript can be found in the KITLV (Collectie Dubois).

3. Dubois MS, Letter III, H281, KITLV.

4. Old Javanese for "king of" (*nata ing*).

5. Dubois MS, Letter II, H281, KITLV.

6. As further evidence, he notes in a letter that he sent someone to Klungkung to explore the possibility of buying recruits from the Déwa Agung, explaining that he did not go himself because of the "great distance" and the difficulty of journeying on "roads inaccessible for horses, as Klungkung lies in and on the mountains" (Letter to Resident of Besuki and Banyuwangi, 24 April 1829, ANRI Bali 6.51).

7. Dubois MS, Letter III, H281, KITLV. He was, however, less than flattering concerning the actual ruler of Klungkung, as the same letter also notes:

The present *Dewa Agong* is about 45 years old; he is on the whole a hypocrite as a king, who spends his life as a sybarite, sometimes in his seraglio and sometimes in his temples, which are only in fact haunts dedicated to sensual pleasures. . . .

. . . It is the custom that a *Dewa Agong* visits, however, at some time in his life the princes with whom he is in political alliance, and it appears that this is even a duty. . . . The one who occupies the throne of *Klonkong* at present made his promenade to several regions of the island about 15 years ago, after his inauguration as *Dewa Agong.* He came on this occasion to overwhelm by the importance of his dignity the court of *Badong,* which was much more burdened than honored by his presence. Of the rest, his appearance in the capitals which fall within his itinerary is an event which remains in the memory of the people up to their last breath.

8. For Lange's role in mediating between the colonial government and Balinese rulers in the 1840s, see chapter 6. For more about Lange, see Nielsen 1927, Geertz 1980, and Schulte Nordholt 1981.

9. He also went to Karangasem, whose ruler was kin to those of Lombok.

10. ANRI Bali 4.51.

11. Schulte Nordholt claims that the Déwa Agung's reference to himself as the Susuhunan of Bali and Lombok in a letter to the Governor General is what raised the question of the Déwa Agung's position for the administration (Schulte Nordholt 1988:153, citing a report by Huskus Koopman dated 30 June 1840 in Geh. Bt. 5 August 1840 K3, ANRI). In fact, Huskus Koopman was already referring to the Déwa Agung as Bali's keizer before this (e.g., Letter from Huskus Koopman to the Governor General, 17 May 1840, ANRI Bali 7). In the sixteenth century, Cornelis Houtman referred to the king of Gélgél, the Déwa Agung's ancestor, as the *kheyser* or *koningh* of Bali (cited in van Kol 1914:281). Nineteenth-century Dutch sources rarely refer to Balinese rulers—any of them—by the word *konig* but usually use *vorst.*

12. I have not been able to determine if the term was used before the Dutch arrived, or if they introduced it. Sidemen et al. (1983:53) claims that the title only appears in treaties with the Dutch, suggesting the latter.

13. ANRI Bali 1.1 and Secret Report #10, 8 April 1874, in V. 31 December 1874 D34, MvK Inventaris 6059, ARA.

14. For example: "On 28 October, a letter with the verbal message that if the Resident might still be present at Gianjar in ten days the answer to his letter would be sent to Gianjar, and otherwise to Boeleleng, as the Dewa Agoeng, on account of the celebration of an offering feast at Sangla Lawak was prevented from giving an immediate answer" (Mail Report #780 in V. 28 April 1903 No. 2, MvK Kol. Res. na 1900, Box 175, ARA). Bangli's ruler often used the same strategy.

15. Letter from Huskus Koopman to the Governor General, 15 August 1840, in Geh. Bt. 6 November 1840 I4, ANRI.

16. Numerous examples may be found in chapters 6 and 8.

17. This report, unfortunately, was not in the archives.

18. ANRI Bali 1.1.

19. Letter from Resident Eschbach to the Governor General, 9 January 1902, Mail Report #711 in V. 28 April 1903 No. 2, MvK Kol. Res. na 1900, Box 175, ARA.

20. Letter #60 from Resident Eschbach to the Governor General, 26 September 1903, Mail Report #189 in V. 27 August 1904 No. 2, MvK Bali/Lombok Series IIIC1, ARA.

21. Kommissorial #116, 30 January 1904, in V. 27 August 1904 No. 2, MvK Bali/Lombok Series IIIC1, ARA.

22. In Dutch, however, such wordplay does not work so well, since the Dutch *geest* connotes "spirit" rather in the sense of ghosts and spooks; a disembodied soul, detached, as in death, from the body.

23. ANRI Bali 1.1.

3. THE VIEW FROM KLUNGKUNG

1. This spirit, or genus of spirits, is known elsewhere in Bali too. In the *Babad Buleleng*, Gusti Panji Sakti, a low-ranking son of the king Dalem Segening, is told that he will have dominion over all the land he can see from the great height of Panji Landung's arms (Worsley 1972). Perhaps it is no coincidence that one of the Klungkung temples at the end of Panji Landung's road is dedicated to Dalem Segening.

2. Outside of the puri in Klungkung he is referred to as Ratu rather than Jero, a higher form of lordship.

3. Many village temples in the villages surrounding the temple complex of Besakih manifest a similar completeness, containing a *sanggar agung* (dedicated to the god of Mount Agung), a seat for the Lord of the Underworld (Ratu Dasar), and shrines to the rice goddess, the deity called Rambut Sedana who ensures prosperity, and the gods of Majapahit (Stuart-Fox 1987:33). As we will see, there are strong connections between Klungkung's court and Besakih.

4. I am fairly confident of this translation, based upon numerous conversations. In addition Warna (1978) glosses *niskala* as "unseen" (Indonesian, *tidak terlihat*); Hobart asserts that *sekala* has to do with what is visible, though more broadly it entails anything perceptible to the senses (1985:112). Note that for Balinese phenomena are distinguished on the basis of how they may be apprehended; but what is known through the normal exercise of the senses is not what is most socially valued.

5. While the topic of offerings is too vast to explore here, they appear to be another way of making visible the invisible order behind the ordinary appearances of things. Take, for example, animal sacrifices. The animal chosen and the color of its feathers or fur depend upon the characteristics of the being to which it is being offered: sacrifices to the negative forces of the east are white and usually consist of geese or chickens; to the south, red four-legged beasts, etc. The skin of the animal and its head are laid on the ground in the appropriate direction;

ritual foods called *saté* and *lawar*, made of its innards and meat, are placed on top of the skin in quantities determined by the number associated cosmologically with the direction in question (thus five is the number of the east). This number is called *urip*, "life." The ordinary form of the animal is destroyed, and what is normally unseen is made manifest: the nonvisible powers that gave the creature life, the essence of its being. One could argue that breaking a living creature into its component parts and then arranging these in ordered form images the goals of the ritual itself.

6. For textual examples, see Hooykaas 1975.

7. There are two major exceptions: the main shrine at the temple of Besakih is a tripartite throne said to be for Divinity manifested as Brahma, Wisnu, and Siwa. There are also additional shrines at Besakih for Wisnu (at the portion of the complex called Pura Batu Madeg), Brahma (Pura Kiduling Kreteg), Iswara (Pura Gelap), Maheswara (Pura Ulun Kulkul), and Siwa (the same tripartite throne, since Siwa represents totality). Shrines to deified ancestors, which consist of three compartments, are also sometimes identified as places for Divinity in its tripartite form of Brahma, Wisnu, and Siwa; others claim such shrines are rather (or also) dwelling places for female ancestors (on the left), male ancestors (on the right), and Betara Guru (in the center). See, e.g., Swellengrebel 1960.

8. Some claim that village deities are local manifestations of the three great Hindu gods. Thus the god of the village "origin" temple (Pura Puseh), associated with the founders of the village, is identified with Brahma, as creator; the god of the village temple proper (Pura Desa, or Pura Balé Agung) is Wisnu, the preserver; and the god of the village "death" temple (Pura Dalem) is Siwa, the destroyer. This neat formulation appealed greatly to colonial Dutch scholars (see Swellengrebel 1960) and continues to be replicated by anthropologists (e.g., Ramseyer 1977). It is also the official position of Parisada Hindu Dharma, an organization that has increasingly taken on the role of establishing doctrine for Balinese religious practices (see Geertz 1973a, Stuart-Fox 1987, and Forge 1980). Under Parisada influence, it is becoming more common to hear such universalizing claims repeated, especially by younger persons who learn them in school or from television. However, there are reasons to question this model. For one thing, many Balinese villages never had three village temples (see Stuart-Fox 1987 on the Karangasem villages near Besakih). Second, it is not Siwa but his consort who is associated with the Pura Dalem, so the parallels are not as neat as they seem (especially as Wisnu's consort is associated with water temples rather than village temples, while Brahma's has nothing to do with temples). Third, it obscures the role of locality and history in the practice of Balinese religion. That one does not worship in any village temple anywhere in Bali as a Christian might comfortably worship in a church outside of his own parish in another town or country is the strongest indication that for Balinese the deities of village temples are not (yet) the same everywhere. Balinese make offerings only in those temples (and more specifically at specific shrines within those temples) where they know their ancestors have done the same, and ideally where their ancestors were involved in the building of the shrine. As we will see, Balinese may also make offerings at less

familiar temples, especially to accomplish specific goals; but here I wish to emphasize the usual practice. Finally, it does not capture the way Balinese experience
their temple gods, nor does it explain the profusion of shrines, offerings, and
ritual practices encountered in most Balinese temples. Among other things, during
rituals Balinese make offerings not only to the deity of that particular temple but
also to the deities of other, more distant temples who have special relations to it.
Lansing (1991) has an interesting discussion of the complex of divinities involved
in temples connected to irrigation. His emphasis on the way such divinities en-
code ecological and social relations captures an important aspect of Balinese ritual,
one first noted by Bateson, who wrote: "We may guess that a Durkheimian analysis
would seem to the Balinese to be an obvious and appropriate approach to the
understanding of much of their public culture" (1970:393). However, it would be
a mistake to think such analyses would be all that obvious to Balinese, or for that
matter very interesting to them.

9. *Raksasa,* monsters or ogres, are also represented in this way. According to
Ida Bagus Jagri, they are a type of *kala.*

10. Balinese sometimes refer to spirits with the Indonesian phrase *orang halus,*
"refined people."

11. Whether or not a luminescence marks the presence of benevolent forces
depends upon its color and location.

12. Larger objects are described as *tenget* or *sakti,* "powerful"; smaller ones, such
as gems or amulets, simply *maguna,* are useful.

13. Texts such as the *Rogha Sangara Gumi* concern royal responsibility for realm
purifications. These, rather than cremations (as Geertz suggests), were the quintessential state rituals (cf. also Forge 1980a and Grader's notes on mouse cremations in Collectie Korn, KITLV). However, royal cremations also played a role in
protecting the realm, since the whole point of death rituals in Bali is to liberate
the soul so that it may merge with the gods. One could say that by their enormous
ritual efforts a king's followers were doing their utmost to get their man where he
could do them the most good.

14. According to Lansing (1987), this is also one role of the head priest of the
temple Batur.

15. Texts like the *Purwa Tattwa* explain such phenomena in detail. Any glowing
object found in the precincts of a temple embodies a divinity and should be
treated as sacred. Precisely which divinity depends upon the object; thus stones
are the god Mahadéwa; gemstones, the god of the temple Ulu Watu; tin, Mother
Earth; gold, the god of Mount Agung; iron, the god Wisnu. However, if a glowing object is discovered outside a temple, and a trance medium claims it may be
honored in the finder's house-shrines, misfortune will follow, for such objects
embody not divinity but demons. To restore well-being it will have to be thrown
into the sea together with expensive offerings.

16. *Nakti'*ing is essentially a form of meditation and hardly unique to Bali. See
Anderson 1972, for a similar Javanese practice; the famous literary example is
Arjuna, in the *Arjuna Wiwaha.*

17. I was told that the full and new moon are auspicious because these times are ruled by the god Smara and his consort Ratih, the deities of attraction. Therefore humans are likely to have good fortune in attracting divine interest. One might also *nakti* on the day *kajeng-kliwon* in the 210-day calendar, which is auspicious for *buta-kala*, especially if one sought powers of the kind associated with sorcery.

18. There is a tacit hierarchy whereby the larger a temple's membership (each state temple is supported in Klungkung by all the farmers in particular watersheds; Besakih, by all of Bali), the more powerful the things associated with it—divine gifts, holy water, or blessings. Not all gifts from the same source, of course, are equally potent. It should be noted that people do not only seek power on such night visits to temples. Almost anything may be sought as a gift from the gods, and the gods of certain temples are known to specialize in fulfilling certain kinds of desires. For example, the temple Bukit Mandéan in East Klungkung is said to be an especially good place for an infertile couple to ask for a child.

19. To "ask for a gift," one might bring the offerings called *pejati* (consisting of a *peras, santun, ajuman,* and *ketipat*) and a *segehan*. A *pejati* offering informs the gods of a place that the offerer has some intention; *segehan* offerings appease lower spirits. *Sakti* keris are always given *segehan* when taken down from their shrines, and people said that whenever the last Déwa Agung returned from a journey his arrival home was greeted with a *segehan* for his spirit entourage. The whole grouping is, by Balinese reckoning, fairly small.

20. For example, a *pemenak*, greeting, *tebasan wawu rauh*, "just arrived," *tebasan merta dewa*, "life- and fortune-giving substance of the gods," and probably a *tebasan pasupati*.

21. Keris are found throughout the Malay archipelago, although there has been relatively little discussion of them by anthropologists. Rassers (1959) on the Javanese keris is one of the few exceptions; of particular interest are his observations concerning the simultaneous identification of keris with both specific individuals and social collectivities, and his comments concerning the role keris play in the social construction of masculinity and the establishment of alliances. Errington (1983) points out that the regalia of Luwu in South Sulawesi embodied potencies and mediated between the divine and human; however, keris per se are not the focus of her discussion, and she only notes that Luwu's regalia consisted of three named keris in a footnote. In a more recent work she offers some interesting remarks on keris as symbols of royal potency in Luwu, but they still play a minor role in her analysis of Luwu polities and politics (Errington 1989:59, 287). Hitchcock (1987) is mainly concerned with the manufacture of keris. There is little attention in any of these accounts to particular objects and stories about them, or to the fact that keris are weapons.

22. See Vickers 1986 for an intriguing discussion of the relationship between sex and war in the poem *Malat*.

23. See chapter 5 for Klungkung, Worsley 1972 for Buléléng, Mahaudiana 1968 for Gianyar, and Schulte-Nordholt 1988 for Mengwi.

24. In Klungkung, *pajenengan* refers exclusively to royal heirlooms such as keris, but in Gianyar the same term is sometimes used for shrines.

25. *Ki* is a Kawi honorific for elderly males or others worthy of respect.

26. Such gems also adorn the *bawa*, or crowns, Brahmana priests wear to perform major rituals, and they are worn in rings by people of all ranks.

27. The poem, the *Geguritan Maligia Padem Warak*, is discussed in Vickers 1991.

28. In general, discourse about kings is strikingly reminiscent of the epic *Ramayana*, according to which the ideal king should possess the attributes of eight forms of Divinity (Worsley 1972:44–45): Agni (fire, a form of Brahma); Bayu (life-force, energy, wind); Baruna (god of the purifying sea); Yama (god of death and judgment); Candra (god of the moon; identical to Ratih); Rawi (god of the sun, identical to Surya and Smara); Indra (king of the gods); Kuwera (god of wealth). I point out the correspondence because the relationship between epic representations of kingship and nineteenth-century ideologies has been questioned by Guermonprez (1985:57), who argues that by the late nineteenth century Balinese kingship was basically secularized. Rather than considering such representations irrelevant, I suggest, Balinese rulers simply took them for granted.

4. MAKING HISTORY

1. One reason Balinese give for keeping dogs is that, as their eyes are not "flawed" in this way, they are still able to see beings invisible to humans. Their barking (or the crowing of fighting cocks) for no apparent reason in the middle of the night may indicate the presence of spirits or of sorcerers in disguised form.

2. While in its more restricted sense *babad* denotes a specific kind of prose narrative, in general all texts about the ancestors of living persons may be referred to as *babad*. For example, Balinese asked to classify manuscripts for the library of the Gedong Kirtya-van der Tuuk included under the category *babad* various poems that had nothing directly to do with genealogical matters (Hooykaas 1979:11–12). These included a genre (*geguritan*) invented in the nineteenth century in which events such as the ritual in which the rhinoceros was sacrificed or the fall of various realms were described. (Klungkung was actually a center for such literature, according to Kanta 1984.) During the same period, I should note, there seems to have been an efflorescence of interest in *babad* too, for these were produced in ever greater numbers, although (for complicated reasons) their production accelerated even more during the colonial era.

On the other hand, tales about the five Pandawa brothers (in *parwa*, prose stories from the *Mahabharata*; and *kekawin*, poetry in the oldest metrical style) or the Javanese prince Panji (the *kidung Malat*, poetry in Javanese meters), which are also considered to be about historically real persons and events, were classified as *itihasa*, "epics" (Hooykaas 1979:11–12). The difference partly is a matter of time—epics are about an earlier time in another place—and partly technical (epics are written according to strict metrical rules).

3. *Kawitan* may also refer to objects that belonged to an ancestor; to the group of persons who all support and worship at temples or shrines dedicated to common

ancestors (see Geertz and Geertz 1975); to the shrines or temples themselves; or even to a *babad*.

4. "History" also includes a newer type of written text, books based upon more Euro-American scholarly conventions.

5. According to some interpretations, a child is formed by a mingling of maternal and paternal substances (see Hooykaas 1975).

6. One should not, however, overstate the differences. The fact that *babad* locate the events they narrate *ing nguni* (in the past) indicates that their authors too only report what they have heard; it is up to the reader to decide what to think.

7. Perhaps related to this is Wikan's claim that in Bali thinking is not regarded as separable from feeling (Wikan 1989).

8. To be more precise, texts were and are written in mixtures of Kawi and various registers of Balinese, depending upon the age of the text and its genre. According to Hinzler (1976), older texts are more likely to be composed in complex forms of Kawi, whereas very recent texts may use Balinese or even Indonesian. Some texts include Sanskrit in their medley of linguistic possibilities.

9. During times of crisis, a portion of such a text may be read aloud during rituals at the group's shrines (Hobart 1990).

10. Vickers (1986) was the first to appreciate that such divergences are typical of Balinese texts and thus part of their construction. Worsley (1972:100, 105) and Hinzler (1976:40) both observe such substitutions in *babad*, without appreciating the challenge they pose for philological notions of texts and their transmission. Kumar (1984) addresses a similar phenomenon in a discussion of Javanese *babad*.

11. While theoretically the opposite could also occur—episodes could be abbreviated or left out altogether—for those versions of the *Babad Dalem* I have examined, later texts are more likely to add narration than to subtract it.

12. Rituals may be accompanied by multiple (often simultaneous) performances in different media. At major rituals it is common to have a shadow play without a screen, and a *topéng* enacted by a single performer, who changes characters by changing masks. Unlike narratives taken from *kekawin* or certain *kidung* (see Vickers 1986), there are, at least to my knowledge, no visual or other plastic representations of *babad* narratives aside from the masks themselves.

13. See Vickers 1989 for a discussion of the relationship between colophons, the events they recount, and the texts to which they are appended.

14. See Day 1904 for an interesting account of the Netherlands government and the colonial administration.

15. Since documents were sent from the pinnacle of the colonial hierarchy, however, they had already been partially processed. Letters from indigenous rulers were sent in Dutch translation, for example.

16. These are distinguished by notation. Documents with designations such as V. 20 November 1988 No. 42 belong to the public series; V. 3 August 1900 A10, to cabinet documents.

17. Besluit 16 July 1872 No. 12, ANRI.

18. The Residency archives themselves are said to no longer exist. Some claim they were destroyed during the Japanese Occupation or during the tumultuous years following the establishment of the Indonesian nation-state. Others hint that many documents have been squirreled away by persons who regard them as a kind of *babad*.

5. THE *BABAD DALEM*

1. The *semetonan*, which consists of all descendants of a particular pivotal figure, is a more encompassing group than the *dadia* described by Geertz and Geertz 1975, which is a local descent group. Until recently only a barely imagined possibility, the *semetonan* is becoming an increasingly important institution for reasons too complicated to pursue here.

2. This theory, and for that matter this text, ignores polygyny. The sons of high-ranking women ranked higher than their half-brothers by lower-ranking women regardless of who was elder or younger. Lower-ranked sons are not mentioned in all *Babad Dalem*.

3. I noted one from Jembrana, four from various noble houses in Kaba-Kaba, six from Sidemen, four from Buléléng (including puris), one from the royal house in Denpasar, and two from Brahmana Buda houses in Budakeling Karangasem.

4. Colophons occasionally identify the copyists of particular manuscripts and the date on which their activity was completed. Sometimes there is information concerning the owner of the original or even a kind of "genealogy" of successive copies, as in K1252.

5. Vickers (1990) thinks the text was written in the early nineteenth century. Stuart-Fox (1987:321) suggests it was written in the eighteenth century, when there is evidence of great Balinese interest in Majapahit: Klungkung's palace, for example, is said to have been modeled on Majapahit's, and in 1730 the Déwa Agung and the ruler of Mengwi visited Java hoping to view Majapahit's ruins (Schulte Nordholt 1988:27–29). Hinzler (1986b) indicates that the text could not have been written much earlier because various personages it refers to are not mentioned in earlier sources. But there may well have been earlier written accounts concerning the dynasty, which were later incorporated into the text now known by the name *Babad Dalem*. There seems, for example, to be a different tone to earlier episodes, less eventful and more lyrical and descriptive. As for Hinzler's argument, the few sources that have survived from earlier periods tend to be not only fragmentary but of a radically different type: largely edicts, incised on copper plates. It is impossible to say that earlier versions of these stories did not exist simply because these sources do not mention by name the major actors that appear in them; there is not necessarily any reason to assume that they would. What survives is hardly representative of what once existed—it is only what has survived. In addition, persons are often referred to by different names depending upon context, making identifications difficult.

6. I pose 1884 as an upper limit on grounds of content. The text begins with the three sons of Déwa Agung Jambé, who established the Klungkung court. But rather than focusing on the heir, it initially speaks of a younger brother who founded a branch line puri in Sukawati, in what is now the region of Gianyar. The text even discusses, albeit sketchily, various branches of this Sukawati house (see *Babad Ksatria* K692, *Babad Ksatria* K693/1, *Babad Ksatria* K958, *Badad Dalem* H2935 and Warna et al. 1986). While in general this emendation is quite different from the earlier portions in discussing branch lines, that it should begin with Sukawati is striking given the political relevance of the Sukawati branch lines to Klungkung's late-nineteenth-century ruler (see chapter 8). By bringing these kin ties to the king's awareness, the author of the text provides a motivation for certain political decisions.

7. Geria Pidada is one of the few Klungkung houses that has participated in the Bali Manuscript Project. Such openness has historical precedents; in the nineteenth and early twentieth centuries, Geria Pidada priests were highly influential in negotiations between the Déwa Agung and the Dutch, and after Klungkung's fall several members of the house held civil service positions in the colonial administration. The present generation leans toward modernity; quite a few members have homes and jobs in Denpasar. Two other *Babad Dalem* also come from Klungkung: K958, a *Babad Ksatria* in the Kirtya collection, is identified as originating from Klungkung, although there is no indication from where, and the colophon of K1252 identifies it as once belonging to a Ksatria Dalem living "south of the puri" in Klungkung. From the evidence of the text itself he would appear to have been a descendant of Déwa Agung Mayun (see genealogy in Appendix), thus a branch member of a branch line that separated from the core some ten generations ago.

8. Belo refers to him as "keeper of the genealogy (babad) of the ruling family of Klungkung" (Belo 1970:28, 38). Another text he wrote, entitled *Pamencangah Dalem*, is now the authoritative text for the core line.

9. In addition to the *Usana Bali*, see, for example, the *Babad Pasek* (Sugriwa 1957).

10. This phrase comes from the opening of the *Babad Pasek* (Sugriwa 1957).

11. *Tapa* refers to the performance of austerities such as meditation; *ulung* is Kawi for a type of bird (Zoetmulder [1982] suggests a hawk) or a dark color. In Balinese *ulung* means "to fall," and this is clearly the way the word is interpreted when people tell the story. Belo, for example, was told that this king, the last Masula, "was very strong in magic power. So strong was he that he was able to take a kris and cut off his own head, and then place it back upon his shoulders again. Often in the palace he would tell his servant to cut off his head and then replace it. But one day he was playing beside the river, and, when he ordered the servant to cut off his head, the servant did so, and the head fell into the stream" (1970:38).

12. See Lansing 1991. Although this is the only text I know that identifies Mayadanawa as Déwi Danu's son, it appears to correlate with the creation of two

aquatic landmarks during the course of the battle between the gods and the ogre-king: the sacred spring Tirta Harum and (from the blood of Mayadanawa) the Petanu River, the water of which was believed to bring misfortune.

13. Endogamy is important to the creation and reproduction of Balinese rank (see Boon 1976; Geertz and Geertz 1975); the significance of royal sisters will be seen later.

14. This passage is found in *Babad Dalem* H2935 from Geria Pidada in Klung-kung and *Babad Dalem A* in Warna et al. 1986. It is not found in *Babad Dalem B* (Warna 1986), *Babad Dalem* K1252, or *Babad Dalem* H3834. *Babad Dalem A* is from the village of Sidemen in Karangasem; since the ancestors of Geria Pidada also came from Sidemen, in the nineteenth century, it is possible that the two texts have a common origin. As already indicated, however, H2935 was copied by Cokorda Anom of Puri Anyar, possibly from a text belonging to his own puri. That the passage is not found in *Babad Dalem* H3834 might be significant, not only because according to its colophon it was copied in 1826, making it the earliest text I consulted, but also because it is from a Brahmana Buda compound in the village of Budakeling in Karangasem, which traditionally provided Buda priests for Klungkung rituals. However, priests from Budakeling in the 1980s all accepted the Brahmana Buda origins of the Klungkung royal house. Without a nineteenth-century text from the Klungkung court itself, it is impossible to say with any certainty whether the attribution of particular Brahmana Buda ancestors to the Klungkung royal family is a recent interpolation. This genealogy is in any event currently accepted by members of the family.

15. Gerdin (1981) was the first to discuss *sidikara* relations. In West Lombok, where she did her research, the signs of such a relationship are slightly different. They involve making a *sumbah*, which she glosses simply as worshipping ancestors, eating *paridan*, here offerings dedicated to ancestral spirits, and *pikul-mamikul*, car-rying each other's dead.

16. According to legend, the two brothers decided to meditate to achieve magical power. The elder brother went to the top of a mountain and performed acts of asceticism—eating only certain pure foods. The younger brother went to the foot of the mountain and did exactly the opposite—eating whatever came his way, however revolting. One day a tiger appeared to the elder brother and threat-ened to devour him. He argued that he was so thin he would make a poor meal, but he suggested that the tiger visit his more corpulent brother at the foot of the mountain. And so the tiger left to confront the younger brother. He said calmly that the tiger was welcome to eat him but asked time to prepare himself for death. The tiger agreed, and the younger brother bathed, dressed, prayed, and then invited the tiger to proceed. Instead of eating him, the tiger—who was actually an emissary of the gods, sent to test the two brothers—ordered him onto his back and set off skyward, toward the heavens. As they passed, the elder brother called out for them to wait and grabbed the tiger by its tail. When they arrived in heaven, the tiger entered a shrine, in which sat a god who instructed the two brothers in the formulas to be used by priests. The elder brother could only hear

part of these instructions, since the shrine was too small to accommodate the tiger's rear parts. This is why the mantra of Siwa priests includes the phrase *samar, samar, samar:* "unclear, unclear, unclear." Versions of the tale may be found in Agung n.d. and Rassers 1959.

17. They are Arya Kanuruhan, Arya Wangbang (who became chief minister), Arya Kenceng, Arya Dalancang, Arya Belog, Arya Pangalasan, Arya Manguri, Arya Kuta Waringan, Arya Gajapara. Also three "wesia," Tan Kobér, Tan Kaur, Tan Mundur.

18. These villages are listed in the text: Batur, Campaga, Songan, Kedisan, Abang, Pinggan, Punti, Pladung, Cintamani, Srahi, Manikalya, Bonyoh, Taro, Bayan, Sukawana, Culik, Tista, Garbawana, Got, Margatiga, Sekul Kuning, Loka Sarana, Puhan, Ulakan, Paselatan, Simbanten, Watudawa, Muntig, Juntal, Carutcut, Bantas, Kuta Bayem, Watuwayang, Kadampal, and Asti.

19. Used by a type of commoner exorcist priest called *sengguhu* (see Hooykaas 1964). When these join in the performance of large rituals they sit on the ground, with Brahmana Buda priests above them. In Klungkung, *sengguhu* never participate in state rituals.

20. I should make it clear here, however, that such differentiation was a matter of representation rather than everyday practice: precolonially, male priests, like all Balinese men, wore keris when they left their compounds, and certainly when they appeared at court. Priests, however, were not identified with their keris, but rather with their ritual paraphernalia. Texts I have seen concerning the origins of priestly lines do not mention the origins of their heirloom keris, in contrast to texts concerning royal lines.

21. The distinctive appearance of keris manufactured in Majapahit might also account for the name. According to Frey (1986), the handle and blade of such keris form a single unit, with the hilt shaped into an anthropomorphic figure, arms stiffly clamped to its side, body and head tilted to one side. Informants glossed the word *dungkul* in ways that suggested such a posture.

22. Agung (n.d.), however, narrates a tale concerning his daughter and the keris Ki Tanda Langlang. This story is discussed in chapter 9.

23. Artists also seek the aid of the god of love: see Hooykaas 1973 for invocations shadow puppeteers make to Kama, another form of Smara, so their audiences will be pleased with the performance, and Zoetmulder 1974 for a discussion of *kekawin.*

24. Arjuna also is represented with a *garuda mungkur* headdress (and his hair in this style); according to elderly informants, the crown prince who died in the 1908 conquest had such a headdress too. It is currently in the National Museum in Jakarta.

25. According to Schrieke (1957), early Javanese kings were also identified with Wisnu.

26. There is an equivalent scene in the *Babad Buleleng* involving Gusti Panji Sakti's salvaging of goods from a shipwreck; Guermonprez (1985) refers to the

scene as a "symbolic node." Such episodes may be typical of *babad*, their differences and similarities might shed an interesting light on how politically prominent clans constituted their identities vis-à-vis other clans.

27. The language of healing is in fact quite military; texts on healing speak of building "fortifications" (*gelar*) and of the "weapons" appropriate to defeating certain illnesses.

28. No one could explain to me why there should be seven layers.

29. According to Cokorda Oka Lingsir of Puri Anyar, the scene carved on the base of this shrine depicts an incident from the *Adi Parwa* in which a *naga* was used to churn the sea with Mount Méru to produce *merta*, the elixir of life.

30. This is also a general attribute of the binding power of snakes. Thus Dayu Alit claimed that a dream of a snake encircling one's body meant someone was in love with the dreamer.

31. For a thorough discussion of Pura Besakih, see Stuart-Fox 1987.

32. According to Stuart-Fox (1987:455), the claim that Iswara, the "pure" form of Siwa who dwells in the east, is the god of Pura Gelap is recent. The *Rajapurana Pura Besakih*, a text written in the early eighteenth century about Besakih shrines and rituals, identifies the god of Pura Gelap as I Déwa Geni (Fire) or Ida Ala Ayu Gumi Akasa (Lord Inauspicious and Auspicious Earth and Sky). However, as Stuart-Fox also notes that the mantras used during the temple's rituals are addressed to Siwa, and Hooykaas claims that there was once a Siwa Lingga in the temple, these may very well be textual euphemisms. Stuart-Fox translates *Pura Gelap* as "Temple of Lightning and Thunder." In Indonesian, *gelap* means "dark, unclear, secret."

33. This is true in all manuscripts. As already noted, there are other similarities between Bangawan Canggu and Lobar.

34. This ritual, apparently directed to the god Brahma, is no longer known in Bali.

35. This, I was rather obscurely informed by Pedanda Gedé Kenitén, was the origin of the custom of killing the *nagabanda* at royal cremations, an act which purportedly was once exclusively performed by Buda priests. Covarrubias (1937) was told something similar.

36. Neither *kadiatmikan* nor *kawibawaan* is the same as *kasaktian*; but they both imply its possession.

37. Agung's *Babad Dalem* fleshes out the reign of Dalem Segening by associating it with the conquest of Nusa Penida. The story goes that Dalem Bungkut, Nusa Penida's ogre-king (*raksasa*) was defeated by a keris wielded by a Gélgél lord (Agung n.d.). The Fanged Lord, Jero Gedé Macaling, formerly Dalem Bungkut's chief minister, transferred his loyalty to the Dalem of Gélgél, which explains why Kapakisan rulers had power over *tanana*. According to *Babad Dalem A* (Warna et al. 1986), however, Dalem Bungkut's defeat occurred during the reign of Dalem Watu Rénggong, so clearly there are different interpretations. The betel-nut container in figure 9 is said to have belonged to Dalem Bungkut. According to Stuart-Fox, a

famous holy man named Dukuh Segening was Dalem Segening's matrilateral grandfather (1987 : 156).

38. The text also includes brief anecdotes about the keris and their properties; however, this passage is very difficult to follow, and I do not at present feel confident in interpreting it.

39. Stuart-Fox derives *Basuki* from the Sanskrit *vasu*, signifying well-being, generosity, wealth, and gold. Besakih is also linked to gold in other ways. For example, according to the *Purwa Tattwa*, a glowing piece of gold found inside a temple embodies the god of Mount Agung.

40. Thus, according to Agung (n.d.), Dalem Ketut Ngulesir built or expanded Pura Dasar (Base or Foundation Temple) in Gélgél, restored Pura Pusering Jagat (Temple of the Navel of the World) in Péjéng, a state temple belonging to his Balinese predecessors, and organized numerous rituals at Besakih.

41. For example, the *Rajapurana Pura Besakih*, in which the Dalem of Gélgél assigns various rights and responsibilities concerning Besakih to particular villages and clans. Many cosmological texts also comment on the kinds of shrines kings should build, the deities to whom they should offer worship, and so forth.

42. During Helms's residence in Bali, Klungkung was ruled by a brother-sister pair (see chapter 6); they were not, however, married.

43. Pura Manik Mas no longer exists; it was polluted when the bodies of those who died in the puputan were brought there prior to their cremation, and its wooden structures were used for their pyres. According to Stuart-Fox, Besakih's Pura Manik Mas was the first stop for Bali's kings when they came to Besakih, before proceeding onward (and upward) to the Penataran Agung (1987 : 123). The *Rajapurana Pura Besakih* suggests a link between this temple and the Naga Ananta-boga. Manik Mas is also one of several temples claimed to be the place where Ida Bagus Manik Angkeran, son of a great Brahmana priest from Java in pre-Majapahit Bali, was burned by the Naga Basuki for trying to steal the jewel from the tip of his tail. (He was restored to life on his father's request and subsequently charged with the care of the temple of Besakih; his descendants were the Arya Sidemen.) Both this tale, and the fact that its ritual date is Tumpek Wariga, the day sacred to trees, are pertinent to Klungkung's Manik Mas, which is associated with both a cremation and trees.

44. Pura Peningar, "Temple on the Heights," is a third temple (more accurately, a shrine), slightly southwest of Pura Manik Mas. It is said to mark the place from which Déwa Agung Jambé saw the luminescent land on which he decided to build his new palace Smarapura.

45. Pura Manik Mas was erected to commemorate a royal cremation organized by Klungkung's queen sometime after 1815, its shrines replacing two trees that sprouted on the cremation site of the two kings for whom the ritual was held—Déwa Agung Putra I and his father (see chapter 6). Pura Taman Sari may have been constructed around the same time (see Kanta 1983). Klungkung's Pura Penataran Agung was supposedly built during a war between Klungkung and Karangasem; as Dubois reports conflicts between those realms in 1829 (Letter to

Resident of Besuki and Banyuwangi, 24 April 1829, ANRI Bali 6.51), my guess is that the entire complex dates from the 1830s.

6. KLUNGKUNG AND THE DUTCH, 1840 – 1849

1. Their names commonly indexed the villages their mothers—and thus her kinsmen—were from, as well as signaling the prince's authority over their inhabitants, his actual or potential subjects (*beraya*, "relatives," but of lower rank).

2. The branch line founded by Déwa Agung Mayun, Déwa Agung Jambé's elder brother, dominated the regions of Tampaksiring and Payangan (see genealogy in Appendix). These houses never became major contenders for power in Bali, but both controlled semiautonomous areas continually contested by Gianyar, Bangli, and Klungkung during the nineteenth century. After Klungkung's conquest, the colonial government placed both regions under Gianyar's jurisdiction.

3. Its name, Puri Denpasar, means "north of the market" and so probably refers to its location: at the cosmologically auspicious northeast corner of the central Klungkung crossroads.

4. According to the *Babad Ksatria*, Bangawan Canggu helped Déwa Agung Madé win the war.

5. For Puri Satria Kanginan, see genealogy in Appendix. Van Bloemen Waanders (1870), whose source was the ruler of Bangli, claims that the war between Klungkung and Nyalian started when Déwa Gedé Tangkeban refused to give the Déwa Agung a keris he owned, named I Lobar. The *Babad Dalem* claims a keris of that name was given to the pivotal ancestor of Bangli's royal clan (see also the *Babad Ksatria Taman Bali*). This was clearly not the Lobar that came from Gajah Mada, but it may have been a duplicate with similar powers. It is unclear why Déwa Agung Putra I would request its return. Lekkerkerker (1926) offers a different version of events.

6. The rule of hypergamy, for example, would make it impossible for a female Déwa Agung to engage in marriage politics (indeed, it would likely rule out marriage altogether); moreover, before menopause, a female ruler could not handle regalia weapons, or so it would seem on the basis of present claims. Nonetheless, precolonially women did occupy positions of authority. For example, a female member of the Brahmana family in whose compound I lived in Klungkung was a royal chamberlain at the time of the conquest. It is also intriguing that unmarried Brahmana women may be consecrated as priests; a Brahmana man who wishes to become a priest, however, must be or have been married—to a Brahmana woman—and have a child.

7. I base this date upon Dubois's claim that Klungkung's new ruler paid a visit to Badung some fifteen years before he came to Bali (Dubois MS, Letter III, H281, KITLV).

8. His descendants know this Déwa Agung as Betara Balé Mas, "God of the Golden Pavilion," after the section of the royal compound in which he died (and presumably had lived) in 1851.

9. See figure 6 for branch lines outside of the capital. In 1840 Nyalian and Bakas belonged to Gianyar. Figure 8 shows branch lines within the capital. In 1840 only Puri Batanbunut did not yet exist; nor did the center for Dutch opium sales.

10. See, for example, the history of Gusti Panji Sakti, founder of Buléléng (Worsley 1972). Members of a commoner clan, Tangkas Kori Agung, likewise claim a royal offspring as their pivotal ancestor.

11. Branch-line *babad*, therefore, are likely to mention the names of women who married into the core line.

12. I am here referring to contemporary rather than nineteenth-century usages. In the last century royal kinsmen very close to the core line were also called Déwa (see, e.g., the *Babad Ksatria*). The matter of titles and their ranking is complicated, since they varied not only in time but in space: *Anak Agung* means something very different in 1990s Badung, for example, than it does in Klungkung.

13. What follows is a very rough summary of the origins of each of Bali's major lords and the state of their relationship to Klungkung in the period in question, reconstructed from a variety of sources. Friederich (1959 [1849–50]), whose information came largely from Brahmana informants in Badung between 1846 and 1848, is a particularly important source, and in certain cases I have consulted *babad*. To assess various assertions about descent it would be immensely valuable to have more information concerning when different accounts were written. As with Klungkung, *babad* for each prominent house contain narratives concerning the acquisition of magical heirlooms, which would be worth comparing in detail. My aim here is merely to sketch a picture of political relations at the time Bali became of interest to the colonial government.

14. Hinzler (1976) claims that Badung and Tabanan's core text was the *Usana Jawa*, in which the emphasis is on their pivotal ancestor, Arya Damar. This Arya Damar was, according to this text, a prince of Majapahit who did most of the actual conquest of Bali. According to Hinzler, the *Usana Jawa* makes no reference to Dalem Sri Kresna Kapakisan. There is a character called Arya Kapakisan: as I understand it, however, Arya Kapakisan is a different figure, generally identified as the ancestor of the Karangasem and Mengwi royal houses (see below). In the *Babad Dalem*, the ancestor of the Badung royal clan makes an appearance on the Gélgél scene during the reign of Dalem di Madé, though Arya Kenceng, its pivotal ancestor, is listed among the Arya who accompanied Sri Kresna Kapakisan to Samprangan.

15. See Vickers 1986 for a summary history of the Karangasem royal house.

16. Schulte Nordholt (1988) discusses various accounts of Mengwi's origins in detail. See also *Pembencangah Arya Dauh*.

17. Dubois MS, H281, KITLV.

18. For versions of Déwa Manggis's rise to power, see Agung n.d. and Mahaudiana 1968.

19. Guermonprez (1985) addresses these issues in greater depth.

20. I myself have not seen any texts asserting such a kin tie; my source was a Peliatan neighbor who is a member of this clan.

21. Stuart-Fox (1987:116) notes that the names of other deities in this complex suggest a relationship to the Batur area.

22. Gianyar artists have been famous since at least the nineteenth century. Cokorda Oka Lingsir explained to me that this was why the decorations in Pura Taman Sari were of unusually high quality.

23. The approximate date comes from Stuart-Fox (1987:570).

24. Letter from Gusti Ngurah Madé Karangasem, ruler of Buléléng, 6 February 1847, in Geh. Bt. 18 May 1847 D2, ANRI.

25. Political metaphors are as pertinent to discourse about divinities as "religious" analogies are to understanding political relations. Certain divinities are spoken of as the kings, ministers, and servants of others.

26. Letter from Lange to Resident Mayor, 8 April 1847, in Geh. Bt. 18 May 1847 D2, ANRI.

27. Letter from Resident Eschbach to the Governor General, 28 December 1901, Mail Report #711 in V. 28 April 1903 No. 2, MvK Kol. Res. na 1900, Box 175, ARA.

28. Both *pura* and *puri* derive from a Sanskrit root meaning simply "place." The distinction between final *a* and final *i* in Balinese is, first of all, deictic, signifying relative distance from the speaker: thus *derika* (over there) versus *deriki* (here). It also sometimes differentiates male and female: *déwa* (male divinity) versus *déwi* (female divinity). The first seems more pertinent to the distinction between *pura* and *puri*, suggesting that temples (dwelling places of invisible beings) are further from ordinary experience than palaces (dwelling places of humans, however awesome).

29. With the exception of Brahmanas, who did not fit into this schema of inner and outer even in ritual contexts. For example, Brahmana priests, while they are often asked to perform temple rituals, generally have little to do with temples; their core rite is performed in their own house-shrines. Stuart-Fox (1987) suggests that even at Besakih commoner temple priests conducted most rituals until this century. Note too that while aristocrats use shrines and cremation towers in the form of many-roofed pavilions with doors—reiterating the symbolism of inside and out—shrines and cremation towers for Brahmanas take the form of an open seat.

30. See Ramseyer 1977 and Swellengrebel 1960 for examples. "Upstream" is Lansing's (1991) gloss; Stuart-Fox (1987) uses "upridge."

31. Dubois mentions that the Déwa Agung occasionally made a tour of the other realms (Dubois MS, Letter III, H281, KITLV), and a Déwa Agung might spend several months at other courts advising about and witnessing major rituals (Mahaudiana 1968; van Bloemen Waanders 1870:31). One Déwa Agung traveled to Badung to marry a princess, but this may have been part of a tour as a new ruler, since the marriage happened in the first years of his reign (Mahaudiana 1968; see chapter 8). Puri Bangli had a special area set aside for the Déwa Agung

to stay during visits (Letter from Dewa Poetoe Boekian, Poenggawa of Bangli, 3 August 1932, OR435 in Collectie Korn, KITLV); this may have been the case elsewhere as well.

32. There is a single exception known to me. Déwa Agung Sakti's sister was taken as wife by the Déwa Manggis of Gianyar, who provided a refuge for Déwa Agung Panji after his defeat by his nephew at Kusamba. Klungkung narrators claim that the Déwa Manggis tricked Déwa Agung Panji into agreeing to the marriage, and that the princess, in protest, placed a polluting substance over the doorway to Puri Gianyar.

33. Van Kol (1903:445) uses *rijksbestierder* to translate the Balinese *mancanegara*; some Balinese sources refer to the *iwa raja*. Geertz (1980:60) calls him the *pemadé*, which means something like "second."

34. "*Ira ngiringang pakayunanne di jabannyane*" is the Balinese (Letter from Déwa Agung Ketut Agung to Mads Lange written about 1850, in the Gedong Kirtya, Singaraja, cited by Sidemen et al. 1983:95). The ruler in this case was female, Déwa Agung Isteri Kania.

35. In the 1990s, it is hard to know how precolonial *manca* differed from *punggawa*. People I knew referred to certain branch-line houses as *manca*, and I have followed their usage.

36. Guermonprez (1985, 1989) finds the diarchy in Balinese kingship reminiscent of eastern Indonesia (van Wouden 1968 [1935]). But I see no evidence of the distinctions between active/masculine power and passive/feminine power that van Wouden describes.

37. He identifies these, based on information received in Klungkung, as Klungkung, Karangasem, Buléléng, Tabanan, Mengwi, Badung, Gianyar, Bangli, and Payangan. Other sources suggest that at this time Payangan was under Bangli's overlordship; in 1842 it became part of Klungkung (van Bloemen Waanders 1870). It is worth noting that in this period Dutch accounts of how many realms there were in Bali and what these realms were constantly shifted. Van den Broek (1835) identified seven: Karangasem, Buléléng, Badung, Mengwi, Klungkung, Gianyar, and Tabanan. Dubois, around 1828–1830, claimed that Bangli was a new realm (Dubois MS, Letter III, H281, KITLV).

38. My source for everything that follows is J. H. Huskus Koopman's notebook, entitled "Dagverhaal 16 Mar.–31 Mei 1840"; ANRI Bali 4.15.

39. It is therefore significant that Brahmana priests often served as envoys for the rulers of Klungkung. From a spiritual point of view the priest may not have been an inferior; but politically he was. Priests made good envoys because they could not, by virtue of their occupation, lie.

40. Arntzenius (1874) identifies a "Cokorda Rai" as a *neef* of the king, a Dutch term meaning either nephew or cousin. Was this the same man? Another puzzle: in Klungkung genealogies the king himself is sometimes named as Cokorda Ketut Rai.

41. Again, the word is *neef*. Déwa Agung Gedé is less a name than a title for the heir to the throne. Since the king had no nephews in the English sense,

children of his siblings, Déwa Agung Gedé must have been one of his many cousins or even a cousin's son. Stories in Klungkung lead me to identify this person tentatively as the eldest son of the founder of Puri Kalér-Kangin, cousin to the king. He did not, however, succeed to the throne; according to some, he was poisoned by kinsmen who had an alternate candidate in mind. As for the Mengwi prince, two princes from Mengwi were in exile in Klungkung around this period (Schulte Nordholt 1988).

42. Lekkerkerker's interpretation of these events hinges upon the Déwa Agung's supposed political ambitions in Lombok. He claims the Déwa Agung invited Huskus Koopman to Klungkung in hopes that the Dutch would help him wage war against Mataram, and Lange encouraged this. The Déwa Agung later changed his mind, for reasons unknown.

43. Thus a letter Lange wrote after becoming an agent for the Dutch noted that he had not been able to speak to the Déwa Agung concerning a certain matter as it was the Balinese "New Year" and "there are no days for doing afaiers [sic]" (Letter from Lange, 26 January 1847, in Geh. Bt. 18 May 1847 D2, ANRI).

44. Lekkerkerker attributes the Déwa Agung's change of heart to several events that occurred in 1841. In January envoys from Karangasem's ruler informed the Governor General that Buléléng and Karangasem (no doubt with Klungkung's consent) were planning an expedition to restore Karangasem-Lombok to the rule of the children of its deceased ruler. Huskus Koopman returned with Karangasem's envoys to Bali the following May with ammunition and weapons, as well as (at last) Kesiman's cannon. Huskus Koopman also encouraged hopes that the Dutch would provide ships to carry troops to Lombok.

45. Mengwi and Gianyar were regarded as Klungkung's "vassals," who therefore would follow the Déwa Agung's wishes; Jembrana was considered a dependency of Buléléng. Reef rights were irrelevant in landlocked Bangli, but it is surprising that its ruler was not asked to acknowledge Dutch sovereignty.

46. Report by the Assistant Resident, 10 October 1844, Bt. 11 April 1845 D1, ANRI.

47. As evidence of both trickery and the lack of comprehension, Schulte Nordholt notes a divergence between the Dutch and Malay texts of the treaties. To explain "sovereignty," the Malay version states that the Dutch will "also own" the lands belonging to Bali; that is, own them together with the Balinese. The Dutch leaves out the word *also*. Schulte Nordholt also cites a secret letter from the Assistant Resident of Banyuwangi (12 May 1845) to the Governor General, accusing Huskus Koopman of violating his mandate. Huskus Koopman had died in the interim (Schulte Nordholt 1988:154).

48. Letter from Governor General to Minister of Colonies, 1 January 1846, Semi-Official Correspondence, MvK, ARA, cited in Schulte Nordholt 1988:156.

49. Buginese, many of them deserters from the 1846 expedition, helped build the fortifications.

50. According to letters from Mads Lange to Resident Mayor, 13 October 1846 and 15 October 1846, in Geh. Bt. 18 May 1847 D2, ANRI. Lange identifies

the kinsman as Déwa Agung Gedé Agung, the king's "brother." More likely, the man was his cousin Déwa Agung Ketut Agung, by then the designated successor to the throne; cousins often refer to each other with sibling terms.

51. The first citation is from Letter #1375, from the Rear Admiral to the Commander of War, 6 December 1846, in Geh. Bt. 18 May 1847 D2, ANRI. The second, cited by Schulte Nordholt (1988:153), comes from van Swieten's report of 6 June 1849 in Geh. Bt. 25 August 1849 D2, ANRI.

52. For example, Lange suggested that the Déwa Agung had Gianyar's ruler poisoned when he tried to secretly "befriend" the Dutch through the intercession of Badung (Letter from Lange to the Resident in the Mayor-Lange correspondence, KITLV, cited by Schulte Nordholt 1988:157). The claim that an envoy arrived from Klungkung to stop the queen of Mengwi from interfering when she tried to arbitrate between Karangasem and the Dutch in 1847 was also probably reported by Lange. At least the claim that the Dutch had to leave immediately in fear for their lives has the ring of Lange to it (Geh. Bt. 28 June 1847 X2, Geh. Bt. 7 March 1847 O2, ANRI, cited in Schulte Nordholt 1988:157).

53. Letter from George King to Mads Lange, 9 December 1846, Geh. Bt. 18 May 1847 D2, ANRI.

54. The first letter from Lange to Resident Mayor is dated 15 Oct. 1846; the second, 16 April 1847; and the third, 1 December 1846. All three may be found in Geh. Bt. 18 May 1847 D2, ANRI.

55. Letter from Lange to Mayor, 15 October 1846, Geh. Bt. 18 May 1847 D2, ANRI.

56. Letter from Lange to Mayor, 13 November 1846, Geh. Bt. 18 May 1847 D2, ANRI.

57. Letter from Lange to Mayor, 17 November 1846, Geh. Bt. 18 May 1847 D2, ANRI.

58. Letter from Lange to Mayor, 21 November 1846, Gch. Bt. 18 May 1847 D2, ANRI.

59. Geh. Bt. 18 May 1847 D2, ANRI, cited in Schulte Nordholt 1988:156.

60. Identified by Arntzenius as the Déwa Agung's nephew/cousin, and probably the same man identified by Huskus Koopman as the secondary ruler.

61. According to the treaty, he brought with him the king's seal. Also signing on Klungkung's behalf were Pedanda Madé Rai and "Ratu Ketut Agung Mengwi" (Arsip Nasional 1964:19). Déwa Agung Ketut Agung was actually the ruler's uncle, although younger than he in age. He did not, in the event, actually succeed to Klungkung's throne; his eldest son did.

7. THE KUSAMBA WAR

1. Although Ida Bagus Rai told me he had read some Dutch publications, even if he had said nothing, his familiarity with colonial sources is clear from his reference to Balinese troops at Goa Lawah. This is not part of oral tradition, and most people, when I asked them about it, expressed surprise that such a thing was

possible. Dutch military histories and newspapers suggest that temples were often used as fortifications, at least in wars against the Dutch. In Jagaraga, Balinese troops held out in the Pura Dalem, and in 1908 there were troops in Pura Dasar. Van der Kraans (personal communication) suggests that this was merely tactical common sense: the thick walls of temples provide excellent protection. Balinese nowadays, however, find such apparent "common sense" deeply puzzling, since a death in a temple would pollute it and necessitate major and expensive rituals.

2. It would not do to overemphasize the influences of colonial rationalities on this man's thinking, however. Ida Bagus Rai told me once that stories about spirits were utter nonsense, but he warned me to watch out for witches. He also remarked that he had read in the *Bali Post*—which had a regular column that often took newsworthy items from such sources as the *National Enquirer*—that there was a problem in America with ghosts. He attributed it to insufficient offerings.

3. This is a branch line of Puri Aan rather than the main puri in Nyalian.

4. Actually, the lowest horizontal bamboo bar in the roof.

5. This term is not in any dictionary; nor did Ida Bagus Jagri or Dayu Alit have any idea what it meant. I tried on various occasions to obtain clarification from those who used the term but still remain in the dark.

6. Literally, *juru jenggot* means "master of the beard." Jacobs (1883:107) mentions a corps of bearded men who constituted a royal "bodyguard" at the time of his visit to Klungkung. They meted out justice on behalf of the king. Moojen (1926:4) claims that members of this guard belonged to the clan of smiths.

7. The number of roofs on the towers used to transport bodies to the cremation ground and the animal shape of the container in which a body is burned are (theoretically) determined by rank, although this was much more strictly enforced when there were still kings. Klungkung's ruler was entitled to an eleven-roofed tower, the highest number, and a bull, which is also the animal used for Brahmanas. Branch-line members of his family were given nine roofs but could still use a bull or cow (depending upon gender).

8. That is, a Balinese month of thirty-five days in the 210-day *uku* calendar (see Goris 1960a).

9. Ida Bagus Rai, remember, referred to an Anak Agung Sangging. There were at least two princes named Sangging in the 1840s, one in Puri Kelodan and the other in Puri Kusamba. Members of the Kusamba branch house argued that it was of course their ancestor who was involved, since he lived, after all, in Kusamba, where the attack took place. But others argued for the Puri Kelodan man, and there are some indications—too complicated to mention in detail—that Puri Kelodan was politically a very significant house at this time.

10. Lange, George King, and the Netherlands Trading Society were all involved in the arms trade in the 1840s. Nielsen (1928:158) estimates there were some one thousand rifles and twenty-five cannons in Bali by 1849.

11. Geertz, whose source was a high-ranking Klungkung prince, claims that Klungkung's heirloom weapons were kept in an area called the Ukiran (which

simply means "carving"). In an episode in the *Babad Ksatria*, Bangawan Canggu is in the king's sleeping quarters.

12. See Dubois, Letter #84 to Resident of Besuki and Banyuwangi, 23 September 1828, ANRI Bali 6.51. He describes Kuta as an "unsavory place."

13. For descriptions of the collection, see Pigeaud 1967–80.

14. H2183, *Kunti-Seraya, Siwa Sumedang,* and texts concerning the Kanda Mpat.

15. The house is of the Manuaba subclan, and its core line is in Sidemen, Karangasem.

16. While the Pedanda definitely called them *regék tunggék,* the word *tenggék,* which is extremely close, means "neck or throat" in Kawi, which would make identification between this spirit and the one to be discussed momentarily even stronger.

17. The syllables are at the same time associated with deities in the *buana agung,* the "big world" or cosmos.

18. Knowledge of the left is also commonly referred to with the Indonesian phrase *ilmu hitam,* "black knowledge."

19. This at least is my impression after examining several texts, including those in Hooykaas 1975. Certain versions may be more common than others, but this might be explained by the history of their transmission. It would be interesting to understand how writers or students come to prefer a particular interpretation.

20. Blood is the symbol of life-force or energy (*bayu*) in the offering called *pang enteg bayu,* "may the life-force be firm, strong."

21. According to texts, these three qualities are characteristic not just of life but of human life. Plants merely have *bayu;* animals lack *idep* (see, e.g., Tonjaya 1981).

22. Recall that dysentery seriously afflicted the Dutch fighting force during this war.

23. An interesting set of substitutions in the ritual speech of vow making explicitly links pigs to humans. I was told if one asked the gods for a favor, and wanted to promise in return for this a roast suckling pig—an expensive offering—one should refer to the pig as a "four-footed cucumber." If the sacrifier promised a pig directly it would be read by the gods metaphorically, as "human being," and they would take the sacrifier himself instead of the offering.

24. This seems to be implicit. *Buta-kala* are invoked by warriors in part because they inspire emotions like anger, objectifying the frame of mind conducive to battle. And so these spirits help in the task at hand, that is, to spill human blood. But in a sense the spirits themselves desire this "food." Thus battles are a kind of demon sacrifice, in which the demons who have possessed the warriors are sated.

25. Unlike the stories about the Kusamba War, this tale exists in written form. See, for examples, Agung n.d. and at least one *Babad Mengwi* (V. 26 April 1940 No. 9, MvK, ARA).

26. It is unclear whether this story was written before or after the Kusamba

War. Whichever came first, both stories exist at present, and so their thematic interrelations are mutually relevant.

27. He was not necessarily a lineal ancestor, though some Mengwi texts claim him as such. Schulte Nordholt (1988 : 19ff.) suggests that the actual connection between Gusti Agung Maruti and the founder of Mengwi may have been tenuous. For a full discussion, see Schulte Nordholt 1988.

28. This *Babad Mengwi*, collected by the colonial government, may be found in V. 26 April 1940 No. 9.

29. On the temple and its goddess, including Batur's relationship to Besakih/Klungkung, see Lansing 1991.

30. Cf. Suryani 1984, a study of the prevalence of *bebainan* among younger women in contemporary Puri Klungkung. However, there were also rumors in Klungkung that certain of the king's wives successfully bewitched their co-wives while he was still alive.

8. THE DUTCH AND KLUNGKUNG, 1849 – 1908

1. V. 28 June 1909 No. 1, MvK, ARA.

2. Letter #2 from Lieutenant-Colonel von Schauroth, commander of the expedition against Klungkung, to the Commander of the Army and the Head of the Department of War, 8 May 1903, in V. 28 June 1909 No. 1, MvK, ARA.

3. According to *De Locomotief*, however, the bombardment had no effect until a shell actually hit the puri (9 May 1908).

4. At that time he was promoted to Resident of Palembang (Politiek Verslag 1863, ANRI Bali 2.3).

5. The politics behind Puri Kaléran's prominence are obscure. The succession had the support of other Balinese rulers. Lange's letters, for example, proclaim Gusti Ngurah Kesiman of Badung pleased with the decision. The best-known tale about Déwa Agung Ketut Agung in Klungkung concerns his conception and birth; its major theme is that Betara Sakti deliberately set out to produce a *sakti* son when Déwa Agung Putra I was killed. According to some in Klungkung, none of his elder brothers was interested in ruling. I was also told, however, that a Cokorda from Puri Kalér-Kangin was designated as heir to the throne but was poisoned. Huskus Koopman mentions a certain Déwa Agung Gedé, a "nephew" of the king and the "crown prince" of the realm, but gives no particulars that might help to identify him further.

6. Although the regulations stipulate that they concern the protocol for visits from the Dutch official in charge of Balinese and Lombok affairs (at that time, the Resident of Banyuwangi), the attention given to etiquette in reports about visits to Bali by lesser officials suggests that the regulations were generally taken as guides to interactions between Balinese rulers and *any* representative of the colonial government.

7. Secret Report #10, "Report on Investigations into the Wrongdoings of Raja Boeleleng," by Chief Inspector of Cultures Zoetelief, 8 April 1874, in V. 31 December 1874 D34, MvK Inventaris 6059, ARA.

8. Ibid.

9. Compare these figures to van den Broek (1835), who estimated over twice that amount. Huskus Koopman was given a figure of about twenty-five thousand in 1840. Van den Broek's figures may have been wildly off, though one would like to know his source for them. Another possibility is that there was an actual loss of population—and territory—between 1817 and 1840.

10. As indicated by his name, Pan Batu. In 1853, however, the Dutch party stayed with a Brahmana, a certain Ida Ketut Sekat (ANRI Bali 4.22).

11. He had spoken none in 1853 (ANRI Bali 4.22).

12. She is here identified as the king's aunt and elsewhere as his mother (ANRI Bali 1.2). She was actually, although much older than he, his first cousin. Most of the royal family claim that she adopted him, but there are dissenters.

13. Letter #3, 31 December 1874 D34, MvK Inventaris 6059, ARA.

14. These quotes, and all further discussion of Zoetelief's recommendations, come from his secret report of 8 April 1874 in V. 31 December 1874 D34, MvK Inventaris 6059, ARA. Unfortunately, the Ministry was sent Dutch translations of the Déwa Agung's letters; I have not seen the originals.

15. There were actually two reports: the Advice of the Council of the Indies, on 28 August 1874, and a secret report from the Government Secretary to the Delegate for Balinese Affairs on 29 October 1874, which duplicates the first (both included in V. 31 December 1874 D34, MvK Inventaris 6059, ARA).

16. According to van Bloemen Waanders (1870), the keris, named I Lobar like the keris Gajah Mada sent to Sri Kresna Kapakisan, had been given to Déwa Gedé Tangkeban's ancestor (see also *Babad Ksatria Taman Bali, Babad Dalem*). Van Bloemen Waanders was told that the keris ended up in the possession of a Brahmana from Banjar, in Buléléng. One wonders if it played any role in the uprising that took place in Banjar in the late 1860s.

I should note that while I heard references to the Nyalian War from a few people in Klungkung, no one mentioned a keris. According to one account, it was a fighting cock that the Déwa Agung requested from Déwa Gedé Tangkeban. The same person suggested that the entire dispute was orchestrated by the Déwa Manggis of Gianyar, to serve his own political ends, an opinion shared by the author of *Babad Kramas* C37:1870. A Gianyar source (Mahaudiana 1968:33) simply claims that Nyalian committed treason or rebelled against the ruler of Klungkung, and Gianyar (no mention here of troops from Buléléng) forced that realm to submit.

17. Van Bloemen Waanders (1870) corroborates this, on the basis of his discussions with the ruler of Bangli in 1856. The tribute was valued at a million kepengs a year, which van Bloemen Waanders estimates at fl.2,500.

18. Letter #3 in V. 31 December 1874 D34, MvK Inventaris 6059, ARA.

19. Missive 8 January 1854 No. 3 and Geh. Bt. 22 March 1854, cited in V. 13 April 1883 No. 14, MvK Kol. Res. 1850–1900, Inventaris 3625, ARA.

20. Letter from Resident Hoos to the Governor General, 17 August 1882,

Mail Report #835 in V. 13 April 1883 No. 14, MvK Kol. Res. 1850–1900, Inventaris 3625, ARA.

21. Ibid. *Tribute* is of course an English translation of a Dutch translation of a Balinese word. Unfortunately, I do not know what term was used by the Déwa Agung in his letter. A clue might be found in a manuscript of the poem *Uug Gianyar* (The Destruction of Gianyar), written by Anak Agung Meregan of Puri Kalér-Kangin in Klungkung during this period. In it Anak Agung Gedé Ngurah Pamecutan of Badung advises Gianyar's ruler to "remember" the Déwa Agung and present him with *tigasana* (2b:9–10). *Tigasana* was generally interpreted by the Dutch to have been a kind of tax; there is a long debate in the colonial literature on precisely what kind.

22. Starting in the colonial period, disputes over the ownership of goods originally obtained by such means have been settled in courts of law. National law generally favors the grantee. I heard of many cases during my fieldwork. For example, the late king of Klungkung gave a white water buffalo to one of his subjects. He was to have complete use of the animal and any of its offspring with the single stipulation that he present buffalo milk to the court for use in rituals whenever needed. Since the original gift, all of the original parties—king, grantee, and beast—have died, and the current owners claim they no longer have any obligations to the royal family. When members of the latter sought to repossess their cow (or rather its descendant), they lost their case.

23. Jacobs writes that smallpox vaccinations were introduced to North Bali in 1859 by van Bloemen Waanders. After an epidemic in 1871–72 took the lives of thousands of Balinese in the southern part of the island, the Dutch offered their help. The rulers were amenable, but the Javanese sent to administer the vaccinations were soon "regarded as Dutch spies. Thus one king after another sent back this 'present' of the Government, with the message that they could manage by themselves" (Jacobs 1883:iii). Badung's rulers remained interested but suggested that the vaccinator for Buléléng simply make an annual visit to the south. Jacobs had written to the Governor General that allowing smallpox to run unchecked in areas bordering colonial territories threatened the health of Dutch subjects, and he suggested that further attempts be made to vaccinate South Bali, perhaps by training Balinese vaccinators. On this journey he hoped to persuade the rulers to select persons they trusted for such training.

24. The mapping project was still incomplete in 1902; during van Kol's 1902 journey to Bali in the company of the Assistant Resident, the latter was again taking measurements.

25. In fact, since certain of these figures wear top hats, they are clearly products of nineteenth-century workmanship. Moojen (1926) also rejects Jacobs's interpretation.

26. Mail Report #835 in V. 13 April 1883 No. 14, MvK Kol. Res. 1850–1900, Inventaris 3625, ARA.

27. Ibid.

28. Letter from Resident Hoos to the Governor General, 5 February 1885, in Mail Report #112, Mailrapporten, MvK 1850–1900, Inventaris 6448, ARA.

29. This period of Balinese history is extremely complicated, and the enormous cast of characters requires the narrative skill of a Tolstoy. For some attempts, see Schulte Nordholt 1988, whose special interest is Mengwi, and Agung 1991, a member of Gianyar's royal clan. Detailed studies of Balinese as well as Dutch sources are needed of all of Bali's realms. My main efforts here have been to think through the sources available to me (in addition to those mentioned, these include Mahaudiana 1968, Agung n.d., a few archival documents, and Klungkung stories) from a Klungkung perspective; needless to say, my account is provisional.

30. Sukawati's relations with the core line at Klungkung were severed after a dispute over heirloom keris between Déwa Agung Anom and his elder brother, Klungkung's king (*Babad Dalem C* in Warna et al. 1986; *Babad Ksatria*; Agung n.d.; for genealogy, see Appendix). Sukawati's lord managed to acquire heirlooms of his own from several sources, including the Great Fanged Lord. Agung (n.d.) claims that the ruler of Sukawati gave these to Déwa Manggis, a courtier in the Sukawati palace, when his own sons failed to show proper filial respect. (The author of *Babad Kramas* C37:1870 claims that the Déwa Manggis's success was due to knowledge of the left, a gift from the goddess Durga.) According to Mahaudiana (1968), the Déwa Manggis received various heirlooms (not, however, identified as those belonging to the Sukawati royal line) from the ruler of Sukawati after the latter's death.

31. Peliatan may also have been a supporter, since Seronggo's lord, Déwa Gedé Kepandaian, spent several days there on his way to Badung according to Mahaudiana (1968:38).

32. He cites colonial documents among his sources. Interestingly, he does not mention Nyalian at all.

33. First of all, since Gianyar ultimately asked for Dutch protection (as we will see), it was important to paint a sympathetic portrait of the events that led to a decision that could only appear negative in the postcolonial 1960s. Some of Mahaudiana's characterizations of situations and persons also suggest that he had other agenda, relevant to the time of the writing. As for the judgments he makes, they would, not surprisingly, be open to debate.

34. When Bangli regained Payangan is something on which I have found no information.

35. There were no tales concerning a failed marriage in Klungkung. Much later the Déwa Agung married a woman from Siangan, a Gianyar branch house.

36. According to van Bloemen Waanders (1870), he was actually the heir to the throne of Payangan, who had fled to Tampaksiring when Payangan was conquered in the 1840s by troops under Klungkung's orders.

37. Letter from Resident Hoos to the Governor General, 5 February 1885, Mail Report #112, Mailrapporten, MvK 1850–1900, Inventaris 6448, ARA.

38. Ibid.

39. Letter from Resident Hoos to the Governor General, 9 February 1885, and Telegram from Hoos, 1 March 1885, both in Mail Report #112, Mailrapporten, MvK 1850–1900, Inventaris 6448, ARA.

40. The heirlooms became a source and symbol of further conflicts between the two realms. Descendants of the Déwa Manggis claim that they were not surrendered voluntarily but on orders from the Déwa Agung. (Dayu Alit's view of the matter is that by his flight to Klungkung the Déwa Manggis was offering his life to the Déwa Agung; the surrender of his regalia was a symbolic expression of that intent.) Mahaudiana argues that the Déwa Manggis was tricked. The Déwa Agung urged the Déwa Manggis to come to Klungkung for his own safety and promised to advise him on the best way of quashing the rebellion. Against his ministers' advice, the Déwa Manggis decided to trust the Déwa Agung, who was, after all, Susuhunan of Bali. Moreover, Déwa Agung Rai had vowed that Klungkung would help him. But when he arrived in Klungkung, he was not permitted even to see the Déwa Agung and spent the next six years as a prisoner in Satria (Mahaudiana 1968:75–78). Clearly Mahaudiana's version is meant to undermine the Déwa Agung's moral legitimacy. While I did not read his book until after my return from the field, and was therefore unable to elicit Klungkung interpretations of these events, in general Klungkung narrators were of the opinion that Gianyar's rulers were absolutely untrustworthy, commonly resorting to slander and trickery, and that by contrast Klungkung's rulers—as was proper to their position—generally acted with *darma*.

41. Letter from Déwa Agung to Resident Hoos, 6 February 1885, Mail Report #112; Telegram from Resident Hoos to the Governor General, 1 March 1885, Mail Report #129; both in Mailrapporten, MvK 1850–1900, Inventaris 6448, ARA.

42. Schulte Nordholt attributes these conflicts to a dispute between Mengwi's chief minister and Badung's ruler. The minister's father, who had a Badung wife, had left Mengwi in disgust after a series of disagreements with other Mengwi lords, in which his son had taken the opposing side. He died in Badung, unreconciled with his son. When the latter asked for his body in order to cremate it, Badung's rulers refused, carrying out the ceremony themselves (Schulte Nordholt 1988:169–70).

43. Ubud was a new branch-line house. Its founder distinguished himself when Mengwi attacked Gianyar in 1874; the Déwa Manggis rewarded him by appointing him *punggawa*. He was succeeded by his son Cokorda Gedé Sukawati, an equally celebrated warrior.

44. The source of the following account is Secret Letter #15, 25 May 1891, from Resident Dannenbergh to the Governor General, Mail Report #458, Mailrapporten, MvK 1850–1900, Inventaris 6487, ARA.

45. While the Déwa Agung said he abandoned opium as a consequence of van Bloemen Waanders's continual harangues against its use, it was not because he shared van Bloemen Waanders's opinions concerning the destructive effect of the drug. As he told van Bloemen Waanders, he gave up the habit in return for the gods granting his prayers for a son (Politiek Verslag 1860, ANRI Bali 1.6).

46. Secret Letter #15 from Resident Dannenburgh to the Governor General, 25 May 1891, Mail Report #458, Mailrapporten, MvK 1850–1900, ARA.

47. Karangasem was still under the authority of a prince from Lombok's Ma-

taram house. Lekkerkerker (1923) claims that Klungkung and Lombok remained on uneasy terms from the 1830s on.

48. The reason for Karangasem's alliance with Mengwi and the basis of its opposition to Klungkung are still unclear to me. According to Mahaudiana (1968), Madé Pasek had talked the ruler of Karangasem into an alliance at the very beginning of the conflicts between Gianyar and Klungkung.

49. A Cokorda in Péjéng resisted without success.

50. Schulte Nordholt cites a report by Controleur J. C. van Eerde from 1 June 1897, in which the Cokorda is described as "faithfully fulfilling his duties to the gods, often remaining in temples at night"; van Eerde notes that "it was believed that the god had granted him his kris" (Schulte Nordholt 1988:183). Déwa Gedé Raka was so dependent upon the Cokorda that he allowed the Cokorda to marry his daughter, even though she was already the wife of his brother's son, a move that was not at all popular. According to Mahaudiana, he was worried the Cokorda might usurp the throne. There were even rumors the Cokorda had poisoned Déwa Ngurah Pahang, although Mahaudiana claims this was merely malicious gossip originating in Klungkung (Mahaudiana 1968:96–99).

51. V. 28 April 1903 No. 2, MvK Kol. Res. na 1900, Box 175, ARA; V. 27 August 1904 No. 2, MvK Bali/Lombok Series IIIC1, ARA; the ritual is described in Swellengrebel 1947.

52. The following year van Bloemen Waanders and the naturalist Zollinger did, apparently, visit Batur. However, they were barred from entering the temple itself, which, they were told, was closed due to the recent birth of opposite-sex twins to a local woman (1870:29). There may, of course, have been changes in ritual practice, but as far as I understand on the basis of my fieldwork, what was prohibited after such a twin birth was the celebration of rituals or the making of offerings. Since in 1904 Nieuwenkamp's efforts to enter this temple aroused the opposition of the local populace (although in the end he succeeded, and he claims he was the first European to have done so; Nieuwenkamp 1922), one suspects this was merely an excuse.

53. These incidents suggest that the Dutch were thought to be polluting. Epidemics might result from pollution, since divinities would remain far from a polluted space. In any event, it is clear that the Dutch were widely associated with negative forces.

54. Mail Report #828, "Political Situation July 1904," in V. 1 May 1906 No. 5, MvK Bali/Lombok Series IIIC2, ARA.

55. His limitations were later recognized by the Dutch, who ascribed them to a "weak personality" (Letter #3006/2 from Resident de Bruyn Kops to Governor General van Heutz, 18 May 1908, in V. 28 June 1909 No. 1, MvK Kol. Res. na 1900, ARA).

56. Unfortunately reports go into no details, though it would be interesting to know if any were regalia. When I mentioned this incident to Ida Bagus Jagri and Dayu Alit, they found it highly significant: no one would to dare steal anything from a *sakti* ruler.

57. Secret Letter #159, 17 March 1902, from Resident Eschbach to the Governor General, Mail Report #711 in V. 28 April 1903 No. 2, MvK Kol. Res. na 1900, Box 175, ARA.

58. In December 1905 the Resident reported: "The Viceroy in his reports has given an incorrect representation of the facts of what occurred and therefore exaggerated the actions of Klungkung's subjects and concealed or glossed over those of his dependents." Moreover, incidents continued to occur even after Klungkung had been "chastised" by the colonial government—for example, an attempted revolt in Angantaka and Jagapati and in a number of villages in the Ubud region in 1905–06 (Mail Report #747 in V. 4 April 1907 No. 45, MvK Bali/Lombok Series IIIC3, ARA).

59. Mail Report #751 in V. 28 April 1903 No. 2, MvK Kol. Res. na 1900, Box 175, ARA.

60. I do not mean to say that these relationships explain everything; almost certainly they do not. It would be essential to know more of local events in each of these regions to properly understand their relationship to Klungkung. However, the Dutch, who completely ignore kinship and other such relations, cannot be taken as reliable sources. There is reason to think that the Resident was also presenting an account that would justify further colonial interference.

61. Letter from the Government Secretary to Resident Eschbach, Mail Report #751 in V. 28 April 1903, MvK Kol. Res. na 1900, Box 175, ARA.

62. Ironically, by going over the Resident's head to the Governor General, the Déwa Agung performed an action that almost precisely recapitulated Huskus Koopman's behavior toward Badung during the first embassy to Bali.

63. V. 28 April 1903 No. 2, MvK Kol. Res. na 1900, Box 175, ARA.

64. Mail Report #68, December 1902, in V. 27 August 1904 No. 2, MvK Bali/Lombok Series IIIC1, ARA.

65. Mail Report #284, "Political Situation February 1903," in V. 27 August 1904 No. 2, MvK Bali/Lombok Series IIIC1, ARA.

66. Mail Report #109B, "State of Affairs December 1903," in V. 27 August 1904 No. 2, MvK Bali/Lombok Series IIIC1, ARA. They could, of course, have been kinsmen of the ruler or even kinsmen of the deceased ruler of Klungkung. The report makes no further identification.

67. Mail Report #972, "State of Affairs August 1904," in V. 1 May 1906 No. 5, MvK Bali/Lombok Series IIIC2, ARA.

68. The Bangli princess was a sister of the man who succeeded to the Bangli throne in 1875, although the Déwa Agung may have married her before this. The marriage with the Siangan princess probably occurred between 1885 and 1893. Officials estimated that the son of this woman, Cokorda Mayun, was about seventeen years old when they exiled him in 1908 (Mail Report #1498, MvK, ARA).

69. I know of at least one other attempted marriage. Late in his reign Betara Dalem was planning to take as wife a young kinswoman from Nyalian. The marriage did not occur due to a fatal breach of custom by the girl.

70. "The Return of Banjarangkan" (Balik Banjarangkan), as the Pedanda re-

ferred to this event, probably occurred in the late 1890s. Schwartz (1901) notes that when he visited Klungkung in 1898 people complained of their onerous military duties, as a result of the war first with Karangasem and more recently with Gianyar.

71. Gusti Gedé Jelantik, ruler of Karangasem, mentioned to van Kol (1903: 430) that he was with his troops during the war with Klungkung.

72. Bukit Buluh, like Goa Lawah, is near the Klungkung-Karangasem border, but in the hills. While not a state temple, it was supported by various lesser lords.

73. A third person, who lived in a village near Klungkung's northern border with Karangasem, remembered hearing a tale about that front. Outnumbered, in desperation the Klungkung troops threw papayas at their enemies, who saw them as bullets and ran away.

74. The word I have translated by the phrase "disobey the command" is *murug*, which Barber (1979, vol. 1:432) glosses as "be stopped up (a hole), be dammed (water); be made ineffective (a law or command)." The idea seems to be that ignoring a royal order was like physically resisting a natural force.

75. Not to be confused with the Déwa Agung Jambé who conquered Gusti Agung Maruti and founded the Klungkung court. No one could explain why the king was known by this name. "Jambé" is ordinarily associated with either the Badung royal house or the Gélgél branch of the Klungkung house, and so would have made sense if his mother was from either place. But his genetrix was from a branch line of Puri Akah, and he had been adopted by the princess of Mengwi. Déwa Agung Smarabawa, his younger brother, was the son of the Bangli princess.

76. Mail Report #824 in V. 4 April 1907, MvK Bali/Lombok Series IIIC3, ARA.

77. Mail Report #1644 in V. 1 May 1908 No. 52, MvK Bali/Lombok Series IIIC4, ARA.

78. Mail Report #474, February 1906, in V. 4 April 1907 No. 45, MvK Bali/Lombok Series IIIC3, ARA.

79. Mail Report #1644 in V. 1 May 1908 No. 52, MvK Bali/Lombok Series IIIC4, ARA.

80. Journal of the Chief of Staff, 24 October–2 November 1906, Mail Report #1682 in V. 1 May 1908, MvK Bali/Lombok Series IIIC4, ARA.

81. Letter from Resident de Bruyn Kops to the Governor General, 5 February 1908, Mail Report #250 in V. 1 May 1908, MvK Bali/Lombok Series IIIC4, ARA.

82. Among other things, he was outraged by the whole matter of etiquette. The correspondent for the *Surabaya Handelsblad* noted: "He once expressed the wish that the controleur of the B.B. [Civil Service], passing his puri, should dismount from his horse by way of showing respect" (*Surabaya Handelsblad*, 21 April 1908).

83. Karangasem was also factionalized over relations with the Dutch. De Bruyn Kops reports that the lord of Selat belonged to a bloc that felt Karangasem's ruler should have taken Lombok's side in its war with the Dutch. According to de

Bruyn Kops, only the presence of a Dutch force at Lebu, Karangasem prevented him from coming to Klungkung's aid. In any event, Karangasem's ruler used the occasion to rid himself of this troublesome lord, who was duly arrested by the Dutch (Letter #3006/2 from Resident de Bruyn Kops to the Governor General, 18 May 1908, in V. 28 June 1909 No. 1, MvK, ARA; also *Surabaya Handelsblad*, 20 May 1908).

84. Letter D from Resident de Bruyn Kops to the Governor General, 8 May 1908, in V. 28 June 1909 No. 1, MvK, ARA.

9. THE DESTRUCTION OF THE WORLD

1. The phrase is also used of less solemn situations. People will shake their heads and mutter, in mock seriousness, *"uug gumi"* in disgust over prices in the market, shoddy merchandise, and the constancy of the rain and its effect upon dirt roads and yards.

2. The contexts in which this term is used are interesting. If a plant's leaves are bleached by exposure to too much sunlight, they are *punah;* if a rooster has been ill and recovers, but its comb ever after is a pale pink, he too is *punah*. The fading of the colors in a painting is described with the same word; however, cloth faded by the sun is not. *Punah* seems to refer to a loss of brightness and vitality. This is certainly relevant to Balinese understandings of power. In many texts, powerful rulers have a *teja* or *cahaya*, a glow (cf. Anderson 1972, on Java). To lose one's connection to the *niskala* would therefore appear as a dulling.

3. The Dutch attacked Klungkung on Tuesday-Manis of the week Wayang, just five days before the 210-day anniversary of the Penataran on Saturday-Kliwon of the same week (for the calendar, see Goris 1960c). Perhaps the Déwa Agung requested five more days to respond to the Dutch ultimatum in hopes the gods would help him then. With the exception of Cokorda Isteri Biang Sayang, however, no one in Klungkung mentioned dates, so clearly the timing is not relevant to Klungkung history making (and her date, calculated on the basis of her father's memories, was a different one altogether).

4. Ida Bagus Kakiang of Geria Bendul had heard yet another story about magic: that sorcery objects were tied to the upper branches of the banyan tree that stood before the temple complex in Senggguan, so that persons and objects passing beneath were rendered powerless. Bundles of white cloth pouches tied with tricolor thread were said to have been discovered when the tree was cut down some years later.

5. Pedanda Gedé Kenitén confirmed when asked that he had heard the story about urine being sprinkled on the weapons, but he did not volunteer it. I suspect he did not find it a very convincing explanation of Klungkung's defeat. One can easily see why: given his own narrative, there would have been nothing left to be polluted by the time the holy water was brought.

6. Déwa Agung Rai, Betara Dalem's brother, died in 1904, about a year after

his brother (Mail Report #972, "State of Affairs August 1904," in V. 1 May 1906 No. 5, MvK Bali/Lombok Series IIIC2, ARA).

7. The word he used, *masihin* (from the root *asib*, "love"), implies more than mere political alliance.

8. Some Balinese ideas about parallels between the "great" and "small" worlds (*buana agung* and *buana alit*) of cosmos and body may be found in Hooykaas 1975. For a somewhat different application of these concepts to Balinese kingship, see Geertz 1980:107−8.

9. In Bali someone who is confused is said not to know east from west.

10. No one knew what *baru* might have meant, although it is a common name for royal weapons; several persons recalled there used to be a court functionary called the *juru baru*—perhaps the person responsible for the royal spears? Zoet-mulder (1982:219) glosses *babaru* as a kind of religious office and *pabaru*, taken from Old Balinese inscriptions, as possibly a kind of tax. The Balinese dictionary edited by Warna et al. (1978) identifies *baru* as a figure in the retinue of a Brah-mana priest.

11. This tale was spontaneously narrated by the administrator at Udayana University who processed my research permit. Unfortunately I did not note his name. The narrator's Badung origins are suggested by certain narrative details, which are reminiscent of a tale about two brothers, ancestors of Badung's royal house, one of whom was skilled in the use of a blowgun and the other equally adept with a whip. The Dalem in Gélgél—presumably Dalem di Madé—was annoyed by daily visits from a raven, and one brother killed the bird with his blowgun. The appreciative king, pleased by the other brother as well, married their sister, who was the mother of the first Klungkung king, and gave the broth-ers authority over Badung (see *Babad Dalem* H2935:70a−72a; Friederich (1959 [1849−50]) heard much the same tale in Badung itself). Members of the Badung's Puri Pamecutan, from the root *pecut*, "whip," trace their ancestry from the whip-carrying brother.

12. The Resident reports the following:

At the time of the Controleur's presence in Gianyar, the Dewa Agoeng of Kloengkoeng sent his son Tjokorda Raka [i.e., Cokorda Raka Pugog] to inform him about the following incident.

One of the Kloengkoeng poenggawas had tried to bring his subordinates in the desa [village] Aan in rebellion against the Dewa Agoeng, because one of the district chiefs, on account of neglect of duties, was to be punished and in the meantime began to bring the desa in a state of defence. By a quick and strong armed action, however, the sedition had no further results. At the appearance of the dispatched troops, the desa inhabitants separated themselves from the poenggawa and asked forgiveness. Only the poenggawa and some followers committed the revolt, but gave themselves up when three of the followers were wounded. The poenggawa appears to suffer from insanity. The plan is to exile him and the village chief to the island Noesa; to the villagers, forgiveness was granted (Mail Report #497, "Political Situation April 1903," in V. 27 August 1904 No. 2, MvK Bali/Lombok Series IIIC1, ARA).

It is curious that the incident was reported to the Dutch at all. What was the Déwa Agung trying to communicate? (And was it in fact the Déwa Agung who sent Cokorda Raka, or his son Déwa Agung Jambé? It is my impression that Déwa Agung Putra III tended to rely on his brother Déwa Agung Rai rather than his son, whereas Déwa Agung Jambé was to employ his half-brother as an envoy to the Dutch consistently). Second, oral accounts identify the narrator, Cokorda Raka, as the leader of the first attack on Aan. Stories also assert that the *punggawa* was killed (though not until a second attack, which perhaps had not yet occurred at the time of this report). The remarks about the *punggawa's* sanity are interesting. I do not know whether Balinese engaged in the Euro-American pastime of using accusations of insanity to disparage political opponents, especially since in Bali madness is understood to be caused by such things as sorcery, a curse, or a period of great tests (by demons) for one engaged in spiritual pursuits (which the Cokorda certainly was). However, it is striking that elsewhere Cokorda Raka Jodog, the son of Déwa Agung Rai, is also said to "suffer from insanity." A colonial report claims that this is why he was not allowed to replace his father as *rijksbestierder* upon the latter's death, so that the office passed to Déwa Agung Smarabawa, brother of the new king Déwa Agung Jambé—curious, since the *rijksbestierder* was usually a brother of the king rather than the son of a prior *rijksbestierder*. As it happens Cokorda Raka Jodog was, like Cokorda Aan, both fond of *nakti'*ing (seeking power at night in temples), and not on very friendly terms with Cokorda Raka Pugog (and other close advisors of Déwa Agung Jambé).

13. Here is yet another way in which Tanda Langlang is a wandering sign, since in these stories about Klungkung's fall it is still in the possession of the core line.

14. The only suicides I ever heard about in Bali were of the "Romeo and Juliet" type, in which a couple had been forbidden to marry.

15. A second princess, Déwa Agung Isteri Ngurah, full sister of Déwa Agung Smarabawa, was drowned for illicit sexual relations at the same time. However, no tragic tales are offered to excuse her behavior, and there are no signs of lingering sentiment concerning her death. Interestingly, while according to colonial sources the executions occurred during Déwa Agung Putra III's reign, this is by no means clear from Balinese narratives (Letter from Resident Eschbach to the Governor General, 28 December 1901, Mail Report #711 in V. 28 April 1903 No. 2, MvK Kol. Res. na 1900, ARA).

16. There is another Pura Pusering Tasik in Bangbang, Bangli (Soebandi 1983:49–52).

17. Secret Letter #1 from Controleur Palmer van den Broek to the Resident in M.G.S. 28 August 1896 No. 1783, ANRI. In many ways, Klungkung stories paint Déwa Agung Smarabawa as the superior brother. People refer with approval, for example, to his opposition to the Dutch. He is reputed to have been popular, in part for public performances as Panji in *gambuh*. His name—Smarabawa, bearer

of love—is also suggestive. Since his son became Klungkung's last ruler (see chapter 11), and since the Dutch no longer rule Bali, his positive reputation could well be retrospective.

18. The first incident is mentioned in Kommissorial #51, Mail Report #711 in V. 28 April 1903 No. 2, MvK Kol. Res. na 1900, ARA. Presumably this is the same woman whose death by drowning is mentioned in the Mail Report in a letter from Resident Eschbach to the Governor General on 28 December 1901.

19. When Klungkung held a ritual at Besakih in December 1907 (see below), the Resident wrote to the Governor General that he would have his "spies" there.

20. Conversely, the colonial conquest informs recent narrations of the defeat of Bédaulu. For example, when Ratu Dalem Pemayun told me the story of the Majapahit conquest, he spoke of Majapahit's desire to "colonize" Bali and to have Bali's ruler defer to Majapahit authority.

21. Not all victors are positively valued. For one, Gusti Agung Maruti's usurpation is not read as a proof of the illegitimacy of the Kapakisans, although this may be because they were reinstated. Interestingly, a version of Déwa Agung Jambé I's conquest of Gusti Agung Maruti I heard from Ratu Dalem Pemayun in an interview in March 1985 is yet another tale in which conquest is made possible by subterfuge:

> Gusti Agung Maruti was very *sakti*, and the source of his *kasaktian* was his tail [note the suggestion of animality]. The lords still loyal to the Dalem held a meeting and decided that to defeat Maruti they had to trick him out of his power. They set out to find the most beautiful woman in Bali. Mantras were chanted over her to render her irresistible, and she was then sent to the market in Gélgél, so she could be seen and her beauty reported to the puri. Gusti Agung Maruti desired her immediately and could hardly wait to be alone with her. But when he tried to consummate the attraction he found himself impotent. She told him that she thought it was due to his tail; the gods would not allow someone resembling an animal to sleep with a woman of her beauty. If he would cut off the tail, no doubt the problem would be solved. He wasted no time but whipped out his keris, sliced off his tail, and gave it to her. She brought it posthaste to Sidemen to prove to the assembled lords that she had succeeded, and they immediately sought an auspicious day to attack. Gusti Maruti died fighting on the beach near Klotok, and his descendants fled to Kramas and Mengwi.

22. What struck Anak Agung Gaci as more significant than the skin color of the Dutch was their "blindness"; cf. the story told in chapter 4.

23. Letter from Resident de Bruyn Kops to the Governor General, 23 December 1907, in V. 1 July 1908 J11, Secret, MvK Kol. Res. na 1900, Inventaris 98, ARA.

24. According to the *Karya Pangelem ring Kakisik*, apparently written by Gusti Putu Jelantik, the colonial government's interpreter and *punggawa keliling*, the ritual was held on 17 April 1907 (Buda Wagé in the Balinese week Ukir).

25. Anak Agung Niang Kudar, the narrator's wife, explained that in precolo-

nial Bali no one—not even the Déwa Agung—was allowed to wear gold to the top of Mount Agung, to the shrine called Tirta Mas (Golden Holy Water). The sanctions for doing so, as the narrative shows, are supernatural. The peak is said to be so close to the heavens/sky (*langit*) that monkeys pass back and forth between them. Another prohibition involving gold marked social hierarchy: only members of the royal family were allowed to wear gold on their heads.

26. Secret Diary of the Troop Commander, 26 August–1 September 1908, in V. 28 June 1909 No. 1, MvK, ARA.

27. The idea that some set period of time—commonly eleven generations—had passed was expressed by several members of the royal clan as well. They alluded to legends concerning this, but no one was very clear about these. Some persons said that the eleven generations were up when the Dutch first appeared, but Déwa Agung Putra II and Déwa Agung Putra III were powerful enough to hold out for two more generations.

28. Letter D from Resident de Bruyn Kops to Governor General van Heutz, 8 May 1908, V. 28 June 1909 No. 1, MvK, ARA. De Bruyn Kops's comments about the Kusamba War suggest that Klungkung stories about that event reflect a Balinese (rather than just a Klungkung) interpretation of that event as it was seen in 1908.

10. "FINISHING"

1. Apart from newspaper correspondents (who were probably not on the front lines), the closest thing to a Dutch eyewitness of Klungkung's puputan was the pastor who accompanied the expedition (Fisscher 1908), but he did not see the actual shootings. The most extended treatment of the event is an article written in 1937 for the Dutch-Indies Officers Association (Anonymous 1937). More dramatic descriptions may be found in van Kol (1914) and Nieuwenkamp (1922). Baum (1937) offers a fictionalized account of the puputan in Badung, based in part on information from colonial officials.

2. Diary of the Chief of Staff, 19–23 September, Mail Report #1516 in V. 1 May 1908 No. 52, MvK Bali/Lombok Series IIIC4, ARA.

3. The Dutch used prisoners as coolie labor on such expeditions.

4. Several people mentioned *bubuh pirata,* "rice porridge for ancestral souls." What were not made were the multiple representations of the various component parts of a person (see, e.g., Bateson and Mead 1942).

5. Hooyer provides no source for this remarkable description, but Weitzel had also described what was involved in a "popootan" (1859:10).

6. Letter #3006/2, 18 May 1908, from Resident de Bruyn Kops to the Governor General, and Diary of the Chief of Staff, in V. 8 June 1909 No. 1, MvK, ARA.

7. Hooyer (1895:312) notes that a troop of men dressed entirely in white and consecrated to death formed the front line for any battle in Bali; other soldiers wore red.

8. Not only did Pedanda Gedé Tembau do so, but there are similar claims in the *Babad Ksatria* in reference to Déwa Agung Putra I's death during a war against Bangli.

11. THE EMPTY LAND

1. A note on twentieth-century Klungkung titles. The highest Kapakisan title is Déwa Agung, which is used for sons of the ruler by high-ranking wives; sons by lower-ranking wives were Cokorda. The son of a Cokorda by a woman of similar rank remained Cokorda; by a woman of lesser-rank, Anak Agung. In theory, if an Anak Agung married a commoner, the rank of their sons would be even lower: Déwa and (if the trend continued) Pungakan. But this does not seem to be more than a theoretical possibility, since I never heard any lower titles used for members of the Klungkung clan who traced descent from the post-Gélgél period. Most members of the clan attempted to maintain the rank of their twig on the family tree by at least trying to alternate marriages generationally: the son of a commoner wife would seek an endogamous wife. The history of the ranking of titles is very hard to trace. For example, the *Babad Ksatria* uses the title Déwa where nowadays people would say Cokorda or Anak Agung. This may have been a purely textual convention, to emphasize continuity with the Gélgél period; then again there may have been a change in the titles used in Klungkung in the twentieth century. Title rankings, by their very nature, could not be stable for Bali as a whole, since they were sensitive to the local political hierarchy as much as to descent per se. Thus in Peliatan, Ksatria Dalem—by Klungkung standards very far from the center—are always Cokorda and Anak Agung. This reflects their awareness that they have Anak Agung neighbors in Gianyar, kinsmen of Gianyar's king.

2. V. 10 August 1911 No. 18, MvK Bali/Lombok Series IIIC7, ARA. See especially the Kommissoriaal #32198, 31 December 1911; the letters from Resident Veenhuizen to the Governor General on 15 March 1910, from Fryling to the Director of the Civil Service on 9 June 1910, and from Hazeu, Advisor for Native Affairs, to the Director of Justice on 24 October 1910 in Mail Report #362; the very secret letter from the Resident to the Assistant Resident on 12 January 1910, and secret letters from the Resident to the Governor General on 7 February 1911, from Controleur de Haan to the Assistant Resident on 26 February 1911, from the Assistant Resident to the Resident on 28 February 1911, from the Resident to the Governor General on 2 March 1911, and from the Government Secretary to the Resident on 27 March 1911 in Mail Report #587.

3. Veenhuizen, Memorie van Overgave 1914:245–46, MvK, ARA.

4. These included most of Klungkung's former ruling class; see Mail Report #1498, 1908, MvK, ARA.

5. Both Cokorda Alit Bagus of Puri Anyar and Ida Bagus Kaot of Geria Pidada, however, thought the primary candidate was the Cokorda of Ubud, a descendant of the powerful lord who had been Betara Dalem's enemy. Ubud was very prominent in the colonial era, and colonial officials and other foreigners were on familiar

terms with the Ubud princes (who were, after all, Ksatria Dalem). The more common opinion held that the prime competitor for the position was one of the experienced civil servants in Geria Pidada, which wielded considerable power in the region until the installation of the new king. A Brahmana king would have reproduced the circumstances of the original Kapakisan ancestor.

6. During this period, Bangli, where Mount Batur is located, was under the jurisdiction of the Controleur of Klungkung, even though it retained a Balinese regent. Therefore, there is some logic to having a Klungkung prince invited to the mountain by a colonial official. However, note that the story implies that the Dutch recognized Klungkung's prince as responsible for the welfare of all Balinese. The Batur story is more popular among commoners than among members of the royal clan.

7. It was impossible to obtain any consensus in Klungkung about the coronation ceremony itself, although it was obvious from what people remembered and Pedanda Gedé Kenitén insisted that the ceremony was very different from the one that occurred in Gianyar in July 1903, described in Swellengrebel 1947. Geertz's claim that what has been called a coronation is really a consecration was flatly rejected by the Pedanda, who was Klungkung's court priest. Kings could be consecrated, he said, but that ceremony was more or less the same as a priestly consecration, and the offerings and mantras differed from those used to create a king proper. To outsiders, various Balinese rituals appear very similar, but in fact the offerings, the mantras recited by the officiating priest, and sources of the holy water used differ, depending upon whether the purpose of the ritual is to install a king, celebrate the anniversary of a temple, exorcise demons, and so on. Balinese royal installations, while called *mabiseka*, have little in common with Indian rituals of that name.

8. Letter to the Governor General from Resident de Bruyn Kops, 29 June 1908, in V. 13 January 1909 No. 42, MvK Kol. Res. na 1900, Inventaris 610, ARA.

9. Ibid.

10. Part of Concept-Nota (draft), May 1938. It is unclear whether the letter was actually sent. I have a photocopy (for which I have Hildred Geertz to thank) on the top of which is written "Dr. Goris: "Rijksbuit op Bali: Rijkssieraden Zelfbestuurders in Bali (Praktisch Advies)." The notation "Poesaka 49b" appears in the upper corner, and the document is stamped "Fakultas Sastra, Udayana University." This suggests it was among Goris's papers (he was affiliated with Udayana after independence), but librarians at the university have no idea where it may be located.

11. These were all titles granted to Bali's rulers by the colonial government.

12. In 1908 the correspondent for *De Locomotief* noted that Gianyar heirlooms were among the booty, and he mentioned that its state lances were being returned to Gianyar's ruler (*De Locomotief*, 11 May 1908, "The Excursion to Kloengkoeng"). This is puzzling in light of Swellengrebel (1947:11–12), who lists lances among the missing regalia.

13. Secret letter from Roeloef Goris, dated 4 December 1937 and entitled

"Nota over de wenselijkheid of noodzakelijkheid van het teruggeven aan de herstelde Zelfbestuurders op Bali van voorwerpen als *krijgsbuit* door onze Regeering verworven." This report was appended to the draft of the Concept-Nota (see note 10), which I presume was written by Resident Moll.

14. In some realms royal keris appear to have been associated with fertility. Schulte Nordholt describes ritual processions of royal keris in Mengwi in connection with local irrigation systems (1988:57).

15. This report was no longer appended to the letter I saw. However, a copy of it, entitled *Beschrijving van eenige tijdens de Zuid-Bai Expeditions 1906–1908 buitgemaakte vorstelijke poesaka-wapens*, is in the library of the Museum Bali in Denpasar. I am grateful to Bronwyn and Garrett Solyom for photocopying it for me.

16. "Arda Walika" may have referred to a keris type. According to Goris's report, the Central Javanese courts of Jogja and Solo included an object called Arda Walika among their regalia, which he identifies as a crowned snake—that is, a *naga*.

17. I have not been able to find any colonial accounts of these incidents.

18. How he could have been so sure, since Klungkung had had Gianyar's regalia since 1884, is a mystery. According to Goris and Grader's report, until he went to Batavia he knew the keris only from descriptions by his court priest.

19. The *Kidung Pamancangah* (Berg 1929), for example, provides only a brief description of the hilts of three Klungkung regalia: Ganja Dungkul had an ivory hilt carved in the style *tanjung kapatihan*, full of gems (*mirah*), set with the gem *mirah adi* (canto 1:51); Tanda Langlang, a gold hilt in the form of Bayu, overlaid with a "cloud" of "water jewels" (*manik warih*), with a band of red and blue gems (canto 2:7); Bangawan Canggu, a gold hilt in the form of Bayu, set with rubies (*mirah bang*) and "sprayed" with "water jewels" (*manik toya*) (canto 2:76–77). Since hilts are transposable, however, these descriptions could not necessarily identify the keris.

The catalogue of the National Museum collection in Jakarta, which seems to have been written by Javanese museum employees, demonstrates an alternative way of knowing such objects: instead of descriptions of hilts or types of gems used, it identifies damascene patterns, enumerates the curves in the blade, and describes the materials used for the sheath, all according to classification schemes well known in Java (Museum Nasional 1972). Dutch catalogues emphasize yet other features: the designs carved into sheaths, and especially measurements (see Juynboll 1912b).

20. That the keris was said to have been lost at sea once again suggests narrators had Bangawan Canggu in mind.

21. When the gods of Besakih process to Klotok, they also stop at Pura Puseh Tabola in Sidemen (Stuart-Fox 1987:329), in recognition of the Arya Sidemen who were given the task of caring for Besakih during the Gélgél era. Unlike Klungkung's Penataran, this temple has a triple lotus shrine (though it is not an exact replica of Besakih's), as well as shrines to other divinities worshipped at Besakih (Stuart-Fox 1987:319).

22. According to Geertz (1980:115), the precolonial royal house-temple included a shrine to Agung, located next to the *padmasana*. His Klungkung informant did not describe its appearance, which suggests it was a *méru*.

23. Examples include three of Klungkung's state temples (Pura Dasar, Pura Goa Lawah, Pura Kentel Gumi), Pura Batur, Mengwi's Pura Taman Ayun, etc.

24. Anak Agung Niang Kudar, who was born there, claimed that Puri Kaléran closely resembled the old Puri Agung. According to her, there was a hierarchy in the kinds of structures allowed branch-line puris. Those belonging to high-ranking royal brothers could approximate the Puri Agung; those inhabited by lower-ranking princes, especially princes with no followers (*panjak*), contained fewer marks of puri architecture. It is difficult to confirm this at present, since so much rebuilding has gone on in compounds belonging to members of the royal clan.

25. The sole exception is Puri Bedulu. Its name might allude to the Gianyar village Bedulu. The *Babad Ksatria* mentions a prince of the Sukawati branch line from this village, whose disagreements with Gianyar's ruler brought him to Klungkung for a time (see also Agung n.d.:138). It is not clear whether these events predated the founding of Klungkung's Puri Bedulu, but it is possible that the puri was originally built by this exile. No one in Puri Bedulu itself could account for its name.

Bibliography

ABBREVIATIONS

BKI   *Bijdragen tot de Taal-, Land-, en Volkenkunde*
TNI   *Tijdschrift voor Nederlands Indie*
C   Balinese Manuscript Collection (4354), Department of Manuscripts and University Archives, Cornell University Libraries, Ithaca, N.Y.
H   Hooykaas Collection, Koninklijk Instituut voor Taal-, Land-, en Volkenkunde, Leiden
K   Gedong Kirtya, Singaraja, Bali
ARA   Algemeen Rijksarchief (General State Archives), The Hague
    MvK   Ministerie van Kolonien (Ministry of Colonies). Series consulted include Mailrapporten, Kolonien Resolutien 1850–1900, Kolonien Resolutien na 1900, Bali/Lombok Series, Memorie van Overgave
ANRI   Arsip Nasional Republik Indonesia (National Archives of Indonesia), Jakarta
    Koleksi Bali, Geheim Besluiten
KITLV Koninklijk Instituut voor Taal-, Land , en Volkenkunde, Leiden
    Collectie P. Dubois (H281), Collectie Mayor-Lange (H1177), Collectie Korn

BALINESE MANUSCRIPTS

Babad Dalem K1252, formerly Collection R. Goris.

Babad Dalem belonging to Puri Nyalian in Klungkung.

Babad Dalem H2935, Geria Pidada, Klungkung (colophon dated 1918); transcribed in 1980.

Babad Dalem H3574, Geria Gedé Blayu, Marga, Tabanan; transcribed in 1982.

Babad Dalem H3837, Geria Tengah Budakeling, Bebandem, Karangasem; transcribed in 1983 (colophon says it was "written" by Sunia Jnyana in isaka 1748, or A.D. 1826).

Babad Dalem Turun ka Bali K732/4, Singaraja (?); transcribed in 1980.

Babad Kramas C4354, Box 37, Manuscript 1870.

Babad Ksatria K692, Buléléng; transcribed in 1941.

Babad Ksatria K693/1, Singaraja; typed in 1940.

Babad Ksatria K958, collected in Klungkung in 1933; transcribed in 1941.

Babad Ksatria Taman Bali H3235, Jero Gedé, Sidemen, Karangasem.

Bwana-Tatwa H3670, Jero Sidemen, Karangasem.

Buwana Winasa. Written by Ida Pedanda Ngurah of Geria Gedé Blayu (Marga, Tabanan) in 1918. Copy made for L. Heyting in 1919 is now in the Collectie Korn (KITLV OR435 no. 270) under the title "Nederlandse expeditie tegen de Bali rijkjes Tabanan en Badung (Z. Bali) in 1906 en enkele feiten daarna t/m 1910 geschreven door Pedanda Ngurah Blayu."

Buwana Winasa K4443, from book in latin characters belonging to I Wayan Reta, Kesiman, Denpasar, Badung; transcribed in 1978.

Gegoeritan Oewoeg Gianjar K458/2, collected in Singaraja in 1930; transcribed in 1941.

Gaguritan Uwug Gianjar K560/3, no information.

Geguritan Padem Warak, Hooykaas Collection (number not available). Original palm-leaf text belonging to Mekel Trena, Puri Kawan Singaraja; typed 1983.

Karya Pangelem ring Kakisik, Gowa-Lawah, Museum Bali No. 351.p.45.l.c. Copied from notebooks belonging to Puri Gobaraja in Singaraja.

Kunti-Seraya, palm-leaf text belonging to Geria Kutuh, Kamasan (copy in collection of M. Wiener).

Mayadanawatatwa, K15/1, Denpasar; transcribed in 1941.

Pambencangah Dauh, written by Gusti Lanang Mangku, Jero Selat, Klungkung (copy in collection of M. Wiener).

Purwa Tattwa, Hooykaas Collection (number not available).

Radjapoerana K1531/12, Sanur, transcribed in 1948.

Ranayajña K370/7, Abiansemal.

Rogha Sanghara Bhumi, manuscript belonging to Ida Pedanda Gedé Tembau, Geria Aan, Klungkung. Printed by Kantor Departemen Agama Kabupaten Klungkung (1978).

Siwa Sumedang, manuscript belonging to Ida Bagus Kakiang, Geria Bendul, Klungkung (copy in collection of M. Wiener).

Tingkahing Ngubuh Babahi, H2183, Geria Telaga, Sanur, Badung.

Tutur Rana-Yaynya H3941, Puri Kaléran, Kaba-Kaba, Kadiri, Tabanan.

GENERAL REFERENCES

"De Actie in de Negara Kloengkoeng in 1908." 1937. *Organ der Nederlansch-Indische Officiersvereeniging* 22 (4): 132–36.

Agung, Ide Anak Agung Gde Agung. 1991. *Bali in the Nineteenth Century*. Jakarta: Yayasan Obor Indonesia.

Agung, Ida Tjokorda Gede. n.d. *Babad Dalem*. Unpublished manuscript, Puri Kaleran Sukawati, Pasikian Semeton Kawit Tunggal Dalem Sukawati.

Agung, Tjokorda Gde. 1976. *Babad Dalem Sukawati*. Unpublished manuscript, Puri Agung, Tegallalang.

Anderson, Benedict R. O'G. 1972. "The Idea of Power in Javanese Culture." In C. Holt (ed.), *Culture and Politics in Indonesia*. Ithaca: Cornell University Press.

Anonymous [Medhurst, Dr. W. H.]. 1830. "Journal of a Tour along the Coast of Java and Bali. With a Short Account of the Island of Bali particularly of Bali Baliling." Singapore: Mission Press.

Arntzenius, J. O. H. 1874. *De Derde Balische Expeditie in herinnering gebracht*. The Hague: Gebr. Belinfante.

Arsip Nasional (ed.). 1964. *Surat-Surat perdjandjian antara Keradjaan-Keradjaan Bali/ Lombok dengan Pemerintah Hindia Belanda 1841 s/d 1938*. Djakarta: Arsip Nasional.

Asad, Talal. 1973. "Two European Images of Non-European Rule." In T. Asad (ed.), *Anthropology and the Colonial Encounter*. New York: Humanities Press.

Bateson, Gregory. 1970 [1949]. "Bali: The Value System of a Steady State." In J. Belo (ed.), *Traditional Balinese Culture*. New York: Columbia University Press.

Bateson, Gregory, and Margaret Mead. 1942. *Balinese Character: A Photographic Analysis*. Special Publication of the New York Academy of Sciences.

Baum, Vicki. 1937. *A Tale of Bali*. Garden City, N.Y.: Doubleday.

Belo, Jane. 1949. *Rangda and Barong*. Monographs of the American Ethnological Society, no. 16. Seattle: University of Washington Press.

―――. 1970 [1935]. "A Study of Customs Pertaining to Twins in Bali." In J. Belo (ed.), *Traditional Balinese Culture*. New York: Columbia University Press.

Berg, Cornelis Christiaan. 1929. *Kidung Pamancangah: De geschiedenis van het rijk van Gelgel*. Critisch Uitgegeven. Santpoort: C. A. Mees.

Beschrijving van eenige tijdens de Zuid-Bai Expedities 1906–1908 buitgemaakte vorstelijke poesaka-wapens. Unpublished manuscript in the library of the Museum Bali, Denpasar.

van Bloemen Waanders, P. L. 1859. "Aanteekeningen omtrent de zeden en gebruiken der Balinezen, inzonderheid die van Boeleleng." *Tijdschrift van het Bataviaasch Genootschap* 8:105–279.

―――. 1870. "Dagverhaal eener reis over Bali. In Juni en Juli 1856." *TNI* 4 (2): 12–27.

Boon, James A. 1977. *The Anthropological Romance of Bali, 1597–1972*. Cambridge: Cambridge University Press.

Bottoms, J. C. 1965. "Some Malay Historical Sources." In Soedjatmoko et al. (eds.), *An Introduction to Indonesian Historiography*. Ithaca: Cornell University Press.

Bourdieu, Pierre. 1977. *Outline of a Theory of Practice.* Cambridge: Cambridge University Press.

van den B[roek, H.A.]. 1835. "Verslag nopens het Eiland Bali." *De Oosterling: Tijdschrift bij Uitsluiting Toegewijd aan de Verbreiding der Kennis van Oost-Indie* 1: 158–236.

Caron, L. J. J. 1929. "Memorie van overgave van den Resident van Bali en Lombok." AA 192, ARA.

Clifford, James, and George E. Marcus (eds.). 1986. *Writing Culture: The Poetics and Politics of Ethnography.* Berkeley and Los Angeles: University of California Press.

Cohn, Bernard. 1987. *An Anthropologist among the Historians and Other Essays.* New York: Oxford University Press.

Cole, William. 1983. *Balinese Food-Related Behavior: A Study of the Effects of Ecological, Economic, Social, and Cultural Processes on Rates of Change.* Ph.D. diss., Washington University.

Collingwood, R. G. 1946. *The Idea of History.* Oxford: Oxford University Press.

Comaroff, Jean, and John Comaroff. 1991. *Of Revelation and Revolution: Christianity, Colonialism, and Consciousness in South Africa.* Chicago: University of Chicago Press.

———. 1992. *Ethnography and the Historical Imagination.* Boulder: Westview Press.

Covarrubias, Miguel. 1937. *Island of Bali.* New York: Alfred A. Knopf.

Day, Clive. 1904. *The Policy and Administration of the Dutch in Java.* New York: Macmillan.

Day, Tony. 1986. "How Modern Was Modernity, How Traditional Tradition in Nineteenth-Century Java?" *Review of Indonesian and Malaysian Affairs* 20 (1): 1–29.

Dirks, Nicholas B. (ed.). 1992. *Colonialism and Culture.* Ann Arbor: University of Michigan Press.

Dubois, Pierre. 1830. "Légère idée de Bali en 1830." Western Manuscripts H281 (Collectie P. Dubois), KITLV.

Errington, Shelly. 1983. "The Place of Regalia in Luwu." In L. Gesick (ed.), *Centers, Symbols, and Hierarchies: Essays on the Classical States of Southeast Asia.* New Haven: Yale University Press.

———. 1989. *Meaning and Power in a Southeast Asian Realm.* Princeton: Princeton University Press.

Favret-Saada, Jeanne. 1980. *Deadly Words: Witchcraft in the Bocage.* Translated by C. Cullen. Cambridge: Cambridge University Press.

Fisscher, H. 1908. "Met de troepen naar Bali." *Berichten uit Nederlandsch-Oost Indie voor de leden van den Sint Claverbond,* 249–68.

Forge, Anthony. 1980a. "Balinese Religion and Indonesian Identity." In J. J. Fox (ed.), *Indonesia: The Making of a Culture.* Canberra: Research School of Pacific Studies.

————. 1980b. "Tooth and Fang in Bali." *Canberra Anthropology* 3 (1): 1–16.

Foucault, Michel. 1979. *Discipline and Punish: The Birth of the Prison*. Translated from the French by Alan Sheridan. New York: Vintage Books.

————. 1980. *Knowledge/Power: Selected Interviews and Other Writings*. Edited by C. Gordon. New York: Pantheon.

Franken, Hendricus Jacobus. 1960. "The Festival of Jayaprana at Kalianget." In J. L. Swellengrebel (ed.), *Bali: Studies in Life, Thought, and Ritual*. The Hague and Bandung: W. van Hoeve.

Frey, Edward. 1986. *The Kris: Mystic Weapon of the Malay World*. Singapore: Oxford University Press.

Friederich, R. 1847. "De Oesana Bali." *TNI* 9 (3): 245–373.

————. 1959 [1849–50]. *The Civilization and Culture of Bali*. [Originally published as "Voorloopig verslag van het Eiland Bali." *Verhandelingen van het Bataviaasch Genootschap* 22 and 23]. Calcutta: Susil Gupta.

Furnivall, J. S. 1944. *Netherlands India: A Study of Plural Economy*. Cambridge: Cambridge University Press.

Geertz, Clifford. 1973a. "Deep Play: Notes on the Balinese Cockfight." In C. Geertz, *The Interpretation of Cultures*. New York: Basic Books.

————. 1973b. "'Internal Conversion' in Contemporary Bali." In C. Geertz, *The Interpretation of Cultures*. New York: Basic Books.

————. 1973c. "Person, Time, and Conduct in Bali." In C. Geertz, *The Interpretation of Cultures*. New York: Basic Books.

————. 1980. *Negara: The Theater-State in Nineteenth-Century Bali*. Princeton: Princeton University Press.

Geertz, Clifford, and Hildred Geertz. 1975. *Kinship in Bali*. Chicago: University of Chicago Press.

Gerdin, Ingela. 1981. "The Balinese Sidikara: Ancestors,. Kinship, and Rank." *BKI* 137: 17–34.

Gerlach, A. J. A. 1859. *Fastes militaires des Indes-Orientales Neerlandaises*. Paris: C. Borrani.

Goris, Roeloef. 1937. "Nota over de wenselijkheid of noodzakelijkheid van het teruggeven aan de herstelde Zelfbestuurders op Bali van voorwerpen als *krijgsbuit* door onze Regeering verworven." Unpublished manuscript, Fakultas Sastra, Udayana University Bali (copy in collection of M. Wiener).

————. 1960a. "The Temple System." In J. L. Swellengrebel (ed.), *Bali: Studies in Life, Thought, and Ritual*. The Hague: W. van Hoeve.

————. 1960b [1933]. "Holidays and Holy Days." In J. L. Swellengrebel (ed.), *Bali: Studies in Life, Thought, and Ritual*. The Hague: W. van Hoeve.

————. 1969a [1937]. "Pura Besakih, Bali's State Temple." In J. L. Swellengrebel (ed.), *Bali: Further Studies in Life, Thought, and Ritual*. The Hague: W. van Hoeve.

————. 1969b [1948]. "Pura Besakih through the Ages." In J. L. Swellengrebel (ed.), *Bali: Further Studies in Life, Thought, and Ritual.* The Hague: W. van Hoeve.

Grader, Christiaan. 1960a. "The State Temples of Mengwi." In J. L. Swellengrebel (ed.), *Bali: Studies in Life, Thought, and Ritual.* The Hague: W. van Hoeve.

————. 1960b. "Pemayun Temple of the Banjar of Tegal." In J. L. Swellengrebel (ed.), *Bali: Studies in Life, Thought, and Ritual.* The Hague: W. van Hoeve.

Graves, Elizabeth, and Carnvit Kaset-siri. 1967. "A Nineteenth-Century Siamese Account of Bali with Introduction and Notes." *Indonesia* 7:77–122.

Guermonprez, Jean-François. 1983. "Le Récit des origines d'un groupe de Pandé à Bali." *Archipel* 25:109–36.

————. 1985. "Rois divins et rois guérriers: images de la royauté à Bali." *L'Homme* 25:39–69.

————. 1989. "Dual Sovereignty in Nineteenth-Century Bali." *History and Anthropology* 4:189–207.

Guha, Ranajit. 1983. "The Prose of Counter-Insurgency." In R. Guha (ed.), *Subaltern Studies 2.* New Delhi: Oxford University Press.

Gullick, J. M. 1958. *Indigenous Political Systems of Western Malaya.* London: Athlone Press.

Haar, J. C. C. n.d. "Memorie van overgave." MvK, Memorie van Overgave, Koninklijk Instituut voor de Tropen Series, ARA.

Helms, Ludvig Verner. 1969. *Pioneering in the Far East.* London: Dawsons of Pall Mall.

Hinzler, Hedi I. R. 1976. "The Balinese Babad." In S. Kartodirdjo (ed.), *Profiles of Malay Culture: Historiography, Religion, and Politics.* Jakarta: Ministry of Education and Culture.

————. 1983. "The Balinese Manuscript Project." *Southeast Asia Library Group Newsletter* no. 25:7.

————. 1986a. "The *Usana Bali* as a Source of History." In T. Abdullah (ed.), *Papers of the Fourth Indonesian-Dutch History Conference: Literature and History (Volume 2).* Yogyakarta: Gajah Mada University Press.

————. 1986b. "Facts, Myths, Legitimation, and Time in Balinese Historiography." Paper presented at the Workshop on Balinese State and Society, KITLV.

Hitchcock, Michael. 1987. "The Bimanese Keris: Aesthetics and Social Value." *BKI* 143:125–40.

Hobart, Mark. 1985. "Anthropos through the Looking-Glass: Or How to Teach the Balinese to Bark." In J. Overing (ed.), *Reason and Morality.* ASA Monographs, no. 24. London: Tavistock Publications.

————. 1990. "The Patience of Plants: A Note on Agency in Bali." *Review of Indonesian and Malaysian Affairs* 24:92–135.

Hocart, A. M. 1970. *Kings and Councillors.* Chicago: University of Chicago Press.

Hooyer, G. B. 1895. *Krijgsgeschiedenis van Nederlandsch-Indie van 1811 tot 1894.* The Hague: De Gebr. van Cleef.

Hooykaas, Christiaan. 1964. "The Balinese Sengguhu Priest, a Shaman but not a Sufi, a Saiva and a Vaishnava." In J. S. Bastin and R. Roolvink (eds.), *Malayan and Indonesian Studies: Essays Presented to Sir Richard Winstedt.* Oxford: Clarendon Press.

———. 1973. *Kama and Kala: Materials for the Study of Shadow Theatre in Bali.* Amsterdam: Verhandelingen van de Koninklijke-Nederlandse Akademie van Wetenschappen, Afdeling Letterkunde.

———. 1975. *Cosmogeny and Creation in Balinese Tradition.* The Hague: Martinus Nijhoff.

———. 1979a. "Preservation and Cataloguing of Manuscripts in Bali." *BKI* 135: 347–53.

———. 1979b. *Introduction à la littérature Balinaise.* Paris: Cahier d'Archipel publié par l'Association Archipel 8.

Inden, Ronald. 1990. *Imagining India.* London: Basil Blackwell.

Jacobs, Julius. 1883. *Eenigen tijd onder de Balier.* Batavia: G. Kolff.

Juynboll, Dr. Hendrik Herman. 1912a. Vol. 3, *Supplement op den catalogus van de Sundaneesche handschriften en catalogus van de Balineesche en Sasaksche handschriften der Leidsche Universiteits-Bibliotheek.* Leiden: E. J. Brill.

———. 1912b. *Catalogus van 'sRijks Ethnographisch Museum. Deel 7: Bali en Lombok.* Leiden: E. J. Brill.

van der Kaaden, W. F. 1938. "Geschiedenis van de bestuursvoering over Bali en Lombok, 1889–1938." *Tropisch Nederland* 11:202–8, 219–24, 234–40, 253–56, 265–72.

Kanta, Madé. 1984. *Kesusastraan Bali pada jaman Klungkung.* Singaraja: Balai Penelitian Bahasa, Departemen Pendidikan dan Kebudayaan.

Kats, J. 1939. "In Memoriam H. J. E. F. Schwartz." *Djåwå* 19:86–88.

Klinkert, H. C. 1870. "De laatste strijd en heldendood van Generaal Michiels." *TNI* 4 (2): 187–215.

van Kol, H. H. 1903. *Uit onze kolonien: uutvoerig reisverhaal.* Leiden: A. W. Slijthoff.

———. 1914. *Dreimaal dwars door Sumatra en zwerftochten door Bali.* Rotterdam: W. J.& J. Brusse's Uitgevermaatschappij.

Korn, V. E. 1922. *Balische overeenkomsten.* The Hague: Martinus Nijhoff.

———. 1932. *Het Adatrecht van Bali.* The Hague: G. Naeff.

van der Kraan, Alfons. 1980. *Lombok: Conquest, Colonization, and Underdevelopment.* Singapore: Heinemann.

———. 1985. "Human Sacrifice in Bali: Sources, Notes, and Commentary." *Indonesia* 40:89–121.

Kumar, Ann L. 1984. "On Variation in Babads." *BKI* 140:223–47.

Lansing, J. Stephen. 1991. *Priests and Programmers: Technologies of Power in the Engineered Landscape of Bali*. Princeton: Princeton University Press.

Lekkerkerker, C. 1920. *Bali en Lombok: Overzicht der litteratuur omtrent deze eilanden tot einde 1919. Uitgave van het Bali-Instituut*. Rijswijk: Blankwaardt & Schoonhoven.

————. 1923. "Het voorspel der vestiging van de Nederlandse macht op Bali en Lombok." *BKI* 79: 198–332.

————. 1926. "Bali 1800–1814." *BKI* 82: 315–38.

Liefrinck, F. A. 1915. *De landsverordeningen en overeenkomsten van Balische vorsten*. The Hague: Koninklijk Instituut voor Taal-, Land-, en Volkenkunde.

De Locomotief. April–May 1908.

Mahaudiana. 1968. *Babad Manggis Gianjar*. Gianjar: A. A. Gde Thaman.

Mayun, Cokorda Gedé. n.d. "Kitab sejarah puputan ring Panegara Klungkung, druwé Cokorda Gedé Mayun ring Puri Anyar Ersania Klungkung (Semarapura)." Manuscript belonging to Cokorda Isteri Oka, Puri Anyar, Klungkung.

Milner, A. C. 1982. *Kerajaan: Malay Political Culture on the Eve of Colonial Rule*. Association for Asian Studies Monograph no. 40. Tucson: University of Arizona Press.

Moojen, P. A. J. 1920. *Bali: Verslag en vorstellen aan de Regeering van Nederlandsch Indie*. Batavia: Uitgave v/d Bond van N. I. Kunstkringen en N. I. Heemschut met steun v/d N. I. Regeering.

Multatuli (Edward Douwes Dekker). 1967. *Max Havelaar; or, The Coffee Auctions of the Dutch Trading Company*. Translated by R. Edwards. Amherst: University of Massachusetts Press.

Museum Nasional. 1972. *Katalogus koleksi ethnografi dan sejarah lokal*. Jakarta: Museum Nasional Republik Indonesia.

————. n.d. "Inventaris koleksi." Typescript catalogue of Balinese manuscript collection.

Narayana, Ida Bagus Udara, Madé Kanta, I Nyoman Kutha Ratna, and I Nyoman Sukartha. 1987. *Terjemahan dan kajian nilai Pralambang Bhasa Wewatekan karya Dewa Agung Istri Kania*. Denpasar, Bali: Proyek Penelitian dan Pengkajian Kebudayaan Bali, Departemen Pendidikan dan Kebudayaan.

van Niel, Robert. 1963. "The Course of Indonesian History." In R. McVey (ed.), *Indonesia*. New Haven: HRAF Press.

Nielsen, Aage Krarup. 1927. *Leven en avonturen van een oostinjevaarder op Bali*. Amsterdam: E. M. Querido's Uitgevers-Maatsch.

Nieuwenkamp, W. O. J. 1922. *Zwerftochten op Bali*. Amsterdam: Elsevier.

Nypels, G. 1897. *De Expeditien naar Bali in 1846, 1848, 1849, en 1868*. Haarlem: De Erven Loosjes.

Penduduk propinsi Bali 1980 menurut kabupaten dan kecamatan: Hasil pencacahan lengkap sensus penduduk 1980. Denpasar, Bali: Kantor Statistik Propinsi Bali.

Pidada, Ida Bagus Rai. 1983. *Buku Puramatatwa Satria Dalem.* Unpublished manuscript translation of *Babad Satria Dalem* belonging to Pedanda Gedé Wayan Pidada, Geria Pidada Klungkung.

Pigeaud, Theodor. 1967–80. *Literature of Java.* 4 vols. Leiden: Leiden University Press.

Price, Richard. 1990. *Alabi's World.* Baltimore: Johns Hopkins University Press.

Ramseyer, Urs. 1977. *The Art and Culture of Bali.* Oxford: Oxford University Press.

Rassers, W. H. 1959. *Pañji, the Culture Hero: A Structural Study of Religion in Java.* The Hague: Martinus Nijhoff.

Regeg, Ida Anak Agung Madé. 1957. *Babad Bali Radjiya. Kaparidartajang.* Klungkung: Pustaka Murni.

Ricklefs, M. C. 1974. *Jogjakarta under Sultan Mangkubumi: 1749–1792.* London: Oxford University Press.

Robson, Stuart O. 1972. "The Kawi Classics in Bali." *BKI* 128 : 308–29.

Rubinstein, Raechelle. 1991. "The Brahmana According to Their Babad." In H. Geertz (ed.), *State and Society in Bali.* Leiden: KITLV Press.

Sahlins, Marshall. 1976. *Culture and Practical Reason.* Chicago: University of Chicago Press.

———. 1985. *Islands of History.* Chicago: University of Chicago Press.

Said, Edward W. 1979. *Orientalism.* New York: Vintage Books.

Sanggka, Madé. 1971. *Babad Timbul Sukawati.* Unpublished manuscript, Yayasan Loka Phala Buddhaya Sukawati.

Sasrowidjaya, Raden. 1875. *Serat poerwatjarita Bali.* Batavia: Landsdrukkerij.

Schrieke, Bertram Johannes Otto. 1957. *Ruler and Realm in Early Java.* The Hague: W. van Hoeve.

Schulte Nordholt, Henk. 1981. "The Mads Lange Connection. A Danish Trader on Bali in the Middle of the Nineteenth Century: Broker and Buffer." *Indonesia* 32 : 17–47.

———. 1986. *Bali: Colonial Conceptions and Political Change 1700–1940. From Shifting Hierarchies to "Fixed Order."* Rotterdam: Comparative Asian Studies Program 15.

———. 1988. *Een Balische dynastie: Hierarchie en conflict in de Negara Mengwi, 1700–1940.* Ph.D. diss., Free University of Amsterdam.

Schwartz, H. J. E. F. 1901. "Dagverhaal van eener reis van den Resident van Bali en Lombok, vergezeld van den Controleur voor de Politieke Aangelegenheden en de Poengawa's Ida Njoman Bandjar en Goesti Njoman Raka naar Karangasem en Kloengkoeng van 11 t/m 26 April 1898." *Tijdschrift voor Indische Taal-, Land- en Volkenkunde* 43 : 108–23.

Scott, James C. 1985. *Weapons of the Weak: Everyday Forms of Peasant Resistance.* New Haven: Yale University Press.

Sidemen, Drs. Ida Bagus, Drs. Anak Agung Bagus Wirawan, Drs. Wayan Dunia, and I Made Kanta. 1983. *Sejarah Klungkung (Dari Smarapura sampai Puputan).* Klungkung, Bali: Pemerintah Kabupaten Daerah Tingkat II Klungkung.

Soebandi, Ktut. 1981. *Pura Kawitan/Padharman dan Panyungsungan Jagat.* Denpasar: Penerbit "Guna Agung."

———. 1983. *Sejarah pembangunan pura-pura di Bali.* Denpasar: Penerbit CV. Kayumas.

Stuart-Fox, David J. 1987. *Pura Besakih: A Study of Balinese Religion and Society.* Ph.D. diss., Australian National University.

Sugriwa, Gusti. 1957. *The Babad Pasek.* Denpasar: Balimas.

Surabaiasch Handelsblad. April–May 1908.

Suryani, Luh Ketut. 1984. "Culture and Mental Disorder: The Case of Bebainan in Bali." *Culture, Medicine, and Psychiatry* 8 : 95–113.

Swellengrebel, J. L. 1947. *Een Vorstenwijding op Bali.* Leiden: Mededeling Rijksmuseum voor Volkenkunde 2.

———. 1960. Introduction to J. L. Swellengrebel (ed.), *Bali: Studies in Life, Thought, and Ritual.* The Hague: W. van Hoeve.

T. 1874. "Bali en Lombok." *TNI* 3 (2): 439–55.

Taussig, Michael. 1980. *The Devil and Commodity Fetishism.* Chapel Hill: University of North Carolina Press.

———. 1987. *Shamanism, Colonialism, and the Wild Man: A Study in Terror and Healing.* Chicago: University of Chicago Press.

Taylor, Jean Gelman. 1983. *The Social World of Batavia: European and Eurasian in Dutch Asia.* Madison: University of Wisconsin Press.

Thomas, Nicholas. 1991. *Entangled Objects: Exchange, Material Culture and Colonialism in the Pacific.* Cambridge, Mass.: Harvard University Press.

Tonjaya, I Nyoman Gede Bandesa K. 1981. *Kanda Pat Bhuta.* Denpasar: Penerbit & Toko Buku Ria.

———. 1984. *Kanda Pat Sari.* Denpasar: Toko Buku Percetakan & Stencils "Ria."

Vickers, Adrian. 1982. "The Writing of Kakawin and Kidung on Bali." *BKI* 138 : 492–93.

———. 1986. *The Desiring Prince: A Study of the Kidung Malat as Text.* Ph.D. diss., University of Sydney.

———. 1987. "Hinduism and Islam in Indonesia: Bali and the Pasisir World." *Indonesia* 44 : 31–58.

———. 1990. "Balinese Texts and Historiography." *History and Theory* 29 (2): 158–78.

———. 1991. "Writing Ritual: The *Kidung Karya Ligya/Gaguritan Padem Warak.*" In H. Geertz (ed.), *Balinese State and Society.* Leiden: KITLV.

Wagner, Roy. 1975. *The Invention of Culture.* Chicago: University of Chicago Press.

Warna, Drs. Wayan, et al. (eds.). 1978. *Kamus Bali-Indonesia*. Denpasar: Dinas Pengajaran Propinsi Daerah Tingkat I Bali.

—. 1986. *Babad Dalem: Teks dan terjemahan*. Denpasar: Dinas Pendidikan dan Kebudayaan Propinsi Daerah Tingkat I Bali.

Weitzel, A. W. P. 1859. *De derde militaire expeditie naar het eiland Bali in 1849*. Gorinchem: J. Noorduyn.

Wiener, Margaret J. 1993. "Dangerous Liaisons: The Sexual Politics of Magic in Colonial Java." Paper presented at annual meetings of the American Anthropological Association.

—. 1994. "Object Lessons: Dutch Colonialism and the Looting of Bali." *History and Anthropology* 6 (4): 347–70.

Wikan, Unni. 1990. *Managing Turbulent Hearts: A Balinese Formula for Living*. Chicago: University of Chicago Press.

Wittgenstein, Ludwig. 1979. *Remarks on Frazer's Golden Bough*. Nottinghamshire: Brynmill; Atlantic Highlands, N.J.: Humanities Press.

Worsley, Peter J. 1972. *Babad Buleleng: A Balinese Dynastic Chronicle*. The Hague: Martinus Nijhoff.

wan Wouden, F. A. E. 1968. *Types of Social Structure in Eastern Indonesia*. The Hague: Martinus Nijhoff.

De Zoete, Beryl, and Walter Spies. 1974 [1938]. *Dance and Drama in Bali*. Kuala Lumpur: Oxford University Press.

Zoetmulder, P. J. 1974. *Kalangwan: A Survey of Old Javanese Literature*. Koninklijk Instituut voor Taal-, Land-, en Volkenkunde, Translation Series 16. The Hague: Martinus Nijhoff.

—. 1982. *Old Javanese-English Dictionary*. 2 vols. The Hague: Martinus Nijhoff.

Zurbuchen, Mary Sabina. 1987. *The Language of Balinese Shadow Theater*. Princeton: Princeton University Press.

Index

heirlooms, 56, 63, 67, 74, 403 n.30; colonial discussions of, 345–47; responsibility for, 97; texts as, 85. *See also* weapons, heirloom; regalia

Helms, L., 131

hierarchy: colonial, 88–89; under colonial rule, 332; keris and, 66; Klungkung and, 155. *See also* rank

Hinduism, Balinese, 332, 350

history: the colonial encounter and, 14; cultural production and, 151; ethnographic, 77, 95; as a Balinese category, 78, 385 n.4; local, 7; official, 7; rhetorical emphasis of Balinese, 12, 185. See also *babad*

Hobart, M., 148, 150, 380 n.4

Hocart, A., 56

Hoevell, W. R. van, 92

holy water, 51, 361; effects of, 75, 282; stories about polluted, 278–79, 283; temples and, 216; types of, 46, 283–84

Hooyer, G. B., 324

Hooykaas, C., 93–94

human sacrifice: rumors of, 216–17; interpretations of European power and, 220; I Seliksik and, 189–98

Huskus Koopman, J. H., 28, 140, 158–72; Badung's rulers and, 159–62; journal of, 137; at Klungkung, 162–70; Klungkung's position described by, 25, 34

hypergamy, 392 n.6

iconography, 50, 239

Ida Bagus Gédé, 20; tales of Klungkung's conquest, 291; on Déwa Agung Oka Geg's coronation, 339

Ida Bagus Jagri, 15–17, 206, 208; collaboration with, 15–20; comparisons to Gianyar and Badung, 45–49; discussions of archival materials, 95; interpretations by, 61, 68, 71–72, 79, 81, 109, 156–57, 208, 211, 311, 323, 327; on interpreting texts, 83, 85; as

interviewer, 187–88, 195–96, 204, 320–21, 326; role in research, 81

Ida Bagus Kakiang Bendul, on the conquest, 408 n.4

illness: attributed to the Dutch, 254; avoiding audiences and, 169, 231, 238, 258, 272; memory and, 48, 214, 218; as a sign, 59; of Dutch soldiers, 179; sorcery and, 223

Inden, R., xi, 148

Indonesia: and Bali, 22; Jakarta hegemony in, 363–64; local history in, 7, 361–62; kings in, 344; religion in, 349–50, 352

innuendo, 80–82

insanity, causes of, 410 n.12

inside: as a symbolic location, 153–54, 158

interpretation: of natural signs, 57–58; of texts, 82–87, 208

interpreters, 163, 167

intertextuality, 21, 87; the *Babad Dalem* and, 101; stories about the conquest and, 298–303

invisibility: Klungkung's, 12–13, 357–58, 362–64

invisible forces: agency and, 73–74; in Balinese history making, 12; Balinese metaphysics and, 50–55; power as connection to, 58–63; presence of, 55–56; speech and the study of, 16, 79–83, 206–7; rulers and, 57–58, 74–75

Islam: Balinese perceptions of, 201–2; magic and, 203–4

Iswara, 46, 51

Jacobs, J., 92; visit to Klungkung by, 236–39

Java: Balinese culture and, 104; British occupation of, 26; colonialism in, 41, 165; as a model to understand Bali, 35, 41, 227, 266; rulers of, 35. *See also* Blambangan; Majapahit; Pasuruhan

Jero Ketut, 340